FRANCE 1940-1955

OTHER BOOKS ON FRANCE BY
ALEXANDER WERTH

FRANCE

1940–1955

by

ALEXANDER WERTH

Senior Simon Research Fellow (1953–5),
University of Manchester

WITH A FOREWORD BY G. D. H. COLE

The French are the monkeys of Europe.—ADOLF HITLER

The worst straggler of all. . .—NEW YORK TIMES

France is a charming country; only the French can never make up their minds about anything. We like people to be our friends or our enemies. We don't like wobblers.—MR KHRUSHCHEV

❈   ❈   ❈

La Vierge est venue en France plus souvent qu'en aucun autre pays.
—JACQUES MARITAIN

HENRY HOLT AND COMPANY
NEW YORK

89311-0116

PRINTED IN THE UNITED STATES OF AMERICA

THIS BOOK IS
GRATEFULLY DEDICATED TO
LORD AND LADY
SIMON OF WYTHENSHAWE

CONTENTS

PART III

THE ROUGH ROAD TO THE "WEST" (1946–8)

PART IV

FRANCE IN THE COLD WAR (1948–50)

PART V

BATTLES AGAINST ARABS, COMMUNISTS AND—AMERICANS (1951–3)

1. The School Quarrel.—2. France "the Worst Straggler".—3. Mendès-France as Cassandra.—4. French Jitters over Preventive War Talk.—5. *Collier's* Jolly Atom War.—6. "This is an Era of Total Anguish."

A*

PART VI
THE END OF AN EPOCH

Tunisia

FOREWORD

I HAVE great pleasure, though also some diffidence, in complying with my friend Alexander Werth's request for a brief foreword to his book. For a good many years now I have been following with admiration his books and articles about contemporary world affairs and particularly about France and the French overseas empire. No one is better fitted than he to render an account of French affairs since the Third Republic collapsed fifteen years ago. If there is a difficulty for him in telling this story, it is that he knows too much and is so familiar with the ins and outs of it that he does not always realize how little most of us actually know about them. We have, of course, our general impressions about Vichy France, about Pétain, and Laval, and about such even more sinister figures as Doriot and Darnand. We know something about de Gaulle—without being able quite to understand him. We are mostly very ignorant about the French Resistance, though we know some of the reasons why, as a coherent force in post-war France, it so quickly melted away. We are better aware of the appalling blunders of post-war French policy first in Indo-China and then in North Africa, and of the long rearguard action the French put up—in my view very rightly—against German rearmament. Most of us, however, have very little idea of how these things appear to French eyes and minds; and it is for this insight and understanding above all that Alexander Werth's book is to be welcomed.

For one thing, I think he brings out very clearly how great has been the French contribution to the cause of peace during the years of "cold war" that began in 1947. At point after point, French stubbornness—commonly represented abroad as mulishness—did a great deal to prevent the cold war from turning into a hot war against Communism. The French knew from the first that France could not endure a third war, or hope to survive one without sheer eclipse; and, dispirited—or even ashamed—as they often seemed, their will to survive as world leaders remained exceedingly strong. This will sometimes led them into adventures—for example, in Indo-China—that were disastrously beyond their real strength. But it was, at bottom, much less a will to military power than a will to cultural influence. Not for a moment, even in their deepest pessimism, did they cease to believe that French culture was the best of all cultures: never, even when they were denouncing the

xiii

"*trahison des clercs*", did they give up their respect for intellectual values. In politics they were for the most part more than commonly petty and intriguing; but France remained, and remains, a country where ideas count and are seriously debated, not merely by a small intellectual élite, but by great bodies of quite ordinary men and women.

Indeed, this endless debate about values, which is the gist of France's contribution to the world, is also largely the cause of its political instability, which goes, as many have observed, with a deep-seated social stability that not even Vichy or the Germans were able to upset. This element of stability, in face of a deeply changed condition of affairs, largely explains the persistent attempt to revert to the ways of the Third Republic. The instability, on the other hand, rests on the fact that, even now, France has not completely absorbed the lessons of its great Revolution of 1789. Whereas in Russia, within a year of the Revolution of 1917, the old ruling classes, including the old bourgeoisie, had completely vanished as a political and as a social force, in France there have been ever since 1789 active reactionary elements within the society, not at most times very numerous, but always influential enough to make a great noise and often able to cause dangerous disturbances, as in the Dreyfus Case and, again, in the crisis of 1934. This latter crisis was indeed, in Alexander Werth's view, which seems to me correct, the real beginning of Vichyism and of the moral collapse of 1940. Today Poujadism is an ominous revival of the same spirit.

Another thing Werth brings out very clearly—and it is important that we in Great Britain should understand it—is that the French view of our country differs widely from our own—especially in relation to the events of 1940. "Dunkirk" is for most of us a word that evokes proud memories; but for most Frenchmen it evokes memories of disaster and even of desertion by the British. It is difficult for us to realize at how bad a psychological moment Winston Churchill made his "grand gesture" proposing common citizenship, or how suspicious of Great Britain many Frenchmen are today in face of British reluctance to take the plunge into a confederated Western Europe. It is, however, of great importance that we should understand this attitude, which Alexander Werth all the more sympathetically lays bare because he is no friend of the Right.

I also find Werth very illuminating about Mendès-France and about the forces ranged for and against him during his all-too-brief tenure of office in 1954–5. During those fateful months Mendès-France did three big things. He wound up the war in Indo-China, started out in North Africa on a new policy and put an end to the projected European Defence Community. For none of these things has he been forgiven by his political enemies. What he had no time to do was to achieve anything notable in the economic field, though this was really his main concern and is today the main basis of his challenge to the powerful groups that are still blocking the way to economic development and social justice. Not of course that Werth is an unqualified admirer of Mendès-France. He fully realizes the curious psychological incompatibility between Mendès-France and certain ways of thinking existing not only on the French Right, but also on the French Left. Perhaps Mendès-France's greatest weakness is his incapacity of being wholeheartedly a man of the Left in his fundamental approach and in his reaction to day-to-day events. On the other hand, there seems, under the Fourth Republic, extremely little room for any bourgeoisie other than that bourgeoisie of the Right which has been responsible for so many of the follies of recent years, above all in the colonial field, and which is still very far from mending its ways. There is thus a danger of the "intelligent bourgeoisie", as represented by men like Mendès-France, proving both a misfit and a contradiction in terms.

The writer of a mere foreword, however, is not called upon to repeat the arguments of the book he introduces, but only to say, as briefly as he can, why he believes it to deserve the widest attention. This I have tried to do, and I can now stand aside and leave the author to speak for himself, as he is very well able to do.

G. D. H. COLE

All Souls College, Oxford
January 1956

INTRODUCTION

I N AMERICA," the *Monde* recently wrote, "there is more friendship
for France than confidence in France." Friendship—and, indeed,
admiration, and the kind of affection that Eluard expressed so well
in his nostalgic war prisoner's dream:

> Un pays où le vin chante
> Où les moissons ont bon cœur
> Où les enfants sont malins
> Où les vieillards sont plus fins
> Qu'arbres à fruit blancs de fleur
> Où l'on peut parler aux femmes . . .

A slow country, especially south of the Loire, old-fashioned and
lovable. Such is a widespread, and not entirely false picture of France
—or of a part of it—that so many foreigners like to carry in their hearts.

On closer examination, however, it is a country full of contrasts and
contradictions. On the one hand, first-class motor roads, and the world's
fastest *rapides* on her main lines; but, on the other hand, a backward
peasant economy, not nearly enough new houses, a *patronat* that is
often mean, shortsighted and overcautious with its industrial "Mal-
thusianism"; a good social-insurance system, first-class engineers,
scientists, and technicians, but under-equipped laboratories; a highly
organized State, with an efficient civil service, but a lame tax-collecting
machine, some corruption, and one of the shadiest police services in any
ostensibly democratic country; a people abounding in decent human
instincts, but capable of the greatest ruthlessness in its overseas territories; a people tired of war and passionately devoted to peace, and yet
tolerating, for eight years, a costly, brutal, and senseless war to be
waged in Indo-China. A people combining a vocal feeling of inferiority
with a quiet but solidly-established sense of superiority. A puzzling
mixture of good and bad, yet not with quite enough of the "good" to
make France a thoroughly efficient modern State. And when a man
like Mendès-France shows too much reformist zeal, he thereby treads
on too many toes, and Parliament prefers to get rid of him.

Apart from the dainty and whimsical "Letters from Paris" in our
better-class journals—Letters full of French words in italics, and dealing

chiefly with the artistic, touristic, gastronomic, wine-sipping, and *haute-couture* topics of Eternal France—neither the British nor the American press has, on the whole, been very kind or very understanding to the France of the last ten years.

Some journals have, indeed, been extremely unkind to the France which is a member of the Atlantic Alliance, a member of the Free World, and one of the Big Four (albeit the smallest of the Four); and have even, on occasion, described her (*a*) as a dame extracting on false pretences no end of billion-dollar bills from her sugar-daddy, and (*b*) after a rapid change of sex, as the Sick Man of Europe.

Even in many of the more sober comments France is still (apart from hungry Italy) the country of the Free World where one person in four votes Communist, where many things are still in a chronic economic, financial, and political mess; where Parliament is frivolous, irresponsible, and even "unrepresentative of the French people" (Mr Attlee *dixit*), and composed, in Sir Winston Churchill's phrase, of so many "vehement and self-centred groups". In the eyes of the British and American publics, it is a place where "governments change all the time", and whose ministers are so many "dear little men", who cannot usually be taken seriously at all. Who, indeed, is a mere Monsieur Laniel to expect to travel in the same car at Bermuda as Churchill and Eisenhower?

This book is not an apologia for the France of the last fifteen years. It is merely an attempt to explain how French minds—all kinds of French minds—work, and what are the deep psychological and historical reasons which have made France, at least until very recently, such an "unsatisfactory" partner in the Free World community.

I know only too well that in the State Department, at the Foreign Office, in British and American universities and newspaper offices, there is a very common view, recently expressed to me by a well-known professor, that what is really wrong with France is that, since the War, she has "failed to find her place in the world". The said professor was generally petulant about "French intellectuals" and "the chaps on the *Monde*" whose influence, during the last ten years, he declared to have been "disastrous". What he meant was that France, as a relatively weak Power, would have done better to have toed the Washington line from the start, instead of striking "pretentiously independent" attitudes and constantly trying to put little spokes in America's wheels. Which, in the end, he said, would only mean that Adenauer's Germany, and not France, would become America's Number One partner on the Continent of Europe.

"True, only too true," I hastened to agree; but ventured, none the less, to suggest that there were perhaps a few profound psychological and historical reasons why France had her own point of view on so many things, and why she had not behaved quite as well as she should have done. Some of these reasons, indeed, go a long way back.

In *La Mort dans l'âme*, the third—and best—volume of Jean-Paul Sartre's *Les chemins de la liberté*, there is the unforgettable description of a French army unit at the height of the *débâcle* of June 1940—an army unit isolated from the rest of the scattered French forces, and preparing either to surrender to the Germans—who might arrive in this village somewhere in Central France at any moment—or put up a last quixotic fight. In the end they fight; but as he looks at all the chaos and bewilderment around him, one of the French soldiers makes the following reflections:

"Odd," Mathieu thought. "Yes, quite ridiculous." He gazed into empty space and said to himself: "I am French." And for the first time in his life he thought it was an absurd idea. *Oui, c'est marrant* . . . "France—we had never seen France.

"We were right *in* it. . . . It was so natural to be French. It was the simplest, most economical way of feeling universal. There was nothing to explain; let the others explain—the Germans, the British, the Belgians—by what stroke of ill-luck, and through whose fault they were not quite human. . . . But now France had overturned and was lying flat on her back: a great big dislocated machine; and now we say to ourselves: 'Well, that was *it* . . .'"

Perhaps Mathieu should not have been so surprised; for ten years before Hitler's lightning invasion, the "dislocation" process of the French machine had gone on. For ten years France had lived in a state of false security behind the Maginot Line and other myths; and even after war had broken out, Daladier boasted of having been "sparing with French blood"—*avare du sang français*.

But one day the Germans broke through; and the collapse was not only a military collapse, but as Marc Bloch wrote at the time, above all a moral collapse. All the myths broke down all at once: the Maginot myth, and the myth of the invincible French Army ("Finest army in the world", Weygand had said only a year or two before, and "Thank God for the French Army", Churchill had said, time and again), and also the myth that this war would not cost many lives.

It was from the moment that France realized that she had been beaten as she had not been beaten before, that the French feverishly began to look for their "place in the world". The first thought was that, strange as it might feel to be "a Frenchman", it was inconceivable that France would die and vanish. *Vernichten*—why! even Hitler could not have *meant* that. And, indeed, the Armistice terms showed, thank God, that he hadn't meant it.

In the circumstances, France's instinct of self-preservation, combined with infinite weariness and a feeling of physical inferiority, proved very strong. But it is probably true to say that just as France had never physically and, indeed, mentally recovered from the first world war by the time World War II began, so she has not fully recovered to this day from the moral shock of 1940, and has tended to be excessively cautious and distrustful of everybody and everything. If the Maginot Line proved a snare and a delusion, it was natural that France should be extremely cautious before placing her faith in anything else—whether it be integration in Hitler's Europe, or integration in the Atlantic Pact, in EDC, or any other alliances.

After the *débâcle* of 1940, everybody in France started looking for France's "place in the world". One does not often see Englishmen brooding over "the destiny of England"; but the Frenchman often broods over "the future of France" and her "place in the world". It is partly because in 1940 France felt so very near annihilation.

Just a little over twenty years before, she had, as a military Power, done as much as could have been expected of any nation; nearly 1,500,000 Frenchmen had died, and long lists of names were engraved in gold letters, that had not yet grown dim, on the war memorials of every town and village. It had all made France sick at the thought of fighting another major war. And, looking back on 1939 after the *débâcle*, there were many who thought that this second world war should never have been fought at all. The conditions for fighting it were far worse than they had been in 1914. Then France had powerful allies; in 1939 her only allies were Britain and Poland; Poland, whom France and Britain could or would do nothing to help, had been wiped out in three weeks; and Britain had few troops on the Continent; and then there was Dunkirk, and France was left alone, face-to-face with what was truly the mightiest army in the world. There had been bad, wicked miscalculations all round. . . .

What *could* happen to France now? Some—and not all of these were "traitors"—thought that her place might well have to be inside an integrated Nazi Europe—*enfin, tant pis!*—others thought that passive resistance, which would still save the "soul" of France, would be the best policy; at least a semblance of independence should be preserved: hence the myth of Pétain and the *Etat Français*. It is true that, internally, Vichy represented a *coup d'état*, and the seizure of power by a new team of men who were cashing in on the defeat of France and of the Republic; but at its best, it also represented the "double game", an attempt to hold out, to "limit the damage", to avoid that "polonization" of France that Pétain dreaded above all things.

And one of the most skilful psychological operations was to make France, at the depth of her national and military humiliation, "feel good", and to paint in large tricolour letters the word VERDUN over the picture of defeat and disaster, and to embark on an orgy of flag-waving and self-glorification.

No doubt, most of all this was bogus, but a large part of France was delighted to indulge in this self-deception, to clutch to this straw of national pride—and hope for the best. Even if, as seemed only too likely at the time, Hitler were to win the war, some kind of France would somehow survive. Even this was a happy thought to many, compared with the nightmares of the invasion days.

But soon it became clear that Germany had not yet won the war. And the French began, on the quiet, to mock the Germans, and to look to England—that England which so few Frenchmen had ever loved.

Anglais, Anglais, hommes anglais [wrote Bernanos from Rio in December 1940] ... Nous autres, Français, nous ne nous sommes malheureusement jamais donné beaucoup de mal pour comprendre les Anglais, que nos ancêtres du XVᵉ siècle appelaient "Godons" et qu'ils huaient au cri populaire de "A la queue! A la queue!" parce qu'ils les soupçonnaient de dissimuler dans leur culotte, en punition de leurs pêchés, cet appendice diabolique ...

But now—

Hommes anglais! vous écrivez en ce moment une des plus grandes pages de l'Histoire, c'est vous qui l'écrivez, Anglais, mais c'est sûrement pour les enfants que vous avez commencé d'écrire: *"Il était une fois une petite île, un grand peuple seul contre tous ..."*[1]

And then began the Resistance, slowly, very slowly; but if, at first not many French hands resisted, nearly all French hearts did, because it was no longer necessary to assume that Hitler had won the war. It was possible now to assume that France would have a better place in the world than merely that of a German satellite. It is only fair to say that the Resistance began in a small way even when Hitler's victory seemed certain—and not only around de Gaulle in London, but even inside France. But those first-hour resisters were still only a handful of men.

Then Russia came into the war and the Communists became increasingly active in the Resistance, and what also stimulated Resistance was the urge to evade deportation to Germany under the Compulsory Labour Service.

Eventually, the Resistance became the political force which tried to lay the political and philosophical foundations of the future Fourth Republic; the word *Revolution* was in the air, and de Gaulle himself uttered it, though perhaps without knowing what it meant.

[1] Georges Bernanos, *Lettre aux Anglais* (Paris, 1946), p. 18.

Two phenomena emerge very clearly from an examination of what is called in this book "the de Gaulle Period and the lost battle for a New France".

One is the extraordinary parallelism between French internal developments and the international situation. "Unanimity"—or *tripartisme*, as it was later called—was based on the assumption that a peaceful and, indeed, friendly co-existence between East and West would continue indefinitely; and for rather longer than international developments justified, the Communists were convinced—or tried to convince themselves—that they would continue, for years to come, to be a constructive and dynamic government party, alongside the Socialists and the MRP—and, no doubt, in due course gain wider and wider control of France. Yet the Cold War, which began with the Hiroshima Bomb and was, as it were, officially confirmed by Churchill's Fulton speech in March 1946 (as well as the Indo-China War which broke out at the end of 1946), made this "peaceful co-existence" on the Government level in France increasingly difficult. Even so, the myth of East-West unity was maintained longer inside France than in the international field. One reason for this was that it was socially and economically *advantageous* for de Gaulle, and then for the MRP and the Socialists to keep the Communists in the Government as long as necessary. But by 1947 it became internationally impossible to keep up the pretence of "unity", whatever its internal advantages. This strange and highly significant episode will be explained in some detail in Part III.

The other phenomenon demonstrated during these years was the widespread French dislike of Revolution. In a selection of the writings and speeches of Saint-Just, published in 1947, Jean Cassou (at that time still very close to the Communists) wrote a significant introduction, in which, after referring to Marat and Saint-Just as "the titans of the French Revolution", he said:

The truth is that the French Revolution has not been completed. Robespierre, Marat and Saint-Just will not be integrated in our national consciousness until the work they undertook has been done. In the history of our country there has been, since 1794, a long period of waiting and suspense, and the men who were defeated in 1794 are still waiting on the threshold of unanimous recognition.... Despite their genius, the French Revolution, *their* French Revolution stopped half-way.... Instead of developing into what they wanted, it became Thermidor and Napoleon.... The bourgeoisie, those who acquired the *biens nationaux*, the *Thermidoriens*, the financiers of the Directoire, the *fonctionnaires* of the Empire—these are the men who are still the masters of our destiny.[2]

What then was France's place in the world? De Gaulle had one

[2] Saint-Just. *Pages choisies. Introduction par Jean Cassou* (Paris, 1947), pp. I–II.

obsession: *grandeur française*; France should, at any price, be included among the Great Powers; she could, he thought, achieve this only if she steered an even course between East and West. This policy failed completely—it failed even long before the breakdown of *tripartisme*.

And then, with the Cold War increasing in violence, France became, willy-nilly, part of the Western *bloc*, a member, first, of the Brussels Pact, then of the Atlantic Pact, and, finally, after the rejection of EDC, of West-European Union, complete with a rearmed Germany.

But between the Brussels Pact and the final ratification of German rearmament, *no less than seven years* were to elapse, and *nearly five* since the United States first officially demanded that Germany be rearmed.

Numerous episodes in this book are concerned with this resistance, ca'canny, hesitation, obstruction, sabotage, and disloyalty—to quote only a few of the unflattering words used in Britain and America to describe France's profound reluctance to take a step which, she was deeply convinced, would immensely increase international tension, and might even—as was the case especially between 1950 and 1952—precipitate World War III.

As in the days of Pétain, a "double game"—of a slightly different kind—was now being played. The governments, always in need of dollars, paid lip-service to EDC (if any, like Schuman and Bidault, believed in it, it was chiefly because it seemed to them a lesser evil than straightforward German rearmament). And if finally, after many years' haggling, France finally capitulated under overwhelming British and American pressure, it was with the consoling thought at the back of her mind that the major danger arising from German rearmament had now passed; that it no longer mattered as much as it did in 1950–52, and that *la question est dépassée*. With H-bombs on both sides of the "curtain", what did 12, or even 20 or 30 German divisions matter! They might, of course, matter; but it was now less likely that they would; for Germany was as scared of H-bombs as any other country, and perhaps even more so; and there was now at least a chance that Churchill might prove right when, only a few days before the final French ratification of the Paris agreements, he said in the House of Commons:

It might well be that, by a process of sublime irony, we shall have reached a stage in this story where safety will be the sturdy child of terror and survival the twin brother of annihilation.[3]

Why had France hesitated so long? Again, the question of her "place

[3] *The Times*, March 2, 1955.

in the world" arose with particular sharpness. No doubt, Marshall Aid and dollars for reconstruction, and dollars for rearmament, and dollars for Indo-China had turned her into a satellite—but only a reluctant satellite, and, at times, a resentful and rebellious one. Dollars were all very well; but there was not only a deep distaste for German rearmament (a distaste which, it was so often said, neither America nor even England, which had never been occupied, was capable of sharing), but also a deep conviction that this rearmament was not necessary, since the Russians, threatened with atomic reprisals, were extremely unlikely to attack Western Europe. If, on the other hand, German rearmament was carried out, certain American Generals might well want to use the German army as a spearhead in their Roll-Back policy. People as responsible as Eisenhower were already talking in 1951 of an early "showdown". The end of 1951 was the time when France fathomed the depths of gloom—a feeling which provoked that "revolt of Europe", so significant a development during the following year.

All this caused strong anti-American currents in France, currents by no means confined to the Communists, with their *US GO HOME* scribbles. The "non-conformist" press, with the *Monde* at its head, and practically the whole of the French intellectual élite, were, in a sense, "anti-American". This word should not, however, be misunderstood: they were highly critical of American policy, and dreaded certain "crazy" people like Carney, Radford and MacArthur. At the same time, they admired America, and were impressed by the tremendous vigour of American economic power, and if the French brewers and *apéritif* manufacturers hated Coca Cola (more, indeed, than the public did), and the intellectuals squirmed at the thought of a million copies of *Reader's Digest* being sold in France, these intellectuals nevertheless took Faulkner and Hemingway more seriously than any modern British writer.

With Britain relations were difficult, too. A large part of France had loved England during the war. But when Britain—which was not even paying the dollars—was sending reminders to France, demanding that she ratify EDC—which "was good enough for Paris, but not for London" (as de Gaulle put it)—it caused anger. Many Frenchmen on both Right and Left started remembering all sorts of unpleasant things about British policy *vis-à-vis* France between the two wars: the British hysteria over "French militarism" and "French hegemony" in the early 'twenties; the abortive British "guarantee" on the Rhine; the disastrous effect on all British—and German—political thinking of Keynes's *Economic Consequences of the Peace*, the British build-up of Germany right up to the time of Hitler; Philip Snowden's description of the good M. Henry Chéron, Poincaré's hugely fat Finance Minister as *grotesque et ridicule* (for the French take it very badly even when their most absurd-looking representatives are called names by foreigners; *cf.* Bevin's description of Bidault as "the dear little man", or Churchill's ill-treatment of Laniel at Bermuda); and then Britain's refusal to do anything about Hitler's occupation of the Rhineland in 1936, and the Anglo-German Naval Agreement signed behind France's back; and so on, and so on, right on to the "desertion" at Dunkirk and the sinking of a large part of the French navy at Mers-el-Kébir in July 1940. . . .

All these bad memories were mingled with a secret feeling of envy. Britain had come out of World War II as a more obviously "Great Power" than France. Also, it was reluctantly admitted that Britain had, since then, handled her home affairs better than France, and had been wise in India and Burma, while France had been wickedly foolish in Indo-China. No doubt, Kenya, Cyprus, and Malaya were a mess—but it was (at least for the time being) a smaller mess than North Africa.

And then there was another thing: the French Socialists and many of the MRP—all those people who sincerely believed, or tried to believe in "Europe"—had hopefully looked to the British Labour Government. But the British Labour Government—whom the French Socialists, like poor relations, adored from afar—was too busy with the Welfare State, and other home problems, and India and Burma, and had, anyway, a passionate dislike for supra-national schemes and any "mucking about" with national sovereignty, as Ernest Bevin used to say. Moreover, Bevin obviously shared the dislike felt by the "common man" in England for the French. They had put up such a miserable show in 1940, whereas England, only a few months later, showed the world how *she* could "take it". That the two situations weren't in the least comparable didn't matter. All this is sad, but true.

Also, there was disappointment, especially among the French Socialists, over the "insularity" of British Labour, and its failure to put up any sort of fight for the socialization of Germany. As a result, the German Socialists declined, and soon the road was clear for an American-blessed Free-Enterprise Germany, complete with Adenauer and the Big Bosses of the Schwerindustrie in charge.

These strange, and often strained relations between France and Britain on the one hand, and between France and America on the other cannot be ignored in any account of the French seven-year "resistance". To this day, this mutual misunderstanding continues.

It may be objected that many Frenchmen were much more wholehearted than the above suggests to the Atlantic Pact, to EDC, to German rearmament even. This, in a limited sense, is true; but the whole tortuous course pursued by the French governments between 1949 and

1955 shows that, whatever their private preferences, they constantly had to reckon not only with critical intellectual groups, a critical press, but also with an equally anxious and critical opinion in Parliament and in the country. The Oradour Trial, and all sorts of other things, seemingly irrelevant to non-Frenchmen, came into it. To the French generally, as all the delays and "sabotage" of those years shows, the American alliance had its uses, but it also carried with it, especially at certain times, very serious dangers to France's security.

On at least one occasion—in December 1950, when Attlee flew to Washington to stop MacArthur from running wild in Korea—the French had the comforting feeling that perhaps Britain's attitude was not fundamentally as different from France's as appeared on the surface. For if France "sabotaged" the roll-back policy in Europe, had not Britain consistently done the same for many years in the Far East? But this tacit solidarity was seldom explicit.

"The history of a nation", it has been said, "is a history of its ideas; and a nation without ideas has no history." What makes French history fascinating—whether 200, 20, or even 10 or 5 years ago—is that the country is, more than any other, in a constant ferment of ideas. Maurrasism, Liberalism, Socialism, Communism, Burnhamism, Existentialism, and the numerous schools of Catholic thought are so many centres of hard—if not necessarily good—thinking, which have all produced a rich crop of writing and discussion under the impact of the world events of the last 15 years. Nearly all the best French writers —all the way from Mauriac and Malraux to Sartre, Camus, Aragon and Eluard—have been *engagés* and have played an active and influential rôle in the political life of the country. It is scarcely conceivable that the controversies over North Africa, for instance, could have assumed such vast proportions without the influence of Mauriac and of journals like *Esprit, Temps Modernes, Témoignage Chrétien*, or *France-Observateur*, journals with practically no equivalent outside France for profound political analysis, courage, and genuine knowledge.

Yet, alongside all this great intelligence, there was also a mass of monumental stupidity, which was hard to cope with. Thus, since 1946, France had been made to spend a substantial proportion of her resources on reconquering a colony over 8,000 miles away. How was this possible? Originally, it was merely a case of de Gaulle and his followers reasserting the existence of France as a Great Power; if, "through the fault of the British", she lost Syria, she was not going to lose Indo-China at any price. Lightheartedly, she embarked on a "little war" of colonial reconquest; at first it was meant to look as merely a major "police operation". And then, as the years passed, and more and more people found the war in Indo-China profitable, France was drawn deeper and deeper into the bog, till she finally found herself involved in what was a major war against World Communism.

If the war was not stopped earlier, it was chiefly because no conscripts were used in Indo-China, which was far away; and the war did not cost very much at first—and so few people cared sufficiently one way or the other. They did not at the time realize that the war in Indo-China was crippling France's own economy more and more and was seriously reducing her weight in Europe, and, above all perhaps, preventing North Africa, as M. François Mitterrand put it in a remarkable book published in 1953, from being turned into "another California", as it so easily might have been, if even a minor part of the 3,000 milliard francs spent on the Indo-China War had been spent on improving economic conditions in Algeria, Tunisia, and Morocco. How much easier it would be today to handle a prosperous and contented North Africa, without a starving surplus population, as in Algeria, and without the hate-breeding *bidonvilles* of Algiers and Casablanca!

Subjects like Indo-China and North Africa frequently come within range of the discussions on France's "place in the world", for the question whether there is, or is not to be, a French Empire in coming years is relevant to the question of whether France will, or not, keep her place in the front rank of the Powers. Even nominally.

It was a mistaken sense of *grandeur* that made the French embark on a reconquest of Indo-China in 1945; and it is the miserly dread of being robbed of their treasures that makes the diehards to this day adopt methods which may, before very long, lead to the loss of North Africa. Short of exterminating a large part of the population (not a purely theoretical hypothesis, for such methods have been used before, notably in Madagascar), it is hard to see how France can keep North Africa without embarking on an imaginative, statesman-like series of sweeping economic reforms and major political concessions. In the next few years North Africa is, in any case, likely to be France's Number One problem.

Or is it too late, especially after what happened in Morocco in the latter half of 1955, to do anything more about it? Will France have to resign herself to losing North Africa? The question is discussed towards the end of this book.

The main theme of this book is France's place in the world, and all the political controversies and discussions that have, directly or indirectly, been connected with this question. I have avoided detailed economic discussions, but since a country's weight in the world is largely determined by economic factors, and since its weight also largely determines its place, I have dealt with questions like the standard of living, wages, and social conditions in so far as they appeared relevant to the main subject of the book.

Thus, the strength of the Communist Party in France has, in some measure, been due to the existence of certain revolutionary traditions in France (traditions singularly weak in Britain and the USA), but also due to the insufficient determination on the part of the bourgeoisie (as has so often been remarked) to "include the proletariat in the national community". As Pierre-Henri Simon wrote in the *Monde* on June 30, 1955:

Without going into all the details of the tendentious and contradictory statistics, and while granting that the signs of "pauperization" are somewhat less obvious in 1955 than they were in 1953, the fact remains that in the last fifteen years the economic conditions among wage-earners *as a whole*, have not improved, and have remained slightly below, rather than slightly above, the 1938 level, despite longer working-hours. On the other hand, during the same period, the index of productivity has increased, and the capitalists have, though not necessarily by increasing dividends, nevertheless greatly increased the capital value of their holdings. It's no use quarrelling over statistics and the arguments for and against including social insurance benefits in "wages"; it is just enough to look around to realize that the economic improvements in France since the war have greatly benefited such elements in the bourgeoisie as industrialists, engineers, top-ranking technicians, bankers, and even part of the liberal professions; here there has been a spectacular increase in luxury living. On the other hand, the *petite bourgeoisie* of employees and government officials, as well as the working-class have been barely maintaining themselves along a horizontal line of well-being.

It seemed, around 1945, that the capitalist order in Europe was crumbling; yet time was to show that, in reality, capitalism was coming into its own again; ten years later it was in a stronger position than it had been for over a quarter of a century. And parliamentary institutions, if anything, had helped capitalism to place at the head of France, Belgium, Germany, Italy, Holland, and the UK either plainly conservative or cautiously reformist governments.

One of the great questions in France today is whether a generous reformist policy can defeat the revolutionary instincts of the French working-class, or whether the bourgeoisie will be sufficiently short-sighted to play into the hands of those Communist leaders who believe in "everything or nothing", and who have denounced reformism as a dangerous heresy, calculated to paralyse the vigilance of the working-class.

In short, the problem of a satisfactory *modus vivendi* between capital and labour, as we see it today—at least in many cases—in the USA,

Britain and even Germany, has not yet been solved in France. In 1954 more than one-half of all wages in France were still below 30,000 frs. a month.

There is, however, another point with a direct bearing on the future of the French Communists and the French working-class generally. Nineteen fifty-five marks the end of an epoch in more ways than one. The Cold War suddenly developed into a Cold Peace, and never in all her history had Soviet Russia seemed less revolutionary and, consequently, less inspiring to foreign Communists, than in 1955. What, in the circumstances, is to be the national and international position of the French Communists and of the working-class movement? It is one of the great question-marks of the next few years. Or is this Soviet "tameness" only temporary?

Parliamentary parties have been dealt with in this book, mostly, though not entirely, with reference to international and colonial affairs. To illustrate their attitudes to this or that home or foreign problem, I have not hesitated to quote at some length some of the more significant parliamentary debates which, I have often felt, gave one a more direct "feel" of how the French think and talk than almost anything else. I frequently used the same method in my three books on the 1930–40 period in France.[4]

On the other hand, many subjects are almost wholly outside the scope of this book: such as the Constitution and the inner workings of parliamentary institutions, which have already been fully dealt with in English by Mrs D. Pickles and Mr Philip Williams; or even more specialized subjects like the Administration, local government, social security, or special economic questions of great importance in France, like the structure of French agriculture, etc. Nor have relatively dormant questions like French Black Africa been touched upon.

Further, in discussing the various international treaties, over which the French have fought in the course of the last ten years, I did not think it necessary (or practical) to quote the actual full texts; these, when necessary, can be found in almost any reference library.

My three main sources have been: direct personal contacts and observation; newspapers and periodicals; and books. The books have been particularly useful for Part I, dealing with Vichy, the Occupation and the Resistance. The evidence on Vichy is often conflicting and contradictory, and the information on men like Pétain, Darlan, and Laval required much sifting, weighing, and comparing; in the highly

---

[4] *France in Ferment* (London, 1934); *The Destiny of France* (London, 1937) and *France and Munich: Before and After the Surrender* (London, 1939).

controversial case of Laval, in particular, I sometimes had to throw my own "instinct" into the scales, an instinct derived from a fairly close personal acquaintance with the man. I always found it hard to believe that he was consciously and deliberately evil.

Apart from talks with numerous Resistance leaders (notably my friend Claude Bourdet), who gave me a clear insight into many of the Resistance "problems" and into the Resistance "mentality", I have not done any "original research" into the innumerable little facts and events that add up to that great thing called *the Resistance*, and have simply borrowed certain facts, figures and organizational details from writers, some of whom have devoted long years of study to this highly complex episode in the recent history of France: notably Mme L. Aubrac, M. Bloch-Lainé, Mme M. Granet, and, above all, M. Henri Michel, whose book, *Histoire de la Résistance* ranks as the fairest and most accurate all-round account of the Resistance. Naturally, I have also used much Resistance literature—articles, memoirs and even "fiction"—written both during and after the war to illustrate various points. I should particularly like to draw the reader's attention to the chapter called "Post-Mortem on the Resistance", based on a collective attempt by ex-Resisters to assess the net results of the Resistance and its long-term significance.

In assessing the rôle played by the Vichy leaders, I naturally found the verbatim reports of many of the "purge" trials of particularly great value—above all, the Pétain trial, itself a gold-mine of historical information covering a wide period; but also many others, such as the trials of Laval, Benoist-Méchin (in reality this was a posthumous trial of Darlan); Pucheu, Darnand, de Brinon, Brasillach, the "radio traitors", "press traitors", and many others. Of the almost innumerable "Vichy memoirs", I found *La Chronique de Vichy*, by Maurice Martin du Gard, the representative of the *Dépêche de Toulouse* at Vichy and the book by Du Moulin de Labarthète, the head of Pétain's *cabinet civil* by far the most interesting, if not always wholly reliable. A good deal of checking and cross-checking had to be done. Of more recent studies of the more disreputable aspects of Vichy, M. M. Vanino's *De Rethondes à l'Ile d'Yeu* is of the greatest value.

As regards the immediate and early post-Liberation period, readers may be surprised to find me quoting *Combat* much more frequently than any other paper. This was quite deliberate. *Combat* represented, and expressed more brilliantly and coherently than any other paper, the hopes, anxieties, disappointment and growing frustration of the non-Communist elements in the Resistance, who had hoped and believed that a New France would really be built on the foundations laid by the CNR Charter.

During later periods—especially from 1949 on—the "stickiness" of

France was primarily represented by the *Monde*, which, in the words of a US Embassy official, was "more worrying to the State Department than the Communist Party," since it *both* guided public opinion and coherently reflected powerful currents of French public opinion in quite a remarkable degree.

No doubt it sometimes went to unnecessary extremes when, at the height of the Cold War, it embarked on its "neutralist" campaign—which was scarcely realistic; but the "delaying tactics" it preached to the French Government were welcomed by most Frenchmen, and even by many members of the Government, who were secretly in agreement with the *Monde*'s line, whatever they said to Washington. More than that, the *Monde* often provided them with welcome alibis in their pursuit of an *attentiste* post-war policy. Though in different contexts, there were still curious points of similarity between Maurras's *la France seule* and the *attentisme* and "neutralism" of the *Monde* and the left-wing intellectuals—so often wrongly accused of being mere crypto-Communists. They were, if anything, extremely French in their "reserve" *vis-à-vis* both Britain and the United States. The same, for that matter, is true of de Gaulle.

As events were, indeed, to prove, both public opinion and Parliament were extremely reluctant to take the plunge; if, finally, they took it, and agreed (with the utmost reluctance) to German rearmament, it was when it *perhaps* no longer mattered very much.

In the chapters on Indo-China and North Africa I extensively used (apart from direct observation in the case of the latter), parliamentary debates, and such valuable studies as Professor Ch. A. Julien's *L'Afrique du Nord en marche* and (for Indo-China) the writings of Paul Mus and the admirable *Histoire du Vietnam, 1940–52* by Philippe Devillers. For the murkier side of the Indo-China War I also used, apart from parliamentary debates, the records of the two parliamentary committees of inquiry, one into the *affaire des généraux*, the other into the *trafic des piastres*.

Although the preparatory work on this book was done for several years past, this book was actually written during my two years as Senior Simon Research Fellow at the University of Manchester. (A large part of this time was, of course, spent in France.)

I want to express my particular gratitude to Professor W. J. M. Mackenzie of the University of Manchester, who guided me in my labours, read most of the manuscript, and made numerous valuable suggestions and criticisms; as well as my friend Dr Brian Chapman, also of Manchester University, whose encouraging comments and bright ideas were most helpful and stimulating.

I should also like to thank my kind Manchester hosts, Mr and Mrs J. Jennens, for having so patiently put up with the litter of torn-out

Journal Officiel pages and thousands of other scraps of paper in their otherwise tidy Chorlton-cum-Hardy home, and with the clatter of the typewriter at some unholy hours of the night.

The French friends who have, directly or indirectly, helped in the production of this study of France are too many to enumerate. But I thank them all. I don't think they will find this study unfriendly to their country, where I have spent the better part of twenty-five years.

A. W.

January 1956

Part I

VICHY, OCCUPATION AND
RESISTANCE (1940–4)

FRENCH PUBLIC SENTIMENT DURING THE OCCUPATION

THE DAY Marshal Pétain, France's Providential Old Man, declared that "the fight must cease", the German war machine was still relentlessly sweeping across France, driving before it millions of refugees, including almost the entire population of Paris. The organization and the morale of the French Army were broken. Already a fortnight before, Britain had virtually abandoned the fight on the European mainland; the fabulous RAF had not come to the rescue in the hour of France's greatest need; at Tours, only a few days before, Churchill had come and gone, and Roosevelt had sent his best wishes, but no more; after which Paul Reynaud and his Government fled to the next—and final—stage. And here, at Bordeaux, in a pandemonium of cars, and of milling crowds of jumpy and angry people, and scrambles for seats in cafés and restaurants, and rumours of new German bombings and new German break-throughs—though there was, by now, little left to break—Reynaud abandoned the future destinies of France to the frail hands of the aged Marshal. And, supported by a Cabinet of fatalists, careerists, opportunists and I-told-you-so's, the Marshal asked for an armistice. There followed a period of four years which is one of the strangest and most complicated in the whole history of France.

Looking back on it, one realizes now even better than one did at the time the extreme complexity of those years. How did people behave? How did people react? Suddenly, within a few weeks, the whole of France was faced with a set of entirely new factors and situations. The simplest, and perhaps least unfamiliar thing was the German Occupation—though even this seemed, at least at first, to be different from what it had generally been expected to be. Established, not in Paris, but in the blatantly provisional, incongruous and historically meaningless setting of Vichy,[1] was not only a new government, but a new régime, claiming

---

[1] The Pétain Government first moved from Bordeaux to Clermont-Ferrand, but it was found to be inadequate as the "capital" of the unoccupied zone. Paul Baudouin, Pétain's first Foreign Minister, explained the choice of Vichy in his Diary as follows: "*June 29, 1940.* At Clermont the chaos is unimaginable. . . . For the Ministry of Foreign Affairs I was offered a half-empty private hotel containing

to represent a "National Revolution". Was this régime simply part of the German political machine in Europe? Was it a "purely French" phenomenon? Was one to accept it sincerely, or only in a spirit of opportunism? Was it, or was it not, *the* lawful government of France? Was it right to collaborate with the Germans, and if so, how much was permissible, and where did treason begin; or was it not treason at all to co-operate with Germany? Did one take part in Resistance—with a small r or a big R—against the Germans only, or against Vichy as well? Where did France stand in relation to Germany, in relation to England and—a question important to the Communists—in relation to Russia? Who was de Gaulle? Was it conceivable that France and the French Army could have continued the war in North Africa?

Apart from these questions, almost everybody was obsessed by some personal problem or tragedy, like sons or husbands killed or taken prisoner; in many cases there was the question of whether to return to the Occupied Zone or not; and, last but not least, *how* was one to live? Not all these issues presented themselves to the French people all at once. Yet as they emerged one by one, all these issues, all so new and bewildering, wove themselves into a baffling new pattern of unforeseen, or almost unforeseen conflicts, dilemmas and new ways of thinking.

Few things are more difficult to decipher than the minds of Frenchmen during the 1940-4 period. In almost every utterance of those years one can suspect mental reservations and genuine or artificial alibis of one kind or another; the all-out Vichyite did not necessarily exclude an early end of Vichy, and the Gaullist may at heart have felt that Vichy was serving a useful international purpose, however offensive its home policy. There were anti-Vichyites with a soft spot for Pétain. Even in the active Resistance there were men with pure motives, and others with impure and selfish motives. To use Péguy's famous distinction, the Resistance in its later stages tended to turn from *mystique* into *politique*. There were the profiteers of Vichy and the profiteers of the Occupation and the Black Market; and there were

seven rooms in all, and without electricity or a telephone. . . . It is impossible to concentrate the government at Clermont-Ferrand, which is too small and too encumbered with refugees. . . . I told the Marshal why I thought the move to Clermont seemed to me a mistake. He replied that he realized that, but the responsibility rested with Laval who for several days had been pressing for the establishment of the government at Clermont where were his newspaper, his printing works and a good many of his interests. I told the Marshal that only . . . Lyon was possible, where the government would not be isolated. The Marshal bluntly refused, for he did not wish to come into contact with M. Herriot, the Mayor of Lyon. As his refusal seemed to me final, I suggested Vichy, where the big hotels would enable us to establish ourselves comfortably. The Marshal agreed with this proposal." *The Private Diaries of Paul Baudouin* (London, 1948), p. 153.

millions of "ordinary" people who simply "waited"—hoping passively for a Liberation which, pray God, would be as quick and painless as possible. There were those young people who, while the fighting was going on in the Boulevard St Michel and around the Préfecture de Police during the Liberation of Paris, were quietly bathing and sunbathing alongside the Pont St Michel—as related by Dansette in his *Histoire de la Libération de Paris*. Or, to quote an even more blatant example of this kind of *attentisme*: the French couple living in the expensive Parc Monceau area of Paris who, when asked what they had been doing during the street fighting in Paris, said: "We spent all those days with friends across the street playing bridge." Also remarks like this are not uncommon: "Of course I was in the Resistance." "How do you mean?" "Well, I was consistently anti-German." The remark is, in reality, not as silly as it sounds. One of the main purposes of the active Resistance—indeed, for a long time, its principal purpose—was precisely to create a mood of passive resistance throughout the country; the very fact of *being* anti-German was, in a sense, a contribution to the Resistance effort. The fact that virtually the whole of France was, at least in this very limited sense, "anti-German" was important in itself.

Apart from those mental reservations in which France abounded during those years, there are some other difficulties in the way of deciphering the working of French minds under Vichy and the Occupation. Quite inevitably, many people saw things in 1940 or 1941 or even in 1942 in a perspective that was different from the perspective in which they saw the same things in 1944 or later. Under the effect of the shock of June 1940 Hitler must have seemed to many a giant and a superman; England must have seemed very, very small and vulnerable, and Russia and America on a different planet. Certain fatalist reflections during that period by André Gide, for instance, on the invincibility of Germany and on the indifference to it all of the French peasants as long as they went on making money are no doubt an extreme example of a fairly widespread defeatist mood in France soon after the collapse; yet among certain intellectuals the desire to look at the disaster *sub specie aeternitatis*, to recall the absorption of the Franks by the Gauls, and to argue that it might work out very well in the end this time too, was a fairly common reaction. "No doubt Gide would like freedom", wrote one of his intimates, Roger Stéphane, in his wartime diary (December 10, 1940);

but would not freedom today, he wonders, simply mean disorder? He would like France to revive; but he does not believe in such a revival; politically, he says, France is destined to be *protected*, either by Germany— or by the Anglo-Saxons. But after the victory of either of them, will not all the problems still be left unsettled? On the other hand, Gide continues to be impressed by the grandiose dimensions of the Hitler Plan. And will not

Hitler, he wonders, having won all along the line, suddenly become transformed into Augustus, a prisoner of his own greatness and of the grandeur of his mission?[2]

Small wonder that Gide was not very warmly received when he turned up at Algiers in 1943 as a belated "Gaullist"! And there were those who followed Maurras in welcoming the military *débâcle* as a "divine surprise",[3] as the inevitable prerequisite to the "National Revolution", which would sweep away the last cobwebs of the Popular Front and of parliamentary democracy. There were also plenty of people who "accepted" Vichy either for personal gain (thus, it was very easy for certain ambitious young men to attain ministerial rank in Vichy without having first climbed the tall parliamentary ladder), or for the benefits it conferred on their class or age-group; or as a skilful political expedient that would "limit the damage", or even purely emotionally—Pétain representing, in the days of national catastrophe, the badly needed "father symbol". Finally, Vichy represented, in the minds of practically all government officials, *the* government and the continuity of the French State. It is significant, for example, that only *one* French judge should have refused Pétain his oath of allegiance.[4]

Lastly, the period from 1940 to 1944 is difficult to disentangle because, in the years after the Liberation, a vast mythology was built round it—a mythology partly derived from the earlier Resistance and BBC propaganda and partly from the desire to interpret actions, not in the light of contemporary conditions, but in the light of what these actions *should* have been in terms of the patriotic principles of 1944. If Maurras saw the France of 1940–1 out of focus, many of those who looked back on the same period, after the lapse of a few years, also made it appear different from what it was at the time. People who had lacked foresight, were now credited with foresight; many Vichyites were now crediting themselves with motives which were made to look much purer in retrospect than they had been in reality; here the most was made of more or less artificial alibis; for political reasons relating almost entirely to the aims of the RPF in 1949, de Gaulle was, at that time, to give a very different interpretation of Vichy from that which he had given it in 1940 or 1941. Retrospectively, as seen through the pages of Aragon's *Les Communistes*, the behaviour of the Communists

---

[2] Roger Stéphane, *Chaque homme est lié au monde* (Paris, 1946), pp. 94–5.

[3] Maurras later argued that by "divine surprise" he had not meant the military defeat, but the "gift" that Pétain had made to France—namely, that of his own person.

[4] There was much discussion after the Liberation on the validity of this "compulsory" oath of allegiance. Some of those who, for reasons of their own, now treated it lightly, liked to recall certain officials in the past who had sworn allegiance between say, 1812 and 1853, to several régimes in succession.

in 1939–40 was more consistent, clear-sighted, and more impeccably patriotic than it appeared at the time; according to him, they had shown a far shrewder understanding of the Soviet-German Pact than they had really done; for in 1939 the Pact had thrown most of them into a state of the greatest confusion.

The rôle played by the Resistance was, for political reasons, immensely magnified in 1944 and stupidly "debunked" a few years later, when the Vichyite Right began to treat the FFI as though they had been merely an army of cut-throats. The "myth" of the Liberation of Paris solely *by* the people of Paris was severely dealt with as early as 1946 by the revelations concerning General von Choltitz, who just did not want an all-out fight; another "myth" was the solid unity of the Resistance movement, as embodied by the CNR (*Conseil National de la Résistance*) which, for international reasons, and in order to make it easier for de Gaulle to show the Allies that a united France stood behind him, and so to obtain recognition for his government, was made to include M. Laniel and a few others who had not been outstandingly active in the Resistance, and who were wholly out of sympathy with the social and economic "revolution" provided by the CNR Charter.

Similarly, there are innumerable instances of men interpreting their past behaviour in a doubtful and tendentious manner. The example of M. Herriot's ambiguous behaviour at Vichy in July 1940 and of his final flirtation with Laval only a few days before the Liberation of Paris, is a striking case of the "half-acceptance" of Vichy by many of the leaders of the Third Republic—an attitude which they later did their best to gloss over.

Indeed, about the only people in France on whom there were no two opinions, and who themselves scarcely made any attempt to justify themselves, were the all-out *collabos* and traitors—the French Gestapo men, for instance, or the people who, for purely mercenary reasons, or, in a few rare cases, because of a fanatical belief in Hitler, staked everything on the German horse. A few, like Drieu La Rochelle, committed suicide; many of the others fled to Germany under the contemptuous protection of the German army. These included men like Doriot, the ex-Communist leader, who had now become a Nazi and who proudly wore his SS uniform; plain careerists and money-makers like the ex-Socialist Marcel Déat, editor of the Paris *Œuvre*; "Ambassador" Brinon; Hérold-Paquis, the head of the German-controlled radio in Paris; and Jean Luchaire, the head of the *collabo* press in Paris, as well as his film-star daughter, Corinne, for whom Paris under the Germans had been just one continuous round of champagne parties, receptions at the German Embassy, and German dinner parties *chez Maxim's*. This "Paris group", which, for the most part, was, indeed, thoroughly disreputable was, at all events, a convenient scapegoat for the Vichyites, many of whom also tended, in order to demonstrate their own greater purity, to identify Pierre Laval with this group.

And, of course, the biggest "myth" of all was that the Resistance leaders had come, once and for all, to replace the Vichyites and the men of the Third Republic, and that a new France, totally unlike the Third Republic, would rise from the ruins. But, for one thing—and this perhaps explains a great deal—the ruins were not as extensive as they might have been. The human losses were about three times smaller than in the 1914–18 war, and although the total destruction of property was greater than in 1914–18 (chiefly by Allied bombing) it was more widely spread out and captured the imagination less than names like Reims, Arras, and Verdun (after all, the mass destruction of cities was still very *new* in 1914); and neither Paris, nor any other major city (except Caen, Brest and Le Havre) had been destroyed or even half-destroyed. It was possible to "return to normal" without resorting to ultra-heroic methods.

This, indeed, made it easier in a few short years, to return to a "normality" that was, on the face of it, not unlike the normality of the Third Republic.

One of the most interesting questions—though one particularly difficult to answer for the reasons enumerated above (mental reservations, changed perspectives, distorted vision, "myths", and the rewriting of history and the distortion of facts by *both* Left and Right, sometimes in a manner that would make both Trotsky and Stalin green with envy) —is what *the state of French public opinion really was during the Occupation and the Vichy régime*. There were, of course, no proper opinion polls; and "public opinion" and "public sentiment" are very broad terms; they cover groups comprising people who could not possibly have felt about everything in the same way. Yet there are still at times some clear indications of not only how this or that section of the public felt, but also of how the majority of opinion felt, even in conditions when the greatest caution in expressing one's feelings was advisable. The sources of information are numerous, but the more valuable ones are relatively scarce. Much of what was written *after* the Liberation is of little value; on the other hand, Resistance literature published *during* the Occupation is too full of wishful thinking and propaganda. It is more valuable, therefore, to look for *admissions*—however cautious— made by pro-Germans and pro-Vichyites that not all was well.

In this respect one of the most valuable sources is the *Journal de la France* by Alfred Fabre-Luce, known before the war for his determined advocacy of Franco-German collaboration, his belief in the greatness of Hitler, and his rapturous approval of Munich. In 1940–1 he was an all-out collaborationist rather than a Vichyite, and he openly accused the anti-Laval clans at Vichy of consciously sabotaging the rapid and highly profitable integration of France in Hitler's Europe.

Volume I of his "diary"—it is not so much a diary as a periodical survey of currents of opinion in France between 1939 and 1942—published in Paris in January 1941, actually ends triumphantly with a description of France in July 1940, after the setting up of the Vichy régime. He is frantic with delight at Hitler's victory, which, he argues, is something for France's ultimate good. A large part of the book is concerned with ridiculing and denouncing those who rushed France into the war against Nazi Germany; and this would not have happened but for what Drieu La Rochelle had described to him as "the tragic failure of French Fascism" in 1934–5.[5] What kind of country was it, he gloated, with a constantly falling birth-rate, with minds which were all fuddled with drink, with an army where, during the "phoney war" in Lorraine, soldiers were mutilating themselves and committing suicide—what kind of country was it to stand up to Hitler's Germany? "This military France of 1939 was like a nation of ghosts." (*Ibid.*, pp. 193–4.)

And if Daladier was its leader during those months, he seemed to embody the country's feeling of resignation and despair ... In newsreels he always looked like the chief mourner of his own country's funeral.

Anti-Germanism, Fabre-Luce said, was "the biggest racket of our time". And now Germany had won, and, before very long, England would give up the "hopeless struggle". Her latest blunder was Mers-el-Kebir.

Now the quarrel between France and England is final and complete. In one day England killed more French sailors than Germany did during the whole war. It aroused in the hearts of the French old hatreds and grievances—Joan of Arc, Fashoda ... Less than three weeks after the Armistice a thirty years' alliance was broken. The physical solidarity of the European continent had proved stronger. Inexorably, Europe is rapidly coming into being. (*Ibid.*, p. 361.)

There followed sneers at

de Gaulle, Reynaud's under-secretary, telling us through the Daventry microphone that he was the "leader of all the Free French" and inviting his countrymen to join in an international brigade, now in England's service, the wreckage of all the defeated armies of recent years.

Analysing the mood of 1940, Fabre-Luce wrote:

There are some who say of Pétain: "Here is our Hindenburg. But where is our Hitler?" True—France has made a revolution without revolution-

---

[5] Alfred Fabre-Luce, *Journal de la France*, vol. I (Paris, January 1941), p. 216.

aries. Universal suffrage has been scrapped. The secret societies have been dissolved. Men in responsible positions may be punished or dismissed. Strikes have been prohibited. Education has become French. Laws have a new opening sentence *"Nous, Maréchal de France, chef de l'Etat Français"* ... But what we still lack is a new *élite*. In Germany the struggle for power brought the new *élite* to the surface. Our institutions, on the other hand, were totally reformed overnight by a parliamentary vote of 569 men, stunned by the country's defeat. This short cut does not mean that we need not make a greater effort.... We've got the framework. Now is the time to organize France, and put new life and substance into her. It is from this great task that the leaders of the future will emerge.

They talk of *national revolution*.... But is it not, above all, a *world revolution* that is on the march? A world revolution, of which France forms an important part. It is not for her to give orders any more, but to collaborate, to inspire herself [by the example of Germany] and, above all, to *be*. Here, on the threshold of the new world, one is filled with a feeling of reverent awe. (*Ibid.*, pp. 403–4.)

To Fabre-Luce, clearly, the "national revolution", as seen by Pétain and Maurras, was nonsense. There could be no *"France seule"*. Vichy —or rather France—made little sense except as part of a vast Nazi world. To him, in July 1940, the victory of this Nazi Europe was not in doubt.

But look at Volume II, written in part at the end of 1940, and in part during 1941 and the early months of 1942. How the whole tone changes! Neither the French people, nor even Vichy, for that matter, were ready to follow the sublime and inspiring course pointed out to them in the apotheosis of the last pages of Fabre-Luce's first volume.

The sequence of events, as described by this collaborator, or "European", as he liked to call himself, is highly illuminating. What was this July 1940, when he stood in "awe and reverence on the threshold of the new world" and when, it seemed to him, France was going to "collaborate, inspire herself, and *be*"? It was, alas! as he already wrote in December 1940,

a midsummer night's dream—a short dream of France looking to Germany for salvation. It was just a short dream between two long dreams in which she had looked, and was now again looking for salvation to England.[6]

The pity of it! And as France was showing herself so wretchedly feeble, the "Europeans", he [Fabre-Luce] and Déat and Doriot—began to despise her. Already in September or October 1940 he wrote:

French opinion is no longer guided by the Government or by any vested interests, still less is it guided by the German occupation authorities. It can be seen obeying anonymous catch-words, and spreading rumours from one

[6] *Op. cit.*, vol. II, p. 91. The second volume was published in Paris in 1942. The two volumes were to be reprinted in a large single volume at Geneva in 1945—with nearly all the above passages omitted!

end of the country to another. . . . During the day your Frenchman sounds *so* simpleminded; one would think he had never read anything but the DNB news; but at night, behind closed doors, and among trusted friends he turns on the BBC . . .

and then:

"Since, by October, there was still no German invasion of England, the old discredited slogans of 1939 came into circulation again. . . ."

If, after the famous Hitler-Pétain meeting at Montoire in October 1940, the Germans showed no hurry to repatriate the French war prisoners, and to cut the occupation costs by half (it was rumoured round the Hôtel Matignon that they had agreed to this) it was, said Fabre-Luce, because *"they were finding that French opinion was again becoming increasingly anglophil"*.

Fabre-Luce was, of course, distressed by this "sabotage" of Montoire. Here, to him, had been a great stepping-stone towards a United Europe. Germany was going to be so good to France; she was going to free the prisoners and cut down the occupation costs, and fully restore to France the Nord and the Pas-de-Calais *départements*; the details of all these arrangements were to be worked out on December 22, but by that time "the great artisan of Franco-German friendship, Pierre Laval" had been dismissed.

And what, Fabre-Luce asked, was Germany to get in return for all these concessions? Here he made a very important point: (and one which explains the relatively lenient terms of the Armistice, providing for a Free Zone). *France was the only major power in Europe that had been defeated and occupied by Nazi Germany. If, therefore, France, whose prestige among the other defeated powers of Europe was still high, took the lead in integrating herself wholeheartedly in Hitler's Europe, then the other occupied countries—Belgium, Holland, Denmark and Norway, Poland and Czechoslovakia, as well as satellites like Hungary and Rumania would collaborate with Hitler all the more readily.* "But if France resists, then there can only be slaves in Europe." If Montoire was sabotaged, and if Laval was dismissed—Laval who *wanted* a German victory, but failing that, fancied himself as a mediator in a negotiated peace—it was, according to Fabre-Luce, because *of the pro-British sentiment that, already by December 1940, was sweeping the country. (Ibid.*, vol. II, p. 68.)

By this time Hitler had failed to invade England, and news was now reaching Vichy of General Wavell's successful offensive in Cyrenaica, and of rapidly increasing American war production. The United States was becoming more and more committed to helping Britain: all this played into the hands of the anti-Germans. As early as August—after Fabre-Luce's "midsummer night's dream"—the French radio, which had started on a series of anti-British programmes, was already receiving floods of letters signed ostensibly by workers and peasants ... (though possibly they were only Jews in disguise). Letters were even sent directly to the Marshal saying "Couldn't you tell the radio announcer in the seven-o'clock news, the fellow with the booming voice, not to speak of Mr Churchill with that irritating snarl?" But now the anti-Germans were going a good deal further: "Why finally quarrel with a country which, for all you know, may yet win the war?"

After that Fabre-Luce told with deep indignation the story of Laval's dismissal from the Vichy government on December 13, 1940—to him, a major setback to Hitler's "European" policy, and one which was to deprive France of the benefits of a friendly Germany. And he also deplored the coolness with which Pétain, under the influence of the Vichy "reactionaries" had received the news of the "noble and generous" gesture Hitler had decided to make to mark the growing friendship and unity of France and Germany.

To coincide with the centenary of the reburial of Napoleon's remains in the Invalides, the Führer was, indeed, giving France the remains of the Duke of Reichstadt, Napoleon's son, who had died, and been buried in Vienna in 1832. The great day was to be December 15, 1940.

Although practically everybody in France seems to have thought the idea incongruous and melodramatic in the worst "Germanic" sense,[7] if not a downright piece of mockery ("what we want is not bones but meat" was the current Paris wisecrack), Fabre-Luce not only commented on the Führer's "gracious and benevolent gesture", but explained on the strength of certain German comments, including a speech by Alfred Rosenberg—the "great political significance" of Hitler's gift to France. On the one hand, he said, there was the anti-German, essentially *Royalist* doctrine of the *Action Française's "la France seule"*; on the other hand, there was the *Bonapartism* of the "Europeans", Hitler being, in their view, the spiritual and historical heir of the victor of Austerlitz, with his dreams of a "European Empire".

But Pétain, suspecting a plot to kidnap him, and suddenly dismissing Laval, refused to go to Paris. Hitler's gesture had been wasted on the ungracious French.

In the circumstances, the reburial of the King of Rome on a cold winter night in Paris was a complete fiasco. There was no Pétain (though he was represented by Darlan) and there was no Hitler. Only a few die-hard "collaborators" were present.

The bronze coffin, [Fabre-Luce wrote] that had arrived that morning at the Gare de l'Est, passed through the high gate of the Invalides between two rows of municipal guards holding burning torches. With lighting effects

[7] Actually, it was Benoist-Méchin who claimed to have first put forward the idea.

and smells, an effort had been made to make this strange midnight mass impressive. According to Drieu La Rochelle, "a whole kilo of incense was burning above our heads in a vessel of such enormous dimensions that we felt like so many Lilliputians" . . . Alas! the whole meaning of the ceremony seemed to have changed; it looked no longer like a celebration of Franco-German friendship but like the funeral of the Montoire policy. (*Ibid.*, vol. II, p. 89.)

The Germans, of course, took Laval's dismissal very badly. Abetz was rushed to Vichy. Pétain had to admit that he had been "misinformed". Offers were made to Laval—but only of minor posts which he refused to accept. Flandin, who had been appointed Foreign Minister, was cold-shouldered by the Germans; his main ambition was apparently to bring about a negotiated peace between Britain and Germany. But fundamentally the change was not as great as the "palace revolution" of December 13 seemed to suggest. The appointment of Darlan on February 10 as Pétain's "Dauphin" was, in Fabre-Luce's view, "at any rate a step in the right direction. . . . *Attentisme* had triumphed for only a few weeks. Pétain had realized that he had gone too far".

What during 1941 and the beginning of 1942 was the feeling in the country? Again Fabre-Luce was full of mournful and scornful admissions. Although he argued that in 1941, less than a year after her defeat, France was already enjoying an "enviable diplomatic position" in the world, he regretfully admitted that "if one consulted the voice of the street, collaboration remained unpopular".

And the French were moody, difficult people: "What France thinks of the Germans during the winter of 1940–1, they thought of the English during the winter of '39–'40." In Paris, in early '41, Fabre-Luce found the people particularly ungracious, despite all the delightful things the Germans were trying to do. Mozart at the Louvre and at the Palais Royal; *Tristan* and *Seraglio* at the Opera. Karajan, the finest German conductor, had been brought to Paris. Yet who was in the audience? "Dinner jackets of the collaborators and of the few remaining Americans, alongside the green uniforms of the Wehrmacht officers." The condition and the morale of the ordinary people were bad:

The people have lost weight. They are thin and tired. They keep worrying about British landings that never come off. And they keep worrying about the Gestapo which they see everywhere.

The French upper-class Fabre-Luce found sitting on the fence, but mostly Gaullist in sympathy; and "listening to the BBC had become a sort of pathological phenomenon with which doctors were becoming increasingly familiar". He sneered at University students who demonstrated in the Champs-Elysées on Armistice Day carrying a fishing-rod (*gaule*)—"being frightfully brave, but still hoping that the Germans wouldn't see the point". Impossible people altogether; the working-class, he admitted, were starving, and were embittered with both the Germans and their own employers; they were, he said, having plenty of evidence that those who had gone to work in Germany were having a good time. And yet they would say: "Go to Germany? Some who went there say it's all right. But we don't believe it. Or even if it's true, they'll still end up behind barbed wire."

And then the war started in Russia. Of course, Fabre-Luce gloated about Communism "soon becoming territorially non-existent"... "The frontiers of our civilization are daily moving further East...." "Doriot sets a glorious example by joining the LVF" [the French Legion for the Russian Front]. But, on the other hand, he talked for the first time about active resistance.

Terrorists... Laval and Déat wounded by a bomb at Versailles... German officers wounded in the streets of Paris... Hostages are being executed—Communists, or others found in possession of firearms... It's an infernal vicious circle.... *It creates ill-feeling that did not exist last year* ... And now the Communists are trying to create *inside France* that Second Front the Russians are clamouring for.... These gangsters do not represent France....

After that, of course, things went from bad to worse from the collaborators' and "Europeans'" point of view, and it is not necessary to concern ourselves with their further reactions. The purpose of this close analysis of Fabre-Luce's *Journal de la France*—a particularly valuable sample of collaborationist literature—was to show that even during the eighteen months that followed the Armistice, when France was living under the shadow of what must have looked to most like a probable German victory, public sentiment remained, in the main, essentially anti-German. There can be little doubt that if a shrewd observer like Fabre-Luce (which he is, quite regardless of his political views) had detected any important sections of public opinion favourable to genuine collaboration with Germany, and to "integration" in Hitler's European Empire, he would certainly have made the most of it. But he found none.

This is an important point that must be borne in mind in all discussions on Pétain and Vichy, Darlan, Laval, the die-hard pro-Germans—and the Resistance.

CHAPTER TWO

VICHY AND THE MARSHAL

1. WHAT IS PÉTAINISM?

On july 23, 1945 Pétain appeared before the High Court of Justice, and declared that it was not competent to try him.

The French people, represented by the National Assembly, invested me with power. The High Court, as it is now constituted, does not represent the French people, and it is only to the latter that the Marshal of France, the Head of the State is now addressing himself.... I shall answer no questions, and this is the only statement I wish to make.

I spent my life in the service of France. Now, nearly 90 years old, and thrown into prison, I still wish to continue to serve France, by speaking to her once more. Let her remember! I led her armies to victory in 1918.

After that I deserved rest, yet I never ceased to devote myself to her. However old and tired I was, I always responded to her appeals. On the most tragic day of her history, France turned to me once again. I asked for nothing. But they begged me to come, and I came. I thus became heir to a catastrophe for which I was not responsible. The guilty men hid behind my back to shield them from the anger of the people. When I asked for the armistice, in agreement with the military chiefs, I performed an act of salvation. The Armistice saved France, and, by leaving the Mediterranean free and by saving the integrity of our Empire, it contributed to the victory of the Allies. My Government was legally formed, and was recognized by all the Powers of the World, from the Holy See to the USSR. I used this power as a shield to protect the French people. In the process I did not hesitate to sacrifice my own prestige. I remained at the head of the country during the Occupation. Will you try to understand the difficulty of governing in such conditions? Every day with the enemy's knife on my throat, I had to struggle against his demands. History will tell you all I have spared you, even though today my opponents are only thinking of reproaching me with what was inevitable.

He went on to say how he had to "humour the enemy", and how he had to

utter certain words and perform certain acts which made me suffer more than you.... Let those who accuse me now search their consciences and try to answer honestly what would have become of them but for me.... While

General de Gaulle, outside our frontiers, continued the struggle, I prepared the ground for liberation, by keeping France alive, though in pain. *What good would it have been to liberate ruins and cemeteries?*

Pétain even claimed that the work of his government had been constructive.

A constitution was drafted. However, I was not given time to promulgate it. And, despite immense difficulties, no government did more than mine to honour the family and, to prevent the class struggle, to seek to safeguard the conditions of work in industry and on the land. Liberated France can change the vocabulary. But in what it builds, it can build usefully only on the foundations I have laid.... No one has the right to break the historic continuity of our country.... I represent a tradition which is that of French and Christian civilization, opposed to the excesses of all tyrannies.... By condemning me, you will condemn the hope and the faith of millions of men. Whatever your verdict may be, there will always be the verdict of God and posterity.

This, in a nutshell, is the case put up for what, after the war, came to be known as "Pétainism". The short statement the aged Marshal made at the opening of his trial must certainly have been carefully prepared in advance, no doubt with the help of his principal defence counsel, Maître Isorni who, in the years that followed, remained the chief spokesman of the Marshal's cause.

It was not a matter that merely concerned the person of the Marshal. Vichy was a social and historical phenomenon of profound significance in French history, and the defence of Pétain also implied the defence of the "system", and a defence of the people who had, in one way or another, identified themselves with Vichy.

One of the chief aims of Pétainist propaganda was, of course, to turn Pétain into a symbol, and to identify him with all that had been "good" about Vichy. For what was bad, others were responsible.

Pétainism, as the above statement shows, claimed

(1) to have saved France from destruction;
(2) to have saved the Empire and to have contributed to the victory of the Allies, one of the main arguments being that but for the Armistice and the establishment of the French Government in metropolitan France, the German army would have invaded North Africa *via* Spain, captured Gibraltar and "closed" the Mediterranean;
(3) to have represented a link in the historic continuity of France;
(4) to have represented both internal and international legality;
(5) to have played a "double game" for the good of France;
(6) to have complemented and supplemented de Gaulle's efforts outside France;
(7) to have been in the true French and Christian tradition;

(8) to have laid the foundations for a better, more virtuous France, with work and the family receiving special protection from the State.

This last claim, which sounded particularly arrogant in 1945, is, nevertheless, one which has a good deal in common with ideas held by all that is anti-Socialist, anti-Communist and anti-trade-union in France. What the Pétain statement meant to convey was that the principles of Vichy were *live* principles—with a future—if France *was* to have a future.

This gross oversimplification of Pétainism had one very important implication; there had been many "impurities" in the history of Vichy, but these had been the work of men who were not pure Vichyites. And it is obvious that one of the main purposes of Pétain propaganda was to create a myth and a legend of Vichy and Pétain which had very little in common with what had actually happened. The impurities of Vichy were thus attributed to two things: the need to play a "double game", and the presence at Vichy of evil men who had nothing in common with the pure essence of Pétainism. This was all the more convenient to do as the Marshal, who had little experience of practical affairs, had, indeed, often been content to let others do the work for him, and to act as an indispensable and inspiring figurehead. If evil things (it could be later argued) were done in his name, it was because his name had been used in vain, because he had been betrayed, because he had been made to sign things which, at his age, and with his lack of political experience, he had not quite understood.

Therefore, if there was anything "wrong" with Vichy, it was not because of Pétain, but in spite of Pétain. And in the process of whitewashing Pétain, the Pétainists have been particularly anxious to create a counter-legend, through the concentration of responsibility for all that was wicked at Vichy on a few individuals, above all on Pierre Laval. From the outset, Laval was deliberately excluded from the benefits of the Pétain myth. It is curious, for example, that Isorni and the other Pétainists should not have raised a finger in favour of Laval, even when they were quite willing to rush to the defence of an all-out Fascist like Brasillach; and that, from 1940 on, the *Action Française* should have treated Laval as somebody totally alien to "the spirit of the Marshal".

One must, of course, be careful not to rush to the other extreme, as some have done, and to see in Laval the quintessence of innate French political wisdom, and to look upon him as a secret defender of the democratic tradition during the Vichy era and the Occupation. One only has to observe the ruthlessness with which Laval engineered the establishment of the Vichy régime (with Pétain remaining discreetly in the background) to realize that Laval's "republicanism" was not exactly in the best tradition. But Laval was, in a sense, an isolated individual, who did not represent, as the men of the "National Revolution" did, a distinct social class, with strong historical traditions. And it is at least partly true that, after laying the foundations of the "National Revolution", Laval found himself outwitted by others who were personally more in harmony with the aged Marshal. There is an illuminating anecdote in Maurice Martin du Gard's *Chronique de Vichy*. The day Laval had got the National Assembly to "vote away" the Third Republic he said to Pétain:

"Well, *Monsieur le Maréchal*, are you satisfied with what I have got for you?"

"Yes," said Pétain, "it's perfect. But now, Monsieur Laval," he added after a short silence, "you will have to learn to obey." For a brief moment Laval thought it a good joke and laughed.[1]

And Martin du Gard added: "Obey—Laval had never obeyed anybody.... And he also had a way of blowing cigarette smoke up the Marshal's nose, which the Marshal couldn't stand."

Indeed, the "National Revolution" was in spirit somewhat alien to him; and though he had laid the foundations for it, he found that his own Third Republic reflexes were incapable of correctly responding to the new régime. He did not like the reactionary personnel of Vichy; and came, more and more, to regard the "National Revolution" as a temporary structure of no lasting value. This, much more than the fact that he was "pro-German", explains his conflicts with Pétain and with Pétain's entourage.

In the Pétainist mythology, Laval is treated as a villain, or, as Weygand said, as "Pétain's evil genius". He wasn't his evil genius at all; others had far more influence with Pétain than Laval—Du Moulin de Labarthète, Dr Ménétrel, and various other cagoulards and *maurrassiens*, such as Alibert, Pétain's Minister of Justice, who, already many years before, had worked out the main lines of the Vichy Constitution, and who also did so much to engineer the 13th of December *coup* against Laval. The truth is that Pétain *used* Laval. He was quite content to let Laval make himself unpopular by negotiating with the Germans. The idea that Laval was Germany's No 1 agent had been started at Vichy, in Pétain's entourage, and by the *Action Française*. So deep was the conviction created by this legend, calculated to keep the Marshal pure, that Britain and America were both taken in by it, and made many serious diplomatic mistakes as a result.

There were also others who—more understandably—were excluded from the benefits of the Pétain legend: the "Paris group" of collaborators—Déat, Doriot, Luchaire, de Brinon—of whom more later. But

[1] Maurice Martin du Gard, *Chronique de Vichy* (Paris, 1948), p. 58. Maurice Martin du Gard (not to be confused with his namesake, Roger Martin du Gard, the novelist) was the representative of the *Dépêche de Toulouse* in Vichy.

how pure was Pétain himself? And who were the "pure Pétainists"? The "pure Pétainists", as will be seen, were above all, the people of the anti-parliamentary Right—members of the Right-wing parties, members of the Action Française, of the Croix de Feu and the other Leagues which had been so active in 1934–5. The Légion was Pétainist: so was the hierarchy of the Church. On a different plane, there was a very widespread pro-Pétain sentiment in 1940–1 in the country, though limited chiefly to the unoccupied zone—which had good reason to be "grateful". For a time, as we shall see, Pétainism became almost a religious cult.

But what sort of man was Pétain? and how did the Pétain myth originate?

2. FROM THE "6TH OF FEBRUARY" TO VICHY

To see how it was gradually built up one has to go a long way back, and, in doing so, one cannot overlook the significant fact that Vichyism was born on February 6, 1934. Pétain the politician was a typical product of the 1930–40 years in France.

Chance would have it that he first came into active politics at the age of 78, as Minister of War in the Doumergue Cabinet, a few days after the 6th of February Riots. What had he been until then, and what did he represent in the eyes of French opinion? He represented one thing only: the glory of the French Army. No doubt, there are many unkind phrases about Pétain to be found in the memoirs of Joffre and Poincaré. It transpired from these that Pétain's great reputation as a soldier had been exaggerated, and it was even suggested that the Battle of Verdun was won not so much thanks to him, as in spite of him, by men of stronger nerve like General Nivelle and General Mangin. According to Poincaré, he was a pessimist and a defeatist by nature, and had it depended on him, the defence of Verdun might have been abandoned. But he had, nevertheless, rendered many great services during the 1914–18 war, and had duly received the Marshal's baton. He had also remained until 1931 a member of the French Army's *Conseil Supérieur* and had continued for years afterwards to act as an expert in military affairs. Only it now seems apparent that he was not keeping up with the times, and that his understanding of military affairs had, by 1934— and indeed before—become out of date.

The offending Joffre and Poincaré volumes were to be prohibited under the Vichy régime, but perhaps more was made by Pétain's critics after the 1940 Armistice of his "innate" defeatism than was warranted. Only one has to distinguish between his prestige as a general of the 1914–18 war and his merits as a technician in the 1930's. It seems (regardless of the Poincaré and Joffre criticisms) to have been the general opinion that he was a highly competent commander in the first world war, though perhaps lacking Foch's greater sureness of touch. Colonel de Gaulle had dedicated two of his early books *Au fil de l'épée* and *La France et son Armée* to Pétain. In the dedication to the second one he wrote: "To Marshal Pétain . . . thanks to whom the last two chapters of this book are the story of our victory."

But as a technician, Pétain had clearly lost touch with the latest military developments during the years immediately preceding the second world war, and this astonishing "backwardness" was to be demonstrated as late as 1938, when he wrote his famous preface to General Chavineau's book, *L'Invasion est-elle possible?*—a preface in which he minimized the importance of aircraft and tanks in the "next" war. However, it is only fair to say that he was in good company!

This "inadequacy" of Pétain as one of the principal advisers of the French Army during the ten years preceding the war was, indeed, one of the facts that clearly emerged from the Riom trial in 1942—and partly led to its "adjournment". An argument also used fairly effectively by men like Reynaud, Blum, and Daladier was that the military unpreparedness of France was due not to the financial "sabotage" of the Army by Parliament, as was alleged by the Vichyites, but to the excessive confidence Parliament had placed in the judgement of men like Pétain and Weygand, whose reputation had been boosted, in the eyes of public opinion, out of all proportion with their real merits. In a different context, the same is, of course, also true of Gamelin who (the story, at any rate, was widely current in 1940) had not even taken the trouble to study the German invasion of Poland on the ground that "it couldn't happen here". Even so, with Foch dead, with Lyautey in his dotage (he died in 1936), with Franchet d'Esperey an invalid, Pétain (and, to a lesser extent, Weygand) represented, during the last few years before the war, the last living symbols of France's military glory. It was that which, paradoxically enough, made it possible for Pétain to carry out his extraordinary political and psychological operation after the military disaster of June 1940.

What did Pétain represent politically? No doubt, *la Grande Muette* was considered in principle to be non-political. But both Weygand and before him, Foch, had trouble with various governments for being ardent Catholics and ultra-Conservatives. Tardieu tells a significant story, illustrating the anti-clerical prejudices that existed against the Army before 1914. It is the story of how Foch was appointed head of the École de Guerre not long before the first world war: Clemenceau—who was very unorthodox in this as in other matters—summoned him to his office and offered him the post. "Don't you realize, *M. le Président*, that I am a practising Catholic? *"Je m'en fous"*, Clemenceau replied. "And that my brother is a Jesuit priest." "I've already told you

—*je m'en fous.* You are appointed." Most of the older leaders of the French Army had, indeed, the reputation of being "reactionaries"— Lyautey, Foch, Weygand, Franchet d'Esperey. I remember how in 1934 the Action Française, the Jeunesses Patriotes and other semi-Fascist organizations all claimed to have the secret support of either Lyautey or Weygand; and they even claimed that "before long" they would come into the open, and lead the revolt against *la gueuse.*[2]

Actually, it never came to that. In the years that followed, it was a shrewd move on the part of certain anti-parliamentary forces to seek the support not of Franchet d'Esperey or Weygand who, from the republican point of view, were highly suspect, but of a seemingly non-political soldier like Pétain. For Pétain had the reputation not only of being non-political, but also of being particularly "democratic", charming, and "human" in his personal manner—much more than any of the other famous generals. Unlike most of the others, he was known *not* to be an ardent and practising Catholic, and it was also known that he had married a *divorcée*. If later, at Vichy, he became a determined churchgoer, the reasons for this were political, rather than personal.

Yet, in 1934, this seemingly "neutral" old man was suddenly bitten by the political bug, when he accepted office as Minister of War in Doumergue's "National" Government.

Of course, one has to remember the atmosphere of the turbulent years that began in 1934, when the Croix de Feu, the Action Française, the Jeunesses Patriotes and the other Fascist and semi-Fascist "leagues" openly challenged the Republican régime. Something had radically changed in France in a very short time. Nineteen thirty-two and 1933 had been the last two peaceful and "normal" years in France, though already in 1933 signs of a gathering storm could be detected.

There was some ground for this in developments abroad. Hitler had come to power in January 1933, and this was bound to have grave repercussions in France sooner or later.

There was something else. The great leaders of the Third Republic—Clemenceau, Poincaré, Briand were dead. Their successors—Chautemps, Daladier, Sarraut, Flandin, Bouisson, were not impressive. Herriot, Caillaux, Tardieu were, each in his own way, fairly big men, but they were, for different reasons, too "controversial" and had too many personal enemies. Herriot had not yet lived down his fiasco as head of the *Cartel des Gauches* in 1926. The only "elder statesman"

---

[2] According to Loustaunau-Lacau, giving evidence at the Pétain trial, the aged Marshal Franchet d'Esperey was in 1937 actively associated with the secret terrorist society, the CSAR (or Cagoule), and considered that Deloncle's plot to "overthrow the State" was France's last hope. (*Le Procès du Maréchal Pétain,* vol. I, p. 254.)

who might have played a salutary part in subsequent years was Louis Barthou, who was Foreign Minister in the Doumergue Cabinet, and the man who was trying to "encircle Germany" with the help of a Russian alliance. But Barthou's life was cut short in October 1934 by the bullet of an assassin in the hire of Mussolini. Barthou was not, however, widely known to the general public (except for being constantly libelled as a thief of valuable books[3] and as a sex maniac— "*fouettez Barthou!*"—in the *Action Française*), and in the emergency of February 1934 the only "grand old man" France seemed able to produce was ex-President Doumergue, a mediocrity and, in reality, a routine Third Republic politician.

Nineteen thirty-four was the year of the Stavisky Scandal, the 6th of February riots and the formation of the Doumergue Government under "street pressure"; and much that happened in 1940 and under Vichy can be traced back to that year:

The ideology of the "6th of February" was a forerunner of the ideology of Vichy.

Vichy was the ultimate triumph of the *Action Française*.

Pétain's Légion Française was like the consecration of Colonel de la Rocque's Croix de Feu *mystique*.

Many of the men who were to play a major rôle at Vichy had won their spurs on the 6th of February, or had come to the surface in the course of the political and ideological quarrels that followed.

Vichy was the *revanche* of the men of the 6th of February who had suffered a defeat under the Front Populaire two years later.

Many men who were most active in the turmoil of those years were also the men who were most active during the years of Vichy. Déat had broken away from the Socialist Party in 1933; so had Marquet, whose quasi-Fascist slogan "Order, Authority, Nation" had "horrified" Blum at the Socialist Congress that year. Déat was, in the years that followed, to become more and more the French "national-socialist" till he finally became one of Hitler's chief hirelings in Paris; Marquet was to become Pétain's first Minister of the Interior. Doriot, breaking away from the Communists, soon became, as head of the Parti Populaire Française, the "purest" French Nazi of all.

Gringoire's circulation soared to 700,000 between 1934 and 1939. It poisoned the minds of millions of Frenchmen with its anti-Parliamentary, anti-Socialist, anti-British, pro-Nazi, pro-Mussolini and anti-Semitic propaganda. Its wrecking activities made it, in a way, the most influential paper in France. It also foreshadowed Vichy. The venom of *Gringoire* and the *Action Française* had eaten deeply into the soul of France and had created a more or less conscious defeatism in the Army. It had also, according to Admiral Muselier, poisoned the minds of the Navy to such an extent that it had helped to render a pro-British movement in the French Navy after the Armistice particularly difficult.

[3] *Cf.* Charles Maurras, *Le Bibliophile Barthou* (Paris, 1929).

The Popular Front was a severe temporary setback for the forces the 6th of February had brought into the open; but these forces kept their powder dry, waiting for the hour of revenge. It was during the Popular Front days that the slogan "*Plutôt Hitler que le Front Populaire*" was launched—no one quite knows by whom. But it caught on. After the end of the Popular Front, it was Daladier who—though at one time a member of this Front—was to personify, poor man, the first victories of the resuscitated 6th of February spirit.

First there was Munich. Then, under his *pleins pouvoirs* of 1938–9, Daladier began, in a half-hearted sort of way, to create something which already foreshadowed Vichy. The chief ideologist of the Daladier régime of 1938–9 was Jean Giraudoux in whose book *Pleins Pouvoirs* one already finds something of the *Famille, Travail, Patrie*, back-to-the-land and let's-have-more-babies ideology. And then, when the war was precipitated by the Soviet-German Pact, there was the outlawing of the Communist Party, complete with persecutions and concentration camps. Whether this was justified or not is another matter. Its relevance is that the Vichyites later never failed to say: "We didn't start it; Daladier did."

It was also during the 1934–9 period that "collaboration" with Nazi Germany was stimulated in a variety of ways. Abetz, the Nazi agent, had been active in Paris since 1933. There was much coming and going between Berlin and Paris. People like Fernand de Brinon, claiming to represent the "Briand tradition", and claiming also to be acting on instructions from Daladier (this was as early as 1933) and to be acting (oddly enough) on behalf of the Jewish Banque Lazard, started publishing Hitler interviews and pro-Nazi articles in the *Matin* and the *Information*.[4]

The Comité France-Allemagne, headed by Fernand de Brinon, was very active during the troubled years of 1934–9, and counted among its members and supporters a substantial number of intellectuals, including many who later cheerfully collaborated with the Germans, or assumed more than ambiguous pro-Vichy attitudes in the United States and elsewhere. The head of the Comité France-Allemagne, Fernand de Brinon—*persona gratissima* with the Germans—was later the obvious Ambassador for Pétain to appoint to Paris. However, he

---

[4] It is true that de Brinon was far from being alone in the field of Hitler interviews. Among the most famous (and historically important) Hitler interviews of the "francophil" and "pacifist" variety was that published by Bertrand de Jouvenel in *Paris-Midi* only a few days before the Germans marched into the Rhineland on March 7, 1936. (See the author's *The Destiny of France*, pp. 217–19.) Later Jouvenel became a shining light and intellectual ornament of Doriot's PPF. In Paris in 1941 he published *Après la Défaite*, a "philosophical" work full of admiration for German methods and Nazi dynamism. However, at some stage of the occupation he retired to Switzerland, emerging after the war as an expert on France in the British press.

went even further than Pétain had expected him to go: he turned out to be simply a German spy who turned over confidential Vichy material to the Germans.

It was into this unsavoury world of domestic and international intrigue, personal ambition and ideological plotting that the 78-year-old Marshal suddenly found himself plunged as a member of the Doumergue Government. He had not been a politician before that. Now in a way hard to determine—except that those were exciting times, and everybody was somehow expected to take sides—it was gradually impressed upon him that he had a major political rôle to play. How could the idea first have been suggested to him? He must have listened to a lot of talk in 1934. He must have heard something of the Doumergue-Tardieu discussions on the necessity of revising the Constitution. According to Loustaunau-Lacau, giving evidence at the Pétain trial, Pétain had taken a sudden interest in Laval, who was his colleague in the Doumergue Government:

The relations between Laval and Pétain before the war were much less important than people imagine. They were, in fact, based on one sentence. One day at a reception at the Quai d'Orsay, in 1934, Doumergue said to Marshal Pétain as he pointed at Laval who was standing near a window: "The Republic is rotten to the core, but there is still *that* one." Pétain has since repeated this phrase to me on more than one occasion during our talks and walks—with a kind of persistence with which old men like to repeat themselves. With them certain phrases become like a reflex.... I think it's an important phrase. There is no doubt that Laval intended to make use of him some day by crowning one of his political combinations with a glorious Marshal's *képi*. Also there is no doubt that Pétain saw in this man with a feline intelligence, in this admirable handler of human material a man who could be valuable as a counsellor on certain occasions. But it never went beyond that.

Only there seems little doubt that in the turbulent world of 1934-5, there were groups who were looking hopefully to Pétain as a figurehead for a Fascist *coup*. Was he aware of it? The first clear sign that somebody was interested in Pétain was the publication in 1935 of a brochure entitled *"C'est Pétain qu'il nous faut"*. Its author was an aged ex-pacifist, who had outraged French nationalist sentiment in the past with his phrase: *"planter le drapeau dans le fumier"*, but who, during the first world war, had become an ultra-nationalist and chauvinist, and who had now obviously become entangled with certain Fascist groups. His name was a well-known one, Gustave Hervé. This brochure foreshadowed in many details the "National Revolution" of Vichy. Paul Reynaud at least was convinced that this boosting of Pétain as the Führer of France could not have been done without his consent. The distribution of the brochure was accompanied by the sale of Pétain badges, which suggested a fairly substantial financial outlay by somebody; it is hard to believe that those who financed the venture should have taken the risk of being disavowed by the Marshal. And yet this story of how Pétain was made "candidate for a Fascist Dictatorship" in 1935 still fails to prove conclusively that he had, by then, finally thrown in his lot with the men of the 6th of February. He continued to be greatly respected by the Left as well, and in November 1935, in an article in *Vu*, even Pierre Cot proposed that, in an emergency, Marshal Pétain be appointed premier![5] Even so, there remains the fact (oddly enough, forgotten by most) that in the 1936 Election Pétain *did* make an eve-of-the-poll appeal against the Popular Front parties. But no major importance was attached to this at the time, and it was not until 1939 that Pétain came into great public prominence again, and this time in a highly spectacular manner.

After the collapse of the Spanish Republic in February 1939, Daladier appointed Pétain Ambassador to Franco Spain. "A stroke of genius!" Daladier's friends, and all the Extreme Right shouted, and Daladier became wonderfully popular even with *Gringoire*, which for years had treated him as the "butcher of the 6th of February". One of the few to protest against the appointment was Léon Blum—on the ground that it was wrong to send to Franco "*our noblest and most human soldier*"!

In a sense the whole idea was incongruous. Pétain, who was now 83, had never been an ambassador in his life. He was suddenly to learn the job of Ambassador just as, a year later, he was to learn the job of head of state, broadcaster and writer of *communiqués*. It was asking a lot from a man in his middle eighties.

The appointment and the views expressed about it on all sides perhaps helped to inflate the old man's vanity—and to give him the idea that he was the Man of Providence. No doubt Daladier's motives were respectable: it was important, regardless of ideological considerations, to flatter a victorious Franco into a state of non-belligerency—if a European war were to break out soon, as seemed more than likely.

Although he had never been Ambassador before, Pétain seemed to enjoy his new rôle and was fully conscious of the internal and international implications of his new post. Nevertheless, it seems that his relations with Franco never went beyond a *protocolaire* stage, and that Franco, on the few occasions he saw Pétain, treated him with marked coolnesss. Even so, Pétain was patient and did nothing to antagonize the new Spanish régime, and indeed, hastened to return the Spanish gold to Franco and carry out other promises made in a moment of panic by M. Bérard under the Bérard-Jordana agreement just after the Republican collapse. According to M. Gazel, who was Counsellor at the Embassy, Pétain even refrained from "bothering" the Spaniards more

[5] *Procès Pétain*, p. 992.

than necessary about Frenchmen who were still held prisoner in Spain. Some significance was attached to the fact that, even after the outbreak of war, Pétain should have shaken hands at an official reception with the German Ambassador and should also have opposed the publication in Spanish by the French Embassy of an anti-Goebbels pamphlet.

Was Pétain already then defeatist? And was he also planning to play a major political rôle in France before long? According to the same M. Gazel, Pétain was, even before the outbreak of hostilities, already thinking of the great political part he was going to play:

Twice in one day, he showed me lists of the cabinets he was planning to form one day. Both lists contained the names of Laval and Lémery. I did not have the impression, all the same, that he was at that time plotting against the Republic. He once even said: "The politicians are trying to make use of me. I am going to disappoint them."

But, in fact, he was not going to disappoint them. According to M. Lemarle, another Counsellor of the French Embassy in Spain, close contacts were established, especially after the outbreak of war, between Pétain and Laval. Thus Laval sent a message to Pétain in the latter half of September 1939 saying that he would help him to form a government "free of any people you don't want". This may explain why, when Daladier summoned Pétain to Paris about the same time and asked him to enter the Government, the Marshal refused, as he would not enter any government that did not include Laval—whom Daladier would not have.

Pétain returned to Spain; but there is enough to show that he continued to maintain close contacts with certain politicians in Paris. His Counsellor Lemarle told at the Pétain trial two curious stories: one of the French press attaché who, during a visit to France at the end of '39, had been found spreading defeatist propaganda, and saying that his view that this was a "useless, hopeless war" was fully shared by Pétain —whereupon Pétain upbraided him, not for his defeatist views, but for having quoted him. The other was the story of Lemarle's visit to Paris in February 1940 where he was startled to find a widespread defeatist mood, with all the defeatists referring to Pétain as their man.

What was Pétain's attitude during the months immediately preceding the German invasion of May 10? There is much to show that he was preparing to play a big part. For some time he had been dropping hints as to the political rôle he would soon have to assume. Thus he said on March 30 to de Monzie: "In the second half of May they will need me."[6] And on May 5, five days before the German offensive, he said to Darlan whom he visited at the naval headquarters at Main-

[6] A. de Monzie, *Ci-Devant* (Paris, 1941), p. 207.

tenon: "We must stay shoulder-to-shoulder. May I count on you?" Darlan later remarked: "I must say that, at that moment I did not quite understand the importance of the offer he was making me."[7]

Then came the invasion. The story of this has been told a thousand times, and there are also numerous accounts, told from the most different angles, of the complex negotiations and intrigues that preceded and surrounded the fall of the Reynaud Government at Bordeaux.

No one who, like the present writer, "followed" the French Government, first to Tours and then to Bordeaux in June 1940, can deny for a moment that France and the greater part of the French Army were completely bewildered and demoralized by the suddenness of the catastrophe that had overtaken them. The collapse of the Maginot Line myth, on which France had been fed for years, followed by the almost unobstructed sweep of the German tank divisions across France; the collapse at Dunkirk, which accentuated the feeling that France was "completely alone"; the fall of Paris on June 14—all this created a feeling among the panic-stricken population that France had been beaten. Continue the fight in Africa? To many politicians, to many other thinking people it seemed the right thing to do; but to the shopkeeper of Tours, to the farmer of the Limousin, to the winegrower of the Midi it was all remote and unrealistic. What had happened was a bitter blow to France's pride, but if a referendum had been taken, say, on June 15, on whether France should try to negotiate an armistice, there is no doubt that the vast majority would have said yes.

There was a clear conviction among the people of France that, with the existing alignment of forces, *nothing* could destroy the German Army. It had cut through France like a knife through butter. And who was there to lead France to victory at this stage—Reynaud? Daladier? Herriot? the lachrymose President Lebrun? If Pétain and Weygand (whom Reynaud had called in as "the last chance") had proved helpless, no one else could do anything. France's duty to England? That also seemed a purely academic point. Nor can there be any doubt about the bitter feeling of resentment against Britain that existed in France during the June *débâcle*. England had "deserted" at Dunkirk, leaving France to her own devices, and even the famous RAF had done nothing to help. The damage had been done on all sides. The generals had miscalculated the chances of preventing a German invasion; the Quai d'Orsay, trying to combine military alliances with a purely defensive strategy, had in the end wrecked collective security; and nothing had been done to prevent the slow but profound demoralization of French opinion; for years, *Gringoire* and the *Action Française* and the Fifth Column had sapped French morale.

[7] Béraud's interview with Darlan, published in *Gringoire* in 1941 and quoted in *Le Procès du Maréchal Pétain*, pp. 79–80, and many other books.

Even a man like Vincent Auriol, bitterly opposed to the Armistice, felt that France's chance of resisting much longer could not be great:

In June, the Army had no leaders and the nation had no guides. Everything had been dispersed: the Government, Parliament, the Army Headquarters, the Army itself. For all this mess the Government and the civil authorities were to blame.... No doubt Paul Reynaud had tried to create national unity. But in the absence of organized and disciplined parties, he merely picked up "personalities", here, there and everywhere.... Most of his ministers were in disagreement with him on the major foreign problems.... Before him Daladier had stopped proceedings against the Fifth Column; and Abetz and the politicians and journalists in his pay had been tolerated far too long. Perhaps he was also wrong not to have rejuvenated the higher *cadres* of our Army and not to have associated the Army more closely with the nation ... as the leaders of the USSR had done... Daladier had also taken all vitality out of Parliament, and had, through governing by decree, deprived it of all feeling of responsibility. And when the tragic hour struck, the nation looked in vain for an embodiment of its sovereignty. The broken crown had been swallowed up by the abyss. And when the legal government finally disintegrated at Bordeaux, under the pressure of Pétain and his team, the representatives of the Nation failed to avert the political adventure that had been prepared by the traitors. And only the team of defeatism and dictatorship, sheltering under the Marshal's oak leaves, was there to plot and triumph.[8]

Herriot, as Auriol was to realize, felt that the authority of Parliament had fallen too low to interfere with the Marshal's plans. When Auriol told him that he should call Parliament to approve or reject Pétain's Armistice move, Herriot gazed at him in amazement.

"*Grand Dieu! Pourquoi faire?*"
"Very well," I said, "have them meet in secret session. The Pétain Government has no constitutional basis. It represents nothing. Parliament must decide on the Armistice request..." "No," said Herriot, "it's too late. The request for the Armistice is already in Hitler's hands." (Auriol, *ibid.*, p. 79.)

Herriot added that if the Armistice terms were unacceptable, then, of course, the battle would continue in North Africa.... He showed Auriol a letter addressed to Pétain warning him against abandoning the Navy, the Air Force, and France's naval and air bases. In short, nothing should be done that might lead to acts hostile to France's allies.

Oh, [Auriol wrote] it was couched in noble terms, worthy of Herriot; but what use was it against the will of Pétain and against the audacity of

[8] Vincent Auriol, *Hier ... Demain*, vol. I (Paris, 1945), pp. 76–7.

those who were at the political "club" which was meeting in the Town Hall of Bordeaux?

As Auriol tells the story, they were all there—Laval, Bergery, Bonnet, Déat, de Monzie, Montigny and others—"most of them members of the Comité France-Allemagne, presided over by Scapini and inspired by de Brinon, Abetz's and Goering's liveried flunkey. . . ."

Then there was the episode of the *Massilia*, on which President Lebrun, any members of the Government, and any senators and deputies, who wished to do so, were "invited" to travel to North Africa; cars would be placed at their disposal to take them to Le Verdon. At one stage, Pétain asked Chautemps to act in North Africa as his "deputy"; but he [Pétain] would, in any case, remain in France. The *Massilia* affair was a particularly shady one, and, in the end, only a small number of people sailed, among them Mandel, Campinchi and Mendès-France. But why did not more go? On the one hand, Laval decided not to allow President Lebrun to go: he was needed in France, and he bullied the poor man till he finally surrendered. But why did so many others, who could have gone, not board the *Massilia*? Was it because they suspected a trap? Was it because they thought Pétain and Laval wanted to get a large number of deputies (particularly anti-Armistice deputies) out of the way? Or was it not simply because few had any real faith in the possibility of setting up any sort of effective French government in North Africa—whether under the authority of the Marshal or not? It is, at any rate, significant that Auriol, for instance, should have had this reflex:

On the evening of the 19th, the departure for Algiers had, in any case, been settled. As an ordinary deputy I was going to follow the *bureau* of the two Chambers and the head of the State. But it occurred to me that I was Mayor; the area would be occupied; it would be my duty to remain among my people and not to leave them face-to-face with the army of occupation. My dear friends could defend in Algeria our common ideas. . . . I went to say good-bye to Herriot. . . . He had just heard that Lyon was about to be occupied by the Germans. And his first words were: "I ought to do like you and stay among my own people."

Auriol pointed out that as President of the Chamber of Deputies, it was his duty to go to Algiers. "We then embraced each other." Auriol did not say whether Herriot had agreed with him or not. He obviously hadn't.

The reflex of nearly everybody in France during the Armistice week —and after—was not to embark on doubtful adventures, but to stay put.

3. THE DEATH OF THE THIRD REPUBLIC

It was on June 17 that Marshal Pétain broadcast the words *"Il faut cesser le combat"*, which, on the following day, were repeated in the revised version: *"Il faut tâcher de cesser le combat."* President Lebrun had just appointed him Head of the Government, after Reynaud had resigned and had recommended that Pétain succeed him—thus implicitly surrendering to the Pétain policy. On the 20th, in another broadcast, Pétain announced that the French Armistice Delegation had gone to meet the Germans.

"Weaker than we were twenty-two years ago," he said, "we also had fewer friends. We did not have enough children, we did not have enough arms, and not enough allies—these are the reasons for our defeat.... We shall learn our lesson from our lost battles. Since our past victory, the spirit of pleasure has been stronger in us than the spirit of sacrifice. We asked for much, and we served little. We wanted to spare ourselves great efforts, and now we are face-to-face with adversity.

"I was with you in the days of glory. At the head of the Government, I shall remain with you during the dark days. Stay by my side ..."

And, on the 22nd, after telling Churchill in a broadcast that he was "no judge of either France's interests or France's honour", he concluded:

France has spared neither her blood nor her labour. She is conscious of having earned the respect of the world. And she looks to herself for her own salvation. Let Mr Churchill remember this.... We have survived other trials. We know that our country remains intact so long as her children love her. Never has this love been more fervent. The land of France is rich in promise and in glory. Our peasants have seen their harvest destroyed by hail. They do not despair of next year's harvest. With the same faith as before they plough the same furrow for future seed.

All this, it must be said, was brilliant propaganda, it was like balm to the wounds and to the injured pride of France; the Father Symbol had been created. And equally effective was the broadcast announcing the Armistice.

The terms of the armistice are hard; but at least honour has been saved. No one will use our planes and our Navy.... The Government remains free; and France will be administered by Frenchmen only. Now a new order begins.

And again the "soil" *motif*:

You have suffered. You will suffer still more.... Your life will be a hard one. I shall not rock you to sleep with words of deceit. I hate lies—they have done you so much harm in the past. But the earth—the earth does not lie.

It remains your refuge. The earth is our homeland. A field that goes fallow is a piece of France that has died.... Do not expect too much from the State, which can only give what it receives. Rely on yourselves for the present, and, for the future, rely on your children whom you will have brought up with a sense of duty.

And so on. A new France, a better and more virtuous France would emerge after the great ordeal.

In these early broadcasts Pétain already set the tone of what was to become the "Vichy ideology". But before the new régime was properly set up, some dirty work had to be done. For the next ten days Pétain retired into the background, and Laval took the limelight.

In a later chapter it will be shown how Laval engineered the "surrender" of Parliament to Pétain. But it may already be said here that the result was acquired with much less violence and intimidation than was to be suggested by some people later.

The famous law of July 10, 1940, which was the outcome of Laval's labours, read:

The National Assembly gives all powers to the Government of the Republic under the authority and signature of Marshal Pétain to promulgate in one or more acts a new Constitution of the French State. This Constitution shall safeguard the rights of work, the family, and the country.

This far-reaching law was voted by 569 votes to 80. Why this overwhelming majority? There is no doubt that, in the midst of Vichy chaos, most of the deputies and senators were passively willing to hand over to Pétain, while many others did so with real enthusiasm. Some, no doubt, as Léon Blum later claimed, had been "terrorized" into voting for the "end of the Republic"; but probably a much more typical reaction was that of Herriot and Jeanneney, presidents of the Chamber and of the Senate.

As Vincent Auriol was to write:

On July 9 the Chamber of Deputies met in the morning to examine the draft resolution for the revision of the constitutional laws. It started with a short speech by Herriot; first, a tribute to the deputies who had given their lives for France; then a tribute to the Nation. He sounded like a mourner at the funeral of the Republic, and then, alas! he concluded: "Let us all rally round the Marshal." Why, why such resignation in the man who in 1935 abandoned the presidential chair in protest against Caillaux's little financial *pleins pouvoirs* bill? (Auriol, *op. cit.*, vol. I, p. 114.)

What Auriol kindly omitted to say was that Herriot had gone even further in his "Vichyism" and in his implicit denunciation of the Republic's "guilt". For he said, on that same 9th of July:

After great disasters, one looks for those responsible for them. The responsibilities are of different orders. They will be shown up, the hour of justice will come. France will want this justice to be severe, precise, and impartial.

"Rally round the Marshal"—it was like a gregarious reflex, which few could suppress. Some, who were not so sure that it was the right thing to do, still thought it safer to agree. Others were planning to "cash in" on the New Order—whatever it turned out to be. And Laval had assured them that it wouldn't be so bad. There would be jobs for deputies who behaved themselves.

On July 11, Pétain announced in a broadcast that he had asked the Germans to liberate Versailles and the government districts round the Palais Bourbon in Paris—so that the Government could be moved there. Versailles! This had very precise implications. And, on the same day, the first *acte constitutionnel* was published, opening with the words "*Nous, Philippe Pétain, Maréchal de France*", followed by a second *acte constitutionnel* beginning: "*Nous, Philippe Pétain, Chef de l'Etat français . . .*"
The first one appointed Pétain Head of the French State; the second one endowed him with practically unlimited monarchical powers.
In the third one, Pétain appointed Laval his successor.
Later, Laval claimed to have been double-crossed: all this "*Nous, Philippe Pétain*" stuff was not what he had expected at all. However, he does not seem to have complained at the time. It would have been unwise to do so. The Pétain myth was at its height; and, around Pétain, the "authoritarians" and monarchists of the "National Revolution" were very active. It is true that in the first government that was formed under the new régime, the old parliamentarians (such as they were) were still numerous; there was Laval as Vice-Premier; Marquet at the Interior, Ybarnégaray in the characteristic ministry of *Jeunesse et Famille*; Piétri as Minister of Transport, and Lémery as Minister of Colonies. But there were others too—Alibert, very much a National Revolution man, with an Action Française background, as Minister of Justice. There was Weygand—notoriously anti-Republican—as Minister of Defence, Belin, the trade union leader, as Minister of Labour. The "technicians" were represented in the government by Yves Bout-hillier, Minister of Finance, an *inspecteur des finances* with a passionate loathing for deputies.[9] Baudouin, of the Banque d'Indochine, continued his short-lived career as Minister of Foreign Affairs, and Darlan was Secretary of State for the Navy. As a result of France's military defeat, a new régime had come into being. As some of the Marshal's followers used to say: "It was worth a military defeat."

[9] *Cf*. Moulin de Labarthète, *Le Temps des Illusions*, p. 152.

4. HOW LEGAL WAS VICHY?

Before describing the parliamentary events which led to the adoption of the famous constitutional law of July 10, 1940, it would seem useful to examine the constitutional aspect of the "Vichy régime". During the Occupation, and later, during the years immediately following the Liberation, there were to be endless discussions in France on the "legality" of Vichy. Had the Marshal "usurped"—as was widely alleged—the authority of the French Republic? It was in the interests of the enemies of Vichy to deny that the Vichy Government was the legal government of France. The most valid argument in support of this view was that those who had installed the Vichy régime had done so under indirect German pressure, i.e. by making use of the fact that two-thirds of the country was occupied, and that what was done in the exceptional conditions of Vichy in July 1940 could in no sense be binding on a free France. It has also been argued (notably by Léon Blum) that the law of July 10 was voted by many deputies and senators as a result of downright physical intimidation. Even so, practically all jurists, looking back on 1940 in a detached way, agree that, *formally*, there was nothing invalid about the law of July 10. It is obvious that the great majority of senators and deputies who voted this law did so without any coercion.

A very different attitude is, however, taken by most jurists today to Pétain's Constitutional Acts signed in virtue of the law of July 10. These they consider constitutionally very much more dubious.

There were twelve Constitutional Acts signed by the Head of the State:

Act No 1. (July 10, 1940) appointing Pétain Head of the State and implicitly abolishing the function of the President of the Republic;

Act No 2. (July 10, 1940) fixing the powers of the Head of the State;

Act No 3. (July 10, 1940) proroguing and adjourning the Chambers;

Act No 4. (July 11, 1940) concerning the successor of Pétain; this Act was to be revised five times: 24/9/40, 13/12/40, 10/2/41, 17/11/42, and 13/11/43;

Act No 5. (July 30, 1940) concerning the Supreme Court of Justice [of no importance, since it is implicitly contradicted by Act No 7];

Act No 6. (December 1, 1940) supplementing Act No 3;

Act No 7. (January 27, 1941) reinforcing Act No 2 with reference to the Ministers' and high officials' responsibility to the Head of the State;

Acts Nos 8, 9, and 10. (August 14 and October 4, 1941) increasing the subordination to the Head of the State through the introduction of the compulsory loyalty oath among soldiers, magistrates, officials, etc;

Acts Nos 11 (April 18, 1942) and 12 and 12-*bis* (November 17 and 28, 1942) setting up the "diarchy" system under which power is divided between the Head of the State and the Head of the Government (namely, Laval).

These Acts were, *contrary to the obligation contained in the law of July* 10, never.submitted to the Nation for ratification, but were treated by their author, the Marshal, as final and unquestionable, subject to revision only by himself.

As an eminent jurist, Professor Marcel Prélot was to write later:

Yet this ratification was all the more imperative as this transfer of its authority to the Nation had alone persuaded the Assembly to accept the Government Bill of July 10, 1940.

It is true that no time limit for these ratifications was fixed, but this could on no account be interpreted as meaning indefinite delay. The conditions in which the Bill was voted indicated that there should be only a very short time limit, since otherwise it would have been unnecessary for the Assembly to delegate its powers to the Marshal. It was, on the contrary, felt that the circumstances of the moment required a procedure of *extreme urgency*. The military leaders, notably Weygand, had convinced Parliament that London would be occupied by August 15, and that it was therefore necessary to elaborate and ratify the new constitution before the autumn, so that the new régime in France should be in place, ready to embark on the peace settlement. The deputies and senators, therefore, did not have in mind a long transitional stage, but, on the contrary, the early adoption of a complete new system of new and final institutions. (M. Prélot, *Précis de Droit Constitutionnel* (Paris, 1953), p. 257.)

Here, indeed, is a striking example of the extreme tortuousness of so many of the things that happened at Vichy. Here was Pétain setting up, as it were, an authoritarian régime for all time, and yet, after securing seemingly unlimited powers for himself, delaying the elaboration of a complete constitution—at least partly because England had *not* been invaded by the Germans! In other words, much that was being done, assumed, even at the height of the "National Revolution", a provisional nature, Pétain leaving many loopholes open—including that of falling back, in an extreme emergency, on the parliamentary machinery of the Third Republic! That this is not an idle supposition may be seen from the attempt he was to make at the end of 1943 to call the Parliament he had disbanded—a plan that provoked a furious letter from Ribbentrop. The plan had to be abandoned; but one can imagine the major complications that would have arisen in the de Gaulle camp at Algiers had it succeeded!

Already in October 1940, after the apparent failure of the invasion of England, Baudouin announced that, instead of being "the foundations of the new edifice, the Constitution would be its roof". The Marshal himself said that the Constitution would not be promulgated until France was free. The Constitution as a whole would be submitted to the Nation's ratification, but not the separate Constitutional Acts. Of course, Germany's failure to end the war quickly was not the only reason for this misapplication of the law of July 10; it is obvious that the Pétain régime intended, for as long as possible, to usurp the powers of the Assembly, and to eliminate, if possible, any sort of ratification procedure.

In this, as in so much else concerning Vichy, we find a reflection of this dual phenomenon: the opportunism, and, indeed, the incoherence of its foreign policy and the desire, by hook and by crook, to set up a lasting authoritarian régime. With this end in view Pétain and his personal advisers—who, in this matter, did *not* include Laval—did their utmost to disregard the legal implications of the law of July 10—implications clearly set out in its preamble (the *exposé des motifs*), as well as in the preamble of the draft resolution on Constitutional Revision, passed by both Chambers almost unanimously on July 9![10] The two preambles, as well as the assurances given by Laval "in the Marshal's name", were to the effect that, though their activity would be "inevitably reduced", the two Chambers would continue to exist until the new Chambers came into being. "There will be no hiatus," Laval said, and their committees, at any rate, would, he added, co-operate in preparing the new Constitution. Yet on July 11, Pétain virtually suppressed the Chambers and put an end to the Republic—by scrapping the President. Instead, supreme authority was invested in the Head of the State, the very word "republic" was suppressed, except when accompanied by insulting adjectives. Its mention in the press and public speeches was prohibited. On coins, stamps and public buildings the words *République Française* were changed to "*Etat Français*", and "*Liberté, Egalité, Fraternité*" to "*Travail, Famille, Patrie*". The Republic was referred to as "*le régime déchu*" or "*l'ancien régime*". The Chambers, after Constitutional Act No 3, could no longer meet, except when summoned by the Head of the State. This "freezing" of the Chambers was extended a month later to their Committees; in October 1941 deputies and senators' salaries were stopped, and the Marshal reserved the right to expel Members of Parliament. Parliamentary immunity became a dead letter: numerous parliamentarians were, at the Marshal's sole discretion, sent to prison or placed under house arrest. In legal terms, Pétain's *derived* constituent powers were turned into *original* constituent powers.[11]

To the theorists of the authoritarian state—which had taken the place of the Democratic Republic—the Vichy meetings of the National Assembly on July 9 and 10 had merely been a "formality" destined to regularize and legalize a revolutionary operation which had in fact

---

[10] To certain legal purists, the law of July 10 could not, in any circumstances, invalidate the constitutional law of 1884 which said that "the republican form of government cannot be the object of any proposal for revision".

[11] Prélot, *op. cit.*, p. 260.

already been performed during the days immediately following the Armistice. According to a pro-Pétain jurist, Roger Bonnard, the question had arisen at Bordeaux of simply proclaiming by means of posters (*affichage*) the change of régime; on second thoughts, it was decided that it would be more expedient to follow the legal procedure that was adopted at Vichy in July. This was certain, at least for a long time, to assure the new régime the support of all those French groups which are traditionally attached to the concept of *legality*: the Army, the Navy, the police, the clergy, the greater part of the bourgeoisie, the civil service, and most of the peasantry.

If the negative aims of the National Revolution were obvious (anti-liberalism, anti-democracy, the destruction of the parliamentary system and the disavowal of the whole French constitutional tradition since 1789), its positive aims and achievements were much more confused. For one thing, there were at least two, or rather three conflicting schools of thought. There was the "Vichy" school which was essentially reactionary, monarchist, corporatist and clerical. (Even in this "school" there was endless disagreement, since each of its members had his pet solutions and his pet aversions: for example the post of Minister of Education changed hands five or six times in two years, each Minister having ideas of his own.) Some organizers of the National Revolution placed the emphasis on the "Frenchness" of the said Revolution, followed closely in the footsteps of the *Action Française* (Alibert, Laval's great enemy, was one of them); they liked to talk in terms of *la vieille France* and its ancient and earthy virtues; others looked to Italian Fascism; others still to Franco Spain, with its clericalism, as their model.[12] What was Pétain himself trying to do? According to Du Moulin de Labarthète, the Marshal looked upon Renan and even La Fontaine (!) as "ancestors",

and many of his ideas were derived from Joseph de Maistre, Le Play, Taine, Tourville, Bourget, La Tour du Pin, Maurras and Salazar. And maybe even Barrès.... Pétain was a popularizer (*vulgarisateur*) of many of their ideas, rather than an inventor of new ones.... In the mind of the apolitical old man the *Body Politic* took the place of the *sovereign people* (sovereign towards whom or what?) complete with a hierarchy of families, *communes* and professions.... He discovered, with the help of Gillouin and François Perroux, that the "enterprise" was, as it were, the initial cell ... of all professional organization ...

And Du Moulin de Labarthète, after criticizing the extreme vagueness of Pétain's conception of the "common good", went on:

[12] According to Du Moulin de Labarthéte, Pétain, who had been cold-shouldered by Franco in 1939, personally admired the Salazar, rather than the Franco régime.

The Marshal thought he could replace the anarchy of individualism ... and the coercion of Socialism by a smooth, well-constructed, well oiled system of Newtonian precision. Only it didn't work for lack of water, oil, and air. Because the Corporation, which was Pétain's pet idea, was just an anachronism in 1940 ... Even so, the Corporation had its defenders ... Above all the members of the *synarchie*, who, though not greatly interested in the Corporate State as such, were determined to maintain the *Comités d'Organisation*, provided by the law of August 16, 1940. They even persuaded the Marshal that these *Comités d'Organisation* and the future *Comités Sociaux* of the *Charte du Travail* would become the two pillars on which the Corporation would rest ... I argued with him in vain in my attempt to show that the *Comités d'Organisation* were the expression of the harshest and driest type of capitalism and could only paralyse his generous [pro-labour] plans.... (*Op. cit.*, pp. 60–2.)

The Paris group, on the other hand, followed much more closely the Nazi model, considering that, in a German-dominated Europe, France had better conform to German practice as closely as possible. The emphasis was on National *Socialism*, "Europeanism", and anti-clericalism.

Besides the numerous sub-varieties of these two schools (especially the first one) there was also the purely pragmatist and opportunist third school (if it may be called that), represented by Laval. This school was, in reality, out of sympathy with both the other two, though it was "pro-Paris" rather than "pro-Vichy" so long as a German victory seemed the most probable outcome of the war. This opportunist kow-towing to Nazism did not exclude a certain nostalgia for the Third Republic. This group had no real sympathy for the "National Revolution", and would not take it seriously.

The "Paris Group" fled ignominiously to Germany in 1944; at Vichy, first Pétain and later Laval were prepared to write off the National Revolution as a "temporary experiment", and they made their abortive attempts (Pétain in November 1943, Laval in August 1944) to re-establish the Third Republic—Pétain no doubt hoping that some features of the "National Revolution" would still survive in a "national reconciliation" between himself and de Gaulle, a reconciliation from the benefits of which the Communists alone would be excluded. In 1944, such a "reconciliation" was a psychological impossibility. Fortunately for those who would not compromise with Vichy, the Germans prevented both Pétain and Laval from calling Parliament. Nevertheless, Herriot was to remain convinced that such an attempt in 1944 was favoured by the United States Government, and that it had suggested to Laval that he engineer the calling of Parliament, and that he thereupon hand over the leadership to Herriot. (*Cf.* E. Herriot, *Episodes*, 1940–4 (Paris, 1950), p. 199.)

5. THE MONARCHISM OF VICHY

The myth of an "independent" Vichy France could obviously thrive only during the two years between July 1940 and November 1942.

It was during this period that the "authoritarian state" was built up. The State was "restored in its sovereignty", as the phrase went. Special legislation was enacted against those who were reputed to be the enemies of this sovereignty, notably against what Charles Maurras called "*les trois états confédérés: l'État-juif, l'État-métèque, l'État-maçon*". A variety of restrictions were placed upon personal freedom, and "individualism" was denounced as pernicious fallacy.

This individualism [Pétain wrote[13]] which the people of France treated as a major privilege is at the root of the troubles from which we nearly died... There is no creative virtue in individualism... Individualism receives everything from society and gives it nothing in return.

It should, of course, be borne in mind that neither such articles, nor Pétain's famous broadcasts were, in the main, Pétain's "own work"— chief among his ghost writers were Gillouin (philosopher, wit and literary critic, and reputed by some to be a "secret British agent"[14]), Bergery ("father" of the Popular Front in 1934,[15] and later Vichy's Ambassador in Moscow) and Lucien Romier (for many years *Figaro* editorialist and later, a member of the Vichy Government).

A peculiarity of the Vichy régime was the almost "theocratic" nature of Pétain's position; in him, in the words of Constitutional Act No 2, was embodied "the plenitude of governmental power", the Cabinet therefore becoming, in terms of responsibility, merely an advisory body, every member of the Government depending entirely on the Chief of State, who could appoint and dismiss them at will. The Head of the State was not responsible to anyone: "the ministers are responsible to me; I can only be judged by History"; or, as he put it on another occasion, he was responsible only to "his own conscience and to God". Or, as Roger Bonnard put it:

In the authoritarian state political power stems from its holder, which means that it is outside and above those who are governed. The Head of the State alone holds and exercises power. The value, authority and legitimacy of this power has not been delegated to him by the people, it emerges from the person of the Chief himself.... The authoritarian state springs from the emergence of the Chief who imposed himself as such in view of historic circumstances, and in view of his personal value, his prestige and his authority, and also because he was at that moment the necessary man.[16]

[13] Pétain, *Revue Universelle*, January 1941, quoted by Prélot, *op. cit.*, p. 262.
[14] Maurice Martin du Gard, *op. cit.*, p. 87.
[15] *Cf.* the author's *France in Ferment* (London, 1934), pp. 288-90.
[16] Quoted by Prélot, *op. cit.*, pp. 111-12.

In theory, therefore, fractions of power could only be delegated by Pétain to his ministers and officials; but the ultimate responsibility to "History", to his "own conscience" or to "God"—but not to any man or men—was only his. The Chief embodied both executive and legislative power and could, indeed, at his own discretion, have people arrested and condemned to life imprisonment, as was the case notably of Reynaud, Blum, and Daladier. The only thing Pétain could not do was to declare war "without the approval of the Chambers"—an illogical exception, due entirely to the "criminal" declaration of war on Germany in 1939 by the Daladier Government without the formal approval of Parliament—an episode which figured prominently in all Vichy's "war guilt" propaganda.

It is not necessary here to examine the whole machinery of the Vichy Government or to see in what respects the Vichy theory of the Chief's "plenitude of power" resembles or differs from the French absolute monarchies of the past, the Caudillo principle in Spain, or Hitler's *Führer Prinzip*. Although the royalist implication of Pétain's "divine right" was the most obvious one in the eyes of the anti-republican Vichyites, with their nostalgia for a mythical "ancient France", certain features of the régime showed that the *Führer Prinzip* had not been altogether neglected. Déat's Nazi-inspired plan for setting up a single party in France was rejected by Vichy in 1940, but the Marshal's Légion Française was soon to become a potential "single party", with the idea of *le Chef* ("*Maréchal, nous voila*") as its underlying principle.

The monarchy of Vichy was, under the stress of circumstances, later to be abandoned, or rather diluted, in favour of a "dyarchy". When Laval became head of the Government again in April 1942, he insisted on being invested with proper personal authority, "which would enable him to direct effectively and personally the home and foreign policy of France". (For one thing, he feared a repetition of the "13th of December" *coup*.) After the German occupation of the "Free" Zone, Laval was also given extensive legislative powers. For all that, Pétain alone continued to hold constitutional power, and was therefore in a position to revoke the Constitutional Acts of April and November 1942 setting up the Pétain-Laval "dyarchy". This Pétain did not dare do, but he secretly deprived Laval of his succession in the Constitutional Act No 4 *sexies* (i.e. the fifth revision of the Succession Act), which was handed in a sealed envelope to the Vice-President of the *Conseil d'Etat* and to the *Procureur Genéral* of the *Cour de Cassation*; by this secret Act, Pétain set up a College of seven men which was to call the National Assembly in the event of his (Pétain's) death or "incapacity". The seven did not include Laval.

In theory, the Vichy State was a "strong" régime, which had abandoned the pernicious road that France had (with a few intervals) followed since 1789; its theorists praised it to the skies, and built up a naïve mythology of a better and purer France. In reality, of course, no French régime was weaker. In the occupied zone, its authority was little more than nominal, all decisions being subject to German approval or control; the same was true in the rest of France, after November 1942. Nevertheless, France was, at least nominally, ruled for four years —and more than just nominally for over two years—by a régime which, though weak, artificial and ineffective in most respects, still represented, in political, social, ideological and even emotional terms a historic reality of lasting significance. Vichy was not an accident; Vichyism goes far back into the past, and has also projected itself far into the future. "We are back in Vichy France", was the kind of melancholy remark that could quite commonly be heard among left-wing intellectuals in France in 1952 and 1953. Counter-revolution is a permanent reality in France, and its outwardly complete, though temporary, triumph at Vichy is much more than a historical curio.

6. PÉTAIN THE FATHER

There was, of course, a sharp difference between the reality of Vichy and the mythology of Vichy. Neverthelesss the mythology is not without importance. The cult of Pétain was genuine. It was he who gave respectability and an emotional content to the National Revolution; on the other hand, it was his personal prestige which covered so many crimes and misdeeds and so many shady *combinazioni*. We shall see later what sort of man Pétain really was; but it is useful to dwell briefly on the myth of Pétain—which was of considerable interest and has no obvious parallel in French history. The resemblance with Thiers in 1871 is only very superficial, except in an elementary "class" sense. There is no doubt that in 1940 and 1941, at any rate, Pétain was popular, though popular for two different sets of reasons. The people of the Southern Zone were, above all, grateful to Pétain for having spared them the German Occupation; also, *it was thanks to Pétain that at a period of France's deepest national humiliation she should have been able, paradoxically enough, to embark on an orgy of national self-glorification.* In a way, it was a curious expression of her powerful instinct of self-preservation. On the other hand, Pétain was the man— probably the only man—who made it possible in July 1940 to launch the "National Revolution" at all—and make it, moreover, look respectable.

The feeling of gratitude to Pétain, though chiefly in the Free Zone, was very genuine—and understandable. The Armistice had limited the damage, and had—so it then seemed—saved France from utter destruction. In 1940 and 1941 and throughout most of 1942 (after the German

Occupation of the Southern Zone the myth rapidly faded out; there
was no limit to the adulation and deification to which Pétain was subjected by a chorus of propagandists who were joined by some enthusiastic amateur poets. Thus, the *Revue Moderne* published in 1941 a verse
anthology called *Credo à la France*, with gems like this paraphrase of
the Lord's Prayer—addressed to Pétain:

> *Notre Père qui êtes*
> *A notre tête,*
> *Que votre nom soit glorifié,*
> *Que votre règne arrive,*
> *Que votre volonté soit faite*
> *Sur la terre pour qu'on vive;*
> *Demeurez sans retour*
> *Notre pain de chaque jour;*
> *Redonnez l'existence*
> *A la France;*
> *Ne nous laissez pas retomber*
> *Dans le vain songe*
> *Et le mensonge;*
> *Et délivrez-nous du mal,*
> *O Maréchal.*[17]

Similarly, Le Franciste, in April 1942, published an "act of faith" of
the Pétain religion: "*Monsieur le Maréchal*, I believe implicitly all the
truths that you teach, for you cannot be wrong, and you cannot deceive
your people." Seemingly reputable writers like René Benjamin (*de
l'Académie Goncourt*) filled whole books with fulsome sentimental
trash about the Infallible Guide. Other examples of this deification of
Pétain could be quoted; for instance this "Prayer by a French Woman
to Marshal Pétain", with its final lines:

> *Si vous avez au coeur la divine espérance*
> *De rapprocher un jour, en un même idéal,*
> *Les hommes divisés ... qui sait? ... par ignorance,*
> *Soyez notre Bon Dieu, Monsieur le Maréchal;*

or this touching story of the peasant child who, after writing to the
Marshal, received a photograph from him:

> *Son coeur battait la charge et son regard tendu*
> *S'accrochait a la fière image vénérable;*
> *Il la porta d'un bond sur sa petite table,*
> *Près du Christ indulgent qui, déja, souriait,*
> *Joignit les mains comme le soir quand il priait,*
> *S'approcha doucement dans le plus grand mystère*
> *Et radieux, tremblant, murmura: "Notre Père!"*[18]

[17] Quoted by *Esprit*, September 1951, p. 383.
[18] Both poems are given in the appendix to d'Argenson's *Pétain et le Pétinisme*
(Paris, 1953), pp. 177, 179.

This kind of thing belongs, of course, to the "lunatic fringe". But a peculiarity of Hitler-dominated Europe was precisely the existence of broad lunatic fringes in most countries—while in Germany the "fringe" absorbed almost the entire nation.

One might say that in France there were two lunatic fringes—one on the "Left", represented by Déat and Doriot; the other on the "Right", represented by the *"la France seule"* ideology of Vichy. There were, however, a number of variants of this: on the one hand the "negative" hate propaganda of Maurras, on the other, the kind of "positive" but unrealistic "pietism" and tearful French self-glorification, with its call to return to "France's ancient virtues", and the rolling together of cows, pigs, trees, Joan of Arc, God, *le Maréchal* and an expurgated Charles Péguy.

Both groups were equally impressed by the *"Nous, Philippe Pétain, Chef de l'Etat"* style of official writing; one, because it suggested to them the revival of the Monarchist principle, the other, because it suggested a kind of benevolent paternalism which had been lacking under the Third Republic. But actually, it is very hard to draw the line between the "paternalists" and the *maurrassistes*. The two groups overlapped; both were equally pro-Marshal, and men like Henri Massis and Thierry Maulnier created an ideological bond between them. Massis was one of those chiefly responsible for enlisting Charles Péguy in the service of Vichy as a sort of ideological saint of Pétainism, and for attributing to him all kinds of ultra-conservative Action Française virtues which Péguy had never possessed. For Péguy, with his anti-clericalism, his Dreyfusism, his anti-capitalism, his hatred of Germany, was a much more complex character than was suggested by the *morceaux choisis* with which he was introduced into the Vichy world. No doubt his *Tapisseries*, his *Mystère de Jeanne d'Arc*, his cult of the cathedral of Chartres as a symbol of the "real" France, corresponded to certain moods existing in France—especially in Unoccupied France —during the months that followed the Armistice. Péguy's *Tapisseries* made Frenchmen—and especially French women—"feel good"; it made them feel that they belonged to an ancient and superior civilization—which no military defeat with all these vile, modern weapons of war could destroy.

The France of Péguy [wrote Henri Massis] is the France we have to re-learn.... The France of Péguy is not an idea, a notion, a spiritless body; it is a great, living, real people. The France of Péguy—it is our provinces, our lands, the Loire, the Beauce, it is Paris. The France of Péguy means persons: Joan of Arc, Ste Geneviève, St Louis, Our Lady, and God. It means our trees, our fields, our church towers. And Thierry Maulnier was right to welcome Péguy as "the only poet of our wheatfields", as the only one who was truly aware of our French skies, of our French soil, of our French work....

And Péguy was also recommended by Massis to Vichy France as a teacher of France's "ancient virtues" which must now be re-learned. In his book, significantly entitled *Les Idées restent*, Massis quoted from Péguy such passages on the French people as this:

> When one says *people* today, one uses merely a literary cliché—and of the lowest kind, too; an electoral, parliamentary, political cliché. The *people* as such no longer exists. Everybody is bourgeois now. The little that was left of the ancient aristocracies has become a low bourgeoisie. The ancient bourgeoisie has also become a low bourgeoisie, a bourgeoisie of money. And the workers—they also have only one idea—and that is, to become bourgeois. It's what they call becoming Socialist. The peasants alone have remained profoundly peasant, have remained *themselves* ... Believe it or not, but in my youth I knew workers who had a desire to work.... Work was their joy and the very root of their being. An incredible honour was attached to work, the greatest of all honours, the most Christian of honours, the only one that could always keep its head erect. (Henri Massis, *les Idées restent*, Lyon, 1943, pp. 50–5.)

This was the sort of thing that helped to inspire the *Travail-Famille-Patrie* ideology, the *retour à la terre* and other "bucolic" features of Vichy. It should, of course, be remembered that, in July 1940, there existed the idea of the "pastoralization" of France in a Hitler Europe dominated by an industrial Germany (a kind of inverted Morganthau Plan); and, what is more, this whole concept was not as unpopular as one might imagine among those who still remembered with a shudder the days of 1936, when the industrial worker of France threw his weight about, and when the stay-in strikes staged by the turbulent industrial proletariat of Paris put the fear of death into the *bien-pensants*. And, sure enough, Laval had clearly hinted at Vichy in the early days of July 1940 at the possibility of France becoming a primarily agricultural annex of a primarily industrial Germany (or, as Déat put it more cynically, "Germany's vegetable garden and Luna Park"). This was, no doubt, an unpleasant aspect of the whole thing, and Maurras, with his *France Seule*, and Massis with his "ancient French virtues" preferred not to think about that side of it.

But that the *retour à la terre* was not perhaps taken quite seriously by the man-in-the-street in France is suggested by this amusing passage in Maurice Martin du Gard's *Vichy Diary*:

> In the street, outside, I heard somebody remark: "Well, one has to joke a bit. For if one started thinking too hard ..." And suddenly a newsboy ran past, crying: "*Demandez* Le Jour-L'Echo de Paris! *Le retour à la terre. La charrue avant les boeufs!*"[19]

[19] The *retour à la terre* policy did produce a few tangible results, some of them dictated by the needs of the moment when France was cut off from most of her colonies: for instance the extensive development of rice-growing in the Camargue country.

Putting the cart before the horse (or "the plough before the oxen", as they say in French)—was not this wisecrack by the Vichy *gavroche* a most vital criticism of the Vichy philosophy, in terms of practical possibilities? Did it not also suggest—although the newsboy may not have thought of that consciously—that the military *débâcle* and the Armistice had not, in themselves, settled anything yet? For London had not yet been conquered by Hitler.

7. VICHY AND THE INTELLECTUALS

"Soyez notre bon Dieu, Monsier le Maréchal..." an amateur poetess of the "lunatic fringe" had written. And yet did not Herriot's "Let us all rally round the Marshal!" have a much wider appeal than many today like to admit? The Church hierarchy wholeheartedly supported Pétain; the civil service more or less voluntarily submitted, partly for reasons of professional sentiment, partly for ordinary bread-and-butter reasons. And the intellectual *élite*? The great majority of this, either wholeheartedly or with mental reservations, also followed suit. This was true, above all, of the over-forties. The French Academy, with the sole exception of Mauriac (and the partial exception of Duhamel), was wholeheartedly pro-Marshal. France's two most celebrated poets, Claudel and Valéry were Pétainist, Claudel writing a particularly fulsome *Ode* in his honour:

Monsieur le Maréchal, voici cette France entre vos bras et qui n'a que vous et qui ressuscite à voix basse.

France, écoute ce vieil homme sur toi qui se penche et qui te parle comme un père...

Was this pure opportunism on Claudel's part? According to Maurice Martin du Gard, it was rumoured in Vichy that Claudel had merely hoped to succeed Pétain as Ambassador at Madrid, and was still hoping to succeed Piétri, should the latter be recalled. Claudel, as Ambassador of the Third Republic, was now treating his former masters as "madmen"—"enough," said Martin du Gard, "to make Philippe Berthelot turn in his grave". And he suspected Claudel of having written the whole thing with his tongue in his cheek. One wonders. Claudel—whom Bernanos described as a "ventriloquist"—was the very antithesis of the Liberal Catholic. However, in 1944, he hastened to write an equally fulsome *Ode to de Gaulle*.

Valéry had "received" Pétain at the French Academy in 1931, and they had remained great friends. He often came to see Pétain at Vichy. In Paris, as late as 1943, he published what Maurice Martin du Gard called "new and admirable pages on Pétain". Jean and Jerôme Tharaud and all the smaller fry of the French Academy were all Pétainists—if they were not all-out German collaborators, such as the "two Abels", Abel Hermant and Abel Bonnard, or *les gestapettes*, as they were popularly known. Much of the Paris *beau monde*, with Sacha Guitry at its head, was both Pétainist—and "*collabo*" on occasion. Pétain often received Guitry, whose company he found flattering and highly entertaining. On one occasion, Guitry presented Pétain with the proofs of a *de luxe* anthology dedicated to the glory of France, and entitled *De Jeanne d'Arc a Pétain*.[20] A few like Jean Cocteau, Duhamel, Giraudoux, Gide, and some others, it is true, assumed a more non-committal attitude to Vichy; but even abroad, Pétain had enlisted the support of some well-known writers—even the anglophil André Maurois among them,[21] and in Paris, Ambassador Abetz prided himself on having so many French writers "on Germany's side", among them Drieu La Rochelle, Fabre-Luce, Céline, Suarez, Brasillach, not to mention the smaller fry; and never ceased to boast of the "intellectual life" that continued to "flourish" in Paris, especially around the NRF (*Nouvelle Revue Française*) under the German occupation. An even higher proportion of painters and musicians (not to mention theatre and cinema people) "collaborated". Often no clear line could be drawn between Vichyism and plain "collaboration".

All things considered, real opposition to both Vichy and the Germans among the recognized intellectual *élite* of France was strikingly small. The famous names in active opposition could almost be counted on the fingers of one hand: Mauriac, Bernanos, Malraux, perhaps Roger Martin du Gard; and, of course, among the Communists, Eluard and Aragon. Nearly all the rest of the intellectual opposition was composed of the younger people in the Resistance; of the official *élite* of the French Academy, Mauriac was, in fact, the only real rebel.

The influence of Mauriac's non-conformism was very great both before the war and during the war—just as it was to be great for years afterwards. Like Bernanos, he had taken an independent line against the Maurras-tainted conformism of the *bien-pensants* in relation to Abyssinia and to the Spanish war. In 1940 he did not "accept" France's defeat, and therefore he could not "accept" either Vichy or Pétain. In the part of his famous *Cahier Noir*, which was written in November 1941, he debunked in these cruel lines the myth of Vichy:

As I write, so many, many of my countrymen are moved by this one elementary passion: Fear. They will not admit it; and they are making a great song and dance round the Marshal, and they keep invoking Joan of Arc; but, on the quiet, it all boils down to this one and only simple need:

[20] M. M. du Gard, *op. cit.*, p. 315.
[21] Of André Maurois, who had made for years a highly profitable business of Anglo-French friendship, Mr Churchill is alleged to have said in 1941: "We thought him a friend; but he was only a client."

to save their privileges, to avoid a final reckoning. "While the Germans are there ..."—a reassuring little phrase which Taine and Renan already muttered at the sight of the burning Tuileries Palace ..."

And later, in 1943, he wrote:

When the Government of Monsieur Pétain subscribes to the racial laws, and hands over to the Gestapo foreigners who had trusted France's word, and when the Nazi hangmen find among the Vichy police, among the men of Doriot and Darnand enough helpers and flunkeys to make it almost unnecessary for them to dirty their own hands, who can deny any longer that these wretches are overloading the conscience of that living being, of that living soul, the French nation?

And Maurras—with his *nationalisme intégral*, Maurras, the prime ideologist of Vichy?

Alas, everything one can say in defence of Maurras comes down with a crash in this appalling *finale*: without having wanted it, Maurras and his disciples woke up one day to find themselves in the enemy camp, on the side of the German hangmen and their French flunkeys ...

Mauriac's *Cahier Noir*, to be dropped from British planes over France, already belongs to the Resistance—the *real* Resistance, just as his editorials in the *Figaro* on Abyssinia and Spain and Munich already belonged to the Resistance *avant la lettre*; just as his passionate pleading for a Fair Deal for North Africans in 1952 and 1953 were to continue the Resistance on a different plane. But his passionate defence of certain human, Christian and national French values, with its underlying revolt against "Machiavelli", was something that only aroused the wrath of all those who, in the name of the Marshal, sang praises to the "ancient virtues of France". Mauriac, like so many others in the Resistance, refused to swallow the humbug, the hypocrisy of Vichy pietism with its undertones of "*tant que les Allemands sont là ...*" And if the Germans were to be beaten, then perhaps the Americans ...

No, Mauriac did not think highly of his countrymen as a whole:

Too many Frenchmen are giving the enemy a pretty ignominious spectacle of themselves—this French police, which is like the faithful watchdog of the black-market profiteers, all these business men and all these men of letters who are being enriched by the Army of Occupation—they belong to an undying species. Already in 1796 Mallet du Pan wrote: "Everybody is trying by a thousand different means, and at any price, not to have to share in the general distress. People think only of themselves, themselves, themselves ..."[22]

In the last analysis, Maurrasism was, to Mauriac, nothing but a pre-

[22] François Mauriac, *Le Cahier Noir* (Paris, 1947), pp. 22–69. (The book is composed of two essays, one written in 1941, the other in 1943.)

tentiously ornate intellectual cloak covering up the ugly nudity of the reactionary bourgeois Caliban.

8. THE CASE FOR AND AGAINST PÉTAIN

The Fourth Republic's case against Pétain is both straightforward and, in many cases, ambiguous. He was charged with being defeatist, with having accepted, at least for a time, the "satellization" of France by Nazi Germany; and with having hypocritically aided Germany in her war against both Britain and Russia. After Montoire he had declared: "this policy [of collaboration with Germany] is my policy," and had added that he was taking the fullest responsibility for this:

History alone shall judge me. Up till now I spoke to you as a father, now I speak to you as a chief.

He had also given his blessing to the LVF, the French Legion on the Eastern Front, clad in German uniform.

In home affairs, he had headed a "reactionary conspiracy", and as late as July 17, 1944, when there was no purpose any longer in playing the much-vaunted "double game" (but then *had* Pétain played any "double game" in *home* affairs?) he had written to Maurras:

We have all benefited from your lessons. You have been consistently right. I thank you and congratulate you on the great service you have rendered the country.[23]

His whole entourage at Vichy was, in the main, ultra-reactionary, with a good sprinkling of cagoulard elements, among them Alibert, Ménétier, the chief of his bodyguard, and another man called "the killer" —not to mention a bigger and better killer like Darnand, whom Pétain did not disavow until the very last moment. Even the more "reasonable" people around him, such as Du Moulin de Labarthète, were, for the most part, Action Française men.

It was argued at Pétain's trial that, even though he was nominally "responsible to History", he could not be expected to be responsible for the atrocities committed by the Milice, often in collaboration with the Gestapo; or that he could not be blamed for the treatment suffered by the *volontaires étrangers*—a particularly disgraceful affair. These were the foreigners who had joined the French Army as volunteers in 1939 and who, after being demobilized, were herded into camps as so many suspects and undesirables who had "volunteered to fight for Daladier".[24] Many died in horrible forced-labour camps in Africa, where they were made to build stretches of the Trans-Sahara railway.

---

[23] *Procès Pétain*, p. 898.   [24] *Cf.* Vanino, *op. cit.*, pp. 298–318.

All that can be said about Pétain in this connexion is that if he did not
actively "order" atrocities to be committed, he consciously adopted towards the most revolting aspects of the Vichy régime an attitude of
laissez-faire and was, if anything, rather favourable towards the anti-
masonic and anti-Jewish legislation and, at any rate, tolerant towards
the executions carried out by the Milice.

Other charges against Pétain include his failure to allow the French
Navy to join the Allies or, at least, to seek refuge in a neutral port, after
the Germans had invaded the Vichy Zone, and the extremely tricky line
he adopted in respect of Darlan in Africa. Did he not, like Darlan
himself, try to drive a wedge between the Americans and the British
for Germany's benefit, perhaps, and, in any case, to the greatest detriment of the Resistance?

The defence of Pétain follows closely the statement made by Pétain
himself, and quoted at the beginning of this chapter. There has always
been a tendency, on the part of Pétain's apologists, to say that Pétain
did his utmost to give Germany not the maximum, but the minimum.
If more was given away, "it was Laval's fault". As a demonstration
that Pétain was "better" than Darlan, the Marshal's apologists like to
show that he turned down the Huntziger-Warlimont protocols of May
1941, and agreed only to "co-operation" in Syria, but not in Africa; he
notably opposed the surrender of Bizerta and Dakar to the Germans as
bases. Also, despite Darlan's very serious ambitions in that direction, he
had, in the main, managed to prevent any joint Franco-German military operations against the British and the Gaullists in Africa. As for
encouraging the LVF in Russia, this, it is alleged, was of no real significance. It pleased the Germans, but there was not much in it: the
LVF were only a very small unit—mostly a bunch of riff-raff, more
noted for their raping and drinking activities in Russia than for their
military achievements by the side of the *Wehrmacht*. And perhaps also
—who knows?—Pétain, or some of his friends, did not think the glori-
fication of the anti-Bolshevik Crusade such a bad thing—for future
reference, whatever the immediate outcome of the war.

In foreign affairs Pétain was, as Ambassador Leahy put it in one of
his dispatches to Roosevelt, "a frightened old man". His whole behaviour clearly suggests that he was desperately frightened of the Germans—even after the Germans had obviously lost the war. Why did he
not rebel in November 1942? Why did he not escape to North Africa
himself? Why did he submit to the German occupation of Vichy
France? Why did he not order the Navy at Toulon to join the Allies?
It was because he was afraid of German reprisals. He was afraid, as he
was to tell Maurice Martin du Gard, of the "polonization" of France.
He imagined that, in all circumstances, he could still "protect" France.
And similarly, as is apparent from his interview in *La Gerbe* with

Alphonse de Châteaubriant, he dreaded war with England "because the British might destroy Paris—and that I don't want".

The fact remains that, even to a devoted supporter of Pétain's like Jérôme Carcopino, at one time Minister of Education at Vichy, Pétain's decision to stay on at Vichy as "Head of the State" after the German occupation of the Southern Zone was a fatal mistake, and made complete nonsense of the much-vaunted "double game". For, after November 1942, Pétain inevitably became increasingly subservient to the Germans, and was even obliged to appoint as Ministers men like Déat and Henriot—which was unthinkable before. If, as Carcopino claims, there was a genuine understanding under the "Rougier agreement" between Pétain and Churchill that France would join the Allies if Germany violated the terms of the Armistice, then Pétain merely ignored this agreement.[25] In the last analysis, Pétain's senile desire to keep his exalted job—even under the Germans—had something to do with it, too.

9. HARD AND SOFT VICHYITES

Despite the verbal majesty and solemnity of the National Revolution, despite the personal prestige of Pétain, at any rate during the first year or two of his reign, the flimsiness of the whole Vichy structure could scarcely escape anybody's attention. The area of the Vichy Zone was limited to one-third of the country; it had very little industry, and large stretches of it were unfertile and thinly populated. No large-scale national planning was possible within these narrow limits. The Occupied Zone was only nominally under Vichy *rule*, though it was under Vichy *administration*. And if it was possible, in the Vichy Zone, to forget (or to pretend to forget) that the real master of France was Hitler, everybody was fully aware of it in the Occupied Zone, where the Marshal and his whole "National Revolution" carried little weight. Here it was realized that if Germany won the war, no one could tell whether she would allow the authority of Vichy to extend over the whole of France, or whether she would tolerate Vichy at all, unless it were completely subservient to Berlin. If Germany lost the war, then Vichy as such was doomed; perhaps Vichy's only chance of prolonging its existence was in a compromise peace—which was Flandin's ideal solution, and perhaps also Laval's, though he seldom, if ever spoke of it. In any case, in the Occupied Zone, Pétain's stock was never high—and people from the Occupied Zone who came to Vichy were startled at the Vichy *"mystique"*. We thus have an interesting account of a visit to Vichy in January 1941 by a Socialist, Jean Texcier, of Libération-Nord, who was one of the principal Resistance propagandists in the Occupied Zone.

[25] Jérôme Carcopino, *Souvenirs de sept ans* (Paris, 1953), p. 601.

In Paris [he wrote] one can never get away from the vision of our wounded and insulted country; every moment in the street you can hear its tormentor's voice. Everywhere, too, his flags are flying . . . But Vichy is different . . . By listening hard, by watching closely, one realizes that a subtle political game is going on, full of cunning and diplomacy . . . Everything here seems to be shifting and—shifty. There is a general epidemic of caution . . . There is a lot of coming and going, by officials, and officers and soldiers in uniform. There are large tricolour flags flying over the entrances of all the grand hotels. But in the conversations one overhears there is no life, and none of that warmth which marks our daily talks in Paris. There are no fighters here, there are only diplomats . . . And they all seem far more concerned with the various Court rumours than with the present or the future of France. "Hell!" says the Paris visitor to himself, "they don't really imagine that the fate of France has been finally settled?"[26]

Yet he could not help being impressed and even touched by the outward nobility, and even the pathos of the Pétain symbol. Of course, it was not majestic to him—but pathetic.

This comic opera capital [he wrote] is also a Holy City. With its Marshal in flesh and blood, with its Marshal on prints, posters, photos, postcards, calendars, pipes, paper-weights, and, before long, no doubt, on cough lozenges, Vichy has become a sort of tricolour Lisieux. . . . You realize that a man coming here straight from Paris cannot help being touched by all this display of red, white, and blue. I will not deny it: he even looks with a touch of emotion through the shop window at the sad and delicate face of the Head of the French State, so different from the grotesque snouts of the Axis thugs.

Yet, looking at all these patriotic knick-knacks, he could not help wondering with some anxiety whether all this religious imagery was not a dangerous sign of a great mental laziness, and of a certain spiritual cowardice.

The Marshal's strength comes from the very idea that he is the Man of Providence, that it is best to submit to Providence, and so much easier than to think for one's self.[27]

In Occupied France, on the other hand, he said, the issues were perfectly clear. What mattered to most men there were the daily results of a war that was still being fought; they could see only one possible solution: the liberation of France through the defeat of Germany. And their innermost thoughts went daily to Britain and to America, now wholly committed to Britain's support.

Compared with the military clash between Germany and Britain, what does the National Revolution of Vichy matter, or, as Hitler's scribes in Paris would have it, France's National-Socialist Revolution? Are not all

[26] Jean Texcier, *Ecrit dans la nuit* (Paris, 1945), p. 75.   [27] *Ibid.*, p. 77.

these big and small measures taken at Vichy just a *pastime of a gang of prisoners*? (*Ibid.*, p. 78.)

Everything tends to show that in the Occupied Zone, and especially in Paris, where Germany's ultimate defeat was all that really mattered, the Pétain mystique did not cut much ice. Daily hardships had not killed the *gavroche* spirit, as illustrated by the case of two schoolboys—whom I personally know—who, while doing their share in the *Secours National* money collections, would stand on the Pont d'Austerlitz selling postcards of Pétain to passers-by, crying: "*Secours National! Secours National! Achetez le portrait du vieux c...*" A jest scarcely conceivable in Vichy France!

Despite appearances, Vichy was not a homogeneous régime. The historical circumstances in which it was born made it inevitable that with it should be associated men of widely varying political tendencies and temperaments. Its supporters ranged from fanatical "right-wing" Fascists (Darnand), Action Française royalists and anti-Semites (Maurras, Darquier de Pellepoix), "respectable" semi-Fascists with the typical *ancien combattant* and "good middle-class" outlook of La Rocque and his Croix de Feu (it was this outlook that characterized the Légion Française at its earlier stages, before part of it became "gangsterized" by Darnand and turned into the Milice), and the greater part of the Church hierarchy, down to the ordinary "classical" Right—conservative and clerical—the greater part of the Radical-Socialists, and even part of the Socialists.

A curious aspect of Vichy is provided by the continued existence of a paper like the old Radical-Socialist *Dépêche* of Toulouse, which continued to appear with the sub-title "*Journal de la Démocratie*", with Maurice Sarraut continuing as its editor—until his murder by Darnand or Doriot's gunmen in 1943. Maurice Sarraut's argument in favour of keeping the *Dépêche* going—and the *Dépêche* had been and, in a way, continued to be, the most influential paper in the South—was that, in spite of the censorship and a variety of restrictions, it might still be able to "moderate" the Vichy régime, by playing off the "moderates" against the "die-hards". To Pétain, the support of the *Dépêche* was, of course, of the greatest value, because the small-town politicians, and with them, a large part of the peasant population which, in the South, still had something of the old republican tradition, tended to take their line from the *Dépêche*. It was not until 1943, with the Maquis developing, that a large part of the peasant population, notably in the Massif Central and the Dordogne, began to support the Resistance.

And here again, we come up against one of the major paradoxes of Vichy: although the *maréchalistes* treated Laval as a flunkey of the Germans, the *Dépêche* still thought him basically more "republican" than the people surrounding the Marshal. Its Vichy representative, Maurice Martin du Gard was on particularly good terms with Laval. The latter's reflexes were still those of a Third Republic politician, and there were certain features of the "National Revolution" which he found particularly distasteful, as we shall see later. He was, notably, opposed to excessive interference with the small-town traditions and habits of provincial France, to the dissolution of the *conseils généraux*, to the "purge" among mayors, and to the blacklisting of harmless individuals—local chemists, school-teachers and shopkeepers—on the ground that they were anti-clericals or Freemasons. The accounts of Laval's frequent fraternization with the local worthies in provincial France ring true, and his back-slapping habits maintained his popularity among these people even at a time when he was thought by so many to be responsible for all the surrenders to Germany.

With so many different tendencies existing at Vichy, with Pétain largely under the influence of men of the "National Revolution"—ranging from cagoulard thugs to "moderate" Royalists like du Moulin de Labarthète,[28] with the constant scramble for Cabinet posts among a lot of young people who had not had a chance under the Third Republic; with the Germans constantly trying to interfere in Pétain's frequent government changes,[29] with men like Pucheu, while Vichy France was still "free", trying to enforce the Fascist principle of the "Single Party", very much in the manner of Déat (who, for his own part, was heartily detested by the Vichy conservatives and left Vichy in disgust in 1940)—with all these elements pulling in different directions, Vichy was far from being the solid authoritarian state which the Marshal and the more naïve *maréchalistes* liked, at least until November 1942, to imagine it to be.

Apart from the far-reaching constitutional reforms with their *Nous, Philippe Pétain* style, the rest of the reforms were rather sketchy, and, in many cases, represented scarcely coherent compromises—such as the famous *Charte du Travail*, the most striking feature of which was the domination of the whole system by "corporative" *comités sociaux*, and the absolute prohibition of strikes and lock-outs. It was corporatist and paternalist in character, and was one of the first things to be scrapped by Algiers.

The truth, of course, is that, for all its "corporatist" jargon, Vichy

[28] Du Moulin had been head of the Action Française in the sixteenth *arrondissement* of Paris. The exceedingly "reasonable" book he was to publish in 1946 with its rather condescending tone towards Pétain, makes ironical reading.

[29] Thus, according to Carcopino they were anxious, in January 1941, to have one of their stooges, Abel Bonnard appointed Minister of Education—and even announced the appointment on the radio in order to force Petain's hand—instead of Carcopino, whose appointment was two days later presented to the Germans as a *fait accompli*.

France was, in fact, essentially capitalist, with the trusts, financial oligarchies and big business being their own masters as seldom before. The *comités d'organisation*, with their full control of raw materials, were in the hands of big business; Lehideux, representing nine big firms, with a capital of over one milliard pre-war francs, was at the head of the governing body of these committees. He was later succeeded at this post by Pucheu. The Engineering Committee was, in fact, composed of all the bigwigs of the old *Comité des Forges* (Jules Aubrun, Théodore Laurent, Maroger, Humbert de Wendel, Baron Hely d'Oissel, Baron Petiet, etc); similarly some of the biggest capitalists ran the Coal Committee. Pétain declared on one occasion that these men "should have sufficient authority to negotiate with the Germans" —which they did, with considerable profit to themselves. A good deal of "concentration", "conversion", and "rationalization" was done with a view to "Europeanizing" French industry, which, more often than not meant the subordination of the French trusts to the German trusts. No doubt, here also a "double game" was being played; and Bouthillier resisted against an excessive penetration of German capital into French industry. Even so, the chemical works of Rhône-Poulenc, for example, became subordinated to I. G. Farben, and formed a group called "Francolor", in which 50 per cent of the shares were German. The *Pariser Zeitung* declared with much satisfaction in November 1942 that 70 per cent of French exports went to Germany.

Perhaps all this was more or less inevitable under German pressure; only what is certain is that the much-vaunted cult of *travail* was so much window-dressing; the conditions of labour, both in the occupied and the unoccupied zone were unenviable in the extreme (despite the theoretical introduction of the "vital minimum" principle), while Big Business continued to thrive with the Marshal's blessing. And in these Big Business quarters there were many—especially the younger men— who played about with long-term plans of a Nazi-dominated "Europe", as we shall see later from our account of the "Synarchie" group.

Nevertheless, it is fully recognized today that Vichy did succeed in enlisting the services of some of the ablest economic technicians— notably men like Bichelonne, Bouthillier, and many others, and that, considering the terrible strain on French finances created by the daily payment of 400 million francs to the Army of Occupation, France came, financially, better out of the four years of Occupation than might have been expected—though largely, no doubt, at the expense of the wage-earners. Even so, the depreciation of the franc between 1940 and 1944 had been less rapid than in the years that were to follow.

Not very long before the German Occupation of the Vichy Zone, Wladimir d'Ormesson wrote these typically self-congratulatory lines in the *Figaro*:

Let us think what France was like in June 1940, when all was lost, when all was topsy-turvy. Let us also consider the state in which we still are today, with our country cut in two, or even in three.... And yet, it is a *tour de force* that, in such conditions, the financial and economic life of the country should, even in this relative and fragmentary way, continue to function....

There followed a warm tribute to the work of Yves Bouthillier, the Minister of Finance and an enumeration of various other achievements: the return of the refugees to their homes, the reduction in unemployment, the smoking factory-chimneys, the repairs to roads and bridges, the "programme of great public works", the financial, social and agricultural legislation, the organization of rationing, etc. France had gone through the greatest crisis of her history without having had to enforce a financial moratorium. And he concluded:

No doubt, there have been difficulties, and many of the measures taken are provisional measures. One had to improvise all the time.... And yet— when Siéyès was asked what he had done during the Revolution, he replied: "I lived." It would be a good thing if France could say the same after this terrible crisis....

I lived—I survived—was not this, in the last analysis, one of the most important aspects of Pétainism?

10. THE MIND OF A NONAGENARIAN

In the midst of all those contradictions and all this confusion there was Pétain, nearly ninety, incredibly vain and fancying himself the Man of Providence. He knew that the greater part of France had loved him in 1940, and that many, notably the peasantry, still had a soft spot for him, even after others had become disappointed. What makes it so difficult to analyse the mentality of Pétain is that very few people in the world have had the experience of being nearly ninety; and how, indeed, does the mind of a nonagenarian work—in so far as it works at all? It has often been said of Pétain that although he was "completely lucid" during a few hours of the day (chiefly in the morning), he was somnolent and gaga, in varying degrees, during the rest of the time.

In his lucid moments he could be likeable and even entertaining. He enjoyed his long walks in the morning, followed by a hearty meal ("his appetite", Du Moulin wrote, "is terrific"); there was still about him something of the army officer, with a taste for dirty stories; and he also loved the company of very young women. According to Du Moulin, he once confessed to Laval:

If only I could make love several times a week, I would be a perfectly happy man. But I still have my good spells. . . . What I have really loved in my life are two things: infantry and love-making.

To Du Moulin, who reported these indiscretions to Maurice Martin du Gard, the latter remarked:

"Why, for propaganda purposes, does he have to be represented as a stuffed dummy kneeling in church? The French would much prefer to know that he is still a devil with the girls!" To which Du Moulin replied: "Yes, I know. But there's the Church, and there's *la Maréchale*, which makes it awkward."

And Martin du Gard added:

"He's a soldier; he's pure of heart. Only Laval doesn't think so." "He's ambitious," Laval said. "He's quite impossible."

Laval also said, on another occasion, that the old man, full of childish vanity over his exalted position, had become totally insensitive to the injustice that was being done to so many in his name.

A strange old man, full of vanity and ambition, callous in some important respects, but human in other, less important ones. He liked dirty stories, and he liked La Fontaine and Racine, he enjoyed the company of Valéry and Sacha Guitry, and liked children and pretty young women; and in his conversation he often repeated himself, and though his memory was bad, he had a few pet ideas which he continuously repeated—for instance, that France ought to be more serious-minded, and have a lot more babies, and that France was culturally superior to other nations, and that, in future, she should "impose herself" on others by producing more Racines, and Molières, La Fontaines and Valérys. He was genuinely attached to the soil of France, and his belief in some magic virtue of his own person, as well as a very old man's reluctance to take any positive action, perhaps explains best his negative decision *not* to escape or to rebel when the Germans occupied Southern France.[30]

The preaching of "discipline" and "more babies" was part of that "pure Pétainism" which no doubt appealed to the Church; but, behind it, there was also the "ideology" of Vichy, which was something less simple and less pure. It is worth examining in some detail these two peculiar aspects of Vichy—the rôle of the Church which supported Pétain *the man* throughout, but gradually rebelled against

---

[30] I am not mentioning the "prophetic" conversation he had in June 1941 with Maurice Martin du Gard (*op. cit.*, p. 197) in which he foreshadowed the division of the world into a Russian and an American bloc. It is possible that Martin du Gard—who had a liking for Pétain—was tempted to attribute to him a degree of foresight which he did not in reality possess. The date of the "prophecy" makes the value of this piece of Vichy "Boswellism" doubly questionable.

Vichyism; and, on the other hand, the Action Française, for which Pétain had the greatest regard, but which was perhaps more responsible than anything else for giving Vichy its particularly vicious and "un-Christian" character. It supported "Vichy" to the bitter end, Germans or no Germans, till in the end it became in effect allied to Hitler!

CHAPTER THREE

THE CHURCH UNDER VICHY

Like the civil service, the judiciary, the police, and the armed forces, the Church "accepted" the Vichy Government as the legal government of France, and did it, indeed, with relish—at least for a time. But in this, as in all matters concerning Vichy France, one must guard against over-simplification. All-out clericalism had its strong supporters at Vichy, but it would be untrue to say that Vichy France became overnight a sort of French version of Franco Spain. The fact that the post of Minister of Education changed hands so many times clearly shows that there was a struggle in Vichy among the different tendencies, the peak of clericalization being reached in the very early stages of the Vichy régime, especially under Jacques Chevalier, who hastened to clericalize all the State schools by throwing them open to the *curé* and even by expecting the *instituteurs* to give religious tuition to their pupils. That these measures were impractical, and were bound to create everlasting conflicts beween the *curés* and the 130,000 *instituteurs* of France was so obvious that when Jacques Chevalier was replaced at the Ministry of Education by Jerôme Carcopino (the well-known ancient historian, Director of the Ecole Normale Supérieure, and for a short time, at the end of 1940, Acting Rector of the University of Paris), the latter hastened, in January 1941, to revoke the whole of the Chevalier programme, and proclaimed the "religious neutrality" of the State in respect of education. By "neutrality" he meant, of course, that the *laïque* schools (with about two-thirds of the school-children) would not be in the privileged position in which they had been before; and that the so-called "free" schools, if in financial difficulties (and in 1941 they all were) would also benefit from State subsidies. He was not, however, willing to impose the teaching of catechism on the *laïque* schools, which could usually only have been done against the will of both parents and teachers, though he insisted that religious tuition should be available outside the schools, and at convenient school hours.

The fact, nevertheless, remains that the long republican tradition of refusing subsidies to religious schools was broken by Vichy, and, in doing so, it set up a precedent which was not to die with the Vichy régime. The famous Barangé Law of 1951 was, in a very large measure, inspired by Carcopino's laws of 1941. Pétain himself, according to Carcopino, was under strong clerical influence; "he was haunted by the dream of restoring in France the forces of Christianity, and, if he had not been stopped in time, he would have crushed the Church under the enormous weight of his favours".[1] And Carcopino suggests that it was with Pétain's approval that the more absurd innovations of Chevalier were introduced during the early stages of the régime. Chevalier was not only determined to clericalize the whole of education, but, in doing so, he proceeded to carry out a ruthlesss purge among school-teachers—a purge which was largely stopped by Carcopino; also many of the persons dismissed were reinstated. This part of Carcopino's story is supported by sufficient evidence to make it convincing.

The hierarchy of the Catholic Church was, from the outset, favourable to the Pétain régime, and felt that, even though it was not possible to look very far ahead, it was thanks to this régime that they could help to bring about certain changes in France, which would last, whatever ultimately happened. And in this they proved to be substantially right. Although Cardinal Suhard, the Archbishop of Paris, is quoted by Carcopino as saying that he was totally opposed to looking upon Vichy as an opportunity for a *revanche* against the *école laïque*, he was still eminently in favour of extending to the religious schools the benefit of State aid.

The Church became incomparably more prominent in all official ceremonies at Vichy than it had been for more than a century. The Church not only did its best to "annex" the Marshal, but it was also very much in evidence in all the specifically *maréchaliste* activities of the Chantiers de la Jeunesse and other youth movements; and the Légion was surrounded by the incense of clerical approval.

Vis-à-vis Pétain himself the Catholic hierarchy, with the full approval of the Vatican, assumed the warmest possible attitude. As early as July 30, 1940 Cardinal Gerlier, Archbishop of Lyon and Primate of the Gauls, almost welcomed the defeat of France as a blessing in disguise:

If we had remained victorious [he said] we would probably have remained the prisoners of our errors. Through being secularized, France was in danger of death.

It was, indeed, soon after the Armistice that the hierarchy asked Pétain to revise the *laïque* laws and to grant subsidies to the religious schools. On July 15 Cardinals Gerlier, Suhard, and Baudrillard sent Pétain a "note" explaining "the unanimous wish of the Assembly of Cardinals and Archbishops of France".

[1] Jerôme Carcopino, *op. cit.*, p. 318. Carcopino quotes in this connexion a post-war issue of *La Croix* saying that, after all, Pétain was neither a sincere Catholic nor had his private life been "irreproachable".

These recommendations provided, *inter alia*, that the teaching of catechism be made compulsory in all schools, "and should be inserted in school programmes in such a manner as to safeguard effectively the practical application of this measure". (It was this "note" which, it seems, was closely adhered to by M. Jacques Chevalier in his abortive "reform" of January 1941.) The Cardinals further advocated the "teaching of morality" as an essential complement to religious tuition, and the "elimination of organizations which create conditions unfavourable to the children's morality". The note also asked for "equitable" subsidies to "free" education and (what is more) for freedom to open schools and to "teach there any French child whose good morality and capacity have been recognized". This implied not only the abolition of all the old laws against the religious *congrégations*; it also, apparently, was intended to set up severe competition with the "State" schools.

Although, under Ripert and especially Chevalier, attempts were made to satisfy all these demands, the danger of creating everlasting strife between the *curé* and the *instituteur* was too great—as Carcopino at once realized; and it seems—judging from Suhard's "no *revanche*" remark—that the hierarchy also reluctantly recognized the need to go more slowly about it. It is, nevertheless, certain that among certain influential people both in the Church and inside the Vichy Government, a return to the Loi Falloux of 1850 (which put all State schools under the authority and control of the Bishops) was for a long time looked upon as an ultimate target. Carcopino goes so far as to say that after he had abandoned his post in April 1942, with Laval's return to power, and with Abel Bonnard succeeding him at the Ministry of Education, both the Extreme Right and the "Left" at Vichy combined their efforts to increase greatly the financial privileges of the "free" schools— the one side out of pigheaded ultra-clericalism, the other, "in order to compromise the Vichy régime in the eyes of the régime that was sure to succeed it before long".

But although the Church hierarchy and the ultra-clericals at Vichy did not succeed in enforcing an all-round clericalization of education (perhaps "times were too uncertain"), they still succeeded where they had failed during the last thirty-five years of the Third Republic— namely, in undermining the principle of "separation".

That the Church tried to make capital out of Pétain can scarcely be doubted; and the hierarchy took the grave responsibility of trying to make millions of Catholics believe that Vichy and Pétain represented the resurrection of a full-blooded Christianity in France. The Church certainly held a privileged position at Vichy, as may be seen, for instance from the Convention signed on June 20, 1941 between the General Secretary for Youth in the Vichy Government and Mgr Chollet, Secretary of the Permanent Committee of the Cardinals and Archbishops of France. Under this Convention the Church assumed a leading rôle in the management of youth organizations like the *JOC*, *JEC*, *Coeurs Vaillants*, and others, while the Church agreed to identify them with the cult of the Marshal. The Abbé Paul Grosse, who headed two such youth organizations, totalling 1,200,000 children, declared at Algiers on March 20, 1942: "Our youth are in the service of the Marshal, and they will make a more beautiful and more Christian France."

Here again we come up against one of the seeming contradictions of Vichy. On the one hand, the youth organizations seemed in danger of becoming a sort of Pétain Jugend on Nazi lines; on the other hand, if one is to believe M. Carcopino, men like Borotra, the former tennis champion, who was Vichy's Secretary for Sports, and General Porte du Theil, the head of the Chantiers de la Jeunesse (the Pétainist "scout" movement of over-eighteens, with a membership of 80,000) were, in reality thinking of both "sport" and "scoutism" in paramilitary terms—for the future *revanche* of France over Germany. (It is true that both Porte du Theil and Borotra were suspect to the Germans, and were deported to Germany in 1942.) It looks as though there were, in all these movements, at least three distinct currents— a "pietist" current, a "Fascist" current, and a "nationalist" (anti-German) current. The first two, rather than the last, were Pétainist in inspiration.

With the Church hierarchy, Pétain was highly popular—for a variety of reasons. In a message to the Pope the Assembly of Cardinals and Archbishops declared at the beginning of 1941:

We practise, in the social and civil realm, the most complete loyalty towards the established government of France, and we call upon the faithful to do likewise.

In another message, dated July 24, 1941, they were even more explicit:

We revere the Head of the State and we urge that all Frenchmen rally to him. We encourage all our faithful to come to his side in the work of national revival and to co-operate with him without fear.

As in Franco Spain, so in Vichy France, the Church played the leading part in any ceremonial attended by the Head of the State. In every town he visited, the great ceremony took place usually in or outside the church or cathedral. Thus, at Auch, on August 30, 1941, Archbishop Béguin welcomed Pétain with the words:

The Catholics and their Clergy are with you with all their heart. *Monsieur le Maréchal*, we pray that God may allow you to fulfil to the end your difficult but sublime and holy task.

Anti-clericals have made, since the war, a pretty impressive collection of such "plums".[2] And no doubt the old man was highly flattered by this adulation, verging on canonization.

It should, of course, be added, that the Vatican took exactly the same line on Pétain, as could be observed from the frequent utterances of the Papal Nuncio at Vichy. As Maurras was to remark at his trial, the phrase *"le miracle Pétain"* had not, as was widely supposed, been coined by him, but by "somebody much more authoritative in the matter of miracles, namely, the Pope himself".

This Pétain worship, preached and practised consistently by the entire Church hierarchy (with the exception of the Archbishop of Toulouse and a number of Bishops) was, of course, a great embarrassment to the anti-Vichy Catholics, who were numerous not only in the Resistance, but also among a part—some say the greater part—of the lower clergy. M. Pierre-Henri Teitgen, one of the Catholic leaders of the Resistance (and a future leader of the MRP) was later to speak of the "appalling complexity of the dilemmas with which every Frenchman during the Occupation was faced"; the line taken by the Princes of the Church no doubt greatly complicated the dilemmas before many a good French Catholic, and tended to discourage their wholehearted support for the Resistance.

But especially after the middle of 1942 the French Church hierarchy were faced with some new problems (or rather problems which had become acute in the whole of France). French opinion, including Catholic opinion, was increasingly revolted by the extension of the compulsory labour service in Germany and, secondly, by the mass deportation of Jews from France. On the question of the Jews, there is no doubt that the Church hierarchy did not mince its words: it was the one "concession" made by the Vichy régime to Germany against which they protested vigorously, though it may perhaps be argued that, on the whole, the Protestant Church was even more outspoken on the subject than the Catholic Archbishops.

The leading figure of the Protestant Church, Pastor Boegner, protested at Vichy not only against the numerous measures of discrimination taken against French Jews under the *Statut des Juifs*, but, above all, against the savagery of the deportation of the non-French Jews, and, from his talks at Vichy he derived the most unhappy impression:

In September 1942, [he wrote] during a long conversation with the Secretary-General of the Police, I recalled once more these abominable deliveries of Jews (including children separated from their parents) to the Nazis and again I got the same reply: "Reasons of State . . ." What struck me, indeed, during that visit to Vichy, was the passionate anti-Semitism of

[2] Notably the Communist writer, Roger Garaudy, in *L'Eglise, le Communisme et le Chrétiens* (Paris, 1949), pp. 91–131.

several of the ministers; and their anti-Semitism was something quite out-side German pressure.... When I talked about it to Admiral Darlan, he said that, in order to save the French Jews, they had to give way on the question of deporting non-French Jews.... As for Laval, the Germans had convinced him—or so he pretended—that the Jews were being deported to Poland to do agricultural work.

And Boegner reported the following dialogue with Laval:

"So you are in favour of this manhunt?" I asked Laval. "We shall look for them wherever they are hiding." "Would you let us save the children?" "The children must remain with their parents." "But you know they have been separated from them." "No, they haven't." "But I tell you they have." "What do you want to do with the children?" Laval then asked. "French families will adopt them." "No, I don't want that. Not one of them must remain in France...." But it was no use talking to him. I talked of mas-sacres of the Jews in Poland; he talked about "gardening" in Poland...."[3]

But it is also true that, after a period of reticence and reserve, the hierarchy of the Catholic Church, impressed by the indignation caused among rank-and-file Catholics by the mass deportation of Jews to the East and by the unspeakable conditions in which children were separated from their parents, and by all the horrors of the transit and concentration camps, wrote letter after letter to Pétain, calling on him to put an end to all this inhumanity. Thus the Cardinals, Archbishops, and Bishops of the Occupied Zone sent Pétain a "declaration"—the text of which was to be sent to all priests; it protested against the sufferings inflicted on the Jews, notably on their women and children, for example in the Paris Vélodrome d'Hiver, into which they had been herded. Even Cardinal Gerlier, for all his devotion to Pétain, ordered on September 6, 1942 the following Pastoral Letter to be read in every church of his diocese:

The execution of the deportation measures now taking place against Jews throughout the territory is giving rise to such tragic scenes that it is our painful but imperative duty to protest from the depth of our conscience. We are in the presence of a cruel dispersal of families, and neither age nor illness is taken into account. It makes one's heart bleed to think of the treatment suffered by thousands of human beings, and even more so to think of all that may yet be in store for them....

And Cardinal Gerlier ended his Pastoral Letter with the words, which were like a disavowal of Vichy:

The new order cannot be built on violence and hatred.

These persecutions—in which the French police and other French authorities played a highly unenviable part—caused great distress to

[3] Cf. Maurice Vanino, *De Rethondes à l'Ile d'Yeu* (Paris, 1952).

the Church; the very Princes of the Church who had all but canonized Pétain, were up in arms against the persecutions. No doubt it took Mgr Salièges, the Archbishop of Toulouse to say even more than the others were prepared to say:

That children, women and men should be treated like vile cattle, that members of the same family should be separated and then sent to an unknown destination—that is the sad spectacle reserved for our time to see. Why does the right of asylum exist no longer in our churches? Lord, have pity on us. Our Lady, pray for France. In our diocese, in the camps of Noé and Récébédou there were many scenes of horror. Jewish men are men, Jewish women are women. Foreign men are men, foreign women are women.... They are part of the human race. They are our brethren. A Christian must not forget it.... France, our beloved country, France, in the conscience of whose children there is the tradition of respecting the human person, chivalrous and generous France: I do not doubt that thou art not responsible for these abominations...

Vichy was getting alarmed by this Catholic reaction. The press department at Vichy, the so-called "Service Arbellot", issued the following directives to the press on September 4, 1942:

A good deal of excitement has been caused in various parts of France, in connexion with certain events in which Jews of various nationalities and living in France as refugees, were involved. An insidious propaganda, the sole purpose of which is to compromise the work of the Marshal and his Government, has succeeded in spreading to the Catholic world. These hypocritical lamentations should be opposed by the doctrine of St Thomas and the Popes.... Catholics must not be deceived by this treacherous agitation encouraged by the enemies of the National Revolution.

But Pétain and Laval claimed that they "could do nothing about it", while Xavier Vallat and later, Darquier de Pellepoix of the Commissariat Général aux Questions Juives, which had ordered a "census" of all French Jews, and whose ultimate purpose was to make France *judenfrei* as soon as possible, went on as before. The Action Française, though no longer excommunicated (the thirteen-year ban had been raised at the beginning of the war) threatened the Church with "a major row".

On the deportation of thousands of Frenchmen under the STO (the compulsory labour service) to Germany, the Church also took a clear anti-Nazi line; according to a statement made by the Archbishops of France after their meeting on April 7–8, 1943, the STO did not constitute an "obligation to their conscience" (i.e. it was not a sin to dodge the compulsory service in Germany) but "if they [the Catholic workers] wished to be strong, they would give their ordeal all its redemptory value".

This statement, the first part of which alone really mattered ("no sin to dodge the STO") was not at all what suited the Germans; and the Church became more outspokenly anti-German as Hitler's defeat came to look more and more inevitable. Even so, apart from that, and apart from the very strong stand taken by the whole Church on the Jewish question, many priests in the Resistance were apparently far from satisfied with their Church leaders. Thus a priest wrote in a Resistance paper, *Défense de la France* in July 1943:

> When we are called upon to state the attitude of the Church, we feel a certain humiliation in having only Belgian, Dutch, and German Bishops to quote.... Their statements express the traditional Catholic doctrine with a clarity which contrasts strangely with the silence of our own prelates, and with those timid objections and reservations they sometimes make, wrapping these up in ample protestations of loyalty.[4]

This was, of course, unfair. There still was the Archbishop of Toulouse, who was later to be deported to the German camp of Compiègne, and there were the Bishop of Clermont-Ferrand and other priests who were to be deported to Germany, and many of whom were to die in captivity. Altogether, over one thousand French priests and thirty French pastors were deported, and two hundred priests and twelve pastors never returned. Also, the Church certainly did, for example, a great deal to save the lives of Jewish children, whether French or non-French.

All the same, the *bien-pensant* conformism of the Church in matters other than the STO and the Jews was unquestionable; and to the end it continued to profess loyalty to the Vichy régime and especially to the person of Marshal Pétain. As late as November 1943 Mgr Martin, Bishop of Le Puy, appealed to the faithful not to lose faith in Pétain (in itself an admission that they *were* losing faith).

> The attitude of the Church [he said] towards the National Revolution and its chief is the same today, in the autumn of 1943, as it was in July 1940. There are Catholics who may falter, and priests who may deviate; but they are not the Church. The immense majority of the faithful will turn away from their bad advice and their bad example and follow the straight road along which Marshal Pétain is carrying the flag of French unity.

As late as April 1944 Cardinal Suhard, the Archbishop of Paris, welcomed the Marshal to the capital "with emotion and gratitude": and this, and even more so, the fact that he had conducted a service at Notre-Dame in memory of Philippe Henriot, the savage pro-Nazi propagandist, after his assassination by the Resistance, caused de Gaulle at the time of the Liberation, to refuse to attend a *Te Deum* at Notre-Dame if Suhard were present. This was perhaps rather hard on Suhard, because, contrary to what was said at the time, he had *not* spoken words

[4] Quoted by Roger Garaudy, *op. cit.*, p. 106.

of praise in honour of Henriot.[5] But de Gaulle's demonstration was significant as a rebuke by the Resistance to the Church hierarchy for its more than tolerant attitude to Vichy, if not to the Germans.

However, it blew over, and de Gaulle's demonstration against Suhard had no lasting effect. In later years, while again professing full loyalty to the new established order, the Church hierarchy did not fail to exploit certain precedents which had been happily set up in the Vichy days, thanks, indirectly, at any rate, to the death of the Third Republic.

[5] Paradoxically, it was Cardinal Suhard who, though widely considered a "reactionary", had during the war started the *prêtres-ouvriers* movement, later to be denounced as being "pro-Communist".

CHAPTER FOUR

MAURRAS: THE "PURE" DOCTRINE OF VICHY

O NE of the (unconsciously) funniest pieces of writing to come out of Vichy is the description of a dinner-party given by the Marshal to Charles Maurras, and contained in one of the most lunatic-fringe books, *Le Grand Homme Seul*, by that "poet laureate" of Vichy, M. René Benjamin, *de l'Académie Goncourt*. He watched Maurras enter the Hôtel du Parc.

He bowed deeply to the guards, respectful as he is of all authority.... He was clad in a strange cloak which seemed to have been made of lion skin ... and on his head he wore a small round hat, of the existence of which he was hardly aware. For Maurras attaches little importance to the things he buys. He bought this hat because laurel wreaths are no longer sold in shops.... And then he entered the Marshal's apartments....
The moment the Marshal saw Maurras he rose. Maurras leapt forward, put his hand in the Marshal's, bowed with deep reverence, then smiled radiantly. Their eyes met. They were like two flashes of lightning.... The light of respect. The flame of admiration. The Marshal was saying to himself: "Here is the mind that for forty years has been guiding and giving courage to the best men in France," and Maurras wanted to cry out: "Saviour, oh, magnificent saviour!"

There followed a "conversation":

"What should be taught," said the Marshal forcefully, "is honour." Maurras closed his eyes in a state of grateful beatitude.
"Honour," he cried, "that is the most beautiful thing. There is nothing to add to it."
"But it should be defined," said the Marshal.
"A matter of teaching," said Maurras.
"We could start," said the Marshal, with a smile.
"I accept, provided I may follow you humbly," said Maurras, entranced.

After a few more remarks on the same lines, Benjamin concluded:

It was truly like a dialogue by Plato. Maurras was in the seventh heaven. For thirty years he had been calling for the Sovereign: now he had seen him for a whole evening!" (*Op. cit.*, pp. 41-9.)

The dinner party, the ladies, the "Socratic" conversation—the whole

66

thing was, of course, largely an invention—if only because Maurras was stone-deaf! But there is no doubt that Benjamin, who was one of Pétain's most faithful hangers-on, could only have published this with the Marshal's full approval; also, there is plenty to show that Pétain had the greatest regard for Maurras and the *Action Française*. Thus, in 1941 Pétain gave Maurras a copy of his speeches, inscribed: *"A Charles Maurras, le plus Français des Français"*, and even in 1944 he thanked him again for his invaluable guidance!

The very fact that Maurras, after forty years of violent political agitation, now came to consider himself the exponent of the Pétain ideology at its purest, that he treated Pétain as the ultimate triumph of his own monarchist philosophy, and that it was he who created the myth of *La France seule*—which played so great a part in shaping the "Vichy mentality"—makes it necessary to examine the rôle of Maurras in Vichy France as closely as possible, all the more so as Maurrasism had existed long before Vichy and—even survived it. For Maurrasism, as Mauriac has so often argued, has been the cloak of intellectual respectability worn by the French Right, with their egoism, their *méchanceté*, and their anti-social, and at times even anti-patriotic instincts.

When Maurras came up for trial at Lyon in January 1945, he was seventy-eight years old, and had been stone-deaf during the greater part of his life. In the interminable statement at his trial he was to recount the main phases of his activity during the previous fifty years, as a writer and journalist. He went all the way back to Boulangisme, the Dreyfus Case, in which he had been one of the most vitriolic anti-Dreyfusards and anti-Semites; he recalled his Monarchist and anti-republican campaigns; the establishment of the *Action Française* as a daily paper in 1908, and also as a "movement"; but without dwelling too long upon his frantic anti-republicanism, he went on to emphasize the profound distrust he had always felt towards Germany. He was a believer in "Latin civilization" as against Germanic barbarism; his book, *Kiel et Tanger*, written in 1907, but not published until 1910, was like a clarion call to the people of France, warning them of the inevitability of war with Germany. He was looking forward to this first world war—for he had been brought up in the best *revanche* tradition; and it was essential, he argued, to prepare France psychologically for the final struggle. France, according to him, was rotten with pacifism and anti-militarism; and it was the *Action Française* which, he claimed, had whipped up a sufficient degree of enthusiasm for the "next war" to make France prepare for it in all seriousness, despite all the "defeatism" coming from men like Caillaux and Jaurès, and to withstand the invasion when, in 1914, it finally came. Together with his fellow-royalist, Jacques Bainville, he never ceased to exalt the wisdom of

Richelieu's Testament, and the virtues of the Treaty of Westphalia of 1648 which resulted in a lasting partition of Germany, and "knocked her out for 150 years". He claimed that Barthou's three-years' service Conscription Law of 1913 would never have been possible but for the psychological preparedness for war that the *Action Française* had created in France. He also claimed the greatest credit for the ultranationalistic propaganda conducted by the *AF* during the first world war, and quoted men like Poincaré who, though generally unsympathetic to the Royalists, were nevertheless obliged to pay a tribute to their patriotic conduct during the years of 1914–18, and to their vigilance, thanks to which they had brought to heel "traitors" like Caillaux and Malvy.

Though they had enthusiastically supported Clemenceau during the war, they were bitterly disappointed by the Armistice of 1918 and wished, like certain French generals, that the French Army had marched all the way to Berlin, and had dictated to Germany a Carthaginian peace. The *Action Française*, guided by Maurras, Léon Daudet and Bainville, had strongly supported the partition of Germany, and notably the separatist movement in the Rhineland, backed by General Mangin. They were, however, disappointed in Poincaré, who, in 1923, could still have crushed Germany and marched on Berlin, but who had resorted only to the half-measure of occupying the Ruhr— which at the very moment when this occupation was about to bear fruit, he then abandoned under British pressure.

As Maurras saw it, the most disastrous man between the two wars in France was, of course, Briand, who allowed himself throughout to be bamboozled by the Germans. Finally, the rot had eaten so deep into the foreign policy of France that even a man like Tardieu, a close associate of Clemenceau's, and a man with no illusions about Germany, could no longer resist the "defeatist" current, and ordered the final evacuation of the Rhineland in 1930. And then, of course, the fun started. Very shortly after the last French soldier had left the Rhineland, the German electorate returned 106 Nazi deputies to the Reichstag.

In his survey of the *Action Française*'s policy during the ten years preceding the war, Maurras said as little as possible about the part played by the "anti-German" Camelots du Roi who, together with the distinctly pro-Nazi and pro-Fascist "leagues", endeavoured in 1934–5 to overthrow, or, failing that, to undermine the Republic; of the *Action Française*'s philosophical views during those years, of their conflicts with the Vatican and the Church, and of their ferocious anti-Semitism, notably during the "reign" of Léon Blum's Popular Front Government. What he dwelt on instead was that, throughout those years, he (Maurras) never lost sight of the deadly danger of Germany, and was therefore constantly campaigning for a *rapprochement* with Mussolini's Italy, and for the recognition of the Franco régime in Spain. In retrospect—while omitting his savage press campaign against "Freemason Benes"—he claimed that he was pro-Munich because France was not sufficiently strong to risk any other policy; what he really felt—or so he claimed in 1945—was that a victorious war against Germany, and the ultimate partition of Germany, should be France's constant objective, but that, in 1938–9, she was not sufficiently strong, and it was best for her to save up and build up her strength for a more propitious occasion.

All this needs recalling if one is to understand by what process of mental jugglery Maurras came to welcome Pétain's armistice of June 1940, and how he embarked on the incredible mental tightrope dance which he was to continue until the day in August 1944 when he fell off the tightrope—with the detested Germans on the run . . . and himself about to be sent to prison as a traitor.

What then was the attitude to the outbreak of World War II in September 1939 on the part of the future ideologist of the Vichy régime? In Maurras's view, the 1939 war was *unnecessary*. The French people didn't know what the war was all about. Nobody really knew much about Hitler(!), for he had not even allowed his book, *Mein Kampf*, to be published in France. Fascism versus democracy: both words, Maurras said, were equally meaningless to the man-in-the-street:

In the circumstances, we laid down four rules.
Rule I: We must not make war on Germany.
Rule II: If this war is still imposed on us, despite all our advice, and through the fault of the French Government, then let us make war, but make it thoroughly, with all our strength, and let us *arm*, ARM and A R M.
Rule III: If we win it, then no more nonsense this time. Germany must then be completely and finally crushed . . .
Rule IV: The war must be a 100 per cent national war, with a national aim: no use playing about with any sort of unintelligible anti-Hitlerism or with obsolete democratic slogans; the one and only aim must be the decomposition of Germany.[1]

But the "decomposition of Germany" seemed rather a remote objective, and Maurras felt that France was unfit to fight. "Let us die by all means," he wrote on August 28, 1939, "but . . . a gallant death must serve some purpose. To die helplessly is pure inanity and pure imbecility." But Daladier introduced "a premature censorship" even before the war was declared, and the *Action Française* was severely hampered in its anti-war propaganda.

At his trial Maurras, however, strongly denied that, once the war had started, his "defeatism" had continued. He quoted an article written

[1] *Le Procès de Charles Maurras* (Paris, 1946), p. 84.

at the height of the German invasion, on June 12, 1940, in which he still placed all his faith on France's military resistance. If during the darkest moments of 1918, he wrote, it was still possible to conceive a settlement, an armistice with the Kaiser, nothing of the kind was possible with Hitler:

Today there can be no pact, no treaty, nothing, nothing; only the German yoke. Today we have before us a bestial horde, led by an individual who is the most complete expression of this bestiality.

However, when Pétain asked for an armistice, Maurras fully supported the Marshal. The Germans weren't so bad after all, he reflected. If Pétain and Weygand thought the Armistice inevitable, everybody should submit.

We were surprised by the speed with which the Marshal's words were endorsed by the country. Our forecasts on the Germans' savage fury had partly been contradicted by the facts. The Armistice was not going to deprive us of everything. Along with the Free Zone, the Navy, and the Empire, it was going to leave us juridical and moral sovereignty. The Marshal's Armistice left room for negotiations with the Germans—which was more than could be said of any other country defeated by Hitler.... It created a situation which could be profitably used by France. This was better than anything like Gambetta's *guerre à outrance*, the fallacy of which has been pointed out by M. de Gaulle himself. (*Ibid.*, p. 93.)

On the principle of the all-out war, the *guerre à outrance* Maurras reflected that Gambetta's "quixotic behaviour" had cost France far more in both money and territory than if she had accepted Bismarck's original peace terms of September 1870—only a slice of Alsace and two milliard francs, instead of, a year later, the whole of Alsace and part of Lorraine and five milliards. Also,

if the European enemies of Napoleon had prematurely fought a *guerre à outrance*, they wouldn't have had a gun or a soldier left for their *revanche* of 1812, '13, '14, and '15.

In short, the 1940 Armistice "safeguarded France's future", and left her also something "in the present".

These Maurras arguments are, of course, familiar enough, and have been used by many others in one form or another. Before long, however, the Maurras "philosophy" became a political tightrope dance inside a kind of mental vacuum created by the old man's *idée fixe* of "*la France, la France seule*"—which almost immediately after the Armistice, became the official slogan of the *Action Française*. At this stage the Maurras approach became an extraordinary mixture of anti-German scholasticism, the elevation of the Pétain cult to something going even beyond the *Führer Prinzip*, and the cultivation of a sort of hot-house Vichyism. Its "national revolution" deliberately ignored all the realities of the international situation; it was ferociously anti-de Gaulle, anti-British, anti-Russian, and in effect hysterically hostile to active anti-German resistance inside France, on the ground that it was *also* directed against Vichy and Pétain.

Speaking at his trial in 1945, Maurras tried to deny that he had deliberately deified Pétain. The phrase, "Pétain, the man of Providence" had, he pointed out, been coined by the Papal Nuncio. "Marshal Pétain, your national hero" was the phrase used by Admiral Leahy, the US Ambassador at a banquet at Clermont-Ferrand in the winter of 1941–2. Also, had not Roosevelt congratulated Pétain, on one occasion, on his "magnificent work"? So what was wrong with "adulating the Marshal"? And Maurras went out of his way to show that, despite "the terrible British provocation" of Mers-el-Kebir, where 1,500 French sailors had been killed by the British, and despite all the trouble in Syria, and French Central Africa, despite also the insulting stream of propaganda coming all the time from the "Free French" in London, Pétain had been loyal throughout to his undertaking not to make war on Britain.

Nevertheless, in Maurras's view, France had, apart from Germany, two enemies: Britain and—the "Franco-German Party", represented in the Vichy Government by Laval, and also extremely active in Paris where, he recalled, Déat and Doriot never ceased to attack the *Action Française*. Laval, Maurras said, was a stupid and ignorant man: he had told him in July 1940 that it was no use being offensive to Germany, because he was sure that, within three months, "the Germans would become irresistibly popular in the Occupied Zone". (*Ibid.*, p. 100.)

For four years Maurras and his team waged what they thought to be a very effective war, in the name of "*la France seule*" against Laval and the "Franco-German" clans in both Paris and Vichy.

Thus on September 2, 1940, Maurras wrote to Tixier-Vignancour, at that time chief of the Vichy radio, whom he was accusing of broadcasting pro-German propaganda:

Very well then, the independence of the Free Zone *is* a fiction. Alas, we know it as well as that cretin Déat; we know as well as he does that the Boche can do with it whatever he pleases.... Only let's not say publicly to the Boche that the Armistice is something he can transgress and violate in any way he likes... We must, on the contrary, stick to the least little stipulation of the Armistice, without allowing for a moment anyone to believe that we are not taking it seriously.

And Maurras claimed, indeed, for his press campaign, the credit for having fully persuaded Pétain to get rid of Laval in the famous "palace revolution" of December 13, 1940. Only, Maurras and his followers had some awkward moments. Their line was that France must follow the Marshal blindly; but, if so, how could they accept Montoire? The following dialogue was published just after Montoire in the *Action Française*: a typical Maurras quibble:

Are you in favour of this collaboration with Germany?
I haven't got to be in favour.
Then are you against it?
No, I haven't got to be against it either.
Neutral, then?
No.
You mean you approve?
I have neither to approve it nor to discuss it.

And then he explained that it was the duty of France to follow the Marshal—even when he collaborates with Germany! All the same, Maurras, in his defence, later made great capital out of the charges of *attentisme* constantly brought against him by Laval, Déat and the all-out collaborators.

But while the *Action Française* was in favour of "waiting" in the international field, it

fully supported the Marshal and his devoted ministers—all of those men of talent and experience who elaborated the Labour Charter, the Peasant Corporation, and all those other measures in the building of a new France, and embodied in the words "*Travail, Famille, Patrie*".

This approval of the "new France" extended to the persecution, not only of Freemasons, Jews, and Communists, but also of anyone, including good Catholics like Champetier de Ribes, Bidault, and Francisque Gay, who were against the Marshal. These Catholic leaders of the Resistance were attacked by name in the *Action Française* and denounced to the police; Gaullism was identified with high treason, and the formation of Darnand's Milice—the Vichy equivalent of the SS, and soon to be noted for their savagery—was hailed with loud approval by Maurras. More than once did the deaf old man, radiating hatred, as he had radiated it all his life, call upon the authorities from his editorial chair at Lyon to be merciless against the Resistance, and to shoot hostages. No doubt Maurras still continued to be anti-Boche; but he did not oppose the *relève* and later the compulsory labour service in Germany; and although, as already said, he did not give his blessing to the French anti-Bolshevik Legion, he clamoured for the shooting of Communist hostages inside France: only later, at his trial, did Maurras try to explain that his argument about "better fighting the Communists inside France" was an indirect way of saying (for there was the Vichy censorship) that no Frenchman should join the German Army in Russia. But this again was a quibble.

What then was the psychological process which had made Maurras demand an all-out war against the anti-German Resistance? His main argument was that, but for men like Laval, there would have been no Resistance to speak of!

From the moment Laval returned to power [in April 1942] we were to witness one new disaster after another. America became hostile to us. Moreover, the pro-German policy of Laval and of the Paris clan was exasperating French opinion more and more, and it is deeply unfortunate that, instead of rallying to the national flag carried by the Father of the People, [i.e. Pétain] public opinion should have rushed to the opposite extreme in an endeavour to cancel out Laval's collaborationism by favouring dissident movements more and more. We did all we could to stop this calamity from spreading; but it went from bad to worse, and France was finally divided into two foreign clans.... Till the bitter end we fought against this disaster, the direct outcome of Laval's mistakes; for these mistakes were to lead to the surrender of North Africa, and to the extension of the German occupation to the whole of France's territory; they also led to the disappearance of our little Armistice Army, the scuttling of our Navy, and to the destruction of practically the whole of the material strength that we had managed to preserve as a result of Pétain's wise and salutary Armistice.

Hence his furious campaign against the Resistance, a campaign which, with its innuendoes against individuals and even direct denunciation to the police was much more "practical" in its results than his academic "anti-Boche" position. What Maurras really wanted was to perpetuate the Vichy of July 1940—but neither Laval, Déat and the Germans on the one hand, nor the Resistance and the Allies on the other were leaving the precious hot-house alone. And even after North Africa had fallen into Allied hands, and the Free Zone had been occupied by the Germans, Maurras still continued to bleat *"La France, la France seule"*, unwilling, on the face of it, to take sides. But, in reality, as the Prosecution was to show at his trial, his hatred for the spoil-sports of the Resistance was such that he turned a blind eye to the help given to Darnand's Milice by German units in the extermination of the Maquis of the Plateau des Glières in the Haute-Savoie in February 1944, and simply rejoiced over the extermination of so many "bandits" and "terrorists".

For what had been the battle of the Plateau de Glières? It was the most famous of the open battles fought by the French Maquis. On this plateau, surrounded by steep mountains between Annecy, Bonneville, and Petit Bernard, and not easily accessible, a Maquis unit of some

500 to 600 men had been organized towards the end of 1943 under the command of Lieutenant Morel, of the 27th Battalion of the Chasseurs Alpins. The first series of attacks launched by Darnand's Milice on this little oasis of Free France, over which was flying the flag of the Cross of Lorraine, were repelled. These repeated set-backs were making a bad impression in Germany, all the more so as it was known that the Glières Maquis had been supplied with arms by British planes—however insufficiently.

This is how M. Thomas, the Public Prosecutor at the Maurras trial described the military operations:

General Marion, the Prefect of the Haute-Savoie, was appointed to conduct the operations; he gathered together his troops—the Milice and the GMR. But apart from some skirmishes, in which the Maquis inflicted some losses on the Vichy forces, nothing serious happened. It was then that the Germans came to the rescue, turning their big guns against the Maquis; I don't know how many thousands the Germans sent; but, in any case it was an unequal struggle for the men of the Maquis—perhaps one against twenty, against German artillery and German planes.... Remember with what anguish we followed on the wireless the details of that tragedy. We knew that every time a Maquis post fell into enemy hands there were men who were being tortured and killed. Yes, the Germans were there, followed by the Milice—who were perhaps there to finish off the wounded, and to shoot the farmers who might have given shelter to those who had escaped the massacre.... Over 250 men of the Maquis were killed....'. Soon afterwards the Vichy Information Centre at Lyon published photographs; most of us saw them.... All foreign papers exalted the heroism of the men of Glières, above all the Swiss press.... But what did these gallant men get from their countrymen? Mud and insults from Philippe Henriot—insults to these Free-French prisoners on the point of being executed by the Germans.

And Maurras? He treated them as "bandits" who were disturbing the "order" of Vichy—of the creaking and German-occupied Vichy of February 1944! The rôle played by the Germans in the wiping-out of the Glières Maquis was conveniently overlooked in the *Action Française*. "Not only deaf, but always with blinkers on," the Public Prosecutor said of Maurras, adding, however, with that curious French veneration for the intellectual: "though admittedly a very great writer, and a genius..." "*Un génie, c'est certain.*"

The intellectual dishonesty—or should one say, the monomania—of Maurras was clearly revealed by his reactions to the extermination of the Glières Maquis. Similarly, he had welcomed with cries of joy the constitution of the Milice, that Vichy SS Force which was to fight the Resistance with the utmost savagery. "*O bonheur—une nouvelle institution nous est née...*" he wrote. And he advised men of the Action

Française to join it. Later, however, he declared himself "disappointed" in Darnand, the head of the Milice, when the latter had come to an agreement with the Waffen SS for joint action against the French Resistance. He might have foreseen this; but the anti-German pose had to be kept up at any price; so after the Milice SS agreement Maurras claimed to have told his followers not to join the Boche-tainted Milice any more.

His savagery against the Resistance and the Jews took the form of direct denunciation and demands that the death penalty be more frequently applied to men of the Resistance, and on September 1, 1943, i.e. even long after the formation of the National Committee at Algiers, he wrote:

If the death penalty is insufficient for putting an end to Gaullism, hostages should be taken from among the members of their families and duly executed.

Several attacks were also made, as already said, on the Catholic leaders of the Resistance, with the usual innuendoes, and less well-known persons were also denounced by name. At his trial Maurras argued that if the whole family of a certain M. Fornier of Bourg were deported or shot as hostages, it was not as a result of the denunciation of these people as "Gaullists" in the *Action Française*. But their arrest, following closely on the attack on them in the *AF* was, in that case, a most remarkable coincidence, unfortunate for Maurras. There were several similar cases.

How seriously, one may well ask, was the *Action Française* taken at Vichy? How official was it? This is hard to estimate. It is certain that the Vichy radio quoted Maurras at great length, though, no doubt, the maniacal tone of some of his ravings and the excessive "schematization" of the world was often hard to take seriously. Only some of the very young and some of the very old could take Maurras at his face value; nevertheless, for all its absurdity, its deafness and political blinkers, the Maurras "doctrine" was important in two respects: it helped for a time to give the illusion to many people that Pétain had come to embody the monarchical principle of the Action Française; and, above all, it helped to create an emotional climate of hatred at Vichy, to give an "ideological" basis to the police state, to stir up hatred against the Resistance, which might otherwise have passed off as being primarily anti-German, much more than anti-Vichy; and to encourage Vichy extremism in home affairs—such as its anti-Semitism which, for all Maurras's arguing to the effect that it was "intellectual" and "social", and not "physiological", tended to become something remarkably like Hitler's anti-Semitism in practice.

In short, although few people swallowed his "doctrine" hook, line, and sinker, Maurras's interminable hate sermons day after day and year after year were, nevertheless, to prove a poison that even the Liberation did not eliminate entirely out of France's system. Partly because he was an "intellectual", while some, including the Public Prosecutor, were convinced that he was a "genius", he carried more weight in France than he would have done in any other country. In England he would have had little chance of being taken for anything but a half-demented old bore.

And yet in France Maurrasism continues to be a vital, though destructive force, which has survived its Vichy fiasco. Not even the "final" disgrace of continuing to publish the *Action Française* under the German occupation of the Vichy Zone proved really final.

For some years after the Liberation, it is true, Maurrasism seemed hopelessly discredited. But later it revived, if only in a small way, in the form of two new weeklies, *Aspects de la France* and *Rivarol*. This showed that even with Maurras in his dotage, or with Maurras dead (he died in 1952) Maurrasism and its orgy of reactionary invective and mudslinging were still capable of appealing to numerous French minds, despite the ideological bankruptcy of the *Action Française* in the course of its Vichy "apotheosis".

But it goes far beyond these two weekly journals (with their circulation of about 40,000 each). For Maurrasism represents a French tradition and a French intellectual attitude which will perhaps never die, and which has numerous echoes and ramifications. In a concentrated and "uninhibited" form, it represents the ideology of the Right—a French Right which, in Mauriac's view, has not been "reputable" for a very long time now—if ever it was (Mauriac sometimes doubts it).

And, paradoxically enough, echoes of Maurrasism can sometimes be detected in the most unexpected quarters. Thus, de Gaulle's "federalist" attitude to Germany in 1944–6 and his Ruhr-and-Rhineland policy were largely Maurrasist in inspiration (de Gaulle was certainly brought up in a *milieu* where *Action Française* ideas were familiar); there were also striking points of resemblance between de Gaulle's policy of *grandeur* and aloofness and Maurras's *la France seule*, not to mention many features of the home policy of the RPF, with which Maurras would not have disagreed. More than that—there are certain Maurras ways of thinking (arising from a superiority complex *plus* distrust towards the outside world as a whole) which have their parallels even far to the Left in France: thus, is there not a striking parallelism between *la France seule*, the aloofness and *grandeur* of the post-Liberation de Gaulle, and the "neutralism" of the *Monde* and of the non-conformist Left? In short, *la France seule* is something profoundly

French, and something of which one sometimes meets variants in the most surprising places and contexts.[2]

[2] Like many others, I have always held the view that what made the great success of the *Action Française* as a paper were not the repetitive, long-winded and one-track articles of Maurras, but the brilliant daily "pamphlets" of Léon Daudet, with their fireworks of witty satire and parody and Rabelaisian invective. If Maurras loved Racine and the classicism of the French seventeenth century, Daudet was much more at home in the full-blooded sixteenth-century world of the French Renaissance with its Montaigne, Ronsard and particularly Rabelais. Léon Daudet was the last great "pamphleteer" of the French Right, and such pieces of Rabelaisian invective as "*le Don Juan de lavabo*" (Paul-Boncour) and "*l'hermaphrodite circoncis*" (Léon Blum) were more effective in ridiculing the leaders of the Third Republic than the millions of ponderous words written by Maurras. Alphonse Daudet's son was also a literary critic of the highest order. He was already a very sick man during the summer of 1940, and he died in 1942. In *Léon Daudet vivant*, published in 1948, M. Paul Dresse argues that Daudet would certainly not have followed Maurras to the end, had he lived.

"What would have happened to the Daudet-Maurras friendship if Daudet had seen the French zone, which was still free, invaded by the Germans? His whole past suggests the answer. Being a sick man, he had reluctantly agreed that the *Action Française* continue to appear in the Vichy zone; but to agree to collaborate with the enemy was something very different. Rather than publish the paper under German control, and to become one of those "flunkeys of the pen", whom he has so often denounced in the past, he would have rebelled, and firmly demanded voluntary silence from his friends. If necessary, he would have imposed this silence on Maurras."

This seems a piece of rather idle speculation, since for viciousness, scurrility and political irresponsibility there was usually little to choose between Maurras and Léon Daudet.

CHAPTER FIVE

THE FORGOTTEN ADMIRAL

Nᴏᴛ only in popular memory, but even in most of the writings on the period of 1940–4, Vichy and the Occupation are primarily associated with two names—Pétain and Laval. The fact therefore tends to be overlooked that during almost exactly one half of Vichy's "half-freedom" (i.e. before the occupation of the whole of France), namely during fourteen months out of twenty-nine, Vichy's policy was shaped (apart from the Marshal) not by Laval, but by Darlan.

In so far as Laval's dismissal had anything to do with foreign policy, it was a victory of the *attentistes* over the "collaborators"—though what was much more decisive in his downfall was his lack of sympathy for the "National Revolution". Laval was, at that time, convinced that Germany had won the war, and he tended to think in terms of a New European Order, in which the "Ruritania" of Vichy could not be taken seriously. It is not at all certain that *anybody* at Vichy seriously believed in December 1940 in an eventual German defeat, any more than Laval did; and in most cases the quarrel between Laval and the *maréchalistes* was a quarrel between "integration" in Hitler's Europe and a sort of French "autonomism" under which the National Revolution could develop, within the framework of this Europe, along "traditionally French" lines. In the last analysis it was a quarrel between a quasi-Fascist Right and a quasi-Nazi Left—though, in the case of Laval (who, perhaps in spite of himself, continued to be attached to certain freedoms of the Third Republic) the line to follow was still not as clear-cut as it was for Déat and Doriot.

But although in December 1940 the *Action Française* and other *maréchalistes* visualized a German defeat no more clearly than Laval, they still favoured a "waiting game", all the more so as French opinion (as already shown in the first chapter of this book) was already jubilant over Hitler's failure to invade Britain, had been impressed by Wavell's victories in Libya and was making the most of the increasingly hostile attitude taken by the United States *vis-à-vis* Germany. And there was also Russia, non-committal and a little mysterious, despite the semblance of still fairly "correct" relations between Moscow and Berlin.

If ever there was a time when France should logically have played a waiting game, it was not before December 1940 but after December 1940—that is, precisely during the period when Darlan was Head of the Government. In other words, Laval was Head of the Government for five months after the French collapse, i.e. during a period when Hitler's victory could reasonably be taken for granted. The Montoire meeting (except that it took place already *after* Hitler's failure to invade England) was a logical expression of the belief that France would have to make the best of Hitler's victory in Europe. On the other hand, during Laval's second term of office, from April 1942 till the Liberation, the tide had already turned against Germany; and it was no longer a case of "collaborating" in the establishment of a New Order in Europe, but simply of limiting to a minimum, while pretending to "co-operate", the cynical exploitation of France for the benefit of an increasingly hard-pressed German war economy. This Laval did, though perhaps less effectively than he later claimed.

But between the two "Laval" periods—the first, when a "realistic" policy in favour of "integration" in Hitler's European Order could be defended as being the course least dangerous to France; and the second, when a no-longer-triumphant Germany had to be humoured and, if possible, double-crossed—there was the intermediate period when *attentisme* was by far the most obvious course to follow.

Throughout 1941 and the early part of 1942—which was the Darlan period in France—there were no longer the same arguments as in the second half of 1940 for taking a German victory for granted. By the beginning of 1941 it was already fairly clear that there was nothing *final* about Hitler's great victory of June 1940. The international situation was full of question-marks, with England resisting with greater determination than ever, and with neither America nor Russia showing any signs of having accepted Hitler's European Order as an unalterable *fait accompli*.

Laval was a pacifist by nature, and in his negotiations with the Germans at Montoire and elsewhere, he had carefully avoided committing France to any *military* collaboration with Hitler. The question of such collaboration in Africa had arisen, but both Pétain and Laval (though for different reasons) had always been extremely vague in their replies.

Darlan, on the contrary, was the man willing to co-operate with the Germans in this exceptionally important field; so much so that it may reasonably be argued that, far from pursuing a policy of *attentisme* (at a time when it was the most logical course for France to follow) Darlan (and not Laval) reached—or rather, tried to reach—the peak of Franco-German collaboration. If it did not amount to more than it did, it was for two reasons: resistance on the part of Pétain; and loss of interest by the Germans themselves, who, by the middle of 1941, had other fish to fry.

Darlan was in favour of adopting the famous Huntziger-Warlimont protocols of May 1941, which would have laid the foundations for a Franco-German military alliance had they—or rather, most of them—not been rejected by Vichy. Maurice Martin du Gard quotes a curious remark made by a German, who said: "When we ask Laval for a chicken, we get an egg; when we ask Darlan for an egg, we get a chicken." And all the records that have come to light tend to confirm the impression that, of the three Vichy periods—Laval's July–December 1940, Darlan's February 1941–April 1942, and Laval's April 1942–August 1944—it was during this middle "Darlan" period that the Head of the French Government hankered most for the least excusable kind of collaboration with Germany.

The case of Darlan is interesting for a number of reasons.

(a) As a French naval man, he was anti-British, and so represented a certain French caste reflex;

(b) He was morbidly ambitious; and it was this *personal* quality which, more than anything else, explains his acceptance of the plans for military collaboration with Germany; having persuaded himself of a German victory or, failing that, of a negotiated peace, under which Germany's power would still be immense in Europe, he already seemed to fancy himself as a sort of First Sea Lord of a United Europe;

(c) His attitude to Vichy was cynical; he let the die-hards of the National Revolution do pretty much as they pleased, showing a certain indifference to what they were doing. When Laval returned to office in April 1942, he claimed to be "horrified" by the progress made by the reinforcement of the police state and by the development of the various forms of persecution (Freemasons, Jews, etc.) during the Darlan régime;

(d) If, in November 1942, Darlan went over to the Americans, it was a class reflex on his part, combined with anglophobia and russophobia. The tide of war having, by this time, turned against Germany, he thought he could not only assure with American help the perpetuation of the Vichy régime, but also checkmate, all at once, the British, their protégé de Gaulle, and also the Resistance, which, to Darlan, looked like a monster born from the unholy union of Gaullism and Communism.

What kind of man was Darlan who had for years been the real head of the French Navy? A curious description of him is given by Du Moulin de Labarthète, Pétain's *directeur civil*, who had no love for the Admiral:

This *méridional* was a cold and self-absorbed man, extremely distrustful, and surprisingly coarse in his whole manner and tone, without the halo of nobility which characterized the Marshal. No doubt he was a good sailor. . . . But it has also been said of him that he was a politician. I find this hard to believe. Seldom had I seen a man so little qualified for political life, so unused to parliamentary methods and to handling people, despite ... his years of contact with Government personnel.... All he seemed to have gained from this was a certain low cunning—and some stripes and decorations.... He loved power, and could not stand competition. He brusquely eliminated Laval, and later he brought Weygand crashing down.[1]

That this personal ambition was his primary motive may be seen from a hundred little details of Darlan's behaviour; and, on the whole, he compares unfavourably with Laval who, for all his personal ambition, seemed more obviously than Darlan to put the interests of France first—at least as he understood them. He sought, as it were, to secure for France a quiet little place in the world—whatever this world might be—and was, unlike Darlan, reluctant to see France become involved in Hitler's grand strategy, whatever the benefits he might have derived from this himself. As somebody said of Laval: "He never looks much beyond Châteldon."

Darlan, on the other hand, fancied himself at a certain stage a great military or naval personage in Hitler's Europe.

But first a few words about his anglophobia. It was something innate and had, according to his son, Alain Darlan, been intensified, first by the "scurrilous" way in which Britain had treated France at the various naval conferences between the two wars, and then by Dunkirk, Mers-el-Kebir, and Dakar. Alain Darlan quoted some particularly "waspish" letters written by his father to his family at the time of the London naval conference of 1930:

Here we were, assembled in the House of Lords; on one wall, the Battle of Trafalgar, on another wall, the Battle of Waterloo—charming, I must say! About a thousand people crowding round a vast platform where I had the honour of being. Draughts, photographers, loud-speakers.... Then the King made his entry. He stood in front of his throne. Somebody handed him a paper. He fumbled for his glasses, then read the paper, and then sat down. We also sat down.

On the following day he wrote:

Mr Ramsay MacDonald explained to us that England alone was qualified to use the sea.[2]

And so on, all in the same facetious, slightly venomous style. As head of the French Navy, he co-operated in the Dunkirk operation, and his dislike of the British became even more acute. "The prospect of getting out suddenly make the crawling British grow wings...." And he added that but for the two French admirals on the spot, Abrial and Platon, the Dunkirk evacuation could never have succeeded. After

[1] Du Moulin de Labarthète, *Le Temps des Illusions* (Geneva, 1946), p. 140.
[2] Alain Darlan, *Darlan parle* (Paris, 1952).

Dunkirk he had no doubt felt even more anti-British than most Frenchmen.[3]

It is unnecessary here to deal with the "massacre" of a large part of the French Fleet by the British at Mers-el-Kebir on July 3, 1940, and with the somewhat conflicting evidence on the rôle played by Darlan in this tragic episode. Did his anglophobia, as Baudouin was to suggest, drive him to such extremes that he deliberately allowed the French Navy to be "massacred", by concealing from Pétain the real terms of the British ultimatum until after this ultimatum had expired? Darlan's son, on the other hand, later explained that it was the fault not of his father, but of Admiral Gensoul, who had failed to communicate to Vichy the exact terms of the British ultimatum. Whatever the truth, the frantic anglophobia that Darlan was later to display in connexion with Mers-el-Kebir tended to make him *persona grata* with the Germans.

Darlan's relations with the Germans can be examined under two heads. First, there was his apparent belief in the possibilities of a New Order, in which France would be given a worthy place—possibly even the place of a "brilliant second", instead of Italy. Secondly, to achieve this object, Darlan was willing to take very serious risks, and even get France involved in a war against Britain.

As regards the New Order, it may be interesting to recall that Darlan had largely surrounded himself at Vichy by people who were not typical "National Revolution" men, but believers in an economically efficient, Nazi-dominated Europe. Thus, one of Darlan's closest advisers was Benoist-Méchin, one of the few Doriotists in the Vichy Government, and a man with a somewhat romantic faith in Franco-German friendship, and in Hitler's greatness. Before the war he had written a well-known *History of the German Army*, and also a book in favour of the absorption of the Ukraine by Germany. At Vichy, Benoist-Méchin was Secretary of State in charge of Franco-German relations. Another close associate of Darlan's was Paul Marion, also a Doriotist, and, in 1941, head of the Vichy propaganda machine.

Although some scepticism has been expressed about the very existence of the "synarchie", the "secret society" to which Marion and Benoist-Méchin were supposed to belong, it is worth noting, all the same, that two such entirely different witnesses as Du Moulin de Labarthète and Otto Abetz should have, in one way or another, referred to the "crowd of brilliant young economists and technicians" with whom Darlan had surrounded himself, and who were apparently thinking in terms of France's "integration" in Hitler's Europe.

According to Du Moulin de Labarthète, this synarchie (the word

[3] *Cf.* the author's *The Last Days of Paris* (London, 1940), recording the bitterness widely felt in France over Britain's "desertion" at Dunkirk.

meaning "simultaneous government", functioning alongside the official government) was a sort of secret society with ramifications not only in the higher strata of the administration and of Big Business and High Finance in France, but also among Big Business in other countries, including Germany. The "Big Five" of the synarchie who became influential in Vichy in the days of Darlan were, according to Du Moulin de Labarthète, Leroy-Ladurie, Pucheu, Barnaud, Bichelonne, and Lehideux, all working in close contact with the two "Vichy Nazis", Benoist-Méchin and Paul Marion. They had far-reaching political ambitions, economic plans, and a strong backing from Big Business. Pucheu, the most brilliant and ruthless of them all, "grabbed" the Ministry of the Interior, and proceeded from there to "control and terrorize" a large number of other government departments; the others, all *normaliens* or *polytechniciens*, similarly gained control of most of the economic ministries at Vichy. Du Moulin then traced the association of these men back to the Banque Worms in Paris which, in 1937, had become the headquarters of a "secret society" headed by Barnaud, the only "Aryan" director of this Jewish bank. It was Barnaud who, according to Du Moulin, began to publish in 1937 a magazine called *Les Nouveaux Cahiers*, and who attempted, as a reaction to the Popular Front, "to assemble intelligent people all the way from the Left to the Extreme Right" who would study the French and international situation "in a spirit of French pragmatism". Without recounting all the details given by Du Moulin on the strange activities of this group, it is fairly clear that a lot of fishing went on in the troubled waters of 1938–9, and that the future members of the synarchie represented something of a link between Big Businesss on the one hand, and highly dubious defeatist and pro-Nazi organizations like Doriot's PPF (to which notably Pucheu belonged) on the other. Words like "technocracy" and "managerialism" were already in the air, and together with them went a "hard-boiled" approach to the problems of peace, war, and coexistence with Nazi Germany.

It was this team [wrote Du Moulin] who in February 1941 embarked on the highroad of power. In reply to my remark: "Heavens! you are bringing along the whole of the Banque Worms!" the Admiral [Darlan] replied drily: "It's better to have them than to have the young male virgins of the sacristy with whom you people [at the Marshal's office] have surrounded yourselves. None of your generals, and seminarists—but young fellows, as hard as nails, who will come to terms with Fritz and make us eat good roast chicken." (*Op. cit.*, p. 347.)

Without specifically referring to this group as a "secret society" or a "synarchie", Otto Abetz, the German Ambassador in Paris, also speaks in his very curious book, *Histoire d'une politique franco-allemande*, of "the young technicians and economists round Darlan" as "men of very great ability"; and he relates, notably, how in April 1941, they submitted, with Darlan's approval, a memorandum to Hitler, advocating the integration of France in the New Europe. France, the memorandum said, was Europe's great rampart on the Atlantic, and both in military and economic matters there should be "a harmonious distribution of labour" among the nations of Europe, and "the defeat of France should turn into a victory of Europe".

According to Abetz, the memorandum to Hitler also said:

> The historic meeting of Montoire has shown that Germany is inclined to be magnanimous to France. But this meeting was only of a symbolic nature. Now we want this symbol to become a reality, and we are determined not to fraternize with those who have dragged our country down the abyss. ... We want to save France, and ask the Führer to grant us his confidence.

These were not just words; according to Du Moulin, the "synarchs" used to travel almost every week to Paris and hold conferences with the German occupation authorities, and notably with the economic experts among them, at the Hotel Majestic—not that they found these talks quite as satisfactory as they would have found similar talks with the Krupps and Cunos and other bosses of Germany's *Schwerindustrie*. Hence perhaps this appeal to Hitler. What the "synarchie" wrote to Hitler was not just words; and Abetz even got worried "lest Darlan and his friends were going *too* far"; he warned Berlin to be more forthcoming, as Pétain was "beginning to look with suspicion at Darlan, just as he had looked at Laval before the crisis of December 13".

And Darlan himself? He appeared to be in full agreement with his "brilliant young economists", and was willing to go to almost any lengths to win Hitler's favours. Thus, according to Abetz, he went to Berchtesgaden on May 11, 1941, and in greeting Hitler, remarked that that was "truly a great day" for him to be received by the Führer—a truly symbolic day: it was the Fête of Joan of Arc, the great anti-English heroine of France.[4]

But Darlan did not have much luck with the Germans, though not for want of trying. On May 11, Hitler was much too preoccupied with Hess's flight to Scotland the day before; also, he was busy planning his war against the Soviet Union. If he wanted to see Darlan at all, it was, not for any major constructive purpose, but in order to extract military and naval concessions from him. It was, indeed, during the Berchtesgaden meeting that the foundations were laid for the Syrian agreement and for the Bizerta and Dakar protocols. In return, according to Abetz, Hitler merely said that the German Government would be willing, from time to time, to "grant concessions and facilities to the French Govern-

[4] Abetz, *op. cit.*, p. 201.

ment in return for such services". But on what these "facilities" were to be, Hitler was very vague indeed. Indeed, he specified that, with the war continuing against England, Germany could not make any concessions to France that could, in any way, weaken the Reich politically and economically; he wanted to maintain the demarcation line between the two zones, for it limited espionage in the Occupied Zone; nor was he inclined to cut occupation costs or to release many French war prisoners: they might, for all he knew, join some resistance movement or de Gaulle.

Although Darlan got little out of his Berchtesgaden visit, he still went ahead with the concessions to Germany in Syria, Tunisia, and Dakar. To quote the indictment of Benoist-Méchin, as read out at the opening of his trial on May 29, 1947—an indictment which was in reality that of Darlan—this is what the concessions to Germany amounted to:

When in May 1941 a revolt, led by Rashid Ali, broke out in Iraq against Britain, Darlan's... policy of collaboration came into full force... The Franco-German agreement, which was ratified on May 21, provided for (1) the surrender to Iraq of three-quarters of the French war material in Syria; (2) the placing of Aleppo at the disposal of the Luftwaffe as a refuelling point; (3) the use of ports, roads and railways in Syria for the transportation of German equipment to Iraq; (4) instruction to be given on Syrian soil to Iraqi soldiers in the use of French war material; (5) the transmission to the German High Command, on a reciprocal basis, of all information concerning British forces in the Near East; (6) the transfer from North Africa to Syria of a number of French fighter planes, etc.... On May 8 Darlan asked General Dentz to give German planes on their way to Iraq all facilities.... As a result of these and other moves, 100 German and 20 Italian planes reached Iraq....

On June 8 the British struck out against the Germans and the Vichy French; this led to a clash between the Vichy troops on the one hand and the British and the Free French under General Catroux on the other. It ended on July 15 with the Convention of Saint Jean d'Acre....

While the fighting was going on, Darlan did his utmost to facilitate the Germans' task, and sent Benoist-Méchin to Turkey to obtain transit facilities for the troops in Syria. In the process he declared himself profoundly convinced of Germany's victory.

This wasn't everything. Following his meeting with Hitler at Berchtesgaden on May 11, Darlan made himself responsible for the famous "protocols" of May 28, the purpose of which was "to consummate on a much wider scale the military collaboration between France and Germany".[5]

These protocols provided for the use by Germany of Bizerta as a supply base for the German forces in Libya; the French Navy was to protect the transport of German reinforcements in French merchant ships from Toulon

[5] *Le Procès Benoist-Méchin* (Paris, 1947), p. 22.

to Bizerta; the Bizerta-Gabès railway was to be placed at the disposal of the German armies in Libya; also, France was to supply 1,500 lorries from Tunisia to the German forces.

The protocol on French West and Equatorial Africa provided that the port of Dakar be placed at the Germans' disposal, as well as an airfield in the same area. The protocol clearly implied eventual joint Franco-German action against the British and the Free French in the Chad territory and elsewhere.

In return, Darlan was hoping to obtain important economic and political concessions, such as the abolition of France's payment of the Wehrmacht's occupation costs in France, the re-establishment of French sovereignty over the whole of France, including the Nord and the Pas-de-Calais, a "special statute" for Alsace-Lorraine until the Peace Treaty; the gradual liberation of all war prisoners, etc—the whole implying the wholehearted incorporation of France in the New Order. (*Ibid.*, p. 200–1.)

The great Darlan argument was, in his talks with the Germans, that the Syria, Bizerta and Dakar "concessions" presented a certain risk of war with Britain and eventually America; and that France must, therefore, be "paid" for her services. But, as Benoist-Méchin rather cynically remarked, it wasn't so much that; it was more a case of making the thing acceptable to French public opinion. As for the risks, well—as Benoist-Méchin was to say:

We weren't really at that time running any risks. In May 1941 the United States wasn't in the war; there were no American armies anywhere, and the position of Britain was so precarious that, as Mr Churchill said, "she just managed to keep her head above water". She was on the defensive. In the Middle East she still had some forces, but she couldn't intervene effectively anywhere else at that time, least of all in French North Africa. (*Ibid.*, pp. 193–4.)

If the Bizerta and Dakar protocols came to nothing, it was because certain members of the Vichy Government and, above all, Weygand—who threatened to resign—would not have them at any price.[6]

One very important fact emerges clearly from all Darlan's talks with the Germans: and that is that the French and the Germans had a very different conception of what constituted *collaboration*. In 1940, with the war "practically" won, Hitler was perhaps anxious, with French help, to consecrate and consolidate the New Order. Whether this could have given France any lasting benefits is, of course, doubtful. But French "co-operation" at that stage obviously had its uses from the German point of view.

[6] It is true that Benoist-Méchin later claimed that Weygand had not been "quite so categorical"; nevertheless, the fact remains that the Bizerta and Dakar protocols were not approved by Vichy.

In 1941 the situation was no longer the same. The war was dragging on, and was likely to last for years. In the circumstances, the Germans were not in the least interested in French collaboration on the give-and-take basis that Darlan and his "brilliant young economists" were advocating. Germany, preparing to invade Russia, was only interested in *taking* from France, not in *giving* to France. In 1942 this became completely obvious, as Laval did not take long to discover; but, in fact, the German attitude was not very different in 1941. That was where Darlan made himself so ridiculous, not only in French, but even more so, in German eyes. It was with some astonishment that the Germans reacted to Darlan's eagerness to co-operate with Germany in the military field—for here was truly a case of his "giving them a chicken when they had only asked for an egg". In this connexion Abetz quoted a very curious document, the minutes of a meeting at Ribbentrop's house on June 1, 1941, at which the Franco-German protocols (on Syria, Bizerta, and Dakar) were discussed:

Ribbentrop made it clear that he did not want France to enter into a war against England. It would make things very difficult in North Africa, and would intensify the British blockade of Vichy France in the Mediterranean. ... Anyway, Germany had plenty of other things to worry about at present. Events were in the offing which would change the face of the world. [A reference to the coming war against Russia.] He thought the services to be rendered by France to Germany at Bizerta and Tripoli "quite natural", and they did not call for any kind of compensation. I asked whether some assurances could not be given to the French about their position in Tunisia and Morocco. Ribbentrop said "No; the Italians have claims on Tunisia and in Morocco we might have to give something to Spain".

But the most interesting passage concerns Ribbentrop's attitude to France and the Vichy Government generally:

Ribbentrop added that he personally had no confidence whatsoever in the French. Darlan was perhaps genuinely convinced that Germany would win the war, but the pro-British feelings of the French and their traditional dislike of Germany were too strong to make it possible to trust them. Besides, what respect could anybody have for Frenchmen who were running after the Germans in order to join in the fight against their former allies? This distrust of France was fully shared by the Führer, who considered Italy a true friend who was to be preferred to a doubtful ally like France.

On July 14, 1941, after the war had begun in Russia, Darlan, according to Abetz, made another attempt to join the Axis in a more "worthy" way:

If France was expected to defend herself and all her territories against Britain, and to reconquer, as far as possible, the territories Britain had taken away from her, it was morally essential that France have her proper place in Europe officially confirmed: Darlan therefore asked that a *provisional peace treaty* between France and Germany replace the Armistice. Under this treaty France would wholeheartedly support the New European Order, help in the economic organization of Europe, and join a Three-Power Pact for the creation of this New European Order. But the Axis powers must progressively allow the sovereignty of the French Government to extend to the Occupied Zone; there must be no territorial demands on France and her possessions, apart from the return of the former German colonies and an eventual exchange of territories in Africa; prisoners should be released, and the question of Alsace-Lorraine should be settled in such a manner as not to allow it to "constitute a problem in future". Militarily, France would defend herself against England and any other aggressor, and try to reconquer the dissident colonial territories; her Navy would be used for defending metropolitan France and her colonies against any attacks.

Hitler turned down the offer with disdain as a feeble attempt at blackmail; the French were trying to cash in on the concentration of Germany's main forces against Russia and he was not interested in Darlan's offer to use the French Navy and Army for fighting the British in Africa, any more than he had been interested in the proposal by the Vichy group of Young Ministers, a few months earlier, that France be allowed to "defend the Western rampart of Europe on the Atlantic".

Three weeks after Darlan's proposal of July 14 Ribbentrop instructed Abetz to tell Darlan next time he saw him that the German Government was too busy, for the present, with other things.

It was not till the end of October that contact was re-established between Darlan and the Germans. In return for reinforcements allowed to France's colonial troops, Darlan (Abetz wrote) gave the German Navy information in his possession on the movement of British convoys in the Atlantic; he allowed German torpedo boats to be transported through Vichy France to the Mediterranean, besides giving Germany numerous other "proofs of goodwill". Weygand, whom the Germans distrusted, was recalled from North Africa, and replaced by General Juin, and on December 22, 1941, the Vichy Government informed the German Government that if Rommel's troops were compelled to retreat into Tunisia, they would, far from being disarmed, be well received by the French, and the French troops in Tunisia would be ordered to resist the British if they tried to pursue the Germans into Tunisia.

It is true that, at his meeting with Goering at St Florentin on December 1, 1941, Pétain tried to obtain important German concessions in France itself, and had asked, in Goering's—and indeed, Darlan's —opinion for "far too much". However, not discouraged by the Pétain-Goering meeting, Darlan was still anxious to pursue the discussions on a different basis—and although he was told that the German Government did not wish any "preliminary peace treaty" to be discussed,

Hitler would receive him in Paris, notably to follow up the French proposal for a Franco-German plan of joint defence in North and West Africa. But, at the last moment, for tortuous psychological reasons advanced by Abetz in his book, Hitler cancelled the meeting. Abetz's lamentations are particularly worth quoting in the light of Darlan's claim to have been *attentiste* throughout (a claim strongly denied by "pure" Vichyites like Du Moulin de Labarthète):

> After the generous proposals Darlan had made and the even more generous ones he was preparing to make, Hitler's decision not to see him was a blow from which he never recovered. His attempt to arrive at an agreement with Germany had finally failed. His desire to reconquer Syria by starting out in Tunisia [with Rommel's troops and Juin's troops] all the way across Libya and the Suez Canal was not to be fulfilled. He became the laughing stock of all the *attentistes* in Vichy and of the whole of France.[7]

What seems to have precipitated Darlan's replacement as Premier by Laval was the Riom trial, even though he was not directly responsible either for the idea of holding it, or for the fiasco it was to prove in the eyes of the Germans. But the Germans thought it disgraceful that in a country claiming to be carrying out a "National Revolution", an easy-going trial should be held at which the accused were allowed to mock the Head of the State, and to speak insultingly of Germany. In countries such as Russia and Germany, where they take their revolutions seriously, such a trial would have been inconceivable. The Vichy French, Abetz wrote, had proved themselves incapable, on this occasion, of "wielding the weapon of Terror, without which no real revolution can succeed".

It is unimportant whether or not Riom was the immediate cause of Darlan's downfall. What is important, though, is that Darlan had courted the Germans in vain for over a year, misinterpreting the German meaning of the word "collaboration" and willing, in hunting this mirage, to involve France in the most dangerous military adventures.

One may well wonder whether the contempt and ingratitude with which the Germans had treated Darlan did not have something to do with his decision to go over to the Americans in November 1942—all the more so as, by this time, the tide of war was clearly beginning to

---

[7] Abetz, *op. cit.*, p. 242. All this phase of Darlan's negotiations with the Germans is left practically blank in his son's book. The Berchtesgaden meeting is given a few lines and the North Africa protocol scarcely mentioned. A striking example of "rewritten history". Abetz's story, on the other hand, is substantially confirmed by the evidence produced at the trial of Benoist-Méchin, Darlan's closest associate in his talks with the Germans.

turn. Not that he was basically anti-German; on the contrary, all accounts agree that he was, for instance, tremendously flattered at being received by Hitler; he also seems to have fancied himself something of a Man of Destiny: thus, on his way back from Berchtesgaden, he stroked the handle of his sword, which had been given him by an aunt of his when he graduated from the Naval College. The handle was decorated with the figure of a dolphin. "Prophetic, eh?" he remarked. "Could the old girl have foreseen that I would be *le dauphin*?"

Only the Germans had proved ungrateful; and were they not also going to lose the war? It was beginning to look like it at the end of 1942. Besides, there were other considerations in favour of joining the Americans. If Laval was providing for France the "insurance" on the German side, was it not "patriotic" to "insure" France on the American side, too—*and "insure" Vichy at the same time—which was precisely what de Gaulle was NOT doing*? Moreover, by securing American protection for "Vichy" (whether with or without Pétain's official approval was immaterial), Darlan was also satisfying a *class* instinct against Russia and the Communists. In France, judging not only from the growing ruthlessness towards the Resistance, but also from Darlan's own comments on the Resistance, as reported by his son, he grew increasingly alarmed by the danger of Communism after June 1941.

Thus he said in 1942:

Before the Communists had joined the active anti-German Resistance in France, the Gaullist Party lacked real dynamic vigour and was merely engaging in wishful thinking. Now, thanks to the Communists, who constitute by far the most highly organized Party, and the best-armed Party, and counting among their members real experts in the art of underground propaganda, sabotage, guerrilla warfare and murder, the anti-German movement has acquired the dynamic vigour which it lacked. Instead of appearing to be vulgar terrorists (which they are) they have now acquired, through their association with the Free French, a patriotic halo. But de Gaulle is not using *them*; it is *they* who are using de Gaulle. . . .

This was scarcely a commentary that could please the non-Communist Resistance who always tended to claim at least parity with the Communists in the Resistance movement generally. (Claude Bourdet: "We were more numerous in the Resistance than the Communists.") Darlan's anti-Communism, however, constitutes a significant starting-point in his rapid evolution towards pro-Americanism.

The rôle of Darlan in North Africa has been described and discussed so often that it need scarcely be mentioned here. It is enough to say that, as it turned out, Darlan had miscalculated his timing; in the state of world opinion at the end of 1942, his assassination was perfectly logical and, at the time, spared the Allies a great deal of trouble and embarrassment; for public opinion in all the Allied countries was outraged by the "hobnobbing with Vichy"—however expedient it might have been, for a few days, from a purely military point of view.

Fundamentally, however, Darlan was right in assuming that there were very strong political forces in the United States which were not only opposed to the Communists, but also to de Gaulle, in so far as de Gaulle could, at that time, be considered an ally of the Home Resistance, including the Communists. It was, indeed, these forces which, for many months after Darlan's death, were still to support Giraud, the respectable conservative, against de Gaulle, the "adventurer", who seemed to have the *sans-culottes* on his side, and who glibly talked of "revolution"—at least while he was still at Algiers. That de Gaulle later also became "respectable" though never entirely, from the American point of view—is another story. But it is certain that, in 1942 and 1943, the men of Vichy were more "respectable" in the eyes of Robert Murphy and—by a strange aberration—even in the eyes of Roosevelt, who, apart from anything else, could not stand de Gaulle personally.

That America was on the side of counter-revolution, the Resistance knew only too well. Thus in June 1944 the clandestine Radical-Socialist *Aurore* wrote, under the title "The American Card":

These Vichy gentlemen have now found the Road to Damascus. They are playing the American card. It is their supreme hope. At Vichy they go on whispering all over the place that, being afraid of the USSR, America will facilitate the creation, in the West, of an anti-Bolshevik barrier composed of France and of a Germany camouflaged to look like a democracy.... These gentlemen imagine, above all, that if this marvellous stunt were to come off, they would have nothing to fear from the courts-martial of a Free France, and might even take their seats in the Government![8]

In short, as a sociological phenomenon, the case of Darlan is easy to explain. The mistake he made was to imagine that in 1942 he could make with the Allies the grand career he had failed to make with the Germans. Others who, like him, had first been "anti-Ally" and then become "pro-Ally" had the good sense to assume non-political airs, at least for a time. That was the case of General (later Marshal) Juin, who in North Africa, after the Allied landing, merely became "a soldier"—even though, a year earlier, he had been appointed to North Africa, with German approval, to replace the "anti-German" Weygand. Similarly, thousands of other soldiers and officers in North Africa—including many who had fought the British in Syria—went "Gaullist" during 1943, altering, it is true, the nature of "Gaullism" in the process, as will be shown in a later chapter.

Few generals, apart from Dentz, were to suffer for what they had

[8] Quoted by *L'Observateur*, 28 August 1952.

done in the war. Many of the admirals were to be dealt with much more harshly; it was partly because their caste was too closely associated not only with the "Darlanist" phase of Vichy politics, but also with the tragic series of blunders which had led to the complete destruction of the French Navy—a destruction which Darlan, owing to the tortuous political game he never ceased to play, and even more so, owing to the anti-British "climate" he had created in the Navy, had failed to prevent.[9]

[9] Admirals, more than army leaders, had played an active part in the "National Revolution" and had held prefectoral and other high administrative and government posts under Vichy. They were considered more "reliable" than the generals. Vichy had been nicknamed the *Société pour la protection des Amiraux* or, *anglice*, Society for the Prevention of Cruelty to Admirals.

I have not dealt with the short "Flandin interlude", i.e. with the rôle of M. Flandin as Vichy's Foreign Minister during a few weeks after Laval's dismissal. He was Foreign Minister only in name, since the Germans, greatly displeased with Laval's dismissal, boycotted him, and even refused him a pass for crossing the demarcation line. All the major negotiations with the Germans were conducted during this short period by Darlan, who saw Hitler at the end of December. It would, however, be rash, to say the least, to conclude from this that Flandin represented "open resistance" to the Germans, as is asserted, most surprisingly, by M. Robert Aron on p. 367 of his *Histoire de Vichy*:

"In forcing Flandin to resign," M. Aron wrote, "after having dismissed Laval, the Marshal clearly indicated his attitude: he chose not to choose—he wished neither military collaboration with the Reich, nor open resistance."

Apart from the fact that Laval was not favourable to military collaboration with Germany, it is, surely, absurd to apply the word "resistance" to Flandin. Ambassador Leahy wrote of him to President Roosevelt on January 25, 1941: "Flandin is a compromiser and he leans pretty far over to the German side." As a Munichite, who had sent a telegram of congratulations to Hitler after the Munich settlement, he was notorious as an "appeaser", and his "anglophil" reputation rested on little more than his friendly relations with a number of ultra-Chamberlainite British press lords. At the end of 1940 Flandin differed from Laval—whom, with a display of sickening hypocrisy, he had helped (see Vincent Auriol's *Hier, Demain*, vol. I, pp. 123–39) to push through parliament Pétain's plenary powers—in one respect only: he still thought there might be a chance for an Anglo-German negotiated peace in which he might conceivably be called upon to play a part.

The Germans objected not so much to the person of Flandin—who had given them every satisfaction in the past—as to the manner in which Laval's dismissal was generally interpreted in France and in the world at large as an act of defiance by Vichy towards Germany.

CHAPTER SIX

LAVAL: A REASSESSMENT

WHEN, some years after the Liberation, M. François-Poncet was being "received" at the French Academy, he delivered a long address in which he exalted the virtues of Pétain and de Gaulle, and put the blame for all the shame and ignominy of what had happened on Pierre Laval. Laval's daughter, Mme de Chambrun, thereupon sent every Paris newspaper a long statement which included quotations from various letters which she said were written to her late father by His Excellency, M. François-Poncet, in which the latter had not only expressed his undying devotion to *le Président*, but had also praised his policy as the quintessence of political wisdom. Not a single paper published a line of this document, drawn up with filial piety by a woman who was convinced that her father had been the victim of a miscarriage of justice. That Laval's trial was irregular and scandalous in every way, even Laval's enemies are prepared to admit; whether he deserved or not the rough justice that was meted out to him is a debatable point; but what is certain is that there was, for years after his death, a conspiracy of silence round Laval—a conspiracy for which the most ardent supporters of Pétain were more to blame than anyone else. Communists and Socialists had broken with Laval long before the war, and they owed him nothing. But he *was* a Vichy Minister, and it is his Vichy colleagues who, for years, have been whitewashing themselves at his expense.

Laval was the politician *par excellence* of the Vichy régime, and a Third Republic politician at that. Personally he was *antipathique* to the Marshal and to the people around him, just as the National Revolution did not appeal to Laval himself. But Pétain used him, and, at heart, considered him more capable of dealing with the Germans than anybody else. If, by dealing with the Germans, he was making himself unpopular, so much the worse for him. And, at heart, Pétain must also have remembered that in June and July it was Laval who laid the foundations for the Vichy régime by coaxing and bullying Parliament into giving him (Pétain) his plenary constituent powers.

Yet if ever there was a man who was not all-black and not all-white, it was surely Laval. Even so, the legend of an all-black Laval had been built up by both his enemies and his colleagues throughout the Vichy

93

régime—so much so that, to the outside world, he looked like the blackest of all villains. In his long book, *Crusade in Europe*, General Eisenhower makes only one reference to Laval, and dismisses him simply as "Hitler's notorious puppet".[1] Admiral Leahy, the US Ambassador at Vichy, was conditioned by the *maréchalistes* into considering Laval as such, and although, in reality, there was no reason, in April 1942, why the replacement of Darlan by Laval at the head of the French Government should be considered a major disaster by the Allies (Darlan was, if anything, more dangerous), the US Government uttered grave warnings to Pétain against the re-appointment of Laval. To most of the outside world, Laval was simply a German agent—a view which, for example, Sir Winston Churchill seems to accept to this day as self-evident; yet this is precisely what it is not. In the history of France of those years very few things indeed are "self-evident", and Laval's treason is not one of them. Also, Laval was represented as being morbidly ambitious and financially corrupt.

On the other hand, Laval's apologists have argued that he was a "pure" man, a real French patriot, with a profound understanding of the needs and desires of the French people, and one who did his best to save France from war, and who, when war came, did all he could —first by working for the Armistice, then by setting up the Vichy régime, finally by bravely dealing with the increasingly exacting Germans—to keep France's head above water. He was by birth a peasant (his apologists argue), a Little-France man, not world-conscious, not even very Empire-conscious ("France is really all I care for", he would say); he wanted to keep France out of any war and, unlike Darlan, was not interested in joining the Germans in any military adventures. Even his old "Briandist" federalism was skin-deep.[2] In April 1942 he reluctantly took office, it was said, not because he was ambitious, but because he thought he was better fitted than others in his dealings with Germany, to limit the damage to France. Nobody was less militarist, or less bloodthirsty than Laval. And, at heart, he was not Fascist at all, but a Republican and a democrat, and continued, even under Vichy, to be democratic, friendly and easy-going in his manner, and "to blow smoke up the Marshal's nose", and hobnob with the peasant folk of Châteldon, who loved him.

There is a little truth both in the criticism of Laval and in the defence of Laval. But taken separately, neither the criticism nor the defence explains him.

[1] *Crusade in Europe* (London, 1948), p. 145.
[2] He often liked to refer to his visit to Berlin in 1931 when patronizingly and rather aimlessly he and a doddery Briand talked to Brüning of Franco-German friendship.

LAVAL AS GRAVEDIGGER OF THE REPUBLIC

Several books have been published in defence of Laval, notably *Laval parle*, a collection of documents with a preface by his daughter, Josée de Chambrun; and two books by his lawyers, Y. F. Jaffré's *Les Derniers Propos de Pierre Laval* and Jacques Baraduc's *Dans la cellule de Pierre Laval*, all of which are pathetic human documents and constitute a valuable addendum to his own admittedly brilliant defence at the Pétain trial and later at his own trial—as long as he was allowed to speak.

But they do not, strictly speaking, answer the very severe criticisms of Laval's pre-war policy; still less do they explain very adequately why Laval showed such ruthless determination to scrap the Third Republic in July 1940.

At his trial he argued that he was double-crossed by Pétain and the *maréchalistes*; but was he? The testimony of three witnesses, one a pro-Nazi, Georges Suarez, another, a close parliamentary associate of Laval's, Jean Montigny, the third a political enemy of Laval's, Vincent Auriol, all written in 1940, agree on one point—on the passionate determination of Laval to start a "new order" in France.

The interesting thing about the three books is that, although some of the speeches made by Laval to the deputies and senators in preparation for the "overthrow" of the Third Republic were delivered at secret meetings, and even without stenographers, the accounts of these speeches are substantially identical. The difference between the pro-Laval and the anti-Laval books is chiefly in the accompanying comments, Suarez, for example, saying:

Pierre Laval was conducting the funeral of the régime with supreme mastery,[3]

while Auriol was expressing in nearly every line his indignation at the behaviour of "that crook and twister ... Everything about him is black: his clothes, his face, his soul".[4]

Auriol, needless to say, was taking a pretty jaundiced view of Laval. For one thing, he was clearly infuriated at the skill with which Laval was handling Parliament, playing on men's resignation, fears, ambitions and weaknesses.

L'Audace—Danton's word—he was applying it to Laval and to what he called *le club de l'Hôtel de Ville de Bordeaux*.

Here, since the 15th of June (a day before Pétain's Armistice broadcast) a certain number of parliamentarians had been meeting every day—men who, since Munich, had grouped themselves round Laval, Bergery, Bonnet, Déat,

---

[3] Georges Suarez, *Le Maréchal Pétain* (Paris, 1940) p. 107.
[4] Vincent Auriol, *Hier ... Demain*, vol. I (Paris, 1945), p. 100.

Montigny and de Monzie ... The head of this "Bordeaux Commune" was Laval. Having set up his headquarters at the town hall, he was receiving parliamentarians, journalists and diplomats. ... To give himself the maximum freedom of movement he had refused a post in the Marshal's government. His sole purpose was to change the régime and make France collaborate with Nazi Germany. ... The "club" was in continuous contact with Pétain and with foreign Embassies, and exercised continuous pressure on the presidents of the assemblies, on hesitant deputies and senators and on the President of the Republic. ...

When, on June 25, the Armistice was signed,

Laval was triumphant. He had won the first round of his devilish game. ... It was then that he, and his crony Marquet, joined the Marshal's Government. ...

Soon afterwards Parliament was called, and was to meet at Vichy. The Marshal had retired into the background, and from now on, until the vote of the law of July 10, Laval held the stage. He spoke at several meetings, stressing continuously that he was "the Marshal's spokesman".

At a private meeting at the Petit Casino he explained the meaning of the Constitutional Bill:

The lesson taught us by our defeat is that there must be a change of régime through order and legality ...

Moreover, "the economic life of France must be given a new orientation; it must become an agricultural country integrated in the continental system of production and trade".

It should perhaps be remarked in this connexion that *the overwhelming majority of people at Vichy at that time were convinced that Germany had won the war*; and it is in that context that one has to read Laval's speeches—all versions of which substantially agree. These were the main points he made that day:

(1) France had been defeated, and it was folly to think of continuing any sort of resistance in North Africa. Any further resistance would mean *the total occupation of France*. This was the view held by France's greatest generals; and that was why France had sued for an armistice.

(2) The Germans were only a few miles away; but it was no use despairing. One must face bravely the future, and create the proper conditions for a French revival. It was no use worrying any more about the fate of England; England had caused this war, and dragged France into it, and had then deserted her. France had been tied too long to England's apron-strings. England was going to lose the war. It was essential that France should be first to make peace, and make England pay; otherwise England might make peace with Germany at France's expense.

(3) He (Laval) had good grounds for saying that Chancellor Hitler would

grant France an honourable peace, provided she practised a policy of loyal collaboration with Germany and Italy and integrated herself in good faith in a reorganized continental Europe. "I was always in favour of this policy."

(4) But Chancellor Hitler would only grant France favoured treatment if her Government and her institutions were strong and reliable.... "Just as after 1918 Germany adopted the system of the victorious nations, so France must adapt her political institutions to those of her victors.... Parliamentary democracy, whose greatest crime was to declare this war, lost the war; it must disappear and give way to an authoritarian, hierarchized, national and social régime."[5]

He then dropped a hint that if Parliament did not follow him, and prevented him from safeguarding "the predominance of civil authority", the alternative might well be a military dictatorship. (Was this an allusion to General Weygand, whose troops were stationed a few miles outside Vichy and which, it was whispered at Vichy, might simply disband Parliament?)

In conclusion, Laval tried to gild the pill: if the deputies and senators behaved themselves, there would still be work and jobs for them.

I have received from the Marshal the formal undertaking to let the present Chambers continue until the new Assemblies, created under the new Constitution, have been ratified by the latter. No doubt the present Chambers' activity will be reduced. But we shall certainly use the numerous men who have demonstrated their competence in various fields, we shall consult the major Committees, and shall entrust parliamentarians with important missions.

Even after Laval had agreed to include in the Bill an undertaking to submit the new Constitution "to the ratification of the Nation" (whatever exactly that meant), there was still some resistance from the so-called "Ex-Servicemen's Group" in the Senate who produced a counter-proposal suspending the Constitution of 1875 only until the peace treaty, allowing Pétain plenary powers, but stipulating that constitutional laws are to be drawn up "in co-operation with the relevant parliamentary committees" and that the new institutions be "submitted to the approval of the Nation as soon as conditions permit free consultation".

But when the two sponsors of this Bill, M. Taurines and M. Dormann tried to speak, they were howled down by Laval's supporters. After days of manœuvring, Laval, now fully supported by a previously hesitant Flandin, got a large majority to vote for the Government Bill —569 voted for, 80 against, and 17 abstained.

These 569 were not all crooks and profiteers [Auriol wrote]. The great majority of them were honest men, but without character, without foresight,

5 The references to Hitler are quoted by Auriol but not by Suarez or Montigny.

trembling for their jobs and their future.... There were some also who thought Laval would get them elected to the new Assemblies. Others still were blinded by the dazzle of the Marshal's stars, dejected by the misfortunes of France, and believing that the Marshal's prestige would save her....

Direct intimidation, according to Auriol, had also something to do with the size of the vote: a whispering campaign was started to the effect that "those who voted against wouldn't sleep in their beds tonight"; there were also many troops in the streets of Vichy, and, worse still, Doriot and his thugs had been let loose, and were directly threatening a number of deputies with violence, notably Blum and Dormoy.

A poor show altogether, Auriol thought; and what upset him perhaps most was that *of the 175 Socialists*, there were only 36 who had voted "No". Some, it is true, weren't at Vichy; a few were still in Morocco; but the others? Even many of those who were at Vichy voted for Laval.[6]

In short, Laval had triumphed. From Auriol's point of view, he had deliberately killed the Republic; while Laval's admirers, such as Montigny and Suarez, exalted the "superb mastery" with which he had conducted "the funeral of the régime".

Yet one cannot emphasize too strongly Laval's conviction that Germany had won the war and that France must "adapt herself". Speaking as a witness at the Pétain trial, he said:

Do you believe that in 1940 any man of common sense could have imagined anything other than a victory of Germany? ... France's interest at that time was quite obviously to find with Germany a formula that would have allowed us to escape the consequences of our defeat.[7]

And to this point of view he stuck throughout his first terms of office under Vichy. Hence his enthusiasm for the Montoire meeting which, he persisted in saying, had been sprung as a pleasant surprise on him by the Germans, who, he thought, needed France as a *willing* partner in the organization of Nazi Europe, as a shining example that the rest of the occupied countries were going to follow. He also stressed that

---

[6] There has been some speculation on how the Communists would have voted, had they been there. But thanks to M. Daladier, who had disbanded the Party (and by this time most of the Communist ex-deputies were in gaol)—they were spared this awkward choice. It is hard to say how they would have voted; the Soviet-German pact was still in force, and Mr Bogomolov was soon to arrive at Vichy as Soviet Ambassador to Pétain. Also, they had been "anti-war"—like Laval, like Pétain, like the *Action Française*—though in a rather different way! At the same time the Thorez-Duclos statement, purporting to have been published on July 10, 1940, was certainly hostile to Vichy. (See Chapter IX.)

[7] *Le Procès du Maréchal Pétain*, pp. 539-40.

Pétain *raised no objection whatsoever* to going to meet Hitler at Montoire. Later, in 1945, he was blamed for having lacked faith in the ultimate defeat of Germany, for not having had a "Gaullist" mentality. His answer to this was to the effect that de Gaulle had taken, in 1940, a noble but reckless bet, but that, *as things were at the time,* the only thing to do was to try to save France from the dire consequences of defeat. This "unromantic", "feet on the ground" mentality, this mentality of what Laval called *common sense* was extremely typical of the man—and of a very large part of the French nation.

In December 1940, Laval was thrown out of the Vichy Government; and he did not re-enter the Government again until April 1942. It is only fair to point out that *Laval's attitude to Germany was not the same in 1942 as in 1940.* This is what he wrote in prison in 1945, and his words ring quite true:

The war had taken a new turn in 1942. Russia and America were now fighting against Germany. In 1940, the German Government, at least until Gauleiter Bürckel started expelling the French from Lorraine [in November 1940], had behaved decently, as one would expect a victor to behave if he respected his enemy.... In 1942 everything was different. After my talk with Goering (in March 1942) I knew that Germany was going to treat us roughly, ruthlessly, without taking the slightest account of the future relations between our two countries. . . .[8]

In July 1940, however, Laval was convinced of Germany's victory, and so were most people in France. It was for that reason that he got a not very "resistant" Parliament to grant plenary powers to the Pétain Government. If his manner was truculent, if, to some, like Auriol, he was like a personification of black villainy, it was for two reasons. He was convinced that there was no time to lose; Britain would soon be defeated, and France should hurry to make friends with Germany; and secondly, Laval thought himself particularly well-qualified to assume the task of "guiding" Parliament, because he considered himself one of the few people who had been right throughout. He had been against declaring war on Germany in September 1939; he knew it could only end in disaster; and he also made most of the "crime" of declaring war without the explicit approval of Parliament, the vote on the military estimates on September 2, 1939, being only an "implicit", but not an explicit declaration of war.

His argument was that if France did not oppose the German reoccupation of the Rhineland in 1936, and surrendered both Austria and Czechoslovakia in 1938, it was mad to go to war over Poland in strategic conditions infinitely more unfavourable. "*En '39 il fallait faire autre chose,*" he said.

[8] *Laval parle* (Paris, 1948), pp. 199–200.

LAVAL'S PRE-WAR FOREIGN POLICY

Where Laval took considerable liberties with truth was when he later argued in his defence that he had done his utmost to build collective security round Germany and so to prevent Germany from "expanding". Barthou, before his assassination in October 1934, was well on his way to resuscitating the Franco-Russian alliance, which was to be the cornerstone of a vast encirclement of Germany, including the Little Entente, and, if possible, Britain and Italy. Laval's first act, in becoming Foreign Minister in October 1934, was to put the Russian alliance in cold storage. In a book written a long time ago, I record a meeting with Laval just about this time, and Laval's significant gesture of pointing to the middle of the map of Europe, and saying: "Now, listen, what security can we have unless we come to terms with *that*?"—*that* being Germany.[9] Laval gladly surrendered the Saar to Germany in 1935; he is not known to have protested against the German reoccupation of the Rhineland; and if, as seems likely, he became increasingly alarmed at the growing strength of Germany, and tried to make up for his miscalculations in that direction by courting Mussolini's Italy, there is very little to show that he took the Russian alliance of 1935—though it was he who signed it—very seriously. For one thing, he did his utmost to delay its ratification. (This was done by the Sarraut Government after his fall in January 1936.) It is true that in March 1939, after the German occupation of the whole of Czechoslovakia, Laval made a highly alarmist speech before the Foreign Affairs Committee of the Senate:[10] but here again, his main complaint was that his plan for an alliance with Mussolini's Italy—always something of a mirage—had been sabotaged. But his claim that he had, throughout, tried to form a "chain" round Germany—a Paris-Rome-Belgrade-Bucharest-Prague-Warsaw-Moscow coalition—was a quibble. Nevertheless, he was right in one respect: it was when he reminded the Senate that day of having said that Munich would inevitably lead to a German-Soviet pact. His great mistake had, of course, been, first, in a false "Briandist" spirit, to strive after an agreement with Nazi Germany; then to concentrate his efforts on a Franco-Italian alliance; and, in the process, to have virtually abandoned the Barthou plan based on the solid reality of an East-West alliance against Hitler. The Stalin-Laval Pact had been concluded with the greatest mental reservations, especially on the French side; a Russian remarked at the time: "It will mean just as much as the French intend it to mean"; and if, in March 1939, Laval suddenly reminded France of this "trump", it was rather late in the day; and one cannot help wondering why Laval had never protested against Munich much earlier,

[9] *Cf.* Alexander Werth, *The Destiny of France* (London, 1937), pp. 99–100.
[10] Appendix No. 6 of *Laval parle*, pp. 255–8.

and why he had not tried to remind French opinion of the Franco-Soviet Pact before it had already been rendered as good as meaningless by Bonnet in 1938.

And even in 1939 Laval dwelt far more on the necessity of another attempt to detach Italy from Germany than on the Soviet alliance. There is no completely rational explanation why men like Laval should throughout the last pre-war years have attached such great importance to having Italy as a military ally, as if—were it to come to a show-down—Nazi Germany were automatically going to be deterred by the military power of Italy. Yet for the sake of the Italian alliance, Laval and others were willing to paralyse the League of Nations, to neglect the eastern alliances, and to strain relations with Britain. A sympathy for Fascism and a hankering for an all-Fascist Europe may account for it in the case of some pro-Italians (e.g. the ferociously anti-British *Gringoire* group), but, in Laval's case, what mattered perhaps more was a temperamental and sentimental attraction towards a Latin country, especially one where Laval had enjoyed what he thought to be his greatest diplomatic triumph (the Rome agreements[11] of 1935), where he had been fêted by Mussolini, and where the Pope had made him a Papal Count. "Ah, if my dear mother could see me at this moment," the newly created Papal Count is said to have remarked, as he walked down the steps of St Peter's. (Anyway, that was the story at the time.)

And Laval shared Mussolini's distaste for England. He later denied ever having been anti-British, and even produced as proof of his loyalty to England letters from the British Minister in Paris showing that he had done his best for England to help her out during the great sterling crisis of 1931. That, no doubt, was a long time ago. But later he had come to distrust Britain. He was understandably furious over the Anglo-German naval agreement of 1936, but, above all, he could never forgive Britain and (as Léon Daudet used to call them) *les vieilles folles du Peace Ballot*, the sabotage of the Hoare-Laval Plan, in the preparation of which, he said, a very active part had been taken by the then Prince of Wales, who had a number of long talks with Laval, and who, according to Laval, had later also enlisted the full support of King George V. But British opinion was against it. To Laval, all this British self-righteousness and League-of-Nations purism, which had wrecked the Hoare-Laval Plan, and so also the Rome Agreements (and had finally led to the downfall of Laval's own cabinet in January 1936)

---

[11] "In Rome," Laval said, "Mussolini and I did far more than come to an agreement on the colonies; we concluded a regular military alliance. Secret military agreements, which were never divulged, had been signed by General Gamelin and General Badoglio, as well as secret air agreements which were signed by General Vallin, the Italian Minister of Air, and General Denain, our Minister of Air." (*Le Procès du Maréchal Pétain*, p. 502.)

were disastrously unrealistic. That, in the long run, Mussolini could not be relied on as a friend and ally of France somehow never seems to have crossed Laval's mind. Right up to the war and even later, the Italian alliance was to remain the cornerstone of Laval's foreign policy and his *idée fixe*.

The Germans were not unaware of it, and were, even during the years when he was widely considered *their* man, to treat him with some mental reservations. These reservations would come to the surface whenever relations became strained between Laval on the one hand and de Brinon and the other all-out pro-Germans of the "Paris group" on the other.

LAVAL'S CLASH WITH "VICHY"

But, as already said, Laval accepted Germany's victory as a dead certainty in the summer of 1940, as "any man of common sense would have done". If, on December 13, 1940, he was abruptly dismissed by Pétain, it was, according to him, *entirely* for domestic reasons, as Pétain was going, in any case, to continue the policy of "collaboration" with Germany, which Laval had started.

This is true, and yet—not quite true. There had been a change in public sentiment in France after Germany's failure to knock out Britain in the autumn of 1940; and Laval had come to symbolize in the eyes of public opinion, the policy of all-out collaboration. Although Darlan was, in 1941, to go much further than Laval might have done, Darlan's game was much less obvious than Laval's, and he remained a dark horse for a long time. Also, Montoire, where nothing had really been settled except the principle of collaboration (to which Pétain had fully subscribed), was to be followed up by "technical" Franco-German talks on December 22; Pétain may have become frightened of the prospect, and Laval's dismissal, at any rate, postponed these talks.[12]

[12] What was to be discussed on December 22? According to Laval (*Procès Pétain*, pp. 538–9) who was obviously trying to justify the Montoire policy, Abetz had informed him that Germany would be willing to cut down the 400 million francs a day in occupation costs to 180 million francs; that the Nord and Pas-de-Calais would be reintegrated in France; that the demarcation line between Occupied and Unoccupied France would be "relaxed", and that the question of war prisoners would be discussed, Abetz foreshadowing the release of successive batches of 150,000 French prisoners. On what Germany was to get in return Laval was extremely reticent; but, according to Abetz and other sources, Franco-German "co-operation" was to be extended to Africa; Hitler played with the idea of "redrawing" the map of Africa, France's losses to be compensated at Britain's expense; although Laval claimed that he was against any sort of joint Franco-German military action against Britain and the Free French, it is probable that the Germans would have pressed for it on December 22 or would, at any rate, have foreshadowed the demands they were to make five months later on Darlan.

How far Laval would have gone in these talks in "integrating" France in a Nazi Europe is difficult to say because we do not really know how much importance Laval actually attached *at that moment* to Germany's failure to defeat England. Perhaps not much; after all, Montoire had taken place already *after* Germany had lost the Battle of Britain. But the chief, though not the only reason for Laval's dismissal on December 13 was the lack of sympathy that existed between him, on the one hand, and the Marshal and the *maréchalistes* on the other. The reasons for this were very numerous, and Laval was later to make out a fairly convincing case which was meant to demonstrate that:

(*a*) The Marshal had gone much further with his *actes constitutionnels* than was warranted by the law of July 10.

(*b*) Numerous features of the Republic, and indeed the Republic itself had been abolished against Laval's will, and contrary to the promises he had made to the Chamber of Deputies and the Senate before they had passed the Law of July 10. A most important breach, in Laval's view, was the abolition of the *Conseils Généraux*, the dismissal of mayors, etc.

(*c*) Discriminatory measures against Jews and Freemasons had been introduced much against Laval's will, and without his being able to prevent it; he claimed that his powers as Vice-Premier were extremely limited; he had to fight a stiff battle to limit the damage of this legislation.

(*d*) Parliament had been virtually abolished, deputies' and senators' salaries stopped, all entirely against Laval's will; and later a *Conseil National* was set up.

(*e*) The Légion, which became a State within the State, had been set up, and constantly interfered with the workings of local government, the appointment of Prefects, etc.

At the Pétain trial, as well as at his own trial, and in the notes he wrote while in prison, Laval brilliantly explained the motives of his behaviour during his second term of office (1942–4) and argued, not unconvincingly, that he had, during those two years, "sacrificed himself" for France. He did not, on the other hand, explain very convincingly why he had taken it upon himself—apart from the fact that "Germany had won the war"—to extract the plenary powers for the Pétain Government from Parliament in July 1940; and when a witness claimed to have heard him say with some glee after Pétain had signed the first Constitutional Acts: "That's how one finishes off the Republic!" he merely said that he "did not remember having said that", or if he had said it, "it was merely as a joke in rather poor taste".[13] That may, however, well have been his first reaction, and it should be recalled in this connexion that Laval had not been before the war the staunch democrat he later claimed to have been. In 1935 he used to say that "Parliament can work properly only in normal times" and he had also, on

---

[13] *Procès Pétain*, p. 530.

more than one occasion, expressed his special sympathy for the Croix de Feu, and (according to Tardieu) given money to them.[14]

Yet there seems little doubt that, before long, Laval became more and more disturbed by the monarchist atmosphere that developed at Vichy after he himself had cleared the way for the new régime. But he denied having bullied Parliament into voting the law of July 10.

When we got to Bordeaux the Armistice was a foregone conclusion. Ninety-nine per cent of Frenchmen knew perfectly well that we could not go on fighting... As for the Marshal, practically everybody was for him in those days, among them Herriot and Jeanneney. So when you talk of my having "threatened" Parliament into some sort of surrender, you are more unfair to Parliament than you are to me.

And, turning to the judges:

"So you believe I could have led astray 569 deputies and senators? I should like to have such powers of seduction—they would be useful now!

"Only the trouble was," he went on, "that the Marshal applied the law in a manner I had not foreseen, and in a way that was contrary to the undertakings I had given to the Assembly.

"I thought the dissolution of the *Conseils Généraux* particularly scandalous, as was the dismissal of elected mayors. Although there is no shorthand report of the meeting, I am absolutely certain to have undertaken, *vis-à-vis* Parliament, that the *Conseils Généraux* would not be dissolved. The importance of these *Conseils* varies from *département* to *département*. In the Puy-de-Dôme a *conseiller général* is equal in importance to a deputy or a senator. In the Puy-de-Dôme to abolish the *Conseil Général* was tantamount to abolishing the Republic.

"I protested as hard as I could against this suppression of the *Conseils Généraux*. Journalists in Vichy know how much I protested. But the Marshal's advisers were young ministers who had never been elected by anybody."

A member of the jury then remarked that Laval was still in office when the law of November 16, 1940, abolishing the *Conseils Généraux* was passed. This law, he recalled, authorized the Government to dismiss elected communal and departmental counsellors, and it also specified that mayors of communes of over 2,000 could no longer be elected.

LAVAL: "I protested, but I was not Minister of the Interior.... The worst of it was that the *Conseils Généraux* were then replaced by *Commissions Départementales*; and it was particularly shocking that instead of appointing the ex-*conseillers généraux* to these commissions, the Minister of the Interior

[14] Cf. Alexander Werth, *France and Munich* (London, 1939), and *The Last Days of Paris* (London, 1940).

appointed other people.... The Légion played a leading part in this selection; it was the *revanche* of those who had been beaten in regular elections."

Later, in 1942, when Laval returned to office, he reversed the process, and "made amends for the errors of 1940". He set up *Conseils départementaux* "which had almost exactly the same attributions as the *Conseils Généraux*". In this way he reinstated as many of the former *conseillers généraux* as possible—though not, as we shall see, in the Vichy Zone, where he came into conflict with the Légion.[15]

Further, Laval insisted on the abolition of the *Conseil National*, as an organ threatening to deprive the old Parliament of even a nominal existence.

"If," Laval said, "I told Pétain I'd put another *Conseil* in its place, it was because it was the only way there was of persuading him to get rid of the *Conseil National*. I had no intention of replacing it.

I am dwelling on this part of Laval's defence, because it is extremely typical of the man. For all his alleged "pro-Fascism", he was essentially a small-town politician, and when he talked about things like the *Conseils Généraux* he was really in his element. He also sharply reacted against the Légion which, to him, was something profoundly undemocratic, or rather, "unrepublican". And it was on this question of the Légion that his conflict with Pétain was most fundamental of all.

"It was Weygand," he said, "who had the idea of creating the Légion, and he did it in full agreement with the Marshal. This Légion took the place of all the old ex-Service men's associations and it soon became like a single party. The Légion was the main organ of Pétain propaganda. It played an enormous part in the Vichy Zone. My hostility to the Légion was well known, and I was attacked for it by the Germans, by the Marshal, and by the pro-Nazi press. Every Wednesday the leaders of the Légion complained of me to the Marshal; because every Wednesday, in my absence, the Marshal would receive four, five, or six departmental presidents of the Légion. These were real political meetings.

"The Marshal wanted the Légion to become a single party; only it just did not work in France. A proper single party would have been something like the Nazi Party; the Légion, on the other hand, was full of decent people; only their leaders were rather different from the rest.... The Marshal, you see, wanted to suppress all parties; he wanted only *one* party, the Marshal's party—and this was the Légion with its reactionary leadership."

The Germans, Laval said, would not allow the Légion to function in the North of France, but in the South it was really troublesome.

[15] It is worth noting that in his report to Goebbels, de Brinon should have violently criticized Laval for this reinstatement of Third Republic Prefects and other people who were doing nothing to create a proper pro-Nazi atmosphere in France.

"No member of the *conseils départementaux*," Laval said, "could be appointed without the Légion's approval. Pétain insisted on this. For days I had to argue with them in favour of formerly elected councillors. They pressed the claims of their own candidates.... In the Tarn-et-Garonne I stuck to my guns, and refused to have a reactionary, while the Légion would not have my nominee. So in the end no *conseil départemental* was appointed in the Tarn-et-Garonne at all. To support me, I had the prefects; against me I had the Légion and the Marshal."

Similarly, Laval put the blame on the *maréchalistes* for the legislation against Jews and Freemasons. Although, at the Senate, in 1932, his Government had been overthrown by "an almost open Masonic conspiracy"[16] and he had no great sympathy for Freemasons, he was revolted by the persecution to which thousands of completely harmless people were subjected.

One day I received the visit of M. Marron, a senator, 82 years old, who was Mayor of Ceyrat, near Clermont. His only interest in life was his *mairie*. But he had been turned out for being a Freemason. I thought it was ridiculous and odious.... He was one of the thousands to be purged for being a Mason.[17]

Not only Laval, but also supporters of Pétain (like Du Moulin de Labarthète) referred to the Marshal's "phobia" about Freemasons, whom he considered the quintessence of the evil Third Republic; and Laval had much trouble in restraining fanatical anti-Masons, like Admiral Platon,[18] placed in charge of the "Masonic problem". A special anti-Masonic police, similar to the anti-Jewish police, was working under Gestapo control. Lists of 60,000 Masons were drawn up for publication in the *Journal Officiel* and 7,000 arrests were made by the joint efforts of the Vichy and German police, and thousands more were deported and 550 shot.[19]

Laval had taken no part in the drafting of either the anti-Masonic or the anti-Jewish laws of 1940. For the non-French Jews, Laval agreed, the French Government could and would do nothing; its first concern should have been to protect the French Jews, and he thought the "relatively anodyne" law of 1940 tended to protect them against more drastic German legislation. But by the time he returned to power in 1942, he found that the anti-Semitic drive at Vichy had made great headway. Under Darlan, an "Anti-Jewish Police" had been formed, composed chiefly of members of Doriot's PPF and other pro-Nazis, and Darquier de Pellepoix, a half-demented anti-Semite, was now at the head of the Department for Jewish Affairs. Laval disbanded the anti-Jewish police, and also rejected various items of new legislation pro-

[16] *Procès Pétain*, p.526.   [17] *Procès Laval*, p. 78.
[18] *Laval parle*, pp. 106–9.   [19] Vanino, *op. cit.*, p. 117.

posed by certain Ministers at Vichy, and modelled much more closely than the 1940 laws on Nazi practice. For the protection he was giving the Jews ("I saved thousands of them") Laval was violently attacked by Pellepoix in anti-Semitic papers like *Le Pilori* and *Je Suis Partout*, and also had a lot of unpleasantness with the German authorities, notably when he opposed, even after the German occupation of Vichy France, the extension of the "yellow star" rule to that part of the country.[20]

On the constitutional issue Laval claimed to have been double-crossed by Pétain and his advisers. His argument at his trial was that, in view of the exceptional circumstances of 1940 it had been necessary to *suspend* the 1875 Constitution until the new Constitution, presented by the Marshal, had been *approved by the country and ratified by the Nation*. But meantime he had meant the old Parliament to go on existing; its members were to continue to draw their pay, and to be used, as far as possible, both on the major committees and outside Parliament.

After saying that men like Alibert, Bouthillier and Baudouin had far more influence with the Marshal than he ever had, Laval said that the Constitutional Acts were in flat contradiction with the letter and the spirit of the law of July 10.

"The National Assembly," said this law, "calls upon the Government of the Republic to promulgate under the signature and the authority of Marshal Pétain, in one or more constitutional acts, the new Constitution of the French State. What does this mean?" said Laval. "It means that the Marshal *and* the Government had been invested with constituent powers, with this peculiarity that no Constitutional Act could be passed without the approval and signature of the Marshal. But on the very next day, and without being preceded by the legally indispensable words '*Le Conseil des Ministres entendu*' the first Constitutional Act opened with the sentence 'Nous Philippe Pétain....' This was not at all the spirit in which I had submitted the Bill to the Assembly. The thing stank of Monarchy... And none of the subsequent Constitutional Acts were to be submitted to the Council of Ministers. Why didn't I protest? You have to remember Pétain's prestige at the time. He was more than a king, more than an emperor. He symbolized, he embodied France. He did as he liked. Alibert was given the job of drawing up the Constitutional Acts; everybody in Vichy knew it. And Alibert was seconded by Du Moulin de Labarthète and other people, none of them very republican in outlook. I was *never* consulted on the Constitutional Acts.... After the December 13 *coup* (which showed incidentally, how powerless I was) Pétain committed other abuses, notably by setting up a *Conseil National* which gave the impression of having finally replaced the old Parliament...."

Relations between Laval and Pétain were not too happy; Laval

[20] *Laval parle*, p. 101.

thought he had no political experience, but quite a taste for politics and quite "an appreciable liking for personal power".

So I once said to him: *"Monsieur le Maréchal,* do you realize the extent of your powers?" "No," said he. So I said: "They are greater than the powers of Louis XIV; for Louis XIV had to submit his edicts to Parliament, but not you; for there is no Parliament any more." "Yes, that's true," he said. The next day I saw the Marshal, and he said: "Do you know the extent of my powers?" "No," said I. So he repeated what I had told him the day before, forgetting that *I* had told him.[21]

He thought Pétain not only rather gaga at times but also insensitive and indifferent to a lot of the injustice and cruelty done in his name, extremely vain and frivolous, "much too taken up with the childish satisfactions" of his office[22] and thoroughly insincere.

It seems fairly clear that, in his defence, Laval laid on his "republicanism" rather thicker than was warranted by the actual facts of 1940; and his argument that he was appointed *dauphin* by Pétain in one of the first Constitutional Acts in order to "reassure republican opinion in France" does not sound altogether convincing. But that Laval was not a good "National Revolution" man—even though he had laid the foundations for it—is obvious from the acute hatred he aroused among the Vichy die-hards, notably among the cagoulards and the Action Française elements who were principally responsible for his overthrow in December 1940.[23]

LAVAL'S FIGHT WITH THE NAZIS

The story of Laval's second term of office—from April 1942 to the Liberation, when he was, against his will, carried off to Germany, is a very different story, and is, on the whole, a good deal more creditable to him than his record of 1940 which, essentially, arose from his conviction that Germany had won the war.

Many things had changed for the worse between Laval's first and second term of office. Pucheu, as Minister of the Interior under Darlan, had resorted to the most ruthless police methods against "terrorists" on the one hand, against Jews and Freemasons on the other. The deportation of thousands of Communists or alleged Communists to what were virtually death camps in North Africa had been intensified; Darnand had, already in July 1941, organized his SOL, an offshoot of the insufficiently dynamic and fanatical Légion, and was soon to turn it into the

---

[21] *Procès Laval,* p. 72.   [22] *Laval parle,* p. 97.
[23] Darlan also played a part in the overthrow of Laval. It is doubtful, however, that he favoured Laval's replacement by Flandin. "Flandin," he said, "seems to be more detested by the majority of the French people than Laval." Certainly Laval was personally much more likeable.

famous Milice, loosely described as the "French Gestapo", and which, before long, was indeed going to work in close co-operation with the Gestapo, the Waffen SS and other German forces of repression. The SOL was organized with Pétain's full approval, despite opposition from the more respectable members of the Légion, and since Darnand was Pétain's personal appointment, Laval seems to have had particular difficulty in interfering with the terrorist activities of the Milice. As Darnand was to remark at the end of his own trial, it was not until April 1944 that Pétain thought fit to protest against the Milice.[24] Altogether the clear impression emerges that Laval, during his second term of office, had put up with Darnand and his Milice, but that he had sharply resisted whenever he could against the successive promotions by the Marshal of the *maurrassiste* killer, who had, moreover, become *persona gratissima* with the Gestapo. Nominally, no doubt, the Milice came under the authority of the Head of the Government, i.e. Laval, but there is plenty of evidence to show that Darnand was very much his own master *vis-à-vis* Laval, though not *vis-à-vis* the Germans. When, early in 1944, General Oberg, head of the Gestapo in France, proposed to Darnand that he become, as it were, his French opposite number, by taking the post of *Secrétaire Général au Maintien de l'Ordre*, "the Marshal", Darnand said, "was rather in favour of this appointment, but not Laval. In the end he also agreed, but at first he was ferociously (*farouchement*) against it."[25] A clear indication of Laval's acute distaste for the "killer" and for the Milice-Gestapo methods. It is, of course, also on record that Laval had violently protested against a number of Milice atrocities, notably against the savage murder of Georges Mandel and Jean Zay.

The international scene, by the time Laval returned to office, had radically changed. The Soviet Union and the United States were in the war. Neither Laval nor most people were sure any more of a German victory. Why did Laval return? It was suggested, though with no support for this view (except for a violent anti-Vichy article by Marcel Déat—who was, however, playing a game of his own, and was not necessarily a friend of Laval's) that Laval had been inflicted on Pétain by the Germans. Laval, on the other hand, was later to demonstrate with real vigour and passion that that was not the case, and that as a result of his meeting with Goering in March 1942 he was confronted with the most "agonizing choice of his life". He claimed (and this sounds quite genuine) that his whole family were deeply distressed at the prospect of his assuming the responsibilities of office at that time.

He was to explain at the Pétain trial (though not at his own trial—for here he was prevented from speaking) how it had all happened; and although a large number of general charges were made against Laval

[24] *Les Procès de la Collaboration*, p. 282.   [25] *Ibid.*, p. 262.

for his policy throughout the Occupation, there has been no evidence to show that Laval was lying when he spoke:

(1) of the circumstances of his return to office in April 1942;

(2) of the desperate efforts he made in his negotiations with the Germans to limit the number of workers who were being sent to Germany;

(3) of his famous phrase "I want Germany to win the war" which, he said, was an indispensable piece of tactics, and adopted with Pétain's consent;

(4) of his attempts to restrain the Vichy die-hards who were pursuing a ruthless policy of repression;

(5) of the value of his "friendship" with Abetz, whom he used as far as possible to offset the utter ruthlessness of fanatical Nazis like Sauckel and the Gestapo chiefs.[26]

Laval's capital argument, when all is said and done, was that France's choice, from April 1942 on, was an extremely limited one: either she submitted to the rule of a *Gauleiter*, possibly assisted by a puppet government of totally servile Frenchmen like Déat and Doriot, or she had a nominally independent Prime Minister who, though blatantly pro-German on the surface, was still able to dodge their demands to some extent, slow down, if not actually sabotage, the execution of their orders, and add, despite immense difficulties, a certain "human touch" to the relations between conquerors and conquered. Laval had to protest, and argue, and pull wires, and he seems to have succeeded on many occasions in applying, not only to the Vichy die-hards, but even to the Germans, the technique of "personal intervention"—a weapon

[26] There was a good deal of subtlety, perhaps too much subtlety in Laval's earnest attempts to differentiate between "possible" and "impossible" Nazis. Thus he said to Jaffré (and the record of his conversation sounds genuine):

"I don't know if Abetz was a Nazi at heart. It was one of those questions it was better not to put to a German, even if one was on friendly terms with him. . . . I believe Abetz was loyal to his chiefs, and even more so towards his country. But if he was Nazi by conviction—and I am not absolutely sure that he was—he was certainly not Nazi by temperament. . . . On the other hand, I did meet some 100 per cent Nazis—including some well-conditioned thugs and some real loonies. . . . There was, for instance, a chap called Danneker. Almost a youngster, anyway, quite a young fellow. He had come to France to deal with Jewish questions. An S.S. man, of course. They brought him to see me. Before he had talked for five minutes, I realized that the fellow was completely bats. In forty years of public life I had many occasions to meet dotty people but I had never seen one quite as dotty as this one. When he talked of Jews, he foamed at the mouth and his eyes popped out of his head. He would have put the lot of them in a frying pan. I realized I was wasting my time with him. I asked them to send me somebody else. The other one foamed rather less, but wasn't much better. . . . Abetz was different. He was neither a thug nor a fool, and he understood France better than the rest of them. Not that it was always plain sailing with him either. . . . But at least one could negotiate with him. . . . It was a mistake to talk of *the* Germans; there were Germans, not all alike. . . ." Y. F. Jaffré, *Les derniers propos de Pierre Laval*, pp. 128–31.

he had learned to wield, with consummate skill, in the *couloirs* of the old Chamber of Deputies. It was in this way, for example, that he rightly claimed to have saved the lives of many people, including Paul Reynaud and Léon Blum, though whether he restrained the terrorist activities of Darnand's Milice as much as he might have done—after all he *was* Head of the Government—is not certain. Even so, one of Laval's greatest assets, throughout his political career, had been the "personal approach" with its heartfelt tone of sincerity and loyalty (*"loyauté"* and *"loyal"*, uttered with his warm Auvergnat accent, were his two favourite words), and its power of persuasion.[27] Were the Germans taken in by Laval? Laval argued very convincingly that his "I want Germany to win the war" broadcast of June 22, 1942 had given him quite a long lease of life, but that, after a certain time, the Germans still began to suspect that he wasn't quite as "loyal" as he pretended to be. It was then that they started "colonizing" the Vichy Government with men like Henriot and Déat and Darnand, pro-Nazi thugs, who were to keep an eye not only on Pétain, but on Laval himself.

Why, one might ask, did the Germans not drive Laval and the whole Vichy crowd out of office, and appoint a *Gauleiter*? The answer is fairly simple: By 1943—when Laval was no longer much trusted by the Germans—they had rather too many other worries on their hands, and Laval had, it seems, also impressed upon them that if they were going to get too tough with France, the Resistance and the Maquis would become infinitely more extensive. The Germans, already on the run in the Soviet Union, just hadn't any more troops and police to spare for France.

Anyway, it was not without a touch of pride that Laval compared the proportion of Frenchmen who had been sent to Germany with the proportion of, say, Belgians. The proportion of Frenchmen was much lower; and, what is more, as distinct from many other countries of Occupied Europe, no women were sent from France to Germany.

From all the other occupied countries of Europe (Poland, Belgium, Holland, etc) the number of men and women sent to Germany represented between 5 and 8 per cent of the population; in France (not counting, of course, the number of war prisoners who had been repatriated) the figure was 1.3 per cent of the population, or 13 workers per 1,000 inhabitants.[28]

Laval also claimed that, as against the 2½ million workers whom Sauckel wanted to send from France to Germany, he (Laval) managed to limit the gross number to 641,000 between 1942 and 1944, a total

[27] I remember how, for instance, his speech after the breakdown of the Hoare-Laval Plan in December 1935 completely "bowled over" one of the correspondents of *The Times*, until that day a passionate critic of the said Plan.
[28] *Laval parle*, pp. 129–30.

which, he claimed, was at least partly offset by war prisoners who had been repatriated (110,000) and other war prisoners (250,000) who had received, while still in Germany, the status of "free workers".[29] These figures do not appear to have ever been seriously challenged.

But to return to Laval's decision to re-enter the Government in April 1942. For nearly eighteen months he had been out of office, living the life of a private citizen, partly at the Villa Saïd in Paris, partly at his beloved Châteldon. He did not take any very active part in politics, and still felt, it seems, deeply insulted by the way he had been treated by Pétain in December 1940.

On the other hand, he maintained close contact with Abetz and other Germans, and also seems to have been on good terms during this period with Déat and other French "Nazis" in Paris. He had even gone with Déat, at the beginning of the German-Russian war, to Versailles, to review the first troops of the "anti-Bolshevik Legion", the LVF, and it was then that he and Déat were both wounded by a "terrorist". Laval, though seriously wounded, characteristically asked that the assailant be not killed—a request that was granted. At the same time, he was critical of Darlan, and kept saying that the Admiral was giving away to the Germans far more than he (Laval) would have given away in similar circumstances. He is credited with having nick-named Darlan "L'Amiral Courbette".[30]

A few comments made by Laval during this period to Maurice Martin du Gard are worth quoting; they are typical of the man:

> The English—well, they are English, and have a tremendous sense of their own interest. It's an excellent quality, and if I, Laval, were born an Englishman, I would, with my character, be a highly respected citizen in the House of Commons. A fellow who has made a success of his private affairs is not suspect as he is here. It's only here that people who have failed in business are considered best qualified for running the State.[31]

> The French are irritating people. They always have to be defended, not only against their enemies, but even against themselves. They don't want

---

[29] *Laval parle*, p. 129.

[30] From Admiral Courbet; *Courbette* might be translated "Admiral Kow-Tow".

[31] The legend that Laval was both very crooked in business and fabulously rich is not strongly supported by any evidence. He was a shrewd business-man who bought up a variety of half-bankrupt businesses and made them flourish, such as Radio-Lyon, the *Moniteur* of Clermont-Ferrand, etc. The Socialist and Communist press were going to "show him up" in 1936 and—showed up nothing. Maurice Martin du Gard says he was "*avare plutôt que riche*". He used, of course, his political influence for helping him in business, e.g. by promoting the sales of the mineral water of Châteldon which, while he was Prime Minister in 1935, used to be displayed on every dining-car table on the French railways!

to make children; they don't want to fight, and when one wants to save them from war, and, later, from the consequences of defeat, they grumble.

The Marshal: the trouble with him is that he never wanted to *do* anything; he wanted to wait. But wait for what? He would like to have everybody sitting at his feet—the French, the German General Staff, Churchill, Roosevelt, perhaps Stalin, too. He doesn't want to *dirty* himself. Well, if you are always afraid of dirtying yourself, you never get anywhere....[32]

A curiously prophetic remark. In April 1942, Laval knew that he would have to "dirty" himself. After reporting to Pétain his ominous interview with Goering, in the course of which the Reichsmarschall had complained bitterly of the hostility of the French people, and had warned him that Germany would now treat France accordingly, Laval, after long and laborious negotiations, became Head of the Vichy Government; he thought it was something "he owed France".

The Germans were now at war with both Russia and America, and they were obviously determined to mobilize the maximum of Europe's economic and labour resources; that, and not France's "hostility" was the real reason for Goering's warning.

One of the first landmarks in Laval's second term of office was his broadcast of June 22. The original text said: "I believe in Germany's victory, and I want this German victory, because without it, Communism will establish itself everywhere in Europe." Then he had a discussion with Pétain. The only objection, according to Laval, that the Marshal made was that he, Laval, was no judge of military affairs, and that he was therefore not qualified to say whether he "believed" or didn't believe in a German victory! Pétain later said that he was "horrified" when he heard Laval's broadcast; but Rochat, the Secretary-General of the Ministry of Foreign Affairs, who was present at the Laval-Pétain meeting, later confirmed that Pétain did give the "*je souhaite*" phrase his approval.

In his defence Laval argued that this phrase had been a godsend to France.

I knew that the phrase would deeply hurt the French people, that it would act like a drop of sulphuric acid on people's skins.... But it made it incomparably easier for me to negotiate with the Germans.... It was a sort of *passe-partout* in the most difficult and dramatic circumstances.

And Laval told the curious story of how, after the Allied landing in North Africa in November 1942, he was summoned to Munich by

[32] Maurice Martin du Gard, *op. cit.*, pp. 228–9. Galtier-Boissière also attributes this phrase to Laval in 1943: "*Je suis jusqu'au con dans la merde: alors ne faites pas de vagues!*" and quotes Antoine de Saint-Exupéry who, though in the Resistance, still thought that France should be grateful to Laval—he was *le vidangeur* who was doing "the dirty work" which others, like Pétain, were refusing to do.

Hitler. Hitler's Minister in Vichy, Krug von Nidda, had communicated to Laval Hitler's offer of a Franco-German military alliance *"durch Dick und Dünn"*, and Laval was to give the Führer France's reply. He travelled with Abetz by car to Munich, and Abetz was "distressed" to hear that Laval and Pétain had decided to turn down Hitler's offer. Laval was obviously nervous about meeting Hitler; but after keeping him waiting for about four hours, Hitler merely made a number of snarling remarks, and said that France would keep only those colonies she had herself defended. And, by God, he would chase the Anglo-Americans out of Africa. Laval returned to France, now wholly occupied by the Germans, but feeling that "it might have been worse" if he hadn't said that *"je souhaite . . ."* He seems, at any rate, to have told Hitler how deeply distressed he was that France couldn't accept his generous offer.[33]

But his greatest worry during the second term of office was over the deportation of French labour to Germany. His negotiations with Sauckel were the toughest of all, and it was in this field that Laval claimed to have rendered France his greatest service by resorting to delaying tactics, by trying to explain to Sauckel the "psychological impossibility" of some of his demands, by impressing upon him the fact that the "Secret Army"—the AS—and the Maquis were rightly being called by everybody in France the *Armée Sauckel*; by trading skilled workers for war prisoners, by demonstrating the greater effectiveness of making the French workers work *in France* "for the glory of Germany". He went on and on and on. Sauckel was not entirely taken in by Laval, and in the end got thoroughly distrustful of him. In a dispatch to Hitler on August 9, 1943, Sauckel wrote:

Laval has accepted the transfer of a million French workers from civilian production to German war production in French territories. Even so, he tried to eliminate the German directors from the working of these factories. This we firmly refused. . . . On the other hand, Laval . . . firmly refused to let us have 500,000 French compulsory labour people in Germany before the end of 1943. The discussion lasted more than six hours, and Laval was really incapable of producing any valid arguments for his refusal. . . . All he is trying to do is to gain political advantages for France. . . . He keeps frightening us with stories of people running off to the mountains, and of terrorism breaking out all over France. . . . He does not seem to have enough authority to enforce his own decisions. But that's partly his own fault. He has quarrelled with men like Doriot and Bucard, and would even like to dissolve their organizations; yet it is precisely these people who are Germany's most wholehearted supporters, and are supplying the largest number

---

[33] Just because I *had* used that phrase I was able to say to Hitler: "You know **my** feelings for you, but there are certain things that France cannot accept and this is one of them. *I deeply regret it.*" (*Procès Pétain*, p. 561.)

of people to the SS, the LVF, and the Todt Organization. . . . Laval's attitude
is greatly hampering the mobilization of French labour for the Reich. . . .

And in the same letter, Sauckel quoted another letter he had sent to
Schleier, the German *Chargé d'Affaires*, in which he said:

I have lost all confidence in the honesty and good faith of Prime Minister
Laval. His refusal [to send 500,000 French workers to Germany] is, purely
and simply, an act of sabotage of Germany's life-and-death struggle against
Bolshevism. His totally unfounded and incoherent replies to my clear and
precise questions have made the worst possible impression on me. The
French Ambassador, de Brinon, I might add, was almost as painfully
impressed by his Premier's attitude.

This report, quoted and reproduced in photostat in *Laval parle*
(pp. 262–7), came from the American Nuremburg archives. Neither in
the Pétain trial nor in Laval's trial was any use made of this decisive
document; it seems that Laval and his Defence were unaware of its
existence. This, and much else that has come to light since Laval was
put to death, virtually without trial, make him look very different from
the villainous picture that was painted of him by the Public Prosecutor.
Very significant in the Sauckel document are the references to the
growing hostility between Laval and the all-out pro-Nazis—Doriot,
Bucard, and their followers, and the comic reference to de Brinon,
Pétain's Ambassador in Paris, who was purely and simply a German
spy. The said de Brinon addressed, for example, a letter to Goebbels
on May 11, 1943 in which he wrote (for he was in the habit of reporting to the German leaders what was going on inside the French
Government!):

Pétain wants a sort of Conservative Revolution—the sort of thing Laval
loathes; not that he wants a National-Socialist revolution either. All through
his public life . . . he has been a pacifist. . . . Also, while the Marshal has no
use at all for parliamentarians and beneficiaries of the old régime, he considers that Laval supports and protects far too many of these people.

And Brinon added that Laval was also constantly protecting the Freemasons, whom the Marshal hated, and that "the only person against
whom he had taken reprisals was Admiral Platon, the great enemy of
the Masons. And he has placed Platon under house arrest."

"There is, of course, no doubt about Laval's loyalty," Brinon also wrote
in his letter to Goebbels, [a passage omitted in *Laval parle* but quoted in
the Brinon trial[34]] "and no doubt that he wants a German victory. . . . It
is tragic, however, that Laval should always be so handicapped by his
character when it's a case of taking strong action. He has too many contacts

[34] *Les Procès de la Collaboration*, p. 130.

with parliamentarians to shake off his easy-going habits and his political friendships."

Laval had received no thanks from Pétain for "liquidating" the Third Republic; and subsequently Laval—after realizing that there was not necessarily going to be a Hitler Order in Europe—seems to have "gone back to the Third Republic"—by protecting its representatives and even by keeping its revival in reserve. His abortive attempt, just before the liberation of Paris, to engineer a reassembly of the 1936 Parliament with the help of Herriot was typical of his frame of mind. He failed in this restoration of the Third Republic (suggested to him, Herriot believed, by the Americans) not because Herriot refused to co-operate, but because the Germans and their stooges—the Déats and the Doriots—would not have it. When he was forcibly taken to Germany, he persisted in saying that he was a prisoner of the Germans, and he refused to have anything to do with the comic opera "government" of Sigmaringen set up by Brinon, Déat, Darnand, Luchaire, and other French Nazis.

In a strange book, written by Corinne Luchaire, the film-star daughter of Luchaire, who was amongst the distinguished French émigrés in Germany, there is an account of Laval at Baden-Baden in the summer of 1944:

I found Laval particularly changed. He was acutely worried about his daughter who had remained in Paris, and of whom there was no news. He had brought a large number of packets of *Baltos* with him, and was nervously chain-smoking all the time. When I mentioned the political situation, he just shrugged his shoulders and said that he was nothing any longer; that he was in Germany against his will and had resigned when Abetz had compelled him to leave Paris, by force if need be. Whenever he met a journalist, he read out the letters he had written about August 15 to the Prefect of Police and the Prefect of the Seine informing them that he was no longer Head of the Government, and that the maintenance of order in the capital was now their responsibility ...

After Baden-Baden there was the winter at Sigmaringen. And, in the spring of 1945, the French exiles fled still farther from the advancing Allied armies.

The story [Corinne Luchaire wrote] that the fugitives of Sigmaringen were passing through the village of Wangen must have spread through the area; for numerous French workers, who had been deported under the STO had come in large numbers, and roamed around us in a rather threatening manner. They felt that we were the cause of their misfortunes. Was there going to be a fight among Frenchmen? ... And suddenly we saw Pierre Laval getting alone out of his car and going up to a group of angry French workers. And then he spoke to them. I don't exactly know what he was saying, for at first his voice was drowned in booing; and then there was silence, and he made what must have been one of his last speeches. He explained why he had pursued his policy. It was necessary. He had to limit the damage. He spoke of France, of a cause that had to be defended; he spoke of our fields. And these men who had come to boo him, and perhaps to kill him, were silent, and they were visibly approving; one by one they went up and shook hands with him. And Laval seemed happy.... And then a strange thing happened. These men, who foresaw the danger that was threatening him, told Laval to stay with them, and they would protect and defend him. Laval thanked them, but got into his car, and as he drove off, these men waved him good-bye....[35]

If the Pétainists were glad to see the last of Laval, it is probably true to say that, in October 1945, Laval's execution left France with a very unhappy impression. Reporters at his trial were saying that "he made mincemeat of the Court"; and "if he'd gone on with his defence another day, they couldn't possibly have shot him". Rank-and-file members of the Resistance about that time thought he was "the least bad of a bad lot", and that it was a bad mistake to have shot him. The fact that he had poisoned himself, was then revived, and was half-dead when they executed him made it even worse. But the Pétainists did nothing to defend Laval—"the Marshal's evil genius", as Weygand was to say at the Pétain trial three months before the Laval trial. Laval could be sacrificed so long as the Marshal was to be saved. Laval was not *their* man.

In the years that followed, Laval's stock was to rise in the eyes of French public opinion, especially on the Left, where his antipathy for the National Revolution—as well as for the Germans ("*à vrai dire, je n'aime que le France*") was increasingly recognized. It is significant that in serious criticisms of Pétain and Vichy (such as Maurice Vanino's *De Rethondes a l'Ile d'Yeu*) Laval should often be quoted as one of the most acute and reliable critics of Vichy, with its undemocratic and often inhuman and reactionary spirit, and its political incompetence and amateurishness. Though, in foreign affairs, Laval was also exceedingly naïve and amateurish at times, he understood France and the reflexes of the common man much better than so many of the bigwigs of not only Vichy, but also, alas! of the Fourth Republic. "If he had lived, he might have taken a more sensible line on Indo-China and might have stood up very much better to Mr Dulles than that 'dear little man' Bidault," a prominent elder statesman I know remarked one day in the early months of 1954....

Laval is one of the most curious figures in recent French history—a man with many of the characteristic faults and virtues of his people and a Republican who had turned sour on the Republic out of opportunism

[35] Corinne Luchaire, *Ma drôle de vie* (1948), p. 217. There is also a reference to this incident in Laval's prison notes.

and because, as an innate pacifist, he became frightened of the more dynamic régimes that were arising around France.[36] He thought the French, and not the Germans were *gentils*; it took a real traitor like de Brinon to apply the adjective *gentil* to the Germans!

[36] Oddly enough, the "strong man" who impressed him most—at least so he thought, looking back on it—was not Hitler, but Stalin. "I talked a lot to him in Moscow—and informally, more than I ever did with Hitler. Stalin should be particularly distrusted because he was certainly the most intelligent of the lot. His self-mastery and sureness of touch seemed unique, and he never yielded to impulses. . . . If Stalin is a fanatic (and I am not all sure that he is), he is certainly a lucid fanatic. Now, thanks to the Anglo-Americans, he is on our doorstep." Y. F. Jaffré, *op. cit.*, pp. 135–7.

CHAPTER SEVEN

THE FRENCH NAZIS

IT WOULD be in bad taste to say that a good many more Frenchmen collaborated with the Nazis than is generally supposed. Only one has to distinguish between bread-and-butter collaborators, opportunists who thought it expedient to be "pro-German" for a time, and, finally, those who had been bought by the Germans body and soul, or who had committed themselves so deeply to collaboration, either out of conviction, or for mercenary motives, that they could no longer retreat when the tide had turned.

After all, in an occupied country, almost everybody has, willy-nilly, to "collaborate" with the occupying power to some extent. Though against their will, the French working-class still contributed to the German war effort, either by working in French factories or by allowing themselves to be deported to Germany under the STO and only a relatively small proportion—some for personal, others for patriotic reasons—escaped to the Maquis. The French employer class more or less willingly "co-operated" with the Germans; maybe the peasants overcharged the Germans, but still sold them food. Immense fortunes were made under the German Occupation—by contractors who helped to build the Atlantic Wall, by owners of night-clubs, black-market restaurants and brothels that catered for the German occupants; by a vast army of *trafiquants* who sold to the Germans or their agents any commodity they were willing to buy with occupation francs that cost them nothing, but enriched the racketeers, while impoverishing France as a whole. The German Occupation, and the widespread cynicism and the *crise de moralité* it engendered are among the primary causes of the economic disequilibrium and of the maldistribution of wealth from which France was to suffer for many years after the war.

Probably it will never be known how much "collaboration" money went during the war into hoards of gold and hard currency, into Paris houses and *châteaux* in the country. After the Liberation an attempt was made to sort out all this wartime profiteering; but in most cases the offenders either cleared themselves (after perhaps a few weeks or months in prison) by tipping the right person (the "tips" sometimes running into millions of francs) or skilfully camouflaged acquisitions with the help of well-trained lawyers and notaries. Small building contractors or small businessmen (even Jews among them—and the Joanovici case was by no means the only one) built German fortifications or supplied valuable raw materials to the Wehrmacht, and then bought up valuable real-estate all over France in somebody else's name; small farmers and butchers in Normandy who for years sold succulent steaks to the black-market restaurants of a hungry Paris found themselves, at the end of the war, the proprietors of *châteaux* or of *de luxe* hotels in fashionable health resorts. . . . One could go on indefinitely with an enumeration of the rackets which, directly or indirectly, were all helping the Germans. It would be no exaggeration to say that a *whole new bourgeoisie was born as a result of the German Occupation.* Whether these people *wanted* the Germans to win the war or not is quite immaterial; but, in one way or another, and while the going was good, they did "collaborate".

However, when the Liberation came, this economic "collaboration" was treated less severely than political and ideological collaboration. It is significant that the most famous trials after the Liberation were not those of the economic profiteers of the Occupation, but of the men who supported the Germans on the political and ideological plane. It might be argued that the good done to the Germans by some scribe like Paul Chack or by a fanatical little Fascist like Robert Brasillach was insignificant compared with the services rendered them by this or that building contractor or food racketeer, and that the racketeers, rather than the Chacks and Brasillachs should have been shot; but, in the eyes of the public, the intellectuals and politicians who had collaborated with the Germans had, somehow, sinned against the Holy Ghost in a deeper sense than the black-marketeer, or even the policeman who took his orders from the Gestapo. By *signing* their misdeeds, they had, somehow, sinned more consciously—in a way, an absurd distinction, which even resulted in such unfair discrimination as that between say, Henri Béraud, the famous *Gringoire* propagandist, who was sentenced to life imprisonment, and Horace de Carbuccia, the milliardaire proprietor of *Gringoire* who retired for a while to Switzerland, got five years *in absentia*, and then (without serving these) was simply *acquitted* in 1955! But then, one was a writer, the other—though the real head of the gang —merely "a businessman". It was a curiously French tribute to the power of the pen, to the prestige of the intellectual.

Who were the political *collabos*? And what were their motives? As distinct from the Vichyites and the *maréchalistes*, all-out pro-Germans and pro-Nazis were not numerous; and would not perhaps be worth considering but for one curious question; and that is, What French traditions did they represent? What was their political background?

One might argue, of course, that, in nine cases out of ten, their motives were merely mercenary, or mostly mercenary; in short, they were just "traitors". But the matter is not perhaps quite as simple in France as it was in the case of the handful of British traitors. France had been defeated; France had been occupied; many, like Laval, believed at first that Germany was undoubtedly going to win the war.

But even in the case of plain "traitors", there was nearly always at least the semblance of some ideological basis for their treason. If Vichy was born on February 6, 1934, it is true that some of the pro-Nazism in France can also be traced back to the "1934 spirit" and to certain ideas that crystallized then and during the subsequent years.

DÉAT

One of the principal French Nazis was Marcel Déat, the neo-Socialist and author of the famous "Die for Danzig?" article in the spring of 1939, and who, for all his Auvergnat "nativeness", believed in National Socialism of the German variety, complete with a *parti unique*, and basically hostile to the "reactionary" spirit of Vichy. A man of great ambition, Déat felt frustrated under the Third Republic, and firmly believed in a "Hitlerian revolution" in Europe. He liked to think in terms of that "economic discipline" which France had so sadly lacked throughout her history. As editor of the *Œuvre* he thundered daily against Vichy and against Maurrasism, preferring, notably in the case of anti-Semitism, the more "realist" anti-Semitism of the Nazis to the largely verbal variety of Maurras. Déat was a hard-headed politician, wholly unscrupulous, and firmly believing in the ultimate triumph of Fascism—which he liked "left", rather than "right".[1] He also saw himself as the head, or one of the heads, of a real Nazi Government in France which would, at some stage, replace the "temporary expedient" of Vichy. Towards the final stages of the Occupation, Déat got himself appointed, under German pressure, a member of the Vichy Government, though he continued to stay in Paris, which the French Nazis considered "their" capital. In Déat the *maréchalistes* saw their most dangerous rival. The relations between Déat and Laval were good in 1940 (when Laval firmly believed in a German victory) and much more strained during Laval's second term of office, when Laval resisted the Germans. In the end he fled to Germany and became a member of the Sigmaringen "government". He had little choice and, like others, may still have believed in the German atom bomb. He was one of the French traitors who vanished in 1945.

The fact that this great anti-clerical Nazi and his wife had been living peacefully in hiding in Italy for nearly ten years, most of the time at a

---

[1] For an account of Déat's earlier political philosophy, largely borrowed from Henri de Man, the Belgian *collabo*, see the author's *France in Ferment* (London, 1934), pp. 291-4.

monastery near Turin, and under the protection of the local clergy, was not revealed until April 1955, three months after Déat's death. He and his wife had taken to religion and had gone through a religious marriage with the blessing of the Vatican which (like the Italian police) had known all along about their whereabouts. It is hard to believe that the French police knew nothing. But Déat was obviously too well "protected", and it was less trouble to say nothing.

DORIOT

Equally important among the French Nazis—though in a different way—was Doriot. If Déat was an intellectual and even a *normalien*, Doriot was the "thug". The ex-Communist head of the PPF had managed to place at the service of the French "Nazi movement" a fairly substantial number of young hooligans (with a very small sprinkling of "idealists"), drawn partly from the underworld of Paris, Marseilles, Algiers, Nice and a few other towns, and partly from a small working-class following that Doriot had succeeded in acquiring as Mayor of St Denis. Doriot, a giant with dark, curly hair, certainly had "dynamism", personality, a "gift of the gab"—and money. Money, German money—he had had for a long time, ever since he first founded the *Parti Populaire Français*—the PPF—in 1936, to which were attracted not only some working-class riff-raff, but also the more "dynamic" members of the Croix de Feu which, from 1936 on, had, under the leadership of the gentlemanly Colonel de La Rocque become, from their standpoint, excessively "genteel", bourgeois and ineffective. By 1938 the PPF had indeed become the stronghold of every variety of French Right-wing "thuggery"—a refuge for disgruntled Croix de Feu and Action Française men, and for the temperamentally more violent anti-Communists, anti-Jews, anti-Republicans, New Order "revolutionaries", Marseilles gangsters and a few intellectuals in search of *nouveaux frissons* or merely of new poses—people ranging from eccentric young noblemen like Stanislas de La Rochefoucault and Bertrand de Maud'huy and "thinkers" like Bertrand de Jouvenel to Fascist "neo-Romantics" like Drieu La Rochelle and Robert Brasillach. Much of the emotional catastrophism was supplied to all of them by Louis-Ferdinand Céline whose writings were going crazier and more hysterical with every new book he wrote during those last few years before the war; their titles alone were almost as good as a pre-view of Belsen and Auschwitz: *L'Ecole des Cadavres*, *Mort à Credit*, *Bagatelles pour un Massacre*.

The rivalry in the late 'thirties between the Croix de Feu (later the PSF—Parti Social Français), the relatively respectable *ancien combattant* and only vaguely Fascist movement of Colonel de La Rocque on the one hand and the thugs of Doriot's Berlin-subsidized PPF, on the other, had a close parallel, in Vichy France in the rivalry between the Pétain Légion, and Doriot's PPF, with its affiliated "revolutionary movement". The Légion was at first conservative and *maréchaliste*; but later Darnand, who had all the *dynamisme* of his PPF friends, proceeded to extract from the Légion its most cut-throat elements and to turn them into the Milice, essentially *doriotiste* in spirit. The most pro-Nazi among Pétain's ministers were two other *doriotistes*, Marion and Benoist-Méchin, and it was through Darnand, Marion, Benoist-Méchin and some of the "synarches" who were clustering first round Darlan, and then round Laval, that the Germans engineered such innovations as the LVF (the anti-Bolshevik Legion) and the French Waffen SS unit. It is significant that the most extremist pro-Nazi organizations—the LVF, the African Legion, which fought the Anglo-Americans in North Africa, and the Milice should very largely have been composed of *doriotistes*, and that it is these people who should, almost alone among the whole French nation, have volunteered to fight "for Hitler" in Africa and on the Eastern Front. That most of them were a lot of riff-raff with a greater taste for looting than fighting does not alter the main fact.

In his message to Goebbels, of June 1943, de Brinon wrote:

If only National-Socialism were better known in France, it would have innumerable adherents. Many Frenchmen admire Adolf Hitler and what he does.... It is a great misfortune that France has no men of great calibre. The best and strongest party [among the pro-Germans] is undoubtedly the PPF of Jacques Doriot. It comprises many good and gallant elements, who have already distinguished themselves, notably in North Africa. They have supported the old and powerful anti-Semitic League of that country. Only Jacques Doriot is not, unfortunately, a leader whom all men with a constructive mind will follow. What a difference between him and a man like Adolf Hitler![2]

Obviously, to the mass of the French population, Doriot was simply a German agent, who was, together with Déat keeping himself in reserve for the day when the Germans might set up a "Quisling Government" in Paris, in place of Vichy. The possibility was never quite ruled out. But it is interesting that, as the Liberation grew near, the *doriotistes* should have become increasingly active, not only in Paris, but also at Vichy, where Darnand, a former PPF man, should also have been the first Vichy minister to swear an oath of allegiance to Hitler, and to wear the German uniform as a leading member of the anti-Bolshevik Legion. It was Darnand, too, who recruited *doriotistes* into the Milice, which, before long, became the companion of the Gestapo and of the Waffen SS. It was *doriotistes* again who were most

[2] *Les Procès de la Collaboration*, p. 134.

prominent in the French Waffen SS unit. Besides official formations like the Milice, the Waffen SS and the LVF, there were also the unofficial Doriot gangs who murdered among others, the eighty-year-old Victor Basch, head of the *Ligue des Droits de l'Homme* and his wife, and are also believed to have murdered Maurice Sarraut, editor of the *Dépêche de Toulouse.* It was Doriot and Déat who, though at first fairly favourable to Laval, became increasingly hostile to him, and sabotaged, with German help, his attempt to reassemble Parliament just before the Liberation of Paris. Déat and Doriot were among the French leaders who fled to Germany in August 1944, Doriot becoming more openly than ever the Frenchman most closely associated with the Gestapo and the SS. It must be said that Doriot's PPF supplied to the Milice, to the police, to the administration of concentration camps, etc, a very high proportion of those men who were responsible for the terrorism both in France and in North Africa. Doriot, the "French Führer", after quarrelling with all the other traitors who had fled to Sigmaringen, was killed in mysterious circumstances in April 1944— officially, it was said, by an Allied bomb. For the sake of history this is regrettable, for a trial of Doriot might have revealed the inner working of Doriot's mind. Perhaps his dominant characteristic was his taste for violence—whether Communist or Nazi was of secondary importance.

Till 1934 he had been perhaps the most dynamic figure in the French Communist Party; in 1925 he was Abd' el Krim's chief ally against the French "colonialists"; with a great display of personal courage he had led the Communist revolt in the Place de la République on February 9, 1934 (from which Thorez had kept aloof).[3] Then had come his quarrel with the CP, and, almost without transition, he had become the head of the most obviously Fascist and most blatantly Nazi-subsidized organization in France. Personal ambition, plain corruption, or this everlasting thirst for violence? Whatever may have been Doriot's *qualité suprême* (in the Stendhal sense) the most disturbing aspect of *doriotisme* is the fairly substantial following it enjoyed, and the very fact that there should have been enough Frenchmen willing to form even only a small military unit to fight on the dreaded Eastern Front, after swearing an oath of allegiance to Hitler.

DARNAND

The chief link between *doriotisme* and Vichy was Darnand, the head of the Milice and one of the leaders of the LVF and of the French Waffen SS. The case of Darnand is even stranger than that of Doriot, for Darnand was brought up in the best French nationalist tradition,

[3] *Cf.* the author's *France in Ferment* (London, 1934).

and had an exceptionally fine war record both in 1914–18 and in 1940. But he also was a product of the "6th of February" spirit. After belonging to the Action Française, he joined the Croix de Feu, but not finding it sufficiently revolutionary, he went over to Doriot's PPF, and was also associated with the Cagoule. After the Armistice he began by worshipping the Marshal, and by playing a leading rôle in the Légion. But the Légion, like the Croix de Feu in the past, he found too "soft", and at Nice, as Regional Chief of the Légion, he formed a picked body of men "of whose opinion he could be sure".[4] These picked men he then formed into the SOL (Service d'Ordre Légionnaire). With Pétain's approval, this organization was extended to the rest of the Vichy Zone and, in January 1943, it acquired even greater autonomy under the name of the Milice. In the interval Darnand had worked hard (together with Déat and Doriot) in favour of organizing the LVF, and in September 1942 he and Doriot visited this French Légion on the Eastern Front. At the end of 1943 Darnand formed a French Waffen SS unit. As head of the Milice Darnand organized the closest co-operation with the Germans in tracking down the Maquis and was guilty of innumerable atrocities. With Pétain's approval, he arrested numerous hostages, members of leading Gaullist families. It was Darnand, too, who was largely responsible for the horrible conditions prevailing in the "slave camps" in North Africa—not that, before him, Weygand and others were much less to blame. Altogether, the internment as slave labour of thousands of foreigners who, "under Daladier", had volunteered to fight for France was one of the most shameful and inexcusable acts of the Vichy régime.[5]

After the Liberation of Paris Darnand and 6,000 of "the most heavily compromised *miliciens*" fled to Germany, where he was complimented by Hitler, and where Himmler invited him to get at least 2,000 of the *miliciens* to join a unit called the Charlemagne Brigade, which was to fight for Germany in the East. The others were to be used for sabotage in France. He was a member of the "French Government" of Sigmaringen.

LITERARY TRAITORS

The "literary traitors"—Béraud, Brasillach, Drieu La Rochelle, and so many of the smaller fry of literature and journalism were also mostly products of the "6th of February" spirit; after the Armistice many of them, even more openly than before, continued to distil the poison of *Gringoire* and *Je Suis Partout*. Some, like Brasillach and Drieu La Rochelle—one of the Action Française, the other a *doriotiste*—claimed

[4] *Les Procès de la Collaboration*, p. 246.
[5] *Cf.* Vanino, *De Rethondes à l'Île d'Yeu*.

to derive an aesthetic pleasure from being Fascists. Drieu La Rochelle committed suicide about the time of the Liberation of Paris; in a strange document published long after in the *Nouvelle NRF* (he had been the last editor of the old *NRF* under Nazi patronage) he explained his first abortive suicide attempt by producing a jumble of psycho-analytical and mystical arguments, adding, however, towards the end: "Perhaps all this is a lot of eyewash: the truth may simply be that I'm scared of being kicked around by the police."

As for Brasillach, he assured the Court that he had dished out his venomous propaganda in *Je Suis Partout* (for instance, in favour of shooting hostages) in the conviction that he was "serving France"; and his lawyer, Maître Isorni, compared the death of Brasillach to that of André Chénier! He was a good minor poet and critic; but was there any excuse for forgetting all the death and suffering that Pétain, and Pucheu, and Darnand, and the Gestapo had inflicted on thousands—just because the new "André Chénier" had written in his prison:

> Le mur est froid, la soupe est maigre,
> Mais je marche, ma foi, très fier,
> Tout résonnant comme un roi nègre
> Paré de ses bijoux de fer....

But almost from the moment of the Liberation, the *collabos* were busy compiling their martyrology. *Très fier?* Was there really so much for Brasillach to be proud of?

DE BRINON

If Vichy was born on the 6th of February 1934, so also were most of the "traitors". Some had started their career among the Action Française or the Croix de Feu; most—among them the two *Radio-Paris* star speakers, Ferdonnet and Hérold-Paquis—had then joined Doriot's PPF; but there were some *collabos* and some traitors who claimed to have acted in virtue of some much older traditions. And the two patron-saints who were being invoked by some of these *collabos* were—Caillaux and Briand—Caillaux, who had tried so hard, by coming to terms with Germany, to prevent the 1914 war, and Briand who had so passionately believed in "Europe", albeit an anti-Russian Europe.

Some comic relief, in this story of French treason, is provided by at least two of the principal traitors, both of whom claimed to have been "good Europeans" in "the great Briand tradition" long before the Nazis took over in Germany, and who, when Hitler came into power, had merely persisted in their "peace-loving" policy.

Fernand de Brinon was Pétain's "Ambassador" in Paris, while Jean Luchaire was to become the head of the French collaborationist press in Paris during the Occupation. Both of them were, first and foremost, crooks with an irresistible love for money. But each, in his own way, personified the political *milieu* to which he had belonged for years before the war. Brinon had for years lived on the subsidies of high finance, particularly of the Jewish banks of Lazard and Rothschild, the Banque Lazard being specially interested in the financial newspaper, *L'Information*, on which de Brinon, especially after the triumph of Hitler in Germany, was to become the leading light. Earlier, in the 'twenties, he had worked on the *Journal des Débats*, and had, as a stooge of the de Wendels, the magnates of the *Comité des Forges*, been in contact with leaders of Germany's *Schwerindustrie*. In the name of "peace", he had conducted a press campaign against Poincaré. For years afterwards he had supplied political information to the Banque Lazard, which had paid him for his services up to 20,000 francs a month, at that time nearly £200. He had, altogether done well out of Jewish bankers, who, after 1933, were more eager than ever to promote, *vis-à-vis* Germany, a policy of appeasement; and he had even married the widow of a Jewish broker—a lady who, unofficially at any rate, was, as the wife of the Vichy Ambassador in Paris, to be treated by the Germans as an "honorary Aryan"; as such she escaped with de Brinon to Germany, where, in the end, the tidy sum of four million francs in bank notes, besides a considerable quantity of jewellery, was to be found in her possession.

Already before the war de Brinon (like Luchaire) had been of great value to the Nazis. Both these men had "contacts" in French politics; and one of de Brinon's most useful contacts was M. Daladier. Why Daladier took a fancy to him is hard to say; with his long nose and shifty manner, de Brinon looked like a comic opera spy, and his whole reputation was on the shady side. But Daladier had a soft spot for titled people, and de Brinon was a *comte*, and had an uncle who was a real *marquis*.

Even before 1933 he had taken part in organizing various Franco-German friendship meeting and "youth rallies" and had, in the process, come into contact with a very active young man, and a "true friend of France", Otto Abetz. After Hitler had come to power, de Brinon and Abetz thought that the *rapprochement* between France and Germany was more important than ever.

By this time Brinon had acquired another new German friend, a traveller in champagne, of the name of Joachim von Ribbentrop. In the course of Brinon's trial a fantastic story was told, with minor variations, by Brinon himself and by Daladier. Daladier was French Premier in 1933. He was staying with the de Brinons at their villa on the Riviera when suddenly, without warning, Ribbentrop, who "happened" to be on a motor tour in the South of France, "blew in" one night. Daladier refused to see him. Nevertheless, after Ribbentrop (who, by this time, was an unofficial emissary of the Nazi Party) had gone, de Brinon proposed to Daladier a secret meeting with Hitler, the new dictator of Germany whom no French politician had yet seen. He should (as Mr Chamberlain was to do a few years later) fly to Germany and talk to Hitler. The secret visit seems to have struck Daladier as dangerous and incongruous; nevertheless there is little doubt that he was impressed by the idea of sounding Hitler's real intentions and that he fully approved of Brinon's second-best plan of going to see Hitler himself; Daladier even offered, according to Brinon, to send his *chef de cabinet* along with him. Anyway, the Brinon-Hitler meeting was arranged before long, and in October 1933 there appeared in the *Matin* the famous Hitler interview, with its ultra-pacifism and its protestations of friendship for France. The thing had been published with Daladier's full approval, and there is no doubt that if, during the early part of 1933, the bulk of French opinion knew quite clearly what Hitler meant, the Brinon interview was the first thing to throw it into a state of real confusion, by trading on its instinctive pacifism and by stimulating its wishful thinking. By encouraging the publication of the Hitler interview Daladier had unwittingly contributed to the creation of the "6th of February" spirit, which was not unconnected with an as yet unexpressed desire to fraternize with the Nazis.

In the years that followed, de Brinon was to be one of the great profiteers of that vast movement of "ideas" which was to sweep through France, and to a lesser extent, through England, and which was to express itself in a hundred different ways—the various brands of French crypto-Fascism, the Four-Power Pact spirit, Mosleyism, Appeasement, "Free Hand in the East", anti-Communism, anti-Semitism, anti-Socialism, Chamberlainism, and so right on to Munich, "Peace in our Time", and beyond.

In November 1933 Brinon had founded, together with the blind *ancien combattant* deputy, Scapini, the *Comité France-Allemagne* which enjoyed a great vogue, especially between 1935 and 1939, and attracted masses of politicians and intellectuals and representatives of ex-Service men's organizations. Friendship trips to Germany were organized. Parallel with the *Comité France-Allemagne* the Nazis organized in Berlin a "Germany-France Committee", sponsored by Ribbentrop and other leading Nazis. Brinon was constantly visiting Germany, and between 1935 and 1937 he saw Hitler five times; each time, he claimed, with the full approval of the French Government, and as an unofficial contact man between it and the Nazis. During those years he and his *Comité* were rolling in money, and de Brinon was lionized as never before in the homes of the aristocracy and the *haute bourgeoisie*. The receptions organized by the *Comité France-Allemagne* were among the most sumptuous in Paris. Although there are many omissions in the account he gives of the Communists in his novel *Les Communistes* (written in 1950), Aragon certainly draws a very accurate —if highly satirical—picture of the pro-Nazi *salons* of Paris just before the war, as well as during the "phoney war" of 1939–40. For even after the *Comité France-Allemagne* had petered out (though it was never officially closed) in the summer of 1939, these *salons* carried on its tradition.

After the German invasion of Czechoslovakia in March 1939, Brinon was publicly denounced at the Chamber of Deputies by Kerillis, Ybarnégaray and Louis Marin as a German agent. Shortly before the outbreak of war his friend Abetz was expelled from France, and in September 1939 Brinon discreetly vanished from Paris and retired to his *château* in the Basses-Pyrénées. In July 1940, Laval sent for him, and then dispatched him to Paris, first as an unofficial emissary to "establish contact with the Occupation authorities", and then as Ambassador. The Germans liked Brinon, and Pétain later claimed that the Germans had "inflicted Brinon on him".[6]

There was certainly nothing very *maréchaliste* about Brinon; he was, as General de Laurencie put it, *"le traitre intégral"*, the "compleat traitor". He was the moving spirit in all the most blatantly pro-Nazi undertakings, such as the LVF, the French Waffen SS, etc. According to Du Moulin de Labarthète, he "extracted" from Pétain his blessing for the Anti-Bolshevik Legion ("He gave me something to sign, I didn't know what it was; he said the thing was full of good Frenchmen who hated Bolshevism", the Marshal later feebly explained). He betrayed to the Germans not only Pétain, but even Laval. He was "scandalized" by Laval's resistance to Sauckel, and, worse still, he informed the Germans, as early as November 1940, of secret contacts between Vichy and the British in Madrid—a fact which Laval had to admit to the Germans to be true. He also had to promise to the Germans that they would in future be "kept informed". And later, during Laval's second term of office, Brinon repeatedly reported to the Germans what was going on inside the Vichy Cabinet; he particularly criticized Laval for his unwillingness to send more workers to Germany. In his confidential dispatches to Goebbels and others he pointed out the "weaknesses" of Laval, clearly suggesting that he (Brinon) would be a more reliable French Premier. He was later to head the Sigmaringen "government" which he claimed to run with the full authority of Pétain—a claim against which Pétain (living on the top floor of the same Hohenzollern castle) vigorously protested. Whether de Brinon was as deeply moved by Hitler as he claimed to be ("the rare and wonderful thrill of being in the presence of Genius")

[6] Testimony of General de Laurencie in *Les Procès de la Collaboration: Brinon, Darnand, Luchaire*, p. 153.

he certainly made a good thing out of it; even when all was lost, his wife still had the equivalent of some £30,000 in a suitcase. To do him justice, he was not alone; in the days of the *Comité France-Allemagne*, as well as in the days of his Ambassadorship, he had plenty of friends and hangers-on; at his trial he gave none of them away, and scarcely defended himself.

LUCHAIRE

Jean Luchaire, the head of the French collaborationist press in Paris during the Occupation was a typical product of the *République des Camarades*. Like everybody else who frequented the Chamber of Deputies before the war, I knew him. He was the hand-shaking, back-slapping type. I remember saying once to Robert Dell of the *Manchester Guardian* that he shouldn't be so friendly with Luchaire. "I know," Dell laughed, "he is most *frightfully* corrupt—but he's got *such* a lot of children!" It was quite true; he did have four children, including his eldest daughter, Corinne, who, in the 'thirties, became a film star.

Luchaire always wanted a lot of money. I remember how, in 1934, Louis Barthou, who was Foreign Minister in the Doumergue Government, told me how Luchaire had been getting from Paul Boncour "quite incredible" subsidies for his "rag", *Notre Temps*—100,000 francs a month; how this had gone on for years, ever since Briand had taken a fancy to Luchaire, and how he (Barthou) had now at last stopped this nonsense. Briand had, indeed, taken up Luchaire, until then a very minor journalist, in a big way: it was when, in his little paper, *Notre Temps*, he started to support Briand's policy for a *rapprochement* with Germany (it was still the Weimar Republic then); as well as Briand's "European Union". It was also in 1930 that Luchaire had first met Abetz, "then still a little drawing-teacher from Karlsruhe". Abetz was "francophil", and the two made friends. After a time Abetz was to marry Luchaire's secretary, Suzanne, who was to become "Ambassadress" in Occupied Paris. In his defence Luchaire said that he had a true affection for Abetz, and that he was convinced that the appointment of Abetz as Ambassador to Paris was a godsend to France, and that between them, he and Abetz could moderate the rigours of the German Occupation, and prepare the ground for a happy Franco-German union. He suggested that, in effect, he was adapting his old Briandism to new conditions.

Laval was, of course, aware of Luchaire's friendly relations with Abetz, and sent him to Paris in July 1940 to re-establish contact with him. Luchaire also claimed that, if through Brinon and the *Comité France-Allemagne*, Abetz had established before the war a sufficient number of contacts with the Right, Abetz was only too pleased to be put in contact with the "Left" through the "Briandist" Luchaire.

All this was, in reality, so much eye-wash, but it is curious, all the same, that even so out-and-out a *collabo* as Luchaire should have claimed to represent a certain respectable French "tradition"—for it is a tradition in French politics which, under a variety of forms, has existed for a very long time. Historically, Luchaire might, indeed, claim to be a link in a long chain stretching from Caillaux and Briand to Robert Schuman, the Council of Europe, the Schuman Plan and the EDC! At the same time, Luchaire also represented in his own way the more "rightist" anti-British tradition. But, in actual practice, all that Luchaire really did during his four "golden years" of the German Occupation was to dish out Nazi propaganda, to fulminate against England, America, de Gaulle, Russia, Bolshevism and the Maquis, and to sing paeans of praise to the generosity of Germany and the genius of Adolf Hitler; and by the end of 1943 he advocated a "real" collaborationist government, Laval being, in his opinion, "inadequate."[7] Like Brinon, he also made a good thing out of it. As editor of the *Nouveaux Temps*, he drew a salary of 100,000 francs a month, besides "extras", lived in great luxury, lunched at the Tour d'Argent and, according to his daughter Corinne, even started keeping expensive mistresses which, as a good family man, he hadn't done in the past.

However, by 1944, the best was over and he had to start preparing alibis and excuses. If he wrote the most murderous anti-British and anti-American articles after the Normandy landing, it was, he later said, in order to help out the printers and other employees of the Paris press, whom the Germans were anxious to deport under the STO to Germany. "As a *patron* I had great responsibilities towards these people", he said, and a further excuse he made was that "by that time, anyway, nobody in France took what we wrote seriously any longer". Which, in a sense, was largely true, not only then, but throughout the German occupation of Paris. Like Brinon, Luchaire was a crook and a profiteer of the Occupation, and was nicknamed "louche Herr"— the "fishy *Herr*".

With his family he escaped to Sigmaringen and became "Minister of Information" in the "government" there. In her deliciously ingenuous memoirs, his daughter continued to admire even in Germany papa's "tremendous optimism"; this optimism did not die until he was handed over in Italy to the French authorities; once in gaol, Luchaire, this ugly little flower of the Third Republic, took to religion. "*Je me suis fait baptiser et j'ai fait ma première communion*", he

[7] *Cf.* "Indictment in Luchaire Trial" in *Les Procès de la Collaboration* (Paris, 1948).

wrote to Corinne from prison. And she added: "Conquered by Divine revelation, he reached before his death the heights of serenity." To his daughter, at any rate, he was a martyr, he was *papa* "who had never wanted to harm anyone, who was sincere, and who had never thought unkindly of any man."[8]

[8] Corinne Luchaire, *Ma drôle de vie* (Paris, 1948), p. 238.

CHAPTER EIGHT

THE RESISTANCE

IT WOULD be futile to attempt to write within the narrow limits of even a long chapter a history of the French Resistance. Few episodes of World War II are so complex, so confused, so under-explored and, indeed, unexplorable in part. The Resistance consisted of many things all at once: it ranged from a vaguely anti-German attitude or "expression" which tended to make Germans one met in the street feel uncomfortable, and from listening to the BBC, all the way to active Resistance, which assumed the different forms of illegal and clandestine activity, industrial and administrative ca'canny, railway sabotage, and finally, the Maquis and armed rebellion.

Much in the history of the Resistance is still obscure and the existence of thousands of minute facts and the records of thousands of items of "Resistance Activity" are not sufficient to create a completely clear picture. The picture is often obscured by "myths", by contradictory evidence, often hard to check: Many true facts concerning the Resistance have been irretrievably lost, since so many of the most active resisters were killed or died in German concentration camps. Also, the rivalries among the survivors, each group claiming the maximum credit for itself and granting the minimum credit to the rival group, have tended to distort the accuracy of many of the records, particularly those written after the Liberation. To this day, the competition between the Communist and non-Communist elements in the Resistance has not abated, and even when men like Darlan and Abetz claimed that the Resistance was essentially Communist, one suspects that this seemingly handsome tribute to the Communists (as it looks to us) was intended simply to discredit the Resistance *as a whole* in the eyes of Vichy and Berlin. Being, by its very nature, a conspiratorial and secret form of activity, the Resistance could not be seen as a whole even by those who were most deeply involved in it; all they really knew was what they and their immediate associates were doing. And even if the CNR, formed long after the beginning of the Resistance, may have had a fairly good idea of what, in a very general way, was happening in the country it is apparent that neither London, nor, still less, Washington, had any clear picture of the French Resistance. The information from their agents was often fragmentary, or else highly subjective. Even after the Normandy landing, Field-Marshal Montgomery thought very little of it, though General Eisenhower's tribute to it was rather more generous. Admiral Leahy, sympathetic to Vichy throughout, makes in his long book only a few very short and contemptuous references to the Resistance.

What then did the French Resistance amount to, physically and morally?

I. THE DE GAULLE NUCLEUS

Although, long after the war, Léon Blum claimed that the "first resister" was not de Gaulle, but Georges Mandel, who, as a member of the Reynaud Government that had been forced out of office, reacted most sharply against Pétain's armistice appeal, it is generally agreed that the voice of the Resistance was first "officially" heard on June 18, 1940, when de Gaulle, in his historic broadcast from London said: "*La flamme de la Résistance française ne doit pas s'éteindre et ne s'éteindra pas.*"[1] But there was no flame at that time in France; there were only a few tiny smouldering embers, and the amount of inflammable Resistance material inside France was very small indeed. As for de Gaulle, few had any clear notion of who he was; and this, in a sense, was to be true throughout the Occupation. To many active resisters, de Gaulle remained for a long time an invisible radio voice, and then "a general in North Africa", and a "symbol" whose international value was considerable, but whose political and personal value to France was still an unknown quantity.

It is not necessary here to describe in detail the organization of the Free French in London, or the Free French Forces, or to discuss the difficult and ambiguous position of de Gaulle *vis-à-vis* the British Government and the outside world generally. Still less is there any need here to deal with the complex, but not very satisfactory story of the contacts, the help and co-operation that were gradually—very gradually —established by SOE and other British agencies and purely French agencies in London, on the one hand, and the various Resistance groups in France on the other. But a few facts stand out clearly.

For a long time no major French public figure associated himself with de Gaulle in London, and, politically, his "movement" was a small one-man show. In a sense it was just as well for de Gaulle, before he came to be widely known, not to have some heavyweight like say, M. Herriot round his neck, for his presence in London would have given quite a different character to de Gaulle's venture. But, on

[1] The famous phrase: "*La France a perdu une bataille, elle n'a pas perdu la guerre*" was not included in this broadcast, but in a printed proclamation soon afterwards.

the other hand, this made it far more difficult for de Gaulle to get himself accepted by the British Government as being in any real sense "representative" of France. The people around him were a mixed crowd, and not, on the whole, very sympathetic in the eyes of people who liked to talk of the Republic and Democracy. Even some ex-cagoulards were said to have found their way into Carlton Gardens, which was a hotbed of rather unsavoury intrigue; and among the people round de Gaulle, some were playing a double—and pro-Vichy game. Certain French *émigré* groups in London, notably some Socialists who formed the *Groupe Jean Jaurès*, and another group, with Pierre Comert at its head, who ran the daily paper, *France*, financially supported by the Foreign Office, were on the worst of terms with Carlton Gardens. Later, the same was true of the group around Admiral Muselier and André Labarthe.

But despite all the irritation caused to the British Government and to Churchill personally by de Gaulle and many of the people around him, Churchill—and even more so, Eden—never quite forgot the lone stand taken by de Gaulle the day France was lost, and never lost sight of the potential political importance of de Gaulle as a rallying-point for a multitude of anti-German forces. The Cross of Lorraine was, no doubt, as Churchill said, the heaviest cross he had had to bear, but he was careful never to abandon it by the roadside, even though at times (notably after the North Africa landing) relations between Britain and the Free French almost reached breaking point. De Gaulle's position was a difficult one throughout; on the one hand, he was in every way dependent on Britain; on the other hand, he greatly distrusted her. But if he was truculent and "difficult", it was, as he was to explain in his *Memoirs*, published in 1954, precisely *because* he was weak, and could not afford to negotiate on a basis of equality. In other words, the more "pigheaded" he was, the more attention and recognition was he likely to receive—a calculation which was not entirely without foundation, and worked, at any rate, with the British Government—though not quite so well with Roosevelt.

This was not, however, only a matter of tactics. Temperamentally, and traditionally de Gaulle was, if not exactly anti-British, certainly not pro-British, and his distrust of Britain was chronic. He suspected that Britain was plotting to eliminate the French (whether "Vichy" or "Free") from Syria, and was convinced that South Africa had an eye on Madagascar.

In a later chapter it will be shown how de Gaulle developed from the lone figure of June 1940 to the accepted leader of the Free French, and as the (albeit nominal) head of the whole Resistance. Here it is sufficient to enumerate merely a few essential points:

(1) What gave de Gaulle a special status *vis-à-vis* the British (and,

later, the USA and the other Allies)—a status different from that of all the other governments-in-exile (with the partial exception of Belgium)—was the fact that, not long after the Armistice, he succeeded in imposing his authority on a number of French territories. True, he failed in his design to seize Dakar in September 1940; but already in August, under the leadership of Félix Eboué, its negro governor, the Chad Territory had declared for de Gaulle; Colonel Leclerc (who, four years later, was to be the first to enter Paris at the head of his armoured division) had established his authority over Douala; and, almost on the same day, a Gaullist *coup* had resulted in the capture of Brazzaville. Thus, the greater part of French Equatorial Africa went Gaullist very early in the war, followed by other territories which were, more or less, out of Vichy's reach—the Cameroons, the French colonies in the Pacific and in India, etc.

To de Gaulle this was of the utmost importance; he stood, as it were, at the head of a colonial empire, and was not just an *émigré*. He was, therefore, anxious to be recognized as the "holder of French sovereignty"—though this was, obviously, a claim exceedingly hard for the British Government to satisfy. The setting-up, in September 1941, of the French National Committee in London—a sort of embryonic French Cabinet—did not, in itself, make de Gaulle's legal case any stronger. He had not been recognized by any representative French body—whereas Pétain had, after all, secured plenary powers from the National Assembly at Vichy in July 1940. It was therefore essential for de Gaulle to convince at least the British Government (the US Government still seemed hopelessly beyond persuasion) that "the whole Resistance" was behind de Gaulle. But this was not easy, and the fact that there were French soldiers, sailors and airmen fighting on the side of the British, was not, in itself, sufficient to strengthen de Gaulle's claim to complete recognition.

(2) The Resistance in France was very small at first. Moreover, a large part of it was at first reluctant to "recognize" de Gaulle as its leader. The aims of de Gaulle and the aims of the Resistance were still very far from having been "co-ordinated". (In fact, they were never going to be.) De Gaulle, for one thing, looked upon the Resistance as being primarily a factor of military and international importance, and considered the London Committee as being, above all, the supreme authority for manifesting "France's presence" on the side of the Allies through military operations and intelligence work. The Home Resistance, on the other hand, tended to look upon its struggle, as a revolutionary and ideological struggle. For a long time de Gaulle, himself a man of the Right, and largely surrounded by men of the Right, had avoided committing himself to anything like "the restoration of the Republic", and had chiefly dwelt on "national liberation" as his aim.

However, contacts gradually came to be established with various members of the French Resistance, notably with Socialists like Christian Pineau and Pierre Brossolette, who came on a visit to London; and, some time later (in the summer of 1942) André Philip, a prominent Socialist, took his seat, as Commissioner of the Interior, on de Gaulle's National Committee. De Gaulle announced that the "old freedoms" would be restored in France, and that France was "preparing for a Revolution". A Communist, Fernand Grenier, also "joined" de Gaulle, in the name of his Party, about the same time, and contacts were made with Emmanuel d'Astier de La Vigerie and other left-wing members of the Resistance; it was a prelude to the subsequent Algiers Committee, on which all the forces of the Resistance, including the Communists, were to be represented.

(3) It is not necessary here to give a detailed account of the extremely complicated work done by the London Committee as a centre of French and Allied Intelligence in France—even though, *in the eyes of certain members of de Gaulle's organization, as well as in the eyes of certain British authorities, this was its most important and most immediate function*. Colonel Rémy has written numerous books about the various networks he set up in France, and the rôle played by de Gaulle's BCRA (*Bureau Central de Renseignements et d'Action*)—the name that de Gaulle's principal intelligence organization assumed (after numerous previous transformations) in September 1942—is fairly well known. Its head was Colonel Passy (Dewavrin), who also wrote several voluminous works on the BCRA's activities. As M. Henri Michel was to write later in his *Histoire de la Résistance*:

> The rôle played by the BCRA in the organization of the Home Resistance was considerable; it sent it men, equipment and money, of all of which the BCRA was the principal purveyor.... The various Resistance movements in France largely depended on their recognition by the BCRA. It suffered from lack of experience; the amount of work to be done was enormous, and losses were heavy. Nevertheless, it was largely thanks to this organization that the spontaneous and somewhat incoherent resistance of the French people was given shape and equipment.

There were rivalries and competition between the BCRA and other French and British services (some purely French-speaking, other bilingual); and de Gaulle, for his own part, greatly resented the fact that all these organizations, including his own BCRA, should be under the general control of the SOE (Secret Operations Executive), and that the British Services were under no obligation to report their activities in France to the Free French Committee.

Nevertheless, the BCRA greatly helped de Gaulle to achieve, in the course of the war, many of his objectives—such as "unifying" the

Resistance, and securing its official (if not wholehearted) support for de Gaulle against other candidates for supreme power in France.

In the pages that follow it will be shown how all this was done, and also how de Gaulle won his battle against Giraud—in the face of a great deal of British and American obstruction.

2. RESISTANCE IN THE SOUTH

Until the German occupation of Vichy France in November 1942 there was a marked difference in the very nature of the Resistance in the Occupied Zone and in the Vichy Zone, as there was, indeed, in the mentality of their respective populations. Those in the Occupied Zone were in direct daily contact with the enemy, and their resistance was primarily anti-German. In the Unoccupied Zone not the greatest, but the most immediate enemy was Vichy.

It was not an easy battle at first. The Pétain myth was strong; there was a tendency on the part of the population to be thankful for small mercies—to be grateful to Pétain for not having "allowed" the Germans to occupy the whole of France. For the rest, life was not as hard and harsh as in the North. For some time, at any rate, a kind of verbal resistance could be practised without grave risk to life and limb.

What then were the aims of the Resistance in the Free Zone? At first it amounted to little more than "debunking" the Marshal and the National Revolution (some disobliging quotation on Pétain's "innate" defeatism from Joffre and Poincaré—whose books with the offending passages were banned in Vichy France—were useful weapons of Resistance Literature), encouraging pro-British sentiment, and defending democratic liberties against the onslaught by the ideologists of Hitler's New Order and of the National Revolution. Also, it was important to discourage defeatist moods, and to make people believe that Vichy had not come to stay for ever.

After the crash of June 1940, followed by Fabre-Luce's "midsummer night's dream" of France's integration in Hitler's Europe, conditions for effective resistance were not favourable at first. It is, indeed, very hard to determine where and how "Resistance" came into being. It seems that several little resistance groups began to crystallize about the same time—as early as the summer of 1940. To quote a leading authority, M. Henri Michel, author of *Histoire de la Résistance* and other works (with a few minor corrections made by Bourdet):

Among these was a small group of officers under the leadership of Captain Henri Frenay which, at that time, did little more than publish at Lyon a roneotyped "newsletter". Called "Petites Ailes", this group later came to be known as "Mouvement de Libération Nationale", and after joining with another—predominantly left-wing Catholic group, called

"Liberté", adopted the now familiar name of "Combat". At the end of 1941 it had a governing body of seven members: Frenay, Bertin-Chevance and Claude Bourdet (representing "Vérité") and de Menthon, P. H. Teitgen, Georges Bidault and Rémy Roure (later to be replaced by Paul Coste-Floret), representing "Liberté".

The list of names is significant: Bourdet is one of the leading non-Communist left-wing journalists under the Fourth Republic; so is (though much more to the Right) Rémy Roure (first, *Monde*, and later *Figaro*) while Menthon, Bidault, Teitgen and Coste-Floret were all to become, as leaders of the MRP, influential figures in the Fourth Republic.

In the early stages of the Resistance, in 1940 and 1941, there was great reluctance on the part of its members to commit themselves to "recognizing" de Gaulle—of whom not enough was known, and a favourite argument with "Combat" was that there would have been a Resistance in France, whether there had ever been a de Gaulle or not. However, by the middle of 1941, "Combat" was sufficiently impressed by de Gaulle to "join" him.

What was its purpose and its technique? Frenay aimed at creating a sort of "framework" for a wider Resistance movement on a regional and, eventually, national scale, with a propaganda machine, a press, and an intelligence network. In Frenay's view, a Resistance organization like "Combat" was neither primarily a military or para-military machine (as Vichy soldiers, with an eye on an eventual battle for Liberation, imagined), nor primarily an intelligence network (which was, for a long time, the view taken of Resistance activity by de Gaulle and the British). Frenay saw the Resistance as an organized amalgam of numerous activities, with the *mystique* of a "nation-wide movement". It was Frenay's original conception of 1940 which, in a large measure, foreshadowed what was to happen in 1944.

Already at an early stage small "shock units" of thirty men were formed, these units representing the movement's "secret army"—intended for future uses. In addition J. Renouvin organized the so-called *groupes francs* of whom "*sabotage fer*" units [for railway sabotage] became a distinct organization in 1942. At the same time, Claude Bourdet set up at Lyon a service called NAP (*Noyautage des Administrations Publiques*) the purpose of which was to "colonize" the civil service with Resistance people. The various services of "Combat", including one of "forged papers", employed, by the end of 1942, about 150 persons. Earlier in the year 250,000 francs had been given to the movement by Jean Moulin out of his British funds, a measure of the niggardly treatment given even to an important organization like "Combat". After various attempts in that line, the movement produced a paper, called *Combat*. It first appeared in December 1941, and by the end of 1942 it had reached a circulation of 30,000. It appeared, more or less regularly, three times a month. [Henri Michel, *op. cit.*]

For a long time, the production of this paper was, however, the most tangible manifestation of an organization like "Combat".[2]

Less "hierarchized", different in its structure from "Combat", and more "revolutionary"—with a popular revolt and a general strike as its ultimate aim—was the Resistance Movement that ultimately adopted the name of "Libération". Its leader was Emmanuel d'Astier de la Vigerie, a former naval officer and a remarkable writer. His aim was to assemble, in a single great Resistance Movement Communists, Socialists and trade unionists of both the Socialist-Communist (CGT) and the Catholic (CFTC) persuasion, and to "mobilize the masses" especially in industrial centres—which, unfortunately, were not very numerous in Vichy France.

In the spring of 1942 "Libération" decided to form a para-military organization.

The militants who were entrusted with this task [wrote one of the most active members of "Liberation-Sud", Lucie Aubrac] searched inside the movement, and inside every regional and departmental group, for those who could undertake to form these groups which, at the beginning of October 1942, already comprised about 20,000 members. The trade union and university circles among whom most of the members of "Liberation" were recruited, suited fairly well this form of organization which remained in close contact with the "political" section of the movement, and so closely followed the general situation. Among these groups were easily found people who could reinforce this or that strike movement, or organize attacks on trains, carrying new French war material *nach Berlin*.[3]

The university element in "Liberation-Sud" had largely been supplied by students of the University of Strasbourg, which had, at the beginning of the war, been evacuated to Clermont-Ferrand. After the Armistice, most of the Alsatian students refused to return to Strasbourg which, to all intents and purposes, had been incorporated in Nazi Germany, complete with conscription into the Wehrmacht.

Intellectuals, many of whom had come to the Vichy Zone from Paris and the North during the 1940 exodus, played an important part in the organization, and even more so, in the ideological guidance of the Resistance movements in the South—at least until the time when the Resistance became less an intellectual protest than a matter of life and death.

[2] It is significant that of all the resistance movements in Vichy France the four most important ones should have had the names of papers which have survived to this day: *Combat, Libération, Franc-Tireur* and *Témoignage Chrétien*.

[3] Lucie Aubrac, *La Résistance (Naissance et Organisation)* (Paris, 1945), p. 100.

Another Resistance movement in the South was "Franc-Tireur", most of whose leaders also were Paris intellectuals, including many members of the unorthodox Left.[4] In November 1942 "Franc-Tireur" claimed a membership of 30,000, a figure which the leaders of "Combat" thought "inflated".

The "capital of the Resistance" was Lyon; "Combat" and "Franc-Tireur" were particularly active here. To this day, at Lyon, visitors are shown various obscure little cafés and restaurants where men like Bidault, Teitgen, Farge, and others were supposed to have met to discuss "resistance business". One of the heroes and martyrs of the Lyon Resistance was Gilbert Drû, head of the local *Démocrates Populaires* Federation, the forerunner of the MRP, who was to be shot by the Germans in 1942.

Another notable, though somewhat specialized Resistance movement was the "Témoignage Chrétien" group, at the head of which stood a Catholic priest, Father Chaillet, who was one of the main organizers of the rescue of Jewish children. The adoption of these children by French Catholic families or their smuggling into Switzerland—largely through the good offices of a Geneva Socialist—constituted the main task of this Resistance group. Although there were rights and wrongs on both sides, the famous Finaly Case of 1953 left many wondering, when they remembered the risks taken by Catholics like Father Chaillet, whether the Jewish uncles and aunts of the Finaly boys had not acted ungraciously in demanding their transportation to Israel from the Catholic *milieu* in which they had become completely acclimatized.

A smaller Resistance centre was Toulouse, with an organization called "Libérer et Fédérer", which was mainly Socialist, and advocated a federal structure for France and the French Empire. It was in contact with London, and later formed Maquis units. Bertaux, the future Chief of the *Sûreté*, Cassou, the writer, and leading Socialists like Jules Moch and Vincent Auriol were "more or less in contact with this group".[5] In general, however, the anti-Pétain politicians like Auriol, many of whom were living in semi-retirement or complete retirement in Vichy France, were not very active in the Resistance. Partly because they were too well known, and the risk of being arrested was accordingly greater; and partly because their credit with the rank-and-file of the Resistance was not high.

[4] Its leading members included an anti-clerical Radical like Albert Bayet, the tremendously dynamic Yves Farge (noted as a great organizer), the historian, Marc Bloch (who was later to be killed by the Germans), as well as J. B. Lévy, Claudius Petit and the *trotskysant* Georges Altman, who edited the clandestine *Franc-Tireur* and was to become the editor of the post-Liberation paper of the same name.

[5] Henri Michel, *op. cit.*, p. 21.

3. RESISTANCE IN THE NORTH

Before Vichy began to take the Resistance in the South seriously, Resistance was, in the main, an intellectual attitude, plus a little conspiratorial activity, and it did not entail grave risks.

It was different in the North. Here Resistance was dangerous from the outset, except the milder forms of "physiognomic" resistance and the more harmless variety of practical jokes.

The defeat and the Occupation [wrote Lucie Aubrac] gave birth in France to a new national feeling... stimulated among all classes of society by the presence of German soldiers on French soil.... The commandeering of foodstuffs and industrial commodities, the billeting of German soldiers, the curfew, and patrolling of French streets by German soldiers... the sight of greedy and gluttonous Germans bursting with money created a sort of traditional historical *décor* which produced the corresponding traditional reflexes. (*Op. cit.* p. 12.)

It should be added that the issues were not confused, as they were in Vichy France, by the myth of the Marshal and the ideology of "*la France seule*"—none of which made much impression in the Occupied Zone. To quote Lucie Aubrac:

A little like children in the presence of a boorish teacher, the French tended from the outset to make fun of the Germans. Travellers in the *Métro* would deliberately direct Germans to stations miles out of their way; bus conductors would skip stops where Germans wanted to get off; while shop assistants loved to sell Germans all the duddest and most unsaleable articles, after a glowing display of flattery.... The servility of the French press in Paris was so blatant that the critical sense of the French people reacted immediately. The corrupt and notorious pro-German agents and the newly-acquired German stooges filled people with the same degree of disgust. A kind of instinctive national solidarity found expression in innumerable cases where escaped war prisoners needed help. (*Op. cit.* p. 15.)

If Vichyism bred among the population of the South a certain *immobiliste* and *attentiste* attitude, the presence of the Germans in the North stimulated more "activist" reflexes. But to resist actively and in an organized way was infinitely more dangerous in the North than in the South.

Large groupings comprising, like certain Resistance organizations in the South, 20,000 or 30,000 or 40,000 people were unthinkable in the North. Here the Resistance had to be split into much smaller units; and even these smaller units led a very precarious existence, and dozens of them were stamped out by the Germans. Much greater secrecy than in the Vichy Zone had to surround their activity and there were some groups of identical political colouring in the North which were not aware of each other's existence until 1943.

The story of the first well-known Resistance group clearly demonstrates the great difference between the relative impunity with which the non-Communist organizations in the South were able to operate during the first couple of years and the shadow of torture and death that hung from the start over any resistance in the German-occupied zone. This group was formed at the Musée de l'Homme at the Palais Chaillot, and comprised a number of young scientists, such as Boris Vilde and Lewitzky, teachers, lawyers, Dominican priests, and other intellectuals. The group was called the "Comité National de Salut Public", and it established contacts in Brittany and the south-west, where the first issue of their publication, called *Resistance*, was published in December 1940, Professor Paul Rivet, the Director of the Musée de l'Homme, Jean Cassou and Jean Paulhan being among its contributors. Already two months later the organization was rounded up by the Germans, and seven were executed; it was rounded up again in July 1941, and two more were shot; finally, in November the group was almost wiped out; six were shot, six decapitated, and many more deported to Germany.

"Défense de la France" was a Resistance group run by university students, and financially supported by a French industrialist. Their adventures, full of hairbreadth escapes, amusing (if dangerous) stunts like stealing dozens of German army cars, and the printing of a clandestine newspaper in the cellar of the Sorbonne have been gaily described by one of their leaders, René Dunan, in his book, *Ceux de Paris*, published soon after the Liberation. They managed, according to him, to distribute as many as 100,000 copies of their paper, thanks to the good offices of hundreds of other students.

Another notable Resistance group was formed in the North, with Jean Lebas, the Socialist mayor of Roubaix as its central figure. This group came into existence as early as November 1940, and published a monthly paper, *l'Homme Libre* in more than foolhardy conditions—the room in which it was roneotyped was separated from the German Kommandantur by only a glass door. The *maire* of Roubaix supplied the group with its roneo machine, paper, and cars for distributing the *Homme Libre*. But already in May 1941, Lebas was arrested. However, the organization survived, and the Socialists of the Nord had a meeting with Dutch and Belgian Socialists at Namur in May, 1942, the first international Socialist meeting of its kind in occupied Europe. (*Cf.* Henri Michel, *op. cit.*)

There were several other units in the North of France, e.g. "Ceux de la Résistance", "Liberation (Nord)", "L'Armée des Volontaires", etc; indeed, in almost every fair-sized town there was some Resistance group; but most of them led a very precarious existence.

The Trotzkyist or "trotzkysant" wing of the French Socialists formed the "Mouvement National Revolutionaire"; in the Latin quarter, Jean-Paul Sartre took part in a university group called "Socialisme et Liberté"; and there were many more.

Among this mass of small groups, few of them with any clear plan of action, apart from "keeping up morale" and publishing some sort of news sheet, it was difficult for both London and de Gaulle to find their way about. Finally, after many efforts to establish contact with the various groups, and a great deal of sorting-out and co-ordination activity, notably by Colonel Passy's BCRA, three main groups gradually took shape in the Occupied Zone, the "Libération-Nord", the "OCM" (Organisation Civile et Militaire), and the "Front National". Most Resistance groups in the North were at least partly dependent on financial aid from London, and London was able to exercise some financial pressure on them; those which would not co-operate ran the risk of losing financial support, and of disappearing "spontaneously" even without German interference. The three above-mentioned organizations managed to become, more or less, *national* organizations, in the sense that they gradually built up a network throughout the Occupied Territory, and, especially after November 1942, succeeded in extending their activities to the southern part of France.

"Libération-Nord" received its main membership and support from Socialists, CGT members, and members of the Catholic trade unions. Like most resistance movements, its main activity at first consisted in bringing out an illegal paper; its first issues—at the end of 1940—were simply typed at the Ministry of Food in Paris by Christian Pineau (later one of the more prominent Socialist leaders under the Fourth Republic) who held there a civil service post—a good example of the *noyautage* of the administration by Resistance members. A large part of the paper was written by a cartoonist, Jean Texcier, who, as a "clandestine" journalist, became one of the most pungent, epigrammatic and popular pamphleteers of the Resistance press.[6] Before long, it reached a circulation of 50,000 copies a week—one of the most remarkable feats of its kind. At the time of the Liberation of Paris it published its 190th number, and the next issue was already printed on the rotaries of the *Matin* and called *Libération-Soir*. Contact was established in 1941 with the British and the Free French, and early in the following year Pineau travelled to London, after which a *comité directeur* of the movement was set up, composed of Ribière, Pineau, Texcier, and Wallon (Socialist Party), Tessier (Catholic Trade Unions), and Neumayer and Saillant (CGT). (Saillant later became openly associated with the Communists, and was elected chairman of the WFTU, after Sir Walter Citrine's resignation.) From 1943 on the organization was more or less com-

[6] A few samples of his writing will have been found in an earlier chapter.

plete, with a section in each region (and later, in each *département*), headed by a civil and military chief.

"Libération-Nord" refused to amalgamate with the "OCM", which it considered "reactionary" and "militarist".

The "OCM", composed in the main of soldiers and of members of the civil service and the professional classes, established contact with London in 1942 and, through the "Rémy network", received funds. It was fairly valuable to London, as the OCM, which operated chiefly in the Paris region (where it claimed to have a few thousand members), had many of its people inside government offices. After the Liberation, the OCM supplied a fairly high proportion of the new personnel for the higher ranks of the Administration. Its leaders were Blocq-Mascart, J. H. Simon (of the *Conseil d'Etat*) and A. Lepercq, subsequently Finance Minister in the first post-Liberation government.

Larger and more important in the long run was the "Front National". It was the only Resistance movement, both military and political in character, which exercised considerable influence in both zones, though it was Northern in origin. Its ideology was that of a sort of all-embracing Popular Front, and the ambition of its leaders was to absorb, as it were, all the Resistance movements that had already come into being. The Communists were more active in the "Front National" than in any other Resistance organization, and it was, indeed, not until the end of 1941 that the "Front National" became very active. The two leaders of the Front National, Villon, in the North, and Marrane in the South, were joined on their respective committees by men like Joliot-Curie (at that time a Socialist), Justin Godard (one of the "Masonic" and *Ligue des Droits de l'Homme* Radicals), Bidault (Popular Democrat and leader of the "Combat" Resistance group in the South) Altman and Farge (of the "Franc-Tireur" group), Debû-Bridel and even Louis Marin, the well-known "anti-Boche" nationalist deputy of the Right.

But the key positions in the FN were held by orthodox Communists. The claim by the FN to "absorb", as it were, other, and older Resistance groups was not easily accepted by some: there were conflicts between the FN on the one hand and Libération-Nord and OCM, on the other, in the North, and similar conflicts between the FN and the three major Resistance groups in the South, despite the inclusion of some of their leaders on the FN's committee. Later the FN acquired considerable prestige through having organized the famous Corsican insurrection. Its men there had been armed on orders from General Giraud—a typical paradox of the French Resistance: a semi-Vichyite general encouraging a quasi-Communist rising! A characteristic feature of the FN was the creation of "sub-FN's", as it were, especially among the least organized parts of the population, without trade union or party ties—e.g. a "French Women's FN", a "Peasants' FN", a "Shopkeepers' FN", a "Lawyers' FN", etc. Each of these groups published a paper, and the "Front National" succeeded, probably more than any other Resistance movement, in becoming something in the nature of a "mass movement", in which "ordinary people" were included. In reality, not so many belonged to it as one might imagine, but the Communists were no doubt, as early as 1942–3, preparing for the time when the FN *would* become a mass movement. They knew that, all being well, many cautious and careful people would jump on the Resistance band-waggon when it was no longer very dangerous to do so.

For the truth is that, despite the large number of organizations in both the Occupied and Unoccupied Zone the number of *active* resisters was small even in 1942–3 and almost negligible before that. The same persons, though sometimes under different names, reappear only too often in the annals of the Resistance—a fact which has prompted some observers to say, rather unkindly, that the *real* Resistance in France was like a stage army. Which, like most wise-cracks, contains an element of truth, but is not strictly true.

Although many top *leaders* of most of the Resistance movements had some fairly definite political colouring (Communists in the "FN", orthodox Socialists in "Libération-Nord", Liberal Catholics in "Combat," trotzkysant Socialists in "Franc-Tireur", etc) the rank and file had, in many cases, no definite political associations, and joined a Resistance movement, when they felt like it, just because it *was* a Resistance movement, and not because it was Catholic or Communist in origin. This is one reason why, politically, the Resistance movements were never able to organize themselves into anything like coherent political parties after the Liberation (their rank and file had united for anti-German action—and for little else). It also explains why, before very long, they were superseded by the political parties of the old type, and why, while the Resistance lasted, the political parties (other than the Communists, and to a certain extent, the Socialists), were not in great evidence for a long time.

But the Resistance had its fair and noble side: the men of the Resistance often sank all past differences and were united in a single purpose. On a different plane, it created the same kind of ultra-democratic feeling of fellowship and equality, without any social barriers, as existed in London during the blitz winter. Bishops and freethinkers, Royalist snobs and Communist railwaymen, the *curé* and the *instituteur* found themselves, as resisters, in the same boat, as it were, all united by the national shipwreck of 1940.

After 1942 the Resistance movements, having been properly labelled and organized, chiefly by London, acquired more rank-and-file supporters. But the proportion of organized resisters was still relatively small, compared with the passive resistance that went on everywhere, and in a thousand small ways: peasants were slow in delivering their produce; civil servants and industrial workers practised ca-canny, teachers made ambiguous remarks to their pupils; no statistics can measure the amount of this passive everyday resistance, prompted not by any directives from above but by a dislike of being occupied by the Germans. It is true that the clandestine newspapers and the BBC had all helped in creating this state of mind.

4. THE POLITICAL PARTIES "JOIN" THE RESISTANCE

How did the old political parties fit into the Resistance? It may be said that, generally, all that was Right and Centre was solidly behind Vichy; and that the Resistance, in so far as it was supported by any parties at all, derived its main support from elements which were chiefly on the Left—though not entirely so.

The right-wing elements in the Resistance were acting for the most part independently of any party, but in virtue of some old nationalist tradition. The traditions that counted in prompting isolated individuals of the Right and Centre to join the Resistance were: (1) a nationalist "East-of-France" tradition going back to Barrès and Poincaré; (2) a military tradition, which also was essentially "anti-Boche"; (3) a Liberal Catholic tradition, essentially democratic, anti-Fascist and anti-Munichite, as represented by a man like Bidault, who, in a sense, could scarcely be called left-wing (even though the Jeune République, which was affiliated to the Popular Democrats, held views very close to Socialism). Middle-of-the-road groups like the Radicals were much less prominent in the Resistance, and, at first, only a few individuals, acting entirely on their own, took part in it. The Socialists were sharply divided; and the Communists did not officially commit themselves to the Resistance movement until after the German attack on the Soviet Union. But their case is a very special one and will be dealt with in a separate chapter.

Even the Fascist and semi-Fascist Leagues, which had been so prominent in the middle 'thirties, and other Fascist organizations, were not all united during the Occupation and the Vichy régime. The Croix de Feu (which in 1936 had become the Parti Social Français (PSF)) were divided into a large Pétainist majority and an anti-Pétainist minority. The former held a prominent place in Pétain's French Légion, with its "war veteran" *mystique* and a seemingly fanatical devotion to the Marshal; the anti-Pétainists among the Croix de Feu, on the contrary, tended, in virtue of an "anti-Boche'" tradition, to gravitate towards the Resistance. The position of Colonel de La Rocque himself was a very odd one. At first he wholeheartedly supported Pétain, but was later deported to Germany as an American spy. He returned after the Liberation, and died soon afterwards. Nearly all the Camelots du Roi followed Maurras, with his fanatical pro-Vichyism; but there were a few exceptions, and some Royalists, such as Guillain de Bénouville, were prominent in the Resistance. The "Cagoule" (who around 1938 were guilty of various provocations and murders, such as the murder of the two Roselli brothers, apparently on instructions from Mussolini or his police) fell into three groups: one, under the notorious Deloncle, worked for the Germans, at least until 1943; another was pro-American and "Giraudist"; a third one was said to be Gaullist. Colonel Passy, the head of de Gaulle's Intelligence in London, was believed to have been a "cagoulard", though this was denied both by himself and by Soustelle. No evidence exists that he ever was one.

The only groups who remained openly pro-German till the end were the small Fascist organization of "blueshirts", the Francistes (whose leader, Marcel Bucard, was later shot by the French); Doriot's PPF, and some of the people round Marcel Déat, not to mention the die-hards of Darnand's Milice.

As for the "classical" Right, its parliamentary parties were all pro-Pétain. They had been scared by the Popular Front legislation of 1936-7, and Vichy was, to them, as near an ideal as could be imagined. It was authoritarian politically, paternalist in its capital-labour relationships, and was supported by the hierarchy of the Church. Economic power was concentrated in the hands of the *Comités d'Organisation*, which were, in effect, run by the representatives of Big Business and High Finance. Nevertheless there were some men on the Right with old-fashioned "anti-Boche" views, such as the aged Louis Marin, who formed an embryonic *Fédération Républicaine*, and later he even joined the "dynamic" and Communist-dominated "Front National".

Many of the Radicals were considered among the chief culprits of the political mismanagement that had led to the disaster of 1940, and, on the whole, their credit was very low on all sides. The Right despised the Radicals for having had bogus-strong-man Daladier among their leaders, and the Left despised them for Bonnet's kow-towing to Ribbentrop. Although after the Armistice, Bonnet played no important part in politics and retired to Switzerland he was a Vichyite for all that. Daladier, on the other hand, was a prisoner of Vichy. Many Radicals had voted for Pétain, and even Herriot, the g.o.m. of the Radical Party, assumed at first a highly favourable attitude towards Pétain, much to the disappointment of an uncompromising Republican like Vincent Auriol.

Not that the Socialists—at least as a parliamentary party—were any better than the Radicals.

Thirty-six of the eighty deputies who had refused Pétain their vote on July 10, 1940 were Socialists; but many other Socialist deputies and senators co-operated with Pétain—notably Spinasse, formerly Blum's Minister of National Economy, Paul Faure, the leader of the Munichites in 1938, and among the Socialist trade unionists, René Belin, who became Pétain's first Minister of Labour.

There were Socialists in a variety of Resistance groups both in the South and in the North (notably the Lebas group at Roubaix), and Pierre Brossolette—who died a heroic death—was one of de Gaulle's chief contact men in France. But the Party as such did not at first do anything beyond forming a *Comité d'Action Socialiste* (CAS) in January 1941, with H. Ribière as its first Secretary-General, to be succeeded soon after by Daniel Mayer, who was later to become an important figure in the Resistance. Two committees (one for the North and one for the South) were set up. The Socialists' attitude to de Gaulle was very reserved at first. It was not until 1942, especially after Christian Pineau's visit to London, Blum's favourable statement on de Gaulle, and André Philip's inclusion in the Free French Committee that relations between de Gaulle and the Socialists in France became "normalized".

In 1943 the Socialist Party was officially reconstituted—chiefly as a result of the reconstitution of its eternal rival, the Communist Party, which had, by this time, made the proud claim of being "the only Resistance *party*". This reconstitution of the Party was accompanied by a purge—all the Socialists who had voted for Pétain were automatically excluded.

Much more active from the outset than either the Radicals or the Socialists were the Catholic Popular Democrats and especially the Jeune République. Despite the *Pétainisme* of the hierarchy of the Church, members of these two Catholic bodies were at the origin of several Resistance movements, and were particularly prominent in the Resistance movements in the South, especially in "Combat". After the amalgamation of the three main Southern movements, the Popular Democrats in the Resistance aimed at organizing a great Liberal-Catholic Party. Bidault, Teitgen and de Menthon founded the *Mouvement Républicain de Libération*, which later became the MRP.

The Communist Party line[7] did not become clear until after the German attack on the Soviet Union, which transformed the "imperialist" war into an "anti-Fascist" and "anti-imperialist" war. Contact was established, through Fernand Grenier, in January 1943, with de Gaulle; while, inside France, the Communists did their best to turn the Resistance into a "dynamic", "activist" and Left-wing movement, with powerful emphasis on its "national" and "revolutionary" nature

[7] See Chapter IX.

—so much so, indeed, that both the Free French abroad, and certain more moderate Resistance movements inside France became alarmed at the vigour displayed by the Communists. Not that they could be dispensed with; de Gaulle knew as well as Vichy did that the Communists were more likely than other elements in the Resistance to turn it into a mass movement and, eventually, into a striking force of some military importance. Many non-Communists could not help admiring the single-mindedness and the courage of the Communists in the Resistance. Other classes of French society, François Mauriac wrote in 1943, in his celebrated *Cahier Noir*, were all at sixes and sevens; "only the working-class *as a whole* remained faithful to France in her distress and humiliation." ("Seule la classe ouvrière *dans sa masse* aura été fidèle à la France profanée."[8])

But while it is true that the Communists did all they could, as time went on, to "cash in" on the Resistance which had, in the main, been started by others, it is also true that they were to become the most hunted and persecuted party of the Resistance, and also that part of it which, more than any other, took part in active Resistance like railway sabotage,[9] who formed the guerilla units of the Francs-Tireurs-Partisans, and later played a very active rôle in the formation of the FFI. Although they had "adhered" to de Gaulle, they tended not only to ignore orders from London, but also charged the Free French with cold-footed *attentisme*.

A serious charge brought against the Communists by non-Communists in the Resistance is, of course, that their (largely successful) attempts to "colonize" almost every section of the Resistance movement and to "politicize" it, made it even more difficult than it might otherwise have been, to build up a single "Resistance Party".

The Communists had been excluded from the CGT in September 1939, after the prohibition of the Communist Party as such. The CGT that survived was, therefore, limited, at least so far as its leadership was concerned, to Socialists and old-time syndicalists, with Jouhaux as their chief. But the establishment of the Vichy régime created a new situation even for this "tame" CGT, especially after one of its leaders, René Belin, had adhered to the Vichy régime.

The leaders of the CGT formed in the Occupied Zone a *comité d'études économiques* which was allowed by the Germans to publish a fortnightly bulletin. They frequently conferred with the Catholic CFTC.

---

[8] Against this phrase, Mr Charles Morgan was later to protest strongly but not very effectively in an open letter to Mauriac.

[9] There were endless rivalries in the Resistance and the dominant rôle of the Communists in railway sabotage is denied, for example, by leaders of Combat who claim much of the credit for this.

It was through the rank and file, rather than through the leaders, that contact was gradually re-established with the Communists, who meantime had built up a "shadow CGT" (composed of the so-called *unitaire*, i.e. Communist elements) and an agreement for concerted action was reached between the leaders of the two groups in May 1943, complete with the setting-up of a Central Bureau comprising six *confédérés* (i.e. non-Communists) and three *unitaires* (i.e. Communists).

After this, the Catholic trade unions continued to go their own way, and the question of their fusion with the CGT no longer arose.

5. UNITING THE RESISTANCE

De Gaulle, as we have seen, had the greatest difficulty in getting anybody to recognize him as an authority in any way "representative" of France. On the other hand, the Resistance was, for a long time, little more than a collection of small, incoherent and unco-ordinated units of potential, rather than real anti-German and anti-Vichy action. However, by the middle of 1942, the Resistance was showing signs of developing into a force that might in time have to be reckoned with. Only cohesion was still lacking; and what was therefore needed were two things: (*a*) co-ordinate and unify the various Resistance groups in France, and (*b*) show that they were "behind" de Gaulle.

However, it was a long and laborious process before the formation of the CNR (the *Conseil National de la Résistance*) could be achieved. There were distrust and many mental reservations on all sides. De Gaulle tended to look upon himself as a sort of Commander-in-Chief of the Resistance inside France; while the Resistance leaders, seriously doubting de Gaulle's understanding of local conditions in France, were unwilling to submit to his authority which, for all they knew, might be under British direction. The British were, of course, suspected by the Resistance of playing a game of their own—which was not necessarily in France's interests. Why, for instance, were they so cautious about supplying arms to the Resistance? Nevertheless, the question inevitably arose whether the British might not, all the same, be more willing to help the Resistance materially if they were sufficiently impressed by its unity and its growing numbers.

In view of this almost inextricable tangle of rivalries, suspicions and mental reservations on all sides, it seems all the more remarkable that men like Jean Moulin and some others should, in the end, have managed to give not only a certain unity to the Resistance, but should have achieved a sufficient degree of "mutual recognition" between the Resistance and the Free French abroad which was to be of political and international benefit to both.

Jean Moulin, a former Prefect, who had been arrested and tortured by the Germans and had been dismissed by Vichy, first arrived in London in September 1941. He returned to France in January 1942 and began the laborious process of "unifying" the Resistance. The fact that he had money to distribute was of great help to him. It was, of course, hard at first for Moulin to determine the relative importance of this or that Resistance movement; but finally Moulin was "accepted" as de Gaulle's representative by most of the Resistance leaders, and he set up a *Délégation Générale du Général de Gaulle en France* which de Gaulle himself went out of his way to represent as a sort of dome crowning the whole Resistance. This was an idea which, for international reasons, it was important to put across; in reality it was not quite as impressive as all that. The *Délégation* was a sort of central office which had its delegates attached to the various Resistance groups, and it acted as an agency for supplying the Resistance with funds and other "means of action"; it was also important as an intelligence channel between the Home Resistance and de Gaulle. After the arrest of Moulin in June 1943—subsequently he was, without giving anything away, to be savagely tortured to death by the Germans—Bingen took over as Acting *Délégué*, until the appointment of Bollaert in November 1943 as *délégué général*, with Serreulles as his deputy for the North, and Bingen for the South. After the arrest of Bollaert in February 1944, Parodi became de Gaulle's fourth General Delegate, and was lucky enough to last until the Liberation. Bingen was arrested in 1944 and poisoned himself. Altogether, this brief enumeration of arrests—and deaths—shows that it was no sinecure to be de Gaulle's Delegate in France.

The foundations for a united Resistance had been laid by Moulin as early as 1942. By March 1943 he had already achieved the unification of the three principal Resistance Movements in the South through the formation of the MUR (*Mouvements Unis de la Résistance*).[10]

Despite this seemingly coherent unification of the whole Southern Resistance in the MUR, there continued a good deal of rivalry among the various groups; and the whole Southern Resistance was blamed by the Northern Resistance for going in too much for politics, and what complicated matters was that the predominantly, though not exclusively Communist-dominated "Front National" had not adhered to the MUR.

Alongside the MUR and the four "co-ordinated" Resistance move-

[10] In this, its three paramilitary organizations formed a kind of shadow army, the *Armée Secrète*; there was also a unification of the other "services"—"military affairs" (under Frenay) with its four sub-sections: *Armée Secrète*, *Groupes Francs*, *Maquis* and *Parachutages*; then a Propaganda Section (with a number of sub-sections) under J. P. Lévy, and a General Secretariat, with its liaison services with other Resistance movements. In each of the regions, the *Comité Directeur National* appointed a *directoire* of three members.

ments in the North, a *Comité Général d'Etudes* was set up—seemingly an "intellectual" body, but one of considerable political importance, and comprising most of the leaders of the future MRP; its *Cahiers politiques*, discussing the various Resistance and post-Liberation problems, including the eventual nomination of the Prefects of its choice, provided a foretaste of the MRP's political and administrative ambitions.

Since the end of 1942 de Gaulle had considered the formation of a "National Council of the Resistance" (CNR); its purpose would be to demonstrate to the Allies that he had "the whole of France" behind him; this became particularly important when his whole position was challenged by Giraud and the USA after the North Africa landing in November 1942.

The Resistance movements were, of course, being conducted by men whose names meant little or nothing to the Allies; therefore it was useful to add to their names those of certain "representative" pre-war public figures. It was apparently Moulin's idea to include in the CNR even the representatives of political parties which had not been reconstituted, and even of those, the majority of whose members had adhered to the Vichy régime. This "insulting" idea met with fierce opposition from Resistance leaders like Bourdet; but finally they agreed to the formation of the CNR on the understanding that it would have no real executive or governmental responsibility. This was all the more understandable as, in his desire to include *everybody* in the CNR, except out-and-out Fascists, Moulin could find no one in the large right-wing party, the *Alliance Démocratique* except the Marquis de Moustier (the only one to have voted against Pétain)—and he was a Giraudist and anti-Gaullist—and therefore Moulin was reduced to proposing the seat of the AD representative on the CNR to M. Joseph Laniel, a rich Norman industrialist who, though he had voted for Pétain, now seemed in a mood to jump on the Resistance bandwagon.

The other major right-wing party, the *Fédération Républicaine* was not represented on the CNR by its most prominent anti-Pétain member, the aged Louis Marin (who could much too easily be identified), but by a much younger man, Debû-Bridel. He was also a leading non-Communist member of the "Front National". Partly perhaps as a result of his Protestant background, Debû-Bridel had an almost un-French civic conscience; the French statesman he respected most between the two wars was André Tardieu, with his contempt for the easy-going *mœurs* of the Third Republic. Besides being a novelist of some distinction, Debû-Bridel was, as a journalist, associated with Emile Buré of the *Ordre*, which was austerely Republican, rather in the tradition of Poincaré, anti-German and anti-Munich. It was natural for Debû-Bridel to be in the Resistance and to be associated with the most dynamic part of it, the "Front National", even though it was largely Communist. After the Liberation, Debû-Bridel was one of the most devastating critics of the Black Market. Later, still in search of "justice, order and authority", he joined de Gaulle's RPF, where he remained a determined opponent of German rearmament.

It was a risky venture, that first meeting of the CNR, in a house in the rue du Four, in the heart of Paris, on May 27, 1943. The two trade union federations were represented by Saillant (CGT) and Tessier (CFTC); there were eight representatives of the Resistance movements,[11] and six representatives of the "old" political parties.[12]

The meeting was presided over by Jean Moulin who read a message from de Gaulle, saying that France would be restored in her democratic rights as soon as possible. Then, despite some opposition from Villon (Communist), a resolution was unanimously passed "cancelling all the acts of Vichy", and entrusting General de Gaulle with "the management of the Nation's interests" and leaving the management of military affairs to General Giraud—which implied a clear disavowal of Giraud as political leader.

For security reasons there were only two full-dress meetings of the CNR until the Liberation. A permanent steering committee was set up, consisting of five members—Bidault (who became president of the CNR after the arrest of Moulin on June 21, 1943), Blocq-Mascart (OCM), Saillant (CGT), Villon (FN) and Copeau or Bourdet (MUR)—rather with a Communist or pro-Communist predominance. The bureau's chief function was to maintain contact among the more or less scattered members of the CNR with a view to drawing up the famous Programme of the CNR. This was finally completed on March 15, 1944—a few months before the Liberation. The CNR through its bureau, also did a good deal to co-ordinate the work of the secret military and para-military organizations; it debated on the future of the Press, and appointed a number of sub-committees, which prepared a series of measures and reports preliminary to the Liberation. It was on these committees that the Communists were most active. Liberation Committees were also set up in the various *départements,* roughly corresponding, in composition, to the CNR itself, account being taken in each case, of the "political colouring" of the *département* in question. These Liberation Committees, "representing" the Resistance, were to come into conflict with de Gaulle's "central authority" soon after the Liberation, as we shall see.

[11] Villon (Front National), Lenormand (Ceux de la Liberation), Lecompte-Boinet (Ceux de la Résistance), Charles Laurent (Libération-Nord), J. H. Simon (O.C.M.); Bourdet (Combat), Claudius-Petit (Franc-Tireur), Copeau (Libération-Sud).

[12] Mercier (Communists), Le Troquer (Socialists), Rucart (Radicals), G. Bidault (Pop. Democrats), Laniel (Alliance Démocratique), Debû-Bridel (Fédération Républicaine).

The most important CNR Committee was that concerned with the unification and command of the "secret armies"; this was the COMAC (*Comité d'Action Militaire*) composed, in 1944, of two Communists (Villon of *Front National* and Kriegel-Valrimont of *MUR*) and one non-Communist (de Vogüé of *Ceux de la Résistance*).

The attempt to replace the old parties, when the time came, by new groupings that had emerged from the Resistance itself, led to nothing. The *Comité Central de la Résistance* proved still-born—according to some observers, owing to the obstructive tactics of the "Front National" which was unwilling to see itself "drowned" and outvoted in a single Resistance federation comprising seven "bourgeois" rivals. The "Front National" hoped, on the contrary, to swallow up, as far as possible, the rest of the Resistance. Later, the *Comité Central de la Résistance*, more or less sabotaged by Bidault and the Communists, gave way completely to the CNR, which implied the recognition of the old parties. After the arrest of Jean Moulin it was decided that de Gaulle's *délégué général* and the President of the CNR could not be the same person, and the CNR thus shook off the "guardianship" of de Gaulle.[13]

Altogether, the CNR, since the arrest of Moulin, became fairly independent of de Gaulle—even though, for foreign consumption, it continued to support him fully. But there was to be a great deal of friction between the Resistance, and especially its Communist part, and the Free French abroad over practically everything.

And the most paradoxical feature of the Liberation was the support that not the Resistance, but the "old" Parties were now to receive from de Gaulle himself. Was it not chiefly because the Communists had become too powerful in the Resistance?

6. THE MAQUIS

Until the end of 1942 the Resistance was largely limited to people who had been prompted by their political ideals to act as they did, rather than by any immediate material necessity. The STO, the Compulsory Labour Service, directly affected the everyday life of many thousands, and threatened the everyday life of millions; many who, until then, had been "unpolitical" or indifferent, were faced with the dilemma of obeying the Germans or of dodging the Germans and eventually entering into "active" Resistance.

With Hitler's Reich losing more and more men at the Russian Front, the German authorities in France were clamouring more and more stridently and threateningly for French labour in German industry. The two half-measures tried at first—the enlistment of French "volun-

---

[13] See below Bourdet's opinion on Bidault's fraternization with the Communists and the help he gave them in "colonizing" the Resistance.

teer labour" and the *Relève* (the system under which, at least in theory, one French war prisoner was released if three skilled workers went to work in Germany) had proved a failure.

When finally the STO was introduced, "comb-out" committees were set up in French factories, people were rounded up in the street, in theatres and cinemas, the families of dodgers were threatened with reprisals, and ration cards were delivered only on production of a labour certificate. Nothing since the Armistice had given France a greater shock than the law of February 16, 1943, introducing the STO. For it was after Stalingrad that the Germans decided to draft as many of their own industrial workers as possible into the Army; and these had to be replaced by "forced labour", including French labour. In factories, lists were drawn up of those who were to leave for Germany on a given date. Later, the Germans went even further, and tried to enforce the nation-wide conscription of certain age groups—including young French peasants—a psychological mistake of the first order; for, in the main, the French peasant population, a large part of which was still living relatively well, and often thriving opulently on the black market, had given the Germans relatively little trouble. But, by this time, the Germans had become desperate.

Motives in resisting were not all pure, of course. There were those who felt, above all, that Germany was rapidly losing the war, and that it was unpatriotic to help her in her arms production. Others were simply scared. The German and German-subsidized French press screamed about the Allied "terror bombing" of German cities, and the BBC gloried in the infernos of Hamburg and Frankfurt and Cologne. It was no more pleasant to be treated as *chair à bombardement* than it was to be treated as German cannon fodder. The Resistance movements and the shadow trade union organizations did all they could to encourage people to resist what had generally come to be known as "deportation". Only what was one to do? If you left your home and your work, you also lost your ration card.

The most obvious solution was to get away into the country, and get "lost" among the French peasant population. Many French townspeople had family links with the countryside, and cousins and grandmothers could be of great help in granting hospitality to STO deserters. But there were many others with no such connexions, and these had to be helped by the trade unions and the Resistance organizations. Financially both were desperately weak, and *the moneyed classes in France did not do much to help.* Nor was the financial help from London adequate. According to M. Bloch-Laîné, an expert in these matters, de Gaulle's BCRA, which was the principal distributor of funds to the Resistance, succeeded altogether in sending to France 3 milliard francs in notes, and under 1 milliard francs in bonds, as well as 1,200,000 dollars in cash—not a large amount, especially when one considers that two-thirds of the francs sent relate to the April-to-September 1944 period. On the other hand, the revenue raised by the Co.Fi.—the financial organization of the Resistance—by means of selling Algiers treasury bonds and by resorting to other, much more complicated, financial transactions carried out through a few helpful bankers (these were not numerous) amounted to a mere 600 million francs.[14]

The "STO deserters" who vanished into the countryside or became *maquis* nomads did not run into vast numbers—the total seems to have been less than 100,000, and a much greater number *did* submit to "deportation", as became only too apparent when they began to come home—or failed to return—in 1945. Nevertheless, there were more than enough STO deserters and their families to cope with. As far as possible, they were helped by the trade unions, the Resistance movements and the CAD (*Comité d'Action contre la Déportation*) set up by the CNR, as well as by organizations like the "Forged Papers service" of the MUR in the South, which for two years or more became involved in some of the most fantastic activities connected with the Resistance. All this work was a good deal more complicated and more dangerous than the mere production of clandestine newspapers.

In the Southern Zone, Moulin encouraged the creation of organizations like the MOF (*Mouvement Ouvrier Français*) which, however, came to little. More important were the *Comités de Résistance Ouvrière* which tried to set up anti-STO cells in every factory; the chief organizer of this network was Degliame. The MUR also created a special Maquis service, distinct from the *Armée Secrète* service.

One of the immediate results of the STO in the North, where co-ordination among the Resistance movements was much more difficult, was to increase the number of young people adhering to the predominantly Communist Francs-Tireurs Partisans, under the command of Charles Tillon.

At the same time, the CNR succeeded in setting up an organization parallel to that in the South, and also called the CAD, the most important activity of which was also to manufacture forged documents, ration cards, etc, on a very large scale, which would enable the "deserters" to dodge the endless controls imposed by the German occupation authorities. The forging, with its arsenal of letter-heads, French and German rubber stamps, and so on, was done with great virtuosity, and with many humorous subterfuges, such as the rumours spread on various occasions, which unnerved the Germans, that the *genuine* labour cards and identity cards in a given area were *forgeries*.

[14] *Revue d'Histoire de la 2-e Guerre Mondiale* (November 1950), pp. 6–19.

Much less humorous was the CAD's task of supplying the STO deserters with food and clothing. The difficulties were so great and the funds so short that the deserters were at times obliged to resort to methods little short of robbery; peasants were more or less compelled to supply foodstuffs in exchange for somewhat doubtful bonds, repayable after the war; tobacco shops were looted; known collaborators were attacked and robbed; even *mairies* were—though sometimes with the connivance of the Mayor or some other official—invaded and the stock of ration cards carried off. It was these incidents which, multiplied manifold in anti-Resistance propaganda during the war and, retrospectively, by pro-Vichyites after the war, created a legend of large-scale murder and banditry throughout the country on the part of "Communist bands". It is, of course, true that in some cases common criminals operated in various places, parading as the "Resistance". It was more or less inevitable.

To restrict the bad effect this was having on the population, funds had to be urgently raised, either in London or through the Co.Fi. But the money was slow in coming. Banks and post offices had to be raided by the larger Maquis formations: the biggest haul was that of 100 million francs from the Sainte-Claude branch of the Bank of France in the Ain *département*. The bank manager, who was in sympathy with the Resistance, did not resist much. Dozens of post offices also allowed themselves to be "robbed". These "robberies" did much less to annoy the rural population than the forced "requisitioning" of food.

Arming the Maquis was even more difficult; Britain has been accused by many people in the French Resistance of having "let them down", for fear of ill-considered attacks on the Germans, and for fear also of arming too many Communists. It was not until D-Day was in sight that the "Jedburgh" missions were sent to organize and arm the Maquis in a big way. But until then, many small and badly-armed Maquis formations were wiped out by the Germans and the Vichy police.

On the whole, no Maquis of any size could, at least until the spring of 1944, be constituted except in places where there were large forests or mountains; and there were scarcely any Maquis formations in the North of France until 1944, except in Brittany. The very earliest Maquis, in the Alps, seems to date back to as early as the beginning of 1942; there was one Maquis formation, in 1942, composed of a few hundred workmen, who had taken refuge in the mountains round Maurienne, after looting an arms dump. Early in 1943, other Maquis sprang up, largely composed of STO deserters, in the Massif Central. The numbers were still small, running into a few hundred here and a few dozen there. Even as late as January 1944, at the Lyon meeting of the Maquis chiefs from all over France, the total number of *maquisards* was estimated at only some 30,000, most of them in the South. It is true that during the winter of 1943–4 the Maquis had suffered many severe losses at the hands of the Germans, Italians, and the Vichy police.

The Germans, as said before, had made the bad psychological mistake of trying to mobilize into the STO not only workers, but also university students and young peasants—in fact, at one time, all Frenchmen born in 1922.

The resistance of the peasantry and of the educated class to the STO was even more determined than that of the workers; the peasants hated to leave their land, and undergraduates had no desire to work in factories, least of all in Germany. The fact that peasant lads sought refuge in the Maquis was of great help to the others; although peasants were at first distrustful of the *maquisards*, the presence of their own sons among the "outlaws" tended to create better relations between the peasantry and the Maquis generally. The comradeship created by the STO among the various elements who had to seek refuge in the Maquis also made the peasantry rather less distrustful, not to say hostile, towards the "foreigners" who had joined the Maquis—Jews, fleeing from persecution, Alsatians and Lorrainers in Southern France whom the Germans considered as Germans, and whom they intended to conscript into the Wehrmacht; and those Spanish Republicans who, though not numerous in the Maquis, were amongst its most experienced soldiers. These Spaniards, who had lived miserably in France ever since the end of the Spanish civil war, and who, under Vichy, were in constant fear of being extradited to Franco, or of being sent to concentration camps, were among the most dynamic elements in the French Resistance, and among those best suited for guerilla warfare. Some had been *guerrilleros* in Spain. Other foreigners included Belgians, Dutchmen, Poles, Yugoslavs, and even a few anti-Hitler Germans, and, after 1943, some escaped Russian war prisoners.

The creation of the Maquis confronted the Resistance movements with a set of new problems. Most of these Resistance movements had their "secret army"—but these "secret armies" were theoretical, rather than real, in the absence of not only arms and equipment, but also of proper instructors and opportunities for drilling. Now the STO had driven between 30,000 and 50,000 young people into the Maquis—and this provided the most obvious Resistance material. Driven from their jobs and homes, hungry and embittered, these young people could be turned into perhaps the most hardened and most dynamic part of France's "secret army". Apart from supplying the *maquisards* with forged papers, and, as far as possible, with food and clothing, a South of France organization like the MUR, through its "*Service Maquis*" endeavoured, as far as possible, to train the very mixed crowd of *maquisards* as soldiers. Similar (and more effective) work was undertaken by the Communist *Front National* and its guerillas, the FT-P.

The problem that arose was how large a Maquis unit should be. There were those in favour of the widest possible dispersal, with no unit to exceed 15 or 20; others favoured much larger concentrations; Colonel Romans, who organized the numerous Maquis of the Ain, considered 50 the ideal unit—strong enough to put up a fight, but not too large to be easily detected. In practice, most Maquis units were much smaller; though, on the other hand, there were the famous "redoubts" of Vercors, which, starting with 400 men, attained about 1,000; in the Glières Maquis (which came to almost as tragic an end as that of Vercors) there were 500 to 600 men; the Montagne Noire Maquis had 1,000 men, and the largest concentration of all, the three Maquis of Mont Mouchet, totalled as many as 9,000. Mobility—and the ability to move away in nomadic fashion whenever there was a danger of being encircled—was an essential part of the Maquis' life.

The Resistance tried to get professional officers into the Maquis; but this attempt met with no success, with one or two notable exceptions, particularly at Glières, where the Maquis was commanded by officers of the *Chasseurs Alpins*. For one thing, most officers had a distaste for guerilla warfare, and many must have thought it quixotic to join an "army" that had no adequate arms or equipment. Captain Kervenoael, of the Dragoons (one of the few professional officers to join the Maquis), said that his total stock, in the spring of 1943, was 60 muskets, 2 rusty sub-machine guns, 2 grenades, 45 revolvers, and 4 Lebel rifles—for the several hundred men of the Montagne Noire Maquis.

Arms from England? Desperate appeals were sent to England; but not much came—at least not until D-Day was in sight. Thirty planes parachuted, it is true, 580 containers to the Glières Maquis, with 90 tons of equipment; the Montagne Noire Maquis received between November 1943 and June 1944 enough to arm 500 men—but not the 1,000 who were there. Many young men had gone into the Maquis in their town clothes. Their clothes and shoes were soon worn out. The chief source of supply were the raids on Pétain's *chantiers de la jeunesse*, which were numerous in Vichy France; sometimes the watchmen were in sympathy with the Maquis, and allowed "robberies" to be staged—locks broken and the watchmen themselves gagged and tied up. The staged (or sometimes genuine) attacks on *mairies* and tobacco-shops were naturally played up by the Germans and by Vichy as so much Gaullist or Communist "terrorism"—the senile Charles Maurras in the *Action Française* screaming loudest of all, and demanding merciless reprisals. Medical services of sorts were organized in the Maquis with the help of local village doctors and also medical students who had escaped from the STO; medical supplies were provided by chemists' shops in the Vichy Zone, by "contacts" in hospitals, etc. Some priests (and, in the Protestant areas like the Ardèche, some ministers) either lived in the Maquis, or were available when a dying man or a traitor about to be executed wanted spiritual comfort.

The appointment was made by London in May 1943 of a "Chef National Maquis", with six regional chiefs in the Southern Zone; but this whole organization came into conflict with the CAD run by Yves Farge, which looked upon the Maquis as rather a creation of its own. It was not until the beginning of 1944 that the conflict was, more or less, settled after agreement had been reached on the incorporation of both the "Secret Army" and the Maquis in the FFI (*Forces Françaises de l'Intérieur*) later (in June), to be placed under the general command of General Koenig.

The Francs-Tireurs-Partisans were also incorporated in the FFI, after lengthy discussions between de Gaulle and the Communists at Algiers; but they, and the Maquis they had formed were essentially Communist, and desired to remain as autonomous as possible; hence, from de Gaulle's point of view, a good deal of indiscipline on their part. They considered themselves as the "toughest" of all the Resistance groups, and Tillon was something of a romantic revolutionary (Russia 1919 style) who did not easily submit to Algiers.

Partly for this reason, partly because de Gaulle's own representatives were distrustful of the British (who, in June 1944 started forming their own Maquis in France, the so-called *Maquis Buckmaster*); partly also because the French Resistance did not take too kindly even to the highly useful "Jedburgh" missions with their arms, and their French, American and British officers, sent to arm and organize the French Resistance—because of all this (it has sometimes been argued) the Resistance did not show itself capable of the maximum cohesion and discipline at the time of the Normandy Landing.[15]

On the whole, it is almost impossible to generalize about the Maquis. The Maquis units differed in size, in efficiency, in equipment and training. They also differed politically; the FT-P Maquis were the most dynamic, favouring direct action long before the Normandy Landing, on the ground that "you learn to fight only while fighting". The Russians, while glorifying their own Partisans and those of Yugoslavia often complained of the inadequacy of the "Partisan war" in other countries and tended to blame London for its "caution". The Allied general staff and the French commanders of the Secret Army were, indeed, in favour of waiting, and of hitting out "all at once", without incurring punitive expeditions and the piecemeal extermination of villages by the Germans.

However, the Maquis did not always have the initiative. First the Vichy police (gendarmes, GMR, Milice) would attack the Maquis;

[15] Cf. M. Granet, *Dessin Général du Maquis. Revue d'Histoire de la 2-e Guerre Mondiale* (November 1950), p. 64.

when they failed, the Germans would come to the rescue. The gendarmes, recruited before the war, were easy-going and not dangerous; often they came to terms with the Maquis and let them "escape". Much more dangerous were the GMR and especially Darnand's Milice, a *basse police* of thugs, murderers and torturers, partly recruited from the underworld of Marseilles and—from amongst Maurras's young "intellectuals". But even the Maquis' encounters with the GMR and the Milice were seldom fatal, since neither of these were heavily armed.

It was different when the Germans, with tanks, heavy artillery and planes attacked the Maquis, as they did at Glières in February and March 1944. With guns and planes 8,000 Germans dressed in white attacked 500 *maquisards* in their snowy redoubt, after the latter had successfully held out against the Milice for two months. Finally, after resisting the Germans for several days, the *maquisards* decided to disperse on March 26, having lost 150 men, of whom 90, most of them wounded, were savagely massacred by the Germans, while the surviving prisoners were tortured and deported to Germany; the rest of the force escaped over mountain passes, with the help of the local inhabitants. Significantly, Abetz, in his account of the same operation, claimed that the local inhabitants thanked the Germans for having liberated them of the "terrorists", and insulted the few surviving French prisoners.

Although the Glières Maquis had received a substantial quantity of light arms from England, these were insufficient to save it against the major German onslaught at the end of March. But other Maquis formations received even less equipment, and the parachuting of arms did not assume any major proportions until D-Day, or just before.

After June 1944 the activity of the Maquis becomes more or less inseparable from that of the FFI, in which the *maquisards* were, in fact, incorporated. The task of the FFI, including the Maquis, in accordance with the instructions of the EMFFI (General Staff of the French Forces of the Interior), itself in contact with the Allied Supreme Command was, above all, to prevent the Germans, scattered over France, from regrouping, and from joining too rapidly the German forces engaged in the battle of Normandy. There could, of course, be no question of expecting the poorly-armed French forces to annihilate whole German divisions; but the French could interfere with their communications and wage guerilla warfare on them. This the French forces did— and with great effect. Allied bombing and the railway sabotage carried out by the French Resistance had already virtually paralysed a large part of the railway transport in France. The railways in the vital Limoges-Clermont-Brive-Toulouse quadrangle had been virtually put out of action ever since April 1944. Surprise attacks on German army columns moving towards the Normandy beach-head were numerous, and of unquestionable value to the Allies; the infamously notorious *Reich* Division—including the SS-men of Oradour fame[16] took nearly three weeks to reach Normandy from the Toulouse area—at least three times longer than it would otherwise have taken, and it reached Normandy in the end in a battered state. The great mobility of the French forces that had harassed the *Reich* Division was one of their strong points.

On the other hand, the idea of forming a sort of "French redoubt", without much contact with the Allied armies, in the Massif Central proved a tragic mistake. Several thousand *maquisards* were concentrated in the Vercors area about the time of the Normandy landing. For some weeks they tied up a German Infantry division and a panzer division, but being only poorly armed, they were finally wiped out, with the help of SS troops landed by gliders. Over a thousand of the French, including all the wounded, were massacred. Rather less disastrous was the resistance of the Montagne Noire Maquis which, after a major battle against heavily-armed German forces, split up into small groups which continued to harass the enemy, now (July 1944) in a hurry to pull out of Central France. A curious case was that of the three Maquis groups of Mont Mouchet, in the Cantal, Lozère and Haute-Loire area of the Massif Central: these three groups had been formed to absorb the smaller Maquis units in the Auvergne, which had proved too vulnerable to German "punitive expeditions"; they were also meant to form part of General Koenig's abortive plan of a "French redoubt".

This plan [wrote Marie Granet, on the strength of information given her by M. Ingrand, who was *Commissaire de la République* at Clermont-Ferrand after the Liberation] was finally abandoned. But the "redoubts" had already been locally organized. Even a partial mobilization had been ordered by way of experiment. But against the will of the local Resistance leaders, this *partial* mobilization became a *general* mobilization. As soon as the peasants and the townspeople had "unofficially" learned that a "mobilization" had been ordered, they spontaneously started swarming towards Mont Mouchet; all the roads were crowded with people—many of them armed—in cars and on bicycles! The railway stations were crowded with "conscripts". A strange and moving spectacle in a heavily occupied country. But the Germans and Vichy must have known about this mass movement, and the Germans seem to have become particularly alarmed. However, they did not react immediately, and the "mobilization" was carried out peacefully in April and May 1944.... And yet there was such a shortage of equipment that only 9,000 could be enrolled, and the rest had to be sent home... After June 10, the Germans attacked...[17]

[16] It was on June 10, 1944 that the Reich Division, infuriated by the obstruction they had met with on their way to Normandy, exterminated the entire population of Oradour, near Limoges. Over 600 people, including women and children, were murdered, or burned alive in the village church.

[17] *Revue d'Histoire de la 2-e Guerre Mondiale* (November 1950), pp. 69–70.

This "spontaneous mobilization" was significant of the real temper of the people, especially in that part of France.

Two of the three Mont Mouchet Maquis came to a tragic end, complete with the massacre of the wounded and of the doctors and nurses. Only the third of the Mont Mouchet Maquis was to see better days. Formed into small and very mobile groups, it harassed German troops throughout the summer of 1944, and also encircled and captured several of the smaller German garrisons. By July 1944, well supplied by now with parachuted arms, these *maquisards* were able to establish a sort of small "Free Republic" at Mauriac, whose leader, the above-mentioned Ingrand, now recognized by Vichy as representing the "New Government", received a representative from Vichy, who had come to negotiate the terms of Pétain's surrender to de Gaulle! However, it came to nothing, since the Germans hastened to rush Pétain off to Germany. Also the "Free State" of Mauriac received a visit from the Swiss Minister at Vichy, who, though he had a German pass, also asked, to be on the safe side, for a "Mauriac" pass, with which to travel to Switzerland: it showed that, by this time, the FFI were virtually controlling large stretches of France.

A number of other "free republics" sprang up, some of short duration, such as the "free republic" of Nantua and Oyennax in the Ain. With a large German force of 35,000 approaching, the men of the "republic" had to disperse, but regrouped later, after the Provence Landing, and finally liberated Bourg and other towns in September 1944. Throughout the summer of 1944, indeed, the whole South-East of France and the Massif Central were teeming with guerilla war. On one occasion, the Maquis of the Morvan Forest just missed capturing Pétain on his way to Germany.

This guerilla war was of unquestionable value to the Allies; General Eisenhower estimated the value of the FFI at the equivalent of 15 divisions; and said that they had hastened victory by two months.

7. THE FFI

The Maquis was, in a way, the most hardened, if not the most experienced, part of the FFI—the French Forces of the Interior—which represented an amalgam of the Maquis, "secret armies", and the Communist FT-PF (*Francs-Tireurs-Partisans-Français*). The Secret Army (or should one say "armies"?—since it consisted of the "military sections" of the various Resistance movements) was placed by Moulin, after a good deal of argument, under the command of General Délestraint at the beginning of 1943, with Morin (of "Combat") and Aubrac (of "Libération-Sud") as his deputies. As early as June 1943, Kaltenbrunner, the Nazi police chief, estimated at 80,000 the effectives of the French Secret Army. It was, of course, as we have already seen, largely a "shadow army", with few opportunities for regular military training. In spite of this lack of experience, many leaders of the Secret Army strained at the leash, and it took Délestraint some trouble to impose on them the *attentiste* policy advocated by London. Délestraint, after his arrest, was replaced by Jussieu-Pontcarrel; after the latter's arrest the command was taken over early in 1944 by Malleret-Joinville, a Communist. By this time already the Secret Army and all other French Resistance Forces were about to be merged into the united armed organization, the FFI.

The Resisters most impatient with *attentisme* were, besides the men of Frenay and d'Astier, the Francs-Tireurs-Partisans, the military organization of the Front National. Composed at first of Communist *militants*, the FT-PF attracted an increasing number of young people. The FT-PF, though sorely lacking in arms, like the rest of the Resistance, nevertheless were responsible for a good deal of "direct action" during the Occupation—train wrecking, railway sabotage, assassination of collaborators, etc. The railwaymen (Communist and non-Communist), as well as the sabotage groups of the MUR, worked in close contact with them. Working both inside and outside Maquis formations, the FT tended to employ Spanish guerilla methods, and also did their best to manufacture some simple "partisan" weapons such as "Molotov cocktails", tyre-busters, and various rudimentary explosive gadgets. The leader of the FT-PF was Charles Tillon, a future Minister in the first few governments of the Fourth Republic. His "Titoism" in the French Resistance was later (1952) severely criticized by the French Communist Party, which was to accuse him of nationalist deviations, of unrealistic revolutionary romanticism, and of a dangerous tendency to claim some sort of privileged position inside the Communist Party for Resistance leaders—an attitude implying a lack of regard for a man like Thorez, who had spent the war years in Moscow. It is conceivable that Tillon still bore the Russians a grudge for the Soviet-German Pact.[18]

Finally, there was what was left of the Armistice Army, after its dissolution, following the German occupation of Vichy France. The generals of this army did not dare hand over to the "Secret Army" or to the Maquis the arms they had hidden away at the time of the dissolution; and most of these arms were later discovered by the Germans. But the dissolved "Armistice Army" formed, nevertheless, the ORA (*Organisation de Résistance de l'Armée*), largely composed of officers —and with practically no troops. These officers were Giraudist rather

[18] The case against Tillon is described in a later chapter on the 1952 "purge" in the French Communist Party.

than Gaullist, and many of them smuggled themselves to North Africa to join Giraud. Inside France, what was left of the ORA was essentially *attentiste* with no desire to come out into the open until D-Day. The leader of the organization, at that time, was General Revers, the future hero of the *affaire des généraux*.

The CNR for its part, set up, as already said, a special Military Action Committee, the COMAC—which in 1944 became chiefly Communist. Although there was much disagreement on the exact limits of its authority, it was to play an important part on a number of occasions, notably during the Liberation of Paris, when it tried to take advantage of its right to "transmit order for immediate action"—a somewhat ambiguous phrase.

One can well imagine that, with so many different "military" Resistance organizations, some believing in *attentisme*, others advocating direct and immediate action, "after the manner of the glorious Soviet Partisans"; some, like the ORA, familiar only with regular warfare; and all of them complaining of the lack of arms, it was not easy to achieve any sort of organic unity among all the forces.

Nevertheless, after many quarrels and discussions, as already said, it was finally agreed in February 1944, to unify the various Resistance "armies" into a single force, the FFI. It was only after a lengthy period of transition and adaptation, and endless negotiation between the French and the Allies, that the FFI were placed under the command of General Koenig and his EMFFI. And that was not until after D-Day.

The impression of all the Resistance leaders was that, among the British and the Americans, there was great scepticism as to the potential value of the French Resistance movements. It is true that, by D-Day, there were several hundred active wireless stations behind the Atlantic Wall, and French co-operation in this field was much appreciated by SHAEF; but the FFI were, in fact, not expected by SHAEF to take part in operations in the battle area, apart from supplying information. The most that was expected of them was that they be of some help behind the German lines, by wrecking and hampering German communications and by engaging, where possible, in guerilla warfare. Various sabotage plans (*Plan Vert, Plan Bleu*, etc) had been worked out in advance; but right up to D-Day not nearly enough was done, according to all French observers, to arm the FFI for any serious warfare.

To equip the FFI properly, at least 60 tons of equipment a day should have been dropped during several months before D-Day. But even as late as March, only 20 tons a day were dropped. By D-Day, only half the FFI were armed at all; and they had no tanks, no armoured cars, no artillery, no anti-aircraft or anti-tank guns, no organized air-force, and no commissariat.[19]

[19] Henri Michel, *op. cit.*, p. 108.

There were, after D-Day, seventeen German divisions in Normandy; there was not much the Resistance could do there, since, with most of the population evacuated, there were, in the battle zones, more Germans than Frenchmen. This made any "Resistance", other than Intelligence, virtually impossible. In Brittany, on the contrary, the FFI fought for two months an arduous battle against the Germans; by the end of July, with more and more young people joining the FFI, now well supplied with arms, the French forces in Brittany grew to some 20,000. During July alone, 400 German trains had been wrecked in Brittany, 300 telephone lines had been cut; and a guerilla war was conducted all over the country. More and more men joined the FFI: by the end of August, there were already 80,000 Breton FFI's. A large part of the province was liberated exclusively by these French forces. By this time the American forces had left entirely to the French what mopping-up was still to be done in Brittany. The Germans fled to Brest, Lorient, and Saint-Nazaire, where they remained blockaded until the end of the war. In two months the FFI had taken 20,000 German prisoners.

The guerilla war and the sabotage of German communications had by now spread over the whole of France. The railways between the German border and Normandy were practically out of action. German troop movements were often hopelessly slowed down. The keen activity displayed by the French forces was of great help to the Allies, and of immense moral value to France itself. No less important for the French was the feeling that their own forces were liberating numerous towns, and whole provinces, such as almost the entire Alpine part of France, with cities like Grenoble and Annecy. Similarly, practically the whole of the Massif Central and the south-west of France were liberated by the FFI. It was to the FFI that the German garrison of Limoges surrendered. Thanks largely to the constant harassing tactics of the FFI, only one quarter of the German forces in the south-east that had been ordered to pull out got as far as Dijon. Altogether in the south-east, the FFI captured 40,000 prisoners.

By August 1944 it was no longer "Resistance" in the old sense; it was War; and many thousands of volunteers, who, because of the dearth of arms, but also for less respectable reasons, had hesitated to join the Resistance, were volunteering for service in what was already, in effect, the French Army. No doubt there were many timid souls who were now only too willing to show that they *also* were in the "Resistance". It was very easy—too easy—in August 1944, with all the Kommandanturs and Gestapos on the run. In 1944 and 1945 there was hardly a person one met in France who hadn't been "in the Resistance". Genuine resisters usually knew when it was true—and when it wasn't.

All the same, the fact remains that after D-Day the Germans suddenly found themselves in enemy country openly at war. This was no longer limited to Maquis patches in Savoy or in the Massif Central—it was true of the whole of France. Immediately after D-Day 180 German trains were derailed, and there were some 500 railway cuts. During the next few weeks there were 3,000 cuts. One of the more comic stories about those days was the whining account of Corinne Luchaire's "frightful" railway journey from Paris to Germany. The film star, who, unlike her distinguished father, was not given a car for going to Germany, but was dumped in a railway carriage, crowded with other "collabos", started her exodus with a three-day hold-up at the Gare de l'Est— before the train could start on its jerky journey at all; and throughout the slow journey the *collabos'* carriage buzzed with rumours of "terrorists" responsible for all the delays.

The Germans soon had to abandon the use of the railways almost entirely and go by road; but here, too, the FFI caused them innumerable delays. Some were caused by the simple trick of falsifying signposts.

Also, the FFI greatly increased the mobility of the main allied forces; the French could be depended upon to mop up any German pockets to the side of the advancing American armies. The estimate made about D-Day by SHAEF that, in the broadest sense, some 3 million Frenchmen could be depended on to "resist" actively was no doubt roughly correct. The figure included the 350,000 men of the Maquis, FT-P and "Armée Secrète", with perhaps as many in close contact with them; and the couple of million of trade unionists who could be depended upon to start, when necessary, a general strike. The French railwaymen did wonders during those months following D-Day, and often before. They and the postmen had, indeed, throughout been of the greatest help to the Resistance and to the Maquis.

Yet, there were many things that had prevented the Resistance from being a real nation-wide *levée en masse*. There was the shortage of arms. As late as May 1944 the head of the Maquis organization was still giving the number of "well-armed" men in France as 35,000–40,000 —and of these only 10,000 had munitions for more than one day's fighting. But, on the other hand, there are also many who have persisted in stressing the fact that the Resistance was the movement of a *minority*—even though in August 1944 it acquired a good many short-term hangers-on when it suddenly became fashionable and advantageous to be *résistant*.

No doubt, rebellion before 1944 was both impractical and suicidal, and, instinctively, France wanted to *survive* and shared Pétain's dread of "polonization". But if, as the Allied Command reckoned, *the working-class* would, in 1944, fully support the Resistance if necessary it knew that a large part of the peasantry and of the *petite bourgeoisie* were passive in the main, and that under the Germans their protest had been a silent protest—like that of the old woman and her daughter in Vercors' *Silence de la Mer*, the most famous "Resistance" novel written at the time and one which was sharply attacked in the Soviet press. And the upper *bourgeoisie* was, in the main, indifferent, if not downright hostile to the Resistance, with its talk of Revolution and a "New Deal".

In a sense, the Resistance was in the tradition of 1792 and the Commune; but "Versailles" sat tight, waited, and gathered strength. It could afford to wait "as long as the Germans were there", as Mauriac had said. Was this unfair? Yes and no. For after the Germans had gone, it was other forces of Order, and not the forces of Revolution that were to gain control of France.

8. WHY DID FRANCE RESIST?

Why, one may ask, did France—or a part of France—resist at all? To resist was contrary to every primitive instinct of self-preservation; it was contrary also to the philosophy of Vichy which consisted in "sitting tight" and in "keeping out of it", and in "taking a long view of history"—rather with the implication that French lives were too precious to waste, especially after all the losses France had suffered since 1914, and, indeed, since the Napoleonic wars; and that only by "adapting" herself to whatever new Europe might emerge after the war, did she have a chance of surviving at all. All this was mixed up with the cultivation of a sort of spiritual superiority complex, inspired by the reading of Péguy, with sentimentalizing *la vieille France*, with its old sterling values, and Joan of Arc and the Cathedral of Chartres, and with the rather childish idea that if the worst came to the worst the sweetness of French life and the good humour of French wine would, in a few generations, turn the Germans into members of a higher civilization. At heart, not many believed in this—except possibly for a short time after the Armistice; but it was a good screen for *attentisme*—and also for plain cowardice. And yet, before long, there were men and women who *did* resist. This Resistance in the early days of Vichy and of the Occupation was totally disinterested. They resisted because it was, to them, a matter of ordinary self-respect to do so. They were unwilling to accept the final defeat of France; the sight of a Nazi treading on French soil made them squirm; the thought that they would be expected to "accept" Hitler and Hitlerism as part of the French "way of life" was morally and physically unbearable. Equally unbearable was the thought that while London was "taking it", or that while the Red Army was fighting the battle of Moscow or the Battle of Stalingrad, France was "doing nothing".

The noblest French resisters were those who took up the struggle when the outcome of the war was still uncertain; later, after the North-Africa Landing, after Stalingrad, and especially after D-Day, only too many jumped on the Resistance bandwagon, in the hope of being duly rewarded by the winning side. At times, the sight of the politicians rushing to join de Gaulle at Algiers was about as unsavoury as the sight of others running after Laval and the Marshal at Vichy.

How did people come to join the active Resistance? Often it started in a small and almost trivial way; one kept for somebody else a few compromising papers; or one put up somebody in danger of arrest; solidarity led to action: to hiding arms, to going on "missions"; in time, Resistance became to many a full-time job. No doubt there were those who worked inside the Vichy administration, or even in Government offices in Paris, and who still belonged to the Resistance; theirs also was a dangerous life; but it was not as dangerous as that of full-time resisters—those who had to leave their work, their families, and live in hiding, with forged papers, and often without money. All the time the resister had to be on the alert, watch every step he made, and every word he uttered; he had to learn to look calm when the Germans examined his forged papers; when he stayed at an hotel, it was better to leave at the break of dawn, before the police arrived on their daily inspection; he learned to distrust everybody; and the thought that, as a result of his slightest slip, he might be not just killed, but tortured (and who could be absolutely sure that, under torture, he would not speak?) must have been the most haunting thought of all.[20]

No doubt, during the first couple of years, in the Vichy Zone, it was not desperately dangerous to belong to an "intellectual" Resistance movement but, in the North it was dangerous from the outset to resist actively in any way. And later, with Pucheu adding to the numerous Vichy police forces the special "Police des Questions Juives" and the SPAC, the "Service de Police Anti-Communiste", which could operate throughout France, not to mention Darnand's Milice, that French version of the SS, it became almost as dangerous to be in the South as in the North. Henri Michel mentions, for instance, one particularly notorious *Brigade Spéciale* at the Préfecture de Police in Paris—that of the *commissaire* David—which, in three years, arrested 2,611 people, of whom 495 were handed over to the Germans and 125 shot. And everybody knew of horrible places like the "French Gestapo" building in the rue Lauriston, run by a famous French policeman, Bony, who had sold himself to the Germans simply for money, and another, even more notorious policeman, Laffont, clad in SS uniform, the stories of

[20] Henri Michel, *op. cit.*, pp. 120–1. Thus, it was the prospect of being tortured that made Pierre Brossolette kill himself by throwing himself out of a window of the Ministry of the Interior. He knew too many secrets. Another Resistance leader, Bingen, poisoned himself after being arrested.

whose sadistic orgies in the torture chambers of the "French Gestapo" sent cold shivers down the back of even those who kept clear of the Resistance.[21]

The Vichy law of August 14, 1941 set up at every *cour d'appel* a special tribunal that meted out "quick justice" in all cases of "Communist or Anarchist activity". Further, a *Tribunal d'Etat* was set up in Lyon and Paris with judges who did not necessarily belong to the *Magistrature*, and could simply be appointed *ad hoc* by the Vichy Government. In 1944 Darnand set up special Courts-Martial (*cours martiales*) to deal with the Resistance.[22] And all this vast police and legal machinery was there to fight the resistance, in addition to the German police services. These included the Abwehr, the Geheime Feldpolizei, the Feldgendarmerie, and the following four, all popularly known as "Gestapo"—the SD (Sicherheitsdienst), the Sipo (Sicherheitspolizei), the Kripo (Kriminalpolizei), and the Gestapo proper. To these should be added the special French anti-Jewish, anti-Masonic, and anti-Communist police forces.

Although, as is generally known, many French policemen helped people to escape arrest, one of the grimmest phenomena of the years of Vichy and the Occupation is the fact that *so many thousands of Frenchmen should have conscientiously helped the Germans to track down fellow-Frenchmen*. Without the help of these French policemen and plain-clothes men who, more easily than any German could have done, wormed themselves into the confidence of the Resistance, the Resistance would not have suffered such heavy losses.[23] It was the French, and not the German police, who, in the Avenue Henri-Martin in Paris, "questioned" more than two thousand people; it was also the same French police team who claimed the credit for having detected fifty-four wireless transmitters and for having captured twenty tons of parachuted arms.

No doubt, in the Liberation of Paris the "police strike" was a very important episode, and many of the police, particularly of the relatively "harmless" *police municipale* were fully in sympathy with the Resistance; but how many policemen at the Préfecture, one may well wonder, struck, in order to create an alibi for themselves and for their whole

---

[21] Dunan, *op. cit.*, pp. 30–1.

[22] Rather to the embarrassment of the judges, Pétain's defence claimed that the various emergency tribunals had been set up at the request of the regular Vichy magistrates who did not want to "compromise" themselves by trying "terrorists", and preferred to leave this rough justice to the police.

[23] De Gaulle's famous agent, Colonel Rémy, defined with grim irony the word *gestapo* in the "glossary" appended to his *Mémoires d'un agent secret de la France Libre*: Gestapo: German police organism... whose reputation of efficiency was greatly exaggerated. Without the help of the Milice and other collaborators, it would have caused few ravages. (*Op. cit.*, p. 533.)

profession? Although this particular episode and also many genuine good turns done to suspects by French policemen, notably during house searches, have tended to create the impression that there were many "good fellows" among them, the net result of the French police's activity during the Occupation and the Vichy régime has still been to make the *policier*, never greatly loved in France, a particularly distasteful character. Not only that; but since the war, third-degree methods learned from the Gestapo during the years of "co-operation" have tended to ingrain themselves into the daily routine of the French police, not in North Africa only, but even in France itself. A leading jurist like Maître Maurice Garçon has denounced in no uncertain terms, notably in several articles in the *Monde*, the virtual legalization of torture since the war.

Especially since 1942 the Resistance had to live constantly in the shadow of torture and death. The Maquis and the FFI knew that, in case of capture, they would be shot as "terrorists".

It is difficult to understand the Resistance unless one realizes the sinister atmosphere in which it was born and in which it grew up.... It was full of enemy agents. Every arrest not only created a void, but increased mutual distrust and multiplied the dangers. Every release by the Gestapo, every escape was suspect.[24]

Thirty thousand people of the Resistance were shot, and out of the 112,000 men and women deported to Germany only 35,000 returned alive—and many of them physical and mental wrecks.

Once again, it should be emphasized that the real Resistance was only a minority of the French people; for one thing, the material means of extending the Resistance, except after D-Day, were inadequate. It often suffered from lack of unity, from rivalries, and from the inevitable infiltration of racketeers and profiteers. The military part it played was, in the vast panorama of the second world war, a small and modest one; it has lately become fashionable, especially among people with not very good consciences, to attack the Resistance; while many people who were most active in the Resistance, have spoken bitterly of the final result of it all: *that* was not what they had hoped for. The Resistance had failed to create a "new France"—even though it had, at least to some extent, provided France with human material for a new government and administrative personnel. But times change; and many of these people have since become as conformist as though they were elder statesmen inherited from the Third Republic. As Mauriac was

---

[24] H. Michel, *op. cit.*, pp. 125–6. There is a remarkable essay on the subject in J.-P. Sartre's *Situations*, vol. III (Paris, 1948). Also, numerous novels have described the intense nervous strain that Resistance imposed on its members, notably Roger Vailland's admirable *Drôle de Jeu* (Paris, 1945).

to say of Bidault: "What an interplanetary distance between the Bidault of 1939 and our present Foreign Minister!"

And yet the Resistance had not been in vain: thanks to it France was able to look other nations straight in the face. For this the Communists, who, inspired by the Red Army, took very grave risks in the Resistance, claim the greater part of the credit. The very fact that the Maquis and the FFI were partly Communist has made anti-Communists almost identify the Resistance with Communism—and to attribute certain summary executions and other acts of violence to "Communist banditry"—when, in reality, most of these acts of violence were quite understandable in a country that was at last shaking off four years of German and police oppression.

For the country, by 1943–4, was in a violent and exasperated mood. There was tragedy in many homes. France had lost the war of 1940; 115,000 had been killed or were missing; 1,800,000 prisoners were in Germany; and since the introduction of the STO 600,000 more had been sent there. Over 100,000 men and women of the Resistance were dying a slow death in German concentration camps. The country was undernourished; there were the Allied bombings; enemy propaganda and intimidation did all it could to break the people's spirit. Considering the small help received from abroad, and the refusal (with rare exceptions) of the French moneyed classes to help, it is hard to see how the Resistance could have done more than it did.

9. POST-MORTEM ON THE RESISTANCE

It is interesting to see how those who were in the Resistance looked back upon it all after the lapse of several years.

On the eighth anniversary of the Liberation of Paris—in August 1952—the *Observateur* had the fruitful idea of asking a large number of old Resisters belonging to various political groups, to say what they felt about it all. The keynote of it all was bitterness and disillusionment; and yet, at the same time, a feeling that it was *still* worth it, if only because Resistance was a kind of moral imperative—to some!

Roger Stéphane, who was associated with "Combat", denied that the Resistance had any real positive value, but maintained that it had an enormous "negative" value. It was not constructive, whatever either the Catholic or Communist resisters may have believed at the time; but it was valuable as a *refusal*, as a *protest*. And even in the case of the Catholics and Communists, the Resistance was primarily *anti*-something rather than *pro*-anything.

I do not think that any of the Communists seriously believed that, with the departure of the Germans, a Socialist Republic (one had not yet heard in those days of "people's democracy") would be born. The Communists fought without any positive aims; they fought *against* reaction and *against* Fascism. And the Worker, who does not like a foreign occupation, simply fought against the Boche. And the same, after all, is true of the Catholics; they were disgusted with the pharisaical ways of old Pétain and with the totalitarianism of his master, Hitler.

What mattered most, he went on, was not the *action* of these people, but the *attitude* they adopted—what he called *témoignage*—and this applied, fundamentally, to individual, unorganized resisters almost as much as to the Communists and Catholics. No doubt, the Communists had killed a few Germans—a few hundred, perhaps a few thousand; but not enough to make any difference to the outcome of the war. There was the *bataille du rail*; but that, after all, had not made any vital difference either. No doubt, the clandestine press did a good deal to keep up people's morale, *but it was small stuff, compared with the BBC.*

When all is said and done, [Stéphane concluded] the Resistance was not so much an *action* as a *refusal.* Thanks to this refusal, we were able to look the Russian, American, and British soldiers straight in the eyes without blushing.... And, to paraphrase Churchill's famous phrase about the RAF in the Battle of Britain, one might say: Never have so many run so many risks for so little.... It may seem ludicrous; but it is this ludicrous little thing—this refusal to submit—which saved our human dignity.

If to Stéphane, the Resistance was purely negative, Bourdet, of "Combat", looked at it rather differently. He, and many others in the Resistance, did have hopes and illusions that a better France would be the reward for all the sacrifices made. They believed in the Charter of the CNR; yet when, in the summer of 1945, he returned from Buchenwald, he felt that everything had already gone wrong. Partly because of de Gaulle; partly because of the Communists, who had prevented the Resistance from becoming a united force.

Only what was the force that could transform France? [Bourdet wrote]. Some simply said, The Communist Party, and the "Fronts" surrounding it. No doubt if the CP had taken the lead immediately after the capitulation, I, like many others, would certainly have followed. This unique and privileged position of the CP would no doubt have created in the Party itself a new spirit which might have satisfied all the Resisters ... But the Party continued to be confused and bewildered by the Soviet-German Pact, and *as* a Party, it wasted a whole year (June 1940 to June 1941). This was not altered by the intelligence and courage of many individual Communists who joined the Resistance in 1940. The CP continued to be handicapped, even despite all the vast treasures of heroism it spent on the Resistance from July 1941 on.... The CP remained a Resistance organization, one among many others, and we were not inclined to submit to it.

Then, what was the alternative? Bourdet said that there was really only one chance for a new France: the Resistance *as a whole,* including the Communists (but not with the Communists as the leaders), and with de Gaulle at its head, should have built the new France:

A great political force should have been constituted, comprising the Communists, all the revolutionary, Socialist and near-Socialist elements of the Resistance, regardless of their philosophical views, and comprising the entire rank and file and most of the leaders of the Resistance.

No doubt, he went on, there were snags; men like Bidault[25] wanted to reconstitute Christian Democracy on a clerical basis, and some of the Socialists were being sectarian, and thinking in terms of simply re-forming the old SFIO. The Communists, too, might have been hostile —just like the Communist to whom, in 1943, Bourdet had proposed a grand Resistance party on the lines indicated above, and who had told him that there was only "one historical reality, the CP, and that if the others did not follow it, the CP would fight them . . ."

But even these difficulties, he wrote, could have been overcome. Because there was de Gaulle, and de Gaulle's prestige was such that he could in 1944 have got all the necessary support, "had he remained faithful to his mission". But de Gaulle was to turn his back on the Resistance. Time and again de Gaulle had cold-shouldered and insulted the Resistance leaders during his triumphal journeys through France in the autumn of 1944. And on the day of the Liberation of Paris he had uttered the word "Renovation", and had avoided the word "Revolution".

The old bourgeois society was rapidly put back in its place, while the spontaneous, somewhat anarchical, but still terribly vital reforms of the Resistance were cast aside. Later, point was added to this by the catastrophic replacement of Mendès-France by Pleven. . . . For months afterwards I still tried to go on believing in de Gaulle, but in the end I understood that at Algiers de Gaulle had already fallen into the hands of the military and administrative castes of the bourgeoisie, and that in Paris he was back in his own old obsolete *milieu* and that here, in Paris, a hundred thousand "haves" were counting on de Gaulle to save them from the "Revolution"—*our* Revolution, the Revolution of the Resistance.

Having turned his back on the Resistance, having treated with contempt those grandiloquent soldiers in rags, with too many stripes—how like the soldiers of 1793 some of them were!—de Gaulle finally abandoned the ideal of the Resistance to the Communists; "and our dream, which might so easily have come true, was ruined".

Albert Gazier, the Socialist leader, was on the whole, less hard on de Gaulle. If dreams of the Resistance came to very little—though, no doubt some of these became, in a fragmentary way, a reality thanks to

[25] *Cf.* Bourdet's opinion below on Bidault's "surrender" of the Resistance to the Communists.

the social and economic legislation of 1945–6—it was because the French people were not sufficiently interested.

Those who had great illusions in August 1944 were not as numerous as one would like to think. Most of the Socialists, for instance, did not imagine that the disappearance of the capitalist system and the creation of a Socialist democracy were possible in a foreseeable future.... Few Socialists talked of "revolution", even of a "legal revolution", as Bidault had done.... For one thing, the war was not over yet. And people also had too many worries: the deportees and the prisoners had not yet returned, and problems like food, transport, production, the purge, the recasting of the political institutions, the cost of living, inflation, etc, took up people's thoughts....

Agreement with the Communists, according to Gazier, had become very difficult owing to the international situation; as for the "Revolution", of which so many men of the Resistance had dreamed in 1944, it had come up against the desire, on the part of the majority of the people, to "return to pre-war"—with, more or less, the same kind of institutions, political parties, and newspapers.

Rather the same line was taken by Francisque Gay, of the MRP.

"Back to the Third Republic" was the fundamental desire of the old parties. One had to be a pretty learned man to know the difference between the Constitution of 1946 and that of 1875.... No doubt some new things were done—based on ideas inherited from the Resistance: several of the nationalizations had been carried out very well, and the Fourth Republic could be proud of the new system of social security and of family allowances; but, by and large, those responsible for France's financial and economic policy had shown neither great courage nor great imagination. Although the MRP had, at the beginning, faithfully reflected the spirit of the Resistance, it had not done much to carry through the reforms that had been talked about so much. Both the MRP and Gaullism declined, because they had both failed in "renewing" France; and the more "experienced" older parties cashed in on this double failure.

The trouble with the MRP was, according to Francisque Gay, himself a leader of the MRP, that instead of being inspired, as it was at first, by the Christian-Socialist ideals of Marc Sangnier, it tended to take up, instead, the paternalist tradition of La Tour du Pin, Albert de Mun, Henri Bazire and Jacques Piou.

Pierre Hervé, speaking for the Communists, called for a regrouping of the old Resistance forces: he mocked the Gaullists "who have now through their own fault, and because of de Gaulle's own absurd anti-Communism ... been outwitted by the old Vichyites". Had the Resistance stayed together, none of this would have happened. The Resistance, he said, must get together again, not only to carry out more fully the programme of the CNR, but also to prevent the enslavement of France by America.

Blocq-Mascart, of OCM, attributed the failure of the Resistance to the fact that "the Communists knew exactly what they wanted", while the others did not. All the same, France was in a revolutionary temper in 1944, and the non-Communists of the Resistance could still have agreed on a certain minimum programme of "humanist Socialism"—a sort of New Deal. But it all came to very little. "Whereas a new democracy should have emerged from revolution, the fear of revolution brought about a routine democracy, without any profound reforms having been carried out."

The part played by the Resistance, both at home and abroad, against the Occupation, in the Liberation battles, and in the final stages of the war against Nazi Germany constitutes a glorious period between two mediocre periods of our history.

Emmanuel d'Astier de la Vigerie also felt that great hopes had been aroused by the Resistance, and these had found expression in the reforms of 1945–6. But then all went topsy-turvy, under American influence. But what still remained in France was *a Resistance temperament*. The Resistance had been the meeting-place for men of different political views, but of similar temperaments; and d'Astier foresaw conditions in which people with the "Resistance" temperament would get together again for some major national task—such as preventing war.

It is true that something of that kind was to be observed during the years following d'Astier's prophesy: the opposition in the country to German rearmament and to EDC certainly assembled as varied a crowd of people as the Resistance—old-time nationalists, Gaullists, Communists, Neutralists, and, above all, many who had been active in the Resistance.

The theme of the widespread "Nostalgia for pre-war", which tended to paralyse the Resistance, is also to be found in Gilles Martinet's attempt to answer the question whether the Resistance really "believed in its Revolution".

France [he said] wanted a change. But—let's admit it: for many of our fellow-countrymen this change was rather like a return to pre-war. There was a nostalgia for pre-war conditions, which, seen from afar, looked even better than they had been in reality. There was, above all, a desire for peace and well-being. . . . As for the Communist Party, one only has to read the papers it published during the Occupation to see that it was not preparing for a *coup de force*, but was planning to co-operate for a long time in coalition governments. . . . It was very distrustful of any "revolutionary" talk.

Nevertheless, he went on, with the Third Republic discredited just as much on the Right as on the Left, and with Socialism alone capable of making the necessary reconstruction efforts required to put France on her feet, the most dynamic part of France was, in 1945-6, on the Left. These were primarily the men of the Resistance—Socialists and Communists. It was not true that de Gaulle could have set up a personal dictatorship. If de Gaulle suddenly resigned in January 1946, it was precisely because he realized that the Left continued to hold the initiative. Later, the Marshall Plan altered all that; for it took the initiative out of the hands of the Left. It was not a French solution of France's post-war problems; whereas the fundamental Socialism of the Resistance would have been. True, the Resistance was, on the face of it, neither Right nor Left;

but to say this [said Martinet] is to forget the political nature of the enemy, and to ignore the social and economic context of the struggle. There could be no "revolution by the Resistance", but, unless it renounced itself, the Resistance could lead to one thing only—which was Socialism.

And his conclusion is singularly like that of some of the other writers already quoted: the struggle in France for a more "independent" policy in 1952 had some striking affinities with the struggle for freedom fought by the Resistance: again, it was not so much a question of Left and Right as a question of "temperament".

It may be argued that this parallel is far-fetched. Yet there is no doubt that, apart from the formal distinction in France between Left and Right, there is a much deeper psychological distinction between the Resisters and the pro-Resisters, on the one hand, and the different brands of defeatists (using the word in a very broad sense, of course) on the other. Other countries have known similar phenomena; in England the two temperaments have an (albeit superficial) parallel in the Churchill-Chamberlain conflict—but in England the question of independence was never put with quite the same tragic sharpness as in France.

THE COMMUNISTS, THE WAR AND THE RESISTANCE

THE anti-Nazi record of the Communists before the war, the tragic dilemma that the Soviet-German Pact created for them in August 1939, and the exceptionally large place they held in the Resistance make it important to examine the Communist case particularly closely. All the more so, as the post-war political quarrels in France are filled with echoes of the Communists' pre-war and war-time history.

The announcement on August 24, 1939, that a German-Soviet non-aggression pact had been signed in Moscow by Molotov and Ribbentrop threw the French Communists into a state of utter confusion. For years they had been in the vanguard of the "struggle against Fascism"; since 1933 Hitler had been denounced with ever-growing violence as enemy number one of world peace by the whole propaganda machine of the CP; it was primarily "against Hitler" that French Communists had fought in Spain; they had, louder and more unanimously than any other body of French opinion, denounced Munich as a betrayal; to be anti-Nazi had become like second nature with every French Communist; Hitler, to them, as to many others, was the ally of all that was most vile and reactionary in France—of all those people who, on the quiet, were saying: "*Hitler plutôt que le Front Populaire.*"

People still remembered only too clearly the humiliating and sinister Ribbentrop visit to Paris in December 1938, when Hitler's Foreign Minister and the detested Bonnet exchanged ominous compliments on the radio. More and more openly was there talk during the months that followed Munich, of a "free hand in the East" for Hitler, and the *Matin*, with Bonnet's approval, ran a series of articles on the satellization of the Ukraine by Germany.

The greatest firmness towards Hitler seemed to the Communists the only course. When in April 1939 Déat wrote in the *Oeuvre* his famous article "Die for Danzig?", recommending, in effect, a Polish "Munich", the Communist press denounced this line of argument with the greatest violence; Duclos, during the same month, declared: "No further capitulations to Hitler"; and the *Humanité*, some time later, drew attention to the "suspect intrigues of Burckhart, the League of

Nations High Commisioner at Danzig, in which it suspected a revival of the "Runciman technique".

With seventy-two deputies in the Chamber, the Communists had become, since the 1936 election, a major political force in France—among the public generally, in Parliament and in the trade unions. They had been the most "dynamic" element in the great Popular Front movement that had arrested the progress of "Fascism" in France and had extracted from a reluctant and frightened bourgeoisie the labour reforms of 1936. The Popular Front had, since then, no doubt degenerated; there had been Blum's "pause" of 1937; there had been his non-intervention policy in Spain, there had, above all, been Munich, which Blum had accepted "with mixed feelings of cowardly relief and shame". Daladier, another "leader" of the Popular Front, had since gone over almost completely to the other side; he had broken the general strike of November 1938, and had since been behaving in a grim and rather unaccountable way, striking strong-man attitudes which might mean something, but which might also mean nothing at all. Bonnet, the sinister Bonnet, at any rate, continued to be his Foreign Minister.

After the Prague *coup* of March 15, 1939, Daladier seemed in a feverish hurry to conclude an alliance with the Soviet Union, but Bonnet kept on restraining him, and, across the Channel, Mr Chamberlain was not very keen either. True, a British guarantee, in addition to the Franco-Polish alliance, had been given to Poland; only what did it mean without a proper alliance with Moscow?

No doubt, the possibility of a Berlin-Moscow deal was not to be ruled out, especially since Stalin's speech in March, in which he declared that Russia had no intention of pulling other people's chestnuts out of the fire; soon afterwards, Litvinov, who had for years symbolized Russia's desire for collective security and for a closer understanding with the Western powers, was dismissed. The German press openly welcomed this as "a highly significant development".

Even so, the French Communists who, over the past five years, had acquired certain ways of thinking, and who had been taught to look upon the Soviet Union as the stronghold of world peace and anti-Fascist resistance were still unwilling to face the possibility of a Russian *volte-face*—despite the ominous free-hand-in-the-East implications of Munich and of the Bonnet-Ribbentrop meeting. They went on thinking that it was not yet too late to repair the damage done by Munich. Hence the "no more surrenders to Hitler" slogans when Germany, in April, proceeded to turn the heat on Poland.

To see the tragedy of the French Communists—for it was the greatest tragedy in their history—in proper perspective, it is necessary briefly to examine Russia's motives in signing the Soviet-German Pact of August 1939. Moscow had, since Munich, become wholly distrustful of Britain and France. It became Stalin's obsession to keep the Soviet Union out of the war—which, he was deeply convinced, was coming. Russia in 1939 was not militarily prepared to fight Nazi Germany, and had, at any price, to gain at least two or three years' grace. Even in 1941, after two years of feverish rearmament, it was to be touch-and-go. Whether the British and French military missions which, at the eleventh hour, were sent to Moscow had any serious intention of making a hard-and-fast alliance with Russia or not, seems almost irrelevant. The only condition in which such an alliance might still conceivably have acted as a deterrent on Hitler was the free passage of the Red Army through Poland; once this condition was refused, the alliance became altogether pointless. One even wonders whether the Polish refusal to let the Russian Army enter Polish territory was not received by Moscow with a sigh of relief. It postponed for an indefinite time the danger of a clash between the Red Army and Hitler's Wehrmacht. The Russians must also have had a very strong suspicion that if they intervened in the defence of Poland, Britain and France would not be able to do much about it. As it turned out, they were unable to do anything to help Poland; would they have done any more to help Poland-plus-Russia? In 1938, before the Siegfried Line was completed, and while the Bohemian Bastion was still held by the Czech Army, a two-front war against Hitler was still a practical possibility; by 1939 Germany had become practically invulnerable in the West and was also much stronger both on land and in the air than in 1938. To the Russians the dangers of an alliance with France and Britain in 1939 were very real indeed; the chances were that if Hitler struck in the East, the march on Warsaw would be followed by a march on Moscow, with the Western armies doing little or nothing to help, and Chamberlain and Bonnet and many others rubbing their hands on the quiet.

The Soviet-German Pact, on the other hand, carried with it the immediate advantage of being able to push the Soviet frontier a long distance to the West through the incorporation in the Soviet Union of, first, Eastern Poland and then the Baltic States, both of which seemed at that time an unquestionable strategic advantage. No doubt in 1941, all these territories were rapidly abandoned by the Red Army, but may, even so, have been sufficient to use up just enough German military energy to make a difference to the striking force of the Wehrmacht by the time it reached the outskirts of Moscow. Similarly, the Soviet-Finnish war was primarily dictated by the urgent need to reduce the terrible vulnerability of Leningrad. (The biggest Soviet blunder in the case of Finland was, of course, the—rapidly abandoned—attempt to inflict on her a Communist government from outside.) So in a strictly strategic sense the Soviet-German Pact of 1939 was to justify itself fully in 1941, assuming—and that was Moscow's well-considered assumption in the summer of 1939—that nothing could stop Hitler from attacking Poland, except possibly a firm Russian-Polish alliance—but even in this case a dirty deal between Hitler and the West was not to be ruled out. Was the risk worth taking?

Instead, Stalin preferred to "risk" a German attack on Western Europe; and this is where he made his worst miscalculation: he did not believe that France would be smashed in five weeks. No doubt it looked like an ugly revenge for the free-hand-in-the-East tendencies of the Bonnet-Chamberlain school of thought, but, short of stopping the war altogether after the Polish campaign (and an attempt was to be made in that direction) Stalin had not much choice. The decision now lay with Hitler.

But Moscow still hoped that if Germany attacked in the West, it would mean a long war, in which Germany would exhaust much of her strength, after which conditions advantageous to Russia would be created for either a general peace settlement, or a Russian intervention against Germany. That, sooner or later, Russia would have to fight Germany was generally assumed in Moscow; but in 1939 Russia preferred to choose the time, rather than let Hitler choose it. The rapid collapse of France wrecked all these calculations. If Stalin did not pay the penalty for his error until 1941, he largely had to thank the Battle of Britain for it, a point never mentioned in Soviet histories of the war.

As regards the French Communist Party, the truth is that, obsessed as he was with the immediate security of the Soviet Union, Stalin simply decided to disregard their difficulties. If the French Communists were to be let down in 1939, it couldn't be helped. To Stalin, much bigger issues were at stake. The fact that they had been consciously sacrificed by Russia in the name of higher considerations (the survival of the Soviet Union) does not seem to have occurred to them—at least not until much later. But in 1939 the French Communists were certainly put in a psychologically agonizing position.

The German-Soviet Pact came to the Communists, as Gabriel Péri was to say, like a bolt from the blue. Some couldn't believe it. When, however, the news was confirmed, their first reaction was to say that the Soviet Union could not be wrong; it was a good thing—a triumph for peace. The *Humanité*, greeting the Pact as a triumph for peace, clamoured that Daladier fly immediately to Moscow and join the "peace pact". A pathetic *communiqué* was issued by the Communist parliamentary group on August 25 in which Thorez was quoted as saying at its meeting that day that, through this pact, the Soviet Union "had dislocated the bloc of aggressors who had joined forces under the anti-Comintern Pact". But, Thorez added:

If Hitler still unleashes war, then let him know that he will have the people of France solidly united against him, with the Communists in their front rank, ready to defend the security of their country and the freedom and independence of nations.

Also, said Thorez, the Communist Party fully approved the military precautions taken by the French Government and its preparations for going to the aid of Poland if she were attacked. And Thorez concluded:

We desire the conclusion of a Franco-Anglo-Soviet alliance which remains both necessary and perfectly possible. Such an alliance would usefully complete the Franco-Soviet mutual assistance pact which is still in force. . . .

It seems quite obvious that, after the conclusion of the German-Soviet Pact, the Russians had not even taken the trouble to give the French Communists a clear lead. With their idea of turning the German-Soviet Pact into a wider peace pact the French Communists were simply groping in the dark, still hoping for some miracle to happen. But the dice had been cast, and there was to be no miracle. No doubt there were some Communists who got much nearer the truth, but were unable to persuade the leadership that the truth should be told to the French people. Jacques Sadoul, who was the Paris correspondent of *Isvestia* wrote a personal note to de Monzie, a member of the Daladier Government, in which he expressed his dismay at the jubilant line taken by the *Humanité*, adding for de Monzie's information:

To destroy Hitler, we shall need the co-operation of the USSR. We shall have it at the right moment—so Souritz (the Soviet Ambassador) has just told me. *But this help will not come until the USSR is convinced that we mean business; that France and England really intend to fight a total war against Hitler,* till his final downfall. Our task as French Communists should be to see to it that the hour of Soviet co-operation should strike very soon and that this co-operation is not rendered impossible by the blunders of Paris and our excessive distrust *vis-à-vis* Moscow, which it does not deserve.[1]

If this very sensible note was specially intended for Daladier's notice, he did not take the trouble to examine all its implications. He preferred to crash ahead against the French Communists—Moscow might have known. Nor was Sadoul able to impress his views on the French Communist leadership. So they continued the incredible line that the Pact was good news. A few lost all faith in miracles from the start; on the day after the Thorez statement, five deputies resigned from the CP, to be followed in the next few months, by several more, a total of 21 out of 72. But the Communists, with Thorez at their head, continued their patriotic line, even after all possibility of a "wider peace pact" had vanished. On September 2 they voted the military credits, which implied a declaration of war on Germany.

[1] Anatole de Monzie, *Ci-devant* (Paris, 1941), pp. 143–4.

They had been put in an impossible position. The Soviet Union was being accused by everybody of the blackest treachery; and the Communists were losing all their best friends in France. On August 29 the Union of French Intellectuals expressed their "stupefaction at the *volte-face* of the Soviet leaders", and among the signatories were such emphatically left-wing intellectuals as Joliot-Curie, Langevin, Victor Basch and Albert Bayet. Pierre Cot—another future pro-Communist and winner of a Stalin peace prize in 1954—ferociously attacked the Soviet Union for having played the trick of an "inverted Munich" with a "free hand in the West" on France.

The *munichois* screamed loudest and demanded the most savage reprisals against the Communists; Doriot declared:

Stalin has betrayed France! our reply must be the destruction of Communism, the dissolution of the Party of traitors, the imprisonment of their leaders....

Daladier was only too glad to oblige. A few days after the announcement of the Moscow Pact, all Communist papers were prohibited, and a police terror was unleashed against the Communist *militants*. On September 26, after the Russian invasion of Eastern Poland, the Communist Party was dissolved by decree. Those who had remained in the Party formed a new *groupe*, the *Groupe Ouvrier et Paysan*, and it was in their name that Ramette and Florimond Bonte sent Herriot the famous letter of October 1 asking that he call Parliament in order to discuss the Soviet German peace proposals after the collapse of Poland.

We want a just and lasting peace; we believe it can be rapidly obtained, for apart from the Western warmongers and Nazi Germany, there is also the power of the Soviet Union, which will help to build collective security....

In England, Mr Lloyd George took very much the same line—with impunity. But in Paris all hell broke loose. And, paradoxically enough, it was the *munichois*, the people who were most unfavourable to the war against Nazi Germany (which, they were convinced, had been started in the most unfavourable conditions) were the loudest in their denunciation of the Communists' "treason". *Was it because they knew that the country on the whole was not enthusiastic about the war, and that if a peace settlement were made, the Communists would get all the credit for it?*

On October 7, the wholesale arrest of Communist deputies began, except, for the time being, of those who were in the Army. A certain number, Duclos and Frachon among them, went into hiding, but the others were arrested, and forty-four (including some of those who were in the Army) were to be brought up for trial in March 1940.

It was about this time that an event of lasting importance occurred: the desertion from the Army by Maurice Thorez. He escaped to Belgium, and, some months later, found his way to Russia. In a well-documented, but very biased book, *Les Communists Français pendant la drôle de guerre*, A. Rossi denounces as completely unfounded the Communist argument that Thorez deserted, because if he hadn't, he would have been arrested, whereas by "deserting" he could continue, from abroad, to guide the Party. "No arrests", he says, "were made among the *mobilisés* at that time." Quite true—but it was only a matter of time; Fajon, who also was *mobilisé* was to be arrested after the Communists' trial in March. So were the other mobilized deputies.

The Party was in a state of great confusion, and there is a good deal of truth in the argument that if the Daladier Government had not embarked on a policy of repression and terrorism against them, they would have disintegrated to a much greater extent than they did. Even Rossi admits that persecution had strengthened the solidarity among the Communists, if only because of the fear of being thought a coward and a traitor to one's comrades. For all that, the bewilderment was great. No doubt there were some who, like the omniscient Communists in Aragon's novel (written long after the event in 1950) knew from the outset that the Russian occupation of Eastern Poland was "a good thing in the long run"; but in 1939 most people still found the "fourth partition of Poland" (with Molotov's insulting remarks on Poland thrown in for good measure) hard to swallow. All the same, the Communists' proposal for a peace settlement after the collapse of Poland was politically understandable. From a purely French standpoint, it might, for all its apparent cynicism, have been welcomed by a great many people at least as much as Munich was welcomed (in the same cynical spirit) a little over a year before. But just because the proposal was made by the Communists, Bonnet, Laval and all the other future Vichyites who, at heart, considered this war as "hopeless", would not have anything to do with it. *The repercussions on the home front would have been far too great. If there was to be a peace settlement with Hitler, it was not to be under the auspices of the Communists; hence the denunciation of the Communists as traitors, defeatists, etc, and the arrest of the Communist deputies.* (Not that, strictly speaking, there was anything unparliamentary or illegal in the proposal sent to Herriot in the name of the *Groupe Ouvrier et Paysan*, at that time a properly constituted parliamentary group—a point conceded even by M. Rossi.)

It was not then—while there was still hope of a peace settlement on the basis of the Molotov-Ribbentrop *communiqué* of September 28— that the behaviour of the Communists was unintelligible. Whether defensible or not, whether moral or immoral, peace after the collapse of Poland *was*, after all, a policy. It is after the failure of this attempt to make peace in October 1939 that it becomes extremely difficult to make head or tail of what they were trying to do.

Anyway, who were *they*? There were a few leaders in France who had not yet been arrested. There was Thorez abroad. There was the Comintern. There were the *militants* who were still trying, as best they could, to bring out a roneotyped *Humanité*. Who was giving instructions? Who was following the instructions, and to what extent were they being followed?

It seems that the confusion as to what the French Communists ought to do was extreme, not only in France, but also in Moscow, in so far as Moscow cared at all. Through its pact with Hitler, Moscow had not "betrayed" France, as was commonly said (after Munich, Moscow had no obligations to France) but it had certainly "let down" the French Communists by putting them in a quite untenable position. They had not even been warned that the Molotov-Ribbentrop Pact was coming; they had been allowed to go on with the usual anti-Hitler propaganda right through the summer and were then expected, without any preparation, to turn the most neck-breaking somersault. It taxed to the utmost any man's blind devotion to Stalin and to the Soviet Union—all the more so as it was not at all clear how all this could ultimately square with France's interests. It was, no doubt, important to have kept the Soviet Union out of the war—but what was to happen to France? To buy off Hitler with the dead body of Poland—which was what Moscow and Berlin were now suggesting? Surely nothing could be more *munichois* in spirit, and it was difficult for the French working-class, reared in the great anti-Fascist tradition, to be enchanted with the idea. For even though the "Colonels' Poland" was "Fascist", corrupt, and incompetent, the Polish people had fought heroically against the Nazis.

Yet after the failure of the "Polish Munich", things became even more difficult for the French working-class to understand. All they knew was that the French Communists were being persecuted with great relish by Daladier's police—ostensibly for trying to play Hitler's game on orders from Moscow. The persecution was very serious. On November 18 a law was passed giving prefects complete discretion to deport any person they considered "dangerous to national defence and public security". At the end of November, after an abortive attempt by Florimond Bonte to speak at the Chamber of Deputies, the Chamber withdrew the parliamentary immunity of all Communist deputies, except of those with the Army, and Bonte was arrested on the spot, even before his parliamentary immunity had been formally withdrawn; on January 9, after seven mobilized deputies suddenly appeared in the Chamber, where they were bodily assaulted, it was decided that *all* Communist deputies, without exception, were to have their mandates cancelled. In vain, M. de Kerillis, the right-wing deputy, argued that rigorous measures should also be taken against the "other Fifth Column"—the agents of Abetz—the whole fury of Parliament was concentrated against the Communists. There followed other measures, such as the famous Sérol Decree making anyone guilty of "demoralizing the Army and Nation" liable to the death penalty. In industry, workers could be instantly dismissed or conscripted into the Army on the least suspicion of Communist activity. Thousands of Communists were put in prison or deported to North Africa, where many were to die in horrible conditions; and the cadres of the Party suffered some heavy losses.

Probably the most striking aspect of clandestine Communist activity during the "phoney war" was the half-heartedness among the *militants* themselves. It is significant, for example, that during the Resistance of 1941-4, the Communists—and other resisters—were able to print and circulate enormous quantities of clandestine literature; but the Communists did not do so in 1939-40. One would have thought that, despite police activity, the material facilities for doing propaganda were still greater than under the German occupation; and that is probably true. Nevertheless, apart from roneoed copies of the *Humanité* and a few other papers, all the *printed* propaganda material was not made in France, but smuggled in from abroad. A proper printing press requires a large number of reliable accomplices, and everything tends to show that there was, among the Communist *militants*, a lack of enthusiasm for the kind of work that the Cominform and the clandestine leaders of the Party were expecting them to do, and an acute consciousness of the unfavourable and hostile political climate in which they were working. The change of the party line had been much too abrupt as a result of the German-Soviet Pact, and readers of the clandestine *Humanité* were puzzled and worried rather than convinced. There was bitterness both against the French Government and against Russia. Among the Communist leaders themselves morale does not seem to have been very high, judging from the morose atmosphere of the Communist trial in March 1940. Although Bonte, Billoux, and one or two others put up something of a fight, most of the accused were not only in poor physical condition (they had, for one thing, been refused the privileged treatment of political prisoners) but also very much on the defensive.

On a large number of side issues the Communists in their clandestine propaganda—in so far as it was carried on at all—were on solid enough ground; they—and the French working-class—had plenty to grumble about. After the CGT, through the elimination of the Communists, had become a mere shadow of its former self, it carried very little weight with the Government and the employers, and working conditions, with poor pay for compulsory overtime, were very harsh. The soldier's pay, especially compared with that of the British soldiers, was miserable in the extreme; soldiers' families often suffered great hard-ships, and, on the other hand, war profiteering was already flourishing, the clandestine *Humanité* being full of information on fat dividends, bonus shares, etc, in French heavy industry.

Also the war in Finland had raised the big question whether the French *bourgeoisie* were not hoping to turn the war against Germany into a war against Russia. The Communists made, of course, the most of the "Weygand Army" and of the plan, "seriously considered at one time"[2] of bombing the Baku oilfields. There was a lunatic fringe in both France and England who thought it "strategically advantageous" to take on *both* Germany and Russia, the implication of such articles often being that Germany was a less important enemy than Russia.

But on the main issue, namely, on what was to happen to France—the directives of the Party were not at all convincing. First there was the Thorez interview given to a Communist paper in Belgium and reprinted a few days later in the *Daily Worker*, the purpose of which was to show that this war against Nazi Germany was an "unjust imperialist war", and that it should be shown up as such to the soldiers, peasants, workers, evacuees and soldiers' wives. Then came Dimitrov, who, in the clandestine January issue of the *Cahiers du Bolchevisme*, called upon the workers of all countries to struggle against the "im-perialist war". In particular he called on the workers of Britain and France to wage a relentless struggle against their governments, which were alone responsible for the continuation of the war; it could have stopped if they had listened to the German-Soviet declaration of Sep-tember 28. He opposed any fraternization with the Socialists, declared the Popular Front, with its anti-Fascist ideology, to be out of date, and assured the workers that their powers were *"ten times greater than during the first world war, for now they had the Soviet Union behind them"*.

Throughout the hard winter of 1939–40, and with an ominous spring approaching, France, as a whole, was becoming increasingly unhappy and demoralized. The soldiers of the "phoney war" were tired and dis-gruntled; there was much hardship among their families; the Finnish war had come to an end; Britain and France had made themselves ridiculous in the process; and the Norwegian campaign had been an unqualified disaster. Gamelin, in one of his reports, claimed that Com-munist propaganda had much to do with the demoralization of the French Army; but there is nothing to show that all, or most, of the grumbling was specifically Communist. After the German break-through at Sedan there was at least as much defeatism among the officers as among the men—probably more so; and it was not the argument that this was an "imperialist war" that shattered the French

[2] Rossi, *op. cit.*, p. 167.

Army. It was shattered by the collapse of the Maginot Line myth, by the loss of the best French and British troops in Belgium, by muddle and incompetence, by the vast superiority of the Germans in aircraft and armour. The Communist cadres had been thinned out by the waves of arrests and even where they were in action, it still seems that they were not particularly eager to spread the Dimitrov gospel of the "imperialist war"; it was the kind of propaganda which, given the French realities of the moment, could not cut much ice. To feel bitter about war profiteers was one thing; but to be consciously "anti-war" in the hope that, somehow or other, the Soviet Union would defend the French workers against Hitler's armies was to be singularly unrealistic. Was Moscow aware of it, and was the "anti-war" propaganda of Thorez, Dimitrov and others who were putting forward such "directives" intended *not* to be taken seriously by the French CP—and were they not simply in the nature of a sop to the Germans? Rossi who, if he could, would be only too glad to attribute the French *débâcle* to Communist propaganda, admits that this propaganda was in no way decisive; and he also agrees that no one could have been more shocked by the speed of the French collapse than Stalin.

But whether important or unimportant, Communist propaganda about the "imperialist war" *did*, in some measure, however small, contribute to a disaster which was *not* in the interests of the Soviet Union, and which, indeed, might have led to its annihilation but for England's refusal to surrender after the fall of France. No doubt it helped Moscow for a time to remain on good terms with Hitler, to spout platitudes about the "Anglo-French imperialists", and also to congratulate him (as Molotov was to do) on his great victory over France. Gaining time at any price was Stalin's obsession in 1939–40; it was the same even more cold-footed opportunism which, a year later, made him try to gain time—if only a few weeks—by chasing Czech, Belgian, Greek, and other "Nazi-occupied" diplomats out of Moscow, and by recognizing the anti-British Rashid Ali as the ruler of Iraq.

But to play on the loyalty of the French Communist Party, and to condemn it to years of persecution was a much more serious matter. How necessary was it for Moscow to dish out defeatist slogans to the French Communists, instead of letting them follow their first impulse— which was to fight Hitler, regardless of the German-Soviet Pact and regardless of the defeatism of the French Right? It was not till after the war that Stalin admitted that "many mistakes had been made" and that the second world war had been different from the first world war; *from the outset*, he said, it had been an anti-Fascist war of liberation. Was not his sacrifice of the French Communists one of the "mistakes" he had in mind?

The Communists were in a more morose mood than ever when the

German invasion started on May 10. Daladier later claimed that the Communists had done great damage, and quoted in particular one case of serious sabotage in an aircraft factory, after which four men, including a boy of seventeen, were shot. But it had not gone much beyond such isolated cases. During the French *débâcle* the Communists, like everybody else, were in confusion; the Comintern was spouting antediluvian propaganda such as "Just as the German workers, inspired by the Party of Thaelmann, must struggle against German imperialism, so the French workers must bring the French war culprits to heel..." etc. The temptation was great to say "We told you so", and to recall the September peace offer that had been rejected; on the other hand, it seems that some French Communists were impressed by the Russian occupation of the Baltic States—which suggested to them that Russia was very strong and that Stalin could, in some measure, influence Hitler. This perhaps explains the naïve overtures made by some Communist underlings to the German authorities after the Germans had entered Paris.

The truth, of course, is that as the Germans were sweeping across France, the Communists lost their heads as much as anybody else, and perhaps more so.

For Pétain, Laval, Bonnet and the future Vichy clan had their plans more or less prepared. But the clandestine Communist machine was dislocated, with practically all the Communist leaders in prison. Duclos, Péri, and Frachon were among the few who were still at large, but none of these remained in Paris to make contact with the Germans. Impressed by the vague idea that Hitler had Stalin to "consider", some of the local Communists in Paris (including, it is true, Jean Catelas, a deputy and a member of the Central Committee, who was later to be decapitated by the Germans) approached the Germans in an attempt to get the Communist leaders out of prison, and in the childish hope that the Germans would allow the Communist press to appear again. In return for this "legalization", these Communists were willing to help in restoring work in industry. The *Humanité* which appeared clandestinely a few days after the Germans had entered Paris denounced de Gaulle as a British agent, and expressed its satisfaction at the fraternization it had observed between French workers and German soldiers. Whoever was responsible for all this (and Radio-Moscow is supposed to have given some advice about getting the Communist press "legalized" under the German occupation), there is no evidence that this "fraternization" was the result of instructions from the Political Bureau of the French CP.

In any case, the Germans soon made it clear that they were the masters; that Moscow had not been promised anything; and that the Germans were willing to deal with Vichy and to give their patronage not to the Communists (even though they had been "against the war"), but to the Communists' worst enemies—to Doriot and his Nazi ruffians. As under the Third Republic, so under the Germans and under Vichy, the Communists were to remain the most persecuted minority.

As the German armies drove through France in May–June 1940, the Communist deputies and thousands of other Communist prisoners ("tens of thousands", Thorez was to say in 1945) were moved from prison to prison, from camp to camp, farther and farther south. If, as the Communists later claimed, Professor Georges Politzer (shot by the Germans in 1942) sent to Reynaud an appeal at the height of the invasion that all the Communists be let out, that a *lutte à outrance* be organized, and that Paris be defended "house by house and street by street", this appeal was ignored. It is true that a group of Communists, interned in the Ile d'Yeu, did ask that they be released, so that they could join the Army and help in the defence of the country; it is also true that many Communists fought bravely and died in the "imperialist war"; but there is not enough evidence to show that, even though there were many "deviations" on various levels, the Party *as such* changed its policy. The Thorez-Duclos proposals of June 6—which Thorez was to play up in 1945[3] as proof of the CP's consistent anti-Hitlerism (no mention of "imperialist war" this time) do not appear at the time (if ever they were made) to have reached their destination. Nor is there any record of either the Politzer appeal or the Thorez-Duclos proposals of June 6 having been broadcast at the time by Moscow or any other station. Both "documents" seem to belong to that mountain of "rewritten history" in which those years abound. The Communists were not the only "re-writers". It is true that there was the episode of the "Thorez-Duclos appeal of July 10, 1940", of which much was to be made by the French CP after the war. Supposed to have been published on the day of the historic vote of the National Assembly granting constitutional powers to Pétain, this document (in the version published after the war) said that France would never be a country of slaves, and it was not defeated generals, corrupt politicians, and business sharks, but a national movement, grouped round the working-class, that could alone bring about a French Renaissance.

Actually, the Appeal does not seem to have been published until September 1940 in the clandestine *Cahiers du Bolchevisme*, and though it contained everything given in the post-war version, it also included the usual harsh remarks about Reynaud, Daladier, their plutocratic war, British imperialism, etc. It did, however, indicate that if the people of France were highly critical of the pro-British "warmongers", they would not submit to the "present [Vichy] gang" either. At the same

[3] Maurice Thorez, *Une politique de grandeur française* (Paris, 1945), p. 289.

time, it defended once more the wisdom of the German-Soviet Pact, and paid a tribute to the Soviet Union, "that rampart of peace".

Even assuming that the Appeal reached a wide public, it is doubtful that it could have been politically illuminating or inspiring, least of all at the time of the Battle of Britain.

Vichy did not intend, any more than the Germans, to be soft with the Communists; the inhuman treatment of these in Vichy gaols and camps was notorious. When hostages were to be shot by the Germans, Vichy preferred the victims to be Communists rather than other prisoners. Du Moulin de Labarthète tells the story of how Pucheu, Pétain's Minister of the Interior was allowed by the Germans to choose the names of the hostages they were going to shoot after a German officer had been assassinated at Nantes. Pucheu rejected the first list submitted to him—most of these were ex-Service men and "good Frenchmen", but he accepted an alternative list of 50 names, of whom 44 were Communists, including a deputy, Charles Michels, and a boy of 17, Guy Mocquet. They were all shot at Châteaubriant on October 22 and 23, 1941.

On the night of the 23rd [Labarthète related] Pucheu tried to justify himself: "I did what anyone, as Minister of the Interior would have done . . . I could not allow forty good Frenchmen to be shot."

Romier was overwhelmed by this reply: "But how could you, Pucheu? How could you choose the hostages to be shot?" "I didn't choose them. I simply let the Germans give me a different list."

"You had no right to do that, my friend. Whether ex-Servicemen or Communists, they were all good Frenchmen. You had no business to choose; the massacre should have been left entirely to the Germans!"[4]

That was the famous occasion on which Pétain, in a somewhat quixotic mood, decided to protest to the Germans by travelling to the demarcation line and by offering himself to them as a hostage—a plan which, without much difficulty, he was persuaded to abandon. Whether Romier, as related by Labarthète, ever used the phrase: "ex-Service men, or Communists, they are all good Frenchmen"—that was certainly not the opinion prevalent at Vichy. All the evidence shows that the Communists who had been in prison ever since the Daladier days, and others who had been picked up after the Armistice, were treated with great harshness and inhumanity in the Vichy gaols. Drancy, Gurs, le Puy, the Maison Carrée at Algiers and dozens of other gaols, mostly in Vichy France, have been described by some of their inmates. Just a sample from a Communist writer:

The *maison d'arrêt* at Saint-Etienne. It was here that Henry Lagrange of

[4] Du Moulin de Labarthète, *op. cit.*, pp. 354–5.

Limoges, who was 25 years old, Molet of Beziers, who was 22, and Delorme, secretary of the miners' trade union of Saint-Etienne, aged 46, died of hunger at the beginning of 1943. A small piece of bread, a bowl of turnip and six spoonfuls of water called "soup" was all they were allowed. The thieves and murderers could get four parcels a month of three kilos each, but the Communists came under the Ministerial Circular of October 26, 1942, which allowed them only one four-kilo food parcel a month. Eight kilos a month less to eat because they believed in Communism instead of killing their father or raping little girls . . .[5]

And he quoted the report of the prison doctor who said that owing to lack of food, the death rate among the Communists was "exceptionally high". Also, he explained that the author of the circular of October 26 was none other than Professor Barthélemy, Pétain's Minister of Justice, leading authority on constitutional law and one of the most respectable of the "Vichyites", who passionately believed in the "National Revolution".

One of the strangest episodes in the wartime record of the Communists (and one which has been used by anti-Communist propaganda with great effect since the war) was the famous letter from Billoux to Pétain on December 19, 1940. Billoux was one of the leading Communist deputies imprisoned at le Puy—a prison notorious for its horrible conditions. Couched in polite and respectful terms, this letter recalled that the Communist deputies had been irregularly sentenced to long terms of imprisonment in April 1940. The real reason, Billoux said, why they had been sentenced was that the Communists "had been alone to oppose the war and to demand peace". Alluding to some of Pétain's own ministers, Billoux said that there were many who fully agreed with the Communists, but who were afraid to say so at the time, and who "hoped to seize power through the defeat of our country". Since Pétain himself declared that "he hated lies", it would be only right that he should allow the people of France to know how the Communists had done their utmost to save France from disaster. Their letter to Herriot should be published, as well as a full account of their trial in the spring of 1940.

We were dragged before the Court because we alone had had the courage to call upon the people of France to drive out the Daladier Government, with its crushing responsibility for the war. . . . Before the examining magistrate I said: "This war will be disastrous to France; if we lose it we shall be Hitler's slaves, if we win it we shall be Chamberlain's flunkeys. Yet we could have pursued a policy of independence—the policy which has saved the Soviet Union from War."

Why, Billoux further asked, were the Communists, "the only true defenders of the independence of France", being kept in prison, and

[5] Aragon, *L'homme communiste* (Paris, 1947), p. 73.

why were more being arrested? Were they going to be treated as agents of England, as, in the past, they had been treated as agents of Germany? This, presumably, was meant to show that they were not in sympathy with de Gaulle.

To put an end to lies, *Monsieur le Maréchal*, it is also necessary that the Communists be liberated at once, among them the deputies who alone protested against the war. Meantime, pending this act of justice, it would, to say the least, be right that they be allowed the privileges of political prisoners, and that they be spared such acts of meanness as, for instance, these last two:
(1) We are no longer allowed to receive food parcels.
(2) The Minister of the Interior has refused to let my wife and my little daughter, aged twenty months, whom I have not seen since my arrest, visit me.

And what was Billoux offering Pétain in return?

Since nothing was published on the *in camera* sessions of our trial in which we denounced the real war culprits, I ask that I and my friends be heard as witnesses by the Supreme Court of Riom.

This apparently meant that Billoux and the other Communists were willing to testify on the "war guilt" of Daladier, Blum, Reynaud, and others who were going to be tried at Riom. Whenever, in later years, one mentioned the Billoux letter to French Communists, they were greatly embarrassed, and avoided any clear explanation.

Yet what was the real explanation? Perhaps the date of the letter provides a clue. December 1940. The Communists, like most people in France, were probably sure either of a German victory or of a negotiated peace in some not very distant future, possibly with Russia as the arbiter. A desire for a personal vendetta against Daladier cannot have been the real reason for this letter. Was it not rather the thought that the cadres of the CP had been decimated; that the CP had been left almost without leadership, and that there was a grave danger of the Communist leaders being allowed to die of starvation, one by one, in the Vichy gaols? The reference to the food parcels is highly significant in this respect, as well as to the Billoux baby. It is, after all, conceivable that, in purely human terms, even the tough Communist leaders, with no prospect of *ever* being let out, and with no very obvious cause for which to die just at that time, were feeling sorry for themselves. If let out, the Communists might still have a political part to play—perhaps they thought that Russia, still at peace, might exercise some influence on French affairs, in competition with Germany; left to starve in gaol, they were of no use to anybody. What would they have said at the Riom trial no one can tell—it never came to the test. Perhaps they would have made the Vichy leaders as uncomfortable as Daladier. Pétain's defence said that if they were not allowed to testify, it was because they were likely to stress France's "war guilt" and play straight into the hands of Hitler.

Anyway, it was all a shabby business and the apparent attempt to "fraternize" with Pétain was just as naïve as the other Communist attempt to fraternize with the Germans. Yet the whole affair is difficult to judge without reference to two things: the total uncertainty of the international situation and—the starved condition of Billoux and his fellow-prisoners. In any case, unlike much that the Communists were to do after the German invasion of Russia, the Billoux letter was not among the heroic exploits of the French CP during the war. Did Billoux write it on his own initiative? It seems, at any rate, improbable that he could, while in prison, have received any instructions from Thorez or Duclos.

Everything changed for the French Communists with Hitler's invasion of Russia. Although many Communists had joined the Resistance as individuals (thus, Pierre Hervé joined "Libération" before June 1941) the Party as a whole had no clear line to follow. Now, in June 1941, it was clear at last. They were able to make up for all the mental agony and all the humiliations they had suffered between September 1939 and June 1941. They became the most dynamic and vigorous element in the French Resistance, and if anything, criticized London for its reluctance to encourage "direct action".

Both the Germans and Vichy regarded the Communists as by far the most dangerous part of the Resistance after June 1941; they were exceptionally prominent in the Maquis and in guerilla warfare generally, and many of the rank and file—and maybe some of the leaders, such as Tillon—liked to think in terms of a *real* revolution in France. It seems that Tillon, in particular, as leader of the Francs-Tireurs, felt bitter about the counsels of moderation on the eve of the Liberation that were now coming from Moscow; this bitterness may well have been an echo of the bitterness so many Communists had felt over the Franco-Soviet Pact, when Russia's interests *also* had to come first.

In the Vichy mythology, the Communists became the "bandits" and "terrorists"; and the Germans, too, arrested, deported and killed many thousands. Communists were very numerous among the hostages shot by the Germans. There was the shooting of the hostages at Château-briant, in October 1941; hundreds of others were to be shot on Mont-Valerien that "Golgotha of Paris", as Aragon called it, in the next two years; thousands of other Communists were shot in Maquis round-ups both by the Germans and by Darnand's Milice; eight members of the Central Committee of the CP were shot, among them Pierre Semard and Gabriel Péri, the brilliant young spokesman on foreign affairs in the Chamber of Deputies, who had "accepted" the German-Soviet Pact with such ill-concealed bitterness. Half the staff of the *Humanité* lost their lives, as well as seventy people who had been caught distributing the paper.[6] Danielle Casanova and thousands of other Communist *militants* and *militantes* died in German death camps. The CP was to call itself *"le parti des Fusillés"* at the time of the Liberation, and tended to pooh-pooh the part played in the Resistance by others. In exalting their own merits in the Resistance, the Communists tended more and more to monopolize the key posts in all the Resistance movements. In the opinion of one of the non-Communist leaders of the Resistance, Claude Bourdet, it was this unsuccessful attempt by the Communists to *run* the whole Resistance during the final stages that was the chief reason why de Gaulle turned against it.

I venture to quote here a conversation with Bourdet in 1954 as an illustration of the conflicts inside the Resistance, both before the Communists virtually took it over, and after. In Bourdet's view, the Resistance was wrecked by the Communists and by Bidault. This was how he explained it:

We old resisters were, most of us, opposed to the creation of the CNR. It meant, among other things, the revival of the rotten old parties, the Radical-Socialists, for instance. All these parties which were being dragged into the CNR were so many whited sepulchres. However, for de Gaulle's sake, we agreed, Moulin having sworn that the CNR would have no opportunity to command.

Then Moulin was arrested by the Germans—and here was Bidault wanting his job. Already in the past Bidault had had a deplorable effect on Moulin; he had tried to persuade him (and through him, de Gaulle) that the Resistance leaders were all ambitious *condottiere*—except himself. Now, to get himself elected president of the CNR he proceeded to flirt with the Communists, who accepted him on the *comité directeur* of the "Front National". Having been elected president of the CNR he then decided that this was only a "paper appointment" and insisted on setting up a permanent *bureau* of the CNR. This was supported by the Communists.

The purpose of this move [Bourdet went on] was to knock on the head the *Comité central des Mouvements de la Résistance* which we had created in Paris, and into which we had managed to incorporate the predominantly Communist Front National which, though almost non-existent in the South, was strong in the North by now. This proportion of *one* CP movement to *seven* others was, of course, unfair and I tried to correct this. But in the Bidault *bureau* it was the other way round.

On this Permanent Bureau of the CNR, presided over by Bidault, the Communists or near-Communists were in the majority. Similarly, after my arrest (and though I had urged that I be replaced, if I were arrested, by Cheval, so as to keep the balance between the Communists and the others)

[6] *Cahiers du Communisme* (December, 1950), p. 72.

a friend of mine, but a Communist, was pushed forward. I was arrested on March 25; by the beginning of April both the *bureau permanent* of the CNR and the *comité directeur* of the MUR were in Communist hands. After the little *coup d'état* on the MUR, the Communists also grabbed the COMAC by appointing Kriegel-Valrimont as representative of the Southern resistance ... And to think that about 80 per cent of the Resistance rank and file were not Communists! And that is also how Bidault started his political career: first by helping to sell the Resistance to the Communists, and then by separating the Catholics from the rest, to create his own MRP.

No doubt Bourdet felt bitter about both Bidault and the Communists, and tended in retrospect to credit them with greater machiavellism than they had exercised in reality. Nevertheless, he made there an historic point of some significance.

But was he not, all the same, minimizing the rôle of the Communists in the Resistance? For even a man like Beuve-Méry, the editor of the *Monde*, who was anything but pro-Communist, still referred in 1945 to the Communists as the most dynamic part of the Resistance, as its *aile marchante*.[7] Also, the attraction the Communists exercised on many intellectuals (always an important point in France) after the war, is unquestionable. Aragon and Eluard, whose wartime poetry was full of national anti-German and revolutionary inspiration, came very close to becoming the two national poets of France. A poem like Eluard's *Liberté* caught the mood and the innermost feelings of France under the Occupation—or rather, of all those who resisted, actively, or even passively—better than almost anything else. If Vichy had its "intellectual *élite*" and its writers (who were playing for safety), so the Resistance, too, had its *élite* and its writers (who risked their lives)— and among these Aragon and Eluard—Surrealists in the past, but Communists now—were amongst the most famous.

The attraction that, for years afterwards, the Communists continued to exercise on a very large part of the French intellectuals—though less *per se* than as a powerful *corrective* to "bourgeois democracy", and to so many of the Free World shibboleths of the cold war epoch is a reality which cannot be overlooked in any examination of the subsequent course of French history.

Parodying Bourdet who said that everybody in France is "anti-neutralist, but——", one may well say that a very large part of France is "anti-Communist, but——". Among the intellectuals, in particular, anti-Communism is usually of a milder quality than it is in Britain or in the USA. There are many reasons for this. Nearly everybody has *personal* contacts with at least a few Communists, and the Communists they personally know do not eat babies; also, there is no profound conviction that the Communists are *always* wrong; there is a guilt feeling

[7] Hubert Beuve-Méry, *Réflections politiques* (Paris, 1951), p. 152.

vis-à-vis the working-class; and there is the consciousness that the Communists were in the front rank of the Resistance, and received no reward for it.

And, above all, perhaps, there is the conscious or unconscious acceptance of the fact that the French Communists cannot be altogether detached from an historically valid, and even "respectable", French revolutionary tradition. A tradition on the existence of which (it has sometimes been argued) Moscow had merely "cashed in". (The thought that the Communists had "usurped" this revolutionary tradition made a man like Léon Blum wring his hands with rage and despair.)

Despite all this, the fact remains that on the national scale and *politically*, the Communists have always been in the minority, with at least 70 per cent of the people of France "against" them.

Sometimes it has been said that this would be different, if only the Communists were "National Communists". But would it be? There was no "Moscow" in 1848 or in 1871.

*　　*　　*　　*

What many thinking people have felt to be particularly disastrous throughout the post-war epoch was the inability of the Left, partly through the fault of the Communists, but, even more so, owing to the fatality of the Cold War, to remain united and govern the country.

As a result of this failure, it was the men and the ideologies of the traditional Right that in effect dominated government policy, particularly in the colonial field. In the process, these short-sighted and pig-headed men were able to take advantage of the relative ignorance and indifference of the general public in these matters.

This indifference continued until the moment when the failure of these policies became only too obvious to everybody, and even began to affect the ordinary man's life in France itself. For instance, when there was talk of conscripts being sent to Indo-China at the time of Dien Bien Phu, or when conscripts *were* beginning to be sent to Morocco and Algeria in 1955.

But for a long time the outcry among the intellectuals over Indo-China and North Africa fell on deaf ears, and was less effective than their outcry over Germany. For in every Frenchman Germany produced certain well-conditioned reflexes, which North Africa and especially Indo-China did not.

Part II

THE DE GAULLE PERIOD AND THE LOST BATTLE FOR A "NEW FRANCE" (1944–5)

CHAPTER ONE

DE GAULLE, THE NOBLE ANACHRONISM

D E GAULLE is a unique figure, the only monolithic figure in the recent history of France. Perhaps Stalin said at Yalta a truer word on de Gaulle than he fully realized: "De Gaulle—he is not complicated." In the highly complicated world of today statesmen generally reflect the complexity of their epoch. De Gaulle, on the contrary, with his single-track mind, with French Greatness as his *idée fixe*, is like an historical anachronism—a man who is not truly typical of mid-twentieth-century France.

In Volume IV of *The Second World War* Sir Winston Churchill wrote a striking page on de Gaulle; yet if this page is not as penetrating as it might be, is it not because Churchill, while instinctively detecting in de Gaulle certain qualities of greatness which were very similar to his own, perhaps failed to see that both his greatness and de Gaulle's were anachronistic? There was, however, this difference: while Churchill's "anachronism" turned out, for a variety of specifically British reasons, an almost miraculously successful one, de Gaulle's did not.

Both believed in "national greatness"; yet if this feeling of pride was stimulated in England by the ordeals of 1940, the greater disaster that befell France during the same year could only undermine her self-confidence. Throughout the war, Churchill and de Gaulle had to work on very different human material. The victorious island could, five years later, still fancy itself a great power in the world; defeated France (for even in the midst of the Allied victory of 1945 she was still haunted by the memory of 1940) found it hard to believe in her own greatness. Perhaps the "logical" French mind was more aware than the sentimental British mind of the true distribution of strength in the world; perhaps also the fact that England was a "well-run" country, and France a "badly-run" country made a difference. If, in spite of everything, France still believed in her "superiority", this was different from "greatness", as de Gaulle understood it.

This is what Churchill wrote:

In these pages various severe statements based on events of the moment are set down about General de Gaulle, and certainly I had continuous difficulties and many sharp antagonisms with him. There was, however, a dominant element in our relationship. I could not regard him as representing active and prostrate France, nor indeed the France that had a right to decide freely the future for herself. I knew he was no friend of England. But I always recognized in him the spirit and conception which, across the pages of history, the word "France" would ever proclaim. I understood and admired, while I resented, his arrogant demeanour. Here he was—a refugee, an exile from his country under sentence of death, in a position entirely dependent upon the goodwill of the British Government, and also now of the United States. The Germans had conquered his country. He had no real foothold anywhere. Never mind: he defied all. Always, even when he was behaving worst, he seemed to express the personality of France—a great nation, with all its pride, authority and ambition. It was said in mockery that he thought himself the living representative of Joan of Arc.... This did not seem to me as absurd as it looked. Clemenceau, with whom it was said he also compared himself, was a far wiser and more experienced statesman. But they both gave the same impression of being unconquerable Frenchmen.[1]

This magnificent passage has, however, in its reference to France, the Churchillian fault of using too lightly sonorous and abstract words like "pride, authority, and ambition". Where was the France that was proud, authoritative, and ambitious? The words fit de Gaulle perfectly; but do they fit France—the *whole* of France, or even the greater part of it?

Nine years after his triumphal entry into Paris, de Gaulle was to say, looking back on it all:

Think by how many failures my public life has been marked! First I tried to persuade the civil and military authorities to endow France with an armoured force which would have spared us the invasion. I failed. After the disaster of 1940 I urged the Government, of which I was a member, to go to North Africa and evade the enemy. In vain.... I failed at Dakar. After victory I endeavoured to maintain the unity that I had formed around myself. But this unity was broken. Later, in grave circumstances, I again tried, and failed.... If these failures had been mine, they would have been of no importance; but they were also the failures of France. True, from time to time, there were successes.... And yet—during the darkest moments of the war, I sometimes wondered: Perhaps it is my mission to represent in the history of our country its last upsurge towards the lofty heights. Perhaps it is my lot to have written the last pages in the book of our greatness.[2]

And six months later, after another of de Gaulle's press conferences against EDC, Mauriac, who was there, felt what so many others must have felt: "the last Frenchman who had made his countrymen believe that they were still a great nation."

[1] Churchill, *The Second World War*, vol. IV, p. 611.
[2] *Le Monde*, November 14, 1953.

His words [wrote Mauriac] are like a cold wind, coming from very far and very high, from the past when France was a great Nation.... Yes— he persuaded us of this at the darkest and most shameful moment of our history, and there are still millions of Frenchmen who have not forgotten it.... No one asked him: "Do you agree with the [Laniel] Government?" because by his very presence, General de Gaulle makes the dictatorship of Lilliput invisible to the naked eye....[3]

Mauriac also recalled that, at that same meeting, de Gaulle had used this strange phrase—and had used it naturally, almost without arrogance, but with a touch of melancholy pride: "*J'étais la France.*" And no one had protested; because, in a sense, it was true. But only in a very limited sense. He symbolized during the years of the Occupation and Vichy, and for a short time after the Liberation the fighting spirit of a country that was predominantly pacifist and war-weary; he personified also a tradition of military honour in a country that was deeply conscious of its technical, military, economic—in short, its physical— inferiority. De Gaulle also carried the banner of national independence and national unity in a country that was conscious of having, in the main, been liberated by foreign armies, which was deeply divided, and which, not only militarily, but also economically was inclined to be increasingly dependent on stronger and wealthier nations.

De Gaulle had a large following on two occasions: when it was a case of driving out the German invaders, and when it was a case of preventing an (albeit hypothetical) Russian invasion. When the danger passed, he was forgotten by many; and he had only an insufficient following when he attempted a policy of genuine French independence and of *grandeur française*, and proclaimed that France would never be a pawn in the power politics of Russia and America.

As for home affairs, his—albeit unconscious—class loyalties were too strong, and he found no common language with the working-class. Also, he was proud, distant and austere; and if, at times, he was capable of uttering words of contempt or angry sarcasm, he lacked the boisterous wit of a Clemenceau or the lachrymose warmth of an Herriot, and expected hero-worship rather than popularity. His incapacity to make himself popular in a human way did much, in the early months of the Liberation, to estrange him from the Resistance.

Many people have known de Gaulle; countless articles and numerous books have been written about him—yet both to those who have known him, and, still more, to those who have written about him, he has never really "come alive". Some of his enemies in the London days—notably André Labarthe and Admiral Muselier—have spoken of his disloyalty, his low cunning, his capacity for intrigue; but even if, on occasion, he

[3] *Le bloc-notes de François Mauriac. L'Express*, April 17, 1954.

was disloyal, it could only have been in the name of some major political purpose (as he saw it); seldom, if ever, for any base or even plainly personal motive. If de Gaulle was deeply conscious of having a mission, he seems to have derived little *personal* pleasure from his triumphs, lacking completely the plebeian vanity of a Mussolini, a Hitler, or even a Napoleon.[4]

One would think that, since he had political and military friends, they would tell us something of de Gaulle the Man, and bring out at least some warm, human touch in his character. But even in the two large tomes of Jacques Soustelle, one of his closest associates, one would look in vain for anything that seriously conflicts with the slightly caricatural portrait drawn of him by Emmanuel d'Astier, who served under him for a short time at Algiers as a member of the Liberation Committee.

As a leading member of the Resistance, d'Astier had met de Gaulle for the first time during a mission to London.

I went to the Connaught Hotel at 9 p.m.... I waited. Then the Symbol came into the room. He was even taller than I had thought. His gestures were slow and heavy like his nose. His small head, his waxy face were carried by a body of an uncertain architecture. His most usual gesture was to raise his forearms, while keeping his elbows close to his body; attached to a pair of frail wrists, his inert, very white, somewhat feminine hands, with the palms turned upwards, seemed to be raising all the time whole worlds of abstract burdens.

He did not ask questions. We dined. He does not like men; he only loves their history, especially the history of France, of which he was "doing" a chapter himself, writing it in his mind as he went along, like a frenzied Michelet.

Was de Gaulle truly interested in the Resistance; could he understand it? d'Astier, having just landed from German-occupied France, could not help wondering.

I felt I was talking of things that were much too precise, and also much too confused—a mixture of concrete details of everyday existence and of Utopian sentiments. And as I talked, I felt that de Gaulle was picking up only those bits that were fitting into his History.... Not that he was incredulous. He was distrustful, because he despises too many men and too many things in this world; but he was not incredulous, if only because I was just a French ant bringing its bit of straw to his historical edifice....[5]

[4] All the same, it should be remembered that for several years before 1940 he had suffered from thwarted ambition, and from a sense of injustice: the French Army leaders were not taking him seriously and were slow in promoting him. He is also said to have observed, during his early days in London: "*Rien n'est si grand qu'une grande aventure*", which implies a touch of personal ambition, in addition to "pure" patriotism.

[5] Emmanuel d'Astier, *Sept fois sept jours* (Paris 1947), pp. 77-8.

Did d'Astier, on closer contact with de Gaulle at Algiers, get to know him any better? Perhaps not; it merely seemed to confirm his first impression:

I had now seen him ... use his three weapons: prestige, secrecy, and cunning. His ruses were not of a high order; but secrets kept by a natural and icy prestige can lead very far. I have often wondered where this prestige came from—was it merely from his exceptional tallness, or from that unchanging appearance which is like a portrait insensitive to the warm currents of life? Or did it come from that inspired voice, with its broken cadences, emerging from a lifeless body, which lacked all animal warmth—like a voice coming out of a wax figure? Or did this prestige come from that distance that he keeps between himself and other men? Or from that perfect language of his—even when the thought behind it isn't perfect —which is reminiscent of certain famous sermons of the eighteenth century? .... He remains a mystery to me, this man whose only motive force is an historical idea, the greatness of France—and *for whom this greatness of France is a road that replaces all other roads—those of God, of men, of progress, and of all ideologies*.... How often have I regretted not to have known him before, or rather, *during* those days in June and July 1940 when he begot the France shaped in his own image.... He was like a hero of Plutarch who was seeking his place in history and had not found it yet.[6]

This is a cruel account of de Gaulle; and yet, as already said, the writers most favourable to him (including himself) add little to "humanize" him. What does one learn from them? That he was, before the war, a great military technician, that he had an excellent record in the 1940 campaign but could, obviously, do no more than he did, all his advice on the organization of the French Army having been ignored; that he was the first to lead the revolt against the Armistice; that he fought a desperately hard diplomatic battle to get at least some recognition for himself as the Symbol of Free France, this part of the story ending in the grand Paris apotheosis of August 1944.

But even to his closest followers he is something very like d'Astier's "Symbol". He is invariably *"le Général"*—tall, superior, and distant, and reminiscent of that historic anecdote he himself tells in *Le fil de l'épée*, about somebody saying to Bonaparte as he stands before a noble and ancient monument: *"C'est triste."* To which Bonaparte replied: *"Oui, c'est triste comme la grandeur."*

My own limited acquaintance with de Gaulle suggests to me that d'Astier rather exaggerated his "absurd" side: for de Gaulle is sufficiently impressive to get away with even a little absurdity. But his lack of human warmth is, indeed, disconcerting in a man of such powerful political emotions. Not that de Gaulle is "cold" in the ordinary sense; on the contrary, I would say that his "inhumanity" was a *warm*

[6] *Ibid.*, pp. 146–47.

inhumanity, like that of a great prince of the Church. The first volume of de Gaulle's *Mémoires*, published in 1954, bears out this impression, and is remarkably consistent with de Gaulle's writings twenty years earlier.

But was de Gaulle in reality quite as mysterious as d'Astier made him out to be? Eight years before the war, and two years before writing his famous *Vers l'armée de métier*, de Gaulle wrote a brilliant little essay which, read today, not only sounds truly prophetic, but very largely explains de Gaulle's character and the workings of his mind. That de Gaulle had great erudition, a rare classical style of writing, and a superior mind is clearly revealed by *Le fil de l'épée*. But it also reveals a vast superiority complex and almost certainly a faith in himself as a man of destiny. And it explains very clearly, eight years in advance, just *why* he "rebelled" in 1940. Character, Prestige, and a Doctrine, according to de Gaulle, are the three main elements that make a great soldier and leader of men. And in all three chapters we find passages that look like X-rays of de Gaulle's own "mysterious" mind.

The passion to act by one's self is accompanied by a certain roughness. The man of character embodies the harshness inherent in his effort. His subordinates feel it, and often suffer from it. Such a chief is distant, because authority does not go without prestige, and prestige does not go without distances being kept.

In relation to his superiors, he finds himself in a difficult position. Sure of his own judgement and conscious of his strength, he makes no concessions to the desire to please. He . . . is not capable of passive obedience . . .[7]

And then—this prophecy of 1940:

But when the danger becomes pressing . . . a kind of tidal wave sweeps a man of character right to the forefront. . . . And where, indeed, did one ever see a great human task being achieved without a man of character feeling the irresistible urge to act? . . . Nothing would have been achieved if counsels of base caution or suggestions of cowardly modesty had prevailed. More than that: those who do great things must *often ignore the conventions of a false discipline*. Thus in 1914 Lyautey kept Morocco despite orders from above; and after the battle of Jutland, Lord Fisher bitterly commented on Jellicoe's dispatches: "He has all Nelson's qualities, except one: he has not learned to disobey."[8]

De Gaulle's "rebellion" of June 18 was no improvisation or sudden brainwave: he had prepared himself just for this kind of gesture many years before; his defiance of the Established Order in certain conditions had been thought out in advance. Similarly, in *Le fil de l'épée*, in the chapter on Prestige, he explained the reasons why a great military leader must be reserved. "Nothing great was ever done in the midst of chatter," he wrote.

[7] De Gaulle, *Le fil de l'épée* (Paris, 1946), pp. 46–7.   [8] *Ibid.*, pp. 50–1.

Hoche, general-in-chief at the age of twenty-four, and living in a world of rhetoric, nevertheless soon learned to be silent. His impetuous character and his brilliant oratory soon gave way to cold dignity and laconic speech. . . . And who was more taciturn than Bonaparte? . . . . And the generals of the *Grande Armée* followed their master's example.[9]

Alexander, Hannibal, Caesar, Richelieu, Condé, Hoche, Masséna, Napoleon—how de Gaulle loved to roll these names round his tongue! And to this member of a very narrow conservative military caste, the greatness of France and of the French Army was a kind of all-absorbing obsession; and no one was better prepared than he to assume in war-time the rôle of leader of the Free French.

So June 18 was not, as has sometimes been suggested, a lucky BBC fluke; psychologically, on the part of de Gaulle, it was a long-premeditated gesture. *Le fil de l'épée* explains the de Gaulle of 1940; it also explains his haughtiness, his reserve, and even his decision to abandon power in January 1946, as we shall see later. For in 1946 he had to deal not with soldiers or potential soldiers, but with French civilians; and he was out of his element.

[9] *Ibid.*, pp. 74–5.

CHAPTER TWO

WAS DE GAULLE A *GRAND BOURGEOIS* AT HEART?

B Y the time the de Gaulle Government was ready to take over
in France in 1944, Pétain had been removed to Germany. Whatever the Germans' reasons for doing so, they thus created a
political vacuum in France, which suited de Gaulle perfectly.[1] In the
circumstances, his claims to being "recognized" were stronger than
ever.

Thanks to de Gaulle, there had, indeed, been a remarkable four
years' continuity in the institution of a Free French authority (which
was, it is true, nearly wrecked by the establishment of a "rival"
authority in North Africa in November 1942). From the small nucleus
of men around the *Chef des Fraînçais Libres*, recognized as such by the
British Government on June 22, 1940, this authority expanded more and
more. On October 27, 1940, after the capture of some important
African territories by the Free French, the *Conseil de Défense de
l'Empire* was set up; less than a year later, on September 24, 1941,
the *Comité National Français*, already looking remarkably like a regular government, complete with ministers, provisionally called *commissaires*, and with ever-growing contacts with France itself, was created
in London. Although this de Gaulle organization was put in an extremely difficult position for several months after the North Africa
landing, with Darlan and, later, Giraud tending to deny the London
Committee any legal authority, de Gaulle, after "sharing" supreme
power with Giraud for a short time, finally succeeded in securing full
control of the *Comité Français de la Libération Nationale*. This *de
facto* government was set up in Algiers on June 3, 1943, and it took de
Gaulle some months to eliminate Giraud from its leadership altogether.
However, de Gaulle was virtually the sole head of the Government by
the time a Consultative Assembly was set up at Algiers in September
1943; three days before D-Day, on June 3, 1944, the CFLN proclaimed
itself the *Provisional Government of the French Republic*.

The gradual elimination of Giraud, who continued almost to the

---

[1] *Cf.* Prélot, *Précis de Droit Constitutionnel* (Paris, 1953), p. 281.

bitter end to be Eisenhower's *protégé*, required a good deal of clever manœuvring on the part of de Gaulle, not only against the British and American governments, but also against the Vichyites who were in possession of most of the key posts in North Africa, and (at least according to Soustelle) even against all sorts of double-crossing Socialists and Communists who were, in their own way, intriguing with Giraud against de Gaulle.

Where then did, ultimately, de Gaulle's support come from? In so far as the Consultative Assembly at Algiers represented chiefly Metropolitan France, and de Gaulle also had the backing of the CNR, it came from "public opinion" inside France. Secondly, with Vichy more and more discredited, de Gaulle received much of his support from the French troops in Africa—wholeheartedly from the Free French (under Larminat, Koenig, and Leclerc) and, with some mental reservations, from the ex-Vichyites. The mass movement among these to join the Free French was such that by the time Leclerc's famous Armoured Division—which was the first to enter Paris in August 1944—was formed, it consisted of 12,000 "Free French" and of 15,000 "others", including a large number of officers who had been fervent supporters of the Marshal, and some of whom had even fought the British in Syria.[2] As Soustelle remarks, the attraction that "Gaullism" exercised, at that stage, on the Vichyite rank and file was due to the fact that "Gaullism" by now represented a clear-cut issue, whereas continued loyalty to the Marshal involved a man in a highly tortuous form of reasoning.[3] This may be a good explanation; but there must be a better one still: did not the Vichyites, in the summer of 1943, start joining de Gaulle in large numbers because (*a*) he was now obviously going to be on the winning side and (*b*) because he was, in sociological terms, very much "one of our own kind"? And did they not feel, perhaps unconsciously, that the Socialist and Communist *commissaires* surrounding de Gaulle were a temporary expedient, and that, at heart, de Gaulle was not a revolutionary and, though since 1940 a "rebel", could fundamentally be only a man of law and order?

Here again we have a French situation which cannot be explained in a few simple words. On the one hand, de Gaulle had become, by the autumn of 1943, not only the undisputed head of the National Committee, and the "obvious" leader of the New France, who was being more and more recognized as such both by foreign countries ("now at last we know *you* are the man", Eisenhower had said), and by the bulk of public opinion inside Metropolitan France (where even the diehard elements in the Resistance felt that he was at least a "useful

[2] General de Larminat, *Revue de la France Libre*, No. 20, April, 1949, p. 15.
[3] Jacques Soustelle, *D'Alger à Paris* (Paris, 1950), p. 231.

symbol"); but, on the other hand, behind this façade of apparent unity, the struggle for power was continuing.

For a time, it is true, de Gaulle himself tried to maintain the façade of anti-Vichyism and national unity. In his opening speech before the Consultative Assembly at Algiers on November 3, 1943, he spoke as the head of a truly *new* France. Vichy was condemned absolutely as "illegal"—a point very important to de Gaulle—for Vichy was still in existence.

> The invasion and the Occupation [he said] destroyed the institutions that France had given herself. Taking advantage of the distress of a people stunned by military defeat, there were men who established, on the soil of France, and in agreement with the enemy, an abominable régime of personal power, a régime of lies and inquisition. Supported by the invader with whom they boast of collaborating ... these people have, in the truest sense, imprisoned the sovereign nation. The salvation of our country became our supreme law. We had to create a provisional authority to direct France's war effort and to uphold her rights. . . .[4]

There followed a magnificent—almost literally Churchillian—tribute to the Resistance, "the fundamental reaction of the mass of the French people":

> No doubt, it is not like an army fighting regular battles. But it is everywhere, determined and effective. It is embodied by an organization built up in France itself, the CNR. . . . It is in the factories and in the fields, in offices and in schools, in the streets and inside houses, in the nerves and the thoughts of the people. It is in the actions of those heroic units which miss no chance of harming the enemy and of punishing traitors. . . . Never have our banners deserted the battlefield, and today, here in Africa, 500,000 soldiers are waiting anxiously for the chance of meeting the enemy face to face on the other side of the sea. . . . Resistance: that is today the elementary expression of the nation's will.[5]

Grandeur militaire . . . He recalled Bir Hakeim and the Fezzan, and the exploits of French airmen in England, in Libya, in Russia, where the Normandy Squadron was sharing in the glory and the sacrifice of the Red Army.

And France's place in the world, and her *diplomatic importance* were like another *idée fixe* of de Gaulle's:

> France must now play once more a great international rôle. She believes that no European matter and no major world matter can be settled without her; the reasons for this are set out on the map of the world, in History and in the conscience of humanity.

[4] Charles de Gaulle, *Discours aux Français*, vol. II (Paris, 1944), p. 251.
[5] *Ibid.*, p. 255.

He then spoke of a general election in France as the only possible means of expressing the will of the sovereign people; but meantime, much preliminary work was being done.

This first meeting of the Provisional Consultative Assembly is a landmark the significance of which has been noted by world opinion. It marks the beginning of the resurrection of representative French institutions.

Republic, democracy—both words were used by de Gaulle—those words which he had hesitated to use in the early London days. And yet that "national unity" of which he now liked to speak at Algiers was somewhat artificial.

For if it is possible, in spite of a good deal of unsavoury intrigue that went on at Carlton Gardens, to speak of the "purity" of Gaullism in its early stages, much of the old Gaullist *mystique* inevitably suffered from its contact with North Africa. And even if the CNLF and its Consultative Assembly could be looked upon as a cross-section of France itself (not that either of them lacked adventurers, careerists and *arrivistes*, only too ready to cash in on de Gaulle's imminent triumph), the whole atmosphere of Algiers and of North Africa generally was a good deal more dubious. North Africa had never been "typical" of France—neither its French inhabitants, nor its soldiers and officials. Far into 1943, according to Soustelle, government offices at Rabat and Algiers continued to display portraits of the Marshal, with an occasional portrait of "*Moustachi*" Giraud added; and the replacement of these by pictures of de Gaulle was just a little too sudden.

For when one speaks of the "continuity" of the Free French institutions between 1940 and the Liberation, one has to remember that the *Comité Français de Libération Nationale* was by no means a simple "continuation" of the French National Committee of London, but a sort of amalgamation of this Committee with Giraud's *Commandement en chef civil et militaire*, which had been recognized at the Anfa conference by Britain and the USA as the supreme French authority in North Africa. And its original authority can, in a sense, be traced back to Vichy; and it may even be argued that de Gaulle's CFLN had Pétain as one of its ancestors!

The argument runs like this:

De Gaulle's CFLN had received its powers from the "bicephalous" Giraud-de Gaulle CFLN, which, in part, had derived its authority from Giraud's Imperial Council, which had received its authority from Darlan; Darlan, for his part, had received his authority from Noguès, the French Resident in Morocco, who, on November 13, 1942 had handed his powers over to Darlan after having himself been appointed by Pétain two days before (telegram No 59649) sole representative in North Africa of "the Marshal, Head of the State".[6]

The legal value of this "pedigree" may be contested; but there is no doubt that the Free French, once in Algiers, found themselves associated with a very large number of people who had little in common with the "pure" Gaullism of 1940. The elimination of Giraud towards the end of 1943, though welcomed as a great triumph for de Gaulle, did not mean the elimination of Giraudism; on the contrary, de Gaulle had, willy-nilly, to inherit all the Giraudist elements who became a sort of infectious Trojan Horse in the midst of the Free French.

For what did Giraudism mean in the first place? After his escape from Germany, General Giraud, a soldier with a great reputation among all the conservative elements in the French Army, and among most of the officers involved in the Resistance, imagined that Pétain's "Armistice Army" would follow him if the Germans invaded Vichy France. He did not take the "Gaullist" Resistance seriously. American secret services encouraged him, and obviously preferred him to de Gaulle. But when it came to the point, the "Armistice Army" did practically nothing to oppose a German invasion of Vichy France, and allowed itself to be disarmed. Giraud, having been let down by the "Armistice Army"—which he had described to people in the Resistance who had contacted him in 1942 as "the biggest trump in my game"— finally allowed Allied agents to persuade him to go to Gibraltar; from there (having by this time been forestalled at Algiers by Darlan) he went on to North Africa. Here Giraud was recognized as a "resister" by Churchill and Roosevelt, but became in reality the rallying point for all the Vichyites, now only too glad to jump on the Allies' bandwagon.

Giraud had the support of high finance, of big business, of the North African *colons*, of all the upper ranks of the army and administration; in short, of all the "forces of order".

De Gaulle, on the other hand, could claim to have "public opinion" in France behind him, as represented by the CNR; he was also a more cunning politician and a more striking personality, and had a much more effective propaganda machine than Giraud's. But while de Gaulle's victory over Giraud was psychologically and historically understandable, the "forces of order" continued to pull their weight, even after ostensibly abandoning Giraud in favour of de Gaulle.

It was indeed after Giraud's elimination that one observes two very significant developments:

(1) The representatives of the "old society" and of the old "general

[6] *Cf. Combat*, May 26, 1949.

staffs" (military, administrative, political, and economic) joined de Gaulle, the only remaining valid symbol of France's future. These people were not out-and-out Vichyites—they were people who had been careful not to compromise themselves too openly with Pétain. Among these were men of very considerable practical experience, and it became inevitable that they should tend to squeeze out the self-taught amateurs from amongst the Free French.

(2) These people began to "convert" many of the Free French surrounding de Gaulle to their own way of thinking. For it is a curious fact that, for the bourgeoisie, it was not entirely "natural" to be in the Resistance. It meant, to only too many of them, a breach with their original *milieu*. Yet, contact with the "common people" in the Resistance had given many of them a new outlook, and it seemed for a time that these people were going to form the *cadres* of a truly *new* France. In reality, however, the Giraud-de Gaulle "fusion" largely cancelled out this tendency: long before the Liberation many of these "exiles" found themselves in their "natural" *milieu* again—a process which was, if anything, precipitated by the tendency of the Resistance in France itself to come under the spell of the Communists.

No doubt, there was a good deal of antipathy at Algiers between the "London Free French" and Frenchmen who had distinguished themselves say, in Syria where they had fought the British; nevertheless, the gregarious social instinct that drove the bourgeoisie of all shades to join against the revolutionary forces, which were increasingly active in France, was unmistakable.

And the question inevitably arises whether it was not about the end of 1943 that de Gaulle himself, no longer feeling in the least a "rebel officer", became conscious of having got "home" at last. For now he was the head of a traditionalist society; and he was living once again in an atmosphere that was not unlike the world in which, as a member of an ultra-conservative family, he had lived all his life.

The great conflict of the Liberation days between de Gaulle's representatives and numerous elements of the Home Resistance showed that de Gaulle was definitely standing by this time on the side of Law and Order; unlike even Bidault, he would no longer use the word "Revolution", and preferred the vague word "renovation", implying merely a few improvements to the old Law and Order. At Algiers he had still said: "This war is a Revolution, the greatest Revolution in our history." In Paris, in August 1944, he was no longer to use that word.

For all that, he was hailed by Paris as a hero, as the greatest national figure France had had since Clemenceau, and as the undisputed leader who symbolized the "unanimity" of the French people.

The contradiction is more apparent than real. On the day of de Gaulle's Paris apotheosis everybody simply preferred to forget the angry quarrels that had gone on, only a few days before, between his representatives and those of the Home Resistance, and not to look too closely at the difficulties and inevitable conflicts lying ahead.

This was a natural, instinctive reaction, the reaction of personal and patriotic joy at being rid of the Germans at last; and de Gaulle at that moment represented, to the exclusion of all else, the battle against Germany. But the reconciliation was inevitably only a short-lived one.

CHAPTER THREE

THE PARIS INSURRECTION

Wｈᴀᴛ happened in Paris just before the Liberation?

General Chaban-Delmas, de Gaulle's *Délégué Militaire National* tried to restore order. He talked for thirty-five minutes, trying to demonstrate that the truce was desirable. The FFI hadn't enough arms. The "gentlemen's agreement" with Von Choltitz was proving a useful expedient.

Ribière, Daniel Mayer, and Mutter supported him. . . .

But the COMAC had held two meetings that day, and their fury over the truce was becoming more and more violent. Kriegel-Valrimont now said that London was deliberately sabotaging the popular rising; it did not want the people to hold a proper place in the Government. Vaillant said it was monstrous to try to deprive the people of Paris of a battle they had been preparing to fight during the past four years. And Villon screamed at Chaban-Delmas: "I have never in my life seen such a cowardly French general."

The meeting was suspended. When it was resumed, Villon apologized to Chaban-Delmas. He argued, however, that the truce wasn't a question that merely concerned the 600 men at the *Préfecture de Police*—there were the FFI, the *milices patriotiques*, the people generally—who all offered enormous possibilities. . . .

Parodi, representing de Gaulle, thought that a premature insurrection would have been disastrous, but he also thought that an insurrection that was going to start too late would fail in its object. He was obviously bothered by the danger of a new AMGOT taking control. It was absolutely necessary, he thought, that, before the arrival of the Allies, the Resistance be firmly established in Paris.

This small sample from Dansette's admirable *Histoire de la Libération de Paris* almost suffices to give one an insight into that strange atmosphere in which Paris was liberated—an atmosphere of rivalry between the two main forces of the Resistance. Broadly speaking, there were, on the one hand, the Communists—revolutionary and Jacobin in temperament, ready to take the most desperate risks, and reflecting, too, the 1848 and *communard* spirit of the Paris working-class. On the other hand there were the more cautious men—the men of the External Resistance, and the "moderates" of the Home Resistance (the *attentistes*, as the Communists disdainfully called them)—who thought in terms of "military possibilities" and were anxious to avoid Quixotic action that might lead to terrible loss of life and to the destruction of Paris, if the rising were not sufficiently co-ordinated with the advance of the Allied troops. Many of these people were already "government-minded".

It is paradoxical to find that, in Paris, the Communists should have supported the very policy which, in the case of the Warsaw rising ("unco-ordinated with the Red Army Command") was to be so severely condemned by the Russians.[1] The circumstances were, however, different—if only because, around Paris, the Germans were now definitely on the run, and because a major massacre in Paris would, in any case, have precipitated the Allies' advance on the capital; Warsaw, on the other hand, was separated from the Russians by the Vistula, and only a small and blunted Russian spearhead was anywhere near Warsaw; it was, indeed, at this critical moment that Goering's six armoured divisions were thrown into the battle to check the Russian advance. There was little danger of this happening around Paris, and COMAC, on the whole, had guessed right.

At another meeting of the CNR, as reported by Dansette, Villon (the COMAC representative) was saying:

You are frightened of the people; you are stopping the fight so as to steal their victory; the truce you have made with the Germans is like Pétain's Armistice; the spirit of Munich, the spirit of Vichy is replacing the true spirit of the Resistance—you have stabbed the insurrection in the back.

However, with an eye on the advancing Allied armies, de Gaulle's representatives agreed to a full-dress insurrection which was to last two or three days; honour was saved; Paris had been liberated by its own people; there was no excuse for AMGOT to take over; and relatively little damage had been done—if only because General von Choltitz had disobeyed Hitler's orders to destroy Paris.

From the mass of records and evidence on the liberation of Paris, there is one thing at least that stands out very clearly: the working-class of Paris fought the Germans—with old rifles, with pistols, with kitchen-knives even; in the working-class areas barricades were springing up in every street; a large map of Paris appended to Dansette's book shows hundreds of barricades in the 18th, 19th, 20th, 12th, 13th, 14th, and 15th *arrondissements*, very few in the 5th, 6th, and 7th, and the southern half of the 16th (Auteuil), and practically none at all in the Passy, Etoile, Champs-Elysées, and Monceau areas. No doubt they were absurd, these barricades, made of overturned cars and bits of

---

[1] Not that the Russians were blameless. Through lack of co-ordination, their radio, without any reference to the plans of the Red Army Command, was issuing general directives to the Poles "in the enemy rear" to "rise against the Germans".

furniture and a few paving-stones: not one of them could have stood up to an 88mm shell. Yet it "felt good" to be on the barricades; and out of their poor homes men and women and children dragged their cupboards and mattresses. And Colonel Rol, the dynamic regional commander of the FFI, a former worker who had been sacked for Communist propaganda from Renault, Citroen, and Bréguet, issued orders on August 22:

A CHACUN SON BOCHE!

COUVRIR PARIS DE BARRICADES!

Joliot-Curie was making "Molotov cocktails" at the Sorbonne. There was much sniping; there were hundreds of skirmishes; every day, while the insurrection lasted, forty or fifty bodies were being taken to Notre-Dame des Victoires; they were beginning to stink in the heat. Food was desperately short; but the FFI captured 2,500 tons of frozen meat from the Germans, and were able to hand out half-pound rations to the troops.

Barricades in the working-class quarters, but none in the Champs-Elysées area.... The bourgeoisie were worried lest the FFI (les Fifi, they already venomously began to call them) captured the Mairies which the Germans had abandoned. All the profiteers of the Occupation were dreading a "People's Government"—de Gaulle seemed a much, much lesser evil; and they prayed for de Gaulle to come to the rescue of that Law and Order which the Germans were so hastily abandoning.

And then, on the 25th, the Leclerc Division entered Paris from the South; not without considerable difficulty had de Gaulle succeeded in persuading the Allied Command to hasten the rescue of Paris, and to let it be done by a French unit. The Insurrection had not been a terrible thing like Warsaw; but nearly three thousand Frenchmen had been killed, and there were some 7,000 wounded. All things considered, it was a small price to pay for even what some have called a "token rising"; in one sense it was that; the Germans did not fight back as they might have done, and the partial three days' "truce", and the curious negotiations that went on behind the scenes between Mr Nordling, the Swedish Consul-General, and General von Choltitz, the military commander of Paris on the one hand, and the same Mr Nordling and M. Parodi, de Gaulle's representative on the other, all tended to spoil the traditional romantic picture of a great Paris insurrection, with its barricades, 1830 or 1848 style. But was that the fault of the working-class?

A significant editorial on the subject was written a year later in *Combat*—probably by Albert Camus:

For a whole year now we hear some good souls telling us that there never was any Paris insurrection, and that the men of the Resistance did no more than fire a few shots into the air, at the very last moment. It is true that these good souls weren't on the barricades.... For there weren't any at Auteuil and Passy.

Others again paint us a glorious picture of the whole people rising like one man, brandishing their rifles and liberating Paris all by themselves, in a great romantic flourish. The truth is simpler—but no less great. Four or five thousand men, with a few hundred firearms between them, came out, in accordance with a well-worked-out plan, in order to hold up the retreating remnants of the German 7th Army. After less than a week 50,000 Parisians were on the barricades, in the districts of the Revolution, and were fighting with arms captured from the enemy. Thanks to them, Paris slowed down the German retreat ... and spared the Allies some additional battles. ...

Such is the truth. But one should add to it the colours of a Paris summer, the thunderstorm on that Wednesday night, and the young people manning those barricades and laughing at last, for the first time in four years.[2]

De Gaulle's arrival in Paris on August 25, 1944, when he was received at the Hôtel-de-Ville by the members of the CNR, representing the home Resistance, was, of course, one of the great moments in the recent history of France. As he himself said: "It is a moment the greatness of which transcends our lives." Bidault, as President of the CNR, and Georges Marrane, the Communist President of the Paris Committee of Liberation, both paid equally warm tributes to de Gaulle. On the following day, amidst immense public rejoicing, de Gaulle travelled all the way from the Etoile down to the Hôtel-de-Ville and thence to Notre-Dame, where, despite much firing from Germans or the Fifth Column, and some dead and wounded (some shots were even fired inside the Cathedral), he calmly stood through the service, joining fervently in the *Magnificat*. His cool courage made a great impression.

The immense enthusiasm of Paris that day was like one deep, unanimous sigh of relief at the thought that the German occupation was over; and de Gaulle was loved that day because he had come to symbolize the Liberation, and to personify France's soldierly virtues. The Resistance press, which had, during the Insurrection, taken over most of the newspaper offices, was lyrical and romantic in the extreme: the Communist *Humanité*, for example, printing on top of its front page on August 26 these lines of Victor Hugo:

> Aux armes, citoyens! Aux fourches, paysans! ...
> La Marseillaise n'est pas encore enrouée,
> Le cheval que montait Kléber n'est pas fourbu,
> Tout le vin de l'audace immense n'est pas bu
> Et Dieu nous en laisse assez au fond du verre
> Pour donner à la Prusse une chasse sévère ...

[2] *Combat*, August 20, 1945.

And, below these verses, these banner headlines:

Les derniers ennemis anéantis dans la capitale!
TOUTE LA JOURNEE LES FFI ET LES TROUPES ONT
COMBATTU POUR REDUIRE LES ILOTS ALLEMANDS
D'un bout à l'autre de la France encore occupée
levée d'armes du peuple pour exterminer
l'envahisseur

A 15 HEURES, DE L'ARC DE TRIOMPHE
A NOTRE-DAME
LE PEUPLE UNANIME ACCLAMERA
LE GENERAL DE GAULLE

"La guerre continue ... La France doit se trouver au premier rang
des grandes nations!" *déclare de Gaulle à l'Hôtel-de-Ville où il
est accueilli par Georges Marrane ...*

SOLDATS DE LECLERC, AMIS AMERICAINS,
Paris qui s'est libéré lui-même les armes à la main
VOUS ACCUEILLE ET VOUS SALUE!

The other papers were scarcely less restrained in their enthusiasm.[3]

But, like the French officer who said it on Armistice Day 1918, so
de Gaulle could say on the day of his Paris apotheosis: *"C'est
aujourd'hui que ça commence."*

[3] The principal dailies that had begun to appear (all on two pages) during the
Paris Insurrection—and most of them under some "Resistance" banner—were:
Le Parisien Libéré (organ of the O.C.M. Resistance organization); *France Libre*
(Editor, André Mutter, one of the right-wing members of the CNR); *L'Aurore*
(organ of the Radicals); *L'Aube* (organ of the Démocrates Chrétiens, with
articles by Maurice Schumann, Bidault, Letourneau, etc); *Combat* (organ of the
Combat resistance movement; editor, Albert Camus; among its contributors,
J.-P. Sartre, G. Bernanos and other distinguished names); *Le Populaire* (official
organ of the Socialist Party); *Défense de la France* (a former clandestine paper,
which was, before long, to assume the much more commercial title of *France-
Soir*—a revival, in effect, of the old *Paris-Soir);* then, three near-Communist
papers, all of "Resistance" origin: *Franc-Tireur* (run by the leaders of the
Resistance group of that name, notably Albert Bayet (Radical) and Georges
Altman (Socialist); and, similarly, *Libération* and *Front National*: and, finally,
the official Communist organ, *L'Humanité* and the Communist evening paper,
Ce Soir. About the only paper not specifically attached to any Party or particular
Resistance movement (and indeed, Vichyite in its whole tradition) was the
Figaro; but it also had resumed publication during the Paris insurrection, and
most of its contributors (at *that* stage) were, more or less, "Resistance". Most
notable among the weeklies to appear immediately after the Liberation of Paris
were *Carrefour*, with a great front-page article by Mauriac; *Lettres Françaises*
(near-Communist); and the *Canard-Enchaîné* (at that time, though not for very
long, near-Communist, too). The *Monde* did not begin to appear until December
1944.

CHAPTER FOUR

FRANCE AT THE LIBERATION.
THE CNR CHARTER

W HAT were the main problems with which de Gaulle's Provisional Government was faced at the time of the Liberation? First, the application of a number of basic *ordonnances* passed by the CFLN (after an *avis favourable* from the Consultative Assembly at Algiers) concerning the future government of France.

The *ordonnance* of April 21, 1944, provided that elections be held for a Constituent Assembly not later than one year after the complete liberation of French territory; in the interval the "republican institutions" would be "progressively re-established".

Further, it provided that, in the case of the *communes*, the municipal councils which existed on September 3, 1939 be re-established, though after the elimination of those members who "had directly favoured the enemy or the usurper" (i.e. Vichy). If, after such a purge, there was no quorum, the vacancies were to be provisionally filled by the Prefect, after consultation with the regional Liberation Committee. An "all-bad" council was to be replaced by a "special delegation" nominated in a similar way by the Prefect. In the case of the *départements*, a similar procedure was to be applied to the *conseils généraux*, except that the "purging" was to be done, not by the Prefect, but by the Minister of the Interior. In the appointment of new councils priority was to be given to councillors who "had remained faithful to their duty", and to members of the Resistance (male or female) —account, however, being taken of the political majority on the dissolved council and of "the tendencies that had expressed themselves in the department since the Liberation".

A very important provision was the constitution of departmental Liberation Committees, composed of representatives of the Resistance organizations and of political parties directly affiliated with the CNR. These Committees, according to the *ordonnance*, were to "assist the Prefect, but cease their functions after the re-establishment of the *conseils généraux*". As we shall see, it was over these provisions that serious difficulties arose for a time between the de Gaulle Government and the local Resistance committees which often attributed to themselves functions that were in conflict with the *ordonnance* of April 21, thus creating something of a clash between the central and the local authorities.

The *ordonnance* further provided that the Provisional Government and the Consultative Assembly be moved from Algiers to France as soon as possible, and that the Assembly be enlarged. As for the subsequent election of a Provisional Representative Assembly, the *ordonnance* specified that a very considerable number of persons would not be eligible: former members of the Vichy Government; deputies and senators who had voted for Pétain on July 10, 1940; persons who had aided the Germans or harmed France or her allies, or had accepted from Vichy "a portion of authority, or the seat of a national councillor, a departmental councillor or, in the case of Paris, of a municipal councillor".

Another *ordonnance* of August 9, 1944 declared all the acts of the Vichy Government to be null and void.

For centuries France had been a highly centralized country, and it was certain that, sooner or later, the central Paris Government would be accepted as the supreme authority by the population. But the fact that for four years the country had been cut in two, that large parts of the country had been liberated by the FFI and other Resistance organizations with little or no contact with Algiers, was bound to create some temporary difficulties. For one thing, it was not in the first place the Algiers Government, but the CNR that had proposed, in its "plan of immediate action", dated March 15, 1944, the establishment of Liberation committees in towns, villages, and enterprises, under the general direction of departmental Liberation committees, themselves subordinated to the CNR.

In many parts of Central and Southern France in particular, the local Liberation committees followed only the general instructions contained in the CNR programme. Thus, instead of re-establishing the authority of the pre-war municipal councils, in accordance with the Algiers *ordonnance*, they often took over themselves the duties of the municipal councils. Also, in many places, especially where the Communists were particularly active, "civil and republican guards" were formed, and these would often not obey the central government, except through the medium of the Liberation committees. For some time, the de Gaulle Government was to have great difficulty in trying to enforce a strict application of the *ordonnance* of April 21.

In addition to the Prefects, special *Commissaires de la République*, many of them sympathetic to the Communists (Aubrac for Marseilles, Farge for Lyon, Ingrand for Clermont-Ferrand) were appointed by the Government in an attempt to overcome the difficulties.

At Limoges, Toulouse, Montpellier, and some other cities it took some time before the balance was restored between the local authorities that had emerged from the Resistance and the Provisional Government now established in Paris.[1]

[1] *L'Année Politique*, 1944–45, p. 14.

Although the *Commissaires de la République* had been given extensive powers (suspension of officials, requisitioning, etc), it seems that they were instructed to use persuasion, rather than force *vis-à-vis* the Liberation committees. It is certain that, among these Liberation committees, there were people who distrusted de Gaulle, and were hoping to see, before surrendering their authority, how far the de Gaulle Government intended to apply the CNR Charter.

It is unnecessary to apologize to the reader for giving as full a summary as possible of the CNR Charter; for this Charter may be said not only to embody all the aspirations of the great majority of the *résistants* (though not, of course, of all the nominal members of the CNR, such as M. Laniel or M. Mutter), but also to constitute a sort of ideological foundation-stone of the Fourth Republic. The whole subsequent history of the Fourth Republic was largely a struggle between those who wished to see the CNR Charter applied, and those who were determined to ignore it—even though, occasionally, paying lipservice to it. This is particularly true of its economic and colonial clauses.

It must, however, be said that, at least during the first two or three years after the Liberation, some social and structural reforms were introduced in virtue of the CNR Charter; also, those who drafted the two Constitutions always had to bear the CNR Charter in mind. It is true that many of these reforms, such as the nationalization of the banks, were in practice to prove largely nominal. But that is another story.

The CNR Charter began by saying that all those united in the CNR were determined to remain united after the Liberation in order to:

(1) Establish the government of the Republic under General de Gaulle, which would defend the political and economic independence of the Nation and re-establish the strength, greatness and prestige of France;

(2) See to it that traitors be punished and that those who aided the enemy or were actively associated with Vichy be eliminated from the administration and from professional activity;

(3) Demand that the property of traitors and black-market profiteers be confiscated, and that profits made during the war and Occupation be heavily and progressively taxed;

(4) See to it that universal suffrage be re-established; that there be full freedom of thought, conscience, and expression; that there be complete freedom of the press and its independence *vis-à-vis* the State, vested interests and foreign governments; freedom of association, meetings and demonstrations; inviolability of the home and the secrecy of letters; respect of the human person; absolute equality of all citizens before the law;

(5) Promote the following indispensable reforms:

(a) *Economic:* The establishment of a true economic and social democracy, implying "the eviction from the management of France's economy of the great economic and financial feudal forces";

The subordination of private interests to the public interest;

The intensification of production in accordance with a Plan to be decided upon by the State, after consultation with all those concerned with this production;

The nationalization of "all the great monopolized means of production, which are a product of common labour; of the sources of power; of mineral wealth; of insurance companies; and of the big banks";

The development of producer and consumer co-operatives; the right for sufficiently qualified workers to be appointed to managerial posts and directorships inside an enterprise; and a share of responsibility for the workers in the economic direction of enterprises;

(*b*) *Social:* The right to work and rest, to be assured particularly through the re-establishment and improvement of the system of labour contracts;

An adequate rise in wages and the guarantee of a wage level which would bring to every worker and his family "security, dignity, and the possibility of a fully human existence";

The protection of purchasing power on a national scale through a policy leading to monetary stability;

The re-establishment of independent trade unionism;

A complete plan of social security;

Security of employment, with legislation regulating employment and dismissal; re-establishment of workshop delegates;

Adequate old-age pensions;

[Various measures in favour of remunerative agricultural price, in favour of agricultural labourers, etc.]

(*c*) *Colonial:* The extension of political, social, and economic rights to native and colonial populations;

(*d*) *Educational:* The fullest educational possibilities for all French children, in accordance with their ability, and wholly regardless of their parents' social or financial position. The creation, by this means, of "an élite by merit instead of an élite by birth".

This was obviously a left-wing programme corresponding most closely to the Socialist outlook, and representing, as it were, a minimum programme for the Communists, and a maximum programme for the more cautious people in the CNR. A few, like Laniel and Mutter, merely associated themselves with it *pro forma*. They were, indeed, to make this quite obvious as soon as any economic legislation on the lines of the CNR Charter came up for parliamentary discussion.

The CNR Charter was not a revolutionary programme; it represented rather a sort of New Deal, or what Bidault, the President of the CNR had called, on the great day of de Gaulle's Paris apotheosis, "*la révolution par la loi*". But even this "revolution" was to be largely sabotaged—consciously, or through the force of circumstances. What the CNR, in drawing up its optimistic programme in 1944, had not taken into account was the coming of the Cold War and of the war in Indo-China, both of which wrecked, before long, every prospect of a left-wing majority (which the Resistance essentially represented) carrying out a left-wing programme. The French Communists were not the only, or even the main, culprits in this tragic failure.

Needless to say, 1944 was hardly a time suitable for far-reaching structural reforms, requiring heavy capital outlay. The war was going well, with the Allied troops sweeping across France and Belgium, and with the Russians inside Poland and Rumania; but its end was not yet clearly in sight. De Gaulle's main preoccupations were (a) the rôle that France still had time to play in this final stage of the war, and (b) her diplomatic position—and, indeed, the international status of his Government which, at the time of the Liberation of Paris, had not yet received *de jure* recognition from the Big Three. How was the French Army to be enlarged and equipped, so that it could pull its weight? Also, what was to be France's diplomatic "orientation"? De Gaulle's and Bidault's journey to Moscow in December 1944 was an event typical of the diplomatic game of "independence" de Gaulle was trying to play at that time.

Inside France two of the major problems were (a) the "clean-up" and the punishment of traitors; and (b) not so much a coherent economic reconstruction, as a variety of emergency measures for "normalizing" everyday life as far as possible. For life was anything but normal. Over two million men were still in Germany. The country had suffered great damage from the four years of German occupation, from the military operations that were still going on; from the often unnecessarily destructive Allied bombings;[2] from the destruction of railways and bridges; from the shortage of rolling-stock and of all raw materials.

At the time of the Liberation, economic activity was almost at a standstill. Railway transport had been virtually paralysed all over France, and food conditions in the larger cities, and especially in Paris, were extremely bad. All the bridges on the Seine between Paris and the sea, on the Loire between Nevers and the sea, on the Rhône between Lyon and the sea had been blown up. Over a thousand road and railway bridges had been destroyed. Practically all the ports, with the exception of Cherbourg, which was used by the Allies, were either out of action, or still in German hands. Of 17,000 railway engines, before the war, less than 3,000 were left, and railway trucks and carriages were down to about 40 per cent, and many of these in poor

---

[2] The most common story told by people in bombed French cities (Arles, for example) was that British bombers aimed well, but that American bombers often "smashed everything except their strategic target".

condition. By the end of the war, nearly half a million houses had been destroyed and 1½ million damaged; the output of electricity in September 1944 was down to one half, and that of coal to one-fifth of the 1938 level, even though the coal mines had suffered less than might have been feared.

No doubt, the destruction in France was mild compared with that suffered, for example, by Poland or Western Russia; the number of livestock had diminished to only a small extent, and, although owing to shortage of manpower, fertilizers, and agricultural machinery, the soil of France was yielding less than before the war, France managed, even after the wholly "abnormal" summer of 1944 to harvest 6·4 million tons of wheat, or about 80 per cent of the pre-war average. In every Norman village, huge pyramids of *camemberts* were getting higher and higher—in both senses—in the absence of transport. Some parts of the country were bursting with food, while Paris was on starvation rations, and, for a few weeks, even the black market found it hard to cope with transport difficulties. Adult rations were down to 1,050 calories, and though vegetables and other unrationed food could be bought in the "open" market, wages had scarcely doubled since pre-war, while the currency inflation had reduced the franc to about one-fifth its pre-war value.

The working-class were, as usual, having the worst of it. Their anger against the Germans and against the profiteers was accordingly greater than among other categories, such as the peasantry, who had been less severely hit economically, while many had even made large profits.

There was a certain machiavellian cunning on the part of de Gaulle and the bourgeoisie to give the Communists a share of power in the Government; apart from the "sentimental" consideration that they had been very prominent in the Resistance—which made it impossible to keep them out altogether—there was the much more practical consideration that their presence in the Government, and notably in the economic posts, would tend to keep the exasperated working-class both patient and diligent, and as untroublesome as possible. And that, broadly speaking, is what happened so long as the Communists were in the Government. Despite privations, the French working-class worked very hard throughout 1944, 1945, and 1946, contributed immensely to the restoration of the essential services and to the "normalization" of life. Within a year after the Liberation, the mines, railways, and much else were already in relatively good working order. Slogans like those contained in Thorez's speech at the Vélodrome d'Hiver on November 27, 1944 on his return from the Soviet Union had much to do with it: "Make war; create a great French army; work like blazes, rapidly rebuild industry," etc. He was also to be of great help to de Gaulle in other ways: notably by approving, on January 21, 1945, the dissolution of the *milices patriotiques*, attached to the Liberation committees, and by discouraging strikes and "unreasonable" demands for wage increases. The Communist ministers, as Mendès-France was to say much later, may have been "disloyal" to de Gaulle in 1944–6; but, on balance, de Gaulle undoubtedly greatly gained from their presence in the Government.

Two things put an end to Communist co-operation: the beginning of the Cold War and the outbreak of the war in Indo-China, both of which made it impossible for *tripartisme* to be maintained; for *tripartisme*, like the CNR Charter, was based on the assumption that the forces of the Resistance, of which the Communists were an essential part, could remain united. *Tripartisme* became an uneasy partnership from the moment the gulf began to widen between East and West. After that, it was good-bye to the New Deal, to the *révolution par la loi* and all the rosy dreams of the Resistance of a "better" France. We shall see later how much (or how little) the Communists were to blame for this.

CHAPTER FIVE

THE RESISTANCE: FIRST SIGNS
OF FRUSTRATION

THE Government of "National Unanimity" under General de Gaulle was formed a fortnight after the Liberation of Paris; it was, in the main, composed of some former members of the Provisional Government at Algiers, of representatives of the Home Resistance, and of four of the "old" political parties.[1] A first Government list was published on September 5, but the "final version" was not adopted until four days later. M. Bidault, abandoning his post as President of the CNR to M. Saillant, of the CGT, became Foreign Minister, a post he appears to have coveted for a long time; another Demo-Christian, M. de Menthon, took the arduous post of Minister of Justice; M. Mendès-France became Minister of National Economy, a post at which he was soon to come into conflict with M. Lepercq, the "orthodox" Minister of Finance, and, after M. Lepercq's death in a road accident in October, with his successor, M. Pleven. In April 1945 M. Mendès-France resigned. The Ministry of the Interior went to M. Tixier, a Socialist, while the Ministry of Food went to M. Giaccobi, to be succeeded soon after by M. Ramadier, whose management of the Food Ministry was to become one of the worst jokes of the year. Only two Communists were included in this first post-Liberation Government: M. Billoux, as Minister of Health, and M. Tillon as Minister of Air. The Communists felt that they were being discriminated against, but nevertheless accepted the two posts as a small beginning.[2]

No doubt, several of these Ministers had been active *résistants*, notably Bidault, Teitgen, and de Menthon, not to mention Tillon (who as a Communist, presented a special case); but these, no less than the rest of the Government, rapidly became conscious of being "government men", and the latent conflict between the Government and the

---

[1] Radicals, Christian-Democrats (later called MRP), Socialists and Communists.

[2] Among the other important appointments were: M. Diethelm (London group), War; Lacoste (Soc.), Production; Tanguy-Prigent (Soc.), Agriculture; Pleven (London group), Colonies; Parodi (high official), Labour and Social Security; René Mayer (Rad.), Transport and Public Works; General Catroux, North Africa; P. H. Teitgen (Dem. Chr.), Information.

Resistance organizations soon became very apparent. De Gaulle him-self was clearly out of sympathy with the Home Resistance.

One of the most active members of the Resistance, Lucie Aubrac, the wife of Raymond Aubrac (*Commissaire de la République* at Mar-seilles) was to tell me some years later:

The CNR, as you know, was created towards the *end* of the Resistance, just in order to give the world the idea that de Gaulle had "the whole of France behind him". At Algiers, on the other hand, de Gaulle had to collect all sorts of *vieux crabes*, just to create an illusion of continuity—the idea that he was, somehow, continuing the Third Republic.... For a long time the Resistance didn't know much about him. In Normandy, before he arrived, they used to ask: "What's he like—big or small, thin or fat?" During his "triumphal journey" through France after the Liberation, he behaved most unpleasantly. At Marseilles he was given a truly exuberant reception. You know what our Marseillais are like.... There was a tre-mendous parade of the Maquisards, wearing pretty tattered civilian clothes —real *sans-culottes*!—most of them with open collars, for it was a very hot day, and with flowers tied to their rifles. And they dragged along a German armoured car, and on top of it were a lot of young Marseilles women in somewhat frivolous and not quite modest summer dresses, screaming and waving flags—a really nice bit of Mediterranean exuberance. And, do you know, de Gaulle took it very badly indeed; he sat there glumly, muttering: "*Quelle mascarade, quelle mascarade!*" His anti-plebeian instincts came out with a vengeance that day. And, on another occasion, at Lyon, he wanted to sit at a banquet between the Prefect and the *Commissaire de la Répub-lique*. Instead, we put him between two leaders of the local Resistance. He took it very badly, looked like thunder, and didn't address one word to them throughout the meal.

In a sense, it was a triumphal journey; but on more than one occa-sion de Gaulle made it quite clear that the Government was master now, that the Resistance organizations had outlived their usefulness, and that the Liberation committees and their "patriotic guards" were a survival of the past, and should disappear.

It was not very long after the Liberation of Paris that *Combat*, the most characteristic of the non-Communist Resistance papers, wrote: "All the Resistance has now left is the movements and the press." But the "movements", of which, in fact, there were by now only two "federated" movements that mattered, the chiefly non-Communist and partly anti-Communist MLN (*Mouvement de Libération Nationale*) and the predominantly Communist *Front National* were before very long to be "absorbed" in the political parties. The extent to which a "movement" like the MLN became scarcely distinguish-able from a party may be seen from its campaign in search of members: in the Paris metro there were posters saying: "Join the MLN!" and a typical joke of the year was the cartoon of the peaceful middle-aged man coming home, many months after the Liberation, and telling his wife and children: "I have just joined the Resistance." As for the press, its character also changed, though less rapidly, and *Combat*, with its slogan (printed, it is true, in smaller and smaller characters, and finally in almost invisible type) *"De la Résistance à la Révolution"*, tried to carry on the Resistance tradition right into 1949. A few went plainly Communist (like *Libération*); many disappeared altogether; while much of the "Resistance" press simply went "commercial", notably *Défense de la France*, which became *France-Soir*, as well as *Aurore* and the *Parisien Libéré*.

But the fact that not only the Communist, but also the non-Communist Resistance aimed very high at first, and took the CNR Charter very seriously may be seen from the growing bitterness of a paper like *Combat* which, soon after the Liberation, began to complain of the "strange demeanour" of de Gaulle and his Ministers.

At the height of the Paris Insurrection, in its first (regularly printed) number, it wrote:

The fight against Nazi Germany continues; it's the hardest of all, *but it is not the only one*. It is not enough to reconquer that semblance of freedom with which the France of 1939 had to be content. Unlike the old France, the new France must not be under the thumb of the financial powers...

And again on October 1:

We want a liberal policy and a collectivist economy. Without such an economy which will deprive the financial powers of their privileges, and give these privileges to labour, political freedom can only be a delusion.

And on October 7:

We still believe in the truth of the resolution, passed by the Combat Congress at Algiers last March—that "Anti-Communism is the beginning of dictatorship". While disagreeing with the Communists on many points, we firmly reject political anti-Communism, with all its unavowed aims.... And while we agree with the Communists on their collectivism, their social programme, their ideal of economic justice, and their disgust with a moneyed society, we thoroughly disagree with their "political realism".

Already by the end of October *Combat* became outspokenly critical of de Gaulle; first over the dissolution of the *gardes patriotiques*, which was done "without the CNR having been consulted", and in a manner insulting to men who had rendered great services—and were continuing to exercise a salutary vigilance in the country—even though they might latterly have been joined by some "doubtful elements". And, secondly, it protested against the Liberation Loan, which, coming before *any* monetary reform, was like a disastrous surrender to the "financial powers", whose "confidence" was now being sought. The issue was, indeed, fundamental; and Mendès-France was to resign over it before long.

What, in the eyes of *Combat* (run at that time by Albert Camus and Albert Ollivier) was the rôle that the Resistance should have played *vis-à-vis* the de Gaulle Government?

The future of our political life cannot be abandoned to the Parties only.... It's a case of building up a new élite whose authority would be based exclusively on competence and a high moral character—an élite of work and thought. The Resistance can provide this élite, which could form revolutionary clubs.... Remember the power exercised on the Assemblies by the Jacobin and even the Feuillant clubs.... It is not a case of blindly imitating the French Revolution; but these clubs, independent of the parties and of the Government, and directly acquainted with local conditions could usefully inform the Government and the Assemblies. As distinct from parties, the function of a genuine élite is to seek authority rather than power.[3]

What it claimed was, in effect, this: it was no use pretending that the *majority* of France was actively *résistante*; the *real* Resistance was however an *active minority*, which was entitled to exercise an influence in excess of its numbers. In a sense, this idea of the Resistance "clubs" was not a still-born one, though it never came to the formation of any actual "clubs". But it is true, as will be seen later, that intellectual groups, all of which had originally been more or less associated with the Resistance, and which had an important and occasionally decisive influence on public opinion and, indirectly, on Parliament, were to contribute a very great deal to the intellectual alertness and liveliness of France under the Fourth Republic—notably intellectual groups who produced papers like the *Monde*, *Esprit*, *Combat*, *Témoignage Chrétien*, *Les Temps Modernes*, and, more recently, *France-Observateur*, and (in a way) *L'Express*. If they failed to revolutionize the country's economy in accordance with the CNR Charter, they fought effectively against reactionary and authoritarian tendencies on the part of certain French Governments, and exercised considerable influence in opposing EDC, in clamouring for years for peace in Indo-China, in denouncing the Governments' misdeeds in North Africa, and in frequently showing up certain French institutions, notably the police. In the end, the influence of these groups was about all that was left of the Resistance, apart from its specifically Communist wing. But it was highly important, as we shall see.

In 1944–5 de Gaulle came, more and more, to consider the Resistance as merely a nuisance—at any rate those elements in the Resistance which would not "conform". A typical example of their treat-

[3] *Combat*, November 8, 1944.

ment was the Government's refusal to let a CNR delegation visit North Africa in January 1945—lest they saw too much, or said all the wrong things to the natives—whose happy future had also been provided for in the CNR Charter!

Not that de Gaulle was against a "New France" in every sense. Far from it. Soon after the Liberation of Paris a number of highly important nationalizations were decided upon: the coal mines of the Nord and Pas-de-Calais; the Renault works; the Gnôme et Rhône works; civil aviation, and the merchant navy—a different method of nationalization was applied in nearly every case. No doubt, the Resistance "ideologists" were not going to be satisfied with the mere word "nationalization"; what was to happen, they asked, *after* an enterprise had been nationalized? Did not de Gaulle take the view, *Combat* inquired, that it was "enough to recruit a body of state administrators and controllers" to run these nationalized industries, and that it was "a case of forming a bureaucracy that would boss them."

We, on the contrary, think that the management and administration of these enterprises should be placed in the hands of the trade unions, who should provide the technical and administrative staffs.[4]

And already it sounded a note that was to become only too familiar some years later: the danger of "technocracy" and "managerialism":

More or less the same men are running industry as in the Vichy days—when they ran the *comités d'organisation* and the *comités de répartition*. The high officials in France have two prevalent tendencies—either to be ultra-conservative or to go in for what might be called "reformist Fascism". Especially the high financial officials should no longer be the same people, if anything new is to be done in France. For it is not the Ministers who guide the officials, but *vice versa....* There is a real danger of the old *République des Camarades...* being succeeded by a *République de Techniciens*.[5]

Truly prophetic words, as anyone would realize who, in later years, went inside the Renault works, for instance—with its State-appointed Director-General every bit as tough a boss as M. Louis Renault—who died of heart failure back in 1944 at the thought of being nationalized as a penalty for his unpatriotic behaviour during the German Occupation.

[4] *Combat*, March 3, 1945.   [5] *Combat*, February 14, 1944.

CHAPTER SIX

DE GAULLE: EAST-WEST DILEMMA AND THE FRENCH ARMY

D E GAULLE had plenty of other worries between the Liberation and VE Day. He did not like the way France was being treated by the Great Powers. It took several weeks, even after the Liberation of Paris, before the Big Three recognized his Government *de jure*, the USA being particularly reluctant to do so. France had a rather bad press in both England and America, the *Daily Express*, for instance, saying that France had better be occupied by Allied troops, and painting lurid pictures of a large part of France being a patchwork of miniature "Soviet republics", with the Paris government lacking all proper authority. Such attacks continued for several months.

Both de Gaulle and Bidault kept on repeating that they were not in favour of a "Western Bloc"; it would be wrong to "separate Western Europe from the rest". De Gaulle also pressed for a "separate" status for the left bank of the Rhine and for the Ruhr—a significant "Poincaré", not to say "Maurras", approach to the German problem. As he got little support from Britain and America, he sought Russian support. In this respect his Moscow visit was, however, a failure—even though "French military spokesmen" were saying at the time that Stalin and de Gaulle had agreed on Germany's frontiers: France on the Rhine and Poland on the Oder.[1] This was not the case. However, the agreement between France and the Soviet Union to do all they could to neutralize Germany "by opposing any initiative liable to enable Germany to attempt aggression once again", as well as the agreement of mutual aid in the event of German aggression against either of the signatories were an important diplomatic achievement for de Gaulle. That de Gaulle was not altogether satisfied with the personal side of his Moscow visit is another matter;[2] and, worse still,

[1] *Franc-Tireur*, December 19, 1944.

[2] De Gaulle's visit to Moscow, which I witnessed, had some comic sides to it. First of all, de Gaulle made a bad *gaffe* at Stalingrad when he referred to it as a "symbol of allied unity". To the Russians, Stalingrad was, of course, an exclusively Russian victory, nobody else doing much against the German army at the time. (To the Russians North Africa was a "mere sideshow".) Even the equipment at Stalingrad was almost exclusively Russian, the lend-lease material not arriving in appreciable quantities until later. In Moscow de Gaulle was

he was to be furious not only with Stalin, but also with Churchill and Roosevelt at not being invited to Yalta. His bad humour was revealed soon afterwards by his refusal to go to Algiers to meet Roosevelt, on the latter's return journey from the Yalta Conference. Stalin, for his part, was reported to have referred to France at Yalta as being "of no consequence"—a phrase which, one rather suspects, was attributed to him by those wishing to pull France "the other way". Not that, as we shall see, the "other side" was in the least forthcoming to de Gaulle's demands, notably about the Rhineland and the Ruhr.

While the war against Germany was still in progress, the French Army continued to be one of de Gaulle's major concerns, if not the greatest of all. At the time of the Liberation of Paris there were two armies in France: one was a regular army, organized overseas, including the famous armoured division under General Leclerc; the other was the Home Army, the FFI, which had been in action for some months, and especially since D-Day. One was a professional army, the other a revolutionary army, and it was de Gaulle's problem to turn the two into one great national army. There were great psychological and technical difficulties in the way. The professional soldiers, with their outer discipline and their traditions were disconcerted at the sight of these soldiers without uniforms, and accustomed to the hard school of "illegality" and individual initiative.

No doubt [*Combat* wrote on September 24] there is distrust on both sides. But as a school of courage and character, barricades are just as good as trenches. And this people's army will put some fresh blood into the somewhat obsolete traditions of the French Army.

But the problem of *cadres* was a very tricky one. Would the officers of the FFI be able to keep their ranks—the Regular Army officers denying that an FFI Colonel, for instance, not accustomed to the use of heavy modern equipment, was fit to remain a colonel. On September 23 a decree of the de Gaulle Government "amalgamated" the FFI rank and file with the regular French Army; but the question of officers was left open. However, it was decided soon afterwards that

startled to find that the ordinary Russian public took no interest in him at all, and scarcely knew who he was; in the Moscow underground he had his large feet trodden on and was pushed about as roughly as anybody else by clusters of people struggling to get in or out; his and Bidault's determination to attend Mass at the little Catholic Church in Moscow was treated a trifle ironically by many, including the French Minister, who remarked: "*Mon Dieu, ce n'est pas un gouvernement, c'est une sacristie!*" Bidault, for his part, finding that nobody was taking much notice of either him or de Gaulle, complained that this was "*un peuple froid, un peuple inhumain. . .*" Nor did all go smoothly at the Kremlin. Stalin is said to have found de Gaulle "about the stickiest negotiator he had yet come across", and Stalin's attempts at joviality made little impression on "poker face". The latter refused to recognize the "Lublin Committee".

after a few weeks' additional training (when necessary), the FFI officers could be incorporated, with no change of rank, in the Army. There was, however, subsequently to be much friction between these "plebeian upstarts" and the "regular" officers, who had come from Algiers, and many of whom had faithfully served Pétain. The amalgamation of the Regular Army with the FFI in 1944 started in effect something of a class struggle among the French officers and, needless to say, the "old school" won in the end. Already, soon after the collapse of Germany one was to hear stories about the French Occupation Authorities in Baden-Baden having created there "a little Vichy of their own".

A high proportion of the FFI officers were, of course, Communists, including men like General Malleret-Joinville (always referred to after the war in the anti-Communist press as "General" in quotation marks); and their elimination from the Army was to be progressive, but thorough. In 1951 M. Jules Moch, at a luncheon of the Anglo-American Press Association swore that "only two Communist lieutenant-colonels, and nothing above that rank" were left in the French Army, and that even these would be eliminated as soon as possible. With general conscription in France, it was, unfortunately, he said, inevitable that there should be "a certain proportion of Communists" among the conscripts! Whispering propaganda, even in 1944–5, tended to place FFI colonels and FFI generals rather in the same category as Papal Counts.

But that was not de Gaulle's greatest worry while the war was still in progress. Much more serious, from his point of view, was the fact that, despite the available human resources, there was no material means of building up, before the end of the war, a major French army. On October 26, 1944, de Gaulle bitterly complained at a press conference of the Allies' failure to supply France with arms; "not a single major army unit could be properly constituted since the Liberation", he said, and he denied that the lack of landing facilities was "the only reason for this". "It's an extraordinary thing," he said bitterly, "but then this *is* an extraordinary war." Altogether, said de Gaulle, there were "incredible difficulties" about arming and clothing the French Army, and the Allies were in no hurry to help.

To the French, it was becoming like another "phoney war". During Rundstedt's December offensive there were no French troops in the field except the Delattre Army, the Leclerc Division and the Alsace-Lorraine Brigade; some 20,000 FFI had been drafted into them; 70,000 FFI's were used for besieging Saint-Nazaire and other ports still in German hands, but they were too poorly equipped to be able to do much. The others were idle.

The French are not allowed to fight [wrote *Combat* on December 23 at the height of the Rundstedt offensive]. Thousands of volunteers go to recruiting stations, and are sent away. Quite near, a cruel war is being fought, and they are not allowed to take part in it. The French are not used to being treated as outsiders, as football fans, cheering on the teams. . . .

There was a touch of tragic irony about it. In 1939 the French Army, though armed (not very well, it is true), was not very keen to meet the Germans. "Now, in 1944, there is an unarmed nation, straining at the leash, anxious to take a major part in the liberation of French territory, and seeing English, American, and other soldiers die instead. . . ."[3]

With VE Day approaching things were still far from good if France was to hold a worthy place among the victorious nations. On March 1, de Gaulle said that there were altogether 1,200,000 French soldiers, but their equipment and armament were wholly insufficient. The first French tanks would not be produced until the following September. Rightly or wrongly, there were again suspicions, as during the Resistance, that the Allies did not particularly *want* to arm more Frenchmen than necessary—there was rather too much "revolutionary material" among them, with no guarantee that they would prove good, disciplined soldiers—even though de Gaulle himself had said on October 25, probably quite sincerely:

The FFI are nearly all young people of the highest quality, and France can make of them an impressive army. It's only a matter of a few months; you will see what a good mixture it'll make—the old Army and the FFI.

But his hopes of what would happen "in a few months" were to be disappointed.

Perhaps events in Greece, Belgium, and Italy had something to do with it. The Allied Army commanders were becoming increasingly distrustful of the "Resistance", and of anybody connected with it. The shooting-down of a workers' demonstration in Brussels, the resignation of three Ministers from the Belgian Cabinet, General Erskine's threats to "get tough" with the Belgian "trouble-makers", the open war between the British and the Greek Resistance, the "Darlanization" of Belgium, Greece, and Italy—all these were interpreted by both de Gaulle and the French Resistance people as so many danger signals. Although the Allies were, on the face of it, discriminating against France because of the revolutionary temper of the "Communist-infested FFI", de Gaulle, who wanted a big army, and who thought he could keep the Communists in order once they were *in* the Army, took it all very badly.

³ *Combat*, December 23, 1944.

CHAPTER SEVEN

THE SEAMIER SIDE OF PARIS, 1944-5

IT WOULD, of course, be a mistake to conclude from all this that the France of 1944—France as a whole—was in a general mood of heroic exaltation. The night after de Gaulle's great Paris apotheosis, the German airforce carried out a "revenge" air-raid on Paris, one of the worst the capital had experienced, and there were several thousand casualties. Life in the capital was abnormal. There was no transport. The first metro trains did not start running again until September 11; and food conditions were extremely bad for a long time and, indeed, throughout the first post-Liberation winter—worse than under the German occupation. Infantile mortality increased in Paris that winter by 40 per cent, compared with 1943. There was terrible poverty among the families of the war prisoners and deportees. No doubt, during the *Semaine de l'Absent* the "spivs" displayed their feelings of charity and paid lavishly for their entertainments and black-market meals; but there was still the story of the old woman of 72—and thousands like her—whose daughter had, as a *résistante*, been deported to Germany, and who was getting 300 francs a month to live on.

In the Resistance press angry editorials were quoting criticisms from the British press, comparing the fair ration system in England with the wholly inadequate one in France; in France, the black market was making an increase in rations impossible.

It is not the fellow on a bicycle who brings back a few eggs from a village, or even the 150-franc restaurants that are undermining our whole food situation. It's the wholesale "disappearance" of black-market food, it's the restaurants with 1,000-franc menus that are responsible.... It is those who sell medicines at fantastic prices, who stock tons of butter for the *de luxe* restaurants, who divert coal from the war effort—those are the traitors and saboteurs. In a fortnight the whole lot of them could be liquidated.[1]

The *trafiquant* must have laughed himself sick. "In a fortnight!"—it was to take about three years before the black market disappeared and only when there was no longer any room for it.

By the spring of 1945 the food situation got completely out of hand; largely owing to the inept "strong man" measures decided on by the

[1] *Combat*, February 14, 1945.

Minister of Food, M. Ramadier. Swarms of policemen were sent all over the neighbourhood of Paris, to search anyone carrying even a small parcel! It was a case of hunting anyone who was trying to save himself and his family from starvation. In a few days eggs shot up from 5 francs to 17; Ramadier in his anti-black-market hunt had got hold of the wrong end of the stick. For in Normandy the individual cyclist was unable to buy any food: this was all "reserved" for the big sharks of the Black Market. On March 19, when even the miserable ration cards were not honoured, there was an "anti-hunger" demonstration of 5,000 housewives outside the Hôtel-de-Ville. In a number of places there were food-riots and coal-riots; at Denain, near Lille on January 18, 1,200 people invaded a coal mine and carried off 150 tons of coal; and 350 housewives tried to break into a sugar refinery.[2] Shocking reports were published from Le Hâvre, Brest, and Caen. In the last-named, 20,000 people were clamouring for some kind of shelter for the winter. Everywhere hospitals were short of the most elementary supplies. The Ministry of Health was saying that 75 per cent of the urban population was showing signs of more or less severe undernourishment. It was a hard winter—with queues, and no coal, and practically no railway travel. A large part of the time, papers had to appear on one half-sheet. "Worse than under the Germans", was a common complaint. In January, de Gaulle tried to explain these hardships by saying that France's import programme was "far behind schedule".

In November the enlarged Consultative Assembly met at the Luxembourg, but in an atmosphere greatly lacking in enthusiasm. Economic conditions were deplorable, and from all over the country came expressions of discontent and anxiety. The enthusiasm of the Liberation days had died down. On the day the Assembly met, Mauriac quoted somebody who had said at the time of the French Revolution: "*Tout le monde veut bien la République, personne ne veut ni la pauvreté ni la vertu.*"

"Virtue", in the high moral sense, was lacking among wide sections of the population, who had been demoralized by the Occupation. There was a *crise de moralité*. The victory of the Resistance was a Pyrrhic victory in more ways than one; the Government had become thoroughly *governmental*; de Gaulle was obsessed with foreign and military policy, and the rest of his ministers were struggling with painful everyday problems; the Resistance movements were being invaded by thousands of *faux résistants*, so much so that *Esprit*, in its first post-Liberation number in December 1944, was able to write:

The best people in the Resistance have been deported or shot, and what is left is chiefly the cautious fellows, and the eleventh-hour Resisters; so what's left is a mere shadow of the Resistance as it really was.

[2] *Le Figaro*, January 19, 1945.

Even so, important reconstruction work was being done wherever possible, and the underfed working-class was showing the greatest patience and endurance. In many places, notably at Lyon, Limoges, Clermont-Ferrand, and Marseilles, the *Commissaires de la République* were showing tremendous enterprise in organizing the food supply and the public services, with the full co-operation of the trade unions and the Liberation committees. The *Commissaires de la République*, endowed with almost unlimited powers, occasionally even exceeded these powers, as did, notably, M. Aubrac, *Commissaire de la République* at Marseilles, who, on his own initiative, not only blocked bank accounts, but proceeded to apply a whole nationalizations programme on a "regional" scale, scandalizing the Paris Government and, before long, getting himself recalled. But this revolutionary spirit of the Resistance, which was still alive in some of the outlying regions, was no longer strong in Paris, which was rapidly turning into an even worse *panier à crabes* than it had been under the Third Republic.

The moneyed middle-class continued to live fairly comfortably, and a book like Galtier-Boissière's *Mon Journal depuis la Libération*, while reporting at second-hand a few hunger riots and the like, is more concerned with "lunch today with so-and-so", and "*un bon gueuleton* last night with so-and-so". The rest is all gossip of a rather unsavoury kind, with a good deal of sneering at the "decay" of the Resistance, and with daily stories of the widespread opportunism and corruption, and of the political somersaults performed on all sides. Much of it is concerned with purges, arrests and *collabo* trials—all of which provided Paris with no end of material for gossip, and also for an easy exercise of irony—chiefly at the expense of the magistrates who, with one exception, had all sworn allegiance to Pétain.

CHAPTER EIGHT

THE "PREMIERE CHARRETTE"

THE traitors' and *collabos'* trials were, in a sense, the circuses to which an underfed population was treated during that hard winter of 1944–5.

The punishment of traitors and collaborators had, indeed, loomed large in the programme of the CNR, and, immediately after the Liberation there was a wave of arrests in Paris. A number of people were manhandled in the street, and also many women who were known to have associated with Germans, had their heads shorn; similarly a woman who had betrayed her husband to the Gestapo was exhibited for public opprobrium, with a notice, describing her crime, tied round her neck. The arrest of well-known people·was played up in the press with great relish—for instance, the arrest of Sacha Guitry, who had had no trouble under the Germans, and who, though a well-known wit, did not appreciate at all the spontaneous *mot* of the FFI fellows who had come to arrest him: "On whose authority are you arresting me?" "On the authority of the Paris Committee of Liberation."[1] He was taken to the Vélodrome d'Hiver, which was rapidly filling up. On September 1 there were already 1,900 men and 600 women at the Vel d'Hiv, among them the said Guitry, and various associates of Pétain's like General Herbillon, and M. Bouffet, the former Prefect, and the "two Abels" (Hermant and Bonnard), both *de l'Académie Française*, and a German film-actress who had been General Stulpnagel's lady friend (but who was later released, since she had presumably also worked for French Intelligence); and a Russian princess, who was a Gestapo agent, and many more. Alfred Cortot, the pianist, was also arrested, for having worked on the German radio in Paris; and so was a well-known actress, who had been much too friendly with a German. "My heart is French; what does the rest matter?'" she exclaimed (according to the most printable version).

Little prominence was given in the press to the arrest of "economic" collaborators—though these were the most numerous; what interested people was the arrest of Vichy politicians, and of *collabo* writers and journalists, as well as the capture of the more notorious criminals in the French police—notably the *miliciens* who had murdered Georges

[1] *Carrefour*, August 28, 1944.

Mandel, and the members of the "French Gestapo" in the rue Lauriston, with the slimy Bony and the horrible Laffont at their head. Six
hundred arrests were made within a few days in August at Vichy. In
November it was believed that about 10,000 persons had been arrested
in Paris and the Paris area. Dozens of Vichy Ministers were locked up
at Fresnes, while many of the smaller fry were sent to the former
Jewish concentration camp at Drancy, to be taken on from there to
Poissy and other prisons.

During that winter there were a number of famous trials in Paris[2]
—the trial of Bony and Laffont, the French Gestapo chiefs, who were
both sentenced to death and executed; the trials of Suarez, Brasillach,
and Paul Chack—three pro-Nazi writers, who were also sentenced to
death and shot; Henri Béraud, the famous anglophobe editorialist of
Gringoire, was sentenced to death, but reprieved by de Gaulle; Bunau-
Varilla, proprietor of the *Matin*, who used to throw dinner parties in
honour of the Germans, with flowers arranged as a large swastika in
the centre of the table, and Stéphane Lauzanne, his chief editorialist,
got off with very long sentences; some, like Albertini, Déat's assistant,
got off lightly with five years.

There were two criticisms of these trials. The Communists and others

[2] It should be explained that an *ad hoc* machinery of justice was set up to try
cases of treason and "collaboration" under the *ordonnance* of November 28,
1944. Most of the cases were tried by Courts of Justice set up in each *Cour
d'Appel* circuit, as well as subsidiary courts in most of the *départements*. These
Courts of Justice comprised a presiding judge, a jury of four, a Government
representative, and an examining magistrate. Civic Courts were also set up to
deal with many thousands of cases of *indignité nationale*, an offence defined by
the *ordonnance* of August 26, 1944.

Special Departmental Committees were set up to deal with "illicit profits".
These Committees, which included representatives of the Treasury and of the
Departmental Liberation Committees had power to impose fines and to order
the confiscation of such illicit profits derived from black marketing, trading with
the enemy, etc. All this judicial machinery soon tended to become clogged by
the very large number of cases with which it had to deal, and by the shortage of
adequate legal personnel. This personnel was also "purged", though not severely,
only a little over one-tenth of the 2,100 members of the *magistrature* being
"suspended" by January 1945. (For full details, see the excellent account in
Dorothy Pickles' *French Politics* (London 1953), pp. 12–15.) That public opinion
was distrustful of the *magistrature* and tended to be ironical at their expense may
be illustrated by the example of the tremendously self-righteous *Procureur-
Général* Mornet (he was later to prosecute in the Laval and Pétain trials before
the High Court, which was to be specially set up to try Vichy Ministers in virtue
of the *ordonnance* of December 27, 1944). Not only, like practically all his colleagues, had he sworn allegiance to Pétain, but had just missed (through no
fault of his own) being appointed Public Prosecutor at the famous Riom Trial
of Blum, Daladier, General Gamelin, etc.

Apart from the "regular" courts, there were also emergency tribunals set
up by local Liberation Committees—of which more later.

of the Resistance complained that it was all done in much too slow and desultory a fashion; that a lot of the small fry (*le lampiste*) were made to suffer, but that the "big bosses of the Fifth Column" were running around freely. As Albert Bayet wrote in *Franc-Tireur* on October 15:

The wretches who, for four years, betrayed France must be punished; it is not merely a matter of justice, but of national dignity. It does not mean that we have to punish all those who, in good faith, were taken in by "the victor of Verdun". Many believed that the Marshal was secretly in agreement with de Gaulle. Many of these people joined the Resistance after Montoire or Toulon. But there was a genuine Fifth Column of police spies, journalists, ministers, admirals, etc. And only too many of the chiefs of the Fifth Column are still running around—in the French Academy, in fashionable *salons*; you still see them on boards of directors, and in the high ranks of the administration. Just you wait—they'll soon start kicking against the Resistance in the name of Order, Legality, the country's Higher Interests, National Unity, etc.

In another editorial *Franc-Tireur* dealt with the economic *collabos*:

They have made milliards; they bought themselves *châteaux*, and shares, and diamonds, and furs and gold. In the hungry and blacked-out Paris of the Occupation they feasted behind the curtains of night clubs. They spent on one dinner a worker's three months' wages. They rubbed shoulders with the masters of the New Order, with crooks and *collabo* journalists and Gestapo tarts. They sold themselves five times, ten times; with his 500 millions a day the Boche bought up everything ... and most of this money has stayed behind in France, in the hands of these rotten Frenchmen.[3]

Others, notably Mauriac, criticized the trials on quite different grounds; much about them was arbitrary; they were like a lottery, in which you picked a lucky or an unlucky number, and he generally disliked the whole thing on moral and religious grounds.

A middle course, typical of the non-Communist elements of the Resistance, was taken by *Combat*, which deplored not only the practical mismanagement of the "purge", but its very dubious juridical basis—at any rate, in a large number of cases. Collaborators, it argued, should have been tried on the strength of a new legislation with retroactive effect, and setting precise time limits to the offences in question; instead, the Courts went on trying these offences on the strength of pre-war laws, which, in many cases, did not necessarily "fit". At the same time, "we live in a world where dishonourable action does not necessarily mean a breach of the letter of the law"; as a result, strictly legalistic defence was easy, and sentences, though "morally essential", sometimes lacked a proper legal basis. With an adequate juridical

[3] *Franc-Tireur*, October 20, 1944.

weapon at their disposal, the Courts could have acted quickly and effectively, and avoided a lot of quibbling; but

now it's too late. They will still sentence to death a few journalists who scarcely deserve it, while some bigger fry will wriggle out of it. . . . Yet a country that has failed in its clean-up is also liable to fail in its renovation. . .[4]

It is true that, in many cases, there was still the principle of "national unworthiness" that could be applied with some effect, depriving a person of his civil rights for life, or for a number of years, if he had acted "dishonourably", without necessarily breaking the law.

In a later chapter it will be shown just *how* extensive the French "purge" was (most of the principal trials were, indeed, not to be held until after VE Day). It is also then that the question will be examined of the "nation-wide terrorism" and the "thousands of summary executions" of which the Maquis, the FFI and the local Liberation Committees were alleged by pro-Vichyite propaganda to have been guilty during 1944 and the early part of 1945. It is sufficient to say here that these stories were wildly and systematically exaggerated.

[4] *Combat*, January 4, 1945.

CHAPTER NINE

RESISTANCE SPLITS. THOREZ TO
DE GAULLE'S RESCUE

URING that winter of 1944–5 living conditions were hard for most people; there were the greatest transport difficulties; the war was still on; and there was also a widespread tendency to say that the war prisoners and deportees should return to France before far-reaching political decisions were taken. This principle of "waiting" for their return applied not only to the General Election, but even, to some extent, to political activity generally.

Nevertheless, the two great Resistance Congresses, held during the winter of 1944–5, were to prove of far-reaching political importance, and already foreshadowed the breakdown of the "Resistance" as a major political force in the country.

The First National Congress of the MLN (*Mouvement de Libération Nationale*), which was held in Paris between January 23 and 28, 1945, had been preceded by a regional congress of the MLN at Lyon. This had passed a resolution in favour of an organic fusion of the MLN with the predominantly Communist Front National, and in favour of the constitution of a "National Liberation Front" comprising representatives of all "progressive" political parties (including the Communists, Socialists, Radicals, and MRP) and of all the trade unions with a view to agreeing on a minimum programme.

Some days later, the Paris regional congress of the MLN took a much more anti-Communist line, and rejected the recommendations of the Lyon Congress. This was followed by the meeting of the National Congress of the MLN. It soon became apparent that the MLN (now claiming a membership of 500,000, including, no doubt, hundreds of thousands who had "joined the Resistance" after the Liberation) was sharply divided into an "anti-fusionist" majority and a "fusionist" minority, the former gravitating towards the Socialist Party, the latter towards the Communists. Prominent among the "anti-fusionists" were Claudius Petit, André Malraux, and André Philip, each, in his own way a notorious anit-Communist. The "fusionists" included Kriegel-Valrimont, and Pierre Hervé (both Communists) and "fellow travellers" like Albert Bayet, Degliame and d'Astier de La Vigerie. The motion in favour of "fusion" with the Front National was defeated by

250 votes to 119. A *comité directeur* was then set up, comprising representatives of both the majority and the minority; but this did not mean that there had been no split. The split, though not official, was a fundamental one; the majority had rejected the idea of a United Resistance organization, for fear of finding it dominated by the Communists. Not that the Front National was wholly Communist; it included on its presidium Jacques Debû-Bridel, one of the (nominally) right-wing representatives on the CNR; two Catholic priests and a Protestant pastor; M. Max André of the MRP; among other prominent non-Communist members of the Front National was M. François Mauriac, who was, indeed, to be elected to the *comité directeur* of the FN at the end of its congress on February 3. (There were, it is true, some protests, no doubt owing to the line Mauriac was taking over the "purge".) The resolutions passed were high-minded and patriotic—pursue the war, form a great people's army, "unite the Resistance"—if not on a national scale (which the MLN had made impossible), at any rate on a local scale, etc. The FN Congress was visited by delegations from the MLN (its minority members were warmly, and its majority members coolly received) and, on behalf of the Communist Party, by Jacques Duclos, who advocated the unity of "all Frenchmen and Frenchwomen of goodwill, wherever they may come from, provided they desire to work for the renaissance and greatness of France".

By this time the Communist leaders, though distrustful of de Gaulle, were determined to make things as easy as possible for him—at least so long as the war continued, and soft-pedal the revolutionary spirit of the Resistance.

Maurice Thorez, who had returned from Moscow in November (a special decree having by this time been passed, under which his "desertion" in 1939 could be amnestied—which, indeed, it was) came out in favour of "legality", and astonished the Communist rank and file (who had violently protested against the dissolution of the *gardes patriotiques*) when he said before the CP's Central Committee on January 21, 1945, that the Government had been quite right in dissolving them. These groups, he said, had their *raison d'être* before and during the insurrection, but the situation was now different. Public security must now be maintained by the regular police. And he fully endorsed de Gaulle's line on another issue:

Nor must the local and departmental authorities, any more than the CNR, substitute themselves for the Government. The Liberation committees must not administer, but only help those who administer. They must, above all, mobilize, train and organize the masses so that they produce the maximum war effort, and support the Government in its application of the policy laid down by the Resistance.

Thorez was obviously pursuing three objectives: his statement was a sop to the peasants who, in various parts of France, were dissatisfied with the "arbitrary" behaviour of some of the Liberation committees; it was a move in favour of a maximum war effort on the part of France (with all that this implied in the international field); and it was a gesture in favour of de Gaulle. Thorez apparently thought that if all went well, de Gaulle might yet be prevailed upon to make the CNR Charter a reality. There is little doubt that, *at that stage*, the Communists were not only willing, but anxious to stay in the Government, and pull their weight as both a *progressive* and a *national* party. De Gaulle, for his part (as his speech at Nantes on January 14 had already shown), seemed only too pleased to *use* the Communists; by being in the Government, by keeping the working-class quiet and patient, by calling for "arduous work" in the war effort, they were helping him—more even than themselves. They were even taking the risk of some of the discontent among the more "romantic" ex-Partisans, and among the underfed working-class rebounding on them—a point certain Trotzkyist groups in France did not fail to exploit, at any rate among the small audiences at their disposal.

It is certain, however, that Thorez's "anti-revolutionary" orders caused great uneasiness inside the CP itself. The quarrel did not, however, break out openly until much later, when Marty and Tillon were "purged" in 1952—as will be seen in a later chapter.

CHAPTER TEN

THE FIRST EXIT OF MENDÈS-FRANCE

THE fundamental weakness of France after the Liberation was the absence of a constructive financial and economic policy; and it was the misfortune of France that the timid, inept, hand-to-mouth financial policy adopted by M. Lepercq and, soon afterwards, by M. Pleven in the early months of the Liberation should have remained, with minor variations, France's financial policy for years to come.

At Algiers, Mendès-France, then *Commissaire* of Finance, had drawn up a drastic plan of financial and monetary reform; but when the Government moved to Paris, he was appointed Minister of National Economy, and succeeded as Minister of Finance first, by Lepercq, and then by Pleven. The Mendès-France–Pleven clash was the clash of two conceptions, of two "ways of life", and throughout the hard winter of 1944–5, Mendès-France had watched with growing dismay Pleven's easy-going, happy-go-lucky mismanagement of the country's finances—at the very time when the danger of a runaway inflation was immense. Both Mendès-France and Pleven had been in the "Resistance", but Mendès, as a Free French fighter-pilot based in England, had been "in it" in a much more real sense than Pleven, who, happening to be on a business mission in London in June 1940, joined de Gaulle and became one of the most active political busybodies at Carlton Gardens.

Mendès-France was no sentimental *résistant*, looking upon the CNR Charter as his Ten Commandments; he had little love for the Communists, did not look in the least "revolutionary", but he was a highly expert—partly Keynesian—economist, whose opinion was valued in the Radical Party (he was the youngest deputy in the 1932 Chamber)—even though the leaders of the Party thought him "brilliant, but rather wild"—a fault which, they thought, would disappear with age. I remember him as a very young deputy at Radical Congresses in 1932 and 1933. He was then considered as one of the "Young Turks", who often trod mercilessly on M. Herriot's toes, but who were to scatter, in later years, in the strangest way—Pierre Cot becoming a near-Communist, Bergery becoming a cynical Vichyite, Jacques Kayser joining the *progressistes* in 1945, and, soon after, dropping out of politics altogether, and Mendès-France becoming the Cassandra of the

Fourth Republic and then the more or less successful liquidator of the errors accumulated between 1944 and 1954—"the most serious and most lonely statesman of the Fourth Republic", as one of his critics described him.[1]

"Serious" and "lonely"—the adjectives fit well even the Mendès-France of 1944. It was the *manque de sérieux* of men like Pleven who almost drove him to distraction throughout the winter of 1944–5, and finally drove him out of the de Gaulle Government. He was not a "Resistance" fanatic, and was not anti-capitalist; but he was in agreement with the CNR Charter in so far as it stressed the need for stable wages and their pre-condition, a stable currency; he also believed in austerity, and in a fairer distribution of the national income. He was often aptly referred to as "France's Stafford Cripps".

On landing in France in 1944, he felt that nothing was more important than to put her finances in order; if this was not done, she would be building on sand. Little or nothing, in his view, could be done about the black market and about the "illicit profits" accumulated during the war years without a drastic monetary reform. Only a few weeks later, Belgium carried out a monetary reform rather on the lines of the Mendès-France plan, complete with the exchange of notes, the freezing of accounts and an instructive, if not perfect, inventory of wartime profits. One of Mendès-France's principal ideas was that the black market would necessarily be paralysed, if not come to a complete standstill, if the mountains of currency in the possession of the *trafiquants* were frozen or exchanged for new notes only progressively, and subject to various controls and checks, as in Belgium. This monetary reform should, in Mendès-France's view, be accompanied by appropriate measures to balance the budget, and to draw goods on to the official, instead of the black market. But monetary reform was the cornerstone of the whole structure.

But from the start he came up against opposition—not least from the permanent officials of the Ministry of Finance and from the Bank of France who thought that France was "not in a mood" to accept austerity. He argued in vain that the best people in the Resistance were willing, as *Combat* had put it, "to be poor, so that France could be rich". This was dismissed as childish "Resistentialist" idealism, with which the French peasantry would certainly not agree. M. Gutt, the Belgian Finance Minister, who had put through the monetary reform, indeed, himself remarked:

For France, as for all other liberated countries, monetary reform is Problem No 1. If this isn't solved you'll have devaluation and a constant rise in prices. As it is, the French franc is worth only one-third its nominal value

[1] Claude Bourdet in *France-Observateur*, October 7, 1954.

on the Brussels black bourse. Loans and the declaration of currency assets can go together. Only, in France, the assault against the mountain of 600 milliards of hoarded notes affects 18 million peasants—and that, of course, is a major political problem.[2]

It wasn't only a question of the peasantry. The bourgeoisie also liked to "get back to normal", and was too shortsighted to see the need for monetary reform, always a "troublesome" business. Under Lepercq and Pleven the Government had, as already said, launched its Liberation Loan, in itself a gesture of appeasement to the hoarders of notes, and an appeal to the "confidence" of the people with money. True, despite this appeal, the loan, which brought in only 73 milliards of actual *notes* out of a total circulation of over 600 milliards (the rest of the 155 milliards subscribed was in bonds) had been supported in only a very small measure by the big profiteers, who just weren't interested in 3 per cent, and who, moreover, had not yet been fully reassured that they would be left in possession of their ill-gotten gains.

De Gaulle knew nothing about economic matters, and in "arbitrating" the dispute between Mendès and Pleven in January 1945, could not at first make up his mind. At one point he is said to have remarked rather feebly to Mendès: "Yes, but aren't all the experts against you?" To which Mendès-France replied: "I know a certain Colonel de Gaulle who, before the war, had all the experts against *him*."[3]

During the spring, things went from bad to worse, and in April, still receiving no satisfactory response from the Government—who were frightened of "peasant revolts"—meeting with stronger opposition than ever from the Bank of France and the "experts", and receiving only half-hearted support from the politicians (all with an eye on the coming municipal elections), Mendès resigned, not to become a Minister again for ten years.

A few days before, Pleven had announced his "plan" under which all notes were to be exchanged one-to-one, "without freezing or retention", a capital levy (of sorts), and another issue of bonds for "small holders" (*petite épargne*). These last two items were chicken-feed; but the first item meant the final rejection of Mendès-France's plan. Capital was not to be "alienated"; the "co-operation" of capital had to be "voluntary"; only was "capital" really going to "co-operate"?

It will not [wrote *Combat* on the following day]. Circumstances today are such that we are bound to live in a controlled economy, and all this financial liberalism is wholly unsuitable.... The dazzling victory won by the black market over the official market is due to the freedom left to

---

[2] *Combat*, December 26, 1944.
[3] Ronald Matthews, *The Death of the Fourth Republic* (London 1954), p. 189.

money to do exactly as it pleases. . . . Today our economy is rotten from top to bottom, with wages running in vain after prices. . . .[4]

A week later Mendès-France resigned, and at the press conference he gave he went over much of the already familiar ground:

It was necessary to build the foundations without delay. This had not been done; inflation is in full swing, and the black market is triumphing over the official market all along the line. . . . There can be no order in the food supply if there is no normal currency. . . . The working-class is being starved, and the middle class with fixed incomes is being ruined.

And he spoke bitterly of the absolute need to draw up an inventory of French fortunes; 600 milliards had been extorted from France by the Germans; all this money had been spent in France; yet all M. Pleven was hoping to recover in the 1945 budget by way of "illicit profits" was—12 milliards! Pleven's "capital levy", spread over four years was childish; with notes exchanged at par, all the illicit wealth would have time to go into hiding. If he (Mendès-France) failed, it was because the "economic powers that be" and the Bank of France had been against him. Not that he received much support from the political parties, partly because they were thinking of the municipal election, and partly perhaps because the whole thing was all a little above their heads—even though, three years later, the Soviet monetary reform, with many features resembling the Mendès Plan, was to be hailed as "*génial*" by the French Communists.

The resignation of Mendès-France a few weeks before the end of the war was a melancholy prelude to peace, the advent of which was to be celebrated in Paris in a somewhat morose atmosphere. France had not done the right thing to put her financial house in order; the part played by the French Army in the greatest of victories over Germany had been inconspicuous; and now the war prisoners and the deportees (some of them) were returning, and they were not impressed by the New France, with its black market and its ugly contrasts between wealth and poverty, worse than anything that had existed before the war.

[4] *Combat*, March 30, 1945.

CHAPTER ELEVEN

THE PRISONERS' RETURN

EXCEPT for the return from Germany of the war prisoners and the deportees, there was no sudden change in conditions before and after VE Day. The full horror of the German concentration camps was revealed to the French public during those weeks—not that they had had any illusions. It merely confirmed their worst fears. The names of Belsen, Dachau, Buchenwald, Ravensbrück, Auschwitz, and the rest of the death camps were on everybody's lips. Thousands of Frenchmen had died there; others returned from there in American Army planes, crippled in body or mind; many men and women of the Resistance and others were brought back weighing half or less than half their normal weight. No doubt, many of the ordinary war prisoners, who had spent five years in Germany—people of "healthy peasant stock"—simply took it in their stride, and went home, and back to their work, merely cursing their luck at having wasted five years of their lives.[1]

But to many it had "done something". Some, it is true, spoke of the solidarity in the *stalags* and even in the concentration camps; but was this altogether true?

Have we not forgotten that in the camps, too, we had a black market, more ignominious than the black market which we condemn here in France? Have we forgotten all the vile little acts, conscious, half-conscious, sub-conscious that were committed on the path of "premature release"? Or the contrast between the tables at which they were devouring food parcels, and those where others had to be content with the German hunger ration? ... And as we became increasingly conscious of being the victims— the inglorious victims—of a tragedy the mechanism of which escaped our understanding, we declined both physically and mentally, and no amount of self-righteousness *Paris-Soir* blah can make up for it.[2]

These three issues of *Les Vivants* (after that the review seems to

---

[1] Morale was best among those who had worked on the land. I remember some French war prisoners, newly liberated, who claimed that, with all the German men mobilized, they (the French) had "practically run the whole of East Prussia" towards the end of the war, lacking neither food nor—German women.

[2] René Menard in *Les Vivants: Cahiers publiés par des prisonniers et déportés*, III, Paris 1946, pp. 21–23.

have stopped publication) provide a tragic insight into the minds of some of these two million Frenchmen who had returned from Germany—more or less alive. Were these merely the meditations of a few neurotic intellectuals? Hardly. For some of them were to speak of the tragedy of the war prisoners in a more general way.

There is also the myth—and perhaps the most devastating of all to our newly recovered freedom—of faithful and love-sick Isolde.... Yet I am told that in Paris alone, the Courts are dealing with 30,000 divorce cases concerning ex-war prisoners, that 60 per cent of married men who return find that the bonds between them and their wives have, in one way or another, been broken; that most of the *fiancées* back home will not keep their promise; we also know that a new race of bachelors has been formed in the prisoners' camps.... It's no use sniggering; behind all these things there are countless personal conflicts and tragedies....[3]

And the France to which they had now returned was not the France of their *Stalag* and *Oflag* daydreams. Another ex-prisoner wrote:

The ex-prisoner has found an amorphous country, used to its hardships, and incapable of saying no.... The passers-by in the street seemed, before the war, to be going somewhere. Now they look like people walking, but not going anywhere.... The question of money is most revealing. There's a black market on every level. And the worst of it is that it's *an insult to Labour*. Only fools work; the others do their black marketing and eat.... They pity those who don't eat, but don't give a damn. Only pity is the spice to their egoism.... Everything is taken for granted, even the victims. "One has a right to be lucky. If it isn't me, it would be somebody else...."[4]

What then was the way out? The Resistance? This ex-war prisoner, significantly, praised the Resistance, admired the Resistance, and all that it did, but he felt that at the end of the Resistance "there can only be blood".

Instead of sinking into a fatal heroism, we must, first of all, *be*, and measure the dimensions of this being. In saying this, I am not going against the spirit of the Resistance. It is, on the contrary, its most profound lesson.... But we cannot any longer crucify a living being on the dead wood of principles....[5]

Here, at any rate, was one who, deliberately misinterpreting *action* to justify his own *inaction*, was rapidly going "existentialist" in the worst sense; and a characteristic phenomenon—though by no means the most obvious one during the months immediately following the end of the war in France—was this vogue of existentialism or rather, of a kind of pseudo-existentialism for which Jean-Paul Sartre and his

[3] *Ibid.*, p. 24.
[4] Henri Maldiney, in *Les Vivants*, I, Paris 1945, pp. 15–16.
[5] *Ibid.*, pp. 17–19.

group could scarcely be held responsible, but which still did not prevent all the *désorientés* and the disillusioned, and the cynics and the black-marketeers of 1945 from bleating about Sartre, and Existentialism, and Saint-Germain-des-Prés. Were not the ex-prisoners partly to blame for it? Perhaps the worst of it was that it was something morose, wholly lacking the gay irresponsibility of the "early 'twenties". And small wonder that, to the Communists and other *hard* people, Existentialism seemed a major danger to the people's morale, and that in Czechoslovakia, where Sartre had a great vogue just after the war, his books should have been the first to be banned after the Communist *coup* of February 1948.

The mental confusion among the ex-war prisoners and deportees, all their disillusionment, even their failure to receive proper care and food and clothing on their return to France—all this became something of a political issue, and, since two million ex-war prisoners represented a substantial part of the electorate, they became the object of some harsh political quarrelling. The Communists, in particular, launched ferocious attacks on Frenay, the Minister in charge of the prisoners' welfare. The anti-Communists retorted by trying to make capital out of the delays and mismanagement in the repatriation of French prisoners who had been liberated by the Red Army, and who were being sent home by sea *via* Odessa. This propaganda carried little weight, because it was the Russians who had, after all, liberated them. But there were the Alsatians who had served in the German Army, and whose prospects of being repatriated from Russia were much less certain; and this was exploited with some effect in Alsace.

But politically the war prisoners proved of small consequence, and had nothing vital to add to what had already been done by the men of the Resistance. Rather more important were some of the deportees, who belatedly joined the political personnel of the Fourth Republic.

CHAPTER TWELVE

FRANCE'S PRECARIOUS BALANCE
BETWEEN EAST AND WEST

N O SOONER was the war over than there was already "a lot of loose talk about the next war between Russia and the Anglo-Saxons".[1] Nothing very precise yet—nothing quite so definite as the talk that was to be set loose, together with the radio-active fumes of the Hiroshima bomb, three months later; but already there was an unhealthy foretaste of the Cold War. "Stalingrad" had been an immensely stimulating word to the whole of France, and especially to the whole of the Resistance; but those who talked about Stalingrad now were already slightly suspect in the eyes of the *bien pensants*.

De Gaulle, just after the war, was in a difficult position. He was at the head of a tripartite government, and in recent months he had spoken with great warmth—at least by implication—of the Communists; at Rouen, in October, he had spoken of "national union—with all marching towards the same goal, the salvation and greatness of our country, which belongs to us all in an equal degree". Then, in the first foreign debate before the Consultative Assembly Bidault had said that France wished to be allied with both East and West, as well as with the United States; but there could be no question of her being "limited to the West only"; while de Gaulle, after repeating for the *n*th time that elementary security required France's presence along the Rhine, said that "the unity of Europe should be built round these three poles: London, Paris, and Moscow".

But during the closing stages of the war the French bourgeoisie had been rattled by the Red Army's triumphal progress into Central Europe —Russians in Berlin, in Leipzig, at Weimar and Jena—almost at walking distance from the French border. On the other hand, especially among the Catholics, there were qualms about Poland and Hungary, and Churchill was being blamed for having "betrayed" them at Yalta—to which France had not been invited. Not that even bourgeois opinion was always openly anti-Russian or even openly anti-Communist. It was, indeed, well-known that many French businessmen were taking out "insurance policies" on the "other side"—just in case; they were fraternizing with Communists, and even joining the

---

[1] *Combat*, May 20, 1945.

Party (very secretly, of course); and the same was true of some high officials and even some Army generals. Thus, General de Lattre undoubtedly flirted with the Communists and with the Russians during those early post-war months, already fancying himself the head of a French People's Army—if it ever came to that. The speech he made on June 6 at the banquet given at Wendenschloss near Berlin by Marshal Zhukov in honour of Eisenhower, Montgomery, and himself was all the more significant as he was the only one to have stayed for the banquet, "Ike" and "Monty" having left in rather a huff. Vyshinsky had, on that occasion, drunk a toast to France "our only *real* friend", and de Lattre had responded much in the same spirit. Perhaps he and de Gaulle still thought that Russia might help France "to establish herself solidly from one end to the other of our natural frontier, the Rhine".

Just about that time relations with the Western Allies, and notably with Britain, were far from cordial. The trouble that broke out in Syria between France and Britain was to develop throughout June 1945 in a manner most humiliating to France, and no one felt the humiliation more deeply than de Gaulle himself.

But already there were influences pulling the other way. Bidault, on his return journey from San Francisco where (thank heaven) France had at least been given a permanent seat on the Security Council (in those days even that hadn't been certain!), stopped in Washington to see Truman. Again he tried to explain France's position; she could act as arbiter between East and West, and she could be allied with both, but not with one side only; he added, however, that Franco-American friendship was "based on sentiment", and that sentiment "was not without its place in international politics"—which suggested that, whatever France's official policy was for the time being, her heart was with America. But the Americans were still far from satisfied, and the *Washington Post* was quoted in the French press as having said that it was high time France began to share America's views on Russia".

A strange, rather nerve-racking summer altogether, that first post-war summer in France. People were shaken by the sight of the prisoners and especially the deportees, and by so many of their horror stories, and by their weariness and disillusionment. De Gaulle had spoken in March of the structural reforms that would be carried out when the war was over; but for a long time he had other things to absorb his attention—foreign affairs, and the Army, and Syria. "If only he would give a little less attention to the inhabitants of the Val d'Aoste and a little more to the inhabitants of France," *Combat* bitterly remarked on May 22, in commenting on the constant rise in the cost of living, while wages remained frozen. But he couldn't. For a whole month Syria was to become for de Gaulle a full-time job. The "Churchill ultimatum" of May 31 that the French troops be withdrawn to their barracks had outraged him beyond words. It was like a challenge to his whole *politique de grandeur*, and the British—as de Gaulle saw it—were striking at its weakest spot—Syria—whence the bulk of the French troops had been withdrawn to fight in the common Allied cause in North Africa and Italy. "Odd," said de Gaulle at a press conference on June 2, "that our 5,000 men left in Syria should have been thought quite adequate for maintaining order there right up to VE Day; and that after May 8 it should suddenly have been found necessary for the British to take over. Doesn't the whole thing smell of petrol?" And he hinted that an enormous number of people, other than General Spears (who had been recalled at France's request) had been fomenting trouble against the French troops throughout Syria and the Lebanon, and said that on May 8 troops under British command had marched from Palestine into Syria carrying swastika banners.... Syria and the Lebanon had both been persuaded by the British, he said, not to negotiate their independence treaties with the French.... In the end, the French had to abandon all control of the 25,000 Syrian and Lebanese troops under their command, and to withdraw their own 5,000 troops to a coastal strip with a view to early repatriation.

It was a lot for de Gaulle to swallow, and he had to suffer other insults that summer: France, though admitted to Germany as an occupying Power, was excluded from Potsdam. Meantime, both in London and in Washington, France and de Gaulle himself were having a bad press. Mr Sumner Welles was reported by *France-Soir* to have said that the de Gaulle Government was a dictatorship, and that the French "hadn't yet realized de Gaulle's almost morbid distrust of Washington". He thought that Herriot understood the USA much better.

De Gaulle was unhappy about both Britain's and America's attitude. Soon after VE Day he realized that France could not expect to hold any privileged position in Germany. But she still had a great rôle to play in the world, he said at Brest on July 22. This rôle consisted in being "a link between the two worlds". It was essential that France should be that—and "neither a pawn in the game of others, nor their battlefield". It seems that already then he felt that the tension between Russia and the USA was rapidly growing worse.

It was all the more regrettable, the French thought, that the "link between the two worlds" should have been absent at Potsdam.

France isn't at Potsdam, [*Combat* wrote on July 24] but plenty of her rolling stock is still in Germany. We must say that our allies are taxing our friendship pretty heavily.... We still hope to get reparations. And we also hope the world will not be run for ever by the respectable Potsdam trinity.

And in a manner very characteristic of the non-Communist Left, *Combat* shared de Gaulle's sense of grievance, but at the same time reproached him with thinking only of international affairs.

Anyway, France is being accused of arrogance. Perhaps it *is* wrong always to talk of France, with her historic memories, and not to talk of the French people with their terrifying child mortality.

On the whole, France was not pleased with Potsdam, but felt that it might have been worse; there were, after all, a few sops to her pride in the decisions taken, notably her inclusion in the Council of Foreign Ministers. It also seemed that German imperialism and militarism had been crushed for a long time; and that, for better or for worse, Russia's victory had been "consecrated".

But facing her is the great American Empire. The era of empires has begun. Is it a stage towards the establishment of a great human society, or does it foreshadow the death of our civilization?[2]

It was like a premonition of worse things to come; and a fortnight later the first A-bomb was dropped on Hiroshima. The international significance of this did not escape French attention. Anti-Russian papers like the *Figaro* played it up; the Communist press played it down; the left-wing intellectual attitude was more *nuancée*; but on the whole it deplored the fact that more beastliness was being added to the world, and more fear and uncertainty.

It was hard enough to breathe in this tormented world of ours. But here's a new source of anguish, which has a good chance of being the last and final one.... And when one sees Reuter announce that this invention may make all the agreements made with Russia null and void, one can only shudder.... If Japan capitulates as a result of the Hiroshima bomb, that's all right; but it goes far beyond that, we fear....[3]

Already a week later it reported that Truman had announced that the USA would try to obtain by treaty the military bases it needed in the world. "As some of these bases are liable to be in French territory, we can only express our deepest concern."[4] And six weeks later the same paper noted that if, before the A-bomb, President Truman seemed anxious to come to terms with Russia, it no longer looked like it. The world was now divided in two.

Consciously or unconsciously, de Gaulle did not fail to be influenced by Hiroshima; the interview he gave to *The Times* on September 10,

<hr/>

[2] *Combat*, August 5, 1945.   [3] *Combat*, August 8, 1945.
[4] *Combat*, August 14, 1945.

was chiefly concerned with the need of placing the Ruhr and Rhineland at the service of a West-European reconstruction plan, and of
preventing German rearmament at the same time, but he already
seemed to admit the possibility of some sort of West-European bloc—
directed, in the indignant words of the *Daily Worker*, against both the
Soviet Union and the United States! But other observers agreed that
that was precisely what de Gaulle had in mind: the possible creation
of an international "third force", including Britain. Was he not, at
heart, hoping to turn the "link" into a "buffer", in order to reduce
the friction between the Big Two? At the first meeting of the First
Constituent Assembly on November 22 he again said:

Our country, with the position it holds in Europe, Africa, and Asia, and
turned traditionally both towards West and East, can be, and wants to be a
link between the two worlds and, *not at any price, a pawn.*

A curious fact was noted by several commentators who heard
de Gaulle speak that night before the Constituent Assembly: if de
Gaulle's mention of the Soviet Union received tumultuous applause,
and his reference to Britain was cheered, his mention of the United
States met with almost complete silence. It was probably the last
demonstration of its kind, before the Cold War had started in real
earnest in 1946. In December 1945 the memories of Stalingrad and of
Germany's defeat were still fresh, and so was the silent resentment
against the USA for having dropped that atom bomb, the cause of so
many bad dreams. Anti-Soviet feeling was, on the whole, slower to
develop in France than in Britain or the USA.

Moreover, it was well known that de Gaulle's brief visit to the
United States at the end of August had not been a success, despite the
great publicity it had received in the American press, and the usual
noisy reception given him in New York. In his talks with Truman he
had stressed the need for France to control the left bank of the Rhine,
and the need for the Ruhr to be internationalized, Ruhr coal being a
factor of vital importance in the reconstruction of Europe. As for
American bases, what he said was little short of arrogant from the US
point of view; he recalled that the Americans were, in fact, using
Noumea, in New Caledonia, as a naval base; but this, of course, he
added, was only a provisional arrangement, France having full
sovereign rights over it. Naturally, he said, all sorts of precise arrangements would have to be made to organize collective security; but he
showed no interest in leasing any bases specifically to the United States!
In the circumstances, Truman was in no hurry to offer France any
special financial aid; nor did he find de Gaulle very responsive when
he suggested that France would do well to get the Communists out of
the Government. The polite but cool reminder that this was, after all,

an internal French affair was not well received. De Gaulle didn't understand—or didn't want to understand. In the words of the Associated Press correspondent in Washington, the USA made it clear that it did not feel like treating France as a first-class power. De Gaulle had clearly dissatisfied Truman.[5] A curious episode was that of the French journalists: as they were presented to Truman, he said sharply: "I hope you will in future be more loyal to the United States. I have nothing to add."[6]

At the London Conference of Foreign Ministers in September the French obtained no more than that their views on the Ruhr and the Rhineland would "receive further study through the usual diplomatic channels".

[5] Quoted by *Année Politique*, 1944-45, p. 285.
[6] *Combat*, August 24, 1945.

THE EFFECT OF THE PETAIN AND LAVAL TRIALS

THE end of the war with Germany was marked not only by the homecoming of over two million war prisoners, STO workers, and deportees, but also by the capture in Germany, Austria, and Italy of some of the principal Vichyites and *collabos*, among them de Brinon, Darnand, Luchaire, etc. Pétain returned voluntarily *via* Switzerland, and Laval, who had fled to Spain, was "strongly urged" by the Spanish authorities to return to France. The two most famous post-war trials were held during that summer and autumn—Pétain's in July, and Laval's in October. Public interest in these two trials was enormous, and, in the press, they almost wholly eclipsed all other news, including Potsdam and the final stages of the war against Japan. Although few failed to exercise their irony at the expense of the magistrates, and especially of the Public Prosecutor Mornet, who were now trying the very man to whom they had sworn allegiance (a tricky point, however, on which much could be said for and against),[1] the Pétain trial before the High Court was still a fairly orderly affair.[2] As a Celebrities Parade there had never been a trial to equal it.

Apart from a galaxy of admirals and generals (all carefully defend-

---

[1] The Resistance organizations at one time advised magistrates to take the oath, as otherwise there was a danger to the Resistance itself of being invariably at the mercy of hostile judges.

[2] The High Court was set up by the *ordonnance* of November 18, 1944 for the purpose of trying persons who had participated directly in the activities of the Vichy Government (head of the state, head of the government, ministers *commissaires généraux* and *secrétaires généraux*, Residents, Governor-Generals and High Commissioners). The Court was composed of three magistrates and a jury of 24, the names to be drawn by lot from two lists of 50 names. One of these lists was to be drawn up by the group of Parliamentary Resistance of the Consultative Assembly, and the list approved by the Assembly on February 27 contained only names of members of parliament who had voted against Pétain's plenary powers in July 1940. (An earlier list, including nine persons who had voted for Pétain, had been rejected on February 13.) The other list, drawn up by the Committee of Justice of the Consultative Assembly, was composed of non-parliamentary members of the Resistance. The first to be tried by the High Court was Admiral Esteva, the French Resident in Tunisia, who was sentenced to life imprisonment. (*Cf. Année Politique*, 1944–45, pp. 146–47.)

ing the interests of their respective castes), practically all the available celebrities of the Third Republic testified—President Lebrun, Jeanneney, Herriot, Daladier, Reynaud, Blum, etc, all whitewashing both the Third Republic and themselves—as well as a large number of Vichy Ministers, among them Peyrouton, Darnand, Bouthillier and—by far the most interesting—Laval. The jury, as distinct from the Laval trial, included (as luck would have it) only a small number of Communists (only one among the parliamentarians), nearly all the rest being Socialists or Radicals. Nevertheless, Pétain was sentenced to death, but his sentence was commuted to life imprisonment, as was to be expected, especially in view of his age. Moreover, the death sentence on Pétain was considered a necessary "symbolic gesture" implying the absolute condemnation of the régime that Pétain had personified. Whether, as many felt, his highly dubious "double game" had, on balance, been a good thing for France, was irrelevant. Only, as *Combat* remarked, in commenting on the trial, "you will not disarm the Pétain worshippers by setting against him the men of the Third Republic, which, after all, *also* capitulated". And it was quite true that hardly a single man of the Resistance had given evidence at the trial.

There was one interesting moral that Georges Bernanos, the famous Catholic writer, drew from the Pétain trial—and that was the "insolence" (as he put it) with which the military caste, represented by men like Weygand, were determined to survive the disaster, and go on behaving as smugly and as pompously as ever.

The most repulsive spectacle at the Pétain trial [he wrote] was this procession of generals who had come to defend Pétain before magistrates who had sworn fidelity to His Person.... I daresay, Weygand is a gentleman, while Laval is a chimney-sweep—a chimney-sweep who has fallen off the chimney and cannot hurt anything more than his own skin. But Weygand and the other runaway generals of 1940 have perhaps irreparably disappointed those who believed that France might yet have a worthy place in the world. This man of terrifying mediocrity (and not Laval) appeared in the Court as the true symbol of our society.

Weygand may no doubt treat Laval as a chimney-sweep. But it is true, all the same, that the runaway generals of 1940, Weygand included, are just like other generals, while Laval is different from other chimney-sweeps. Under any régime, in any century Laval would have been an adventurer, who takes his own risks. It gives to his whole behaviour, to his voice and expression, to his poignant vulgarity a certain character, in short, a *style*, reminiscent of certain men of the *ancien régime*.... Laval will be *something* in the history of France, just like certain others during past centuries who resemble him, and most of whom came, like him, to a bad end; while Weygand belongs merely to our time, to our period, nothing more.

Laval was out of his element at Vichy, while Weygand fitted in perfectly.... The runaway generals capitulated with the knowledge that their careers were out of danger. They were at home at Vichy and, looking at these dummies now, people are wondering whether the disaster of France wasn't just a hole in her history, a hiatus. . . . Whence the insolence of these generals? And are they going to persuade France to restore the prestige of this caste in preference to principles? Will the solidarity of these mediocrities weigh more heavily in the scales of France than true national union?[3]

One may disagree with Bernanos's interpretation of Laval; for Laval was not, strictly speaking, an "isolated adventurer", but a man in many ways representative of the *République des Camarades*; but the alarm sounded by Bernanos at the arrogance with which the generals—and not only the generals, but the upper strata of the administration, and the Clergy, and Big Business, and even the politicians of the Third Republic—were trying to demonstrate the *continuity* of their caste around the cradle of the Fourth Republic was highly typical of the suspicions so widely felt among the pro-Resistance people in 1945. If Laval was being sacrificed as the Vichyites' scapegoat, Pétain too was, in a way, being sacrificed on the altar of Continuity by the very people who had put him in power, and who were now treating the four years of Vichy as a sort of air-pocket in which they had come down with a bump, but without crashing. And was there not also a feeling among these people that the "purge" shouldn't be taken too seriously? The revolutionary spirit and the thirst for vendettas of 1945 would soon blow over, they thought; all those who were trying to have their trial postponed a year or two knew it only too well, and proved to be right. Laval was among the most unlucky in this respect. Both the Court and the jury were vicious, and, more than in the case of any other trial, it was felt by almost everybody in France that the accused had been denied a proper hearing.

He was insulted and shouted down by the jury, and then killed in the most revolting conditions, after his attempted suicide. The comments on his execution ranged from mild embarrassment to a feeling of anger and disgust. Even those who felt that Laval was getting all he deserved thought that his trial and execution were seriously discrediting the whole of the *épuration*; and, in this particular case, the haste with which Laval was "liquidated" suggested that only too many of his parliamentary *camarades* were afraid of what he might say next. That de Gaulle refused to consider a retrial and that Teitgen, the Minister of Justice, should have been equally adamant aroused the strongest suspicion that even de Gaulle was not altogether above political *combinazioni*. . . . Too many—Vichyites, as well as the Deputies and Senators of the Third Republic who were gradually coming into their own again—had a vested interest in Laval's silence and death.

[3] *Combat*, August 12 and 21, 1945.

In a later chapter I shall examine what the total "purge" in France amounted to. After the Laval trial it continued for several more years, but arousing less and less interest.[4]

[4] Even in 1945 it was increasingly felt that the "purge" had been badly mishandled. Even before the Laval trial, which was particularly nauseating, *Combat* wrote on August 30, 1945:

"The 'purge' has failed and is in bad odour. The whole thing has become odious. It is a thing that should have been undertaken seriously and without screams for revenge. . . . Justice has a hard road to travel between the screams of hate and the pleadings of a bad conscience. Besides, the whole thing has been incoherent. Albertini who recruited Frenchmen into the German Army, got off with five years; Gérin, a literary critic on the *Oeuvre* got eight years. He was a pacifist; and one does not send a man to prison for writing a few literary articles, even though the paper for which he wrote was Nazi and not pacifist. But he had denounced and harmed nobody. It is a class judgment that simply humiliates a man without doing anybody any good."

CHAPTER FOURTEEN

THE COMMUNISTS' AMBITION TO BE A PERMANENT GOVERNMENT PARTY

BELOW the surface of "national unanimity" the struggle grew in intensity during that spring and summer of 1945 between the elements hoping to build a "new France" and those hankering for a "return to normal". But how many were still fired by the *mystique* of the Resistance? By and large, everybody was vaguely expecting the CNR Charter to be applied in some measure, and de Gaulle himself seemed to symbolize in people's eyes an uneasy compromise between a vague desire for "something new" and a conservative fear of dangerous experiments. Already, while the war was still in progress, all the cautious people (e.g. in the *Monde* and the *Figaro*) were saying that the time was not ripe for "structural reforms"; first, one had to wait till the war was over; and then one had to wait till there had been a general election. During that transition period between VE Day and the election and referendum of October 21, 1945, the tendency to abandon ambitious schemes and to relax after years of nervous and physical strain was unmistakable.

Truly exhausting, this period of political transition, which is dragging on interminably [*Combat* wrote on July 12, 1945]. Internally France doesn't seem to know where she stands or what she wants. There were terrible massacres in Algeria in May, but nobody seemed to care; at the Consultative Assembly hardly anybody turned up to listen to the speakers.... A terrible confusion of values and ideas.... Everywhere there seems to be a lack of seriousness and a lack of enthusiasm....

And on the following day:

We are living in a kind of nihilist atmosphere, with no doctrine, but merely muddling along from day to day.... The hopes of the Resistance have been dashed to the ground. For nothing has really changed. The same forces that fought each other before the war are doing so now, even though the struggle is less spectacular, because of the façade of National Unity.

This *manque de sérieux* pervaded not only private life but even public life. French generals in Germany, the press complained, were creating a Ruritanian setting around their headquarters, flaunting their wealth and prosperity at the Germans and Allies (as if they could be taken in!) while France was living on short rations. M. Pleven, the Minister of Finance, was preaching thrift to the people of France, creating a "National Savings Movement" and talking of "every Frenchman becoming a shareholder of his country", at a time when nobody had much faith in the franc, and when *petits rentiers*, pensioners and most of the working-class were either half-starved or spending in the black market what little savings they still possessed. M. Pleven's attempt to show that what he was trying to do was merely what the British had done with their National Savings Campaign was just silly.

Those, like M. Herriot, who were most determined to go back to "normal", back to the 1875 Constitution, were saying that what France was needing was not a constitutional reform, but a moral reform; this sort of thing infuriated the people of the Resistance who referred to a case of robbery "really typical of our time"—the case of a bunch of schoolboys who had robbed the father of one of them—but then the victim of the robbery was a notorious black-marketeer! And who was M. Herriot to talk—with his years of banquets and republican hot air, which all ended with his own kow-towing to Pétain? *Un peu de pudeur, s.v.p.!*[1]

But then who, by this time, were "the people of the Resistance"? They still ran a large part of the press, but its non-Communist part, with the exception of *Combat*—papers like the MRP *Aube*, or the OCM's *Parisien Libéré*—was losing much of its Resistance *mystique* and was going increasingly "governmental", while *France-Soir* (the former *Défense de la France*), run by good businessmen and press "technicians" like M. Pierre Lazareff, were, above all, interested in circulation. The *Figaro*, a "Vichy" paper which had not become specifically "Resistance" even in August 1944, was meantime building up the biggest circulation among the French bourgeoisie, distrustful of the Resistance and sharply anti-Communist.

It was the misfortune of the Resistance during those days to have become more and more closely identified, in the eyes of the public, with the Communists (with the Socialists playing second fiddle, but more and more out of tune). Just after the Liberation it seemed that the Socialists were making a determined effort to pull the same way as the Communists. At the meeting of the Seine Federation on September 10, 1944, Daniel Mayer, Secretary-General of the Party, announced that out of 169 Deputies and Senators, only 54 would be maintained in the Party, all the rest having behaved unworthily under Vichy; the Socialist Party would "energetically apply the CNR Charter"; it would "avoid hitting the rocks of anti-Communism", and it was proposing the creation of a Socialist-Communist *comité d'entente*.

[1] Cf. *Combat*, June 5 and August 23 and 24, 1945.

In December 1944 the Socialist and Communist delegations met at the Communist headquarters in the rue le Peleticr and decided to "create between the two parties an atmosphere of comprehension, cordiality, and friendly co-operation", and to set up a "permanent comité d'entente". This met some days later in the offices of the Socialist *Populaire*. The Communists were already toying with two ideas—both equally suspect to many of the Socialists: (1) the creation of a joint Resistance List for the coming municipal and cantonal elections; this, the Socialists feared, could only play into the hands of the Communists, since a very large number of the Liberation committees, who would have much to do with the elections, were Communist-dominated; and (2) the constitution of a United Labour Party, following the organic fusion of the Socialist and Communist Parties.

This did not appeal to most of the Socialists, and the gulf between them and the Communists became apparent in the virtual split of the MLN in January, which was to become a final split in May, when the MLN minority joined with the Front National to form a new organization called the MURF (*Mouvement Unifié de Résistance Française*), which became, as it were, an annex of the Communist Party, even though it still comprised a number of non-Communists: Debû-Bridel, Justin Godard, Marc Rucart, Pierre Cot, and even— M. Herriot. On the other hand, the majority of the MLN, with the blessing of the Socialists, formed, together with a few minor Resistance groups that had remained outside the "Big Two", a new organization called the UDSR (*Union Démocratique et Socialiste de la Résistance*), which was at first to become closely affiliated with the Socialist Party, and then to become simply a minor political party in Parliament—a mixed bag comprising people of such different outlook as M. Pleven and François Mitterrand, but essentially a "government" party.

The *Etats Généraux de la Renaissance Française*, a congress called several months ahead by the CNR and the Liberation Committees (at a time when the Resistance movements had not yet sharply split on many major issues) was to prove an abortive affair, and there was something slightly bogus in the very name of *Etats Généraux* and the fact that they were to complete their work in Paris on Bastille Day. What was the purpose of this meeting? M. Saillant (who had succeeded Bidault as head of the CNR) said it was to create a "better moral climate" in France, to arouse enthusiasm, and drag her out of her "apathy and indifference"—a curious admission in itself. The *Etats Généraux* tended to copy the technique of their famous 1789 predecessor. Thousands of *cahiers* expressing the "wishes and complaints" of the *communes* (drawn up, in many cases, by local Liberation Committees and sifted and filtered by departmental Liberation committees before being forwarded to Paris) were sorted and examined by several committees at the Paris *Etats Généraux*; and on the strength of this examination resolutions were passed with a view to a "French Renaissance". By and large, these resolutions followed the Communist line, notably with regard to the future referendum. The Liberation committees were called upon to support the vote in favour of a sovereign Assembly. Another resolution tried, in effect, to alter the nature of the CNR. After the formation of the UDSR, the Socialists, MRP, and "moderates" now constituted a clear anti-Communist majority on the CNR; therefore the *Etats Généraux* passed a resolution saying that while the CNR was to remain unchanged, a new body was being formed, comprising, in addition to the seventeen members of the CNR, eighteen members representing the National Liberation committees; in this way the pro-Communists were to be in the majority. The new body was to be called the *Conseil Central de la Renaissance Française*; but it was to prove still-born, as it was more or less boycotted by all the non-Communist members of the CNR.

A very important part in the estrangement between Socialists and Communists was played by two things: the first signs of a rapid absorption of the Socialists by the Communists in countries like Poland, and the return to Paris of Léon Blum.

Blum had great influence in the Socialist Party, and he was almost pathologically anti-Communist. This anti-Communism of Blum's did much to colour the decisions that the Socialists took in 1945, and was an important factor in the growing estrangement and hostility of the two "working-class parties"; in the Socialist drift towards "Third Force" conceptions, and towards a purely Western (and pro-American) line in international affairs. All this was, for years to come, to preserve for the Communists the great bulk of working-class support in France. The Communists had at least that to console them, even though their "conquest" of the Resistance, their determination to press for the strict application of the CNR Charter, their attempts to form a united front with the Socialists, and even to join with them in a great United Labour Party (and perhaps to swallow them up in the end) led to nothing, and finally tended to leave them and the bulk of the industrial workers in a position of deplorable isolation in the political life of France.

The hatred between Blum and the Communists was mutual. This refined and precious Jewish intellectual was, in every sense, alien to the French working-class; and in the eyes of the Communists he had, among other things, wrecked the Popular Front, betrayed the Spanish Republic, and condoned Munich; and if ever he reluctantly agreed to a *rapprochement* with the Communists, as he did in 1936, it was under the pressure of the rank and file, and in a spirit of tactical opportunism. He had refused to be a French Nenni. What "Nenni-ist" tendencies there were in the French Socialist Party just after the Liberation were effectively stamped out by Blum in 1945.

His main argument, which he developed in a long speech at the Socialist Congress on August 12, 1945, was that there could be no Socialism without political Democracy, and *vice versa*. He insisted that the French Socialists must "wholly accept" *both* the Marxist doctrine *and* democracy, "as Jaurès had done". "Without socialism," he said, "democracy is imperfect; without democracy, socialism is helpless." This, and much else that he said that day was a rehash of that little book, *A l'échelle humaine* which he had written during his wartime captivity—a book which had a great effect on the post-war ideology of the French Socialist Party.[2]

The decisions of the Congress were not only against organic unity with the Communists, but in effect also against united action, notably in the General Election. A number of provincial delegates had argued in vain that the Socialist Party had "no right to disappoint the vast majority of the working-class", and Professor Paul Rivet spoke of "the salutary example of Italy". But it was no good. André Philip, for example, warned the Socialists against the danger of being "pushed into the background" in any United Party, and Daniel Mayer said there could be no unity so long as the Communists remained "absolutely faithful to the USSR". So the Congress voted, instead, a motion in favour of unity of action with the UDSR—to which the Communists had declared themselves hostile on the ground that it had "split the Resistance" and represented a "reactionary" force. As for "united action" with the Communists, the Congress voted a Jules Moch motion so full of "conditions" that it was almost tantamount to a sharp attack.

It declared that the Socialist Party was all in favour of "labour unity", but that the pursuit of this aim presupposed "loyalty and mutual confidence", which meant that both sides "frankly stated their doctrine" and avoided opportunist attitudes "which are degrading to the human spirit"; that the rules of complete democracy be observed inside the Party, and defended on both the national and the international scale; that the two parties devote themselves entirely to the service of the world of labour, "whose freedom presupposes the freedom of the nation"—which meant that one must not be tied to any foreign government, or even be under its influence. None of these conditions having been fulfilled by the Communist Party (said the Moch motion) the Socialists could not accept the Communist Unity Charter as a basis of discussion; the *comité d'entente* should

[2] Later, in an article in the *Populaire* shortly before the election of October 1945, Blum foreshadowed the possibility of a democratic front, stretching far to the Right, and by implication, excluding the Communists. *Combat* (October 5, 1945) thought the article "disquieting".

elaborate unity of action in the Election, but let each party clearly defend its own programme; after the election, talks would be resumed about unity of action; and there must be no *comité d'entente*, except on a national level.

It was a slap in the face for the Communists; and the last paragraph made it clear that the Socialist leaders were opposed to any discussions about Socialist-Communist unity on any level other than the top level.

Were the Socialists suffering from a certain inferiority complex *vis-à-vis* the Communists? In 1945 the latter were full of zest and optimism, bursting with nationalist demagogy, and with stories of their Resistance record—a field in which it was hard for the Socialists to compete. The very fact that the Socialists had had to expel or suspend about two-thirds of their deputies and senators was bad for their pride.

As regards doctrine, the Communists in 1945 took a line that was strikingly different from that of the Socialists. Unlike the Socialists, who, through some strange atavism, kept on talking about their "Marxism" and "internationalism" (though what exactly they meant by "Marxism" nobody could quite make out, while their "internationalism" usually meant no more than that they felt friendly to the British Labour Party), the Communists in 1945 avoided speaking of either their Marxism or their internationalism. Instead, they seemed to be grooming themselves for the rôle of a major French government party for years to come. No doubt, the study of Marxism-Leninism should not be neglected:

This incomparable weapon [said Thorez in June 1945] has allowed us to understand clearly the most complicated situations, to foresee the probable course of events, to proclaim the most correct and most appropriate slogans . . . while always, in doing so, taking account of the future interests of the French working-class and of the French people. . . .[3]

But if Thorez said this at the Tenth Congress of the Communist Party in June 1945, it was certainly not his main preoccupation. It was not the speech of a doctrinaire, not even the speech of a party leader: it was more like the speech of a practical politician. After recalling the story of the war years (and, *inter alia*, making the best of the German-Soviet pact, which, he explained, had been provoked by Anglo-French "sabotage"), Thorez proclaimed: *La grandeur de la France est à refaire*. With as much sorrow as if he were de Gaulle himself, Thorez deplored the humiliation France had just had to suffer in Syria, just because she hadn't a big army.

Altogether, Thorez's report is of great interest because even if he was not speaking as a "government man", he was at least speaking as the representative of a Party which would, he seemed sure, be in the Government for a long time, and would exercise its influence in order

[3] Maurice Thorez, *Une politique de grandeur française* p. 352. Paris, 1945.

to make the Government action in France as effective, as energetic, and as "left-wing" as possible, and not just in one particular field, but in all fields. He foreshadowed a sort of *critical co-operation* with de Gaulle (or whoever else headed the Government), but this criticism would always be constructive criticism. For example, he warned the Government against being fully satisfied with the recent Four-power Agreement on Germany. Denazification was all very well, but the Government would do well to inquire into all sorts of funny things that were going on behind the scenes—for instance, the attempts made by the big British and American chemical trusts to save I. G. Farben from being dismantled and decartellized. Again, he defended the policy of employing German war prisoners for rebuilding villages the German Army had destroyed or of using them in the coal mines— despite many "humanitarian" protests from abroad, and even from inside France; he discussed the need of American aid, and stressed the absolute priority that should be given to the purchase of machine-tools, since France's industry lagged far behind Britain and America; he also advocated the development of East-West trade; and the modernization of agriculture, above all in Algeria and other French possessions. "*We must produce*", he exclaimed; and there followed not only a tribute to the French working-class which had already repaired most of the terrible damage done to the railways and to rolling-stock; but also numerous constructive proposals on how to increase France's industrial capacity; machine-tools should be imported, and the Government should not be impressed by the *patronat*'s opposition to this on the ground that it would undermine France's own machine-tool industry; the machine-tools were needed *right now* and French industry was in no position to produce them quickly. Or else:

The heads in the cement industry wanted the trade unions to protest against the import of 40,000 tons of British cement a month. Our comrades refused, because, in view of our immense reconstruction needs, they knew that these 40,000 tons of British cement could in no way hurt the French cement industry. . . .

Similarly, Thorez examined the position in the French coal industry very thoroughly, stressing the tremendous effort made by the miners to raise production, but also explaining the technical reasons for a reduced output, as well as the "physiological reasons"—"the physiological deficiency of the miners after four years of super-exploitation by Vichy and the Germans". The absenteeism was not due to laziness, but to physical exhaustion and insufficient food. Miners had to take days off, simply to rest—or else to look for some extra food in the countryside. And then he quoted numerous examples of sabotage by the "200 families", the Vichyites and their agents in the administration and elsewhere.

The impression Thorez tried to give was that the Communist Party was a fully qualified government party, with an expert understanding of international affairs, international trade, the detailed organization of all the French branches of industry and agriculture; that, in short, with a minimum of goodwill on all sides, the Communists in the Government could help enormously in building up a truly modern and efficient France. With this aim in view, they were willing to ask the working-class to work hard, and make many sacrifices. Only unfortunately—and here he quoted *Temps Présents*, the paper of the Catholic trade unions—the CNR programme was not being applied, and the working-class still had the impression that neither it nor the country as a whole were getting anything out of it, and that the money continued to pour into the same pockets as before.

It is curious to observe that on a large number of industrial questions, notably on the need to modernize and re-equip French industry, Thorez was saying almost the same things as say, Mendès-France. Whatever might have become the Communists' ultimate aim, they were clearly willing, in 1945, to help in the reconstruction of France; it has even been suggested that, had it not been for the intensification of the Cold War and the war in Indo-China which made their position in the Government untenable, they might not only have continued to help enormously in producing a more efficient and better-run France, with a contented working-class, but might even have developed into a genuine National-Communist party largely, if not wholly, independent of Moscow—the real nucleus of a "classical Left"—and perhaps ultimately tied to Moscow, as Raymond Aron said, "only by bonds of love".[4] But the Cold War inevitably encouraged the most virulent anti-Communism in France, for class reasons even more than for international reasons and, equally inevitably, it strengthened the bonds between the French Communists and the USSR. There was no inducement any longer to "help French capitalism".

[4] *Combat*, April 16, 1946. Marty later openly denounced this whole policy as a "mug's game", incompatible with the revolutionary traditions of the CP. The bourgeoisie, he argued, had squeezed the lemon, then thrown it away in 1947.

CHAPTER FIFTEEN

THE OCTOBER 1945 ELECTION

THE Thorez speech was in June; the Socialist Congress, at which, as we have seen, the Communist overtures were rejected, was in August; and then, in October, came the referendum and the General Election.

The Consultative Assembly had ceased to exist on August 3; this Assembly, largely composed of people of great personal merit, many of them heroes of the Resistance, had produced no great parliamentary leader, but had made many sound suggestions—of which de Gaulle did not, however, take much notice; as a result, at least a part of the Assembly grew irritable and quarrelsome towards the end. In its obituary of the Consultative Assembly *Combat* wrote:

In a few years from now people may be fairer to the Consultative Assembly and to the services it tried to render. . . . It was not a great revolutionary Assembly; but it did not make any irreparable mistakes, and it wished the country well. Its powers were platonic, but its idealism was unquestionable. . . .[1]

It is unnecessary here to dwell on all the endless squabbles and negotiations between de Gaulle and the parties and among the parties themselves, over the electoral law, over the referendum, and the various electoral inter-party pacts. It is a long story, and not illuminating. The chief quarrel was over a referendum—de Gaulle, supported by the faithful MRP, wanted a Constituent Assembly with limited powers and a limited (seven months) term of existence, while the Communists were the strongest supporters of a "sovereign Assembly". Only a small minority (chiefly the Radicals) wanted a simple return to the 1875 Constitution, complete with Senate.[2]

Shortly before the election, many, including de Gaulle, tried to create in the country a certain feeling of euphoria. M. Pineau, the Socialist Minister of Food, had the extravagant idea of abolishing bread rationing, with the result that, three months later, on January 1, 1946, it had

---

[1] *Combat*, August 3, 1945.
[2] Also, there was some opposition to the complicated and "lopsided" election system chosen by de Gaulle: the advocates of complete PR were (perhaps unreasonably) dissatisfied; even more disgruntled were the supporters of the *scrutin d'arrondissement*.

to be reimposed—with a reduced ration. Bread was subsidized; and while it was off the ration peasants had gone to town to buy dozens of loaves—to feed their livestock. When rationing was reintroduced, the election was over. It was a piece of low election demagogy if ever there was one.

De Gaulle gave a broadcast on October 17, four days before the election, and despite much unpleasantness during the previous week, he paid compliments to his Ministers, to the *fonctionnaires*, to the French people generally for all the patience and goodwill they had shown during the difficult transition period.

Economic life was reviving, food conditions were improving, ships were arriving, foreign trade was developing. He also declared himself satisfied with France's international position. "*Nos affaires sont en bonne voie.*"

An edifice is rising, stone by stone. The workers building it cannot yet see how beautiful it will be. But when it is completed, they will admire it and will not regret the labour they have put into it.

And he hoped "with all his heart" that the answer to the referendum would be a double Yes. (A new Constitution and a "limited" Assembly.)

Rather a prize-giving ceremony [*Combat* remarked]. We would have preferred a more precise balance-sheet for the year, and a list of tasks and priorities.... What we need is not so much "confidence" as *hope*—hope arising from constructive plans, from a revolutionary will.... De Gaulle is on the defensive, despite appearances.

As for the "edifice", it thought it wouldn't be a bad thing if the architects and foremen had at least an approximate idea of *what* they were building.[3]

Shortly before the October 21 election and referendum there had been much talk of the "inertia" and "political indifference" of the French people. In the cantonal elections of September 30 some 40 per cent had abstained. But the general election was different, and some temporary excitement had, in particular, been worked up over the referendum, which was treated by many as something of a plebiscite for or against de Gaulle. Both in the election and in the referendum only some 20 per cent abstained, the larger proportion of the abstentions being, significantly, in the ex-Vichy Zone—to which Paris politics still seemed a little remote. But, for the first time, women had been allowed to vote in a general election, and, in the main, they seem to have taken a certain pride in this new privilege, and went to the polls, voting mostly like their husbands.

[3] *Combat*, October 18, 1945.

From the Communist standpoint the rejection of the "sovereign Assembly" by a large majority was a surprise and a bitter disappointment. As for the election proper, its results were not very surprising, except that the Socialists had expected to do better. Although, in view of the numerous splinter parties and "affiliations" it is always difficult to say exactly how many votes each party has received in a French election, the following figures appear to be roughly correct[4]:

Communists and MURF, just over 5 million votes, or 26%.
Socialists and UDSR, 4.6 million votes, or 24%.
MRP, just over 4½ million votes, or 23.6%.
Right ("Moderates"), 2.9 million votes, or 15%.
Radicals, 1.1 million votes, or 5.8%.

The election system adopted favoured the large parties, with the result that the Big Three had nearly 80 per cent of the seats between them:

Communists and MURF, 158.
Socialists and UDSR, 142.
MRP, 152.
"Moderates", 67.
Radicals, 25.

Most significant was perhaps the big MRP vote. Their electoral clientele of nearly five millions was clearly not composed of people who had all been fired by the *mystique* of the CNR Charter, or who were truly progressive Christian-Democrats in the Marc Sangnier tradition— the kind of people who, before the war, had voted for the progressive little Catholic party of the *Démocrates Populaires*. A very large part of the "classical" Right had swung over to the MRP, not because these were a left-wing party, but because there was every chance of the progressive "Christians" in this party being swamped by Conservative, clerical, and ex-Vichyite elements. The subsequent history of the MRP shows that this calculation proved perfectly correct; the MRP as the government party *par excellence* was expected to be the conservative wing of the "Resistance" Coalition. How conservative the greater part of the MRP following in 1945 was, was to be demonstrated most clearly by their stampede two years later to support de Gaulle's RPF. In 1945 the greatest MRP successes were in what had formerly been conservative and clerical strongholds—notably in Brittany, Normandy, and Alsace, and in Paris they received the bulk of the conservative vote (28 per cent of the total), the "classical" Right retaining only 13 per cent. Also, part of the former Radical vote went (paradoxically enough) to the "clerical" MRP.

[4] Based on the statistics of the Ministry of the Interior, perhaps slightly biased in favour of the Socialists.

Despite Blum's confident prophecies, the Socialists did less well than he had expected—it was at least partly due to the great hostility shown for the Communists by the Socialist leaders; the Communists were still far from unpopular with the "Left" as a whole. A large part of the Socialist vote came from people who had voted for the Radicals in the past.

The Communists, with 900,000 members, as against the Socialists' 340,000, did well as the most "dynamic" party, and one which had certainly made the most of its Resistance record; also, it had attracted the numerous malcontents in the cities (in the Paris area they had 35 per cent of the poll), as well as a surprisingly high proportion of peasant voters (even including some small landowners), notably in the ex-Vichy Zone. Their opponents attributed these rural successes to the Communists' very large provincial press, with its vociferous demagogy. Another explanation is that local Liberation committees exercised a certain influence on the election, mostly in favour of the Communists. They did particularly well in areas where the Maquis had been active— a fact curiously in contradiction with the theory that "the peasants hated the Maquis".

CHAPTER SIXTEEN

DE GAULLE GOES

Fully a month was to elapse between the General Election and the formation of the new de Gaulle Government. During this month a number of things happened: the Délégation des Gauches —representing the revival of a pre-war committee of Communists, Socialists, Radicals, the CGT and the Ligue des Droits de l'Homme— drew up (with the Radical, it is true, acting only as an "observer") a detailed Government programme, largely based on the CNR Charter; another programme, not very different from the Délégation des Gauches programme (except for a strong emphasis on a "special statute" for the Ruhr and Rhineland and also on special rights for "the family") was drawn up by the MRP. By and large, all the three main parties had accepted the "basic principles" of the CNR Charter, and, in theory, at any rate, a sound basis existed for a tripartite coalition government under de Gaulle.

In spite of this, the Communists suddenly started a press campaign in favour of a Socialist-Communist-Radical coalition (for old times' sake, as it were), from which the MRP would be excluded; the Socialists and MRP, on the other hand, advocated a tripartite Government (Socialists, Communists, MRP). The Communists then announced that they agreed, provided they were given a "worthy" place in it—a demand the meaning of which they were to explain some days later, after de Gaulle had already been unanimously elected Head of the Government by the Constituent Assembly. This vote was accompanied by a motion declaring that General de Gaulle "*a bien mérité de la Patrie*"—a phrase that put him in the category of the great men of the first world war: Poincaré, Clemenceau, Foch, etc. When Félix Gouin, the president of the Assembly, took the Assembly's message to him that day at his villa at Neuilly, he was, according to all accounts, "deeply moved". But only a few days later new trouble started: it was when de Gaulle refused to comply with the Communists' demand that they be not discriminated against, and be given one of the three key ministries—Foreign Affairs, War, or Interior.

This he refused on the ground that, in giving one of these key posts to the Communists, he would thereby upset France's careful balance between America and Russia in favour of the latter. He did not put it quite so crudely; but that was precisely what he meant to convey, rather with the implication that the Communists were not an "entirely French" party, and could not therefore be fully trusted. The Communists expressed furious indignation, but, finding that they were getting no support from the other parties, they swallowed their pride in the end, and agreed to enter the de Gaulle Government, rather than be left out in the cold. Besides, what de Gaulle now offered them was not to be sneezed at: five Cabinet posts, namely, National Economy (Billoux), Armaments (Tillon), Industrial Production (Marcel Paul), and Labour (Croizat), while Thorez was to be one of the four Ministers of State. It meant that all the economic ministries (except Transport and Public Works, and Agriculture) were in Communist hands, and Thorez's appointment implied his complete rehabilitation. This was a lot more than a mere amnesty. For there were still many who liked to speak of him as a "deserter", or as "Le premier *parti* de France", as one wit had unkindly dubbed him.

If De Gaulle handed nearly all the economic ministries over to the Communists, it was not out of sheer love for them; he could have found a majority without them. But the Communists, at that time, were still *useful*; they helped to encourage production and to avoid labour unrest.

From the author's Paris notebook, November 1945:

... Except for the row between de Gaulle and the Communists, nobody seems much interested in politics. Much more interested in food conditions.... Black market in full swing—sugar, wine, coffee, cigarettes.... Life in Paris not quite normal yet. Taxis very hard to get. In principle, they are only for pregnant women. Lots of silly jokes about it.... Lot of metro stations still closed.... They don't seem to sweep even the parks. Walked through the Tuileries today over a rustling eight-inch carpet of red leaves.... Talk with Bidault at the Quai. Rhineland, Ruhr, Ruhr coal are his chief worries.... Furious with Molotov for failing to support France.... To my question about how the Communists fitted into the government, he made a face, and said: "Hm...enfin, ça va...à peu près...." Wretched "black market" dinner in a "workmen's bistrot", Batignolles way—300 francs for two: 30s at the present preposterous rate; they say there's going to be devaluation—480 to the £—even that will be far too little.... Streets badly lit at night. Lots of robberies and burglaries.... GI's responsible for some of them. *France-Soir* came out with big headline; "CHICAGO-SUR-SEINE", telling about misdeeds by the GI's.

Some anti-American feeling almost everywhere; strong anti-Russian feeling among the *nice* people, but still some vestiges of previous admiration for the Red Army, Stalingrad, etc. Good deal of anti-Russian stuff in the popular press.... Half the people I meet claim to have been "in the Resistance". But they also say: "Most unfair to have shot Laval. He did his best. We wouldn't be here but for him..." ... Economic *collabos* (met one who made a fortune building bits of the Atlantic Wall) running around freely and living in luxury. They also talk in a starry-eyed way of Sartre and "existentialism"; very fashionable these days. Called on Jean-Richard Bloch at *Ce Soir*. Found him very pessimistic. "Everything going to hell; all the old (and new) reactionaries coming up on top again."... *Daily X* chap (eyes popping out): "We must, must, MUST get the Communists thrown out of the Government...Fifth Column..." and so on. Same attitude among the rest of the Anglo-American press, who eat beastly American-canned-food lunches (mostly bully-beef hash) at the Scribe.... Quite different attitude *chez* Duff Cooper, who thinks it's *very sensible* of de Gaulle to keep them in the Government. Thinks Thorez a tremendous chap "with great charm" (has asked him to the Embassy to lunch), and thinks that several of the others are "very able and earnest fellows", especially Croizat.

Spent a week in Normandy. The peasants, who made fortunes during the war and had no trouble to speak of, all claim to have been "in the Resistance". Like hell they were. They continue to make fortunes, selling meat to the black market in Paris. Except for a privileged minority, Paris is hungry and down-at-heel; but in Normandy—in the countryside—I was served steaks that hung over the sides of the plate.... The peasants are for de Gaulle and against the Communists. Most of them seem to have voted MRP which they consider "de Gaulle's Party". But what interests them most is the attitude of the parties to the *bouilleurs de crû* [the private distiller of tax-free *calvados*].... Railways running, but slowly, and very few trains. Took nearly ten hours, with a change at Le Mans, to get to Alençon. ... The curator of the "museum" attached to one of the Norman *châteaux*—a dusty little old man, like something out of Courteline—treated me to a long discourse on *la crise morale* which, he said, was *quite* general in France. Even small children were crooks....

Despite the clash between de Gaulle and the CP, the first weeks of the first Constituent Assembly were not fruitless. Since all the three major parties were agreed "in principle" to accept the CNR Charter as at least the "framework" for future legislation, de Gaulle's announcement that the "nationalization of credit" and the nationalization of electricity were to be among the Government's immediate objectives met with little opposition, except from the Right. The principal spokesman of the opponents of nationalization was M. Laniel (even though he had been one of the signatories of the CNR programme).

Insurance was also to be nationalized in some degree, still to be determined. Apart from the Bank of France, which was to be "finally" nationalized, the nationalization of the banks was to be limited to the Big Four deposit banks, the Crédit Lyonnais, the Société Générale, the Comptoir National d'Escompte and the Banque Nationale pour le Commerce et l'Industrie; the question of two other banks, the Banque de Paris et des Pays-Bas and the Banque de l'Union Parisienne was in the end to be dropped. The case against the banks was stated by the *rapporteur général* of the Nationalization Bill, M. Pineau, who accused them of excessive caution in their credit policy, caution often amounting to downright sabotage, and of deliberate attempts to bring pressure to bear on the State.

In the end, the Big Four were nationalized, and their shareholders indemnified (though less generously than the Government had originally proposed). The nationalization of the banks did not, in the end, produce anything like the results the "idealists" of the CNR had expected; for they continued to work hand-in-hand with Big Business.

The first steps were also taken towards the nationalization of gas and electricity, which did not, however, come into effect until the following spring. It was also in April that the 32 major French insurance companies were nationalized. In the discussion that had preceded the passing of the Bill, the Assembly derived some amusement from the disclosure that black market sharks regularly insured their commodities against confiscation.

A widespread impression among political observers in Paris at that time was that all these measures—such as the nationalization of the banks and insurance—were carried out rather half-heartedly, without much faith in a glorious Socialist future, which these nationalizations were supposed to prepare. As *Combat* wrote on December 1, 1945:

> Duclos yesterday said: "The nationalizations are neither Socialism, nor even '*la Révolution par la loi*'." Of course not—we quite agree. But then who today in France has any genuine revolutionary ambition left? Even the Communist Party is no longer revolutionary... "*la Révolution par la loi*" is one of those ambiguous phrases which, in the last year, have been worn pretty threadbare—and now even the Communists have adopted it. The phrase clearly suggests slow change; then why not call it "reformist evolution"?

It added that if the Communists were content with that, or even with less, was it not that they were staying in the Government merely in the hope that they would gradually gain in influence? On December 7 it wrote:

> Everything at the Constituent Assembly is vague, even though its avowed purpose is to build a new society.

And a few days later, it lamented over the fact that "the only new institutions so far produced by the Fourth Republic have been the *comités d'entreprise*"—the workers' committees in industry. But they amounted to very little: the *comités* had some say in the running of canteens, and in other aspects of the workers' "welfare"; but they had no connexion with "workers' control"; they had no say whatsoever in the fixing of wages, and even if they were allowed to make suggestions about production processes, nobody was obliged to take any notice. Altogether, the "revolutionaries" of the Resistance were disgruntled.

Even so, a few things *were* being done—though not exactly in a revolutionary spirit. Thus, on December 21 the foundations were laid for the famous Monnet Plan, through the creation of a Government organism that would elaborate a plan "for the modernization and the equipment of the country". But the financing of this Plan was still very much in the air. The abrupt termination of Lend-Lease on September 2 had placed France (like other European countries) in a highly awkward position. On December 14 France borrowed from the Export-Import Bank 550 million dollars, repayable in 30 years, which M. Pleven described as "an appendix and epilogue to Lend-Lease". Its purpose, he said, was simply "to enable France not to interrupt her convalescence, pending the receipt of foreign aid which we shall need if we are to modernize and re-equip our country".

Meantime, in the foreign field, France was continuing to press for a drastic solution of the Ruhr and Rhineland problems. In November M. Couve de Murville went to the United States to explain the French point of view to the Americans. At a press conference he argued in favour of the creation of a sovereign Rhineland State with Allied occupation of its strategic points, and in favour of the internationalization of the Ruhr. Mr Byrnes merely said, at a press conference of his own, that the French suggestions would be "considered". At the end of the month, M. Alphand, another high official of the Quai d'Orsay, went to Moscow on a parallel mission, where, apart from trade talks, he had talks with Mr Molotov, to whom he submitted a French memorandum on the Ruhr and Rhineland, implying French support against any German attempts to recover the Eastern territories if the Russians were helpful.

Symptomatic of the decline of the "Resistance spirit" was the fact that, in December 1945, the "classical Right" suddenly became vocal for the first time. MM. Laniel, Mutter, Ramarony, and Dupont (the first two, very conveniently members of the CNR) decided that it was time to form a solid new political party, the PRL (*parti Républicain de la Liberté*), the purpose of which was to put up a fight against *dirigisme*, which, they said, was hostile to freedom and to free enterprise. M. Laniel made a long speech in which he said that while he and his friends were "heart and soul" with General de Gaulle, they were completely opposed to the present tripartite government, which he described as "Popular Front No 2", as harmful to the interests of the country as had been Popular Front No 1.

Another straw in the wind was the discrimination that was beginning to be used in the official attitude to ex-Vichyites; thus the rigid rules applying to all deputies and senators who had voted for Pétain in

July 1940 were relaxed, a parliamentary *jury d'honneur* declaring some of them to be no longer ineligible.

How far France had travelled in a little over a year from the "tough Resistance spirit", and from "les lendemains qui chantent" of August 1944 was noted by *Combat* in connexion with the budget debate at the Constituent Assembly, and particularly with the speech on the press by Malraux, the Minister of Information:

The budget of the Ministry of Information came up for discussion. Some of the Opposition people started referring to "occult influences in the Press". So Malraux said: "By occult influences you apparently mean the Resistance; well, let me tell you, the Resistance press is a *fighting press.*" Then came a voice from the extreme Right: "But what about freedom?" To which Malraux replied: "Freedom is for those who have conquered it."

A year ago this would have produced unanimous applause. Now it merely caused embarrassment—nearly everywhere. For if, today, one still willingly pays tribute to the heroes and martyrs of the Resistance, it has already become incongruous and anachronistic to recall its revolutionary spirit.... As for the Resistance, crouching in the shadow of the parties, it hasn't got an existence of its own any more....[1]

This budget debate was the real prelude to de Gaulle's sudden and spectacular resignation. In the course of the discussion of the Army estimates, numerous references were made to preposterous examples of waste—red cloth ordered by mistake at Elbeuf for uniforms, or the 10,000 *brassières* ordered for the AFAT (the French ATS)—and many deputies argued that, in France's economic position, when she had no means of building up a large and well-equipped army, it would be best to cut down military expenditure instead of wasting money on obsolete material. On New Year's night a little-known Socialist deputy proposed an amendment cutting military expenditure by 20 per cent, and his amendment was supported by other Socialists and by the Communists. In the absence of de Gaulle the discussion was adjourned till the following day; the quarrel was finally patched up by the adoption of a sub-amendment, saying that the 20 per cent cut would not come into force if, by February 15, the Government produced new proposals for the reform of the Army. But in the course of this discussion, de Gaulle revealed that he was in full disagreement with the Constituent Assembly as to its rights and powers. He rejected in effect the idea of "governing by compromise", and resented the very idea that the Assembly could disagree with the Government on *any* point.

The Assembly [he said] has shown by its attitude that it prefers a régime in which the Assembly governs. It is not a system that coincides with the Government's ideas on the subject.... Is the Assembly in favour of a real

[1] *Combat*, January 1, 1946.

parliamentary régime, or of an all-powerful Assembly which merely delegates limited powers to the Government for carrying out the Assembly's
wishes? I do not deny that the Assembly has legislative powers, but that is
another matter....

Were not only amendments, but even criticism intolerable to de
Gaulle? It looked, as one commentator put it, as though an amendment were to him "a crime of *lèse-exécutif*".

Does it all mean [*Combat* wrote on the following day] that disagreement
on any point must mean the fall of the Government? One can just imagine
what the Assembly's precious "legislative powers" would amount to at that
rate! What de Gaulle in fact wants is a Consultative Assembly—with the
sole privilege of electing and overthrowing the Government. For the rest, it
will, or will not, be listened to.... This is something different from both
parliamentary government as we understand it, and even from the classical
distinction between the legislative and the executive....
But the present position is wholly equivocal. However, now that de
Gaulle has given his interpretation of the Yes-Yes reply to the referendum,
let us decide whether France requires a dictatorship or not. If that is what
de Gaulle thinks, let him say so. And let's have no more of these menacing
innuendos that have been coming from de Gaulle during the past few
weeks.[2]

It might, of course, be argued that de Gaulle had just as much right
as any other prime minister to make any particular issue a vote of
confidence; but what the Assembly resented was that he should consider any arguing superfluous, and any amendments as unwarranted
interference with the Government; also, since it was widely felt that
the tripartite coalition was hanging together by virtue of de Gaulle's
personal prestige, was he not blackmailing the Assembly into a state
of subservience—for if de Gaulle went, wouldn't the coalition collapse?
De Gaulle, for his part, resented "interference with the Executive"
(an Executive which he personally dominated, rendering its members
"pretty helpless", as the Communists were later to complain) and it
is this resentment which largely explains not only his sudden resignation on January 20, but also his subsequent campaign which was, before
long, to lead to the formation of the RPF. It was, of course, not the
only reason for his departure. On returning to Paris on January 14,
after a short holiday on the Riviera, he was irritated by a number of
other things: at the meeting of the Assembly on the 16th, Herriot
criticized de Gaulle for not having cancelled the decorations awarded
to soldiers and officers who had fought the American forces at the
time of the North Africa landing; de Gaulle retorted that these men,
though misguided at the time, had fought for France. Another source

[2] *Combat*, January 3, 1946.

of annoyance was the sudden *rapprochement* between the Socialists and Communists; the Communists had not forgotten the affront they had suffered from de Gaulle in November; as for the rank-and-file Socialists, who had already caused the famous row over the Army estimates, they were beginning to voice, more and more openly, the discontent in the country, and were even beginning to criticize certain ideas of Blum and Daniel Mayer, with their "subservience" to de Gaulle and his *politique de grandeur*—which was not popular in a cold and hungry country, where bread rationing had just been restored.

But was there not also something much more personal, and almost irrational in de Gaulle's resignation? There is a strangely prophetic passage in *Le fil de l'épée*, written in 1932:

> Reserve, character, greatness—these conditions of prestige involve an effort that most people would find discouraging. The constant strain is hard to bear.... Here one finds the real motive for retirements that are hard to explain: suddenly a successful and popular man is seen throwing down the burden. By isolating himself from others, the leader renounces the joys of relaxation, familiarity, and friendship. He condemns himself to that feeling of loneliness which, in the words of Faguet, is "the tragedy of superior men".... The thing commonly known as happiness is incompatible with domination. A choice must be made, but it is a cruel choice.[3]

His letter of resignation, sent on January 20 to M. Gouin, the president of the Assembly, made little sense: he explained that he had meant to retire after the election, but had been prevailed upon to stay at the head of the Government by the unanimous vote of the Constituent Assembly. However, the transition period was now over; France was no longer in a state of alarm; there were still many problems to be solved, and many hardships, but, in the main, France was on the road to recovery. Economic activity was developing favourably, France had recovered all her territories, except Indo-China, but even here she had gained a foothold.[4]

He was planning to give a broadcast—in which, it was said, he was going to denounce the Party system, and explain his disagreement with the Constituent Assembly; but Vincent Auriol dissuaded him from doing so.

And so de Gaulle went; and, as *Combat* put it, "there was no cataclysm, and the empty plate didn't crack".

French opinion was puzzled, rather than shocked. The IFOP (the French "Gallup") published soon afterwards the result of its poll. The most varied opinions were expressed on why de Gaulle had gone:

[3] C. de Gaulle, *Le fil de l'epée* (Paris, 1946), pp. 82-83.
[4] A reference to the occupation of Saigon and parts of Cochin-China by General Leclerc in December 1945.

Disagreed with political parties, Assembly or Ministers   28%
Unable to carry out his own policy   15%
Unable to cope with economic difficulties   9%
Felt his prestige dwindling   8%
Tired of the political struggle   8%
Disagreed on precise points (food policy, etc)   2%
Influence of foreign powers   17%
Political calculation   1%
Don't know   25%

There were a few other questions:

If de Gaulle became head of a new party, would you vote for him?—
Yes, 31%; No, 46%; Don't know, 23%;

Do you think he will again be Head of the Government?—Yes, 21%;
No, 43%, Don't know, 31%;

Are you glad he's gone?—Yes, 32%; No, 40%; Indifferent or don't
know, 28%.

This poll, for what it is worth, still confirmed the impression that
de Gaulle was no longer, in the eyes of the French public as a whole,
the indispensable national figure he had been at the time of the Liberation. The attitude to him, in 1946, was already a very mixed one. The
"empty plates" had much to do with it.

Even so, eighteen months later, in a greatly altered international
situation, he was going to make a spectacular come-back.

WHAT DID THE FRENCH "PURGE" AMOUNT TO?

SINCE the French "purge" took place chiefly during the months of the Liberation and during the subsequent "de Gaulle period", it seems best, before proceeding with the political history of the post-de Gaulle years, to examine at this point the not unimportant question of what the French "purge" amounted to.

At the end of 1954 I received a publisher's circular from New York, containing the following:

France: The Tragic Years (1939–47). An Eye-witness account of War, Occupation and Liberation. By Sisley Huddleston.
... Told for the first time is the real story of the Liberation and the execution in cold blood of more than 100,000 "collaborators", denounced by the real collaborators now turned Communist.... A writer of the first rank—whose English is a delight to read—Sisley Huddleston died in France in 1952 right after finishing the manuscript of this monumental work, which should become a classic on the disintegration of a once-great nation.

Sisley Huddleston, a rather pathetic and absurd figure in his old age, was the only Englishman who, in conformity with the political line he had taken for several years before, not only wholeheartedly embraced the cause of Vichy and the "National Revolution", but, as a deliberate political gesture, applied for, and was granted "Vichy" citizenship. In 1944 he was arrested and locked up for a short time, and wrote in French, on the strength of it, a book called *Terreur 1944*.

The story of the "execution in cold blood of more than 100,000 'collaborators'" is one of those remarkable legends which, nevertheless, crop up from time to time without any foundation whatsoever. Nobody has yet produced the slightest evidence of 100,000, or anything even approaching 100,000 people having been shot "in cold blood" or otherwise.

In connexion with the various Amnesty Bills and Amnesty proposals, the National Assembly was to discuss the "purge" of 1944 and of the years that followed (including the cases of those who had been shot without trial) on at least a dozen occasions. One of the most important debates—which took up four sittings—was held in 1952, under the

Pinay Government, the most conservative and near-Vichyite Government since the war. And still no information of any sort transpired about the legendary 100,000. It is quite true that the Liberation was —understandably—accompanied by a good deal of rough justice, and even some plain injustice, and even a number of actual "atrocities", and it is also true that, with the rather clumsy juridical machinery and the awkward legal texts at their disposal, the Courts were responsible, in 1944–5 for many incoherent and arbitrary decisions. Yet there was much less repression in France, after four years of enemy occupation and nearly two years of "organic" co-operation between the French and German police forces, than there was, about the same time, in several other countries that had been occupied by the Germans— notably Belgium, Holland, and Norway.[1]

Needless to say, there was a good deal of whining from Vichyites and collaborators, who, in the previous years, had condoned and applauded the "discipline" of Vichy, who had raised no protest of any kind not only against the deportation to Auschwitz and Buchenwald and the other death camps of hundreds of thousands of Frenchmen, and had remained totally indifferent to the abominable conditions existing in the camps and prisons under sole Vichy control—notably those in North Africa. People who had never protested against these things, produced in 1945–6, stacks of books, some published in France, others in Belgium or Switzerland, such as the Abbé Desgranges's *Les Crimes masqués du Resistentialisme*, and Fabre-Luce's *Journal de l'Europe, 1946–7*, with its chapter on "the hell of Poissy"—the prison near Paris where *collabos* underwent much moral, rather than physical suffering.

In the parliamentary debates on the Amnesty, notably in 1952, the actual extent of the "repression" was discussed very thoroughly. Neither M. Isorni, Pétain's principal defender, nor any other Vichyites like M. Roger de Saivre or M. Paul Estèbe, who had every opportunity of showing that 100,000 people had been "murdered in cold blood", even attempted to demonstrate anything of the sort. M. Brune, M. Pinay's Minister of the Interior, no more a "resistentialist" than his chief, declared: "From an inquiry made in 1948 among the Prefects, it transpired that the total number of summary executions of collaborators carried out in France amounted to about 10,000; of these 5,234 were carried out before the Liberation and 3,114 after the Liberation without trial, while 1,325 death sentences were passed after the Liberation by *ad hoc* tribunals."

This total of 10,000 was also to be quoted by M. Bidault.[2]

[1] The number of prosecutions in France was proportionately much smaller; the number of death sentences was, however, higher.

[2] *Débats, Assemblée Nationale*, October 28, 1952.

It is not quite clear from M. Brune's statement what exactly he meant by "summary executions"; the speech made by M. Daniel Mayer, the former Socialist representative on the CNR, at the National Assembly on October 21, 1952, gives at least a partial explanation of the circumstances surrounding these executions.

First, about 1,000 death sentences were passed by the "emergency courts-martial" of the FFI between August 31 and October 15, 1944; secondly, there were the "summary executions proper", amounting to about 3,000, which had taken place between June 6 and August 31, i.e. "during that period of national insurrection when it was every Frenchman's duty to fight the common enemy and his accomplices"; in other words, what was called "executions" was often simply part of a series of local "civil wars". After August 31 the *Comité d'Action de la Résistance* set up emergency tribunals in numerous parts of France; it was these tribunals, partly composed of members of the Liberation committees, who passed a few thousand more death sentences; according to M. Mayer, these trials were in most cases, conducted in a much more orderly and legalistic way than M. Brune's statement suggested, and were a great improvement on the courts-martial before August 31.

As examples of "summary executions" it may be useful to recall at least two cases derived from personal knowledge of the people concerned. At the end of June 1944 at le Bugue, in the Dordogne, a local Resistance group surrounded the local headquarters of the *milice*, captured three of the *miliciens* and shot them in the market square. In an automobile factory in the Paris area, immediately after the Liberation of Paris, a White-Russian engineer was shot by the FFI in the factory yard: he had worked hand-in-glove with the Germans, and although he always spoke to them in German, one of the workers who understood the language, was able to report that he had helped the Germans to detect the numerous cases of ca'canny and sabotage that were going on, and had also continuously advised the Germans on the pressures they were to use to increase output.

The best-known case of a "summary execution" shortly before the Liberation was that of the notorious Philippe Henriot, the Nazi radio propagandist (newly promoted under German pressure to a ministerial post in the Vichy Government), who was shot in his bedroom in Paris one night by a number of Resistance men who, disguised as *miliciens*, had succeeded in penetrating into the house. They drove off in their car, after the "execution". The daring exploit aroused great enthusiasm in Paris and seriously scared the other *collabos*. Another well-known case was that of the prefect of the Haute-Savoie, who had organized the extermination of the famous Glières Maquis, and who, at the Liberation, was (understandably) simply "bumped off" by the Resistance.

No doubt there were, especially in the countryside, some ugly personal vendettas, and even some simple robberies under the guise of "punishing collaborators"; on the other hand, during the insurrection, there were also cases when innocent people were shot simply because the Resistance could not take the risk of being denounced by people of whom they were not sure: such is one of the cruel laws of civil war. But there is nothing to show that, between them, the "summary executions" and the death sentences passed by the different kinds of courts-martial and emergency tribunals amounted to more than a total of 10,000. Where then did the stories of 60,000, or 100,000, or 120,000 "summary executions" come from?—not to mention the completely lunatic assertions of a paper like *Aspects de la France* (successor of the *Action Française*) which was quoted by M. Bidault as saying that M. de Menthon, the Minister of Justice at the time of the Liberation, "had 500,000 corpses on his conscience".[3]

In subsequent years it was part of the French conservatives, and ex-Vichyites, campaign against the Resistance and especially against the Communists to refer to the FFI and the Communist Partisans as an army of murderers and cut-throats. Thus, a man like M. Paulhan, who after going over from the Resistance to the anti-Resistance, published a pamphlet in 1952,[4] in which he claimed that 60,000 people had been shot without trial. He declared that he made this assertion on the strength of "the only serious document" on the subject, namely, a report drawn up by "the historical section of General Eisenhower's headquarters" which had "estimated" that in the Mediterranean sector of France alone, there were 50,000 summary executions in 1944, a report subsequently quoted in the *American Mercury* of April 1946. M. Paulhan also claimed that M. Tixier, the Minister of the Interior, had declared in 1945 that 105,000 persons had been "summarily shot". Roger Stéphane, who was on M. Tixier's staff at the time, dismissed the statement as entirely apocryphal. Another important fact showing that the number of "summary executions" had been grossly exaggerated for propaganda purposes was this:

In 1951 the Ministry of Justice had announced through the press and over the radio that the Government was willing to indemnify morally or materially the families of persons who had been "summarily shot", and asked that these persons communicate with it. The response was extremely feeble: only a few hundred families responded.[5]

Apart from "summary executions" and death sentences by emergency tribunals, totalling, according to M. Bidault, about 10,000, the

[3] *Débats, Assemblée Nationale,* October 28, 1952.
[4] Jean Paulhan, *Lettre aux Directeurs de la Résistance* (Paris, 1952).
[5] Paulhan-Stéphane controversy in *L'Observateur,* February 7 and March 20, 1952.

regular Courts after the Liberation sentenced over 2,800 persons to death, but only 767 sentences were actually carried out. In addition, 3,910 death sentences were passed *in absentia*.[6] There were 39,000 sentences to varying terms of imprisonment, but, by October 1952, according to M. Martinaud-Déplat, the Minister of Justice in the Pinay Government, only 1,570 persons were still in prison, including 275 women. Some 40,000 persons had also been sentenced by the *chambres civiques* or other courts to varying terms of national degradation or *indignité*; but, by 1952, these sentences were still in force only in the case of 10,000 persons.

M. Bidault,[7] like M. Daniel Mayer before him, thought that those who talked of "repression" after the war should keep their sense of proportion. If, he said, there were 39,000 prison sentences in France (population over 40 million), there were 50,000 prison sentences in Belgium (population, 8 million), 50,000 in Holland (population 9 million), and 48,500 in Norway (population 3 million).

One thousand out of our three thousand magistrates [he said] have finished this thankless but necessary task. Compared with other occupied countries (Belgium, Holland, Norway), punishment was meted out in France *with extreme moderation*.

The *cour de justice* of the Seine, for example, he said, had passed 204 death sentences; but only 75 had been carried out; 109 had been commuted; 77 of those sentenced to death were still (1952) in prison, but 32 had already been set free—among them, he clearly suggested, some highly undesirable characters, like a certain Marshal, Doriot's right-hand man, and some of the French Gestapo men of the horrible Bony-Lafont gang (these were no doubt being used by the police for their own purposes).

Like Daniel Mayer, Bidault thought that the sufferings of the *collabos* were not at all extensive, compared with the things done to France by the Germans, in co-operation with Vichy. He recalled that of the 108,000 French "racial" deportees, only 3,500 had returned, and, of the 112,000 Resistance and other political deportees, only 35,000. This was not counting the many thousands who had been shot and massacred in France—the Resistance fighters, hostages, and the entire population of a place like Oradour.

No, doubt, it *was* a thankless task for the French courts to deal with "collaboration". As already said in a previous chapter, there was, except for "national unworthiness" (which had been defined by a special *ordonnance*), no new legislation that had been specially devised to punish "collaboration". Such legislation could only have been

[6] Figures quoted by M. Isorni, *Débats, Assemblée Nationale*, October 21, 1952.
[7] *Débats, Assemblée Nationale*, October 28, 1952.

retroactive; in its absence the Courts tried to apply as best they could the pre-war legislation (notably art. 75 of the Penal Code) on treason and "intelligence with the enemy"—even where it did not strictly fit. It was a case of applying the spirit, rather than the letter of the law: a writer like Béraud, for instance, had had no actual dealings with the Germans: even so, his vitriolic articles against England and de Gaulle *were* treasonable in spirit, if not in a narrow legalistic sense. Nevertheless, all this often made the work of the Courts extremely awkward, and tended to leave a good deal of room for arbitrary judgements and decisions, and did not fail, after a while, to make the whole "purge" procedure distasteful to the public.

Partly owing to the legal anomaly underlying the purge trials, partly owing to the "jury gamble"—especially in the case of the High Court —there seemed no fixed ratio between crime and punishment; some bad cases got off lightly; some fairly innocuous cases ended with very severe sentences, as we have already seen. Also action was taken much more readily against political collaborators than against economic collaborators, partly because, in the case of the former, the evidence was always much more easily available—e.g. in the form of speeches, articles, etc, and partly because economic collaborators interested the public less, and, when necessary, were in a better position than the "political *collabos*" to resort to bribery and corruption. The director of Fresnes Prison was much more nervous about the economic than the political collaborators; the badly paid prison staff, he said, found it infernally hard to resist the temptation of generous "tips"; at one time the question even arose of replacing the warders by deportees, recently back from Germany, who would probably be too bitter and angry to be tempted by money; but it was found that they were not interested in prison jobs, having had enough of prisons. Altogether, there was much truth in the quip that you ran about freely if you built the Atlantic Wall, but that you went to gaol if you ever said that the Atlantic Wall was a good thing.

As for the confiscation of "illicit profits", M. Pleven had—apart from a few exceptions which received great publicity—made it beautifully easy for the war profiteers to dodge confiscation, all the more so as the franc-for-franc exchange of notes had been announced a long time in advance, thus giving the profiteers plenty of time to "make arrangements" for avoiding a proper census of fortunes.

Apart from legal action taken against "collaborators", there was also a "purge" in the administration; but it was not severe. Among magistrates, some 10 per cent were suspended, but many were later reinstated; even in the upper ranks of the civil service, it was usually exceedingly difficult to draw the line between determined *maréchalistes* and the great mass of bread-and-butter Vichyites. Even M. Isorni,

Vichy's principal protagonist in the National Assembly, said it was "very difficult to establish" what the "purge" in the administration, the professions and the trade unions had really amounted to; if it had amounted to a great deal, he would no doubt have been less vague. He deplored, nevertheless, the harshness with which notably prefects and mayors had been treated—men whose duties inevitably involved contacts with the Germans and whose task was "infinitely difficult". De Gaulle, at any rate, though extremely intolerant in the case of most of the top-ranking Vichyites (e.g. Laval, whose re-trial he would not even consider) tended, on the whole, to make allowances for a "change of heart"; we have seen this in the case of the Leclerc Division, more than half of which, by the time it reached Paris, was composed of men who had served the Marshal.

Often justice was meted out incoherently: thus, Admiral Esteva was sentenced to life imprisonment for having allowed the Germans in November 1942 to land in Tunisia—even though he had apparently done no more than carry out the instructions of General Juin, his chief in North Africa. However, at the time of Esteva's trial, Juin was already French Chief of Staff, and one of the great personages of the Fourth Republic.[8]

It was one of the contradictions of the de Gaulle régime to be superficially revolutionary (*"par la loi"*), and secretly conservative at the same time; on the one hand "purges", nationalizations, and plans for a new Constitution, on the other hand, a France that was carrying on with fundamentally the same society, the same administration, and even, in the main, the same personnel. What new personnel there was gradually acquired the habits of the old.

In the main, France was tending to model itself on the Third Republic, with Vichy as a solemn, partly tragic and partly absurd interlude, though not one that had left no trace at all. Vichy ways of thinking were not dead, and there were traces of it even in de Gaulle's own almost innate regard for the Travail-Famille-Patrie tryptich, just as there were echoes of Maurras's *la France seule* in his helplessly proud foreign policy of 1944-5. Temperamentally de Gaulle was closer to the authoritarianism of Vichy than to the nascent Fourth Republic on which he was soon to declare war.

[8] Alfred Fabre-Luce, *Au nom des silencieux* (Bruges, 1945), p. 162, also Pierre Parent, *Le Problème Marocain en 1949* (Toulouse, 1949), pp. 100-101.

Part III

THE ROUGH ROAD TO THE "WEST"
(1946–48)

CHAPTER ONE

1946: A YEAR OF UNEASY TRANSITION

NINETEEN HUNDRED AND FORTY-SIX and the early part of 1947 are a period of transition—of a rapid and, one might say, inexorable transition from de Gaulle's "between East and West" and "be tough with Germany" position to a total abandonment of this German policy and to a glad acceptance of Marshall Aid and a reluctant half-acceptance of its political implications.

During 1946 French Government policy was still, according to British and American ideas, non-conformist in many respects. At the Peace Conference with the Satellites in July–October 1946, Bidault still tried to play the rôle of an "impartial arbiter" between East and West. France's breach of diplomatic and trade relations with Franco Spain, earlier in the year, though giving to many the illusion that France had "principles" which the other Western powers had not, was however, in reality, an "unrealistic" hangover from the anti-Fascist ideology of the Resistance, still dear to the hearts of the Socialists and Communists in the Government. To the French Left, and even to some of the MRP, and even to de Gaulle (or at least so he said) it was morally offensive that, with Hitler and Mussolini dead, Franco should still be thriving—though what could be done about it, in the absence of all British and American support, was never quite clear. But the breach of diplomatic and trade relations with Spain was nevertheless consistent with France's home policy at the time: it was, as it were, an expression of "anti-Vichyism" in the international field. Despite various stories in the left-wing press to the effect that "just one little push" from outside would bring the Franco régime toppling down, it is doubtful whether anybody seriously believed it, especially with Britain and America unwilling to take any serious action against Franco. It is significant that while France and, with her, Poland and Czechoslovakia "recognized" the Spanish Republican Government, the Soviet Union did not do so. It was a point which, at the time, rather puzzled the French Communists.[1]

---

[1] The execution of numerous Republicans in Spain early in 1946 was attributed by part of the French press, including *Combat*, to the "irresponsible" utterances on Spain by certain French Ministers. The MRP *Aube*, on the other

As for Germany, the period was marked for France by one disappointment after another, and de Gaulle's and Bidault's policy was being rejected not only by the West, but also by the East. In Germany, America and Russia had now embarked on a game of hard-boiled power politics, in which France's wishes carried no weight at all. At a luncheon at the American Club in Paris in October 1946 Bidault exclaimed: "In the matter of Germany, France is a voice crying in the wilderness!"

Byrnes's Stuttgart speech shortly before had, indeed, shown a perfect disregard for France's ambitions in the German field; and Molotov was equally unco-operative.

Although the Cold War, which had, in effect, begun at Hiroshima, had not yet reached its peak by 1946, the international atmosphere was already far from healthy. Churchill had made his Fulton speech in March. It was like the first official declaration of the Cold War. No doubt, Churchill was not in office at the time; but he had made his speech in the presence and with the blessing of President Truman; and the British Labour Government had scarcely disavowed him. The Russians, in 1946, were on the defensive, and in March they pulled out of Iran, cutting their losses in Persian Azerbaijan, and throwing their friends, the Azerbaijani "progressives" to the wolves. It created a painful impression among the French Communists, while, in America, it was interpreted as a sign of Russian weakness, and increased the desire to "get tough" with the Russians. In Greece, too, the Anglo-American-sponsored Monarchy got 72 per cent in the somewhat dubious September referendum. Almost everywhere there were signs of the gloves being off. No doubt, a semblance of "Allied unity" continued to be maintained in certain limited fields: there was, notably, the Nuremberg Trial—but this also was like a hangover from the good anti-Nazi resolutions taken before the end of the war. Similarly, at the Peace Conference of the 21 powers in Paris in July–October 1946, no insoluble conflicts arose between East and West; and though there were some difficult moments, agreement was reached on the Satellite peace treaties by the end of the year, and they were duly signed in the following February. Even so, Bidault who, throughout, had acted the tactful host, and had taken pride in often successfully proposing East-West compromises when serious difficulties arose, remarked with some melancholy at the final session of the Conference that the discussions had been seriously hampered by the fact that not only had no peace

hand, said that M. Bidault's more diplomatic attitude to Spain during the previous months had proved much more useful, and claimed that on some fifty occasions Bidault had discreetly and successfully intervened with the Franco authorities on behalf of Spanish Republicans in danger of death.

treaty been signed with Germany, but that even the main lines of an Allied Four-Power policy *vis-à-vis* Germany had not been laid down. Which was only too true.

Apart from the virtual abandonment of the de Gaulle policy on Germany, the central event in French foreign policy in 1946 was clearly Léon Blum's mission to Washington. Although Blum protested ("too much") against suggestions that his talks in Washington had in any sense been *political*, they were, in fact, an important step towards France's integration in the American "sphere of influence", towards the end of *tripartisme* and the elimination of the Communists from the French Government—with striking parallel developments in Belgium and Italy. A year later, Jouhaux visited the United States, and the visit was soon followed by the split in the CGT. Cause and effect? no; but, as will be seen later, there was still a tangible connexion between the two.

How many other seeds, good and bad, were sown during that year of 1946? A large part of the year had been taken up with attempts at arriving at a *modus vivendi* with Ho Chi Minh in Indo-China; but before the year had ended, the French influences that had tried to sabotage all agreement, had triumphed (as will be shown later), and the war in Indo-China had begun. This war began, and failed to be stopped, during the short-lived Government of Léon Blum who, at least once before, had already been the Jonah of French politics. He was Premier when the Spanish civil war began; he was Premier again when the war started in Indo-China. In both cases he helplessly wrung his hands, and did nothing to stop it. And the war in Indo-China in December 1946 was easier to stop than the war in Spain in the summer of 1936.

How interested was the general public in France in what was happening in France and abroad? Here one is faced with some contradictory evidence. It is true, on the one hand, that there was an immense amount of political discussion in France during this transition period between the departure of de Gaulle and the end of *tripartisme* a little more than a year later. The *political* press—the *journaux d'opinion*, as distinct from the *journaux d'information*—still had a very large circulation in France. No doubt, this statement has to be qualified: the increase in this circulation was at least partly due to the fact that, compared with 1945, the paper shortage was less acute; so it is probable that in 1945 the interest in politics was at least as great as in 1946, and probably greater; but if one compares the circulation of the *journaux d'opinion* in 1946 with their circulation during the years that followed, it is obvious that interest in pure politics was greater then than later, especially after things had "settled down" in 1948-9. Also, 1946 was an exceptionally busy year in the publishing trade, which produced an unusually large number of political books—reminiscences, *post-mortems* on the war and the Resistance, reflections on the present and future of France, etc.

There was continuous interest in international affairs, in such manifestations of the Cold War as the Fulton speech and the Bikini bomb, and in other manifestations of increased or reduced international tension, such as the Canadian spy case in March or Stalin's famous "No War" statement to the present writer in September 1946. There was also much interest in the repercussions of the Cold War on French home affairs (notably the increasingly difficult position of the Communists in the Government). But it is much less certain that French opinion was genuinely interested in what was, in fact, the central political event of the year—the new Constitution. Alfred Fabre-Luce, in his venomous book on this period[2] says that, in 1946, instead of trying to cure France of her ills, the Government merely "kept on sticking a thermometer into all her orifices, to see how she was feeling". A referendum in May; an election for the Second Constituent Assembly in June; another referendum in October; a General Election for the National Assembly in November; an election (First Degree) for the Council of the Republic in November, and another election (Second Degree) a month later.

It is, at any rate, certain that the interest in the actual process of Constitution-making was lukewarm, to say the least; according to a public opinion poll during the early stages of the discussions on the Constitution, half the people took absolutely no interest in the Constitution, 30 per cent only a casual interest, and some 18 per cent more or less followed the discussions.[3] This impression is supported by an examination of the press of 1946, which devoted remarkably little space to the Constitution. In so far as that nebulous character, the "average citizen" existed, he was, in most cases, pleased to feel that France was again a Republic; but the question of what were to be the precise prerogatives of the more or less innocuous President of the Republic, or the question whether the Senate's powers were to be slightly, or greatly reduced, or whether there was to be a Senate at all, were not problems that could give him sleepless nights. The only factor that tended, after June 1946, to liven public interest in the Constitution a little was the spanner that de Gaulle threw in the works with his "Bayeux Constitution"; but even then the predominant reaction was still: "Let's have the Constitution such as it is, and try to think no more about it."

The first Draft Constitution was rejected partly because its acceptance implied a threat of *"Thorez au pouvoir"* (an implication for

[2] A Fabre-Luce, *Journal de L'Europe, 1946–47* (Paris, 1947).
[3] *Combat*, April 11, 1946.

which the Communists were as much to blame as anybody else); if the Second Draft Constitution (not very different from the first) was accepted by a small majority, it was largely because people were tired of the whole thing, and did not feel like prolonging the quarrel. Food shortages, food prices, black market scandals, and the successive governments' incapacity to cope with all this absorbed in 1946 far more attention than the Constitution.

CHAPTER TWO

BACK TO "ORDINARY" GOVERNMENT

THE relative indifference with which de Gaulle's resignation had been received in the country was, in itself, symptomatic of the desire to "return to normal". For the de Gaulle régime, between the Liberation and January 20, 1946, had not, strictly speaking, been a "normal" régime. De Gaulle was not only Head of the Government but also, in effect, Head of the State—though his powers had not been clearly defined in either capacity. As M. André Siegfried was to write:

The General's personality had, until January 20 dominated French politics. His immense prestige ... and the gratitude that the country felt for him ... constituted a disturbing factor in the traditional party game and in the very manner in which the Government functioned. The old political hands could no longer find their way about. The General represented the Nation in the highest sense.... But his personality upset the traditional workings of a machine which wished to be republican, in letter, as well as in spirit. The de Gaulle régime, by virtue of its own peculiar logic, was essentially *personalist*.[1]

With de Gaulle gone, there was nothing "personalist" about the Government any more. The general agreement among the parties to have so nondescript a politician as M. Gouin as head of the first post-de Gaulle Government seemed almost like an instinctive reaction against de Gaulle's "personalism". It marked, as M. Siegfried said, "a return to a sort of political and parliamentary normality, reminiscent of something very familiar in the past".

Having an "ordinary" government at the head of France, instead of a de Gaulle government, tended, in itself to reduce interest in what was going on at the Palais-Bourbon; the Constitution, as already said, did not arouse much excitement in the country, and few people could work up much interest in the methodical and dreary financial *exposés* of the new Finance Minister, M. André Philip. For although Philip was a *dirigiste* and had supported Mendès-France's financial proposals in 1945, the great chance for a major financial and monetary reform had been irretrievably lost, and M. Philip (like anybody else in his place) was struggling in vain against the mounting tide of inflation.

[1] *Année Politique*, 1946, p. IV.

And as long as there was a shortage of goods in the country and a plethora of bank-notes, neither M. Philip, nor the successive Ministers of Food—the conscientious and businesslike M. Longchambon and, after him, the irate Yves Farge—could do anything other than fight a losing battle against the black market. There were rackets all over the place: the racket of the motor-car licences that were sold "below the counter" at the Préfecture de Police; the sugar racket, as a result of which at least one-third of all the sugar produced in France found its way to the black market and had to be replaced, for the benefit of ration-card holders, by imported sugar; there were rackets in meat and petrol, in newsprint and various raw materials; unsuccessful newspapers, with inflated circulation figures, would sell in the black market most of their newsprint quota; one day there would be some "sensational arrests" among the *commanditaires* of La Villette meat market; another day the papers would announce the arrest of a director of this or that department store or chain store for some racket in raw materials; once or twice, the question even arose of having blackmarketeers shot after a brief trial; the poor consumer, with no hoard of bank-notes under his bed, was told one day to trust the Government's "draconic measures" and the next day to "fend for himself", to "buy direct from the peasants" or get whatever he could from friends in the countryside; if he hadn't any, it was just too bad. There was, over this question of rationing, a futile quarrel between *dirigistes* and *anti-dirigistes*, the former saying that rationing could not be abandoned, since the poorer classes could at least hope to get something with their ration-cards, whereas, if the ration-cards went, they couldn't afford to buy anything; the latter claiming, on the contrary, that the rations were too miserable to keep anybody alive; that they could not be increased because of the black market; but that the abolition of rationing would abolish the black market and "adjust" supply and demand, and, before long, bring prices down (which, with the existing shortages, was by no means certain). But the question of food subsidies still remained; if "freedom" were to be restored, but bread continued to be subsidized, would there not be a repetition of the disastrous Pineau experiment, when—with ration-cards temporarily abolished—cows and horses and pigs almost doubled the consumption of bread in France?[2]

[2] To justify his disastrous decision, Pineau explained at the Constituent Assembly in February that American wheat deliveries had not been up to schedule, that the Army had grabbed flour earmarked for civilian consumption, and, above all, that practically *everybody* had clamoured for the abolition of bread rationing; bakers, consumers, and the representatives of *all* the parties. Waldeck-Rochet (Communist) said that "one sometimes had to go against public opinion". (For all that, the Communist *Humanité* had, like other papers, joined in the popular clamour for the abolition of bread rationing.)

And this, in turn, raised the acute question of food imports from abroad, and the shortage of foreign currency; and there was political competition between "American wheat" and "Soviet wheat". All this absorbed much more of the public's attention than the Constitution. It helps to explain why France was, psychologically, extremely well prepared to accept Marshall Aid gratefully in 1947. Not that, if she had tried very hard, she could not have managed, in the long run, to feed herself without substantial food imports—under Marshall Aid, or otherwise. But the Marshall way was the easy way. However, that is another story.

It would, of course, be a mistake to imagine from the above that France had, since the Liberation, done little or nothing herself to improve conditions. On the contrary, she had done a great deal. By resorting, in certain cases, it is true, to unorthodox methods (e.g. the use of German war prisoners in coal-mining and agriculture) France had restored her industrial production to a quite remarkable degree between the Liberation and the end of 1946;[3] true, the general index of industrial production was, in September 1946, still only 87 per cent of the 1938 level; but coal, which had fallen from a monthly average of 3·9 million tons in 1938 to 1·1 million tons in September 1944, was up to 2·5 million tons in December 1945 and 4·2 million tons at the end of 1946. Electric power was 20 per cent above the pre-war level by the end of 1946, though iron and steel were still lagging behind. But the coal shortage was serious in spite of the tremendous effort made by the French coal industry, and the most common complaint by the successive governments of 1946 was: "The more coal we produce, the less coal do we get from Germany", or, as *Combat* put it more sharply: "*Que la France crève, pourvu que l'Allemagne vive.*" Coal, throughout the year, was to be a cause of constant friction between France and Britain and whoever else was responsible for the allocations of Ruhr coal. The alleged attempts to strangle France economically by constantly cutting her coal supplies were, needless to say, attributed to sinister political motives—and not only by the Communists.

Inflation continued throughout 1946, the note circulation rising during the year from 570 milliard francs to 722 milliards (it had been 142 milliards in August 1939 and 632 milliards at the Liberation), but, much worse, the price index of *controlled* retail prices in Paris rose from 481 (1938 = 100) in January 1946 to 865 in December 1946, thus nearly doubling in a year; black-market prices were much higher still, and wages were lagging far behind.

In short, immense difficulties were piling up, and the maldistribution

[3] All the figures that follow are from the *Statistique Générale*, the returns of the Bank of France, and the *Inventaire financier*, as quoted by *Année Politique*, 1944–45 and 1946.

of wealth, bad enough at the time of the Liberation, had become not less, but more serious two years later. It was not what the Resistance had hoped for. No doubt, certain basic reforms, such as the creation of an impressive new system of Social Security, were being carried out; and 1946 was marked by a significant "moral" reform—the abolition of licensed brothels. That it did not put an end to prostitution and tended, together with its promoter, Mme Marthe Richard, a somewhat eccentric Paris town councillor, to be treated in a ribald vein is another matter. In short, a certain number of things were being done; an improved Social Security system was being built up: generous family allowances and slightly better old-age pensions than before the war (for which the Communist Minister of Labour, M. Croizat, claimed the greater credit) were introduced; a number of basic industries, notably coal, gas, and electricity, Renault and a few other concerns had been nationalized, and there had also been the official (though, in practice, somewhat nominal) nationalization of the principal banks and insurance companies. But it was a long way to Revolution or even to *révolution par la loi*. Both public and private economic difficulties, and a widespread hankering for "back to normal" had damped the enthusiasm of August 1944. The Communists in the Government, who had "pushed" the reforms as hard as they could, and the Communists in industry who had made many sacrifices in not clamouring unduly for higher pay, were beginning to wonder, more and more, *what* kind of France they were helping to build, with the working-class underfed, and with the Cold War increasing the tension between the Communist Party which was looking East and most of the other French parties, which were either looking West or sitting on the fence.

CHAPTER THREE

TRIPARTISME

ALTHOUGH the de Gaulle Government was essentially a three-party government, it included a few members from parties to the Right of the MRP, and was officially known as a government of "national unanimity". *Tripartisme* as such did not officially come into being until after de Gaulle had gone.

The first Communist impulse after de Gaulle's resignation was to try to take the lead in the Government, and to form a Communist-Socialist coalition. This proposal was firmly rejected by the Socialists, who, aware of the growing economic difficulties, were determined that the MRP should share in the responsibilities of government, and not be in a position to benefit from all the criticism that the Government was sure to encounter. Nor were the Socialists anxious to set up an exclusive partnership with the Communists, least of all as junior partners. As a result of a long series of negotiations between the three parties, a "Tripartite Charter" was drawn up, composed mostly of proposals drawn from the two (largely similar) programmes made public in October–November by the *Délégation des Gauches* and the MRP. Food, though the most unmanageable of all problems, was put at the head of the programme as requiring the most urgent attention; among other items were nationalizations, a reform of the administration, the "development of production", and the breach of diplomatic relations with Franco Spain, in accordance with the wishes already expressed by the Constituent Assembly shortly before. On the awkward school problem the MRP had to give way, by accepting the phrase "maintenance of the school statute of 1939"—not that this necessarily committed them to long-term acquiescence. The Government Charter did not mean that proposals, in contradiction with this charter, could not be made by any of the three partners, for example in discussing the draft Constitution.

The *Charte du Tripartisme* was no more than a short-term *modus vivendi* between three parties which deeply disagreed on many issues. They could, however, agree on a minimum working programme—or, at least, so it was hoped. The three parties also agreed to "avoid oral and written controversies and offensive polemics" and to "endeavour to develop in the Government, at the Assembly, in the press and in the country a spirit of loyal solidarity in defending the decisions jointly taken by the members of the Government". It sounded all right—though it is hard to believe that anybody could take these mutual promises at their face value. Even so, this "charter" was intended, in some measure, to enforce a certain discipline on the three parties—in the absence of General de Gaulle. But with new elections in the offing, and with the world splitting sharply into two enemy camps, it required superhuman optimism to expect *tripartisme* to work smoothly for any length of time.

An interesting episode, before the actual formation of the Gouin Government, was the invitation made by all the three parties to the Radicals to join them, and particularly the very pressing offer made to M. Mendès-France to become Minister of Finance. The Radicals refused to take part in the Government, and Mendès-France, in the circumstances, declined the offer to clean up the mess left by his enemy Pleven, who had consistently ignored all the warnings he (Mendès-France) had given him. André Philip (Socialist), who became Minister of Finance in the Gouin Government, though in general agreement with Mendès-France, proved unable to stop inflation. The composition of the Gouin Government was not substantially different from that of the de Gaulle Government, except that M. Pleven had been dropped, and replaced, as Minister of National Economy and Finance, by M. André Philip; Bidault remained Foreign Minister; and the Communists were given four of the economic ministries and two economic under-secretaryships, among them the important department of Coal Production, which went to a Communist particularly familiar with the coal industry, Auguste Lecoeur.

Again the Communists had been refused any of the three "key ministries" but, as before, Thorez was one of the two vice-Premiers, and one of the jobs he was to do in the following weeks was to draft the somewhat controversial *statut des fonctionnaires*. The statute was to be severely criticized in the press as "totalitarian", *Combat* in particular claiming that the governmental body, the *Secrétariat de la Fonction Publique* provided in the Thorez Plan would tend to deprive the administration of its "indispensable continuity and stability" by "making it conform to the whims and vicissitudes of the party in power". However, after some revision, the Thorez Plan was, in the main, adopted.

Gouin, a typical small-town politician, was a jovial, back-slapping *méridional*, who had been active in local politics for many years, and who, after joining de Gaulle in London, later went to Algiers, where he became president of the Consultative Assembly, a post he retained in Paris. "A man of goodwill, rather than of will", was *Combat*'s comment on de Gaulle's immediate successor, and its first reactions to the new premier were not complimentary:

> While asking the French people to trust him, he assumes at the same time apologetic airs; he can foresee how unpopular he is going to be, and he doubts his own capacities. It isn't very inspiring to see a Premier apologizing for being only a stop-gap.... France's general boredom with politics seems to have spread to the ministers themselves—of whom one might expect rather more than just self-pity. One would prefer a little more self-assurance and a little less humility....[1]

M. Gouin was to make it clear before long that he was placing all his trust primarily in two things: German reparations and American aid; free coal and other raw materials from Germany, he said, were "absolutely essential", as well as "a rapid and satisfactory settlement of the problems of the Saar and the Ruhr". And, furthermore, American credits, which would help France to modernize her lamentably obsolete industrial equipment. "And all this", he concluded his speech at the Constituent Assembly on February 14, "will be explained to America by my eminent friend Léon Blum, whom the Government has raised to the rank of Ambassador-Extraordinary."

[1] *Combat*, February 2, 1946.

CHAPTER FOUR

THE COLLAPSE OF FRANCE'S GERMAN POLICY

MEANTIME Bidault was fighting a lone battle over Germany. At the Constituent Assembly in January he had followed the de Gaulle line by saying that Germany "must be deprived of both her war potential and of her invasion base". The Saar mines, he said, must become French property and the Saar must be integrated in the French economic system. As for the Ruhr,

it must become a territory independent of Germany, and subject to international control. All the countries concerned should take part in this control, and the local authorities, elected by the population, should, in due course, be given a share in the government. An international force, stationed in the Ruhr, should safeguard the integrity of the territory.

Under this plan, the Soviet Union was to take part in the control of the Ruhr. He also demanded that the Rhineland be separated from Germany. There was a good deal of unpleasantness between Bidault and Byrnes some time later over the creation of central German administrations, which the French considered "highly dangerous", and which they firmly opposed on the interallied Control Council in Berlin; and Bidault gave an interview to United Press on March 20 in which he reiterated "the French point of view":

We consider that the Ruhr must be internationalized and the Rhine kept under Allied control. This implies a complete political separation of the Ruhr and Rhineland from the rest of Germany—which, of course, does not mean economic separation. We have, of course, no objection to any exchange of commodities between the Ruhr and Rhineland and the rest of Germany.

Both Britain and the United States were wholly out of sympathy with this "Poincarist" policy, and some people in France began to suspect that this disagreement had something to do with the extreme "stinginess" shown to France by those in charge of allocating the Ruhr coal. On March 24 General Koenig complained to the Control Commission in Berlin, pointing out that of the four million tons a month produced by Germany, France had got only 250,000 tons in

March, and that it looked as if everything was being done "to favour a revival of German industry at the expense of French industry". But, in the words of a French commentator, the British and Americans, "sheltering behind the Potsdam agreements, said it was necessary for Germany to keep enough coal to start up some of her industries".

Partly under the influence of the British Labour Party, M. Gouin decided, in his speech at Strasbourg on March 24 to take a less rigid line. He talked in terms of "minimum demands, on which there was unanimous agreement in France", and spoke of "the creation of an international consortium which would control the coal and steel production of the Ruhr"—which (he significantly added) "did not necessarily imply the political detachment of the Ruhr from the rest of Germany", and advocated a lengthy Allied occupation of Germany "which would give time to examine the situation, before the adoption of a final statute for the Rhine provinces". Having in effect disavowed his Foreign Minister, M. Gouin then asked (more plaintively than angrily) for "more coal for France". Gouin was clearly playing the British card: a few days later, at the Socialist Congress, he proposed a Franco-British Pact on the same lines as the Franco-Soviet Pact; this, he said (no doubt for the benefit of the French Communists) would "create a sort of *tripartisme* in the international field"—a pretty phrase which meant, however, little or nothing. And again he disavowed Bidault, this time even more openly, when he said that "annexation, whether open or disguised, is no solution".

Official reactions in England were favourable to Gouin's proposals for an Anglo-French Pact and—even more so—to his apparent departure from the line followed by M. Bidault, for whom Ernest Bevin had, by this time, developed a hearty dislike. "The dear little man", he would say, with no suggestion that the phrase implied any love.

But Bidault refused to consider himself beaten. A communiqué published after the Cabinet meeting on April 5 reaffirmed "the continuity of France's policy with regard to the Ruhr, the Rhineland, and the Saar", and two days later, in a speech at Lille, Bidault reiterated his views, notably on the Ruhr and the Saar. The Communist line was expressed on the same day by Duclos who supported Bidault against Gouin and suggested that while he had no objections to an Anglo-French Pact, he was against having it "at the price of French security, of which the internationalization of the Ruhr was an essential condition". It is interesting to observe that, in taking this line, Duclos was following a French national line, which was wholly different from the line taken by the German Communists and in no way co-ordinated with Moscow, which continued, at that stage, to be non-committal about the Ruhr.

All these discussions about the "separation" of the Ruhr and the

Rhineland are today little more than historic curios, but they need to be recalled if one is to understand the curious evolution that French policy *vis-à-vis* Germany has undergone in the last ten years. What virtually killed all Bidault's plans was something that happened very soon after his Lille speech: namely, the first clear signs that Germany was about to be divided in two, with the line of separation running between the Soviet Zone and the rest of the country. The division was accentuated by the virtual Russian embargo on food exports from Eastern Germany to Western Germany, and by General Clay's embargo on industrial exports (including reparations) from the West to the East. Opinions differ to this day on "who started it". But, oddly enough, official opinion in Britain and America seemed to favour this development, *The Times* on May 18, 1946 already treating the "regrouping" of the three Western zones, independently of the Soviet Zone, as an interesting possibility. M. Bidault thought this a very alarming development; he was still unwilling to consider the separation of Europe and the world into two hostile blocs, and declared on May 28 that "the division of Germany, as suggested by the Anglo-American press" could not be considered a solution. It could only be considered as a sign of the final breakdown of all attempts between the Allies to settle the German problem. As the Foreign Minister of a *tripartite* government, it was particularly difficult for him to endorse this East-West split. But the truth is that *the Cold War was developing more rapidly than the French internal situation*, in which *tripartisme* still symbolized, in a sense, the joint victory of West and East.

For a time, Bidault earnestly tried to act as a brake on the Cold War. But he was fighting a losing battle. Moreover, he was to receive no encouragement from the Russians. At the Four-Power Conference in July, Molotov not only failed to endorse Byrnes's plan for a twenty-five years' (or, in its revised version, a forty years') demilitarization of Germany (was it because of the "unsuitable" control clauses of this plan, or was it because Byrnes refused to commit himself to recognizing as final the Polish-German border? there has never been full agreement on *why* exactly Molotov did not welcome this seemingly admirable plan), but he also declared himself "centralist" and "anti-federalist", and was also opposed to any political separation of the Ruhr, so dear to Bidault. Nor did he support France's claims on the Saar. In short, there was practically no point (except possibly reparations and the Polish border) on which France and Russia saw more or less eye-to-eye; this made it increasingly difficult for Bidault to manœuvre between the Russians and the Anglo-Americans, and before long France had no choice left but to endorse, more or less gracefully, the successive "solutions" to the German problem elaborated in London and Washington. All the more so as it was on the "Western" side that her bread was buttered, however thinly. Also, she had to consider her position as an Occupying Power in Germany, and it was obviously difficult for her to act independently of Britain and America for long.

But the final French "surrender" to the West was still to be delayed for some time. The Russians, perhaps with an eye on the French internal situation, tried, in July, to cheer the French by saying that under the Four-Power control of the Ruhr (without political separation), as proposed by the Russians, France would have far greater influence there than if the Ruhr were separated and came under British or American domination. Also, they said, four-power control would constitute a far better guarantee than anything else against the revival of German militarism or the rebirth of the Ruhr as Germany's arsenal. This was no longer realistic; for in reality the division of Germany into East and West was becoming more apparent every day.

At the end of July the British Government welcomed the American proposal for the economic unification of the British and American zones. A few days later, General Clay swore to the Control Council in Berlin that it was merely a matter of economic convenience, and that there was "absolutely nothing political" about it; but these assurances deceived nobody. For a time France was, nevertheless, still unwilling to take sides too openly, and at that stage refused to have the French Zone incorporated in the "Bizone".

The last French hopes of securing a special statute for the Ruhr or Rhineland were shattered by Mr Byrnes's Stuttgart speech, on September 5. This time Uncle Sam had kissed Germania on both cheeks with a loud smack. Mr Byrnes wanted to see Germany become a federal state, but with a democratic and national central government, and economically united. Allied occupation and general control would, of course, continue, but this general control would be sufficient, and there would be no need for any special control in the Ruhr or Rhineland, which would only "place them under the political domination of foreign powers". In short, the United States was not even in favour of any "economic internationalization" of the Ruhr; France, in Byrnes's view, could have economic control of the Saar, but if she did, she would have to revise her reparations claims. The USA, on the other hand, could not consider Germany's Eastern border as final; and in conclusion Byrnes proclaimed that the American people wished to hand over the government of Germany to Germans.

The Byrnes speech was the straw that broke the back of the de Gaulle-Bidault policy of the two previous years, and delivered, as it was, in the presence of numerous German "personalities" in the American Zone, it was like the official inauguration of a pro-German American policy. This was, before long, to express itself in a variety of other ways. Before the end of the year, Mr Caffery, the US Ambassador, presented to the French Government a Note asking in a rather peremptory manner that the 600,000 German war prisoners "who had been lent to France by the American Army" be all repatriated within ten months. The French looked upon the labour of these prisoners as "reparations", and, on the strength of it, France's reparations claims had, indeed, been previously reduced. The rapid replacement of this labour, notably in the mines, created a major economic problem.

Mr Bevin, for his part, "almost entirely" agreed with Byrnes's Stuttgart speech, and when, a month later, Mr Byrnes came to Paris, he had nothing to add to cheer up the French, except that, in the Ruhr, the "general control" should be more severe than elsewhere. And again he spoke of his plan for demilitarizing Germany for forty years.

With the United States advocating a united Germany with a central government, with the Russians proposing more or less the same thing; with *both* America and Russia willing to allow Germany to increase her steel production; with *both* talking of demilitarization; with no major disagreement between the two, on the face of it, except on reparations and the Polish border, with *both* equally opposed to French territorial claims, and yet with both sides fundamentally disagreeing on the German problem *as a whole*, this disagreement expressing itself most clearly in the virtual partition of Germany, it is scarcely surprising that France should have been utterly confused by the way the German problem had degenerated in a short time. Supporters of the de Gaulle-Bidault policy felt that they had been treated abominably by *all* the Allies; the Communists, puzzled by the contortions of Soviet policy, scarcely knew what to say, and only part of the Socialists, under Blum's influence, followed something that looked like a coherent policy. It was, in the last analysis, a case of taking the line of least resistance, or rather of non-resistance to the British and American trends, as expressed in Byrnes's Stuttgart speech.

Slowly, but surely, the French Socialists tended more and more to take the view that the real allies of Social Democracy in France (if not in Germany) were the British Labour Government and the Truman Administration. Already in July Blum wrote in the *Populaire* that French foreign policy should concentrate on demanding the "international nationalization" of the Ruhr industries and on securing preferential treatment in the allocation of Ruhr coal, instead of wasting time on asking for the separation from Germany of the Ruhr and Rhineland, to which none of France's Allies was willing to agree. Blinded by the illusion that the Truman Administration was "Leftist" at heart (an illusion widely shared in England) Blum refused for a long time to see that it was not in the least favourable to any sort of "nationalization" in the Ruhr, "international" or otherwise, and that, in this matter, the Labour Government had been driven into submis-

sion by Washington. But neither in the matter of the Ruhr nationalizations, nor in the matter of coal allocations were the French Socialists
going to receive any satisfaction; month after month the haggling over
coal went on; Bevin, in his speech in the Commons on October 22,
stressed the importance of German industry to the whole of the
European economy, and in November the British informed the French
Government that German coal exports would have to be reduced, and,
with them, the tonnage earmarked for France. Coming at the beginning of a hard winter, this communication was very badly received in
France, and aroused some bitter criticism of Britain, despite the terrible
difficulties the latter was experiencing during that winter of 1946–7—
difficulties arising, at least partly, from the burden of trying to keep
the British Zone alive.

It was these difficulties that were to precipitate the final economic
fusion of the British and American zones under the Byrnes-Bevin
agreement of December 2. It was a three-year agreement, under which
Britain and America were to finance Germany, each to the tune of 500
million dollars a year, after which the Bizone was expected to become
self-supporting. This clearly suggested that France need not expect any
generous coal shipments from Germany; it further suggested that
Britain and America were not expecting an agreement on Germany
with the Soviet Union—at least not for three years. The agreement also
meant, in effect, that Germany was now divided into three zones—a
large Soviet zone, a large Bizone and a small French zone which,
though precariously self-supporting, was becoming more and more an
economic and political anomaly.

For a time, however, France still resisted, unwilling to bow to the
fait accompli of the "two Germanies". This French aloofness was not
encouraged by London and Washington; even so, it took nearly another
year before France joined the Bizone, with the economic incorporation
of the Saar in France to compensate her, in effect, for her virtual exclusion from the Ruhr. But this "happy ending" already belongs to a
different epoch of French history; by the autumn of 1947 the Cold War
was in full swing; Marshall Aid was on the way, the Communists
were no longer in the French Government, the division of Germany
seemed final, and nobody in France (except the Communists, who
talked of "unilateral action") cared any more what Mr Molotov
thought about the Saar.

As for M. Bidault, he had, at the Moscow Conference in April 1947,
become finally disgusted with Molotov, notably for not supporting
France on this very question of the Saar; this Conference had wiped
out the last vestiges of the French "between East and West" policy.

CHAPTER FIVE

BLUM, MARXISM, AND WASHINGTON

THAT is the way things were going, but in 1946 France still clung to the illusion that she could "mediate" between West and East, and this illusion was encouraged by the continued existence of a tripartite government. But the westward drift was, nevertheless, becoming more apparent every day. Apart from the extraordinarily rapid *pourissement* of the German situation, the most significant development in French foreign policy was Blum's mission to Washington, and it was important not only externally, but also internally. These two aspects of French history have since the war been seldom, if ever, separable.

The France of 1946 was, in many ways, a crazy place; and it was one of the crazy phenomena of the time to see M. Gouin's tripartite government send to Washington the very man who was the worst enemy of one-third of the very Government that he was representing as its Ambassador-Extraordinary. For there was no man who hated the Communists more than Léon Blum. He had hated them ever since the Tours Congress of 1920, when the Communist majority broke away from the Socialist Party. He considered that the Russian Revolution had been a terrible setback to the cause of Socialism—as he understood it. The social revolution, in his view, could be best prepared by a policy of gradual social improvement, which would prepare the conditions for an easy transition to the New Order. The Bolsheviks, he wrote in his well-known *brochure, Bolchevisme et Socialisme* (the 8th edition of which was published without changes in 1936, at the height of the Popular Front) had confused the end and the means, by considering the seizure of power as an end in itself.

The *conquest of power* for revolutionary ends, which is the condition and prologue to the social Revolution has nothing in common ... with the *exercise of power* within the framework of a Socialist régime. . . .

And he claimed that, the Bolsheviks in Russia, having mistaken the means for the end, had *failed*, though exercising power, *to bring about a social Revolution in Russia.* A bold assertion—yet one without which a large part of his argumentation fell to the ground. And what annoyed

311

Blum most was that, in France, Socialists should for years have suffered from a sort of inferiority complex *vis-à-vis* the Communists.

Communist propaganda has never ceased to accuse us of having deserted the revolutionary cause, and of having become vague democrats, and bourgeois pseudo-reformists.... On the other hand, the power of attraction that Communism exercised on people at the beginning and is doing to some extent even now, and the intellectual and sentimental contagion it has spread are due to its arrogant claim to have monopolized the revolutionary will.... Especially in France, the word Communism exercises a kind of magic attraction on people.... I particularly have in mind the popular masses who have, for a century, worshipped at the shrine of the Revolution.... The Communists have tried to capture this enthusiasm for their own benefit, and to exploit it against us....

Blum also argued that the Communists were against improvements in the life of the working-class, because a hungry and discontented proletariat served their purpose better; that the Communists *despised* the people, and merely strove to extract from it "a professional Insurrection Army".[1]

And, characteristically, he added:

These disagreements between Bolshevism and us have not only made it extremely difficult for us to agree on any common action, but they have produced between the two parties a sort of emotional and moral incompatibility.[2]

There was hardly any departure from this line in *A l'échelle humaine*, the short book—a sort of political testament—which he wrote in 1941 while interned by Vichy (though probably slightly revised later), and which was to become influential among the Socialist rank and file after the war. No doubt, he paid a few compliments to the Russians, and admitted a serious mistake: the war had shown that "Bolshevism had not degraded the Russian people";[3] nevertheless—and here he took a very simple view of what had happened—Stalin had become "Hitler's ally" and had "betrayed peace". No doubt, he added, the Communists were "in the front rank of the French Resistance", but, after victory, the French Communists "could still not be assimilated into the French national community", unless they changed their whole way of thinking.

Either there must be a radical change in the very nature of the link that connects them with Soviet Russia, or else there must be entirely different relations between Soviet Russia and the European community. French Communism must detach itself from Soviet Russia, or Russia must commit itself to being European, or, better still, both.[4]

The rest of Blum's book is concerned chiefly with a demonstration

[1] L. Blum, *op. cit.*, p. 15. [2] *Ibid.*, p. 23.
[3] *Op. cit.*, p. 108. [4] *Op. cit.*, p. 109.

of why France "did not, in her distress, call to Social Democracy" in
1940, even though Social Democracy was "the only vital force"; and
with his familiar argument in favour of the "Marx-Jaurès synthesis"
—no socialism without democracy and *vice versa*.

Here we are chiefly concerned with his attitude to the Communists
in 1946 and, consequently, to the tripartite government that was sending him, hat in hand, to the USA. For, in Blum's view, the two conditions laid down in *A l'échelle humaine* had obviously not been fulfilled
by the time he took the plane to Washington; and, despite his protestations to the contrary, the American press stressed that Blum's talks
in Washington were not only economic but also political—which
obviously meant that the presence of the Communists in the French
Government was going to be discussed.

By the time Blum was ready to leave for Washington (the journey
had been delayed for various reasons) the situation in France was difficult and confused. Jean Monnet, the head of the Plan, reported on
March 16 that France would be able to increase her output by 1950 by
25 per cent above the 1929 level, provided she began to receive much
more coal from Germany or elsewhere at once (she was then getting
only 500,000 tons a month from the USA and 300,000 tons from
Germany—which was less than half of what she needed); provided she
imported in the next few years about 1½ million workers from abroad;
provided also she received foreign credits to the tune of "several millard
dollars" during the 1946–50 period.[5]

The economic muddle was greater than ever. As *Combat* wrote in
an angry editorial on March 26, there was no sign of the army estimates, over which there had been such a hullaballoo, being any
smaller than under de Gaulle; if anything, they were larger; André
Philip, the Minister of Finance and National Economy, was all at
sixes and sevens; now he was asking for subsidies, after having denounced them as financially ruinous, and he was increasing prices
after having used every argument for freezing them; and Gouin, after
a "hugoesque introduction" to his Strasbourg speech ("French
spirituality, the millennial civilization of France, the lofty flight of the
Marseillaise", etc) had then merely plaintively talked about the
iniquities of the German coal allocations. It was thought at first that
Philip would precede Blum in Washington, to prepare the ground; but
soon it was learned that the Americans preferred to talk to Blum direct,
and to Monnet, who was to explain his plan to them. The French news
agency was meantime suggesting that Blum "would agree to concessions on the German question and on France's home policy".[6] The
New York Times said the talks with Blum would be not only
economic, but also political; while Bidault was saying that "they

[5] *Année Politique*, 1946, p. 59.   [6] *Combat*, March 22, 1946.

wouldn't be political at all", and it was suggested that Blum had been instructed on no account to yield on the question of Germany. The Communists, for their part, were making a great song and dance, on the day Blum left for Washington, over the shipments of Soviet wheat now on their way to France; a good election stunt, as Russia obviously intended it to be.

What happened in Washington? In a book of "indiscretions", published in 1954, M. Jean Davidson, who was the Washington correspondent of the AFP (the French news agency) at the time, said that the American papers were openly saying, in connexion with a long private meeting Blum had had that day with Fred Vinson, Secretary of the Treasury, that the latter had "formally asked Blum that the Socialists join an anti-Communist coalition, and so oust the Communists now occupying important posts in the French Cabinet". The AFP phoned the French Desk at the State Department which naturally denied the story, saying that the United States "was trying not to interfere in French internal affairs". For all that, Jean Davidson, who took the State Department's denial with a pinch of salt, described the Blum visit to Washington as the "turning-point in French post-war policy".

The Blum visit to Washington was not without its comic side. Davidson described as follows one of his "awful child" conversations with Blum at the French Embassy:

Looking at this ghost of European Socialism ... I could not restrain myself:

"Are you still a convinced Marxist, *Monsieur le Président?*"

Léon Blum could not conceal his surprise. Suddenly leaning back, and then doubling up, as though he had been kicked in the stomach, and taking my arm, he said:

"Now, *mon ami*, this is strictly between ourselves—our American friends might take this very badly, for they are still a bit muddled about Socialism, Marxism, and Communism, of which they are afraid. ..."

In a nervous and persuasive voice, he continued:

"But of course, *mon ami*, of course I remain a convinced Marxist. Besides, paragraph 2 of the latest Declaration of Principles of the French Socialist Party, says ..." and he rattled off from memory the paragraph in question. ...

Davidson then asked how he could reconcile this Marxist position with the negotiations with the United States, fundamentally hostile to Marxism.

Blum, no longer surprised at my questions, then embarked on a long monologue:

"But, *mon ami*, you surely must know that there are two ways of under-

standing Marxism. Russian Communism is trying to capture and monopolize it with a view to setting up a tyrannical dictatorship. I am convinced
that, thanks to our agreement with the United States, we shall be able to
avoid a Russian invasion, which would be a real catastrophe for Western
Europe, and, secondly, prepare, slowly but surely, a revolution towards real
Marxism. We can use the Americans for that purpose. Numerous American
diplomats with whom I have spoken are sure that Socialism can become
the best rampart against Communism in Europe. Only it is all a matter of
very delicate handling...."

"You realize, of course, *Monsieur le Président*," I said, "that the Americans who talk of Socialism as a rampart against Communism in Europe,
hope in reality that Socialists like you will, above all, form a rampart against
Marxism as such—don't you think so?"[7]

At this point Blum, looking very tired, had a coughing fit, and
politely asked Davidson to come back and continue the talk some other
day. Mme Blum, who at this point, came into the room, gave Davidson a dirty look.

While this satirical account of the Blum visit to Washington may
have been somewhat "touched up", it undoubtedly renders correctly
its "undertones". The American press continued to suggest that the
US Government was making it pretty clear to Blum how it would
like the internal situation in France to develop. Also, while *tripartisme*
continued, the financial aid given to France, under the Blum-Byrnes
agreement, was much less than what French opinion, infected by the
wishful thinking in a part of the French press (which had talked in
terms of "milliards of dollars") had hoped for. The Export-Import
Bank had granted France a loan of 550 million dollars in December
1945; now it was granting her another loan of 650 million dollars, but
on less favourable terms than the first loan. Also, it was noted in
France that the USA had been "incomparably more generous" to
Britain, a point on which M. Bidault commented, a little wistfully, in
the ratification debate on July 31. He also remarked that the Washington agreements implied that France had chosen international trade,
and had finally rejected "autarky". Although there was some very
severe criticism of the Blum-Byrnes agreement on the entry of American films to France—an agreement which, many thought, was "going
to kill the French film industry"—the Washington agreements, including the lend-lease and war debts settlement, were unanimously
ratified.

In the interval, on his return from Washington on June 1, Blum had
given a press conference. With an emphasis that many thought excessive, Blum said that "there must be no misunderstanding. On the
American side no military, diplomatic, or political conditions were laid

[7] Jean Davidson, *Correspondant à Washington: ce que je n'ai jamais câblé* (Paris,
1954), pp. 15–16.

down—none whatsoever, either explicitly or implicitly, either directly or indirectly." As already said, many thought he was "protesting too much".

What we did, however, agree on [Blum said] was that the negotiations should be based on the acceptance of the principle that the development of international trade is desirable. . . . The USSR can join in this. The USA is all in favour of it.

He then paid a tribute to "the remarkable disinterestedness" shown by the USA which, he said, was also favourably impressed by the Monnet Plan.

No doubt, said Blum, one might have hoped that, in accordance with the late President Roosevelt's attitude, the USA might make a clean slate of war debts. "But as time passes, things are apt to change; even so, 1·8 milliards of the French war debt has been cancelled. . . ."

Strictly speaking, no conditions, "implicit or explicit, direct or indirect" *had* been laid down; but the fact remained that neither the extent, nor the terms of the help from America were very generous—and the "implicit" meaning of this was pretty clear to everybody in France; it did not, indeed, take many months before France was again in serious financial straits.

CHAPTER SIX

ELECTION BATTLES—YVES FARGE—CANNES AND NICE—DE GAULLE AND BLUM RE-EMERGE

IT IS outside the scope of this book to examine in detail either the Constitution, or the arguments and disputes among the parties that accompanied its drafting in the First Constituent Assembly and its redrafting in the Second, after the first draft had been rejected by the referendum of May 5. Anyone interested in these details will find them in two important English books on the subject: Mrs Dorothy Pickles's *French Politics* and Mr Philip Williams's *Politics in Post-War France*. The general public in France was not keenly interested. As *Combat* was to write soon after the referendum rejecting the first Draft Constitution:

> When one hears complaints that people haven't even read the Constitution, we must say that neither the Assembly, nor the parties have done much to make people interested in it. It doesn't contain a single fresh idea or a single original new institution.[1]

M. André Siegfried, much further to the Right than *Combat*, also thought that there was nothing in the 1946 Constitution (whether first version or second version) to get excited about.

> The 1946 Constitution has much in common with the 1875 Constitution ... and it may even be argued that the Fourth Republic is simply a continuation of the Third Republic.

The real difference between the Third and the Fourth Republic, in his view, was not to be sought in their respective Constitutions, but in the very different rôle played in the two Republics by the parties.

> What is important is that both the choice of Premier and President and the elaboration of the Constitution was carried out by the parties. Therein lies the great innovation of our post-war period.... For if, before the war, the parties were, for the greater part, weak and "inorganic", with little influence on their members, they became highly rigid and disciplined after the war, and were endowed with powers which, once the election was over, were being exercised without direct responsibility *vis-à-vis* the electorate.

[1] *Combat*, May 17, 1946.

This change had chiefly been brought about by the new election system, so different from the pre-war *scrutin d'arrondissement*, which made a deputy look first and foremost to his constituents, or at any rate to his local committees, and not (as he was to do after the war) towards the bureaucrats of his party.[2]

Although the draft constitution, after endless negotiations between the parties was approved at the First Constituent Assembly by a comfortable majority, there was a good deal of uncertainty about the electorate's reactions in the May referendum. The Communists were the staunchest supporters of the Constitution; the Socialists also supported the "Yes" vote, but had refused to conduct their referendum campaign jointly with the Communists. The main arguments used by the supporters of the "No" vote were that excessive powers were being given to the Assembly under the Draft Constitution; that its approval would mean an endorsement of the Communist line, and might well lead to a realization of the *"Thorez au pouvoir"* cry; also it was pointed out to the peasantry in particular that the Constitution did not specifically safeguard property.

In short, the Constitution was rejected by a fairly narrow majority: by 10·6 million to 9·5 million votes, some 5 million abstaining.

Less than a month later, there was the election to the Second Constituent Assembly, the most notable incident in the election campaign being a violent attack by M. Le Trocquer, the Socialist Minister of the Interior, on M. Thorez whom he treated as a "deserter". The Communists violently protested, while the MRP and the right-wing parties made great political capital out of this ugly row between the two "Marxist" parties. The fact that the Communists lost no votes and even gained some, while the Socialists lost heavily suggested that a part of the electorate, still anxious for *tripartisme* to be maintained, resented the Socialists' blatant breach of the Triparte Charter. But, on the other hand, some of the Socialist votes must have gone to the MRP, for whom this election was a major success, making them the largest party in France.

The MRP vote rose from 4·6 millions in October to 5·6 millions;
The Communist vote rose from 5·0 millions to 5·2 millions;
The Socialist vote dropped from 4·6 millions to 4·2 millions.

There were no major changes in the Radical and Right vote.

After much haggling, the new Government was formed by M. Bidault; this, too, was a tripartite government, and not very different from the Gouin Government, except that the Communists, who were again refused "one of three key ministries" got this time six ministerial posts and three under-secretaryships; moreover, the Ministry of

[2] André Siegfried in *Année Politique*, 1946, pp. IV–V.

Food went to a near-Communist, M. Yves Farge who did not actually win his terrific campaign against the black market, but was to cause for a few glorious days a panic among the "sharks" (especially when he threatened to resign if he were refused the weapon of the death penalty), and who did not hesitate to show up numerous gigantic rackets, including the wine racket, in which members of M. Gouin's staff were found to be directly involved. Although he made no specific charges against Gouin personally, he said enough to make Gouin's position extremely shaky, and completely ruined his excellent chance of being elected President of the Republic. Some months later, when already out of office, Farge wrote a book on the wine scandal, called *Le pain de la corruption*, which led to a somewhat inconclusive, but by no means damaging, libel action against its author. Gouin was never to recover fully from the *affaire du vin*.

Farge had the temperament of a crusader, and was genuinely outraged by the black market which he defined as "a crime which consists, not in stealing 500,000 francs from a rich man, but 100 francs from 5,000 poor people". His book also constitutes a savage indictment of the whole French system of distribution—notably of food—a monstrous system which, he said, nobody had taken the trouble to show up since Zola's admirable *Ventre de Paris*.

Farge got the Constituent Assembly to appoint a Committee of Inquiry, and certainly succeeded in blowing many lids off; but he was in office for only five months, and was not asked to continue: he had obviously trodden on too many toes. Whether he would ever have succeeded, had he been allowed to continue his crusade, is hard to say; perhaps not; even so, the Yves Farge experiment was a stimulating spectacle while it lasted.

It may be useful, at this point, to examine a little more closely not so much the financial, as the sociological significance of the black market, and its lasting effects; for it is true to say that it redistributed the national wealth of France to an appreciable extent, and that, in doing so, it also created a new bourgeoisie, while ruining part of the old one. The detailed inquiry on the subject by Paul Bodin, published in *Combat* in January 1947, produced some remarkable facts. He started with the perhaps somewhat sweeping assertion: "In France today the spivs (*les trafiquants*) alone have got money."

During the last two years one liked to think that living conditions would become easier. One liked to think that economic justice would score some gains; that illicit wartime profits would be confiscated and the black market abolished. What has happened is something quite different.

Whereas to many of us the increase in the price of *métro* tickets is a minor tragedy, others spend a thousand francs on a couple of drinks without turning a hair; and in a few hours in a *boîte de nuit* a few people cheer-fully spend the equivalent of a worker's three or four months' wages. It has all happened before, but never quite so blatantly.

The working part of the population was never worse off.

The big shots in the black market call themselves "wine merchants" or "textile merchants", or owners of "entertainments establishments", or owners of "racing stables", etc. The smaller fry call themselves *courtiers*, *représentants*, *mandataires*, cinema proprietors, journalists, etc. It is these people who patronize night clubs.

As distinct from pre-war, only one-sixth of the customers of night clubs are foreigners today; the rest are the spivs.

Bodin then talked of the contempt with which these "*seigneurs du marché noir*"—these spivs and "pork butchers" were treated by self-respecting hotel proprietors on the Riviera.

But some of these people were determined to remain rich, and, as had happened in French history before, internal commotions had again given birth to a new bourgeoisie. Like its predecessors, it would soon adapt itself, and become before long a *respectable* bourgeoisie—perhaps even in less than a generation. (Already one could notice, in the years immediately after the war, the influx of sons of this new bourgeoisie—such as the meat profiteers of Normandy—into schools like the Sciences Politiques, etc.)

But who had got rich and who had been ruined?

Bodin produced some very interesting estimates. Thus, the old bourgeoisie had sold to the new bourgeoisie about 30 per cent of its estates and of its house property; several hundred milliard francs had changed hands in this way. Not a profitable investment, in view of the low yield of *métayage*, but a short cut to respectability. On the other hand, the old commercial and industrial bourgeoisie, trying to keep up its standard of living, had found itself in great difficulties; it had abandoned stable-income investments and had embarked on specu-lation and many had gone bankrupt in the process.

As against this, the Aristocracy of Banking and Heavy Industry had kept its end up very successfully, and owned, directly or indirectly, half the urban house property of France, and one-half of her solid financial assets, including gold and foreign exchange. Thanks to the indemnities paid, the shareholders of the coal mines, gas, and electricity had done better than they had feared. The economic "purge" resulted in a few milliards falling into the coffers of the Treasury, but showed that only the surface of "economic collaboration" had been scratched.

The place next to the Banking and Industrial Aristocracy, was held, according to Bodin, by the Peasantry; neither of these two groups spent money in night clubs. A large part of the 600 milliards of French notes were owned by the peasantry. The third place in Bodin's "inventory of

French fortunes" was held by the medium and small shopkeepers and industrialists. Few of these spent money at night clubs: "Serious business-people these days buy in order to re-sell; they hoard commodities, buy real estate or gold, or expensive paintings; and most of these transactions remain unknown to the tax authorities."

Since the Liberation, he went on, 300,000 new businesses (a large proportion of them food shops) had been established, and most of the "black fortunes" made during the war, and especially between 1944 and 1947, had been made out of transactions in foodstuffs, textiles, electrical equipment, newsprint, etc. The most profitable businesses were those which, alongside the official business, were also able to conduct a "parallel" business, on black-market lines.

Who, then, were these new businessmen, shop-keepers, and small new industrialists?

A large number of them are workers, labourers and technicians who, during the Occupation had stopped working, and had embarked on clandestine trade. Thus they have been lost to productive work. Many of them used to supply businesses that worked directly for the Germans. The three most lucrative branches were the building trade, the trade in spirits, and the manufacture of war material. A recent trial showed that a certain Sigoyer had made 300 millions selling cognac to the Germans; but thousands of others started "nice little businesses" during the war: e.g. a former workman who invented an anti-freeze device which the Wehrmacht adopted for its motor transport during its campaign in Russia. He is now a respected industrialist worth many millions.

The black market became not less, but more active after the Liberation.

According to the authorities, *everybody* today having anything to do with food or ration cards, or their control, at whatever stage of production or distribution, is certain to gain "illicit profits".

After quoting a large variety of black-market and black-Bourse tricks, Bodin concluded that, out *of a working population of nineteen million people in 1946–7, four million people were more or less living on unproductive rackets*; not only the economic effect, but also the moral effect of this was very bad: it bred contempt for honest work, and created hatred among those who had a hard life for those who had an easy life.

He quoted in conclusion this significant dialogue between a police official and a "spiv" whom he had caught. "You're an optician; you've got a perfectly honourable trade; why don't you stick to it?"

"*Vous en avez des bonnes, monsieur le commissaire!*" the optician exclaimed. "One cannot work honestly these days. We are living in the jungle."

The five months' existence of the Second Constituent Assembly and of the Bidault Government coincided with the Peace Conference with

Germany's Satellites which was held in Paris, and which took up much of M. Bidault's time. Despite the continued ravages of the black market, food conditions had somewhat improved; which gave a feeling of a relative "return to normal", and no doubt the very fact that Paris had been chosen as the place for this Peace Conference also gave people the pleasant illusion that Paris had again become a great world centre. M. Bidault himself obviously enjoyed his rôle as "host" at the Conference and at the final reception at Versailles where, the papers reported, he had "shaken hands with 2,000 people". In July, there was an all-round increase in wages, which provided some temporary relief, and, for a short time, things seemed to be looking up.

Combat published in August an entertaining *reportage* on French seaside resorts in the summer of 1946. Biarritz was "black with people"—but these were mostly peasants from the neighbourhood, and the *palaces* were all empty. Same in Nice, with "hardly a single smart person in the Promenade des Anglais", but with the town swarming with people of "modest means", students, schoolboys, and *congés payés*. But "at the Negresco, only 40 rooms are occupied out of 400; there is a staff of 125 for 70 customers; daily deficit, 50,000 francs; 1 Maharajah the only standby". The Government had shown itself unwilling to issue many tourist visas—"they might get the wrong impression".

In the small Breton ports and seaside resorts, every room was booked. But the real "return to pre-war" was to be found at Cannes. Here milliardaires and *congés payés* rubbed shoulders. Bikinis had just come into vogue; the rue d'Antibes was known as the rue Bikini. Bourbons, Rothschilds, Duke and Duchess of Windsor—and, round the corner, students paying 200 francs a day for their *pension*. "A perpetual fête; endless series of galas and beauty competitions; you've got to come here for a week to believe in the return of any easy, abundant life. Nowhere is there such an obvious return to the pre-war spirit as at Cannes."

But all this pleasantness was neither general, nor did it last very long; for another hard winter was in the offing. The constitutional problem and, indeed, the whole political future of France had become complicated by de Gaulle's re-emergence into public life. He had, in May, disdainfully rejected M. Gouin's invitation to take part in a VE Day ceremony, making it clear that he did not wish to be mixed up with the politicians.

Although he had kept silent during the May referendum and the June election, he came out, on June 18, with his famous "Bayeux Constitution", which advocated a strict "separation of powers", a bicameral parliament and what was in effect a Presidential Republic, and he warned the Constituent Assembly against producing a second Draft Constitution on the same lines as the first. About the time the Second Draft Constitution was adopted by the Constituent Assembly— after the usual highly complex negotiations among the three main parties—de Gaulle, in a speech at Epinal rejected this Constitution on the grounds that it "placed the State below the omnipotence of the parties", did not adopt the principle of the clear "separation of powers", and gave wholly insufficient powers to the President of the Republic. He also said that, caught between America and the Slavs, and living in "a hard and dangerous world", France and the French Union could not safeguard their rights, their independence and security without a strong State. A further complication was added by the creation of a "Gaullist Union", which had existed in only an embryonic form before, but which was now threatening to become, in effect, another political party (though it, naturally, scornfully rejected the name of "party"). This might be a dangerous competitor, especially to the MRP.

The MRP advocated the acceptance of the new Draft Constitution, and the Gaullist Union its rejection, so that the MRP leaders, who had always claimed to be "faithful to de Gaulle", as well as the MRP rank and file, found themselves in an awkward spot. Torn between the contradictory instructions coming from the MRP and de Gaulle, the MRP voters in the referendum of October 13 scarcely knew what to do; and a very large number abstained from voting altogether. The second draft constitution was ultimately approved by a narrow majority, 9·2 millions approving it and 8·1 millions rejecting it. Eight and a half million voters had abstained, part of them owing to the *crise de conscience* de Gaulle had created for them, but probably many more simply through lack of interest.

The election campaign, on the other hand, was a good deal livelier. At Bordeaux, a Radical Deputy, M. Chaban-Delmas, claimed that de Gaulle had told him that the MRP leaders were decent but "dangerously incapable" people. M. Bidault was very offended. Maurice Schumann, for his part, was violently attacked by Colonel Passy, formerly head of de Gaulle's Intelligence in London (who had, earlier in the year, been arrested and held *incommunicado* for several months— the circumstances and the reasons for this arrest remained somewhat mysterious to the general public). He cast aspersions on Schumann's war record. Schumann is then said to have appealed to de Gaulle for his testimony, but to have received a friendly, but somewhat evasive letter. The almost immediate effect of this attack on the MRP by de Gaulle and his friends was for the MRP to take up a strongly anti-Communist and *anti-tripartisme* line; Schumann launching the slogan "Bidault without Thorez".

There followed, among the three Government parties, something like a three-cornered mudslinging contest.

The election of November 10 proved the most successful election of all for the Communists who, with just under 5½ million votes, had gained in a few months nearly 300,000 votes. The MRP, with just over 5 million votes, had lost half a million; the Socialists, down to 3·4 million votes, had lost about 800,000 votes. On the other hand, the Radicals, supported by the Union Gaulliste, gained some votes, and so did the Right.

The decline of the Socialists has been attributed by some commentators to their allegedly pro-Communist tendencies; it is much more probable that Blum's ultra-reformism drove many Socialists to the Communist fold, while others, disgusted with the "wine scandal", preferred to vote for nobody.

Although the Communists were *le premier parti de France* once more, it looked already as if the days of *tripartisme* were numbered. The Communists' spectacular success in the election had scared the other French parties, and caused alarm and despondency in London and Washington. Nevertheless the Political Bureau, at its meeting on November 14, announced that the Communist Party was willing to assume the leadership of the new Government. Thorez thereupon proceeded to groom himself for the rôle of Premier; and among the first things he did was to give interviews to *The Times* and to INS trying to reassure British and American opinion. He told *The Times* that there would be no dictatorship of the proletariat, but that a great French Labour Party would create "a new people's democracy in France" (a phrase that did not have quite the same connotation then as it did two years later). At the same time he told INS that the French Communist Party was not tied to Russia's apron-strings, but was in the great tradition of the French working-class parties that had existed since the middle of the nineteenth century. No Communist programme would be applied, "as the unity of the country is an essential preliminary to a French revival".

The idea was to form a Communist-Socialist-Radical coalition under Communist leadership. It may be seriously doubted whether Thorez was doing anything more than play-acting; for he could have had no illusions about the support he was likely to receive, and it was only too obvious what the international reactions to a Thorez government would be. Only the Communists and the majority of the Socialists (with their tongues in their cheeks) voted for Thorez's *investiture*, which was thus about forty votes short. After an abortive attempt by M. Bidault, and various negotiations and combinations, Blum failed to form a coalition, and then finally formed a purely Socialist "caretaker" Government which was to last only five weeks—till after the election of the President of the Republic in January 1947. It was rather absurd and paradoxical that the party that had been most severely defeated should have formed the first Government of the Fourth Republic under the new Constitution. But it received high praise, even before it had done anything, in the British and American press, if only because, for the first time since the Liberation, there were no Communists on the Government benches in Paris. It was—alas!—in the course of these five weeks that the dynamite that, for over a year, had been piling up in Indo-China, blew up.

CHAPTER SEVEN

BACKGROUND OF THE INDO-CHINA WAR

D URING the Occupation and for two years after the Liberation, France had been so absorbed with her domestic affairs and with the question of the place she was to hold in Europe, that public opinion gave even less than the usual amount of its attention to France's overseas possessions. No doubt de Gaulle himself was very Empire-conscious, and, particularly, Africa-conscious; from time to time, France heard the distant rumblings of the various "native" nationalisms that had become increasingly active, especially since 1942–3. There had been riots and massacres in Algeria in May 1945. These caused uneasiness among those who knew about them; and the virtual eviction of the French from Syria during the same year was a blow to France's pride, and to de Gaulle's *politique de grandeur*; but, by and large, de Gaulle was credited with having done his best, both militarily and diplomatically, to "keep the Empire together"; at the beginning of 1946 he expressed his satisfaction at having achieved this, despite the immense danger of dislocation with which the Empire had been threatened ever since 1940. He then added that the only exception was Indo-China, but here, too, General Leclerc had now gained a foothold. On the status of the overseas territories there were lengthy discussions among those who were drafting the Constitution. Chapter 8, one of the longest chapters, is concerned with the French Union, and the preamble to the Constitution, while avoiding the word "independence", speaks of the "freedom" of the overseas peoples, and rejects "any form of colonial rule based upon arbitrary power"; France, it also says, will lead these peoples "to a state of freedom in which they administer themselves and conduct their own affairs democratically". But, on the whole, France was not deeply concerned with colonial problems. The press, significantly, scarcely gave any attention to them in 1944–6.

It is only fair to say that "Vichy" had done its best to preserve for France the territories under its rule; Noguès at Rabat, Boisson at Dakar, Admiral Decoux at Saigon and the other Vichy Governors had exploited with some effect the "Pétain Myth" not only among the French settlers, nearly all of whom were determined *pétainistes*, but even among the natives, who were more impressed by pictures of

Marshal Pétain than by pictures of the drearily civilian M. Lebrun. In an Indo-China almost wholly isolated from France, Admiral Decoux, who, shortly after the Armistice, had replaced General Catroux as Governor-General, had paradoxically enough, surrounded himself with greater pomp than any of his predecessors; and he had embarked on a skilful policy of reforms, which aimed at flattering the Indo-Chinese and, at the same time, tended to limit the effects of the partial Japanese occupation, and of Japan's Great East Asia and "Co-Prosperity" propaganda.

The transition of the overseas territories from "Vichyism" to "Gaullism" at different stages of the war had taken place more or less painlessly; and when the war ended, France found that, although she was about to lose her hold over Syria, her Empire, with the exception of Indo-China, had remained in her possession.

In 1944 Indo-China was still a problem for the future; the war with Japan had not ended, and the future of Indo-China was dependent on a number of incalculable international factors. Few in France seemed interested—except de Gaulle himself who felt that, for the sake of France's "restored greatness", it was necessary that, in the war against Japan, she also should be able to claim to have played a part. Only by doing so could she save Indo-China for herself. The question of writing off Indo-China never seems to have occurred to de Gaulle; and it was this *politique de grandeur* which is, in reality, at the root of that disastrous war which was to cripple France financially and militarily for eight years.

Before the war, Indo-China had been a land of the most ruthless colonial exploitation; and, for many years, any signs of resistance—coming mostly from young intellectuals under Kuomintang influence, many of them French-trained—were mercilessly crushed. Hunger riots, like those of 1930, were also "liquidated" with extreme ruthlessness, as were also their instigators—the "anti-white" VNQDD, and the Indo-Chinese Communists, who had first made their appearance on the political scene about 1930. Their leader was a schoolmaster, Nguyen Ai Quoc (the future Ho Chi Minh) who had spent some years in China, France, and Russia, and who had attended the famous Socialist Congress of Tours in 1920, where the Communists had broken away from the Socialist Party. In 1930 the Communist Party, like other Resistance organizations, was dislocated, and its leaders executed or driven abroad. In the Chamber of Deputies in Paris, men like Moutet and Daladier advocated, about that time, a more "liberal" policy in Indo-China, but they were voices crying in the wilderness.

Some echoes had reached France of the appalling conditions in which labour from Tongking was recruited for the rubber plantations in Cochin-China, and of the assassination of a certain Bazin, a recruiting officer, by a young Annamite student, a member of the VNQDD, a secret nationalist party. There had also been echoes of the savage repression of the riots of 1930. In a remarkable book, *SOS Indochine*, published in 1931, Andrée Viollis, the special correspondent of the *Petit Parisien*, had compared the façade of Indo-China (she had accompanied M. Reynaud, the Minister of Colonies, on an official voyage) with the grim realities—the famine in Central Annam, the gaols packed with "revolutionaries", the numerous executions and the police terror. After his return from France in 1933, where he had received his education, the new young Emperor of Annam, Bao Dai, had at first raised some hopes among the people; but Governor-General Pasquier soon surrounded him with "safe" people, and the nineteen-year-old monarch before long lost all authority and popularity. After a few illusions had been created at the time of the Popular Front in France, things soon returned to "normal" in Indo-China, and 1939 was marked by a new wave of arrests, among those sent to prison being the wife and the small child of a young revolutionary, Giap, the future Commander-in-Chief of the Vietminh forces. Both his wife and child died in prison in 1943, a fact he seldom failed to recall in his later contacts with the French.

Indo-China was to cause France no great concern at the outbreak of World War II. There was "perfect peace" in Indo-China. The trouble-makers were in gaol. The Trans-Indo-China railway had been completed in 1937; the country was developing economically along classical capitalist-colonial lines; rubber prices were rising, and the coolies were better paid than before. The Bao Dai régime was wholly controlled by the French Administration.

The trouble started after the defeat of France in Europe. There was nothing to fear from Germany, but Japan was active in China, just across the border. As early as June 19, 1940 came the first Japanese ultimatum: the demand that the French close the Indo-Chinese border to American exports to the Chiang Kai Shek forces in China. Other demands followed: transit facilities, air bases, etc. The air bases were needed for bombing the Burma Road. Admiral Decoux yielded what he called "an unavoidable minimum", in exchange for Japanese recognition of French sovereignty over Indo-China. Later, under the Kato-Darlan agreement of July 29, 1941, Indo-China was "integrated" in "common defence", and the Japanese were allowed to use Saigon as an advance base for operations in South-East Asia. Decoux prided himself on having established a satisfactory *modus vivendi* with the Japanese. The latter were using Saigon as an important naval and air base when operations began against Malaya; but their presence was "discreet", and they were content to let the 40,000 French troops in Indo-China keep the country in order. Also, owing to the British blockade, practically all Indo-China's foreign trade was diverted to Japan.

But Decoux knew that Japanese racialism was strong, and he tried to counter the Japanese pan-Asian *mystique* of Co-Prosperity with a *"mystique Indo-Chine"*. His "reforms" went so far as to make the more conservative settlers distinctly nervous. He put forward ideas about an "Indo-Chinese Federalism" cemented by France, and introduced such "revolutionary" innovations as the prohibition of saying *tu* to a Vietnamese, or of beating him; and he even embarked on an anti-illiteracy campaign. Although the Decoux régime was completely auto-cratic (and could claim to have set up one of the most horrible concen-tration camps in the world), it was in some ways, paradoxically enough, more "liberal" than anything the Indo-Chinese had seen under the Third Republic.

Thus the number of natives in medium and upper posts in the administration doubled between 1940 and 1944. Also, the administration, which was passionately Vichyite, tended to eclipse the settlers and Big Business, for whom Decoux had little respect. A paradoxical conse-quence of Decoux's "enlightened autocracy" was to provide the future revolutionary régime in Vietnam with a fair number of trained and experienced native officials.

Gaullism was practically non-existent in Indo-China for a long time, and what little there was of it was stamped out with great energy. However, as Japan's defeat became more and more probable, certain moods, familiar in France, began to develop: notably a "guilt com-plex" at not having fought the Japanese, and the feeling that France would not keep Indo-China "unless she fought for it". The Japanese were alarmed by these signs of a new temper among many of the French, and on March 9, 1945 presented Decoux with an ultimatum, which the Admiral rejected; they then rapidly disarmed all the French troops, and massacred some of them. Bao Dai thereupon congratulated the Japanese; solemnly declared that the French Protectorate was abolished; proclaimed Annam to be an element of Great East Asia, and expressed the hope that it would "prove worthy of its indepen-dence". The people of Vietnam (who, in the previous months, had suffered one of their worst famines) could not take this change of régime seriously. The Japanese were losing the war, and "indepen-dent" Vietnam under Japanese suzerainty could only be something temporary.

The Indo-Chinese Communist Party which, already in 1941 had called on the people of Indo-China to fight "both French imperialism and Japanese Fascism", was becoming increasingly active, and, after Hiroshima, the numerous Vietminh guerillas in the country took the name of "Vietnamese Army of Liberation". In the presence of Ho Chi

Minh a Committee for the Liberation of the People of Vietnam met, and on August 10, Ho Chi Minh called for a National Insurrection. The Japanese, preferring to hand over to "yellows", rather than to "whites", did not interfere when Vietminh took over the administration of Hanoi on August 20, 1945. At the same time, a Student's Congress at Hanoi passed a resolution in favour of the Republic and asking for Bao Dai's abdication. Bao Dai (who, only a few days before, had sent a message to de Gaulle demanding France's recognition of Vietnam's independence "without French sovereignty or administration in any shape or form") abdicated without much hesitation, and recommended loyalty to the Republic. At Saigon, too, the Japanese handed their authority over to the Vietnamese—in this case to their own friends, not to the Vietnamese Communists.

For months past, France had been remarkably ignorant of what was going on in Indo-China; and it is certain that few people realized the depth and breadth of the revolutionary and nationalist movement there. On March 24, 1945, de Gaulle had issued a statement saying that there would be a Federal Government of Indo-China, presided over by a Governor-General representing France, and composed of French and native ministers; there would also be a "mixed" Assembly. It was, roughly, what Daladier had proposed fifteen years before, and less than what Indo-China had had under the Vichy régime!

At that stage, however, de Gaulle was primarily concerned not with internal Indo-Chinese problems, but with French prestige; it was essential for France, in his view, to take part in the war against Japan; everything else was of secondary importance for the time being. But Japan's sudden capitulation created a new situation. Admiral Thierry d'Argenlieu, one of de Gaulle's most faithful henchmen, a former naval officer who had become a Carmelite monk, but had joined the Navy again at the outbreak of war, was appointed by de Gaulle High Commissioner in Indo-China. A small number of French troops, which had been earmarked for fighting the Japanese, were ready to sail for Saigon. On August 22, on his way to Saigon, General Leclerc (who was, soon afterwards, to sign the Japanese act of capitulation, on behalf of France, on board the Missouri) was informed by Lord Mountbatten of the Potsdam decision that Indo-China be cut into two zones, one north, the other south of the 16th parallel; in the North the Japanese were to be disarmed by the Chinese, in the South, by the British. Mountbatten is reported to have said: "If Roosevelt were still alive, you wouldn't stand a chance of getting back to Indo-China—but maybe it can be fixed now."[1] MacArthur, whom Leclerc saw a few days later

[1] Philippe Devillers, *Histoire du Vietnam de 1940 à 1952* (Paris, 1952), pp. 149–50.

in Japan, was in favour of the French landing "as many troops as possible".

September and October were a period of great confusion. De Gaulle parachutists who landed in Vietnam were, for the greater part, massacred by the Vietminh. A de Gaulle emissary, M. Sainteny, however, reached Hanoi and established contact with the Vietnamese authorities. Another, M. Cédile, established himself at Saigon. When he offered to the Vietnamese the de Gaulle statement of March 24, they merely smiled. There followed a few weeks of general confusion, complete with anti-French riots and massacres, the landing of British troops, the rearming of French troops at Cédile's request, and the escape from Saigon of the Vietnam "National Committee". Leclerc landed with some troops at Saigon, soon to be followed by d'Argenlieu, the new High Commissioner. Soon afterwards the British withdrew. D'Argenlieu was promptly surrounded by "conservative" advisers, who also brought into his orbit a number of "pro-French" Vietnamese, such as Colonel Xuan and the head of the "Democratic Party" of Cochin-China, Dr Nguyen Van Thinh. Before long, the idea of an "Autonomous Cochin-China" matured in the minds of these people. Already in February 1946 an Advisory Council of Cochin-China was set up, a body of French stooges.

A point to remember is that if Vietminh was powerful in North and Central Vietnam, it was, at that stage, weak and unorganized in Cochin-China. Leclerc declared on February 5, 1946 that the "pacification of Cochin-China and South Annam" had been completed. This announcement was to prove somewhat premature.

Meantime the Revolution was in full swing in North and Central Vietnam. In August 1945 all the dreams of the Vietnam revolutionaries seemed to have come true. The war was at an end; Japan had been defeated; the country was united, and soon (so it seemed) its independence would be recognized by all the Allies. The revolutionaries around Ho Chi Minh were composed of three elements: the "old guard", largely trained in China and Russia, and used to clandestine work; intellectuals, who had lived in Vietnam, but had received their education in France, and were not, like the first group, basically anti-French; and, finally, students, teachers and technicians, mostly French-trained, some of them under the Decoux régime.

In August 1945 Ho Chi Minh dissolved several rival organizations, notably the pro-Japanese parties; all colonial institutions were abolished, such as the régime of mandarins and *notables*; and everywhere People's Committees were set up. The election of a Constituent Assembly was announced, sex equality was proclaimed, and new reforms were introduced: eight-hour day, minimum wage, employers' duties, and anti-illiteracy laws. Eighty per cent of the population was still found to be illiterate. Popular education and evening classes were organized, and one year was given to young and old to learn to read and write. The revolution, which swept the whole country, was even more violent in the countryside than in the towns. Mandarins and *notables* were massacred in many places; "Fascist" property was confiscated; the atmosphere was not unlike that of Russia in 1917–18.

The Vietnam Communists and Ho Chi Minh himself soon realized that things were getting out of hand; that independence should be No 1 target, and that the Socialist Revolution could wait. The working-class represented only three per cent of the active population, and what was required in the first place was an alliance of the working-class, the peasantry and the national bourgeoisie. On November 21, 1945, a Government circular proclaimed that capitalism had not been abolished. Not only had the French gained a foothold in South Vietnam, but North Vietnam had been invaded by the Chinese who had ostensibly come to disarm the Japanese, but started, before long, to make themselves at home, notably by eliminating the People's Committees in several provinces, and turning Hanoi into one vast Chinese black market. The Chinese, like the Japanese before them, had their Vietnamese stooges, and these proceeded to create immense difficulties for Ho Chi Minh.

The happy illusions of August 1945 had been dashed to the ground; for nobody seemed in a hurry to recognize an Independent Vietnam. Russia was keeping aloof; China was thinking in terms of a Greater China; the United States was non-committal, and distrustful, if anything, of the "Leftist" tendencies shown by the Hanoi Government; and France was now firmly entrenched in Cochin-China. There is sufficient evidence to show that, trapped between China and France, the Ho Chi Minh Government tended to look upon France as a lesser evil, and hoped to obtain from the Fourth Republic at least some degree of independence—now that the hope of being promptly "recognized" by the Powers had vanished.

In January 1946 Ho Chi Minh told a French journalist:

We have no hatred for France. We want to re-establish contact with her, all the more so as others [meaning China] are interfering with our affairs. We can make a settlement. But if we must, we shall fight.[2]

This statement was made on the very day of the election, in which Ho Chi Minh and the Vietminh National Front received an overwhelming majority—a majority which they would, according to all observers, friendly and hostile, have received if the election had been even more "democratic" than it was.

[2] Devillers, *op. cit.*, p. 204.

Leclerc was among those who fully realized that Ho Chi Minh had the greater part of the country behind him, and he was opposed to any suggestion that the French try to reconquer Tongking by force of arms. There was another point to which Leclerc attached some importance: Ho's men were mostly French-trained intellectuals, while the pro-Japanese, pro-Chinese and pro-Americans were in the Opposition. This view was shared by Sainteny, who also thought that Ho Chi Minh was not "basically anti-French". But Leclerc's arguments in favour of negotiating with the Hanoi Government aroused resentment in Admiral d'Argenlieu, who even complained to de Gaulle of Leclerc's "capitulationist" tendencies.

Then suddenly, on January 20, 1946, de Gaulle resigned. What difference was it going to make to the policy of France in Indo-China?

Here is the point at which Paris became the scene of a struggle over Indo-China. D'Argenlieu placed his hopes, not so much in the Gouin Government as in the Interministerial Committee on Indo-China whose majority was still Gaullist, Bidault and Michelet being among its principal members. During the subsequent critical months Bidault was to play an important rôle in making the "tough" line triumph.

Leclerc feared that if the French simply tried to invade Tongking the Vietnamese and the "anti-European" Chinese might gang up against them; he also feared that, if pressed too hard, Ho and his men might "take to the maquis" and embark on an interminable guerilla war. After considering numerous possibilities, all unattractive, the French Government decided to start negotiations with the Chinese, with a view to relieving the Chinese troops in North Vietnam. Finally, on February 28 an agreement was reached at Chungking under which the Chinese Government recognized French sovereignty over Indo-China, in return for the abandonment by France of her Concession in Shanghai and of numerous other territorial and economic privileges in China. During March French troops were to replace the Chinese troops.

But this could not be done without serious risk, unless there was some agreement with the Hanoi Government. Ho Chi Minh's new policy vis-à-vis France was summed up in the words "Independence and Alliance". In his talks with sympathetic Sainteny, Ho insisted on the word "independence" being included in the Franco-Vietnamese agreement, and also on the unification of the country—of the "3 Kys", Tongking, Annam, and Cochin-China. Finally, after much trouble and many new complications (arising, notably, from the reluctance of some of the Chinese generals to leave), a preliminary Franco-Vietnamese agreement was finally signed on March 6, 1946 between Ho and Sainteny.

This recognized Vietnam as a Free State with its own parliament, army, and finances. A later conference would decide on the exact status of Vietnam as a member of the Indo-China Federation and of the French Union, and settle the question of diplomatic representation. The question of the "3 Kys" would be settled by means of a referendum in Cochin-China.

On April 3, a military convention was signed, providing that France would maintain in Annam and Tongking 15,000 troops, to be withdrawn within five years at the rate of 3,000 a year. Pending the referendum, the question of French troops in Cochin-China was left open.

In the interval between the two agreements French troops landed at Haiphong and entered Hanoi. At Haiphong one of the ships was severely damaged by a Chinese battery, and the population rejoiced over the "Sino-Vietnamese victory" over the French. Later it had to be explained that the local Chinese had "made a mistake".

The Agreement of March 6 and especially the arrival of French troops in Tongking made a deplorable impression on the Vietnamese, despite the public display of cordiality between Ho Chi Minh and Leclerc. Giap had to explain in a speech that this was "Vietnam's Brest-Litovsk"; that Vietnam would gain independence in the end, and that the only real enemies of Vietnam's independence were "the French reactionaries". Democratic France, on the other hand, was Vietnam's friend. It was with this happy illusion that the French Socialists and Communists would give Vietnam its independence that Ho Chi Minh was later to travel to the Fontainebleau Conference.

The Ho-Sainteny agreement was welcomed among the Left in France, and created an excellent impression in Britain and the United States: the French, whose colonial record was far from good, had, nevertheless, been the first to make an agreement with an important nationalist government in Asia.

But this did not suit d'Argenlieu and the "Saigon clique" in the least. Cochin-China separatism became their trump card. The hopelessly wobbly Socialist Minister of Overseas France, M. Marius Moutet, was argued by Saigon emissaries into agreeing that the Ho-Sainteny agreement was only "of local importance", an admission that he was well impressed by the arguments in favour of Cochin-China separatism. Colonel Xuan, back from Paris, said on May 26 that both Moutet and Gouin had been "sympathetic" to Cochin-China's aspirations, despite a certain prejudice on their part in favour of the Hanoi Government; on the other hand, he and his colleagues had received the warmest welcome from the PRL, the Radicals and the MRP "where we have a real friend in Mme Bidault, the wife of the Foreign Minister, and the sister of Major Borel, head of the 2ᵉ *Bureau* of the French Expeditionary Force in Indo-China". Xuan had found even Thorez quite satisfactory: he had said that he was not at all in favour of liquidating the French flag over Indo-China. The stickiest of all had been "certain Socialists".[3]

Already in March the so-called Advisory Council of Cochin-China appointed Dr Nguyen Van Thinh "head of the provisional government of the Republic of Cochin-China". About this time, Nguyen Binh, head of the Vietminh guerillas in Cochin-China, started a terrorist campaign, concentrating chiefly on the murder of "collaborators". This scared the separatists, and with Vietminh influence growing in the country, d'Argenlieu hastened to announce that, "subject to subsequent ratification", and "pending the referendum, as provided by the agreement of March 6", the French Government recognized Cochin-China as a Free State with its Parliament, Army, and finances"; and the Thinh Government was duly formed on June 1.

Moutet, who had already said too much, found it hard to disavow d'Argenlieu. Ho Chi Minh, who had attended the "preliminary" conference at Dalat in April–May, without this conference reaching any clear conclusion on any vital question, was on his way to Paris when he heard of the Cochin-China *coup*. He arrived in France on June 12, ten days after the election of June 2, which, as we have seen, had been a great victory for the MRP, and a setback for the Socialists. Pending the formation of the new government, he was asked to stay and meditate at the Carlton Hotel at Biarritz, far from the French political hubbub.

He arrived in Paris a fortnight later, feeling increasingly perturbed by the activities of the Saigon Clique, who were clearly determined to sabotage the agreement of March 6 which had been concluded with Leclerc's blessing. The French election had marked a move towards the Right, and the French delegation, with whom the Vietnamese were to negotiate, was composed chiefly of officials, with little sympathy for the nationalist aspirations of Vietnam and presided over by a diehard MRP Deputy, M. Max André. Ho Chi Minh seems to have overrated the weight of left-wing opinion in France, and to have expected powerful support from the Socialists and Communists; he had also been impressed by the enthusiasm that his presence seemed to arouse among certain sections of the population and among all left-wing intellectuals. In the opinion of an authority like Philippe Devillers, Ho Chi Minh's great mistake was to have got himself identified with the Socialists and Communists in France, instead of having looked for support among the more intelligent members of the Right, like Sainteny and Leclerc. His "Leftism" irritated MRP, Radical, and Conservative opinion, and his insistence on "independence" was unpopular with very wide sections, still smarting from the humiliation France had suffered in Syria, and who identified "independence"

[3] Devillers, *op. cit.*, p. 268.

with "separation" from France. This "flirtation" with the Left parties, which were supposed to exercise a tremendous influence inside Bidault's Government in Ho Chi Minh's favour, was a first-class mistake. The Socialists (as became only too clear from the attitude of M. Moutet) were wobbly on the Vietnam issue, and the Communists, anxious to preserve *tripartisme*, and no doubt thinking it unwise to proclaim themselves too loudly the champions of an independent Vietnam, were less emphatic in their views than might have been expected. No doubt France had too many other worries at the time—economic conditions, Germany, etc—to give her main attention to Indo-China. Also, among the general public, there was an abysmal ignorance of Asian affairs.

The Fontainebleau Conference started badly, with a violent attack by Pham Van Dong, the official head of the Vietnam delegation, on d'Argenlieu's policy of *faits accomplis* in Cochin-China. The agenda was composed of five items:

The integration of Vietnam in the French Union and its diplomatic relations; the elaboration of the Indo-Chinese Federation; unity of the 3 Kys and the Cochin-China referendum; economic problems; the drafting of the treaty.

No agreement was reached on any of these points, except on point 4: economic problems. The biggest stumbling-block was the Cochin-China referendum. Ho Chi Minh felt most strongly about it; as for the French Government, it remained non-committal, and continued to be bombarded with telegrams from Cochin-China *colons* entreating it not to yield to Ho Chi Minh, who, they said, represented "only a small minority of agitators and troublemakers"—precisely the kind of argument to be used later by North African *colons* when they spoke of the Neo-Destour or the Istiqlal.

While the Fontainebleau Conference was in progress, Saigon was continuing the sabotage. Leclerc had by now left Indo-China, which made the sabotage even easier. D'Argenlieu called a conference at Dalat which would lay the foundations for an "Indo-Chinese Federation", the delegates representing Cochin-China, Laos, and Cambodia.

This produced a furious outburst from Dong, after which the Fontainebleau Conference was suspended, much to d'Argenlieu's delight. Meantime de Gaulle, Herriot and others in France were becoming increasingly irritated with the Vietnamese and with Ho's clamour for independence. In the end, Ho Chi Minh realized that only a limited agreement was possible in the circumstances, and a *modus vivendi* was drawn up covering a number of economic and financial clauses. Suddenly Pham Van Dong declared that he would not sign it, and demanded that all the five items on the agenda be covered; he particularly demanded a firm committent on the Cochin-China referendum. Short of this, Dong was in favour of signing nothing. No doubt he reflected that if the talks were to be resumed in January, Giap's army might have gained in strength in the interval, and a more left-wing government might be in power in France. Ho Chi Minh nevertheless decided, after several days of grave doubts, to sign on September 14 the *modus vivendi*, dealing with a number of financial, economic, and cultural questions, setting up some joint commissions to deal with them, calling for a cease-fire between French troops and Vietnamese guerillas in Cochin-China by October 31, and providing for a resumption of the talks not later than January 1947.

Trouble meantime was piling sky-high in Indo-China. There had been incidents at Haiphong over the control of the customs, the French claiming a right to control them, and the Vietnamese claiming that this would be contrary to the agreement of March 6. After his return to Hanoi, Ho formed a new Government which, after the elimination of the pro-Chinese VNQDD members, was more to the Left than the last one. Bao Dai remained the Government's "supreme counsellor". The virtual dictatorship of this Government was legalized by the Vietnamese Constituent Assembly by 240 votes to 2. Hostilities in Cochin-China were effectively stopped on October 31—a fact which Saigon found highly alarming. For d'Argenlieu realized that Ho Chi Minh could afford not to fight in Cochin-China, where his support had grown immensely. The *colons* were becoming increasingly aggressive, and began to treat even Thinh and Xuan as secret Vietminh sympathizers, and demanded that on no account was Hanoi's rule to be extended to Cochin-China. They were terrified at the referendum, which had to be prevented at any price.

Although Ho Chi Minh's negotiations with the French since March 6 had been completely fruitless, the situation in Indo-China continued to develop in a manner favourable to Vietminh. Nguyen Binh's guerillas in Cochin-China were controlling the whole countryside, and would not allow themselves to be disarmed. Cochin-Chinese autonomism had proved a failure. The authority of Vietminh in the North was growing stronger every day, and Ho Chi Minh's moderation had attracted to him numerous bourgeois elements and the whole intellectual élite.

Everything was rotting away, as it were, and there was nothing that Saigon could do about it. Only a military adventure could stop the rot; but the Hanoi Government seemed, under Ho's influence, to be avoiding any policy of violence.[4]

The Saigon Clique were greatly upset by the French referendum

[4] Devillers, *op. cit.*, pp. 328–29.

accepting the Second Draft Constitution; it was a disavowal of de Gaulle, and, from d'Argenlieu's point of view, only the MRP could now safeguard the policy of "national interest". The November 10 election, with its increased Communist vote, brought Saigon no comfort; what, if, by January, there was a left-wing government in France which would start making major concessions to the Hanoi Government? There was no time to lose. D'Argenlieu promptly left for Paris, leaving General Valluy in charge. What instructions he left him may be guessed from what was to happen in the next few days.

The real trouble started at Haiphong which, for months, had been the scene of daily conflicts between the French and Vietnamese troops, police and Customs authorities. For reasons, some of which were good and others bad, the French set up a Customs office at Haiphong, ostensibly to stamp out Chinese smuggling which had taken on such proportions as to endanger the Vietnamese currency. This was, however, contrary to the Agreement of March 6, and to the Ho-Moutet *modus vivendi*, and on November 11 Ho Chi Minh sent a sharp protest to Bidault against the "unilateral action" of the French in setting up their own Customs at Haiphong. He drew attention to the urgency of the matter and proposed an amicable settlement of the dispute. His telegram, significantly enough, was deliberately "delayed in transmission" by the French authorities in Saigon, and did not reach Paris until November 26—after the Haiphong disaster. This is the first example, but not the only one of the deliberate sabotage, on the part of Saigon, of the direct communications Ho Chi Minh tried to establish with Paris.

It is impossible here to relate, with all its details, the story of the Haiphong tragedy. But this is, very briefly, what happened. As a result of a number of minor incidents at Haiphong on November 20, fighting broke out in the port and city between French and Vietnamese troops. The extremely aggressive attitude of Colonel Dèbes, the local French commander, did not make things any easier. The French authorities at Hanoi were, however, doing their utmost to stop the fighting. A joint Franco-Vietnamese Commission were promptly sent to Haiphong, where they arrived on the morning of the 21st. A local cease-fire was agreed upon, but was ignored by Colonel Dèbes. Even so, both the French and the Vietnamese at Hanoi persisted in their efforts to avert major trouble. M. de Lacharrière, a French official and Ho Chi Minh agreed to call immediately a meeting of the joint commission which would deal with the customs dispute. To quote Devillers:

Thus, on November 21 a settlement seemed in sight both at Hanoi and at Haiphong. Unfortunately, Saigon's intervention upset everything. In reply to the proposal that the joint commission meet, General Valluy, no doubt advised by M. Pignon, replied ... that two conditions must first be fulfilled: total evacuation of Haiphong by all Vietnamese military and para-military units; total freedom of movement for French troops in the city.

Since the Haiphong incident had already been practically settled, these conditions obviously could not be accepted by the Vietnamese Government. ... General Morlière (at Hanoi) drew Valluy's attention to the folly of this ultimatum: the Vietnamese would certainly refuse to evacuate the native city. If, therefore, the ultimatum were sent, the French would have to conquer the native city by force, and this could not be done without the use of heavy artillery. It would inevitably generalize the conflict in Tongking.... What Morlière did not know was that General Valluy had already on the previous day directly informed Dèbes of the guarantees that were to be demanded. He had even added that he considered it "indispensable to take advantage of the incidents to improve our position at Haiphong".[5]

Despite the efforts made by the two French emissaries from Hanoi to restrain Colonel Dèbes's ardour, nothing could stop him now. The Valluy message had shown him the way the wind was blowing. On the afternoon of November 22 another message came from Valluy demanding that the Vietnamese be taught "a hard lesson". Inventing one pretext after another, Dèbes proceeded to make more and more extravagant demands on the local authorities, and at 10 o'clock the next morning, after the expiry of his "ultimatum", French troops invaded the Chinese quarter, where they met with stiff resistance from the Vietnamese; at this point Dèbes called on the cruiser *Suffren* to open fire on the Vietnamese quarter. According to Admiral Battet, 6,000 people—men, women, and children—were killed or burned to death in the shelling.[6]

The Vietnamese troops in Haiphong did not surrender as a result of this outrage, or evacuate the city; on the contrary, fighting flared up all over the place. However, two days later Giap asked to see General Morlière, who communicated with Valluy. Valluy was now on the warpath. He instructed Morlière to present Giap with an ultimatum, even stiffer than that of November 22. Not only Haiphong, but a large area round Haiphong was to be evacuated by all Vietnamese troops and the city and area handed over to the French military authorities. There were several other conditions.

This new Valluy ultimatum was obviously even more unacceptable than the first. Ho Chi Minh and Giap could no longer have the slightest doubt that Saigon wanted a breach, if not actually war, and was trying to put the blame on the Vietnamese.[7]

Meantime in Paris d'Argenlieu was putting the fear of death into

[5] Devillers, *op. cit.*, p. 335.
[6] Paul Mus in *Témoignage Chrétien*, February 10, 1950.
[7] Devillers, *op. cit.*, p. 339.

"public opinion". *Le Figaro, le Monde, l'Epoque,* and the MRP *Aube* started spreading the most alarmist stories on how France was going to "lose Indo-China" if she was not firm. The AFP, the French news agency, deliberately suppressed all news of the Haiphong massacre[8] organized by the irate Colonel Dèbes, and it was not until many months later, after irreparable damage had been done, that French opinion first heard of some of the facts concerning Haiphong—which was the *real* beginning of the war in Indo-China.

All the same, there was an interval of over three weeks between the real beginning of the war and the official beginning—the Hanoi massacres of December 19. There was still a chance, even after Haiphong, that the war would not materialize. Much depended on developments in France itself.

A characteristic episode during this fateful interval was that of another telegram deliberately "delayed in transmission" needless to say, by Saigon—a telegram sent by Ho Chi Minh to the new French Premier, Léon Blum. It was sent on December 15—four days before the Hanoi massacre—and did not reach Paris until December 26. Perhaps the timely receipt of Ho's proposals for a general settlement of the Haiphong dispute would not have been of decisive importance, but the incident shows that Saigon did everything in its power to prevent a *détente* during those critical three weeks. For there was, after all, still a hope that, with a Socialist Government in office, the worst might yet be averted. A few days before taking office Blum had written in the *Populaire* of December 10:

There is only one way of preserving in Indo-China the prestige of our civilization, our political influence and our legitimate interests—and that is a sincere agreement with Vietnam on a basis of independence, confidence, and friendship. . . .

These well-meaning sentiments were enough to scare the MRP, Admiral d'Argenlieu and the rest of them. Bidault and Pleven were to be particularly active, in all the discussions surrounding the formation of the Blum Government, in demanding a policy of "firmness" in Indo-China.

Despite his excellent sentiments, as expressed in the *Populaire,* Blum, in order not to annoy the MRP, made one absolutely fatal mistake: the first thing he decided after forming his government on December 18 was not only to send to Indo-China his Minister of Overseas France, M. Marius Moutet, who had already made numerous mistakes in connexion with Indo-China, but, what was infinitely worse, to send d'Argenlieu back to Saigon at the same time. At Hanoi where, especially since the Haiphong massacre, the atmosphere between the French

[8] *Temps Modernes,* August–September 1953, p. 409.

and the Vietnamese was one of acute exasperation, the news that d'Argenlieu was returning was to the Vietnamese like a red rag to a bull. Coming on top of several murderous clashes at Hanoi between French troops and Tu Ve (Vietnam Self-Protection Units, who had been organized by Giap in the previous months) it undoubtedly helped to precipitate the outbreak of war.

And yet the evidence on what exactly happened during the tragic night of December 19–20 at Hanoi is contradictory to this day. Morlière and Sainteny had done their best during the previous days to keep in contact with the Vietnamese Government and to prevent the situation from finally deteriorating. But on all sides nerves were on edge. Ho Chi Minh, seriously ill during that fatal week, but hoping that, with Blum now in office, things might change for the better, was less likely than ever to wish to break off relations, and to precipitate a crisis.

This does not mean that there were not Vietnamese elements "ready for a scrap", and perhaps convinced that if there was no showdown, the Saigon Clique would stage more and more "Haiphongs". In this connexion d'Argenlieu's return must have seemed particularly ominous. Anyway, the question arises whether the French troops at Hanoi or the Vietnamese troops (including the Tu Ve), or both, were preparing for a showdown on the night of December 19. The evidence is so confused and contradictory that no clear answer is possible. But a number of facts stand out clearly. All sorts of secret agents, acting on mysterious orders, were spreading rumours that "the Viets" (or "the French") would "strike tonight". What is also certain is that both sides were on the *qui vive*, and that Giap was keeping his troops and the Tu Ve in readiness to strike "if necessary". There is also evidence to show that when Giap realized that the French troops were in a state of military preparedness that night, he ordered his troops not to budge. But it seems (Devillers, p. 355) that certain Tu Ve units either failed to receive his order, or else acted in defiance of it. According to Paul Mus (*Temoignage Chrétien*, January 6, 1950) the purpose of their attack (which began in the centre of Hanoi at 8 p.m.) was not to "massacre Europeans", but (*a*) to break into European houses and seize what arms they could find; (*b*) kidnap the French leaders, without killing them; (*c*) take away as many Europeans as possible as hostages.

That the "massacre of Europeans" was not the object of the Vietnamese plan may be seen from the fact that, after a night's heavy fighting, only 40 Europeans were found to be dead. But 200 hostages had disappeared.

The French troops, with their armoured cars and small tanks, soon cleared the centre of Hanoi, and at 4 o'clock the next day the tricolour was hoisted on the Vietnamese Government House, whence

Ho Chi Minh, still ill, had escaped barely an hour before. In many parts of the town the Tu Ve were still continuing to fight. That same night, Giap, whose troops were now surrounding Hanoi, launched his appeal for a general war on all fronts.

His appeal was followed the next day by one from Ho Chi Minh himself.

The French colonialist clique are pursuing their plan to enslave our country again.... Fight with your arms, your picks and shovels, your sticks. Save the independence and integrity of our country. Final victory is certain. Long live independent indivisible Vietnam! Long live Democracy!

Within two days guerilla war had broken out all over the country.

It led to what General Morlière and others had feared most of all: the generalization of the conflict, the abandonment by the Vietnamese Government of its capital, and the resumption, on an immense scale, of that guerilla war, of which Leclerc had said—and he knew what he was talking about—that it would exhaust the French Army and make it impossible for it, for a long time, to reconstruct itself in Europe.[9]

Whoever was directly responsible for the Hanoi rebellion of December 19 (and Ho Chi Minh certainly was not), there is no doubt that the Saigon Clique had done everything in its power to create a political and psychological atmosphere, in which such an explosion became inevitable. It was the same people who, for years afterwards, were to do their utmost to prevent the war from ending.

A curious question arises. Was the war, viewed from the Marxist point of view, inevitable—seeing that Saigon represented certain quite definite "class interests"? What, one may wonder, would have happened if not Thierry d'Argenlieu but Leclerc had been High Commissioner? The social, family, and political background of Leclerc was almost exactly the same as d'Argenlieu's. The Comte de Hauteclocque —this was Leclerc's real name—had as Catholic, as conservative and as aristocratic a background as Thierry d'Argenlieu; like the Admiral, he had been a Gaullist from the very beginning; yet in Indo-China, one was carried away by his traditional class reflexes; the other was willing to make allowances for a changing world, in which the rising tide of Asian nationalisms had to be reckoned with, if anything was to be saved for France in Indo-China. Would Leclerc in the end have been overruled—and eliminated—by the pressure of the traditional colonialists?[10] In the long run, perhaps. But it is certain that if Leclerc had been High Commissioner at Saigon in the winter of 1946, there

[9] Devillers, *op. cit.*, p. 357.

[10] It is worth recalling that when Leclerc was killed in an air accident in 1947, it was rumoured that the crash had been "organized" by certain colonialist groups in Indo-China.

would have been no Haiphong, and, consequently, no Hanoi, and history might have taken a different course.

But now the damage was done, and the tragic night of December 19–20 was to mark the beginning of that interminable war, against the danger of which Leclerc had warned his countrymen in vain.

CHAPTER EIGHT

BLUM BLUNDERS INTO THE INDO-CHINA WAR

THE war in Indo-China, which was to become "the Dreyfus Case of the Fourth Republic" could have been nipped in the bud. M. Léon Blum declared, three days after the Hanoi rebellion, that no opportunity would be missed to put an end to the fighting. In his statement before the National Assembly on December 23 he uttered all the well-meaning platitudes of which he was capable, and, at the same time, gave full credit to the French authorities in Vietnam for having done everything to avert the disaster!

When we tell you in detail of all that has happened, you will realize that no stone was left unturned to restore agreement with the Vietnam Government. It was our duty, our common duty, to exhaust patiently all the means of preserving French lives in Indo-China ... and also to spare the blood which is not our blood, but which is still the blood of a people whose political liberty we recognized ten months ago—of a people who must soon take its place in the union of peoples federated around France.... The dire necessities of the moment will not alter these basic principles of our policy. We shall not turn a deaf ear to any possibility of a settlement.... Colonial possession finds its final justification only when a colonial people has become fully capable of living a life of its own, and to govern itself. Our reward will be the gratitude of these peoples who...

And so on, and so on. The truth is that Blum did not know what was happening in Indo-China. The Saigon Clique alone was informing the Government, and the press was fed on Saigon-made news from the AFP. What little other news filtered through (such as the dispatches from the Associated Press correspondents) was invariably "delayed in transmission", often by a week or more.[1] Before long, to prevent even such "leakages", a stiff censorship was introduced in Indo-China.

The trouble was that until July 1946 there had been a certain balance between the peaceful and constructive Leclerc-Sainteny policy and the diehard policy of the Saigon Clique, but thereafter the latter, as we have seen, proceeded to present Paris with one *fait accompli* after another. Public opinion in France, too absorbed with other matters, was not at first interested in Indo-China at all (the press hadn't, for

---

[1] Devillers, *op. cit.*, p. 358.

instance, breathed a word of the shelling of Haiphong in November: perhaps it genuinely did not know about it), and when the explosion came in December, the press gave the impression that the French had been treacherously stabbed in the back.

"Tongking must be freed of the pirates who are shedding our blood," the *Dépêche* of Toulouse wrote, and other papers followed, more or less, the same line. The Communist *Humanité* almost alone cautiously used on December 25 an AP telegram, and paraphrased Blum's well-meaning statement.

Moutet flew to Indo-China, and here he was wholly bamboozled by the Saigon Clique. He paid only a flying visit to Hanoi, staying there thirty hours, and then rushing back to France. General Morlière, who could have informed him of the real facts, had by a very strange coincidence been called to Saigon that day, and the personal letter from Ho Chi Minh offering to meet the French Minister and to open negotiations for a settlement on the basis of the agreement of March 6, 1946 was not delivered to him. Instead, Moutet made a statement implicitly approving Cochin-China separatism, and the d'Argenlieu-Moutet "dialogue" published in the *Monde* on December 29, 1946 already showed that the Minister of Overseas France had been won over by the men of Saigon. The peace offers made by the Vietminh wireless were dismissed a few days later by Moutet as "not serious". At Hanoi, he said, he had become wholly convinced of the premeditation of the Vietnamese *coup* against the French. "When I return to Paris, I shall endorse all that has been done by the French authorities in Indo-China who, following the instructions of the Government, have waited till the very last moment before intervening."

His attention had been skilfully directed to the spilt milk: to the alleged "premeditation" of Tu Ve's "revenge for Haiphong", and had been diverted from what really mattered: the peace offers made by the Vietminh wireless and by Ho Chi Minh himself whose personal letter to Moutet (while the latter was at Hanoi) had also been mysteriously "delayed". Only later was it learned that Ho's letter (when it finally reached its destination) was accompanied by a long memorandum including four precise clauses which, if accepted as a basis for discussion, could have put an end to hostilities immediately.

But Moutet had, in any case, already made up his mind. Both in his statements at Saigon and on his return to Paris, he had taken such a firm official line against Vietminh that Leclerc, who had also gone on a short visit to Indo-China, found himself in an awkward position for making any categorical statements. But three points emerge clearly to show that he was in disagreement with the Saigon Clique—and with Moutet: d'Argenlieu had strongly objected to Leclerc's visit to Indo-China at that stage; in a statement made at Saigon, Leclerc had differed from d'Argenlieu's line in making it clear that it was, in his opinion, useless to harp on "anti-Communism", and that France had better try to satisfy the nationalist aspirations of the Vietnamese (these aspirations being embodied most obviously in Vietminh); finally, when Blum offered him the post of High Commissioner in place of d'Argenlieu, he laid down conditions which were rejected at the insistence of the MRP, who (along with Moutet) had supported the Saigon Clique through thick and thin. For by this time Saigon was already preparing the "Bao Dai solution", the elaboration of which was to become the full-time job of M. Bollaert, who was to succeed d'Argenlieu as High Commissioner in April. M. Moutet was, in later months, often attacked at Socialist Congresses for his stupidity and his subservience to the colonialist clique; but the damage was done.

On January 11, after Moutet had failed to respond to Ho Chi Minh's appeals for an armistice, the Vietnamese Government officially announced that the "war for independence" had become inevitable. Nevertheless, in the months that followed, Ho Chi Minh and the Vietminh wireless continued to repeat that there was still time to stop the bloodshed; but all such proposals fell on deaf ears; the Pignons and the d'Argenlieus had already made up their minds that Bao Dai was their man. On May 14, 1947 M. Coste-Floret, the Minister of War, made his immortal statement that "there was no longer any military problem in Indo-China". M. Coste-Floret, that shining light of the MRP, was one of those French politicians, mostly of the MRP, who were more responsible than anyone for misinforming France on the state of affairs in Indo-China, and for prolonging the war till the final disaster of Dien Bien Phu seven years later.

It was the evil fate of Léon Blum and his Government in December 1946–January 1947 not to have stopped the war when it was still easy to do. But, owing to M. Moutet, no attempt was made even to establish contact with Ho Chi Minh, and 1947 was to open the era of sharp conflicts between France and the nationalist and anti-colonialist movements in several countries of the French Empire. Apart from the war in Indo-China, the year was to be marked by riots and massacres in Madagascar, followed by the expulsion from the French Parliament of the Madagascar Deputies and Senators and their incredible trial at Tananarive; soon afterwards came the famous Tangier speech by the Sultan of Morocco, who soon had it explained to him, through the appointment of General Juin as Resident-General at Rabat, that it was tactless, to say the least, to think, in 1947, in terms of the lofty principles of the Atlantic Charter.

In the eyes of many Frenchmen, the spectre of Communism was now stalking the length and breadth of the French Empire. It became part of the Cold War psychosis.

Little more need be said about the Blum Government. It stayed in office for only a month—until the election of Vincent Auriol to the Presidency of the Republic on January 16, 1947. Blum paid a visit to London, where he was received with almost royal honours, and had particularly cordial talks with Mr Attlee and Mr Bevin, who liked him better than they did M. Bidault; and he contributed towards a further *rapprochement* with Britain by laying the foundations for the subsequent Anglo-French alliance. As *The Times* suggested, in commenting on the rapid success of the Blum mission, it was important for France and Britain to co-ordinate their policies not only in Europe, but also *vis-à-vis* the Arab world, and in South-East Asia, where Burma and Indo-China presented very similar problems. What *The Times* did not yet foresee was that the two "problems" would be handled in entirely different ways.

Significantly enough, in France, the Blum Government made the biggest impression by "decreeing" a five per cent cut in prices, soon to be followed by another five per cent cut. There were enthusiastic comments to the effect that here at last was a coherent government, not cursed with *tripartisme*, and which was at last taking the price bull by the horns. Needless to say, these measures proved of no lasting value. They did, for a short time, tend to check a further rise in the cost of living, but by April it was openly admitted that the Blum experiment had failed.

CHAPTER NINE

"RAMADIER FIRES REDS"

BLUM had repeated, ever since forming his Government, that it was only a stop-gap (but *what* a stop-gap!) and that it would resign after the election, on January 16, of the President of the Republic. This election of the first President of the "Fourth" took place at Versailles on a bright sunny day and in the usual festive atmosphere. The Communists put forward no candidate, and M. Auriol was elected in the first round by an absolute majority of 452 (mostly Socialist and Communist) votes, the MRP candidate, M. Champetier de Ribes, receiving only 242 votes, and the other two candidates fewer still. In subsequent years, the Communists liked occasionally to remind M. Auriol, whenever he was nasty to them, that he owed his job to them.

As an elder statesman of the Third Republic, who stood for "stability", Auriol was, during his *septennat*, to exercise considerable influence on the course of events. He was wholly favourable to the "traditional" Republic; he had his two-volume book, *Hier . . . Demain*, which had been published soon after the Liberation, withdrawn from circulation because as President he thought it too bold on a number of economic and constitutional issues, and too severe in its criticism of certain men and institutions; and, in some respects, he was to become singularly conservative. In particular, his attitude to colonial questions sometimes greatly puzzled his Socialist friends. He was, for example, wholly in favour of the Bao Dai "solution" in Indo-China; he responded in a lukewarm way (or did not respond at all) to "progressive" proposals coming from Tunisia and Morocco; and persistently refused to exercise mercy in favour of Madagascar "rebels" like Raseta, even though the latter had been sentenced to life imprisonment in worse than suspect conditions and was a very sick man.

M. Ramadier (like M. Gouin, a typical rank-and-file politician, but one whose sound "republican instincts" were to prove of considerable importance in the real *crise du régime* that followed the municipal elections in October 1947) was known to the general public chiefly for his appalling mismanagement of the Food Ministry soon after the Liberation. With his grey *barbiche* and his platitudinous oratory, he was not impressive. Nevertheléss, it fell to his lot to form that heterogeneous government—the last French government to include the Communists—which was to prove such an important landmark in the history of the Fourth Republic.

As we look back on it, it seems absurd that the Communists should have insisted as much as they did on being included in the Government, for before long they were to realize that they could neither share in the Government's Indo-China policy, nor could they seriously support the continuation of Blum's policy of frozen wages. But it seems that in January 1947 they had not yet realized the full significance of Indo-China; also, they appear to have been carried away by the momentary popularity of the "five per cent cut" policy; above all, there had not yet been a final breach between East and West, and they probably hoped that they could still exercise influence from inside the Government against the threatening East-West split.

Although Thorez was again one of the Ministers of State, and the Communists also held the Ministries of Health, Labour and Reconstruction, as well as the long-coveted Ministry of Defence, their position in the Government was precarious. For one thing, M. Billoux's post as Minister of Defence was diluted, as it were, by the creation of the three full-fledged ministerial posts of War, Marine and Air held by members of other parties; and a large part of the press went on harping continuously on the "international anomaly" of having the Communists still included in the French Government. Also, before long, a distinction came to be established between the Communist *Ministers* and the Communist *Deputies*, who, on a number of issues, would now abstain from voting for the Government.

M. Raymond Aron, one of the most determined opponents of *tripartisme*, wrote in *Combat*[1] after the formation of the Ramadier Government that although, on the face of it, France had not yet chosen "between East and West", the choice could not be delayed much longer:

The composition of the Government explains the choice of this "middle of the road" policy. The three parties look to London, Moscow and Rome. ... There is a danger of Russian invasion plus American liberation, and

[1] M. Aron's association with *Combat* was a short-lived one; he soon joined the staff of the much more opulent *Figaro*, where he was more at home. It was during the worst of the Cold War years—1947 to 1950—that Raymond Aron exercised his greatest influence on French affairs as a "Western" propagandist, though one with strong Gaullist leanings. Admirers referred to him (somewhat exaggeratedly) as "the Walter Lippmann of France". Nevertheless, his *Figaro* editorials, as well as his books, notably *Le Grand Schisme*, published in 1948, were of some influence and were widely quoted in the British and American press. Though in his preface to James Burnham's *Containment or Liberation* (published in French in 1953) he agreed with its general argument, he still drew the line at preventive war against Russia!

the Government is trying to avoid anything that will aggravate this danger.... But it is not true to say that we depend *equally* on both the giants. For reconstruction we are largely dependent on the USA. Without American credits even the present mediocre standard of living of the French people would be impossible. Without them, there could also be no Monnet Plan. Even if the USSR wanted to, it could not replace the USA. Also, our Empire is dependent on American goodwill. Three-quarters of French opinion favours a Western orientation of our diplomacy.... It is a fact that we are situated in a zone where Anglo-American influence is dominant.

He went on to say that in cases where French interests were not involved, France could afford to remain "neutral", or to propose compromises; but in cases, such as Germany, where France's interests were directly involved, she was in the impossible position of having, in the present state of the French Government, either to agree, or to disagree, with everybody. The only possibility, therefore, was for France to take sides—and she should support Anglo-American policy: for "if Germany is not reconstructed with us, it may well be reconstructed against us"[2]—a classical phrase that was to be used on many other occasions, in slightly varying contexts, in future years!

But this was only a small beginning; by March the process of the Government's disintegration, under the influence of much wider world conflicts, was almost complete. On March 4, the Anglo-French Alliance was signed at Dunkirk by Mr. Bevin and M. Bidault, despite protests from the Communists that the problem of Germany should be settled first; a few days later, there was a violent uproar at the National Assembly over Indo-China, to be followed by two even more violent sessions at which Communists and other "Government supporters" came to blows; about the same time a few hundred young people (mostly Gaullists) demonstrated in the Champs-Elysées against the "Marxist terror"; on March 11 the four Communist Ministers resigned from the Belgian Government—it was an important straw in the wind, especially as it came the day before the announcement to Congress of the famous Truman Doctrine. The President not only asked for 400 million dollars for Greece and Turkey, but also laid down the principle of American support for the "free peoples of the world" who resisted against armed minorities aiming to subject them or "against outside pressure".

The Truman speech, made very pointedly on the eve of the Marshall-Molotov-Bevin-Bidault Conference in Moscow, prejudiced the outcome of this conference on Germany and Austria from the very start. France saw in the Truman statement a promise of American aid for any country "threatened by Communism", and a characteristic comment

[2] *Combat*, January 25 and February 7, 1947.

on the French situation was made (a little later in the year) by M. Mendès-France:

> The Communists are rendering us a great service. Because we have a "Communist danger", the Americans are making a tremendous effort to help us. We must keep up this indispensable Communist scare.[3]

Already, on March 18, Raymond Aron drew the obvious conclusions from the Truman statement on Greece and Turkey.

> The Government, composed of enemy parties, is presided over by Ramadier, a man of small authority. We depend on American aid.... The question is, How much can we get from Washington? ... The international situation has drastically changed. The Truman statement is a factor in the political game inside every country of the world. We knew all along that the Americans saw a threat to their own interests, and an advantage to the Soviet Union, in the progress made by *any* Communist Party in *any* country of the world; only people seldom dared to admit it openly. Now there can be no further misunderstanding. Yet, up till now, the Government, and indeed the whole French régime has been based on this camouflage of insoluble conflicts, and on compromises which were known to be dangerous, and were yet considered inevitable.[4]

And, a few days later, he complained that the "tragi-comedy" still continued, and that the Communists showed no signs of getting out— even though the Belgian and Italian Communists had done so. If the Communists did not wish to go into opposition, and if the other parties were unwilling to face the prospect of ruling without them, and without that trade union support, which so closely depended on the presence of the Communists in the Government,

> ... then it means that this régime has nothing in common with parliamentary government, and that its sole purpose is to camouflage conflicts and to delay solutions.... It's no use counting on the moderation of the Communists. Their going into opposition in Italy and Belgium shows that they are getting tougher. A surgical operation is needed.[5]

The whole situation was now beginning to evolve rapidly, and the much-desired "surgical operation" was not far off. The Communists hesitated for a long time to leave the Government, and were perhaps waiting for the outcome of the Four-Power Conference in Moscow. Things were, however, becoming more and more difficult every day. At the Moscow Conference, especially after Molotov refused to support the French claim on the Saar, the gulf between France and Russia widened. Economic conditions in France were again deteriorating; owing to a very bad winter, the food prospects were worse than they had been for a long time, and the bread ration had to be cut to 250

[3] J. Galtier-Boissiére, *Mon journal dans la grande pagaie* (Paris, 1950), p. 187.
[4] *Combat*, March 18, 1947.   [5] *Combat*, March 23, 1947.

grammes. Dollar credits were the great hope for making ends meet before the spring of 1948, when the food situation might become easier. The conflict over Indo-China inside the Government was growing acute.

And then two other major complications arose. At the end of March, serious riots broke out in Madagascar, and in these riots some 200 French people were killed. The local French troops, carried away by the (understandable) anger and panic of the settlers, reacted with the utmost violence, butchering the native population of a large part of the country: whole villages were wiped out and some 80,000 men, women, and children appear to have lost their lives.[6] Immediately it was asked who was to blame (for the killing of the French, of course); and a number of Madagascar Deputies were widely accused of having had something to do with "organizing" the rebellion. Before long, the question arose of raising their parliamentary immunity and having them tried on charges of conspiracy, etc. Being already in full disagreement with the MRP on French policy in Indo-China, the Communists were finding in the Madagascar affair another serious obstacle to their staying in the Government.

Secondly, de Gaulle suddenly reappeared on the political scene. In the presence of numerous generals, the British and Canadian Ambassadors and some 50,000 people, he presided over a ceremony at Bruneval in Normandy, commemorating the anniversary of a famous commando raid carried out by British, Canadian, and Free French troops in 1942. He concluded his speech with a somewhat cryptic phrase:

The day will come when, abandoning their sterile games and reforming that badly built framework in which the nation is losing its way and the State is discrediting itself, the great mass of Frenchmen will rally to France.

"*De Gaulle au pouvoir!*" the crowds at Bruneval shouted. A fortnight later, de Gaulle made another speech at Strasbourg, this time in the presence of several hundred thousand people, and announced the formation of the RPF, the Rassemblement du Peuple Français. All this was new and rather alarming. Already after the Bruneval speech Duclos remarked (revealing thereby a reluctance on the part of at least some of the Communists to "give up") that "when the Republic is in danger, it is better to be inside than outside". The MRP and the Socialists also got alarmed, not because de Gaulle was threatening the Communists, but because he was a menace to the Republic and to the MRP and the Socialists themselves.

[6] No official figures were published, but when in Parliament the figure of 80,000 was mentioned on several occasions, the government scarcely denied it. The Catholic monthly, *Esprit* has spoken repeatedly of the "massacre of 80,000 Malgaches" in March 1947.

For the last two or three weeks [M. Etienne Borne, the chief theorist of the MRP wrote in the *Aube* on April 13] the political leaders seem to be obsessed by hallucinations. . . . In their midst, they have suddenly caught sight of the ghost of Cæsar. . . .

It was, indeed, a serious matter for the MRP, for their voters were among those most likely to join de Gaulle. As for Blum, he was obsessed by the thought of de Gaulle demanding a plebiscite. True, no general election was due until 1951; but what if de Gaulle were now to claim that he represented *le pays réel*, as against *le pays légal*?

Meantime the Moscow Conference was coming to its fruitless end; but the Communists were still hesitating to leave. True, on April 17 there was a violent clash at a Cabinet meeting. Thorez, losing his temper, referred to Moutet as a "colonialist" and denounced as arbitrary the arrest of five Madagascar deputies and senators despite their parliamentary immunity. Teitgen (MRP) said he would ask parliament to raise their immunity, since the Madagascar Deputies had been arrested, as he put it, "in a state of continuous *flagrant délit*"—a fantastic "interpretation" of the relevant article in the Constitution. In that case, said the Communist ministers, they would leave the Government, as they did not wish to have anything further to do with the Government's colonial policy, in Indo-China, Madagascar or North Africa. They walked out in a huff, refusing to attend the luncheon given by the Prime Minister to celebrate Blum's 75th birthday. However, on the following day they decided to stay in the Government, but made it clear that the Communist Deputies were free not to vote for it in future; and the Communist Party issued a statement denouncing the arrest of the Madagascar Deputies as a violation of the Constitution (which, strictly speaking, it was).

Every day the partnership was becoming more and more uneasy. By May 1, the Moscow Conference had broken up in disorder, Molotov, in the words of one French commentator, "having never got over the Truman Message on Greece and Turkey" and "Marshall's hands also being tied by it".

The division of the world into Two Blocs [he wrote] is becoming more and more accentuated. . . . The nations who lost their freedom will not soon regain it; and the nations in need of bread and credits are no longer quite masters of their own destiny.[7]

And then came the straw that broke the loudly creaking back of *tripartisme*. On April 30, 20,000 Renault workers went on strike as a protest against the rising cost of living. Blum's policy of frozen prices and wages had clearly failed.

What were the Communist Ministers to do in the circumstances?

[7] Marcel Gimont in *Combat*, April 26, 1947.

Already they were more than disgruntled over Indo-China and Madagascar, and the breakdown of the Moscow Conference. To continue to support Ramadier's frozen wages policy, and *not* to support the reasonable demands of the Renault workers was too much in the circumstances. Many of the Communist leaders felt that *tripartisme* just could not continue any longer. There was a danger of their becoming unpopular with the working-class.

Already the Socialist *Populaire* and the MRP *Aube* had embarked on a smart bit of anti-Communist demagogy among the working-class by supporting the Renault strike while the Communist CGT was still discouraging it.

So the Communist *Ministers*—and not merely their *press*—came out in favour of the strikes, thus dissociating themselves officially from the "frozen wages" policy, and declaring the "Blum experiment" at an end, as far as they were concerned.

This gave Ramadier the "technical" excuse he had been looking for for officially "sacking" the Communists from his Government.

RAMADIER FIRES REDS—the headlines screamed throughout the USA—indeed, throughout the whole Free World. It was precisely what Ramadier had hoped would happen.

Yet this great turning-point in the history of the Fourth Republic was not as simple as it was deliberately made to look, and the circumstances in which the "Reds" were "fired" deserve to be examined a little more closely. For there was an economic side to it (as exemplified by the Renault strike), as well as a political one.

This is what a great authority like M. François Goguel wrote at the time:

French industrial production, after having made remarkable progress for eighteen or twenty months after the Liberation, reached a limit which it seemed unable to pass in present conditions. This was due to shortage of labour, and especially to shortage of coal. Because industrial production was insufficient, wages continued to be inadequate. If, for example, Renault could have produced three times as many cars as it has been producing, it would have been possible to increase wages. But the shortage in coal and raw materials made this impossible. . . .[8]

In short, the "coal bottlenecks" were mainly responsible for this state of affairs in most French industries. Secondly, said M. Goguel, the problem of wages might not have arisen in May 1947 but for numerous shortages, especially in bread and meat, as a result of which the effect of the "Blum" price cuts had become largely theoretical, since the working-class (like others) had to resort, for a number of

[8] *Esprit*, May 1947, p. 848.

essential commodities, to the black market. This, naturally, brought real wages down.

As said before, the Socialist and MRP papers had, in a demagogic spirit, supported the Renault strikers, even though the (predominantly Communist) CGT had discouraged the strike. Since the Socialists and MRP had embarked on a short-term anti-Communist manœuvre at Renault's, the Communists took advantage of this to come out in defence of the workers, and to prove their sincerity by quarrelling with the Government precisely on *this* issue, and by openly declaring the Blum experiment to have proved a failure. This at least was a consistent line to take in the circumstances, and was, electorally, a better *terrain de chute* than any other.

Not that, at heart, all Communists were equally favourable to the break-up of the Government. Goguel suggests that Thorez and Croizat, for instance (and probably Duclos) were in favour of continuing *tripartisme*, while Tillon was against it.

It is obvious, however, that the determining factor in the "expulsion" of the Communists from the French Government was the international situation.

What started it all [wrote Goguel] was the Truman Message to Congress.... All information from America agrees that a tidal wave of anti-Communism is today sweeping the country. The USA is undoubtedly determined to eliminate Communist influence not only in Central Europe and the Balkans, but in Western Europe as well.... In Moscow Molotov refused us the Saar, not for any specifically French reason, but simply to avoid even a partial agreement with the USA.... As a result France concluded with Britain and the USA a separate agreement which gives us a slightly larger quantity of German coal.... France's attitude therefore became very different from Russia's, and, to the Communists, this was a disquieting "departure" from Ramadier's Government programme of January 21.

To Goguel it was obvious that what France primarily needed were American credits for renewing her equipment; as well as Anglo-American-controlled coal, and American wheat (the latter till the spring of 1948); he also thought there was a clear connexion between the Truman Message and the beginning of de Gaulle's new campaign, with its primary objective of eliminating the Communists from the Government—to begin with.

In view of France's great economic requirements, it was obvious, Goguel said, that the Communists would in any case not have been able to stay in office much longer.

It is perhaps because they saw it clearly themselves that they provoked the crisis which has now eliminated them from the Government. The great question concerning the future is whether they will simply become an opposition party, within the constitutional framework of the Fourth Republic . . . or whether this elimination will assume much more violent forms. . . .

And, in conclusion, he asked the question that troubled many thinking Frenchmen at the time. Since, he said, the unity of action of the war-time Allies had broken up at almost the same time as the unity of action of the three great French parties, what would be the result of it all in the international field? Would France and Britain become the nucleus of a third international force, between American capitalism and Russian Communism, a force that would try to weaken the antagonism between the Big Two; or would France and Britain simply become "integrated" in an American "Western Bloc" wholly directed against Russia?

In any case, Goguel thought the break-up of *tripartisme* a serious matter; he hoped the Communists would remain a loyal opposition party, and refrain from any rash actions. But the responsibility of the rest of the country was equally great; in a country where $5\frac{1}{2}$ million people had voted for the Communists, the kind of professional anti-Communism practised elsewhere with impunity could, in France, lead only to bloodshed.[9]

We know now what the answer is to Goguel's question. Here also a certain "parallelism" could be observed. Since, in spite of everything, it never came to a shooting war between the USA and the USSR, it never came to a violent showdown in France between the Communists and the rest of the country.

Even so, it came very close to a clash when the Cold War was at its height, notably at the end of 1947. Like the Soviet Union, the French Communist Party also became extremely "isolated" for several years, and its members acutely sectarian and "unsociable", at least on the political (though less, on a personal) plane. But the attempt made by "French McCarthy's" to eliminate the French Communist Party artificially in 1952 produced a very unfavourable reaction in the country, where it was still considered "natural" for the working-class, at any rate, to vote Communist. In the last analysis, a widespread feeling of guilt *vis-à-vis* her working-class prevented France from trying to destroy the Communist Party, as well as the fear that the trouble involved might be too great. Perhaps there was also a certain "parallelism" between the reluctance to destroy the Communist Party and the objections to a preventive war against Russia.

[9] *Ibid.*, pp. 850–52.

CHAPTER TEN

MARSHALL'S "YES": MOLOTOV'S "NO"

BUT to return to 1947. It is not certain that in France the "firing" of the Communists from the Ramadier Government was greeted with the same unanimous rejoicing as abroad. For one thing, it put the Socialists in an awkward spot. Raymond Aron wondered whether the popular discontent "so far restrained by the CGT" would not blow up, and also whether the Socialist Party's "final divorce" from the Communists would not "widen still more the gulf between it and the bulk of the working-class".[1] No doubt, he added, it was an "unnatural" marriage, as could be seen from the extermination of democratic Socialism in Eastern Europe; even so, Aron wondered what would be the popular reaction to the Socialists' going into coalition with the bourgeois parties. He wondered—and so did the Socialists themselves. As for the "extermination" of Social Democracy in Eastern Europe, this was, of course, a theme that, in the following months and years, was to become increasingly topical with the elimination of Ferencz Nagy from the Hungarian Government, the trials of Petkov, Rajk and Kostov, and the Communist *coup* in Czechoslovakia, less than a year after the elimination of the Communists from the French Government.

At the National Council of the French Socialist Party on May 6, 1947, a large minority, led by Guy Mollet, was in favour of the immediate resignation of the Ramadier Government; the Communists, Mollet said, had left the Government because of "left-wing pressure", and he considered that the Socialists would be wrong to ignore this pressure. Blum and Ramadier, however, argued in favour of letting the Government carry on "under Socialist leadership"; it was, they argued, essential to do this if only in order to fight the Gaullist menace; their motion was carried by 2,529 votes to 2,125. This was, of course, fully consistent with Blum's "join up with America" policy; and he was fully aware of the numerous signs of more help coming from the United States in the near future.

Already, a few days later, Raymond Aron wrote:

The more or less genuine news of a vast "lend-lease of Peace" Plan that

[1] *Combat*, May 6, 1947.

America is about to produce has already let loose something of an ideological battle in France. Will Uncle Sam's dollars mean our loss of independence? ... The question asked is whether the USA hasn't any ulterior
motives....[2]

Meantime there were many significant new developments. Although
Bidault continued to say that he did not consider the split between East
and West to be final, and denied that there had been a "French volte-
face" at the Moscow Conference, the direction in which the world was
going was unmistakable. On May 14, Churchill made his "Europe
Arise" speech, and advocated the formation of the "United States of
Europe", Europe, in his words, meaning "Freedom, justice, honour,
duty, charity". He talked of France and Britain being Europe's principal "foundation members", advocated the "reintegration of Germany, with her industrial genius", in the Western world, and a
Franco-German reconciliation.

The speech was received in France with mixed feelings; to many
minds it savoured too much of a final split of Europe and of the world
into two hostile blocs.

Bidault remarked that "Europe" was "a very old idea"; Churchill,
he suggested, had invented nothing new; the great question was how
the scheme was to be "applied in practice". And he was still reluctant
to subscribe to Churchill's proposal that France join the Bizone. "The
deplorable prospect of peace being torn up must not yet be taken for
granted." As for Germany, as Albert Camus remarked at the time,
France's hatred had been succeeded by "an odd feeling of distrust and
vague resentment, mingled with weary indifference". Before being a
menace in itself, he wrote, Germany was now, first and foremost, a
pawn in the game between Russia and America; "the greatest problem of this century is the hostility between *these* two Powers".[3]

Finally, on June 5 came Marshall's Harvard speech. It was, naturally,
welcomed in France, as it was bound to be in a country in the throes
of economic difficulties and growing labour unrest. The intellectuals,
nevertheless, wondered what the proposals implied. Marshall's words
had sounded generous, but——. It must be said that economic conditions had, for some weeks, been exceptionally difficult despite the new
loan of 250 million dollars France had secured from the Bank of
Reconstruction (in payment, as Zhdanov was to say, for the expulsion
of the Communists from the Government). The food situation was
bad; bread rations had been reduced, and the black market had become
more active than ever. *Combat* ironically remarked that it was being
"struck at the very heart"—the Police were "rounding up the dangerous profiteers selling flowers, *croissants* and shoe-laces in the Metro".

[2] *Combat*, May 15, 1947.   [3] *Combat*, May 7, 1947.

President Auriol had addressed an impassioned appeal to the peasantry to "deliver, deliver your wheat, all your wheat. . . . We have no dollars, we have no coal. . . ." etc. On May 23 Ramadier had said that France would have to eat maize bread; owing to the frost that had ruined the winter wheat, the *crise du blé* could not be overcome until July 1948. In a number of places there had been food riots. At Lyon crowds of workers had invaded the Préfecture, crying *"Du pain, du pain!"* An *"anti-dirigisme"* offensive had been started by shop-keepers and small manufacturers, and for several days most shops were closed. On May 20, 80,000 dockers were on strike. A few days later, a strike broke out in gas and electricity; the railway strike, which had flared up at the end of May, broke out again all over France on June 8, not to end until a week later. The American press, minimizing the economic hardships of France, screamed about "the hand of Moscow"—an idea that had been prompted by M. Ramadier's own references to an "invisible conductor" of the strikes.

The Government had to make some minor concessions to the strikers, but they were only a temporary expedient. At any rate, it was clearer than ever that Blum's *politique de baisse* had completely failed. While making some concessions to the strikers (largely in the expectation of early help from the USA) the Ramadier Government also made some concessions to the enemies of *dirigisme*; thus the rationing of textiles, fertilizers, and tobacco was to be stopped on July 1, and that of petrol three months later.

The thing that, already by the middle of June, began to be referred to as the "Marshall Plan", though generally welcomed on ordinary bread-and-butter grounds, nevertheless gave rise to a good deal of mental confusion from the start. What was behind it? Taking their lead from *Pravda* which had said that the Marshall Plan was "merely a new version of the Truman Plan", the Communists were at first openly hostile. Thorez described the Marshall Plan as a "Western trap", while Pierre Courtade in *l'Humanité* wrote that the Truman doctrine and the Marshall Plan were inseparable:

Is this supposed to be that friendly aid which, as Marshall suggested, had no connexion with any ideologies? Whom have we got to believe—Truman or Marshall? Surely the two go together. To subscribe to the Marshall Plan without any guarantee is to accept that "world leadership", that Truman talked about. The Quai d'Orsay is not asking for even the most elementary guarantees.[4]

Non-Communist left-wing intellectuals thought it might be an excellent thing—if it really meant the organization of Europe, and not just of half-a-Europe, and if the scheme produced something more than

[4] *L'Humanité*, June 18, 1947.

merely a *coopérative de quémandeurs*—a "scroungers' co-operative", as Bourdet put it. But then *did* America intend Russia and Eastern Europe to be included in the Marshall Plan? Marshall had said so, but was not this, surely, in contradiction with the Truman doctrine?[5]

For a few days nobody could see quite clearly what was intended. Then Bidault declared that neither Britain nor France wished to see Europe "shrink", and he announced that he and Bevin had invited Molotov to come to Paris for three-power talks. Molotov's acceptance raised high hopes at first. The Communists suddenly began to pull their punches, and Thorez even denied having referred to the Marshall Plan as "a Western trap"—even though he had said so publicly only a few days before. Had he "spoken too soon"?

But it was no good. Unable or unwilling to treat Marshall Aid separately from the Truman doctrine, and suspecting that its purpose —as far as the East was concerned—was chiefly to extend American influence to Poland, Czechoslovakia, etc (hence his constant objection, throughout his five meetings with Bevin and Bidault, that the whole thing was incompatible with the Soviet conception of "national sovereignty"), Molotov said No. On July 2 he and his army of experts and advisers (whose very numbers suggested that Moscow had at first been willing to consider the matter seriously) flew back to Moscow. Before leaving, Molotov said that the talks might continue at UN.

Among the French non-Communist Left, the first reaction was to criticize Molotov severely: he had wrecked European co-operation; he had wrecked international solidarity: the Russians had no imagination; they were insular and preferred to lock themselves up in their own sphere. If they were proposing to discuss the matter at UN, it was only because they could use the veto there.[6] Opinion further to the Right was, however, relieved, rather than disappointed by Molotov's spectacular exit. The reaction of papers like *l'Aurore* and *Le Figaro* was that this "greatly simplified matters". On the whole, all that was anti-Communist in France heaved a sigh of relief. It was "simpler that way".

And yet this relief was, in many cases, not entirely free of a certain anxiety. Was there not something "un-French" in having to abandon all thought of compromise, all thought of holding some kind of "middle" position in the world, and in having to "choose"? This reluctance to commit France to an all-out pro-American policy, of hitching France to the American atom bomb—a highly characteristic French mood which was to be (somewhat inaccurately) described in future years as "neutralism"—already began to be expressed soon after Molotov's famous exit on July 2. Claude Bourdet, one of the most coherent exponents of this mood, wrote in *Combat* on July 6:

[5] *Combat*, June 17, 1947.   [6] *Combat*, July 4, 1947.

We are told that "we must choose"—choose between the USSR and the USA, between East and West, between the Right and Left, between de Gaulle and the Communists. Must we give up our desperate desire to represent a civilization on the narrow margin between the two worlds? . . . Very well, they say, but what are you going to do in case of war?

But since, Bourdet said, war was "still improbable",

it is perhaps much better not to "choose" yet. There is no reason why we should hurry to increase violent feelings by throwing into the scales, on either one side or the other, all our hopes and fears. . . . Perhaps this flimsy, this Utopian barrier formed by a few million Europeans, who wish to be neither with the "West" nor with the "East", may yet prove the insuperable obstacles to the disasters that threaten our epoch. . . .

As will be seen later, this state of mind, sometimes described as "neutralism", though never, at any time, an organized political force in France, was, nevertheless, something for which there was at least a little corner in the heart of nearly *every* Frenchman. "Neutralism" symbolized a curious French instinct of self-preservation at the height of the Cold War, and with the threat of a shooting war between Russia and America suspended over the world. Paradoxically enough, "neutralism" was, in its own way, as typically a French mood as were, before it, Maurras's *la France seule* and de Gaulle's "between East and West" foreign policy during the two years after the Liberation, with both of which there is a clear *psychological* (though *not* a political) link. Like the other two, "neutralism" was a simultaneous expression of France's physical inferiority complex and of her intellectual superiority complex.

On the whole, however, the time was not yet ripe for "neutralism". This became increasingly vocal and coherent in 1948 and 1949. But 1947 was a year of acute fears and violent hatreds. "Neutralist" moods were smothered by the urgent and desperate desire for American economic aid, by a sudden anti-Communist frenzy that seized the country, by the desire for *revanche* on the part of the bourgeoisie and the *petite bourgeoisie* after years of *tripartisme* and ineffectual *dirigisme*, and by de Gaulle's immensely successful, if only temporary, attempt to canalize all this anti-Communist rancour and this periodic French outburst of anti-parliamentarianism into the RPF, the Rassemblement de Peuple Français.

Never in the whole of French history had a municipal election been of such national and international significance as the municipal elections in October 1947 when suddenly nearly forty per cent of France went what was loosely called "Fascist". It was, in a way, the strangest and most baffling of all political phenomena in a country that was reputed to be politically mature. . . .

CHAPTER ELEVEN

THREE-CORNERED FIGHT: DE GAULLE, COMINFORM, "THIRD FORCE"

THE months that followed Molotov's exit from the Three-Power Conference on July 2 were the most difficult and confused in the whole post-war history of France. America had promised aid, but the aid was slow in coming, and economic hardships and discontent were growing. The bread ration, which had been reduced from 300 to 250 grammes on May 1, was again cut to a ludicrous 200 grammes, or less than half a pound. *Esprit* published an anonymous letter which it thought significant of certain "defeatist" moods in the middle of 1947, and in which the writer said he was looking back "with nostalgia" to the days of the German occupation, and which he concluded by quoting a phrase he had seen scribbled on a wall: *"Donnez-nous du beurre ... ou rendez-nous les Boches."* No doubt most people did not want the *Boche* back, but they wished Uncle Sam would hurry up.[1]

What is the state of mind in France? [*Combat* wrote in July 15]. The country seems to be divided into two. There are those who say that Marshall has "saved Europe". Dollars and machine tools, wheat and American cigarettes will pour into Europe now; and they don't care a hang what price we have to pay for this aid. And if you suggest that the USA might lay down political and economic conditions, you are immediately classed as a Communist sympathizer.

The *anti-dirigiste* offensive organized by the retail trade and by M. Gingembre's Federation of Small and Medium Manufacturers, the Communist losses in the Social Security elections, the new law introducing proportional representation on the *comités d'entreprise*, the emergence of new mushroom growths in the trade union movement such as the CNT or the dissident postal workers' federation; the Marshall Plan which had been joined by France without Russia participating, and the stampede of the middle class throughout France, and especially in Paris and the urban centres, to join de Gaulle were so many signs of a reaction against the post-Liberation tendency to give (at least on paper) preferential treatment to the working-class, and

[1] *Esprit*, May 1947, pp. 841-42.

against the aspirations towards "economic democracy". This reaction, though, on the face of it, directed against the Communists was, in reality, also directed against the working-class generally.

The tide has turned against the working-class [wrote Bourdet on July 19] and we are witnessing the gradual reappearance of the bourgeoisie in all its strength.

The French Socialists, fully aware of this drift, were more determined than ever (a) not to share in the unpopularity of the Communists and (b) to seek, in this way, to win over from the Communists as much as possible of their working-class support. In this, however, they failed.

Anti-Communism was the keynote of the Socialist Congress that met at Lyon in August, and if there was some disagreement between Mollet and Daniel Mayer on the conditions in which the Socialists should take part in the Government, the anti-Communism was general. "Unity of action", which was still talked about a year before, no longer meant anything. The presence of "fraternal delegations" composed of Hungarian, Rumanian, and Polish Socialist refugees was enough in itself to work up feeling against what began to be called "Stalinism". More and more frequently were the Communists referred to as *les staliniens*. Kravchenko's *I Chose Freedom* had become the most widely-read book in France, closely followed by *Darkness at Noon* and other Koestler books. The Kravchenko-Koestler era had opened in France, as elsewhere in Western Europe and America.

In September Petkov was sentenced to death and he was hanged a few days later. It was the first of a long series of post-war trials, which few failed to describe as "Koestlerian". Throughout France this anti-Soviet sentiment rebounded on the French Communists—or *vice versa*. Often it was hard to say at which end the resentment had begun. Most people swallowed Kravchenko uncritically, and were scarcely aware of the fact that Kravchenko's book was a mighty propaganda weapon in the hands of the State Department, in France as elsewhere.[2] No doubt this frantic anti-Sovietism and anti-Communism in France could not always be taken wholly at its face value. Like Mendès-France, many were saying: "Thank God for the Communists: the bigger a fuss we make over the 'Communist menace' the more dollars we shall get."

Socialists like Jean Texcier, no longer frightened of "capital enslavement", were willing to abandon *le patriotisme de la misère* for "Atlantic solidarity",[3] thus taking a more cheerful view of it than his fellow

[2] I remember a Western diplomat telling me in 1948 of the "excellent job" in which he had just taken part: "We have arranged to get two million copies of Kravchenko printed in Arabic, to be distributed to the whole Arab world."
[3] *Combat*, September 13, 1947.

editorialist, Claude Bourdet, who deplored the fact that so many Frenchmen were "getting silly" with their "frantic Americanism", but agreed that France would, unfortunately, "have to play up to the anti-Soviet demagogy in the USA if she wanted to get all the help she needed."[4] But American aid was slow in coming. There was some talk of "interim aid", but it seemed doubtful whether Congress would decide on any major aid until January 1948. M. Ramadier and his other Ministers were tying themselves in knots to prove to the American "Marshall Plan" emissaries how urgent France's needs were. I remember a humorous Italian diplomat telling me with a touch of gay cynicism of how he had been instructed by his Government to see Mr Clayton one day. "I went there. Waiting-room full of people. Like a dentist's waiting-room. An old chap sitting in a corner, looking as if he had bad tooth-ache. He'd been waiting fifty minutes. By Heaven, it was Ramadier, the French Prime Minister!"

Things were, indeed, in a mess. On September 30, M. Tanguy-Prigent, the Minister of Agriculture, admitted that the bread ration was shockingly low; the present wheat harvest was 33 million quintals, less than half the normal harvest; France's "immediate need" was 26 million quintals, and the Government was hoping to get 6 millions from the USA; talks had been started with the Argentine and the USSR, but "the latter has not yet replied". Measures had been taken for enlarging the area under wheat, and, all being well, things would improve by October 1948, but meantime——. (Which did not prevent the Government from keeping the municipal elections foremost in its mind: thus, during a few weeks before the elections, the "collection" of both wheat and taxes was greatly slowed down in the countryside, in anticipation of American wheat deliveries!)

Both internally and internationally the atmosphere was unhealthy. On both sides of the "curtain" people seemed to be in a state of jitters. The omniscient Madame Tabouis wrote in *France Libre* on September 18:

> We want to stop at any price the Third World War, which may break out at any moment. Even so, I don't think two million Russians will invade Western Europe. One of Marshall's right-hand men told me that he had warned the Russians: "Sixteen out of our 160 atom bombs will be dropped on you if——"

And Galtier-Boissière quoted on August 30, 1947, "one of France's greatest scientists" saying to him that the Americans now had about 60 atom bombs, and that there was only one way of "postponing the end of the world by a hundred years", and that was for the Americans

[4] *Combat*, October 1, 1947.

"to wipe out Russia immediately". Galtier-Boissière seemed to regret that there were still "democratic inhibitions" that made it difficult to do this.[5] A few die-hard Conservatives in England (for instance, Sir Andrew Duncan) were saying, about the same time, exactly the same thing (at least in private); and the ultimate purpose of a book like Kravchenko's (and many others) was to suggest the same idea to millions of people. In all kinds of ways an "atom bomb psychosis" was being worked up, and it is scarcely surprising that this psychosis in the West should have had a parallel development in the East.

While the Soviet Government was doing its utmost to minimize the danger of the atom bomb (the Soviet papers published articles about that time to show that the casualties at Hiroshima were so high only because Japanese houses were "made of plywood and cardboard") the first meeting of the Cominform in September 1947 "somewhere in Poland" showed that, in the eyes of the Kremlin, World War III was, if not certain, at any rate, probable, and that the Communist Parties of the West should do what they could to prevent it.

Its Declaration stated that the world had become divided into two camps, one "imperialist and anti-democratic", the aim of which was to bring about the world domination of American Imperialism, and "the destruction of democracy", and the other, "democratic and anti-imperialist" which must "undermine imperialism, strengthen democracy, and liquidate the remnants of Fascism". The "Truman-Marshall Plan" formed part of the imperialist technique of enslaving the world; and right-wing Socialists like Blum, Attlee and Bevin were merely providing a "democratic mask" for American imperialism. The Communist parties of the capitalist countries, the Declaration further said, "must now firmly carry the banner of national independence and sovereignty"; they must not "under-estimate their strength" and must not allow themselves to be "intimidated or blackmailed". There was "an immense distance between the imperialists' desire to start a new war and their possibilities for unleashing it"—because "the peoples of the world do not wish war".

Zhdanov, the chief Soviet representative at the Cominform meeting, dwelt on American air bases in a large number of countries (France was not among those he enumerated), on the Marshall Plan, which was merely a "camouflaged" version of the Truman Plan (which, he said, had created such an "unpleasant" impression in Europe that it had to be followed up by the Marshall Plan): on the fact that American "aid" almost automatically meant a change in the home and foreign policy of the "beneficiary" of this aid (e.g. France and Italy), and on the American plans for "reviving German militarism".

[5] Jean Galtier-Boissière, *Mon journal dans la grande pagaie* (Paris, 1950), p. 138.

Particularly in France and Italy [Zhdanov said] the Communist Parties must resist the plans of imperialist expansion and aggression all along the line—politically, economically and ideologically—and ... rally to them all the patriotic and democratic elements of their people.

He declared that he was not against American credits—provided these were not a means of enslaving the countries receiving them.

Duclos, who had gone to the Cominform meeting, together with Fajon, sounded uneasy, gloomy, and apologetic, despite a final flourish. He admitted that the French Communists had not denounced American imperialism with sufficient vigour, and had not shown up sufficiently the real reasons for which Ramadier had eliminated them from the Government. He admitted that the Communists were now faced with a vast anti-Communist coalition, stretching all the way "from de Gaulle to Ramadier", but said that they could "reasonably hope" to find some allies among the Socialist rank and file and "some others".

Duclos, who was the wittiest, most "moderate", "human", and "parliamentary" of the French Communist leaders, dwelt, during the greater part of his speech, on all the good the Communists had done to France while in office. He was clearly out of his element at the Cominform meeting, and seemed to feel singularly uneasy at the thought of all the hard days lying ahead for the French Communists, with the "tough" policy on which the Cominform was now expecting them to embark.

He must also have known that the presence of two French Communist leaders at the Cominform meeting would play into the hands of all the anti-Communists in France. Moreover, he knew that France sadly needed American aid, and that it was difficult to impress upon the French people that Marshall Aid was a bad thing, and his phrase, at the Cominform meeting, to the effect that "the demonstration of the possibility of dispensing with American aid would undoubtedly make a big impression" sounded particularly hollow. He almost openly admitted that while the French people were hostile to "enslavement", they were favourable to Marshall Aid, and that it would take some doing to explain to these people that the two were inseparable. In short, it was an unpopular sort of propaganda on which the French Communists were now being expected to embark.

The Communists in France had become increasingly isolated, and Duclos was fully conscious of it.

A three-cornered battle was now going on in France between the Government (which was soon to become the "Third Force"), the Communists and de Gaulle. De Gaulle, as leader of the RPF, had proclaimed the Communists to be Enemy No 1. This was strictly compatible with the internal and especially the international atmosphere of the latter half of 1947, and he was expecting his concentration on anti-Communism to yield rich dividends to his movement.

The rapid rise and almost equally rapid decline of the RPF is one of the strangest episodes in the history of post-war France. Looking back on de Gaulle's career, François Mauriac was later to say that the RPF was "the biggest mistake he had ever made". Mauriac admired de Gaulle as a man and as a great national figure, and it jarred on him to see de Gaulle—a noble, lonely figure—suddenly assuming the rôle of a cheap demagogue, exploiting to the utmost his personal prestige (rather than popularity—for he never succeeded in becoming really *popular*), the economic discontent in the country, the hankering for dollars, the temporary spell of anti-parliamentarism (a periodic ailment in France) the great anti-Communist vogue of 1947, and the desire for a "come-back" on the part of certain elements of the French bourgeoisie who had been, more or less, excluded from public affairs since the Liberation. It was one of the ironical jokes of French history that the men of Vichy should have looked to de Gaulle for their rehabilitation.

CHAPTER TWELVE

FULL SPEED TO THE RUBICON—BUT
NOT BEYOND

IT WAS André Malraux, the greatest intellectual ornament of the RPF (though, in electoral terms, a wholly useless ornament) who is credited with having said in 1949, when the great Gaullist movement was already in decline: "De Gaulle marched us full speed to the Rubicon, and then told us to get out our fishing-rods."[1] The disillusionment of a "revolutionary romantic" like Malraux is understandable enough, when one considers the spectacular rise of the RPF within a matter of a few months in 1947. Not since the days of Boulanger had anything like it been seen in France. But the truth is that a very large number of those who marched to the Rubicon decided, on second thoughts, that they would rather not cross it. The indecision was much less de Gaulle's than that of his followers. For there never was a more motley crew in France than the RPF's following in 1947, and if the RPF was "Fascist" in some of its avowed aims, and especially in its propaganda methods, the greater part of its following lacked the Fascist temperament. Among de Gaulle's followers there was only a very small minority of people who had much in common with the pre-war "leagues" like the Camelots du Roi or the Jeunesses Patriotes, and if de Gaulle received in 1947 the support of certain elements who had previously belonged to the Croix de Feu or to Pétain's *Légion*, this was not the most characteristic feature of the RPF. For one thing, de Gaulle had not yet made peace with Vichy even unofficially—though he was to do so before very long.

The most typical feature of the RPF in 1947 was its *mass* following; but, unlike the mass following of Hitler in 1933, it was half-hearted and full of mental reservations. The reasons for which nearly 40 per cent of the French people suddenly voted for de Gaulle were almost entirely *negative*: they voted for de Gaulle because they were discontented with economic conditions, or angry with the Communists, or so convinced that war was round the corner that they preferred to face the music under de Gaulle than under a mere M. Ramadier. It was not that they expected de Gaulle to save them from war; the strange thing is that de Gaulle did not, at any time, suggest that he could save them

---

[1] Jean Galtier-Boissière, *Mon journal dans la grande pagaie*, p. 258.

from it; the suggestion was rather that if war was to come (and de Gaulle seemed to think it highly probable) it would be better for France if he were in charge. In short, the sudden rise of the RPF was, at least in part, the manifestation of a widespread war psychosis, and of an obsession with the presence in France of a "Fifth Column". This was combined with a general disgruntlement over economic conditions, for which also "parliamentary government" and, by implication, the Communists were, in some way, to blame.

With economic conditions improving, with the danger of war receding, and with the Communists being driven into a sort of political ghetto, the decline of the RPF became inevitable. People began to think more coolly, and hard as they tried, could never quite discover what the advantages of a Gaullist régime would be—for, as a constructive programme, nothing was less precise than the programme of the RPF. But it made at least one thing clear: it would mean abandoning many old habits, freedoms and traditions which, after all, had a good deal to be said for them. Also, the very process of setting up a new régime might lead to no end of complications.

The most puzzling aspect of the RPF is this: What were the motives that prompted de Gaulle to embark on this venture? He was not a demagogue by natural inclination; yet the impression one had of him in 1947 was that he had made up his mind to go through all the motions and contortions of a demagogue; it was an unpleasant spectacle to those who had been impressed in the past by de Gaulle's austere dignity. Why did he do it? Was it his conviction that France was in mortal danger, and that as the Man of Destiny, he must go through these motions, however distasteful they were to him? Or did it all, at some stage, begin to flatter his vanity to think that a man with so little natural "political sex appeal" like himself could still succeed in carrying the people of France before him?—even though he knew, in reality, so very little about them. And lastly, did he think that since the American alliance and American aid were (as it then seemed to him, as to so many others) the most important thing for the survival of France, he was the best man to represent France and France's interests? If so (and a good deal suggests that he did think that), he miscalculated his chances very badly. Yet there is no doubt that, despite all the unpleasantness he had with the Americans during the war, he assumed in 1947 that Truman's America would gladly "accept" him. A part of the American press had given him that impression, and he spared no effort, during his 1947 campaign, to flatter America and to spout anti-Russian and anti-Communist propaganda.

If at Bruneval and Strasbourg he still pulled his punches, his attacks on the Parties and the Communists and his overtures to the United States were wholly "uninhibited" in the speeches he made at

Lille on June 29 and at Rennes on July 27. Each of his meetings, with its many thousands of people, its flags, beacons and elaborate ceremonial, was becoming more and more like a little "Nuremberg" (with the Cross of Lorraine being used in much the same way as the swastika); the organizers of the RPF meetings had obviously learned a few simple tricks from the late Dr Goebbels.

At Lille de Gaulle preached "*la concorde*" which, he said, would obviously exclude "*le jeu des partis*". The RPF was a "framework" into which all Frenchmen and Frenchwomen eager to serve their country—i.e., all other than the "separatists"—should flock. This was a totalitarian conception, if ever there was one. He exalted the freedom and democracy of the United States, whose intervention in Europe had been "provoked" by the aggressive designs of the Soviet Union.

At Rennes, he took great pains to explain why he had taken the Communists into his Government, why he had given them a chance to behave like decent French citizens; he admitted that they had played an important part in the Resistance, and that the Russian Army had been of decisive importance in the defeat of Nazi Germany; but, since then, things had changed:

Everything makes me believe that those who had the road of patriotic service thrown wide open to them, have now chosen to follow another road.

The Communists, he explained, had now become a Fifth Column, plotting to enslave France by totalitarian methods, and to turn her into a satellite of the Soviet Union. And he tried to make his listeners' flesh creep by the fact that a "vast bloc of 400 million people" was at less than 300 miles from the French border—a distance covered in two days by the cyclists of the *Tour de France*! The danger was immense. And meantime the "separatists" (as he called them) were doing their utmost to undermine France's diplomacy, her economy, and the unity and loyalty of the French Union. (For on Indo-China, North Africa, not to mention Madagascar, de Gaulle continued to hold the most die-hard views—and if anything was wrong in these places, it was easiest to blame the Communists.)

Of all de Gaulle's speeches that year, it was the Rennes speech that made the greatest impression. Among the other parties—from the Right to the Socialists inclusive—the anti-Communist Crusade was welcomed. It was instinctively felt by many that de Gaulle had struck the right note: in the conditions of 1947 it was popular to be anti-Communist. Only there was this snag: it was dangerous for the parliamentary parties to allow de Gaulle any sort of monopoly in extreme anti-Communism. They must therefore try to be as anti-Communist as he.

An interesting question was how the Socialists would react to the "anti-Communist crusade". It soon became apparent that if the Socialists disagreed with de Gaulle, it was not on this score. The Rennes speech gave rise to some melancholy reflections on the part of some of the Resistance leaders of the past.

A year ago [Bourdet wrote] such a speech would have strengthened the bonds between the Socialists and Communists. Now ... it will make no difference. The Rennes speech has come at a time when the enthusiasm of the Resistance has vanished, and when the most active political elements in the country are either discouraged, or have become integrated in the old parties. The RPF can therefore in no way become that revolutionary party of the Resistance, for which we prayed in the past.[2]

Far from representing the spirit of the Resistance (Bourdet added), the RPF tended to represent its very opposite, namely, conservatism. De Gaulle's worst mistake was to think all the time in terms of "unanimity". There might be "unanimous" anti-Communism in the country (apart from the 5½ million Communist voters) and even this was far from certain; but there was certainly no "unanimity" on anything else.

This was where de Gaulle's misunderstanding of France was greatest.

This notion of unanimity is an intellectual or a military concept; and, to de Gaulle, all divisions are artificial. Unfortunately for him, the existence of Parties is much more deeply engrained than he seems to think. The nation is, after all, divided into haves and have-nots, and, roughly speaking, the condition of the various groups is reflected in the parties. Also, among persons of the same social category, there are the sharpest moral and temperamental differences; and in the end we shall find that only people of a certain *type* will support his "Party".[3]

This is what should, logically, have happened; but in reality nearly 40 per cent of the French people "rallied" to the RPF in October 1947; which gave de Gaulle the illusion that he was right. However, he was right only on a short-term basis, thanks to the exceptional internal and international conditions of the time; in the long run, he was wrong, because "unanimity" in even slightly less abnormal conditions was not natural in France—not even among 40 per cent of her people.

The fact, however, remains that for at least three months it looked as if France might turn "Fascist" in a very short time. When, on August 25, the RPF announced that it would run candidates everywhere in the coming municipal elections, there was great excitement and bewilderment among the political parties. The Communists appealed to the Socialists for joint action—unsuccessfully, except in a

[2] *Combat,* July 30, 1947.   [3] *Combat,* August 26, 1947.

small number of constituencies. A part of the Radicals and of other centre groups hastened to jump on the Gaullist bandwagon; but the greatest alarm of all was caused among the MRP, who saw themselves losing a huge proportion of their voters. They attacked de Gaulle's "divisionist tactics", and denounced the assertion that the RPF was not a "party" as a piece of demagogy; of course, the RPF was a party —indeed, a *parti unique*, a thoroughly totalitarian conception. As the election approached, the Socialists also grew alarmed at the prospect of losing votes to de Gaulle; Guy Mollet denounced as a mockery the RPF, in which, he said, both people of the Resistance and former *collabos* had now found a common home; even so, he feared that, with economic discontent growing, many Socialists might be lured away by the RPF.

Meantime de Gaulle was speaking to ever-growing crowds all over France "proposing quasi-metaphysical remedies to cure all our ills",[4] while numerous Vichyites, sensing a turn of the tide thanks to de Gaulle, were beginning to publish arrogant articles and books, in which they almost claimed to have been good Gaullists—before de Gaulle!

There were, it is true, a few exceptions. A die-hard pro-Nazi like Maurice Bardèche, not so ready to forgive and forget, published at that time a malevolent, but unquestionably witty, book in which he wrote:

Your General de Gaulle now considers war with the USSR inevitable. Since the defence of honour and civilization is an acetylene torch you can apply to anything, he will turn it on the USSR, and we shall be asked to cheer. Needless to say, the Russian tanks will be at Bayonne in three weeks, or maybe in six days. General de Gaulle will then sing his famous aria about "the lost battle that does not mean defeat" and will ask us to shoot Russian colonels in the Paris metro. In this way we shall become heroes of the Resistance, and will give the Soviet command an excellent reason for sending a few million Frenchmen to Siberia in their desire to safeguard law and order in their occupied zone, while the rest of us will cheer our heads off as the atom bombs of the Liberation drop on our towns and factories; after which General de Gaulle will have a good chance of marching at the head of the Victory parade from the former site of the Arc de Triomphe to the wooden Memorial Hut marking the site of Notre-Dame, and of ruling over a tundra without towns or people, and highly suitable for supporting the edifice of the Future City.[5]

The most interesting point about this passage is the assertion that de Gaulle considered war with Russia inevitable; and there is much to show that if he did not think it inevitable, he at least thought it highly probable, and so did many of the 40 per cent of the electorate who voted for him. And Bardèche went so far as to accuse de Gaulle

[4] *Combat*, September 9, 1947.
[5] Maurice Bardèche, *Lettre à François Mauriac* (Paris, 1947), pp. 177–78.

of provoking the Russians and of encouraging the Americans to treat France as their "expendable" bridgehead in the anti-Russian Crusade. It is curious how, on this occasion, the ex-*collabo* saw eye to eye with the extreme Left; thus, the near-Communist *Franc-Tireur* (as it then was) denounced the RPF as "France's War Party—something we hadn't had up till now."[6]

For all that, the "landslide" was coming, and nothing seemed to be able to stop it. It was, according to traditional French standards, a quite baffling sight. On October 3, Bourdet wrote in an editorial, entitled *Le temps des imbéciles*:

> France is losing her last stronghold: that common sense and quiet irony through which the French voter always used to filter the more outrageous utterances of the various candidates. Now all posters are like patent-medicine advertisements promising to cure all ills. Communism, anti-Communism, and, above all, the Great Man. ...

And, a few days later, after de Gaulle's incendiary speech at Vincennes:

> De Gaulle had abandoned his "superior person" airs and is now playing for all he is worth on the sensitive nerves of the multitude. This crowd of artisans and small shopkeepers reacted with real ardour when he fulminated against the "separatists".... They are delighted when de Gaulle talks about "free enterprise" and makes fun of the parties.... Yet the RPF *is* a party; and Vincennes has perhaps shown what kind of party.... De Gaulle is preparing to conquer the middle class and a part of the peasantry. ... At Vincennes he also made it clear that he favoured the American bloc.

His anti-Communism, indeed, was going down particularly well with the *petite bourgeoisie*. Many wondered what he was proposing to do. Would he follow the American line of starting with an anti-Red purge in the civil service? Would strikes be prohibited and the trade unions dissolved? And would newspapers defending trade union freedom be muzzled? It looked like it. More and more, as the election campaign progressed, he was appealing to emotion, rather than to reason, encouraging fears, encouraging hatred. By the middle of October, a few days before the vote, even some of de Gaulle's severest critics took a de Gaulle dictatorship for granted. They talked of "historic fatality", of "everything being in de Gaulle's favour"; becoming emotional and mystical himself, Herbart proclaimed in *Combat* two days before the municipal elections: *"Il est en état de grâce historique"*, which was going rather far! But it *was* an emotional election—the nearest French approach to the German election of 1933; the electorate was voting for a *man*; against Communism and, by implication, for

6 *Franc-Tireur*, November 13, 1947.

the American Alliance and, only in the second place (if at all), for a change of régime.

The result of the election was, in the circumstances, highly paradoxical: the Communists, against whom all the thunder and lightning of the election campaign had been directed, both by de Gaulle and by many of the other candidates, held their own, while the MRP, the Radicals and the Right were almost wiped out: the RPF had simply taken their place—by catering, in the main, for precisely the same social groups! The Socialists alone among the Government parties suffered relatively small losses. The RPF gained control of the municipal councils of practically all the main cities of France; in Paris they secured 52 out of the 90 seats on the town council and the General's brother, M. Pierre de Gaulle, was to be elected its president. In Paris proper (with the support, it is true, of the Radicals and the Right) they had nearly 56 per cent of the votes, as against the Communists' 29 per cent, the Socialists' 9 per cent, and the MRP's 6 per cent.

Exact statistics are much more difficult to compile in municipal than in general elections in France, but most accounts agree that the Gaullists gathered between 38 and 39 per cent of the votes, the Communists 30 to 31 per cent; the Socialists 18 to 19 per cent, while the MRP were down to a mere 9 per cent, and the Radicals down to even less, most of their habitual voters having gone over to de Gaulle. The exceptionally high Gaullist vote in Paris was attributed partly to the exasperating bus and metro strike, just before the election, as a result of which, it was said, even some habitual left-wing (Socialist and even Communist) voters—especially the women among them—voted for "law and order". But, in the main, de Gaulle failed, hard as he tried, to get much working-class support. It is also significant that in the countryside, in which de Gaulle had not staged any "little Nurembergs", where living conditions were easier, and the Russia-America quarrel more remote, the Gaullist vote was smaller than in the cities.

By and large, almost the whole Right, most of the Radical voters and the bulk of the MRP had followed de Gaulle. After the municipal elections of October 19 (followed by the second ballot—which made little difference—a week later) there was some talk of the MRP having now been "cleansed" of all its "reactionary" elements, and of its having returned to the "Early-Christian" purity of the démocrates-chrétiens, Marc Sangnier's Sillon and the pre-war Aube. Those who said so were deceiving themselves, and were closing their eyes to the political professionalism of the Bidaults, Teitgens, Coste-Florets, Schuman(n)s and Letourneaux. There were also some who imagined that, since the Socialists could not possibly join up with the Communists, there could now be a truly democratic Third Force, a sort of "Socialist rassemblement" comprising the good and truly republican

Socialists, and the "socially-minded" MRP's, and the Radicals who were still "in the Jacobin tradition". All this was mere wishful thinking. There *was* going to develop a "Third Force", but not of the kind the well-meaning Left intellectuals were hoping for.

It was, of course, de Gaulle's bad luck that the elections of October 1947 should have been municipal elections, and not a General Election. No doubt, the result of the voting caused a sensation; the papers talked of the "De Gaulle Miracle"; the *New York Times* declared it to be "the victory of the Marshall Plan over the Fifth Column" (naturally, in saying so, it did not mean the MRP), while the New York *Daily Mirror* rapturously described it as "the best piece of news since the end of the war".[7]

Constitutionally, however, nothing had changed. De Gaulle had no claim to power. The National Assembly had been elected in 1946 for five years, barring an improbable dissolution. Still, it was awkward. The National Assembly no longer faithfully represented the country— except for the Socialists and Communists whose support in the country was roughly the same in 1947 as in 1946. Malraux, apparently on the spur of the moment, declared after the election results were known that the General would demand a nation-wide plebiscite or referendum; however, this was later denied. Short of a new election, the Gaullists could not rule the country—unless a sufficient number of Radicals and members of the Right joined the Gaullist *intergroupe* (on the "bigamy" principle) and won enough support from the MRP to form a "Gaullist" majority. But the MRP seemed, in the main, still hostile.

What finally wrecked de Gaulle's chances was his *manque de psychologie*. At the National Assembly there were plenty of people who were willing to make a deal with him; but the result of the elections went to his head, and he proceeded to behave with an intolerable arrogance which annoyed practically everybody in the National Assembly—even those who had been willing to consider some compromise. In a statement he issued on October 27 he declared that "an immense power had risen" in France; that the "régime of division and confusion" had been finally condemned, and that the Government now represented only a "feeble minority". A General Election was therefore necessary, and a drastic reform of the Constitution. The international situation was very serious and France could not wait.

Everybody knows that the State, as it is now constituted and conducted, is

[7] The British press was more reticent, the *Daily Mail* alone going into raptures. Even so, both *The Times* and the *Manchester Guardian* were more pleased than one might have expected. Reuter's chief correspondent in Paris, Mr Harold King, was known as a passionate admirer of General de Gaulle.

in danger of going to rack and ruin and of falling into a state of anarchy, the usual prelude to invasion.

Anyone who, for fear of the results of an Election, tried to dodge the issue by quibbling over the Constitution would, he said, merely make himself ridiculous. And anyway, the Constitution, for all its absurdity, made it possible for the Assembly to call for a new Election by a two-thirds majority. The statement ended with a vague threat that, whatever the Assembly decided, the RPF would continue to expand and organize itself for the salvation of France.

Such truculence was too much. In addition to de Gaulle's "ultimatum" came a (perhaps deliberately violent) speech by Duclos. Was he shooting a "Cominform line" on instructions? Or was this speech, in which he accused the French Government of having sold itself to American capitalism, and in which he said that Ramadier had ganged up with de Gaulle "in promising Washington the death certificate of the French Communist Party" deliberately intended to save Ramadier as a *lesser evil*, and calculated to encourage a Third Force course?[8] Many people at the time wondered—if only because, coming from an accomplished parliamentary debater like Duclos, the speech sounded almost deliberately stupid and clumsy. In any case, the Duclos speech, coming on top of the incredible de Gaulle ultimatum, saved the Ramadier Government. Some also wondered whether de Gaulle, too, wasn't playing a double game. What if he *intended* his ultimatum to be rejected, so as to gain time to gather even more strength, and not to make a bid for power until the American dollars had started pouring in? But the "ultimatum" was too much in character. One felt that for months de Gaulle had been itching to make just such a statement.

And then a curious thing happened, something "profoundly French", as many observers remarked at the time. It was the sudden awakening at the National Assembly, on that night of October 28, of a certain old "Third Republic" *mystique*—with Ramadier and Herriot saying they would defend the National Assembly against all threats and summonses. "*Notre Constitution . . . les lois républicaines . . .*" and so on. Absurd? Yes and no. Men like Herriot, who knew their provincial France much better than de Gaulle, foresaw what a disastrous effect his "ultimatum" would produce there. As Bourdet was to write on the following day:

De Gaulle has shocked the rank and file of our people—all those to whom a bad republic is still preferable to a good tyranny. In the days of the Resistance we sometimes sought refuge at Lyon and in the Mâcon country in the houses of people who still had pictures of Jules Ferry and Waldeck-Rousseau in their dining-rooms, and for whom the battle against Hitler and Pétain

[8] *Cf. Combat*, October 29, 1947.

was a continuation of the old *lutte républicaine*.... To us, who had been reared on Marx, Maurras or Maritain, this came as something of a revelation. Yet last night, Ramadier, that unwieldy old man, somehow reminded me of all this.... His unoriginal words seemed to echo across the decades, and reminded the young of the great crises the Republic had survived in the past. De Gaulle must no doubt be offended at the thought of being considered Enemy No 1 of the Republic he had helped to resurrect. Only he should know that one does not invent a régime by sheer intellectual processes in an old country like ours.[9]

Thus, bad timing and bad psychology on de Gaulle's part, as well as the impulsive and emotional nature of the vote of October 19 helped to produce this strange result: the RPF's influence began to decline almost from the moment it had achieved its greatest triumph. Many of its supporters had failed to be fascinated by the "little Nurembergs"; many were offended by the arrogance of de Gaulle's "Message" to Parliament, and, in so far as the RPF had a programme, it was disquieting in far too many respects. The implication that the Communist Party (still representing 30 per cent of the voters) would be dissolved, and the prospect of *lois d'exception* suggested the possibility of the "muzzling" being extended far beyond the Communists. It soon alarmed many of the Radicals who had supported de Gaulle on October 19; also, the virtual abolition of trade unionism and its replacement by a system of "capital-labour association", was ominously reminiscent of Vichy's *Charte de Travail* with its "single, apolitical, compulsory" syndicalism and of the paternalist formula of the "*syndicat-maison*".[10]

Also, there were disturbing omissions in the de Gaulle "programme", as revealed by his speeches. For fear of offending the peasantry and the middle class, he seemed to have ignored food profiteers (an important element among the middle class who supported him) and the crucial question of food prices and the cost of living; moreover, for fear of offending big business, he had not said much about the *féodalités*, rather suggesting that only those vested interests and pressure groups would be treated as *féodalités* which were anti-Gaullist. In so far as de Gaulle had any support from the Left (and men like Capitant, Soustelle and some others claimed to be "socially-minded") it still seemed obvious that he was now enjoying the support of all the elements *least* interested in social reforms; that, in 1944–5, de Gaulle had missed his chance of a great social New Deal, and that the most that could be expected from him now was a sort of paternalist policy in industry. When he spoke of cutting expenditure, there were many critics who now recalled that the inflation from which France

[9] *Combat*, October 29, 1947.
[10] F. Goguel in *Esprit*, December 1947, p. 886.

was suffering was very largely due to de Gaulle himself: he had started the rot by his refusal to endorse Mendès-France's plans for monetary reform, and had aggravated the financial situation still further by embarking on a policy of military *grandeur*.

Already by the end of the year, barely two months after de Gaulle's great triumph, and after the collapse of the great strikes of November–December, it was clear that a very large proportion of those who had voted for de Gaulle had given him only their temporary support. Notably, the "liberal" bourgeoisie, which had supported him both politically and financially, was not, as *Combat* put it, in a mood to hand over to him—"not unless it is finally convinced that the Communist threat is very serious indeed. *It will not call in the de Gaulle fire brigade unless it is absolutely sure that the house is really on fire*"—a remarkably shrewd diagnosis which was to prove strictly correct in the years that followed. Already the Schuman Government had, in December, put out the little fire of the strikes and had, thereby, weakened the Communists. Another fact that contributed to the weakening of the Communists was the split in the CGT, carried out with the blessing and encouragement of the Socialists.

In the increasingly orderly bourgeois democracy of 1949–52 the Gaullist grip was growing looser and looser; the RPF's success in the 1951 election was nothing like what de Gaulle had expected, and soon afterwards, there was a split in the RPF, a large proportion of its deputies rushing to the rescue of the most conservative government of the Fourth Republic, that of M. Pinay.

But long before that, Big Business had abandoned de Gaulle in favour of the "Third Force", and another factor of de Gaulle's decline was the fact that he gave the impression of considering World War III imminent.

As François Mauriac put it so well as early as November 23, 1947 in an interview in *Combat*:

We are in the middle of the Cold War between the USA and the USSR. Both our home policy and our foreign policy are bound up with it. But if it is to be War, then we are already living in the Apocalyptic Era—in which case it doesn't matter what we try ... and all political dialectics at this stage become irrelevant. I was for de Gaulle, as long as I thought that he could prevent us from taking sides in the Cold War. Now I am disconcerted, because de Gaulle seems to think that war is inevitable. If France and the world are to be saved, it can only be by people who do *not* consider war inevitable.

Mauriac also dreaded the prospect of "the Army being let loose [by de Gaulle] against the people", to commemorate, as it were, the centenary of 1848. Not that he had any great illusions about the Third Force, composed of small and mediocre people, who would today

... prove incapable of embarking on a dialogue with the French working-class which, though politically very mature, is apparently still under the Stalinist spell. ...

Actually, the Army was "let loose" against the "people" only a few days later—in a small way, it is true, and not by de Gaulle, but by the Socialist Minister of the Interior, M. Jules Moch.

CHAPTER THIRTEEN

THE SPLIT IN THE FRENCH WORKING-CLASS

O NE cannot emphasize too strongly the importance to the whole
future course of the Fourth Republic of the grave events of
November and December 1947; yet there is no recent French
crisis on which commentators, both French and foreign, were less lucid
and coherent.

Almost the entire press was in a state of incoherent emotional excitement, and even the most intelligent of the French papers at the time,
like *Le Monde* and *Combat*—which *did* try to provide a reasoned
analysis of what was happening—were often unable to see the wood
for the trees. As a writer in *Esprit* was to say in January 1948, one of
the tragedies of France during those crucial months was the absence of
a responsible press; all the papers did was either to scream about filthy
strikers in the pay of Moscow or (in the case of the Communist papers)
of filthy strike-breakers in the pay of Wall Street. Only *Franc-Tireur*
and *Combat*, it said, had taken the trouble of pointing out a few
elementary facts: the failure of all the governments since the Liberation to bring about a more equitable distribution of the national
income, and the fact that in the last six months of 1947, *wages had
risen by 19 per cent and prices by 51 per cent.*

It is, indeed, quite true that not only the press, but the general public
were carried away by slogans, by the fear of de Gaulle or admiration
for de Gaulle, by Communism and anti-Communism, by Communist
riots at Marseilles, by the applause and the execration that were produced by the military operations on which M. Moch ("Cavaignac" or
"Bloody Noske") embarked against the strikers; by the days and
nights of continuous uproar at the National Assembly, by railway sabotage and the disaster of the Paris-Lille express, which was derailed by
saboteurs (Communists or *agents-provocateurs?*) on the night of
December 6, and in which twenty people were killed.

The Ramadier Government, unable to cope with the situation any
longer, had given up on November 20, and after an attempt by Blum
to "save the country" (he was turned down by a small majority) a new
Government was formed by M. Robert Schuman a few days later; it
mobilized 80,000 soldiers and got the Assembly to pass, despite days

of violent obstruction from the Communists, a Bill which was calculated to break the strikes.

But all these events were no more than the outward manifestations of a profound crisis which was to shatter French working-class unity, and extend to the French working-class the conflict between America and Russia. As a result of it all, the French working-class was weakened; the Communists were driven into political isolation, and the Fourth Republic at last acquired all the characteristics of a bourgeois republic, at least outwardly wholly "integrated" in the American sphere of influence.

The sequence of events that brought about this fundamental change deserves to be closely examined. The quarrel between the Communists and the anti-Communists was, among other things, over the *nature* of the French strikes of November–December 1947. The Communists claimed that they were economic; the anti-Communists said they were political, and directed by the Cominform or the "hand of Moscow". But the truth is that the strikes were both economic and political. We shall presently see why.

In October 1947 the cost of living had sharply increased and most wages were well below any reasonable "vital minimum". The retail price index had risen officially between January and November from 856 to 1336; in practice, allowing for the black market, to an even higher figure. Wages, as already shown, were lagging far behind. This had happened many times before since the Liberation, but this time it was even worse than usual. All the French Governments had failed to try out any of the remedies that were proving effective in other countries: the "freezing" of assets, as in Belgium; the heavy and almost water-tight income-tax, as in Britain; or the virtual cancellation of unproductive bank-notes, as in Russia. Inflation had created in France a vicious circle in which a large part of the working-class grew to believe that ordinary strike methods were becoming wholly ineffective. Strikes could no longer be effective unless they exercised strong pressure on the State. In other words, it was not enough simply to ask for higher wages (which would soon be swallowed up by inflation); it was necessary to compel the Government to make major changes in its economic and financial *policy*. The only effective weapon, in such circumstances, was the general strike.

Ramadier had avoided, during his six months in office, a generalization of the strike movement, by yielding to the more "aggressive" of the trade unions. But this was a short-term hand-to-mouth policy, which merely contributed to a further rise in the cost of living, and to economic chaos.

As long as the Socialists and Communists were both in the Government, they could, despite many profound differences, still pull, more or less, the same way where the interests of the working-class were concerned—towards "greater social justice" and a progressive reform of the State in a manner favourable to the working-class. After the departure of the Communists from the Government, the "revolutionary" nature of the Communists and the "reformist" nature of the Socialists became accentuated. To the Communists, now in opposition, the general strike was a weapon to be seriously considered; the Socialists, now full of cautious "Third Force" ideas (encouraged by Blum who was warning them not to play into the hands of de Gaulle, "the most immediate enemy") were dead against the general strike. As Paul Fraisse was to write some time later:

These two tendencies clearly emerged at the CGT meetings on November 12 and 13. The [Communist] majority ... proposed a plan the immediate purpose of which was to get the government to discuss the "vital minimum", and other general financial and economic problems, in short, the very basis of the Government's wages policy. But since they had no great illusions on the Government's willingness to agree to this, they ... also favoured a nation-wide agitation which would intimidate the Government.... As against this ... Cappocci, the spokesman of the [Socialist] minority declared that he considered the general strike "excessive", since it would not, in itself, create conditions for adjusting wages and production in 48 hours or even a week.... "If you really want to achieve something else [by means of the general strike] then say so. It will mean throwing the doors wide open to one or another kind of dictatorship."[1]

This was already the prelude to the split in the CGT between the majority, chiefly representing the industrial proletariat and the minority, chiefly representing the employee and the small Government servant class. The respective attitudes of the two to the Cold War also differed widely.

Two days later, on November 14, the Ramadier Government, scarcely knowing what to do, decided, of all things, to start "defending the franc"—by abolishing the coal subsidy (with the result that the price of coal rose overnight by some 40 per cent), and to increase the price of gas, electricity and all transport fares. This started a wave of strikes, in Paris, in the coal-mining country, and other areas. At Marseilles the strikes assumed the proportions of a major insurrection.

The new Government, under M. Schuman, thought it would kill two birds with one stone: get very tough with the Communists, and so make an excellent impression in the United States, and, at the same time, steal de Gaulle's trump card—his anti-Communism. Aware of the offensive that the Schuman-Moch Government was preparing, numerous CGT federations tried to stimulate the strike artificially, launching strike orders indiscriminately all over the country. The

[1] *Esprit*, January 1948, p. 4.

socialist minority, alarmed at the prospect of a "Communist victory", tried, on the contrary, to restrain the strike. Jouhaux, the leader of this minority, went so far as to hope that "if the working-class showed its moderation, the Government would not prove ungrateful".[2]

The Government, and particularly M. Moch, now made it obvious that it was not fighting the strikers, but "the Communists"; it was hoping to take advantage of the divisions among the working-class and also of the strikers' poverty, and their inability to hold out for long. There was heavy fighting in the mining areas between strikers and the CRS guards, who had been sent there to "guarantee the freedom to work"; further, the Schuman Government proposed an anti-strike Bill, the scope of which was so wide that the Assembly refused to pass it without drastic amendments. In the course of the discussions, which were by far the stormiest in recent years, the Communists not only treated Schuman as "Badinguet" (Napoleon III) but also recalled that he had served in the first world war as a German officer, calling him *Boche* and *Pickelhaube*. The anti-strike Bill was such that, for a few days, the Communist and non-Communist strikers were about to sink their differences. There were riots at Valence, Marseilles and elsewhere. In some places the Communist strikers invaded public buildings, notably at Marseilles, where the capture of the town council by the Gaullists as a result of the municipal election had caused intense resentment.

However, by December 9, the strike was broken, the number of men still on strike had fallen from three million to one million, and the National Strike Committee, representing the CGT majority, published a long statement in which it recognized its defeat. It pointed out that some minor concessions had been extracted from the Government, but that the latter had not committed itself to any measures guaranteeing the stability of real wages. It spoke bitterly of the unprecedented mobilization of troops and police against the strikers and said that the dead and wounded among the latter "ran into thousands". It also spoke bitterly of the strike-breakers, and stressed the need to fight for trade-union unity.

This unity had, indeed, been broken. It was, in the last analysis, the fault of both the Communists and the anti-Communists, who had both put their political considerations first and their trade-union interests second.

The Communists, more concerned with international affairs than with the internal situation, suddenly decided to exploit the strikes, for which they had not been prepared, and to force the pace. Thus they tried to involve many workers in the strike against their will, which is always unpopular with the French working-class.

[2] *Le Peuple*, December 9, 1947, quoted by *Esprit*, January 1948, p. 6.

The anti-Communists, on the other hand, scared of this Communist "activism", tried to pretend to themselves that reformism could settle everything and that the general strike was "excessive", without realizing the reactionary nature of the Schuman Government.... It was a mistake to disavow the strike movement, even though it had started in unfavourable conditions. It was also a mistake to forget that it is useless to try to fight on two fronts, losing sight of the fact that the real enemies of the working-class were not the Communists.... Their mistake was at least as great as that of the Communists.[3]

The split in the CGT had now become inevitable. The anti-Communists had, for a long time, complained of the tendency by the Communists to capture all the key positions. Although the new trade union federation, the CGT-Force Ouvrière was likely to be, internally, more democratic than the old CGT,

... it is liable to be handicapped by the predominance in it of the employee element over the *ouvrier* element, and especially by its resentment against the Communists, which will make it hesitate to embark on the necessary united action with the CGT either in favour of better conditions or against any neo-Fascist activities.[4]

The CGT-Force Ouvrière Federation was duly set up soon afterwards. French trade unionism, in which the CGT and the Catholic CFTC had co-operated fairly well after the Liberation, was now split into three groups, each corresponding to its political counterpart in the National Assembly: the CGT was now almost purely Communist; the CGT-FO, though claiming to be "purely syndicalist" was in reality an annex of the Socialist Party, while the CFTC was linked with the MRP—though, it must be said, much more "Leftist" than the bulk of the MRP's parliamentary group. On December 4, when the strikes were nearing their end, Mr Foster Dulles (who was one of the US representatives at the abortive Four-Power talks in London) arrived in Paris, and had talks with members of the Government and with de Gaulle. At a press conference he declared that "what was happening in France was far more important than what was happening in London" (at the Four-Power Conference on Germany). He seemed pleased at the way things were going. American papers reported that during the Dulles-de Gaulle meeting the question had been discussed of "reviving Germany" which both (it was reported) "considered essential"; they also agreed on the necessity of an Anglo-American-French military alliance—rather suggesting that war was highly probable.[5]

By a curious "coincidence", Franco-Soviet trade relations were

[3] *Esprit*, January 1948, p. 9.   [4] *Ibid.*, p. 10.
[5] *Cf. Combat*, December 10, 1947.

broken off during the same week; the initiative for this had come from the Russians in reply to the "hostile attitude" of the French Government which, on November 27, had asked the Russians to withdraw their military Repatriation Mission, and have it replaced by civilians, the Russian military having been engaged in "subversive activities". Also, during the same week, swarms of police, preceded by Sherman tanks raided the Soviet repatriation camp of Beauregard, on the ground that persons of French nationality were being smuggled to Russia, and that there was an "arms dump" in the camp. All this military display was quite absurd, and the reasons given wholly irrelevant, as it turned out; but it made the "right impression". This raid on the Beauregard Camp was preceded by Moscow's decision to withdraw the Soviet Repatriation Mission in France altogether, and by the demand that the French Repatriation Mission in the USSR be withdrawn. The head of this Mission, Lieut.-Col. Marquié, at a press conference in Moscow, disavowed the French Government, saying it was deliberately sabotaging the useful work done by the Repatriation Mission simply in order to please the Americans; Jean Champenois, the AFP correspondent in Moscow, who had expressed his agreement with Marquié, was promptly sacked by the Agency: Marquié, on landing in France some time later, was sent to prison. The Cold War was in full swing, and on December 16 Reuter's Washington correspondent stated, much to the delight of some of the Right-wing papers in France, that, according to well-informed American sources, France was about to break off diplomatic relations with the USSR.

It did not come to that; but, in the eyes of Washington and Mr Dulles, the French were behaving just as America was expecting them to behave; getting tough with the Communists and being thoroughly rude to the Russians. The split in the French trade union federation seemed to delight the USA particularly. Although it was strongly suspected that American funds had had something to do with it, it was not until some years later that this was openly admitted. In the winter of 1953 Mr George Meany, the new leader of the AF of L declared, in a speech at the Washington Press Club:

We also have a great part to play abroad, as important, if not more important, than that of the State Department. I am proud to tell you—for we may reveal this now—that it was thanks to the money of American workers—the workers of Detroit and elsewhere—that we were able to create a split, important to all of us, in the French CGT, by creating the Force Ouvrière Federation.[6]

During the Cold War years, the State Department, either directly or acting through the AF of L, was going to subsidize a good many other

---

[6] Jean Davidson, *Correspondant à Washington* (Paris, 1954), p. 56.

"Left-wing" organizations in France. The Socialist *Populaire*, in particular, openly admitted that it had received funds from American trade unions "and other friends abroad".

At the end of 1947 the stage was set for what was to be known for a time as "Marshallized France". Thanks to Marshall Aid, the Fourth Republic was "returning to normal", and was in many ways scarcely distinguishable from the Third Republic, eating and drinking more than she did in the crazy years of *tripartisme*; neglecting her working-class (who were, however, also picking up some crumbs from the Marshall feast), and neglecting her capital investments, but feeling relatively contented, though not too proud.

Part IV

FRANCE IN THE COLD WAR
(1948–50)

CHAPTER ONE

THE GAP BETWEEN OFFICIAL POLICY AND PUBLIC SENTIMENT

A T THE time of the Liberation, France had embarked on a rough and unfamiliar road, which was to hold many surprises in store. Looking back on it, at the beginning of 1948, she could recall some of the principal landmarks: the defeat of "revolution" by "status quo"; de Gaulle's sudden exit; the rise and fall of *tripartisme*; the breakdown of de Gaulle's German policy and of his policy of "mediation" and *grandeur*; the beginning of the war in Indo-China; the Truman Doctrine and the Marshall Plan in the West; and the creation of the Cominform in the East; the re-emergence of de Gaulle, now as the leader of a totalitarian movement, the birth of the Third Force, and the great strikes at the end of 1947, followed by a split in the trade union movement and the half-voluntary, half-forced withdrawal of the Communists into a political "ghetto".

The mountain road now emerged on to a long, wide plain, the road became less rough, and there were fewer landmarks. It was a long and windy plain where, for years, France was to be tossed by the winds of the cold war. Internationally her rôle had now become almost entirely passive; in home affairs, she had started on a period known as *immobilisme*, in which government after government preferred to shelve problems, rather than try to solve them—a method in the pursuit of which they were greatly helped by American Aid. Without Marshall Aid, a relatively quiet year under the premiership of the somnolent M. Queuille would have been inconceivable.

If, between the two world wars, the major decisions of French Government policy were of world-wide importance, the same was no longer true—if only because the principal decisions—except in the colonial field—were not taken by Paris, but by Washington. Also, if it did matter to the world during the first few post-war years what kind of political and social system was to crystallize in France, the answer to this question had—at least provisionally—been supplied by the beginning of 1948. The Fourth Republic, though still sharply criticized by the Communists on the Left, and openly challenged by de Gaulle on the Right, was now a bourgeois democracy, in which the Socialist veneer of 1944–7 had worn very thin indeed; and it was, on the face of it, a satellite of the United States, its policy largely and sometimes wholly dependent on Washington.

During this "flat" period of *immobilisme* which may be said to have stretched right on to the middle of 1954, the political personnel of France was not outstanding. Apart from de Gaulle—whose prestige was to decline slowly but surely from the time of his spectacular triumph of October 1947—and (at the other extreme) a few of the Communist leaders, notably Thorez and Duclos—there were very few striking personalities in the political arena. Cartoonists wrung their hands in despair. Before the war they had at least a dozen to choose from—but who were the familiar figures now? It wasn't very funny to draw a tiny Bidault with a heavily-shaded nose, or a Schuman who looked like Donald Duck; anyway, the shaded nose was a libel, and Schuman couldn't help *really* looking like Donald Duck. As Foreign Minister during a large part of the time, Bidault was inevitably "known", both in France and abroad, but he was not considered, either at home or abroad, a mental heavyweight. The thought of it made him suffer, and with his petulance, his "bad conscience", his frustrated ambitions, his "split personality" and his "kinks", Bidault is one of the strangest and perhaps most tragic figures of the Fourth Republic—a man whose good intentions somehow always turned sour.

Schuman was, for a time, built up—especially in the American press —as a major statesman, and as "European No 1"; but he was scarcely popular in France (for one thing, his Luxembourg accent was distressingly Germanic), and few responsible statesmen have uttered so many emphatic words as he (for instance, on German rearmament being "out of the question", or on the coming "independence" of Tunisia) which, soon afterwards, had to be eaten without further ado.

Léon Blum, now the darling of Washington and of the anti-Communist bourgeoisie, ended in 1950 his life of personal success and immense political failure in an atmosphere of ill-concealed frustration.

There were also a few other survivors of the Third Republic, who could be impressive at times—Herriot, when he impersonated the "grand traditions" of the Republic; or Paul Reynaud when (despite the unpleasant associations his name inevitably aroused) he gave one of his incisive analyses of France's economic troubles or of the strategic implications of the "atomic age". There were also a few others—Jules Moch, an almost pathetically unlovable figure, but whose administrative ability and whose bitter intensity in dealing with both Gaullists and Communists could not fail to impress.

The rest of them were not very interesting. "Old man" Queuille was quiet, dull, and reassuringly old-fashioned; Pleven, for all his ambition to be the blue-eyed boy of Washington, and his love of intrigue both against Britain and his fellow ministers, was singularly colourless—a slightly "Americanized" business man who, by a lucky fluke, happened to be in London in June 1940, and had had the sense to "join" de Gaulle. Then there was René Mayer, the chief exponent of economic liberalism, the "colonialist" and the "gravedigger of economic democracy", as somebody described him. He was a curious mixture of the "Jewish banker" belonging to the Rothschild family, and the high official of the Conseil d'État, well-groomed and pompous.

Some of the younger politicians, like Bacon and Buron of the left wing of the MRP, or Edgar Faure and François Mitterrand looked promising—but they were still only beginners. Then there were a few like Teitgen, Lecourt, and de Menthon among the MRP, or Christian Pineau and Daniel Mayer among the Socialists, who were still remembered for their Resistance record; but the Resistance was now a thing of the past, and to have been in it was almost becoming a liability. A unique place was held by Mendès-France, who, around 1950, re-emerged as the sharpest critic of the entire Government policy of France, and whose infrequent speeches came to be regarded as political events.

And yet, despite the mediocrity of the political personnel France still carried a great deal of weight in world affairs—not so much because of her governments, as in spite of them. Historically, this was one of the most significant features of the Fourth Republic.

For what mattered in practice were less the speeches made by M. Queuille or M. Schuman than the corrective pressure exercised on the governments by *public sentiment*, a sentiment partly reflected, and partly created, by the French intellectuals and, to a lesser extent, by the administrative *cadres*, who kept their ears to the ground.

Thus M. Pleven could kow-tow to President Truman till his back ached; this kow-towing brought in dollars which, on a short-term basis, were helpful; it did not fundamentally alter the opposition of French public opinion to war and to satellization. *For, in the last analysis, the most important thing that France did during the Cold War years was (a) to put up a certain passive resistance to the pursuit of any dangerous foreign policy which might lead to war, (b) to reassure the Russians that Europe was not seriously contemplating a "Crusade", and that it was therefore unnecessary for them to take preventive action; and (c) to render "dynamic" generals and Senators in the United States sufficiently distrustful of France and of Europe generally, to make them think twice before confidently embarking on World War III.* For if, in 1948, Russia still seemed the biggest war menace, by 1949 the danger coming from "dynamic" U.S. generals seemed as great, if not greater. MacArthur was to confirm these suspicions soon afterward in Korea. On the other hand, it was the relative indifference to the war in Indo-China ("The

French public, I regret to say, doesn't give a damn about it—*il s'en fout éperdument"*, Guy Mollet once remarked) that enabled the MRP ministers to go ahead with their disastrous policy.

No doubt, if one is to judge, for instance, by the press, there were people who, either sincerely or for purely financial reasons, were 100 per cent pro-American. And yet, although their frantic anti-Communism was perfectly sincere, it is impossible to assert that even the most die-hard anti-Communists in France wanted a show-down with Russia—if only because there was never an absolute conviction that Russia could be defeated without France having, in the interval, become the atomic battlefield between the Big Two. Average bourgeois opinion—which, it must be said, stretched far to the Left, right into the ranks of the Socialist Party—was anti-Communist and "pro-Western", but, at the same time, "anti-war"; the Communists, for their part, were "anti-war", but pro-Russian; at the same time, their hold on the working-class, and the partial influence they still succeeded in exercising on much wider sections of public opinion, came precisely from their skilful exploitation of the anti-war feeling in the country. But perhaps the most significant phenomenon in France during those years—1948–50—when, in Thorez's phrase at the Genevilliers Congress (two months before the outbreak of the Korean War) peace was "suspended by a thread"—was the outbreak of what is popularly known as "neutralism".

Neutralism, as a strategic and political doctrine, had its exponents, notably Claude Bourdet, first in *Combat* and later in *L'Observateur*. But it was not these theories and doctrines about turning Western Europe into a big Sweden, with an "armed neutrality" covered by a US guarantee, that mattered in practice. What mattered was that these "neutralist" theories represented a rationalization, perhaps an over-rationalization, of the sentiment prevalent among an immense number of people in France—their plague-on-both-your-houses attitude, their *qu'on nous foute la paix*; their eagerness to accept American aid, but their fundamental dislike of the counterparts of this aid, such as the Atlantic Pact, complete with the highly distasteful establishment of American bomber bases not only in Morocco but in the very heart of provincial France. To have Americans established at Bordeaux, and La Rochelle and even Châteauroux—no Frenchmen could *like* it.

For a time, especially in 1948–9, the press tried to work up popular interest in "Europe"—in "Western Union", the "United States of Europe", the European Assembly, the Council of Europe, and "Federalism" generally. Traditionally, France had had, since Napoleonic days, a soft spot for "Europe"; yet it was an excess of credulity and an excess of wishful thinking if M. Bidault and M. Spaak really expected France to burst into enthusiasm the day they announced: "Today

Europe was born". For what kind of Europe was it? Was it a consecration of the final division of Europe in two? Did it mean ganging up with Germany, as recommended by Churchill, whose own country would, in practice, have little or nothing to do with this "Europe"? Or was it to be a Little Europe, a sort of ideological Fritalux-plus-Adenauer under Vatican supervision? The memory of Briand had made the conception of "Europe" seem Utopian to many, while the memory of Hitler had made it suspect. In the eyes of the Communists, Briand's Europe was indeed little better than Hitler's, since Locarno, in their view, already carried the germs of Munich and of the "free-hand-in-the-East". If the late Professor Joad liked to describe himself as "the only sincere British Federalist", there were not so very many more in France—even though, at the height of the Federalist boom in 1948 there were at least eighteen Federalist societies in the country! As Emmanuel Mounier was to write in *Esprit* at the end of 1948, European Federalism was an excellent idea; it had, nevertheless, to be feared that it was being treated as something of a Cold War racket by rather too many highly suspect characters, and that caution was therefore to be recommended.

The Schuman Plan of April 1950 was much more concrete than the Federalist hot air; but it still failed to arouse the interest it perhaps deserved, if only because it was technically too obscure for the layman, and was rendered suspect in the eyes of many by the "Big Business" atmosphere surrounding it, as well as by Britain's refusal to have anything to do with it. However, the Schuman Plan belongs to a different period, and is only remotely connected with the amateurish or idealistic Federalism of 1948-9.

This highly critical attitude of the greater part of the French intellectuals not only to this "federalism", but also to the Atlantic Pact and to the "Free World" as a whole, with its Hiss Trial, its witch-hunts (which, in a small way, were beginning to spread to Western Europe), and its nascent McCarthyism was something that both reflected *and* instructed public opinion. Numerous papers tended to be "neutralist" —i.e. anti-war, and critical of the Atlantic Pact, and kicking against the dangers of the economic, political and cultural satellization of France (among them *Combat, Une Semaine dans le Monde*—then edited by Beuve-Méry—*Esprit, Temps Modernes*, and, from the beginning of 1950, *L'Observateur*). Their influence—as well as that of Jacques Gascuel's *Perspectives*, an elaborate and expensive economic and political "news-letter", that went to every newspaper and every important business firm, as well as to all leading politicians—was out of all proportion to their limited circulation. But by far the most important influence in this respect was the *Monde*, with its "neutralist" articles by Beuve-Méry, Jacques Madaule, Etienne Gilson, Maurice

Duverger, J. J. Servan-Schreiber, Jacques Kayser, and other well-known writers, as well as by its staff of brilliant editorialists and foreign correspondents. The influence of its 150,000 copies was exercised not only on its readers (who comprised the whole politically educated class of France, and practically everybody in the upper ranks of the administrative and political personnel of the country) but, in varying degrees, on the rest of the French papers, whether they agreed with it, or not. Bourdet's ironical formula, describing the attitude of mind of an immense number of Frenchmen: "I'm not a neutralist, but——" hit the nail on the head. For even if nobody was neutralist, World War III and satellization were opposed by practically everybody; and there were also widespread doubts about the possible implications of the Atlantic Pact. And when it was learned, first, that the Russians had the Atom Bomb and next, that war had started in Korea, this feeling grew stronger than ever.

Of all the things in France that worried the State Department during those years, the *Monde* was about the worst; it was "neutralizing" much of the American propaganda, and was "poisoning the mind of France", as a US Embassy official told me one day in a moment of candour. And he added: "It worries us far more than the Communists do."

And when General Eisenhower, as the first head of SHAPE, arrived in Paris at the beginning of 1951, and 3,000 Communists demonstrated against him, he remarked: "It doesn't matter about 3,000 Communists demonstrating *against* me; what *is* serious is that there shouldn't have been 3,000 or even 300 Frenchmen to demonstrate *for* me."

In the last analysis, was this attitude to American aid, to the Atlantic Pact, to the dangers of World War III so specifically French, after all? Was it not an attitude widely shared by the rest of Europe, and not least—in its quiet way—by British public opinion, whose pressure, for example, sent Mr Attlee one night flying to Washington to stop MacArthur from running amok in Korea?

But if in England there was, for the greater part of the time, a sort of tacit understanding about all these things, in France, a "tacit understanding" was not enough. In view of the existence of a large Communist Party, America expected from official France a greater display of anti-Communist and pro-American zeal than from England; also, the French Left had to be vigilant all the time, if only because for the less intelligent and more anti-social part of the French bourgeoisie, anti-Communism, pro-Americanism and social and political reaction went together, and there was always a certain danger of their overlooking the serious risk of war inherent in any excessive "right-wing drive", either internally or internationally. Hence the great need felt by the intellectuals to act as a brake on such tendencies—even at the risk of sometimes seeing eye-to-eye with the Communists. That was what Beuve-Méry meant in 1951 when he feared it might soon become dangerous to say it was raining, in case a Communist had just said so, too.

And yet, when we speak of the "gap" between official French policy and public sentiment, we do not mean to express in different words the old Maurras distinction between *pays légal* and *pays réel*. It is probably more accurate to say that the French governments during this period played *vis-à-vis* America something of a "double game" (shades of Pétain!), and were steering an uneasy course between America's expectations and the fears and suspicions of French public opinion. So much so that, in 1949, de Gaulle's RPF actually displayed posters in Paris in which it accused even M. Pleven of being a neutralist! It is a funny, but not entirely absurd thought that—all things being equal— M. Queuille and M. Pleven should have behaved with Mr Truman as Pétain and Laval behaved with Hitler! In their own way, they also were *collabos*—with tricks, and a "double game", and mental reservations of their own.

As for the National Assembly, it was fairly representative of public sentiment, but with these qualifications: questions of home policy counted more with it than questions of foreign policy; the governments implicitly demanded that they be given a fairly free hand in "diplomatic talks"; the shortage of funds and the need for American aid was always to be considered; and, finally, in Parliament the cleavage between Communists and non-Communists was sharper than in the country at large.

CHAPTER TWO

HEART-SEARCHING OVER MARSHALL AID

W E HAVE seen in an earlier chapter how the "Marshall Plan" was at first received with relief and gratitude by practically the whole of France, and how difficult it was for the Communists to persuade their listeners that it was a bad thing. Marshall's Harvard Address of June 5, 1947 was followed, as we have seen, by Bevin's and Bidault's invitation to Molotov; by Molotov's spectacular exit from the Three-Power conference on July 2; by the meeting of the "16" soon afterwards, who set up the CEEC (forerunner of OEEC), which, in September, submitted its recommendations to the State Department. In December, Congress, well impressed by Moch's "tough" handling of the Communist strikes, granted France (as well as Italy and Austria) interim aid totalling 522 million dollars; finally, after a little more interim aid to the three countries, Congress, on April 2, 1948, approved the European Recovery Program for the next twelve months—a total of 5·3 billion dollars—which was about two billions less than what the European experts had asked for. By the time Marshall Aid, or rather, as it was now called, ERP, came into action, the world situation had already undergone many important changes, and the very nature of this aid no longer looked quite so attractive as at the time of the Harvard address.

No doubt, taking a short-term view of it, it was a great blessing. It had, indeed, been partly prompted, in the first place, by signs of a real economic collapse in Europe in the early months of 1947, with the crops ruined, industrial production stationary, foreign trade shrinking, and purchases in the dollar zone in danger of being reduced to zero. In 1947 Europe had received from the USA, in one form or another, 5·7 billion dollars; and now 5·3 billions more were to come. It was a tremendous help, on the face of it, but——. There were many *buts*.

For one thing, now that ERP was "in the bag", many began to wonder why it was that France had failed to put her house in order without this help. Especially since 1946 France had suffered from this strange contradiction: on the one hand, it was being constantly said that, like Britain, France must "export or die"; but, on the other hand, it was equally emphatically asserted that, in order to stabilize prices, it was absolutely essential for France to import food in large quantities. This anomaly had, as we shall see, a curious, characteristically French, social background.

After the Liberation, and with full encouragement from the Communist members of the Government, industrial reconstruction tended to be considered the cure for all ills. But, in fact, this did not prove to be the case. Although, by 1947, industry had practically returned to the 1938 level; this miserable "1938" target (which was far below the 1929 level of production) proved an inadequate one; and the shortage of coal and raw materials was preventing any further expansion. But what created the greatest difficulty of all was the chronic food crisis, which, in 1947, threatened to assume catastrophic proportions. It was not that food was non-existent in France; but the French peasantry were being obstructive.

The shortage of food available in the cities, and the inequalities created by the black market had resulted, especially since 1946, in a constant rise in food prices. Hence the continuous clamour for higher wages. No doubt, the food shortage was partly due to a number of specifically post-war causes: labour shortage on the land, and shortages of agricultural machinery and fertilizers; moreover, the peasants had acquired "new habits"; their diet was more plentiful and varied; they had days off, and took holidays, which they had seldom done before. They had grave doubts about the franc, and were reluctant to sell their produce for doubtful notes, unless they could immediately "reinvest" the money; otherwise a sort of "insurance premium" against further depreciation was added to the price. The practice of hoarding is best illustrated by the fact that livestock in 1947 was more plentiful than before the war, but meat prices kept rising unceasingly. Although the successive governments attempted to "regulate" certain agricultural prices in this or that sector of production, they never produced a *general* plan acceptable to the peasantry.

This failure to bring about a *dirigisme agricole* was considered by many economists as the primary cause of France's economic difficulties throughout the first years after the Liberation, and especially from 1946 on.

Since the beginning of 1946 things indeed went from bad to worse, and prices rose even more rapidly than the note circulation. Financially, France was not in a desperate plight at the time of the Liberation; if Mendès-France's advice had been followed, endless trouble would have been avoided; instead, a policy of compromise and half-measures was adopted, which rendered the subsequent succession of devaluations inevitable. But with prices constantly rising, and with "necessary" social expenditure adding itself to all the "indispensable" expenditure, no budget could stand the strain.

As P. L. Simon was to write in *Esprit* in April, 1948:

We had no clear economic policy. We practised a sort of *dirigisme hon-teux*. Our governments failed to create a "national myth", and even the modest objectives of the Monnet Plan were never made the object of a "national campaign"... They hesitated between a verbal *dirigisme* to which everybody learned, more or less, to adapt himself, and an authoritarian *dirigisme* which would have been a gamble in an undisciplined nation of tax-dodgers and rule-breakers.

The curious thing was that *dirigisme* was unpopular with practically everybody in France—but for *different* reasons. The consumer was against it because it was hopelessly inefficient; on the other hand, it was unpopular with bankers, shopkeepers, and the peasantry because, in spite of everything, it still foreshadowed the possibility of an efficient *dirigisme* developing sooner or later, with all its "Socialist" implications. If *dirigisme* was inefficient in 1945–7, it was due less to its inherent faults, than to the lack of a proper personnel and a suitable administrative machinery; regulations were enacted without a proper knowledge of concrete conditions; the administration had no experience of this sort of work, and too much was left to improvisations.[1] Further, France had, during those years, practised what Simon called a *socialisme de façade*; there had been no redistribution of the national income in the absence of a modern fiscal system; instead, the governments salved their consciences with a series of sops: an extension of the social security system; increased family allowances and old-age pensions, and the creation of a new category of citizens called the *économiquement faibles*, who, together with some other categories, were allowed various tax exemptions, reduced rents and railway fares, etc.

All these were half-measures, which did not substantially affect the huge profits made in agriculture, trade, and the black market. Far from being crushed by this "bogus socialism", the small shopkeeper found Socialist deputies taking the greatest care of him, and begging him for his vote. And the same was true of the profiteering peasant. All of which made any revolutionary experiments with the economic structure of France virtually impossible. (It is doubtful whether even M. Pierre Cot ever said to his peasant voters what, in a moment of starry-eyed enthusiasm, he said to me one day in Moscow: "France will remain a backward country until we get our peasants into *kolkhozes*!")

At any rate, by the beginning of 1948, with Marshall Aid on the way, it was increasingly apparent that this was being hailed as a victory for the "liberals" and as the final defeat for the *dirigistes*; it was expected that life would become much easier as a result of it; and only the more

[1] *Esprit*, 1948, No. 4, pp. 534–5.

thoughtful Frenchmen knew that, in the long run, it would not settle much as far as the faulty economic structure of France was concerned.

There was another, even more serious aspect of the Marshall Plan, as many Frenchmen realized by the beginning of 1948. In the first place, Marshall thought of it in terms of a general plan comprising the Soviet Bloc, as well as Western Europe, but it was extremely doubtful whether Congress would have approved of ERP if Molotov had agreed to join in the Plan. Some US senators were taking this line even before Molotov's exit from the Paris Conference. Later the *New York Times* described ERP as "the practical application of the Truman Doctrine" —which meant, in effect, that its purpose was to create a *cordon sanitaire* in Western Europe; a view fully confirmed by Mr Bernard Baruch in January 1948. If Mr Forrestal, for his part, thought that the Marshall Plan represented an excellent substitute for increased American military expenditure, this theory was soon to prove erroneous, since ERP soon showed that it was part of a much more extensive American plan in Europe.

French intellectuals did not take long to realize it. As early as April 1948 *Esprit* wrote:

The transformation of the Marshall Plan into a Holy Alliance against Communism means that priority is to be given to military aid, and that the European countries will also be expected to increase their military expenditure, thus adding to their inflation. Secondly, it means the intensification of the Cold War.... What its advocates represented a few months ago as America's way of saving peace at the lowest possible price has now become one of the greatest war dangers since the Liberation.

And it quoted the *Wall Street Journal*'s complaint about the enormous military expenditure that the USA would now have to incur "to protect itself against the dangers that its activities abroad imply".[2]

Was this overdramatizing things? French economists, it is true, were chiefly concerned with the question whether ERP would really help to get the Monnet Plan at last out of the bog—into which Ramadier, fearing further inflation, had pushed it, by cutting down drastically in October 1947 all expenditure on capital investments. There were, according to them, two dangers: one, that ERP would before long degenerate into a programme of primarily *military* aid— which is, precisely, what soon happened; and, secondly, that the French Government might now take the line of least resistance, and spend most of the Marshall money not on capital goods, but on consumer goods.

But others went further in their gloomy forecasts. François Goguel[3]

[2] *Esprit*, 1948, No. 4, p. 552.   [3] *Esprit*, 1948, No. 4, p. 621.

feared that ERP had awakened in France the old *collabo* spirit—which meant "sacrificing the country's political independence to the benefits of a protection extended to the interests of a privileged class against the revolutionary danger". And he called for the organization of "*political* resistance" against any attempt to "vassalize France"—the mere *technical* resistance put up by the French technicians negotiating with the State Department not being sufficient.

Paul Fraisse, in the same issue of *Esprit*, had no illusions of what ERP would mean in practice.

It represents a policy that is already in full swing.... The failure of the London Conference was followed by the unification of Western Germany, and the economic revival of Germany under the aegis of the USA.... The Prague Revolution was followed by the Brussels Pact, followed by the promise of an American guarantee.... If Italy votes Communist, she will get no further aid.... Our foreign policy now blindly follows the State Department, whether over Germany, Palestine, or Spain.... The British, not obsessed by Communism, as we are, have kept the sense of their own economic interest, and the Marshall Plan is, in London, the object of a very close examination. The official French attitude, on the other hand, is simply to "take what's offered—and damn the consequences".

Fraisse went on to say that conditions in 1948 were particularly favourable to European federalism; but, unfortunately, there were two kinds of federalism: one was a European Federation run on Socialist lines—but this would certainly receive no encouragement from the State Department; it was up to the French Socialists and the British Labour Party to press for this solution; the other version—which unfortunately, had a much better chance of succeeding—was the Churchill-Truman solution, symbolized by the Brussels Pact and aiming to turn Western Europe into an American bridgehead.[4]

These critical comments and gloomy forecasts in the foremost progressive Catholic journal, with its great influence in French intellectual quarters, are typical of the arguments which, among French left-wing intellectuals, were to become increasingly frequent and vocal during the next few years. Coming in the midst of Marshall Aid euphoria in the spring of 1948, this special "Marshall Plan" number of *Esprit* was, as it were, one of the starting-points of a major campaign which was to continue right up to the rejection of EDC—and beyond. It was a hard battle against mountains of propaganda, most of it American-subsidized.

By a curious coincidence, it was during the same month that one of the most influential exponents of the diametrically opposite view, M. Raymond Aron, brought out his well-known book, *Le Grand Schisme*.

[4] *Esprit, ibid.*, pp. 625-6.

His argument was simple enough. He denied the existence of American imperialism; on the other hand, Soviet imperialism had to be "contained"; while the French Communists were a Fifth Column with whom no compromise of any kind was possible:

American influence implies neither assimilation nor imperial domination. ... The choice between a reactionary policy, supported by Wall Street and a Stalinite despotism mellowed by the promise of reforms may exist in other parts of the world; it does not exist in Western Europe (p. 8).

For the rest, he scarcely concealed his dislike of "containment" as a cold-footed half-measure and his hope that the time would come when the Russians would be driven out of Eastern Germany—to begin with:

The best thing would have been to prevent the sovietization of Eastern Germany; the best method is still to demand evacuation by the Russians. But this would imply a degree of resolution of which the British and Americans have proved incapable. Perhaps Churchill would be capable of it, but not Attlee or Truman.[5]

These heroics of M. Aron who, in his neo-Gaullist ardour, was prepared to drive the Russians out of Eastern Germany, and, more or less, to outlaw the French Communists, were in flat contradiction with the views of the left-wing intellectuals of *Esprit*, who refused to admit that the *grand schisme* was final, either internally or internationally, or to accept the view that America and Western Europe were God and the Soviet world the Devil. For one thing, there was Indo-China; there was Madagascar; and also, the French working-class was being starved; and to be as self-righteous as M. Aron was, in their opinion, to be intellectually misguided. However, M. Aron thought them a lot of "fools and ignoramuses" (p. 78). And so the quarrel between two of the main non-Communist schools of thought was to continue for years.

Later, in 1955, Aron published a long book, *L'Opium des Intellectuels*, in which he tried to explain the regrettable behaviour of the intellectuals by attributing it to their morbid craving for Marxism (which was a simple way of explaining everything).

[5] *Le Grand Schisme*, p. 67.

CHAPTER THREE

"WORKING-CLASS DEFEATED"

WITH the failure of the Communist strikes at the end of 1947, the split in the CGT, the consolidation of the Third Force under M. Schuman, and the great financial help about to come from Washington, things seemed, in the early days of 1948, to be returning to "normal". M. René Mayer, M. Schuman's Minister of Finance, was a champion of "Liberalism". His "liberalism" was, indeed, so unsqueamish that he even sought the "confidence" of the war profiteers and the black market aristocracy. Among his numerous financial measures to "restore confidence" was the assurance given of hoarders of gold and foreign currency that they were being "amnestied" in advance, and that if they exchanged their holdings, they would have nothing to fear other than a small fine. Also a free market in dollars was established, ostensibly to help exporters who might be handicapped by the overvaluation of the franc; it was a case, as Professor Hawtrey put it, of "making the black market respectable".[1] Among other measures were the abolition of subsidies to the nationalized industries (only to be reintroduced soon after) and the dismissal of 150,000 civil servants (a figure which, soon afterwards, had to be "revised"), and a further devaluation of the franc; Mendès-France was meantime being sent off to America to ask for a little more interim aid. As a sop to the Socialist members of the Schuman Government, who were shocked by some of M. Mayer's proposals, the latter agreed to an exchange, under certain conditions, of all the 5,000-franc notes, since these were supposed to be the unit most favoured by hoarders and black-marketeers, and represented one-third of the total note circulation. This measure was to prove a failure; for one thing, it was wholly arbitrary: "why not", *Combat* wrote, "pick on holders of all notes with odd or even numbers; or why not limit this control of currency holdings to bald men?" And, anyway, the "sharks" who had most to fear from tax deductions or confiscation, merely sold their 5,000 notes in the black market at the "official black-market rate" of 3,000, while thousands of harmless people had to queue for hours to get their one, two, or three 5,000-franc notes deposited, and then changed.

[1] *Cf.* Pickles, *op. cit.*, p. 87.

All this was mere window-dressing; and throughout the year, and despite Marshall Aid, prices steeply rose, month after month, literally doubling between July 1947 (index 965) and October 1948 (index 1887), and wages, as usual, lagging far behind.

And, naturally, in the circumstances, the black market sharks weren't taken in by M. Mayer—who might have known better. As Léon Blum remarked in January:

> If foreign exchange and gold come out of their hiding-places as a consequence of a general restoration of prosperity, it is highly improbable that they will come out *before*.

In August 1948, *Combat* asserted that although everything was "looking much better"—industrial production was growing month by month, the harvest was the best for years, and the bread ration was going up to 350 grammes—*real wages* were now lower than they had ever been since the Liberation, with the real wages of a skilled worker in the Paris area representing only one-half of his pre-war wages; and the same was true of office workers and government officials (except those with large families, where family allowances made a considerable difference).

But the truth is that *the French bourgeoisie had won a resounding victory over the working-class*, and the Communist bogey had greatly helped it in achieving this result. As Jacques Armel, a brilliant young economist, put it:

> All this hullabaloo over changes of governments is neither here nor there; whether Schuman or André Marie is Prime Minister, or whether René Mayer or Paul Reynaud is Minister of Finance is of secondary importance. The truth is that what looks like a political crisis is in reality a profound social crisis.... The French bourgeoisie has been very skilful in dividing the French working-class and in getting itself incorporated into the framework of international capitalism. In three years it has accomplished an astonishing revival. Having made one concession after another, the French working-class has now its back to the wall. Thanks to it, production has risen, and industrial and agricultural prices are rising.... Having always trusted the Government's promises, which were never kept, it is now helplessly seeing itself suffocated by frozen wages, having already witnessed the most unfair redistribution of the national income. In the name of a freedom, from which it derives no benefits, our working-class is conscious of having won the battle of production and of having lost the battle of wages.... It is watching the parliamentary antics (with the Radicals and Socialists pretending to "defend" the worker) with deep scepticism and distrust. All these "protests" and "reservations" are only a pale reflection of the real hardships of everyday working-class life. (*Combat*, September 4, 1948.)

That, indeed, was the relationship that had become established between the working-class and those Third Force governments which had led France back to "normality". Armel observed in conclusion that "maybe the bourgeoisie can rule without the working-class; but it cannot rule against it" Only, as the story of those years was to show, there was a half-way solution, which was to keep the working-class just an inch or two above the line below which despair and revolt began.

Except that, at times, they were allowed to fall even below that level, and then came things like the strike of the French miners—which began on October 4, 1948, and ended in complete defeat on November 29—a strike in which M. Moch (as a year before) set the CRS loose in the minefields, and brought the *gendarmerie* from Germany, who behaved with even greater savagery. Low wages and the *décrets* Lacoste (the Socialist Minister of Labour) which were considered a violation of the Miners' Statute, were at the origin of the strike; nevertheless, the Government proclaimed that the strike was "political", and M. Moch even claimed that it had been started on direct instructions from the Cominform—failing, however, to produce any solid evidence. It made even an anti-Communist like the famous lawyer, M. de Moro-Giafferi, lose patience: "If you have the evidence, produce it; if you haven't, shut up." M. Moch hadn't any, and all he had to say in the midst of an infernal uproar was that it was *"une hypothèse"*. All of which produced from *Esprit* this comment:

Why did the Government show such reluctance to negotiate with the CGT and why such tremendous zeal to "clear" the mines? One wonders whether it has ever occurred to those who talk about Cominform interference to compare the Government's great display of energy with certain recent statements by Mr Hoffman and Mr Harriman? Also, was there not some connexion between this unusual energy and the coming election to the Council of the Republic, considering that it is in the interests of certain parties, notably the Socialists and the Radicals, to show how "tough" they are with the Communists in order to catch a few votes that would otherwise go to the Gaullists? (*Esprit*, No 12, 1948, p. 857.)

That wasn't the end of it yet. By the time the strike ended, 2,000 miners were in prison, and 6,000 had been dismissed. For two months, a police terror had raged in the mining areas. J. M. Domenach wrote:

The leaders or those alleged to be the leaders were systematically hounded by the police—trade union delegates, town councillors, former Resistance members. This vast system of repression and blackmail was directly aimed at the miners' trade union. Several "ring-leaders" were dismissed the day the strike ended: "you'll be sent for when wanted". In some mines an attempt was made to replace a CGT delegate by an FO man. Under the double pressure of poverty and fear the strike gradually collapsed. . . .

The realists will no doubt say that it's no use getting sentimental, since it all started with a "secret order" from Zhdanov.

It seems to me that people are beginning to think too much in terms of plots on a world scale—which is an easy way of forgetting that people who are near you are ordinary human beings. But what beats me is that Socialist ministers could have conducted their fight against the strikers in this manner, forgetting that they were dealing with human beings—except that one had known for some time now that coldhearted technocrats had taken over the heritage of Jean Jaurès. (*Esprit*, January 1949, pp. 123–4.)

That one was for M. Jules Moch, *polytechnicien*, and M. Queuille's Socialist Minister of the Interior.

CHAPTER FOUR

PAX AMERICANA, PAX SOVIETICA, OR NEITHER?

THE Cold War was eating into people's minds. The story of "Zhdanov's secret orders" to the French miners—even though he had died more than a month before the strike began—was just one example in many of how people's minds worked. In 1948 the Cold War was at its height. It was scarcely surprising. In the West, Bevin and Bidault had begun the year with a scheme of "Western Union"; there was more and more talk of an Atlantic Pact and of German rearmament; Churchill was advocating a "roll-back" policy, even before the Americans had mentioned it, and saying that there could be no lasting peace as long as "the frontiers of Asia were on the Elbe". Soon the same ideas were reported from Washington; an agency story said that America desired a free hand in Eastern Europe, the Balkans, North Korea, and Manchuria; it wanted the Russians to evacuate Eastern Germany, and wished to see the French and Italian Communist Parties dissolved. "The story was only half-denied by the State Department." (*Combat*, February 14, 1948.)

That was in the West. In the East, a few days later, a Communist dictatorship was set up in Czechoslovakia. And, before long, Jan Masaryk threw himself out of a window of the Czernin Palace. The war scare was now at its height, and was being whipped up in the press with great gusto, the evening papers in particular, both Communist and anti-Communist, conducting their war of nerves as hard as they could go:

STALIN'S DILEMMA: ADVANCE QUICKLY OR STOP?
(*France-Soir*, March 19)

EISENHOWER WANTS 1,300,000 MEN ON WAR FOOTING
(*Ce Soir*, February 17)

WASHINGTON TO MOSCOW: "STOP!"
(*France-Soir*, March 6)

USA READY TO ARM 40 FRENCH DIVISIONS
(*France-Soir*, March 28—which added, in very small characters: "according to Drew Pearson")

TERROR IN AMERICA
    (*Ce Soir*, March 28—which added, also in small characters: "says
    Henry Wallace")
GERMAN ARMY OF 500,000
    (*Ce Soir*, March 21)

Almost immediately after the Prague *coup*, the Brussels treaty was
signed in an atmosphere of jitters and uncertainty. There was shoulder-
shrugging over the "little soldiers" of General Revers, Queen Wil-
helmina, the Regent Charles, and the Grand Duchess of Luxembourg
stopping the Red Army for more than a few hours, "while Britain
will have other fish to fry in all parts of the world"; and *Combat* published a cartoon showing Bidault saying to Bevin: "Never mind, we've
still got Marcel Cerdan [the boxer] with us."

De Gaulle was in a more fire-eating mood: "Prague should put an
end to that great weariness which has smothered the souls of so many
Frenchmen . . . Old Europe and the USA must put our poor world
back on its feet." And he hinted that he was ready to take over and
that, if he did, the Russians would not dare invade France; while
Malraux, in a mood of catastrophic exaltation exclaimed that "the
European must light himself with the torch he carries, even if the
flames are burning his hand!"

Why all this uproar over an "imminent" Soviet invasion? In reality,
few people seriously believed it; nobody was preparing to move out
of Paris, though, true enough, many private capitalists—then, as
before—preferred to invest their money in Morocco, rather than in
France; it seemed safer in *every* way, and also promised better returns.
And reports from the French provinces showed that the Prague *coup*
had not aroused there half as much excitement as in Paris.

Even so, the arguing over Western Union, the rearmament of Germany, the advisability of talking, or not talking, to Stalin was growing
hotter every day. Mauriac, genuinely alarmed by Prague, thought a
Western Europe-USA alliance was the only hope; no danger, he
argued, could come from it; and the stronger it was, the more likely
was it to discourage the Soviet Union from going to war.

Bourdet replied that he agreed with Mauriac that most Frenchmen,
if they had to choose, would still prefer the *Pax Americana* to the *Pax
Sovietica*:

But that is not the problem. The problem is to avoid war. . . . It is true
enough that the American Army in 1944 saved France from being overrun
by the Russians. . . . But it is a mistake to assume that no danger can come
from America and that the firmer the USA is *vis-à-vis* the Russians, the
better will be the chances of peace. That is the sophism that dominates the
whole of the pan-Atlantic argument. It is a mistake to identify Hitlerism

with Stalinism. Stalinism is not at all attractive, but the Russian leaders aren't raving lunatics. They may assume that war is inevitable; but they also know that if the Russian people's defensive reflexes are very strong, their aggressive reflexes are very weak.... They may go to war only if they are convinced that American power has become an immediate menace.

And he added that while Marshall was a reasonable man, the people of the USA were being fanaticized by the press and egged on by people like Forrestal and Kenneth Royal; and whoever started the war, Western Europe would be first occupied, and then "liberated"; so her only hope was to avoid war, to add no fuel to the flames, and, if possible, adopt a policy of "armed neutrality" (*Combat*, March 31, 1948).

"Armed neutrality" was to prove Utopian in France (even though it *was* seriously considered as a practical policy in other European countries, notably in Norway and Denmark by the advocates of a neutral Scandinavian Bloc). More fundamental, however, was the debate between the wholehearted supporters of the American alliance, regardless of the risks involved (such risks were denied by them, or minimized) and those who reluctantly accepted the American alliance, but argued that France should do her utmost, even as a member of this alliance, to act as a moderating influence, and reduce tension, wherever possible, between Russia and America. This debate was to continue in France, with minor variations ever since 1947-8. It was accompanied by mutual accusations; the "neutralists" were accused of playing into the hands of the French Communists and of encouraging an aggressive Russia in her belief that the Atlantic Pact was an incoherent, half-hearted alliance; on the other hand, the "pro-Americans" were accused of encouraging America in her "roll-back" fantasies, with all the dangers that these involved. It was also alleged that the "Communist bogey", and the perpetual identification of the USSR and the French Communist Party were being used as instruments of social reaction in France by the most obscurantist of capitalists. Was not this particularly true of the *Figaro*, for instance, with its half-million circulation among the conservative bourgeoisie?

The *Figaro*, while the most important, was, however, only one of the many publications which specialized in this combined anti-Soviet and anti-Communist campaign. But although the pattern of all these publications did not vary much from year to year, there is no doubt that the reactions of public opinion towards the French Communists and towards the Soviet Union underwent many changes which could be well observed, for example, from the behaviour of other publications which were not *specifically* anti-Soviet, and which, if only with an eye on circulation, kept their ears well to the ground. To take the simple example of a purely commercial paper like *France-Soir*; this tried to follow public opinion in some measure in being more anti-Soviet at one time, and less anti-Soviet at other times. If, in 1948–9 it was frantically anti-Soviet, by 1951, when it published Michel Gordey's very *nuancé* series of articles from Moscow with their "human interest", and with their suggestion that the Russian people were *not* against the régime, it obviously felt that the anti-Soviet hysteria (never, in any case, as great among the public as in the press) had greatly abated. Similarly, the reactions of public opinion could be observed from the varying attitudes towards Russia and the French Communists on the part of the left-wing intellectual groups in France, and, to some extent, even on the part of the political parties—even though, in this case, electoral competition left only a very narrow margin for variations— this being particularly true of the French Socialists, who hated the Communist leaders with all the hatred of a spurned rival.

Despite widespread alarm over the implications of the American alliance and over the American solution given to the problem of Germany (with Nazi industrial magnates coming into their own in the Ruhr, and German rearmament not far off), it must be said that, in 1948–9, the "non-conformist" French Left was violently anti-Communist. For this there were many reasons. The political strikes at the end of 1947 had been highly unpopular in the country (the reaction to the miners' strike a year later was rather different), and there was a tendency, even among the left-wing intellectuals, to look upon M. Schuman's "Third Force" as at least a temporary barrier to civil war between the Gaullists (now at their zenith) and the Communists.

Further, Russia, through the Cominform, seemed to have taken the line that war was more or less inevitable, and the liquidation of the Benes régime in Czechoslovakia in February 1948 was considered a confirmation of this view. Czechoslovakia had, until then, seemed a living symbol of the possibility of an East-West compromise and of East-West co-existence within a single country; now it had been ruthlessly scrapped. The succession of trials in the satellite states, complete with the classical confessions that seemed to follow uncannily the Koestler pattern; the propaganda of books like Kravchenko's, besides innumerable articles in the press about 25, 30, or even 35 or 40 million people in "slave camps" (much of this propaganda coming from people ostensibly on the Left, like M. David Rousset)—all this seemed to eclipse the old glories of Stalingrad. The camps (even when allowance was made for all the exaggeration) were the thing that shook the left-wing intellectuals more than anything else, and created those *crises de conscience* so well described in Simone de Beauvoir's novel, *Les Mandarins*. Also, in the field of art and literature, Zhdanovism was upsetting French intellectuals more and more, and even Communist intellectuals like Pierre Courtade and Pierre Hervé (though suffering in silence, at least in public) were not feeling too happy about it. Lysenkoism and other "infallible" theories were rubbing too many people the wrong way, even to the point of making them overlook all the major achievements of post-war Russian reconstruction. Also, the arrogance of a man like Fadeyev, the chief exponent of Socialist Realism at the Wroclaw Congress of Intellectuals in August 1948 made a most unfortunate impression on non-Communist delegates from the West. Hence the emergence, during these years, of all sorts of (more or less ephemeral) movements in favour of "real democracy" in France, in favour of a vast non-Communist (or rather non-Stalinist) Left like Jean-Paul Sartre's abortive RDR (*Rassemblement Démocratique Révolutionnaire*).

Hence also the feeling of relief (mingled with an excessive dose of wishful thinking) with which Titoism was welcomed as a sort of invaluable corrective to the "Stalinite" version of Communism. Tito suddenly seemed like the answer to the left-wing intellectual's prayer for a Communism or Socialism (it didn't matter what it was called) which would be Socialist, democratic, national, anti-Stalinite and, in international affairs, neutralist. Could anything be lovelier! The writings of Tito and Djilas and Moshe Pijade soon came to be studied by Paris intellectuals as serious contributions to political thought! Belgrade became for them a place of pilgrimage. It soon was learned that, inside the French Communist Party, especially among the intellectuals, Titoism had created some acute *crises de conscience* which resulted in the desertion by a handful of people, and total submission to a rigid anti-Tito party line by the rest, whatever their private mental reservations. It took some months before the announcement of American aid to Yugoslavia put an end to the pangs and the heart-ache.[1]

---

[1] If Stalin's quarrel with Tito upset many of the French Communists, Khrushchev's spectacular apologies to Tito seven years later, on the ground that it had all been a mistake ("Beria's fault") puzzled them, ideologically, even more. The repercussions of this episode are discussed in a later chapter.

CHAPTER FIVE

THE TRAGI-COMEDY OF FRENCH SOCIALISM

THE Schuman Government, which had been in office since the previous November, resigned in July 1948, as a result of a quarrel between it and the Socialists over a relatively minor question of military estimates. Relations inside the Third Force Government had been deteriorating for some time; already the Government very nearly disintegrated over the famous Poinso-Chapuis decree, allowing state grants to "family associations" for distribution among families needing such aid for educating their children; to the Socialists, this measure, signed by Mme Poinso-Chapuis, the MRP Minister of Health, was tantamount to a camouflaged subsidy to religious schools. Without going into the details of all the endless discussions and negotiations that this decree aroused, it is sufficient to say that the Socialist Congress in July passed a motion firmly demanding its revocation; it went back on this motion only as a result of a frantic appeal by Léon Blum, who claimed that the alliance of the Socialists and MRP had "saved the Republic", and that it would be folly to break up this fruitful association over a minor matter like this. Not without some grumbling, the Socialists gave way, many of them muttering, however, that the decree was "Vichyite" in spirit, and marked the beginning of a "clerical offensive". Among other resolutions passed by the Socialist Congress which were totally ignored by their MRP partners was one in favour of negotiations with Ho Chi Minh, at a time when M. Bollaert, the French High Commissioner in Indo-China, had already signed with Bao Dai the Along Bay agreement of June 5 laying the foundations for the future puppet state of Vietnam. The Socialist rank and file were conscious of their ministers being the prisoners of the MRP and the Radicals in the Government; they knew that their ministers were helpless to enforce upon the government to which they belonged any principles of a Socialist doctrine—whether in the economic, social, or colonial field; at best, they could try to restrain the Government from going "too far to the Right".

Apart from their liking for office, the Socialist ministers looked upon the "Third Force" as a lesser evil; if this broke up, there might be a dissolution of the Assembly, and then the election might lead to a Gaullist victory. But in the Third Force majority, consisting of the whole of the MRP (including its most reactionary elements), most of the Radicals and some "Moderates" on the Right, it was no use screaming for major social reforms or colonial reforms (M. Bidault was following, in the matter of North Africa, the traditional line of the Quai d'Orsay of sticking firmly to the obsolete protectorate treaties with Morocco and Tunisia) and the Socialists had to be content, as *Combat* put it, "to dish out a lot of vague blah about the 'defence of the Republic'".

On the main trend in foreign affairs, there were, however, no major conflicts inside the Socialist Party. After the expulsion, early in the year, of the "Bataille Socialiste", a small "fellow-travelling" group, the Socialists were unanimously anti-Communist; nor were they favourable to any attempts at "intermediate" solutions, such as Sartre's "Rassemblement Démocratique Révolutionnaire"; Jean Rous, who had joined this "movement", was eliminated from the Socialist Party's *comité directeur*, and members were warned against joining the RDR. On the whole, the Socialists were "pro-European" and "pro-American". If they went to The Hague meeting of the "United States of Europe", only as individuals, and not officially as representatives of the Party, it was only in order not to be too obviously out of step with the Labour Party which was suspicious of this "Churchillian" Congress.

Not that relations with the Labour Government were particularly cordial; the Labour Party, with its large majority in the House of Commons, tended to treat the French Socialists as poor relations; and many of the French Socialists, for their part, were unhappy about Mr Bevin's extreme reluctance to commit Britain to any sort of "federalism", which would involve the surrender of any tangible fraction of national sovereignty. Also, it was widely felt among the French Socialists that both Britain and France (and especially Britain, which had a powerful Labour Government ever since 1945 and was not hamstrung, as France was, by de Gaulle and his *politique de grandeur*) had failed to "radicalize" Europe, and had missed every opportunity of strengthening Socialism and Democracy in Germany. The days had gone when America was still not vitally interested in Germany, as she now was, and when Mr Bevin could still talk of "socializing" the Ruhr industries. Now in Germany, America, and America only, was calling the tune, and every thought of Germany was bound to fill every well-meaning French Socialist with a sense of frustration and of lost opportunities. There was also a good deal of bitterness over the "insularity" shown by the Labour Party ever since the war, and over its striking lack of interest in "organizing" a Socialist Europe. Now it was too late even to think in such terms; and it was increasingly obvious that Western Germany, when finally organized into a State, would not be

Socialist. Everywhere in Western Europe the political centre of gravity was shifting to the Right. It was one of the direct results of the Cold War and of Marshall Aid.

One of the things to be affected by all this was the French press. The Socialist Congress passed a resolution in favour of the protection of the "free press", which had come into being at the time of the Liberation; and one delegate observed that the Radicals in particular were "busy reviving the old capitalist press—with its unsavoury *mœurs*". But here, too, the situation was more complicated than was suggested by the well-meaning speeches at the Socialist Congress: a part of the "Resistance" press had disappeared altogether, and another part of it was passing through a sharp crisis as a result of the acute hatreds that had developed between Socialists and Communists; thus, in 1948, there was a split on *Franc-Tireur*, its Communist or near-Communist members resigning, and the paper becoming increasingly "Atlantic"; the US Embassy was thereupon extremely pleased to record the existence in France of an "Atlantic" paper so far to the Left!

And then there was the awkward problem of the *Populaire*, the official Socialist paper, which was run at a heavy loss, and was known to be subsidized from American—ostensibly AFL—funds (later it admitted it openly). When in the violent debate at the time of the miners' strike at the end of 1948 M. Moch accused the Communists of being paid by Moscow, Duclos proposed the formation of a parliamentary Committee of Inquiry which would not only look into the funds of the Communist Party, but also into the funds of the Socialist *Populaire*; there was an awkward moment when M. Queuille rejected this motion, and the Socialists voted against it, amid cheering and jeering from the Communist benches.

On the whole, the Socialists were favourable to Marshall Aid, and undeterred by comments like this one in *Esprit* (December 1947, p. 278):

One should like to know how Blum and Jouhaux can seriously claim that the Marshall Plan is no danger . . . to Socialism. A child would see that if you want to carry out a Socialist policy, it's no use staking everything on the financial aid from a country run by people who are the most determined enemies of Socialism. But the French Socialists want to hear nothing about it, and . . . it will make no difference even if we quote what the Socialist *New Statesman* wrote on November 8: "Since Léon Blum wrote his *A l'échelle humaine*, it is clear that the party of Jaurès has finally turned its back on the methods and aims of Socialism."

Of course, it made no difference. A great ceremony was organized at Bordeaux in May when "the first Marshall Aid ship'" arrived.

It was a grand day of Franco-American friendship. Speeches were made in the Place de Quinconces by Mr Jefferson Caffery, the US Ambassador, M. Pineau, [then the Socialist Minister of Transport] M. Coudé de Foresto, [the Minister of Food] and M. Monnet. The ceremony was followed by a dinner at Château Margaux. M. Pineau said that, but for this interim aid, the French bread ration would, owing to the bad harvest, be down to 100 or 150 grammes. Thanking Mr Caffery, M. Pineau added: "France owes her revival to the United States. This ship is symbolic of the common prosperity of the Free West. We are on the threshold of a prodigious adventure." And M. Pineau added: "We have never been asked for anything in return".... And M. Schuman said on the same day: "The USA has supplied us with 13 million quintals of wheat, of which 10 million has been given us free." (*Combat*, May 11, 1948.)

Certainly the Socialist M. Pineau was falling over himself. Only what else could he do? Since there was no chance for Socialism (short of ganging up with the Communists) he might as well have the higher bread-rations. For these, at any rate, meant, among other things, that the Third Force had a better chance of steering its uneasy course between Communism and Gaullism, with the prospect of both of them losing in influence.

CHAPTER SIX

DE GAULLE GOES "THUGGISH"

IN THE case of Gaullism this was certainly true. The time between the great Gaullist triumph in the municipal elections of October 1947 and the end of 1948 were, in reality, the only time when the RPF represented a real danger to the Republic.

Several factors contributed to its rapid decline. First, the United States, in spite of some hesitation at various moments, decided to support the Third Force, rather than de Gaulle, who was arrogant, unreliable and moody, and might well precipitate a civil war in France. His behaviour throughout 1948 was becoming wilder every day, and was beginning to alarm wide sections of French public opinion. Some RPF leaders like Malraux were indulging in a sort of cosmic catastrophism, while others, like General de Bénouville, almost went so far as to advocate preventive war against Russia, for which the more responsible people in the United States were not prepared. Such "Free World" zeal was becoming excessive.

Also, de Gaulle *would* put forward his own ideas of *grandeur française* which did not fit in with American plans; for instance when he said:

Since Prague has followed the others into the outer darkness, the West must join up for economic and military co-operation. The physical and moral centre of this grouping must be France. Germany can work with us, though not as a Reich, but as a series of sovereign federal states. . . . We would consider it criminal if our policy and strategy consisted in deliberately abandoning France, first to invasion and then to liberation by means of an atom bomb. (*Combat*, April 18.)

He obviously had his own ideas on strategy, and would be as awkward a partner for the USA as he had always been.

The London Recommendations in June 1948, which were to lead to the abandonment of the Ruhr to Germany, to the early formation of a West-German State, to the absorption of the French Zone in the Bizone and to the Berlin blockade (provoked by the monetary reform in the West) de Gaulle opposed with the greatest vigour as being in every way dangerous to France. He sharply criticized the whole of US policy, as it was now shaping in Germany.

If he was beginning to annoy the United States more and more, he was also beginning to alarm many people inside France who had been fairly sympathetic to him only a few months before. For one thing, every de Gaulle meeting now tended to assume the character of a para-military rally, with thousands of cars bringing supporters from distant parts, and scores of armed men surrounding the General; at the de Gaulle rally at Grenoble in September, there were serious disorders; one Communist was killed and many other anti-Gaullists were wounded by bullets, while the Gaullists were merely beaten up. Jules Moch, who had shown how tough he could be with the Communists, declared himself equally determined to stand no nonsense from de Gaulle. He said that all the shooting had been by the Gaullists, and that a feature of these de Gaulle rallies now were the numerous jeeps crowded with Marseilles gunmen (nervi)—precisely the kind of people who used to surround Doriot in the past. And Moch complained that all these de Gaulle rallies were costing the Government a lot of money and trouble; numerous police cars and a platoon of gendarmes had to accompany him all over the place; altogether, all these security measures had already cost the Government 10 million francs and 57,000 litres of petrol. Whereupon M. Ramadier, the Minister of Defence, said that he was withdrawing from de Gaulle his usual Guard of Honour; "let the Minister of the Interior take care of de Gaulle, as of any other citizen."

All this business about the taxpayer's money and the Third Force government's petrol did not fail to make de Gaulle slightly ridiculous, and he was certainly furious when at a press conference a few days later, he kept referring to M. Moch as *ce personnage* and embarked on a somewhat absurd piece of arithmetic, when he said that since he had received one million letters from his supporters, each with a ten-franc stamp, the Government had been "refunded" its expenses.

He claimed that the RPF had a membership of 1½ millions. It is true that he was still popular; his meetings drew enormous crowds, and in the election to the Council of the Republic of November 7, the RPF did very well, the Council now being composed of 320 members of whom 130 were either members of the RPF or senators adhering to the *"intergroupe RPF"*. It is characteristic that the whole "Classical Right" had now joined up with the RPF. In short, the main support for de Gaulle was now coming from the Right, from all that had been Vichyite in the past. His public meetings were acquiring the characteristics of meetings of the old Pétain Légion, with a certain element of pre-war "League" and "Doriotist" thuggery added: and in his appeals to the working-class to join him (notably at his Vel' d'Hiv' meeting in Paris in December 1948) he used arguments which strongly savoured of all the old Vichy corporatism and paternalism. The audience, however, was mainly bourgeois, with only a small working-class sprinkling.

If he got no change from the working-class, he also failed to secure any support from the Third Force. President Auriol was violently opposed to him, and the MRP and Socialists were determined not to let de Gaulle "pass". It is true that M. Pleven tried to bring about a *rapprochement* between the Third Force and de Gaulle, but he met with no encouragement—even though a few of the MRP sometimes squinted towards the RPF.

There was, however, the "Reynaud episode" of August 1948, which deserves a few words. The fall of M. Schuman on July 19 following a relatively minor disagreement with the Socialists, was followed by the formation of a government under an obscure Radical, called M. Marie, who made, however, the by no means obscure M. Paul Reynaud, his finance minister. This Government broke up very soon, since the Socialists felt that M. Reynaud's financial reforms were only too clearly calculated to favour the peasantry and the middle class, and were doing nothing to protect the working-class against the effects of inflation. But there was more to it than that. To have included M. Reynaud in the "Third Force" was, in fact, to turn a Third Force government into one largely dominated by the Classical Right—and the Classical Right was, at this stage, scarcely distinguishable from the Gaullists. Was it not a case of letting de Gaulle in by the back door?

The overthrow of Reynaud brought on a paroxysm of fury from de Gaulle, who, uttering dark threats, now declared that he was "ready to take over", and, oddly enough, there was a chorus of recrimination against the "hopeless system" from the British press (a large number of whose Paris correspondents were frantically pro-de Gaulle). Not only the *Daily Mail*, but even the *News Chronicle* now started clamouring for a "strong man" in France. This frenzy caused some surprise in Paris, where it was noted that the Swiss press, for example, was proving much more level-headed.

After an abortive attempt by M. Schuman to form the next government, M. Queuille took over, and the Socialists could congratulate themselves at least on having prevented the Third Force from degenerating into a plain right-wing government—or worse. To this extent the Socialists could still render the Republic a service. It was not negligible. And it was soon after the Queuille Government took over that de Gaulle was deprived of his "guard of honour", as a result of the shootings at Grenoble. It was an important landmark in the self-assertion of the Third Force and in de Gaulle's decline.

CHAPTER SEVEN

VICHY ON THE ROAD TO REHABILITATION

PRACTICALLY all that had been Vichyite in France flocked in October 1947 towards de Gaulle's RPF. This created for de Gaulle something of a dilemma. To whitewash Pétain was to attract to the RPF more and more people from the Right, and there was also a danger that certain "left-wing" elements, whose support the RPF was hoping to gain, might be discouraged. Therefore, in 1948, while de Gaulle was still counting on "working-class support", he was careful to steer a middle course, which satisfied nobody. Speaking at a great meeting at Verdun on June 20, he combined a glowing tribute to Pétain "that great war chief, who rendered the country the unperishable service of winning the battle of Verdun" with words to the effect that Pétain could scarcely be held responsible for what he did later, having by this time become completely gaga; or, as de Gaulle put it more nobly: "Owing to old age, he was carried away by a torrent of surrenders." It was a disappointment to both Vichyites and anti-Vichyites. It was not until nearly a year later—when all hope of acquiring left-wing support had vanished—that de Gaulle concentrated entirely on his Right clientele by advocating a general amnesty for collaborators and for Pétain himself; but more important in this respect (though it had the weakness of not coming direct from de Gaulle) was an article by Colonel Rémy in one of the Gaullist publications recording a talk with de Gaulle, in the course of which de Gaulle was quoted as saying that, during the war, France had had two strings to her bow: one was Pétain, the other was he (de Gaulle), the two complemented each other, and both were equally essential for France's survival. There is no record that de Gaulle denied this statement, any more than the words he was supposed to have uttered on another occasion, about "Pétain the shield and de Gaulle the sword". All the same, he hesitated to be too openly pro-Vichy himself.

However, by 1949 it no longer mattered what he said: the Classical Right no longer needed de Gaulle in the same measure as in 1947–8. The "Communist menace" had been averted; there was no longer the same need for the "Gaullist umbrella", and the Classical Right were coming into their own again, "within the framework of the Republic", and were already on their way to power. They felt that the

Third Force could not resist this pressure from the Right indefinitely, and would have to co-operate. A significant symptom of de Gaulle's desertion by the "Classical Right" was the publication in the *Figaro* in 1949 of the violently anti-de Gaulle *Memoirs* of General Giraud.

Just as M. René Mayer had made the black market "respectable", so Vichyism was trying to make itself respectable. It all went together: the rehabilitation of the black market, of "liberalism", of Germany, and, before long, of the Nazis. Already the American authorities in Germany had amnestied Ilse Koch, the "bitch of Buchenwald", who was said to have caused the death of 50,000 people and had made lampshades from human skin. If it was "fair and just" to let out Ilse Koch, how could a mere Flandin still be discriminated against? He hadn't done anything half as bad as making lampshades out of human skin. So discredited Vichy politicians like M. Flandin started throwing their weight about at banquets attended by hundreds of ex-Vichyites, who now went out of their way to demonstrate how right they had been about Communism all along, and to show how monstrous it was to have branded them with "national unworthiness"; and they clamoured for complete rehabilitation. The Radical *Aurore* placed several columns at Flandin's disposal, and he filled them with pieces of "advice from a statesman".

Sacha Guitry, until then under a cloud for his unheroic record during the war, put on, early in 1948, a show called *Le Diable Boiteux*, with Talleyrand as its hero, which was a very transparent apologia for Vichy. The enthusiastic bourgeois audience, as the *Canard Enchaîné* put it, "totalled many centuries of *indignité nationale*". Also, dozens of books by Vichy ex-ministers and other apologists started appearing, explaining the virtues of Vichy and the services it (or, at any rate, the particular group to which the writer belonged) had rendered the country. The spiritual heir of Charles Maurras, the fanatical Pierre Boutang, who was soon to start a weekly paper, *Aspects de la France*, the true successor of the *Action Française*, was giving lectures in the Latin Quarter to the glory of the National Revolution, and so was the son of Léon Daudet. "Movements" were started in favour of the release of the "martyrs", especially Pétain and Charles Maurras. Even the heirs of the more extreme Paris *collabos*, like Maurice Bardèche, brother-in-law of the executed Robert Brasillach, spoke up in defence of collaboration with Germany. His *Lettre à François Mauriac* is a model of its kind.

This rehabilitation or self-rehabilitation of the *collabos* and Vichyites went together with a "counter-purge" among the Resistance, and a witch-hunt against Communists, especially in responsible positions. A major press campaign was started against Frédéric Joliot-Curie, head of the Atomic Energy Commissariat, from which he was soon dismissed. In industry, CGT officials and even rank-and-file Communists were beginning to be victimized more and more frequently, and Communists were being eliminated from responsible posts in the civil service and the Army. Communists could be heard saying: "If you go on like this, you'll soon be treating Communists the way Hitler treated the Jews." And ex-Vichy policemen and magistrates had now, with the Government's blessing, embarked on a major "counter-purge" against alleged crimes committed during the Resistance. To quote *Combat*, which, though wholly anti-Communist, protested violently against this counter-purge:

Not a day passes without the papers announcing sentences passed on members of the Francs-Tireurs-Partisans or of the FFI for reprisals which they carried out against traitors during the Resistance or during the national Insurrection in 1944. Not only excesses and crimes, but even many inevitable acts of war are now being punished. It was both a civil war and a war against the Germans, a fearful war in which not every blow could be correctly aimed. . . . And the most abominable thing is that many of these lads of the FTP and the FFI should now be charged on the strength of forms they had themselves filled in in perfectly good faith after the Liberation, recording what they had done. From all sides we hear of charges being brought against members of the Maquis, of arrests and sentences. . . . [A long list of cases followed.] Guerilla war is different from any other. . . . It involves a terrible psychological strain, and the guerilla fighter cannot even fall back on those "laws of war", whether they are respected by the enemy or not. The partisan has nothing to fall back on; that is why regular soldiers hate so much these *sans-culottes* and their heroic improvisations. . . .
And yet it was not Army discipline that made the Resistance the great thing it was. Its strength was derived from the courage and the spirit of initiative of individuals. Gradually the hated "Fifis" have been eliminated from the Army, and are now being prosecuted by the civil courts. The poisonous whispering of 1945 about "terrorists" is now being officially accepted. . . . Thus two heroes of the Maquis of Rouquerolles, in the Oise, were beaten and tortured by the police the other day for having, on June 17, 1944, shot a Polish woman, Helena Ludwierak, who was a notorious Gestapo agent. (*Combat,* February 19 and 29, 1948.)

While all this fitted into the general anti-Communist pattern of the home policy of the Third Force, it should still be emphasized that, at least until 1952, the legal existence of the Communist Party, though made difficult in many ways, was never to be openly challenged on a government level. The Party was, however, being driven into a "ghetto"—and the personal demeanour of the Communists underwent some curious changes in the process. Their sectarianism, for one thing, became more pronounced than ever.

As for the Vichyites and their clamour for rehabilitation, the Third-Force governments, though granting amnesty after amnesty to those still in prison, were in no great hurry to bring the Vichy politicians back into the front rank of politics; for one thing, the MRP leaders, in particular, looked upon "Resistance" as a title of nobility, the privileges of which should not be readily shared with men with no Resistance "titles"—even though their political outlook was now scarcely different from that of these one-time Resisters.[1] This discrimination by the ex-Resisters against the ex-Vichyites was a convenient convention which the former were determined to observe as long as possible; even if it had no longer (in most cases) a deep sociological significance, it was still a convention that directly affected the question of government personnel, influence, and well-paid jobs. And even M. Pinay, the first *conseiller national* of Pétain to become Premier under the Fourth Republic, failed, in 1952, hard as he tried, to get M. Flandin elected to the Council of the Republic. Both inside and outside Parliament, there still continued to be a certain popular prejudice against admitting prominent Vichyites into politics; this prejudice, however, scarcely applied any longer to the Army, the police, or the professions.

[1] The most notable exception among the MRP leaders was M. Robert Schuman, who had, technically, at any rate, been a minister of Pétain's in the early stages of Vichy, when he was placed in charge of the painful problem of the refugees from Alsace-Lorraine. He later claimed that it had been a "humanitarian", and in no way a political appointment—which was partly true.

CHAPTER EIGHT

FRANCE ABSORBED IN THE ATLANTIC WORLD —THE "NEUTRALIST" HERESY

ALTHOUGH, on the face of it, the greater part of 1948 and the whole of 1949 were an uneventful time in France, apart from the bitter miners' strike at the end of 1948 and the partial strike of dockers and railwaymen, this period was decisive in organizing Western Europe, as we see it today in 1955. The bourgeoisie had won its great victory over the working-class, and everyday life seemed to be settling down, and acquiring a pattern superficially reminiscent of the quieter days of the pre-war era. *Dirigisme* had largely gone out of everyday life with the abolition of the last vestiges of rationing in 1949, and Marshall Aid had killed the black market in ordinary commodities, though the franc was still in a precarious state of health, and the semilegal "parallel" market in gold and foreign exchange continued to thrive. The inefficient "Socialist" rationing system had given way to the "liberal" system of rationing *"par le porte-monnaie"*.

In the international field, this whole period was marked by three distinct, but closely connected phenomena: the hard-headed and "realistic" organization of Western Germany by the United States—a task in which only a purely formal minimum of interference and "advice" was tolerated from France; a much less realistic and, indeed, extremely wishy-washy myth of "Europe", which was being built up by the French Government, and particularly by M. Robert Schuman—a myth which was calculated, in some measure, to make the Atlantic Pact look more palatable, as though it were no more than an indispensable precaution against outside interference with the noble work of Europe-building; and lastly, a strong ferment of ideas in France itself. This, roughly speaking, took the form of a three-cornered clash of ideas between (*a*) the Communists, (*b*) the all-out anti-Communists and pro-Americans, and (*c*) the "intellectuals" who, in varying degrees, were highly critical of the Communists (more than they were to be a few years later) and critical, too, of the Atlantic Pact and of the mumbo-jumbo over "Europe" which, in the opinion of most of them, was still lacking any serious foundations.

Since this book deals primarily with France, and since France was scarcely consulted in the matter, little need be said on the creation of Western Germany in 1948-9—even though it was, internationally, one of the most important landmarks in the post-war history of Western Europe. But some of the main facts should be recalled, if only as "background" to the reactions they produced in France.

In the foreign policy debate at the National Assembly in February 1948, Bidault still argued that France's German policy could be summed up in two points: federalism and the exploitation of the Ruhr for the benefit of the whole of Europe. For an hour, as *Combat* put it, "he read out his piece in a funereal tone of voice", boring to death both his listeners and himself. He also talked of "Europe": Italy had "become a friend again", and had responded favourably to France's appeal in favour of a Customs Union, and in favour of joining a new thing soon to be known by the absurd name of "Fritalux", which sounded ominously like the name of a new refrigerator. Anyway, Fritalux—a France-Italy-Benelux union—never came to anything.

More interesting to the French was the announcement, soon afterwards, that the Saar had become "definitely integrated" in the French economic sphere, but that, in spite of this, the allocations of Ruhr coal for France would not be cut. But these concessions to France were not altering in any way the main trend of US policy in Germany. As early as April the United States made it clear that it wished a West-German Government set up. At the Six-Power Conference in London (USA, UK, France and Benelux) in May no final decision was taken about the West-German Government, but France was strongly urged to let her zone join the Bizone; but there was little doubt that the West-German Government would soon be set up. The monetary reform was agreed on, despite serious apprehension among the French delegates. Papers like *Le Monde* and *Combat* were particularly critical, and suggested that General Clay—and no longer Marshall—was now calling the tune in Germany; that Bevin "had not been at all helpful to France", and that France, in short, had been made to "capitulate". Not only had the Russians been definitely excluded from the Ruhr, but the Ruhr, clearly, was not going to be "internationalized" in any sense. Moreover, it was felt in France that, with their insistence on monetary reform in Western Germany, the Americans were being reckless: it clearly meant the final division of Germany in two; and what would they do if the Russians were to "react violently"? Some French commentators spoke of the "wages of sin"—France's sin in having pursued after the war a policy of *grandeur*, instead of helping to build up Social-Democracy in Germany.

At the National Assembly on June 16, Bidault protested feebly against the suggestions that France had "capitulated":

In the Ruhr [he said] Bevin and Marshall had been opposed to any "special régime" so long as the Occupation was in force; was France to stay out in the cold? Germany [he added wistfully] was now being courted by both sides, and was less inclined than ever to take any notice of French demands. It was necessary, all the same, that France should continue to be "present" in the Ruhr—even though it was being increasingly run by "German technicians".

All this did not sound very convincing. In the debate that followed, M. Paul Reynaud advocated a policy of "realism" and the acceptance of the London Recommendations; he thought it was time that, in the Atomic Age, old-fashioned security considerations should be abandoned; and anyway, he added, it was absurd of France to go on looking for danger "in the wrong place"; the danger came *not* from Germany. "Nor must we leave Germany in a state of chaos; if we do, it will merely be attracted to the East." Other speakers on the Right (as well as some Government supporters) used one of those classical arguments which, time and again, have re-emerged in various contexts in France's post-war history: "If we don't agree with the Anglo-American Plan, we shall be *isolated*." Pierre Cot, Billoux, and others naturally protested against this "imminent revival of German militarism and industrial power", and stressed that, despite Bidault's remarks that reparations to France must continue, there was nothing in the London Recommendations to show that they would; while P. O. Lapie, for the Socialists, talked somewhat irrelevantly and idealistically about "Germany in Europe and the Ruhr in Europe". The motion finally carried by 300 votes to 286 makes pathetic reading.

It reaffirmed the necessity of internationalizing the mines and the basic industries of the Ruhr; it reiterated that there must be effective French participation in the control of German industrial potential, complete with the expropriation of the former German magnates of heavy industry; it reaffirmed France's claim to security and reparations; it insisted on a "long occupation" of all the key areas; it rejected any possibility of a centralized and authoritarian Reich being revived, and recommended a Four-Power Agreement on Germany and further attempts to be made to "organize Europe politically and economically".

M. Moch, for all his anti-Communism, was worried about the possible consequences of the monetary reform, which he considered a blatant breach of previous agreements with Russia, and, at the Cabinet meeting about the same time, he still argued in favour of an attempt being made to reach an amicable settlement with the Russians on this question, and against confronting them with a *fait accompli*.

But it was no good. General Clay was on the war path and would suffer no delays; with the consent of the three Governments, the Deutsche Mark was put into circulation on June 20 (for currency purposes—to begin with—the French Zone was included in the rest of

Western Germany) and a week later, after declaring that, since Four-Power government had been abandoned unilaterally by the Western Powers, the Russians alone were now legitimately in Berlin, Moscow started the Berlin Blockade. Even far to the Right in France there was an uneasy feeling that, legally, the Russians had a strong case.

The French press was alarmed; it said that Clay was now itching to have a showdown—and to force the blockade with tanks or an armoured train.

He thinks he can call their bluff [Marcel Gimont wrote] and the Americans are also talking an awful lot about the A-bomb. Surely, it is not for us, Brussels Powers, to embark on adventures of that kind. All these threats of violence in the midst of a ruined Europe make it clear that our old Continent must find a solution other than blind obedience to either one or the other of the Big Two. (*Combat*, July 20, 1948.)

Fortunately, the screaming against Clay in Europe proved not without effect: before long, it was reported that Truman had decided against Clay's policy of trying to force the blockade. There followed the Air Lift—which proved a success not only technically, but also in showing that the Russians were not prepared to go to extremes. This, however (as was to be expected), strengthened the view that the Russians were "scared"; and there is little doubt that it was American "toughness", supported by Bevin, that prevented a compromise on Berlin from being reached during the Moscow talks in September and October, between the Western representatives and Molotov and Stalin. Stalin was to say on October 28 that "on two occasions" the Berlin crisis could have been ended—an assertion with which Mr (now Sir) Frank Roberts, the British *chargé d'affaires*, who had conducted the negotiations on behalf of the UK, almost certainly agreed. There was much talk in Whitehall at the time of Frank Roberts having been disavowed by Bevin, just when a settlement was in sight. But the prestige value of the Berlin Air-Lift, though costly and risky (in spite of apparent Russian acquiescence) was too great to be abandoned on a "compromise" basis. It was not until the following May, when the Russians admitted defeat that the blockade and the air-lift ended.

For one thing, Clay was determined to postpone any agreement with the Russians for as long as possible, if only in order to give himself time to organize Western Germany. The Berlin Blockade, for one thing, was creating the right atmosphere for this; any talks with Russia, as Clay saw it, would mean suspending "all the important work going on at Frankfort". (*Combat*, July 12, 1948.) The unification of the three zones of the West was rapidly progressing; after the French Zone had been included in the Deutsche Mark area, the foreign trade of the three zones was also unified in October.

A fortnight later something happened that the French had dreaded for a long time; the British and American Governments decided simply to "return the Ruhr to Germany"; and they agreed that it was for the future German Government to decide to whom the mines and the heavy industry belonged. It was the object of the famous Law No 75—which put an end to all the French illusions about the "internationalization" of the Ruhr, in one way or another. M. Schuman "violently" protested to the British and US Ambassadors, and President Auriol made an indignant speech at Compiègne on November 11 (Armistice Day, as it happened) in which he said that it was "unpardonable" to allow "the arsenal of the Ruhr to be restored, and to be placed in the hands of Hitler's accomplices":

Only a status under which the Ruhr property would be placed under international control can safeguard the security of Europe and protect the German people themselves against their own impulses.

On the same day M. Herriot made a similar speech at Lyon.

M. Schuman, before leaving for Washington a few weeks later, tended to dilute the whole question in "European" syrup:

No final settlement is possible without our consent.... The German trustees will, in any case, remain for a long time yet under Allied control.... Anyway, security is not a matter for one country only; either Europe will be the result of joint co-operation, or there will be no Europe; the future Germany must take part in the building of Europe, first on an economic plane, then on a political plane. Such is France's vision of the European problem and of its solution, of which at present we still only see the general outline; but this solution will come, despite all our present hesitations.

He assured the Assembly that he could be trusted to defend France's interests in Washington, and received its blessing. What alternative was there, anyway?

In Washington, as was to be expected, Schuman achieved nothing as far as the Ruhr was concerned; it is not even certain that he tried very hard to follow an Auriol-Herriot line; he was already thinking in terms of a "Little Europe"; and, on the other hand, the Atlantic Pact was already in an advanced stage of gestation. It was, obviously, something more substantial than the Brussels treaty, which had been signed in a moment of panic, without an American guarantee, and without anything to show that it could stop the Russians from reaching the Channel ports in a few days.

If one was to assume that the Russians were determined to invade Western Europe, it was, of course, a good thing. But—was it not to be feared that Europe would, from now on, have to give priority to military, rather than to economic reconstruction? The Atlantic Pact finally consecrated the division of Europe in two, and aroused great opposition particularly in France, Italy, and Scandinavia.

In March 1949 the "neutralist" uproar reached its height, with the *Monde* in the vanguard of the "neutralist" campaign. There were two sets of arguments against the Atlantic Pact: the first, that it was militarily ineffective; the second, that it was dangerous. The campaign was opened by Professor Etienne Gilson in the *Monde* on March 2, 1949. After quoting a *New York Times* editorial, which had said that America was willing to spend dollars on her security, rather than actually go to war, Gilson thought that this meant that the countries of Western Europe would again have to bear the brunt of a world war; and he advocated armed neutrality as a much better solution. His argument was that, without the American alliance, Western Europe's chance of being invaded would be much smaller.

As Bourdet put it, in commenting on Gilson's article:

The neutral bloc could include Western Europe, Sweden, Italy, and probably Switzerland and Yugoslavia;

Unlike the Atlantic Pact, armed neutrality would create no internal divisions; it would be a case of defending a neutral Europe against invaders, and not "American bases against heroes of Stalingrad".

Essential decisions could be taken by Europe and not by Washington, as they were today.

Armed neutrality might diminish America's eagerness to send arms to Europe, but it would also reduce Russia's temptation to invade a Western Europe studded with American bases.

If war between America and Russia became inevitable, America might concentrate on air war and leave Europe out of it; in Europe, the US Army would inevitably get involved with the Red Army and with Communist guerillas; it might also be more expedient for Russia not to occupy Western Europe; in 1940 Switzerland would naturally have been occupied by the Germans if she had been allied to France. (*Combat*, March 16, 1949.)

At the same time, M. Boulet, an MRP Deputy, tabled a motion at the National Assembly in favour of a "neutrality declaration"; but it met with no support from the Government.

In the *Monde* on March 17, M. Beuve-Méry renewed the attack. To him the Atlantic Pact increased the risks of war.

To some people, the essential thing is to win the war if it cannot be prevented; the essential thing, for others, is to prevent the war from taking place at all.

And he asked the awkward question what the countries of Europe would have to do, supposing the USA was attacked by Russia on the Pacific; would they have to start marching into Eastern Europe?

For all that, the Atlantic Pact was ratified without any difficulty (other than violent Communist obstruction) at the end of July, only the Communists, near-Communists and Algerian Nationalists voting against it—plus the above-mentioned MRP Deputy, M. Boulet. There were a few abstentions, including that of M. Mendès-France.

There was a feeling of resignation about this vote, rather than enthusiasm or eagerness. No doubt, the motives that prompted the majority of the Assembly to vote for the Atlantic Pact were very mixed. It was, first of all, an anti-Communist demonstration, at a time when anti-Communism, either for international reasons or, much more important, for domestic reasons, was at its height.

That alone would be enough to account for the Socialist vote. Moreover, the Government had stressed, time and again, that the Atlantic Pact was defensive, and nothing but defensive; and that it would also facilitate the organization of "Europe"—a vague idea which, nevertheless, exercised a certain attraction on both the Socialists and the MRP. M. René Mayer, the *rapporteur* of the Ratification Bill, also stressed that the Atlantic Pact was perfectly compatible with the UN Charter, with the Franco-Soviet Pact and every other commitment France had entered into—all of which was no doubt calculated to overcome the grave doubts expressed on the desirability of the Pact even by Mr Trygve Lie, Secretary-General of UN. And, above all, it was *easier*—easier *vis-à-vis* the United States, on whose bounty France was so dependent. Moreover, the more disagreeable aspects of the Atlantic Pact—the fact that it would, before long, inevitably lead to German rearmament (as the *Monde* was prophesying) and to the early establishment in France of American bases, were not quite tangible yet. And M. Robert Schuman, to destroy any doubts on the subject of German rearmament, declared with the greatest emphasis:

Germany will not be admitted to the Atlantic Pact. The question cannot even arise. There is no peace treaty; *Germany has no army, and cannot have one; she has no arms, and she shall have none.* (*Débats,* AN, July 25, 1949.)

These were the kind of Big Lies, uttered with a great display of authority and conviction—always more effective than small lies, which overcame the last scruples of many of those who, at heart, were not so sure about the Atlantic Pact. It is quite certain that if M. Schuman had told the truth that the Atlantic Pact would inevitably, before long, lead to German rearmament, it would *not* have been approved. At least, not in 1949. But Schuman presented it as being merely a straightforward choice among three things: America, Russia, and disastrous isolation. Presented in this way, the American alliance, *without* German rearmament, was the obvious thing to choose.

CHAPTER NINE

TOWARDS A "BANKERS' EUROPE"?

T HE ratification of the Atlantic Pact by France and Italy (where Nenni had clamoured in vain for a referendum which, he was certain, would reject the Pact) marked a further stage on the road to the political and strategic integration of Western Europe in the "American sphere of influence". During the few years that followed, French commentators used to reflect on the "degree of satellization" of France and Britain respectively, and liked to show that Britain still managed to act more "independently" than France, both in its economic and financial policy and in the conduct of its foreign affairs, notably in respect of China.

Not that this was strikingly obvious in 1949 after the lone battle that was fought and lost by "Stafford Cripps, the last sentry of the British Socialist bastion" (as *Combat* described him).

Socialism? Liberalism? Which way was Europe going? In France there was more heart-searching on the subject in 1949 than in any other country. In a series of articles in the *Monde* which attracted much attention, Jean-Jacques Servan-Schreiber closely examined all the possibilities and all the different facets of the new Europe that was now in the making. He agreed that it was "in the making", and that nothing very concrete had yet been made. But Socialism (represented by Cripps) was being rapidly defeated by "Liberalism" (represented by the United States and, in Europe, by de Gasperi and by the Belgian leaders). The "Socialist" M. Spaak himself was saying in private: "You see that the Labour experiment in England is well down the drain."

Europe [Servan-Schreiber wrote] now seems ripe for a return to the *status quo ante.*... The Europe that emerged from the war was a Europe of the *"lendemains qui chantent"*, of a joyful march towards Socialism. But one by one, all the features of this Europe are rapidly disappearing. What is coming is a Liberal, a "Radical-Socialist" Europe ... (*Le Monde*, June 23, 1949.)

No doubt it was America's fault; but then it was America, Servan-Schreiber thought, which, after all, was trying to "put guts" into a distrustful and defeatist Europe; it was America, and not Europe that was standing up to the Russians and had organized the Berlin airlift; and his conclusion was to the effect that Western Europe was becoming, as it were, another Latin America, enjoying the benefits of a new Monroe Doctrine.

But it wasn't quite so simple. Europe had her own hostile reflexes, which were more complicated than those of Guatemala; and Mr Harriman seemed both puzzled and distressed. For one thing, there was an absurd lack of standardization in Europe's mental processes. Its anti-Communism, for instance, varied in degree, and there was no doubt that the Communist Peace Campaign was affecting large sections of the population normally out of sympathy with "Stalinism".

There was also much heart-searching on another question, based on the assumption that the United States was going to "save" Western Europe from Communism. But how? Servan-Schreiber quoted two widely differing opinions. General Bradley, US Chief of Staff, had said:

Our plan must be on no account to abandon Western Europe to the invader. Our defence line must be as far inside Europe as possible, so that we don't have to start a new landing.

But in reply to the following question:

Is it our policy to organize the military defence of Europe in such a way that we can defend her on the spot, or are we simply going to protect Europe by promising to avenge and liberate her if she is attacked?——

Senators Connally and Vandenberg both replied: "We cannot possibly guarantee that Europe will be defended within its own frontiers." (*Le Monde*, June 9, 1949.)

That, in a way, was the real crux of the matter. Was there not a danger that America, though not yet "imperialist" in 1949 (according to Servan-Schreiber) might become increasingly pugnacious—and "risk" the "temporary" loss of an expendable Europe as part of her world strategy?

It was considerations like these which stimulated the "neutralist" currents in France, particularly strong in 1949–50; one of the main arguments against "neutralism" (apart from the over-facile charges of "defeatism") was that a "neutral Europe" was all very well—provided it was an economically and politically coherent entity, capable of an independent existence—but nothing was further from the truth. (*Cf.* J. J. Servan-Schreiber in *Le Monde*, April 5, 1950.) And, on more than one occasion, M. Beuve-Méry complained in the *Monde* that it was the lack of imagination, the lack of "guts", the lack of a constructive policy, of an *œuvre virile*, as he put it, that was to blame for the state of satellization into which France was rapidly sinking.

The victory of "Liberalism" over "Socialism" in 1949 caused a great deal of discussion in France. Not only were the various Socialist *dirigistes* and the French admirers of the Labour Government disturbed, but also the more "progressive" elements in the Catholic MRP. In the *Aube* (August 20, 1949) M. Etienne Borne, the principal ideologist of the MRP (who was later to get such a raw deal from its conservative wing[1]) deplored the decay of both Socialism (as known just after the war) and of that French *travaillisme* which, he thought, might have come into being if the MRP-Socialist coalition—now freed of the Communist partnership—had been given a chance. In Germany, as in France and Italy, he wrote, Liberalism was now triumphing over Socialism all along the line.

This situation is not without dangers. A wholly "liberal" Europe may embark on a purely negative anti-Communism ... and forget that the most effective weapon for defeating Communism is social generosity. A liberal Europe is also likely to yield too easily to penetration by American capital and American ideology.... Look how Mr Acheson rejoiced at the results of the German election as a triumph of Free Enterprise. ...

And Etienne Borne pointed to another, even greater danger—a danger which, as subsequent events were to show—was ignored by those very MRP ministers to whom Borne's warning was primarily addressed:

This rise of Liberalism confronts the democratic parties of a Christian inspiration with a fearful problem. Here and there we already see them ganging up with the forces of social conservatism, partly in order to acquire certain advantages in the realm of education, and partly because they are finding it difficult to come to terms with Socialists who are too intolerant in their *laïcité*. Yet they must not forget that their major mission is to ... integrate Socialism, freed of some of its purely material ballast, into a wider humanism.... Without this, there can be no free Europe, conscious of its own originality ...

A good forecast of the MRP's subsequent course.

At the beginning of August the Council of Europe met at Strasbourg. Much of the press was sceptical. In the *Monde*, M. Duverger wrote: "The greatest danger for Europe is to imagine that it has been born; it has not even been conceived." Far from having stimulated the "European" spirit among the nations of Europe, he said, Marshall Aid had merely strengthened the autarkist tendencies in every European country. De Gaulle's RPF also dismissed the Council of Europe as "just another fiction", and proposed that there be, instead, a Euro-

[1] They did not raise a finger to save his excellent (but unduly "Leftist", extra-governmental and anti-colonialist) monthly, *Terre Humaine*, which died in 1953. It was, to M. Bidault's taste, far too much in the *Sillon* tradition.

pean referendum on "genuine unity", and advocated that France be the *leader* of this Europe.

For all that, at the Council of Europe and at the European Assembly numerous self-congratulatory speeches were made. The Socialists, despite the rapid progress of "liberalism" in Europe, sounded pleased with the results. On September 10, Guy Mollet, the Socialist leader, said at Strasbourg:

Europe has been born. We shall also create the United States of Europe. A Socialist might wonder whether he should rejoice, since the Socialists here are in the minority. Still, without hesitation, I say: yes, we are glad.

And he concluded, amid discreet smiles:

We know that events will rapidly sweep Europe along the road to Socialism. (*Combat*, September 10, 1949.)

Other French Socialists spoke on the same lines, while M. Bidault, M. Spaak and others proclaimed that "Europe had been born".

Washington, directly, or through Mr McCloy, the US High Commissioner, had been repeating, throughout the Strasbourg meetings, that Germany must be admitted before long to the European Assembly and to the Council of Europe. Things were, indeed, rapidly moving in that direction, and Germany, having voted a Right-and-Centre Government into office in August, was being increasingly patronized by the USA.

Even before the German election, the USA had demanded that the dismantling of German war plants be stopped. The Social-Democrats were isolated, and Adenauer formed, on August 21, his Right-and-Centre Coalition Government. On the next day Mr Paul Hoffman said that American experts would help to "activize" German reconstruction. Encouraged by all this, Adenauer declared on September 7: "Germany must take part in the military defence of Europe."

If ever there was a "double game", it was being played over this question of German rearmament.

On November 1 a State Department spokesman, commenting on an alleged US proposal to France and the UK that a German Army be created, dismissed the story as "fantastic". (*Combat*, November 2.)

On November 10, in the course of the Acheson-Bevin-Schuman talks in Paris, the French endorsed US policy in Germany—less dismantling, and higher steel production.

On November 12 the French press reported an alleged "Acheson Plan": "US defence line on the Elbe. Impossible to have a no-man's land between Elbe and Rhine; progressive German rearmament therefore logical."

Two days later, on his return from a visit to Germany, Acheson said: "I was given a magnificent reception in Germany."

On the next day, November 14, Schuman said at a press conference: "There has been no decision on German rearmament."

On November 16, on his return to Washington Acheson said he had been deeply impressed "by the serious-mindedness of the German people"; and the French press reported that "despite Acheson's denials, everybody in the USA is talking of German rearmament". (*Combat*, November 18.)

On the same day it was announced that dismantling had been stopped at the Thyssen Works and five other major plants in the Ruhr.

A week later, there were the Petersberg agreements, under which Germany became "a member of the Western Community".

Meantime, the French National Assembly had embarked for several days on a dreary and *désabusé* discussion of the "German problem", in the course of which M. Schuman again said that a German army was "completely out of the question". He was being taken less and less seriously; and even among the French, there were now some who openly advocated German rearmament, notably M. Paul Reynaud; while, at the Council of the Republic, General Billotte (who had been hobnobbing with US generals during the previous week) said:

Let's not be hypocrites. Defence on the Elbe will make it necessary to create a German Army. (*Combat*, December 10.)

For all that, on December 15, Acheson was reported to have said: "We are against German rearmament." Mr Morgan Phillips, too, came to Paris to assure the French Socialists that, although he couldn't be certain about the Tories, he could assure his French friends that the vast majority of the British Labour Party were against German rearmament. The more statements were made about it, the less convincing did they sound.

Towards the end of the year there were more and more military meetings in Paris—Chiefs of Staff of the "3"; Chiefs of Staff of the "12"; War Ministers of the "12", etc. It was stated that US arms deliveries to France were about to start. The press was reporting that France would supply *the infantry* for Western Defence (which produced a howl even from the anti-Russian *Aurore*: "What, again!??"), and that, in five years' time, she would have 20 fully-equipped modern divisions in the field.

The *Aurore*, indeed, wrote on January 18, 1950:

We can only have a genuine feeling of revolt at the thought that the French *biffin* will again be the chief victim in a new war. While the Anglo-

Saxons are going to conduct a *de luxe* war in the air and on sea, 50 French infantry men will be killed to one American airman.

A highly characteristic French reaction—not confined to any single party.

Also, the papers were full of reflections on the total abandonment of any idea of "internationalizing" the Ruhr; on "convertibility", on American investments in France, and on the OEEC meeting where M. Petsche and M. Van Zeeland were in full agreement with Mr Hoffman on the best ways of organizing the "capitalist, militarist and bankers' Europe", as *Combat* called it—a Europe based on a Franco-German "marriage", from which England would be virtually excluded. This "Little Europe", with its cartellization, its regional agreements, its international financial machinery was looked upon with great favour by Washington; it implied, as *Combat* said, "the submission of the proletariat and the liquidation of all progressive ideas". The Vatican (Servan-Schreiber wrote), with an eye on a Little—predominantly Catholic—Europe, had become "one of the most active centres of diplomatic activity in the world", with de Gasperi, Schuman, and Adenauer as "its men". Cripps, according to the same writer, took a gloomy view of all this planning which, he said, was tolerating inhuman living conditions, particularly among millions of people in Italy. The Schuman Plan, which was to come a few months later, was to become the essential feature of this "Bankers' Europe", as it then looked to many.

This large-scale and long-term capitalist planning did not, paradoxically enough, exclude the possibility of war. Only what kind of war? Truman said, early in September, that the Cold War must end with the "unconditional surrender" of the countries under Communist influence (a statement which even the *New York Times* thought rather foolish), only to be followed, on September 23, by the Truman announcement that the Russians had the atom bomb! Was this going to make war more likely or less likely? Vishinsky blew hot and cold: he proposed a Big Five Peace Pact (which was turned down), and then said that Russia had "enough atom bombs" for all emergencies. Thereupon an American Senator announced that the USA had atom bombs six times more powerful than the Hiroshima bomb and would soon have one 1,000 times stronger. The French press talked of "nuclear psychosis in Washington", and liked to recall how earlier in the year already, Forrestal had gone nuts, screaming that the Red Army was invading the USA.

The atmosphere wasn't healthy, either in Europe or the USA. Still, whatever was in store, there seemed no immediate war danger. Things, throughout 1949, looked less ominous—at least in the immediate future

—than at the time of the Prague *coup* or the Berlin blockade. But was this only an illusion?

On the other side of the fence, the gloom seemed much deeper. In November Nenni said: "It cannot be denied that we are on the threshold of World War III", and, a few months later in April 1950, Thorez declared: "Peace is suspended by a thread." And then came the Korean War.

CHAPTER TEN

KRAVCHENKO—THE COMMUNISTS' GREAT PEACE CAMPAIGN

"On a parlé des camps russes, dit Nadine. Vincent est bien de
mon avis. Il dit que c'est dégueulasse, mais que si on fait
campagne contre, les bourgeois seront trop contents."
—*Les Mandarins.*

THE Communists were in a peculiar position between the failure
of the Great Strikes at the end of 1947 in France and the outbreak of the Korean War. They had, as already said, been pushed
into a "political ghetto"; the Strikes had alarmed wide sections of the
French population; then came the Prague *coup*, which whipped
up anti-Soviet (and, at the same time, anti-Communist) sentiment
in France; there was alarm over the Berlin Blockade, and a good
deal of anti-Communist hee-hawing over Moscow's quarrel with Tito.
The Mindszenty, Rajk, and Kostov trials in 1949 played into the hands
of anti-Communist propaganda, and there was much talk of "Titoism"
undermining the Communist position in all the "satellite" countries.

In 1948 the ground was well-prepared in France for a major anti-
Communist propaganda drive. The United States was in favour of this,
and the Kravchenko libel action against the Communist weekly, *Lettres
Françaises*, had been heralded for many months before it actually
opened in January 1949. The anti-Communist press and both the
French and American governments were going to make a field-day
of it. This was quite irregular since French law requires libel actions
to be heard *in camera*, but it somehow didn't matter: the maximum
publicity was going to be given to the "Kravchenko Trial". The Soviet
Union was going to be shown up as one vast concentration camp, in
which everybody was living in a state of terror and abject misery.
Kravchenko, a Soviet official who, in 1944, while the war was still in
progress, had "chosen freedom" in the USA, was now going to show
it up as it had never yet been shown up before. *Lettres Françaises* had
called Kravchenko a traitor to his country, a liar, and an American
agent, and had claimed that he had not written the book himself.
American Communists had made similar charges against him; but he
had ignored these and openly declared, both before and during the

Paris trial, that he had decided to bring his action in France, because here there was a Communist Party that mattered; he did not deny for a moment that the whole thing was intended to be a major political operation, primarily against the French CP.

For three months the papers in France were full of the Kravchenko Case. The *Figaro*, the *Aurore* and some others published more or less full verbatim reports running into several pages every day. The importance attached to the case was such that witnesses both for and against Kravchenko came from England and America, and the Soviet Government took the unprecedented step of sending several witnesses to Paris, including a Red Army General and Kravchenko's ex-wife, who showed him up in a somewhat unsavoury light. Although no one could deny that there *were* concentration camps and arbitrary arrests in Russia, the trial did not make it at all clear that the "slave labour" ran into tens of millions, as Kravchenko was trying to show, or that everyday life in Russia was horrible and terrible in every way.

But what, above all, made the whole thing disappointing to those who were going to make tremendous anti-Communist capital out of the Kravchenko trial, and also made the whole thing increasingly distasteful to wide sections of the public (including numerous readers of the *Figaro*) were two things: Kravchenko's highly unattractive personality and the fact that the US Government and the Queuille Government had, between them, agreed to turn this libel action into a major political operation. This distaste was, in the end, to be reflected in the judgement of the Court which awarded Kravchenko ludicrously small damages, and contrasted in its judgement the fine Resistance record of the two defendants, Claude Morgan, and André Wurmser, with Kravchenko's own behaviour during the war. There were all kinds of other "irregularities" which made a bad impression: the American passport with its fictitious name which the State Department had issued to Kravchenko for going to Paris, the fact that American "ghost writers" had helped to produce *I Chose Freedom*, and the wholly irregular publicity, complete with phone cabins for the press, with which the libel action was conducted in Paris.

Maître de Moro-Giafferi, one of France's foremost barristers, and by no means pro-Communist, wholly condemned the "stunt":

> I still don't understand all this publicity given to the case. This publicity is absolutely contrary to the law.

And the correspondent of *Picture Post* wrote that the whole thing was a political stunt conducted by the French authorities: "that's what makes the whole atmosphere at the trial so repulsive." He thought it was serious that, with the complicity of Kravchenko, the French Government should put a law court to such strange uses.

Technically, Kravchenko won his case and was awarded £150 damages, instead of the £10,000 he had asked for. But on balance the case caused more damage to Kravchenko than to the French Communists, and although the Soviet Union and its police system did not come too well out of it, the Kravchenko Affair did not in any way interfere with the vast Peace Campaign the French Communists were planning to launch upon the world.

The French Communists were, indeed, very prominent in 1949, even apart from the Kravchenko trial. They had decided, very shrewdly, to play the Peace card. Already, some time before, the French CP had adopted the slogan: "*Le peuple français ne fera pas, ne fera jamais la guerre a l'Union Soviétique.*" But, on February 22, 1949, before the Central Committee of the CP, Thorez was even more explicit and made a statement which was to cause an infernal shindy:

The Soviet Union [he said] has never been and never can be, in the position of an aggresssor towards any country whatsoever.... The Soviet Army, the army of the glorious defenders of Stalingrad ... has never attacked any people.... The French Government is actively collaborating with the aggressive Anglo-Saxon imperialists. There is a foreign General Staff at Fontainebleau, and France and her overseas possessions are being turned into bases of aggression against the USSR and the People's Democracies....

And then came the bombshell:

If, despite the joint efforts of all Frenchmen, devoted to freedom and peace, they still fail to lead France back into the camp of peace and democracy, and if our people are dragged, against their will, into an anti-Soviet war, and if, in these conditions... the Soviet Army is forced to pursue the aggressors on to French soil, could the people of France do anything other than what was done by the peoples of Poland, Rumania, and Yugoslavia?

But the Thorez statement was only one part of the Communist operation. The second part consisted in Duclos' simultaneous announcement that the CP was embarking on a Peace Campaign.

It must be said that the deputies were rather less outraged by the Thorez statement than might have been expected. Bidault thought it was "a grave statement", but its wording was "conditional". René Mayer dismissed the whole thing as "an absurd hypothesis", and Defferre (Socialist) thought the statement less precise than the earlier "*Le peuple de France ne fera jamais la guerre a l'USSR*", and that it was no use making a martyr of Thorez. Paul Reynaud thought there was "bitter irony" in the suggestion that anyone should want to attack the Soviet Union.

At the National Assembly, on February 24, there was, however, something of an uproar. M. P. André, a right-wing deputy, demanded that the CP be outlawed. M. Scherer, an MRP Deputy, shouted at Thorez: "Do you want to succeed Laval?" Thorez proceeded to demonstrate "America's will for war", quoting *Reader's Digest* and other publications. René Mayer declared that the CP received orders from Moscow. *"Menteur, voyou, canaille"*, the Communists cried, "and what about the Rothschild Bank?"—a somewhat irrelevant retort, which caused M. Mayer to claim (equally irrelevantly) that the Rothschilds had helped Jaurès around 1900 to found the *Humanité*! However, it all ended fairly amicably, with the rejection, by 500 votes to 52, of a Gaullist motion that Thorez be charged with high treason and with the adoption of a Government motion "noting" that the Communists considered that France would inevitably be the aggressor in any war against Russia. M. Queuille assured the Assembly that he would never allow the Army's morale to be undermined.

The peace campaign, inspired by the Communists, was at its height in 1949–50. The great international congress of the Partisans of Peace was held in Paris at the Salle Pleyel in April. The French, Soviet, and Italian delegations were the strongest, but there were also numerous delegates from about 50 other countries. It was the Congress for the benefit of which Picasso painted his famous Dove of Peace.

Both the French Socialists and the British Labour Party looked upon the Congress as a Communist and Moscow-inspired stunt, and their members were sharply warned against giving it any support. The Congress, presided over by Professor Joliot-Curie, as well as the "mass demonstration" at the Stade Buffalo, which marked its conclusion, were nevertheless a great propaganda success for the French CP.

No doubt, much about it lent itself to a good deal of irony. Was it not in the midst of a great pro-peace speech that the Congress suddenly burst into frantic cheers at the news of the great *military* victory of the Chinese Communists, who had entered Nanking? Only that was *different*—it was a war of liberation, it was *une juste guerre*, a victory not *by*, but *over* American imperialism.

Still, it was a little awkward. And Mauriac, in the *Figaro* (May 2, 1949) was being so infernally ironical about Picasso's Dove:

Pablo Picasso, ô contempteur de la face humaine, vous qui detruisez le visage de l'homme avec une haine inspirée, vrai communiste, communiste authentique quoi qu'on dise, qui vous acharnez génialement contre l'image et contre la ressemblance du Père... Picasso, vieux diable admirable...

Yes—the "admirable old devil" had painted just a dove, an ordinary, photographically ordinary dove.... But, said Mauriac, it wasn't really an ordinary dove, for it had the claws of a bear, and around it were lying the bones of Estonia and Poland.

But it didn't matter. It wasn't so certain that Poland *was* "bones"; as for Estonia, who cared? On balance, the Peace Partisans did well; they spoke for days of American Imperialism, of the Atlantic Pact, and, above all, of the atom bomb, and prepared the ground for the Stockholm Appeal some months later—the appeal for the prohibition and the outlawing of the atom bomb—and the appeal was to be signed in France by fourteen million people. The more determined anti-Communists thought the figure alarmingly high, even assuming that many people had signed more than once.

The keynote of the Partisans of Peace Congress was struck by Pietro Nenni who declared:

If the promoters of the Atlantic Pact drag us into war, the peoples of Europe will respond by breaking into revolt.

Paul Robeson sang poignantly—it was like the voice of all the coloured peoples in revolt against imperialism and colonialism. Zilliacus (who soon afterwards was to be expelled from the Labour Party, chiefly for attending this meeting) deplored that the Labour Party had refused to be represented at the Congress, and he attacked Churchill as the spiritual father of the Atlantic Pact. The heroism of the Soviet people was personified by the mother of Zoya Kosmodemianskaya, the young Komsomol girl, who was hanged by the Germans in 1941; and the Metropolitan Nicholas of Moscow, in golden robes and tiara, gave his blessing to the Partisans of Peace. A good deal of genuine emotion was worked up and the danger of an American "press-button" war was keenly felt; and this anxiety was recorded by a number of non-Communist papers in Paris, which noted, however, that the Partisans of Peace had failed to extend the "forces of peace" much beyond the Communist Parties.

It was in 1949 that a little war began between rival "peace congresses". A fortnight after the Pleyel Congress a "Day of Resistance to Dictatorship and War" was held in Paris by a number of *trotzkysant* Socialists, ex-Communists and other "anti-Stalinites", among them David Rousset, Marceau Pivert, Ignazio Silone, and Fenner Brockway; messages were received from Mrs Roosevelt, Messali Hadj, the Algerian nationalist leader, and Gary Davis, the eccentric promoter of World Government who had torn up his US passport and who wasn't permitted to speak at the Congress of the Partisans of Peace in case he said the wrong thing about scrapping frontiers and national sovereignties.

In the summer, a few months later, there was the Budapest Youth

Festival; in Brussels, to counter it, a Democratic Students' Rally was held; here were students from both "white" and "coloured" countries, including a Vietnamese, who kept referring to Bao Dai as "*Sa Majesté Bao Dai*"; also students from Nigeria, the Gold Coast, Madagascar, India, etc. One of the few countries not represented was the Belgian Congo; it was explained that natives of the Belgian Congo were not allowed either to go to universities or to enter Belgium! The anti-Communists also had their awkward moments.

The anti-Communist drive was making itself felt in all fields. In July 1949, the Vatican excommunicated all Catholics "aiding, or taking part, directly or indirectly, in Communist activity". It created something of a problem in Italy, where many Communist voters were also churchgoers; its effect in France was more limited. *Combat* quoted an estimate which said that among the MRP voters 92 per cent were (more or less) practising Catholics; 51 per cent among the Socialists, and only 17 per cent among the Communists. The question asked was, of course, whether the Vatican's decree was aimed at "progressive Christians", and notably against the Worker Priests, an institution that had, in the past, received every encouragement from the French hierarchy.

On July 15 *Combat* commented:

It's curious that the Vatican should have refrained from attacking the Communists in 1944–5 when they were powerful, and when a lot of people thought that the CP and the Front National might gain the upper hand in France.... The only effect now will be to play into the hands of the conservatives, who will go out of their way to tell the Catholic trade unions that any united action with the CGT is sinful.

At Grenoble, Thorez spoke more in sorrow than in anger:

I do not wish to say anything that would offend the faith of our Catholic friends. In the case of the Communist Parties and the People's Democracies, the Vatican is not observing the rule—"Render unto Caesar ..." Yet the Vatican applied it to Hitler, to Franco, to Mussolini—but then these were themselves Caesars.... The hands that were joined in the battles of Liberation will not be torn asunder ...

How much fight was still left in the Communists, despite all these attacks, and despite their partly voluntary, but partly enforced political isolation? It is certain that, in spite of this isolation, the victory of the Communists in China gave them new energy. In Parliament they put up a stiff fight against the ratification of the Auriol-Bao-Dai agreements, when these came up for discussion in January 1950: it was one of the most violent of all parliamentary meetings since the war. And, with the passing by Congress of the Mutual Defence Assistance Act, the Communists in the CGT embarked on an adventure, which was to loom large in subsequent years in the mythology and the martyrology of the French working-class movement. It was when, in January 1950, the CGT gave orders to dockers and railwaymen to refuse to unload and transport American war material, and particularly to prevent war material from being sent to Indo-China.

Even the sharply anti-Communist *Année Politique* (1950, pp. 8–9) admitted that this was, psychologically, a clever move:

For several months, and in' all countries of the world, the Communists had made "the defence of peace against American imperialism" their dominant theme.... Here was a question on which they could see eye-to-eye with a much wider public than the usual *clientèle* of the Communist Parties, and it is a fact that their campaign deeply affected wide sections of the population, impervious to the other themes of Communist propaganda. ... It was also particularly shrewd of the CGT to concentrate its campaign against the war in Vietnam, and to exploit the growing distaste and weariness that this interminable war was causing to ever-growing sections of the French people.

At the end of January, "incidents" in the French ports grew in number. At La Pallice the dockers refused to load a ship carrying war equipment to Indo-China; there were similar incidents at Marseilles, Lorient, Brest, and Dunkirk. In February riots broke out at Toulon, where several hundred dockers attacked the CRS, and at Nice, where 2,000 "demonstrators" burst through the police cordons and pushed into the water an object which, they thought, looked like a V–2 launcher. However, not all the dockers were willing to risk their skins and their jobs; notably at Cherbourg, they refused to follow the CGT instructions not to unload American war material.

Obviously, this attempt to prevent American equipment from being landed, or war material from being sent to Indo-China could not be maintained for any length of time; it was bound to come up against the ordinary bread-and-butter considerations of the dockers and railwaymen themselves. But it was a gesture; and the riots in the ports and the various other clashes produced by this campaign during the first few months of 1950, complete with "heroic gestures" (like that of the *militante* who lay down on the rails in front of a train carrying American war material, and defied the engine-driver to run her over)— all these episodes were going to supply material to Communist propaganda and subjects for Communist novels like Andre Stil's *Le premier choc*, and many others. But it was not enough in itself, either to stop the war in Indo-China, or to prevent "Atlantic" equipment from landing or American bases from coming into being, before long, in numerous parts of France.

When, in April 1950, the Twelfth Communist Congress met at

Genevilliers, the Communists were, nevertheless, in a fighting mood. It was hard to stop all work in the ports; it was impossible to stop all trains and ships: "much still needs to be explained to the workers", Thorez said. But he seemed deeply conscious of the CP's "world mission". "*La paix tient à un fil.... La France au bord de l'abîme ...*" He demonstrated that France was in a state of economic stagnation— and had been for forty years (this part of the speech was strangely reminiscent of Mendès-France); that real wages were still far below pre-war wages, and that social security and family allowances were insufficient to make up for it.

And the Fourth Republic under the "Third Force", under Schuman, and Queuille and Bidault? It was, said Thorez, "a police régime, a régime of mud and blood". Rather a hard way of describing it? Perhaps, but after all—Thorez was speaking only a few weeks after the *affaire des généraux* had blown up—an *affair* that formed part of the shady and dirty background of the Indo-China War. This war was still going on; for four years, blood was being shed there; and the mud? Here was the piastre swindle, the corruption, the shady deals between a crook called Peyré and important personages of the Republic; the Socialist politicians who were trying to hush up leakages; the puppet régime of Bao Dai set up by the MRP politicians and President Auriol; the Socialists and the MRP who were jockeying for places in the gigantic swindle of the Indo-China war; and the rival and "parallel" police services who were cutting each others' throats in Paris and Saigon, and the Saigon gangs, with their dollar rackets and their piastre rackets and their trafficking in military secrets.

The Communists, said Thorez, were the only party none of whose members had ever been mixed up with this mud. Its deputies were living like workmen on 25,000 francs a month (giving up the rest of their salary to the party), "while others cannot manage even on 100,000, and have to supplement their income by resorting to corruption". No doubt Thorez was laying it on thick, amid jeering from the *militants*. But that wasn't the main point of his speech. The main point was the danger of war. With the Chinese Communists in possession of the whole of China, there was a new danger: "What they are planning now is to turn Vietnam into an American springboard against the New China.... Here they may start World War III." In short, every- thing looked ominous. *La paix tient à une fil....* It was, indeed, only too true that Indo-China was now in danger of becoming a major international issue, besides having been, for four years, a source of financial trouble to France, and a source of corruption to her political parties.

Yet the "thread" was to break two months later not in Indo-China, but in Korea. And even then—it did *not* become World War III.

CHAPTER ELEVEN

THE BAO DAI EXPERIMENT

WHAT had happened in Indo-China since the "Hanoi Insurrection" of December 19, 1946, and Blum's failure to nip the war in the bud?

On September 8, 1949 the Government of M. Henri Queuille issued a self-congratulatory statement to celebrate its twelve months in office. Among other things, it claimed to have, in the main, "solved" the problem of Indo-China by setting up the Bao Dai régime. This was no more than wishful thinking. The establishment of the Bao Dai régime had settled nothing at all in the long run, and the war in Indo-China was continuing, eating deeper and deeper into France's finances, and threatening to develop from a war of colonial reconquest into a war of international importance—with the Chinese Communists about to reach the borders of Tongking.

Ever since the end of the war in Europe, France had had trouble with her overseas possessions. In 1945 there had been massacres in Algeria. In 1947 there had been the Madagascar insurrection, followed by a ruthless punitive campaign in which many thousands were massacred. Algeria, Tunisia, and Morocco were in a state of ferment. General Juin had to be sent to Morocco to keep the Sultan in order; the latter had, in 1947, made his famous Tangier speech, in which he had demanded independence and almost openly appealed for support to the Arab League. During the years that followed, North Africa was to be a source of constant worry; in Tunisia the crisis came to a head at the end of 1951; in Morocco, at the end of 1952; in Algeria—though on a smaller scale—in 1954. The awakening of Arab nationalism, and the latent revolt against colonial exploitation and against economic hardships were coming to grips with a colonial system reluctant to relinquish any of its obsolete privileges and tending, more and more, to abandon the paternalism of Lyautey (let alone the liberalism of Blum and Vienot, which was never favoured by the *colons* and the administration), in favour of an unavowed, but nevertheless genuine new way of thinking which was at least partly inspired by the example of Malan's South Africa.

But Indo-China was an even greater, and daily worry to the French

444

Governments ever since the end of 1946. Although the general public in France was, at first, singularly indifferent to Indo-China, the politicians and business interests were not. There was, in reality, a constant mutual influence between political developments in France and the course of events in Indo-China. Thus, as was shown in an earlier chapter, the departure of the Communists from the Ramadier Government was at least partly determined by their unwillingness to be associated with the Government's Indo-China policy; and in the years that followed, the policy adopted in France *vis-à-vis* the Indo-China war and the Indo-China "problem" generally was very largely dependent on the political composition of the French Government at a given moment. For example, the refusal of the French Governments in the early stages of the Indo-China war—in 1947-8—to negotiate a settlement with Ho Chi Minh—which, at that time, was still perfectly feasible—was chiefly due to the growing predominance in the French Governments of the MRP who, moreover, made sure that the Government post concerned with Indo-China was to be held by one of their men, first Paul Coste-Floret, and then Letourneau. These were tough members of the right-wing of the MRP, little Oliver Lytteltons, who were a million miles away from the Christian humanitarianism of the old Démocrates-Chrétiens.

As a result of the "Hanoi Insurrection" of December 19, 1946, the Vietminh Government with Ho Chi Minh at its head "took to the jungle". In the opinion of the far-sighted General Leclerc, who dreaded, more than anything, years of large-scale guerilla fighting, this was the worst thing that could have happened to the French.

That was not, however, the view taken by the men of Saigon. Admiral d'Argenlieu, back at Saigon by the beginning of 1947, hastened to declare that no talks with Vietminh were possible; he spoke of "the former Government of Hanoi", and, before long, came out openly in favour of returning to "the traditional monarchist institution". He sent an emissary to Hong Kong to establish contact with Bao Dai, who, it must be said, at first treated these overtures with the greatest distrust.

The case of Bao Dai is a very strange one, and serious students of Indo-China tend, on the whole, to disagree with the simple view that Bao Dai was merely a figure of fun (*"empereur de boîtes de nuit"*), or a mere French puppet, who would do anything the French asked of him in return for money. That he was not only a pleasure-loving potentate (he has even unjustly been called the "Farouk of the Far East"), but also a cautious and calculating politician may be seen from the simple fact that the French had to court Bao Dai for over two years before he agreed to play their game—which, even then, he thought to be his own game, the main purpose of which was to rid Vietnam of French domination.

In any case, at the beginning of 1947, Bao Dai was wholly unwilling to consider any offers coming from d'Argenlieu, the most detested man in Vietnam. Nor was he willing to come out openly against Ho Chi Minh, whom, in theory, he continued to serve as "Supreme Political Counsellor".

In February 1947 d'Argenlieu, who had become unbearably unpopular with the Socialists and Communists in France, was at last recalled. Ramadier, more or less following the Blum line, now declared that France was willing to "negotiate with the authentic representatives of Vietnam". This phrase was something of a quibble, and represented a compromise between the Communists and part of the Socialists who wished to resume talks with Ho Chi Minh (who at that time was reiterating his desire to "talk") and the MRP who would not hear of it.

No less equivocal was the appointment of M. Bollaert as d'Argenlieu's successor. He was a man with a fine record in the Prefectoral Corps and in the Resistance, was now a Radical Senator, but he had no experience of Asia. What he was likely to do nobody knew at first, not even himself.

In Vietnam, the replacement of d'Argenlieu by Bollaert nevertheless aroused hopes of an early peace settlement. This seemed all the easier to achieve as Vietminh was, by this time, losing ground. It was neither strategically nor politically in a strong position. Most of the towns were now in French hands, and the extremism of the Tu Ve was turning the Vietnamese bourgeoisie and even the peasantry against Vietminh. On March 21, 1947 Ho Chi Minh made a statement in which he "solemnly declared" that the Vietnamese people only desired unity and independence "within the French Union", and he guaranteed "to respect French economic and cultural interests in Vietnam";

France only has to say the word, and hostilities will stop.... But if, despite our sincere desire for peace, the French intend to continue the war, then they will lose everything and gain nothing ... as a result of this bloody and senseless conflict....

Never were the chances for a settlement better. But things were complicated by the creation of a new political grouping, called the "National Union Front", largely composed of anti-Vietminh émigrés in China, and encouraged by the Kuomintang, by the Chinese War Lords and the United States; it soon established contact with certain conservative and "separatist" elements in Cochin-China, such as the Cao-Dai, the Hoa-Hao, and the "Social-Democratic Party of Cochin-China". These various groups, most of them pro-Chinese and xenophobe, held a congress at Canton in March 1947; they withdrew their support from Vietminh and "adopted" Bao Dai. They had no great popular following in Vietnam, but it suited certain French interests to inflate their importance.

So when Bollaert arrived at Saigon on April 1, 1947 he was confronted with two main groups: on the one hand, the "legal" Government of Vietnam, now in the jungle, and, on the other, these various nationalist parties, plus the Cochin-China Government. And in the background, there was Bao Dai, mysterious and non-committal—the ex-emperor, who had "collaborated" with the Japanese, who was still Ho's "Supreme Counsellor", and who was now hailed by the anti-Vietminh elements as their future leader.

On April 19, 1947, Hoang Minh Giam, Ho Chi Minh's Foreign Minister, made a formal peace offer to Bollaert; but the French laid down such stiff conditions—free movement for French troops throughout the country, surrender of half the arms held by Vietminh, etc—that the French terms were inevitably rejected. A curious aspect of this incident was Ramadier's failure to inform the French people of this Vietminh peace offer.

The chances of any further talks with Vietminh were immensely reduced by what happened in Paris soon afterwards: the elimination from the French Government of the Communists, the only Government party that had been wholeheartedly in favour of direct negotiations with Vietminh. On May 17, in an inspired article, the *Journal de Saigon* declared: "Ho Chi Minh represents nothing at all"—a striking phrase which has recurred over and over again, in different contexts, in recent French colonial history.[1]

Meantime the "National Union Front", largely composed of anti-French nationalists like the Cao-Dai (notorious for their collaboration with the Japanese in the past) and the VNQDD, many of whom continued to be Chiang Kai Shek stooges, and now supported by part of the Vietnam Catholics, were continuing to advocate the "Bao Dai solution". The French administration, aware of Bao Dai's love for gambling, sport and women, thought he was weak and malleable, and could be easily tamed—as he already had been once, in 1933, as a very young man. As Devillers put it (*op. cit.*, p. 397):

A "united and independent Vietnam" under Bao Dai seemed a simple solution. He had the traditionalists and the right-wing nationalists behind him, as well as the mandarin class. Bao Dai seemed the best guarantee for French capitalism, and also for anti-Communist opinion in America, whose anti-colonialist prejudices could be overcome by a "solemn proclamation" of independence on the lines of the Bell Act in the Philippines.

[1] Thus, in 1953, I was repeatedly told by French officials in Morocco that the Istiqlal "represented nothing at all".

What was, however, being constantly overlooked was *Leclerc's opinion that, militarily, Vietnam could not be "pacified" without an increase of the French forces in Indo-China by several hundred thousand men*. But, full of wishful thinking, the MRP in France imagined that, with Bao Dai on the throne, Vietminh resistance would soon disintegrate. As for the French Socialists (or most of them), they somehow imagined that Bao Dai might act as a "mediator" and tempt Vietminh to join in the "National Union Front".

It should be remembered that we are still in 1947, i.e. long before the Chinese Communists had reached the borders of Tongking, and that, though the struggle against Vietminh was represented as something "ideological", the war led by the French was essentially a war of colonial reconquest. The establishment of a "puppet régime" was merely intended to facilitate this reconquest, and make it "respectable" in the eyes of the Free World.

Vietminh was, at that time, not entirely sure of itself, and was also divided into "moderates" and Communist diehards. In the summer of 1947 it had, significantly, a dual reaction to all the agitation in favour of Bao Dai. Its official paper, *Cuu Quoc*, took the offensive and warned its readers against the "bogus independence" that the French were now planning to grant to Vietnam; but, on the other hand, to make further negotiations easier, important changes were made in the Vietnam Government. Giap, widely held responsible for the Hanoi massacres, was eliminated from the Government, but appointed Commander-in-Chief; many other "extremists" were dropped, and in the end, there remained only three Marxists in a government of twenty-seven. Bao Dai was confirmed as "Supreme Political Counsellor".

This moderation did not change the attitude of the French, and merely worried them, lest Ho Chi Minh and Bao Dai found a *terrain d'entente*.

The MRP in Paris were up in arms against any possibility of Ho Chi Minh "cashing in" on their Bao Dai experiment, and insisted that henceforth he be wholly excluded from all negotiations in Vietnam.

Under French influence, the "National Union Front" now openly appealed to Bao Dai to form the central government which would "struggle against the red terror", and twenty-four delegates of the "Front" specially flew to Hong Kong to put their proposals before him. But he still hesitated.

Meantime Bollaert had visited Paris, and on his return, his line had appreciably stiffened; in the long-awaited and oft-revised speech he made on September 10 he spoke of "liberty", but avoided the word "independence". His speech was violently attacked by Vietminh, and it also greatly disappointed the "Right" nationalists, who rejected Bollaert's terms, but reaffirmed their allegiance to Bao Dai.

Bao Dai had by this time become impressed by the violence of the Cold War in Europe, and realized that, with the MRP calling the tune on Paris, there was no chance any more of the French coming to terms with Vietminh. Though, at heart, he had probably hoped for an agreement with Vietminh, which he thought the most vital force in Vietnam, he now declared himself against it. He secretly hoped that this would encourage the Americans to support him against the French; he had indeed been impressed by the support given by the USA to the Indonesians against the Dutch.

The autumn of 1947 was marked by a strong French offensive against Vietminh on whom they claimed to have inflicted heavy losses (8,000 dead and 1,500 prisoners); and though it was of no major consequence, the offensive was expected to have a certain prestige value with the actual and potential supporters of the Bao Dai "solution".

This was the solution most favoured by the MRP; some of the Socialists, on the other hand, were experimenting with another, "middle-of-the-road" solution: they thought that, with the help of General Xuan, the former head of the Cochin-China Government, they might get their own people into the key positions in Indo-China. Xuan, who had lived in France since being replaced at the head of the Cochin-China Government by Dr Hoach, returned to Saigon in September 1947, and was soon afterwards reinstated by the Cochin-China Council in place of Hoach. It was one of those bits of political *indochinoiserie*, reflecting the underground struggle between the Socialists and the MRP in France, in which local Vietnamese politics abounded during those years. Xuan, who fancied himself a "mediator" between Bao Dai and Ho Chi Minh, also played about with the idea of a sort of "federal" Vietnam, in which Tongking would in effect be ruled by Ho, Annam by Bao Dai (the nominal ruler of the whole country), and Cochin-China by himself. None of Xuan's projects came to anything at that stage, except that he remained head of what he now called no longer the "Government of Cochin-China", but the "Provisional Government of South Vietnam". Nevertheless, Bao Dai thought he savoured of separatism. The most interesting aspect of Xuan's career was his subsequent downfall as a result of the famous *affaire des généraux*, which broke out at the beginning of 1950. Xuan's downfall was a triumph for the MRP.

By the end of 1947 Xuan's "middle-of-the-road" policy, implying the possibility of a deal with Ho Chi Minh, was out-of-date, anyway. The drift to the Right in France was becoming increasingly apparent, and when the Ramadier Government was succeeded by the Schuman Government, Paul Coste-Floret and, after him, Jean Letourneau, established themselves firmly at the Ministry of Overseas France. These MRP ministers were all-out colonialists, and made no secret of their uncompromising hostility to Vietminh. They were determined to keep Vietnam for France, use Bao Dai as a façade, and imagined that they could crush Vietminh before long.

Bao Dai, for his part, and with eventual American support against the French at the back of his mind, agreed at long last to meet Bollaert on board a warship in Along Bay on December 6. A protocol, containing the magic word "independence", was initialled by the ex-emperor and the High Commissioner, after the former had been assured that the document was merely a "record" of their agreement, and did not finally commit him. This document, over the initialling of which Bao Dai soon got into a panic, marked the beginning of a curious comedy which was to last nearly eighteen months, and in the course of which Bao Dai would travel backwards and forwards between Hong Kong and Geneva, Cannes, or St Germain, dodging the French, or trying to extract more precise assurances from them, and allowing the French to beg him, to cajole, humour, or threaten him in their determination to recruit his services.

Thus, while at Geneva in January 1948, Bao Dai had five meetings with Bollaert, in the course of which he informed him that unless the Along Bay Protocol was amended, he would not return to Vietnam. From Geneva Bao Dai went to Cannes, and then to Paris in order to see which way the wind was blowing. Here he realized that Indo-China was the bone of contention and the object of acute rivalries among the different ministries, the political parties, financial groups and various individuals, each with his own axe to grind. For a time he was scared at the prospect of the Gaullists coming into power, these having declared that they would on no account endorse the Along Bay Protocol, which gave far too much away. Still unwilling to commit himself finally, Bao Dai returned to Hong Kong on March 13, 1948. The main impression he received in Paris was that Bidault considered the Along Bay protocol excessively "generous"; he did not wish Vietnam to have an independent diplomacy, and considered the word "independence" dangerous in view of its possible repercussions in North Africa. If the word was left to stand, it must be surrounded by various "guarantees".

It was Xuan who forced the pace by forming a "central government" of Vietnam on May 27, 1948; the government travelled to Hong Kong where it swore a sort of oath of allegiance to Bao Dai—without his having asked for it. Finally, Bao Dai was persuaded to have another meeting with Bollaert in Along Bay on June 5, 1948.

The "Declaration" published after this meeting said that France "solemnly recognized the independence of Vietnam" which was free to "bring about its unity". As for Vietnam, it proclaimed its adherence to the French Union "as a State associated with France. . . . Its independence has no limitations other than those imposed on it by its membership in the French Union". It further undertook to "respect the rights and interests of French nationals, to assure constitutionally the respect of democratic principles and to give priority ... to French counsellors and technicians". The Declaration further said that after the formation of a provisional government, Vietnam and France would make the "various appropriate arrangements concerning cultural, diplomatic, military, economic, financial, and technical matters".

The reactions that this Declaration produced were remarkable. Vietminh was furious—and uneasy. It felt that if Bao Dai, who had extracted from the French the magic word "independence"—for which Ho Chi Minh had fought in vain at Fontainebleau—succeeded, on the strength of it, to give some substance to the word, Vietminh might lose much of its support. But Vietminh was wrong to worry. The *colons* were making sure that nothing of any importance would be given away to Bao Dai. Their press was up in arms against Bollaert's "surrender", and even advocated the separation of the "colony" of Cochin-China from the rest of Vietnam, which, they said, should be turned into a protectorate; and in Paris Coste-Floret hastened to reassure them by declaring that the war had not necessarily ended; that Vietnam would not be granted either diplomatic or military independence, and that the unification of the 3 Kys was "not necessarily automatic".

The MRP leaders were clearly determined to continue the war, and despite the desire expressed by the Socialist Congress some time later that the French attempt to negotiate a cease-fire, Bollaert was instructed on no account to establish contact with Vietminh. Through some mental aberration, the MRP leaders thought Vietminh would eventually disintegrate through physical exhaustion and through the demoralization caused by the "concessions" made to Bao Dai. A less charitable view is that many people close to the MRP found a prolongation of the war highly profitable.

Bao Dai, for his part, again travelled to Europe. He now took the view that the Along Bay Declaration was only a "declaration of principle", and at St. Germain, on August 25, he informed Bollaert that he refused to return to Vietnam so long as the colonial régime in Cochin-China had not been abolished, and so long as he had received no proper guarantees for the independence of Vietnam. French ministers were saying in Paris the next day: "*Il commence vraiment à se foutre de nous.*"

It is sufficiently clear from the foregoing that Bao Dai was very far from being the "French puppet" and the "night club emperor" of popular imagination. Nevertheless, he yielded in the end, and after several months' further hesitation, signed the famous Auriol-Bao Dai agreements of March 8, 1949. What finally persuaded him to do so?

Apart from the advantages of being a well-subsidized puppet king (not that this ever appears to have been Bao Dai's first consideration at any stage),

it gradually became clear to him [wrote Devillers in 1952] that so long as he resisted, Xuan could not govern in any real sense, and would have no finances, no Army, and no police of his own. The French officials would stay where they were ... and the Xuan Government would be considered more and more a mere screen for the French administration. ... Vietminh's authority would grow daily. ... The last chance of making peace in Indo-China and of establishing a non-Marxist régime might soon go. ... The French authorities were, in any case, determined to go on with the war.

Should Bao Dai simply withdraw? That also was no solution. For if he did, the French Government, with an eye on Mao's advancing armies, would merely back Xuan ... and start a new "Cochin-China experiment" with a puppet government run from Paris by the French Socialists, and sur-rounded at Saigon by the same French colonial administration. (Devillers, *op. cit.*, pp. 442–3.)

To avoid all this, Bao Dai decided to take the plunge, in the hope that, once an "independent Vietnam" was set up, it could play an international game of his own, and come to depend, more and more, on British and American support. Mr William C. Bullitt, whom he had met in Switzerland in September 1949, had encouraged him to sign any "reasonable" agreement with the French; after that the United States could intervene in his favour (*ibid.*, p. 443). On the face of it, at any rate, Bao Dai had finally broken with Vietminh—though, had he been allowed a freer hand by the French and been a man of greater character, he might, once on the throne, have come to terms with Ho Chi Minh. But by now he was a prisoner of the French, and a pawn in the game between France and America.

Under the Auriol-Bao Dai agreements of March 8, 1949 France again

"solemnly recognized the independence of Vietnam", leaving its unity to be decided by a popular consultation. Vietnam's diplomatic independence was still a limited one, since it could be directly represented only in Siam, India, China, and at the Vatican, and its diplomats would have to be accredited by both Bao Dai and the French President. Vietnam would have its national army, but the "French Union" would have bases, garrisons, and full freedom of movement in the country. French property rights were fully safeguarded under the agreement. The only real concession Bao Dai extracted from the French was the complete incorporation of Cochin-China in Vietnam.

Perhaps the most curious development of all after Bao Dai had signed his agreement with the French was his attempt to come to terms with Ho Chi Minh. Xuan said a few weeks later, on May 1, 1949, that

Ho Chi Minh would not be excluded *a priori* from the new Vietnamese Government. Bao Dai, for all his tricky manœuvring with both French and Americans, had always borne in mind that a truly representative Vietnamese Government could not be set up without the participation or, at least, the tacit approval of Vietminh, for which, in spite of everything, he continue to have a sneaking admiration. Once back in Vietnam, he now refused to declare himself hostile to what he himself called "the Resistance".

M. Léon Pignon, a d'Argenlieu man, who had succeeded Bollaert as High Commissioner, grew alarmed, and, as early as May 1949, intimated to Bao Dai in no uncertain terms that "sovereignty would be transferred only to a Government in which France had the fullest confidence". (Devillers, *op. cit.*, p. 445.)

It was in this way that Bao Dai's good intentions were gradually smothered in the months that followed, and that "independent Vietnam" became a mere protectorate, a kind of extension of the colonial régime of Cochin-China to the whole country. Even the right-wing and anti-Vietminh "nationalists" on whom the Bao Dai régime was originally supposed to be based were increasingly "kept in order" by the French administration. But, as time went on, even they became increasingly troublesome. They tried to play off French influence against American influence, and even their loyalty to Bao Dai became more and more uncertain. By 1954, Bao Dai himself was far from sure whether he was more interested in living peacefully at Cannes or in becoming a Vietnamese Syngman Rhee.

CHAPTER TWELVE

THE "AFFAIRE DES GÉNÉRAUX"

1. CHINESE COMMUNISTS REACH VIETNAM BORDER

ALTHOUGH 1949 was one of the least eventful years in France itself, it was of crucial importance in Indo-China. It was at the end of this year, barely six months after the signing of the Auriol-Bao Dai agreements, that the Chinese Communists arrived at the northern frontier of Vietnam, having finally routed Chiang Kai Shek's forces and captured from them immense quantities of American war material.

The Indo-China war, started by the French administration and the "Saigon Clique" was a war of colonial reconquest, in which Bao Dai was to serve as a screen of respectability, had now become in official propaganda part of the Free World's struggle against World Communism.

The whole attitude of Vietminh inevitably changed. Most of the Vietminh leaders, including Ho Chi Minh himself, always distrustful of Chiang Kai Shek's China, had shown the greatest willingness to come to terms with the French whom, in 1946–8, they still considered a "lesser evil". The Communist diehards in Vietminh, greatly helped in this by the French attitude ever since 1946, now, however, gained the upper hand on the councils of Vietminh, and its war became an ideological war not merely against the French Colonialists, but against "Franco-American Imperialism".

In the summer of 1949 Ho Chi Minh still told an American correspondent, Andrew Roth, of *The Nation* that Vietnam could remain a "neutral or semi-neutral" state between the two blocs. By the end of the year, his tone changed. He now declared that the "independence" of Vietnam, and the sovereignty transferred to the Bao Dai régime were just a farce, so long as the French troops were not withdrawn from Vietnam. He also denied any legal existence to the Bao Dai Government, and emphasized that Vietnam had only one legitimate Government, that of the Resistance, and he offered to establish diplomatic relations with any foreign countries wishing to do so. On January 18, 1950 China recognized the Ho Chi Minh Government, and a fortnight later the Soviet Government did likewise. The Moscow press, with its tongue in its cheek, explained that Russia was merely recognizing a government which France had recognized in 1946! Why the Russians had not recognized Ho Chi Minh in the interval was not explained.

Whether, on the other hand, as was suggested at the time, Peking had forced Moscow's hand seems relatively unimportant.

With the Cold War in full swing, and with the Chinese avalanche rolling inexorably towards the borders of Tongking, France, in 1949, had at last become "Indo-China-conscious". The politicians and Big Business had been that for a long time, but not the general public— thought the Communists, at any rate, did their best to work up indignation over *la sale guerre*. Their posters said that with the 100 milliard francs a year that the *sale guerre* was costing, so many thousand houses could be built in France; but, after all, it was still "only" 100 milliards. Before long, it was going to cost incomparably more.

The prospect that the Chinese Communists would soon be in a position to help Vietminh, and perhaps even to intervene directly made the French military scratch their heads. General Revers, the French Chief of Staff, was sent on a mission to Vietnam, and brought back a report which was not only at the origin of the great Peyré Scandal or, as it soon came to be known, the *affaire des généraux*, but it contained important military proposals which the French Governments at the time were determined to ignore, in their eagerness to pose as the champions of the "Free World's Crusade against World Communism". What Revers proposed was, briefly, this: since Vietminh was bound, before long, to receive reinforcements (or, at any rate, military equipment) from the Chinese, France could not, short of putting all her eggs in the Vietnam basket, hope to hold the whole of North Vietnam, and should pull out of the mountainous and other outlying areas to the north and west of the Red River Delta, and concentrate on turning this delta, including Hanoi and Haiphong, and its invaluable rice-fields, into an impregnable bastion. Moreover, he suggested that there could, in the long run, be *no military* solution, but only a *diplomatic* solution to the problem of Indo-China.[1] This advice, as already said, was to be ignored, and in October 1950, Vietminh launched an offensive against the mountain fortress of Caobang, killed or captured 3,000 French soldiers, and forced the French command to pull out of Langson and the greater part of North Tongking adjoining the Chinese frontier. The Vietminh radio was already announcing that Hanoi would be occupied by December 19, 1950, the fourth anniversary of the Insurrection. Marshal Juin was rushed to Tongking and saved Hanoi in the nick of time. The Pleven Government finally got rid of Pignon in December 1950, and appointed one of France's most distinguished generals, Delattre de Tassigny both civil and military chief in Vietnam. Through-

[1] *Année Politique*, 1949, p. 84.

out 1951 he succeeded in consolidating the French positions in the delta. Broadly speaking, he was at last doing what Revers had recommended in his ill-fated report of July 1949.

All these events—the Auriol-Bao Dai agreements, the victory of the Chinese Communists, the "leakage" of the Revers Report, the recognition of the Vietminh Government by China and the Soviet Union early in 1950, the clamour for American aid to the French forces in Indo-China, the sharp increase in Vietminh "terrorist activity" throughout Vietnam, the repercussions in Indo-China of the war in Korea, and the disaster of Caobang in October 1950 (a forerunner of the final disaster of Dien Bien Phu four years later)—all these events tended to make Vietnam France's Number 1 problem in 1949 and 1950.

2. "GERMANS IN INDO-CHINA"

Already in April 1949 there were some violent debates at the National Assembly over the incorporation of Cochin-China in Vietnam, which was the condition laid down by Bao Dai before signing his agreement with President Auriol. Not only the Communists, but even the Socialists challenged the Government's assumption that Bao Dai—who had abdicated several years before—represented anything more than himself. Two months later, on June 10, in a debate of exceptional violence, the Communists raised the awkward question of who exactly, on the French side, was doing the fighting in Indo-China. It was known that the Foreign Legion, with many Germans among them, was fighting in Indo-China; but it was Mme Marie Lambert, a Communist Deputy who proceeded to dot the i's. Addressing the Queuille Government, she exclaimed:

You are now trying to justify the war in Indo-China by talking of murders allegedly committed by the Vietnamese armies. But when you started this war for the benefit of a handful of bankers and rubber-planters, and in defiance of the agreements you had signed with President Ho Chi Minh at Fontainebleau, you had none of these pretexts. . . . But you are not going to deceive French mothers any longer. They know that you have sent there not only German SS-men, but also French SS-men, bandits specially let out of prison. . . . You have sent to Vietnam all this scum and riff-raff to loot and rape and murder. . . . Worse than that; these SS-men are trying to turn our own boys into criminals like themselves.

And M. Pierre Villon, another Communist, referred to a Government circular authorizing the Army to recruit volunteers for Indo-China among the *miliciens* in prison camps and among German war prisoners, including the SS.

Then another Communist, Yves Peron intervened :

Can the Secretary of State for War say yes or no to the following question: Is it true that at least two of the butchers of Oradour-sur-Glane are now serving in Indo-China?

The Secretary of State said he had no knowledge of this; on the contrary, he knew that the military justice of the country was looking for these murderers everywhere.

CHARLES TILLON: But you are not denying that you've been recruiting murderers.

YVES PERON: Forty of the murderers of Oradour are known; eleven are in prison at Bordeaux; and two are in Indo-China.

CRIES FROM THE CENTRE: What are their names?

YVES PERON: These are the people you are defending with your howls.

The Communists failed to produce any names; but they did not give up.

ANDRÉ TOURNÉ: Would the Minister confirm that a *milicien*, a traitor who murdered the eighty-year-old Victor Basch [President of the Ligue des Droits de l'Homme] is now serving in Indo-China?

There was no reply. But instead, M. Teitgen (MRP) tried to embarrass the Communists by recalling that the military measures taken against Vietminh after the December Insurrection had been signed by Thorez, as one of the members of the Ramadier Government. Tillon, finally replying after the uproar had subsided, merely said that "there was no holding back of Bidault—he just wouldn't listen to any counsels of moderation"—a remark suggesting that the Communists could not go against Bidault in a Coalition Government without breaking it up.

TILLON: And, what is more, in that government we opposed this war, which you have now turned into your *sale guerre* . . . and now you find nothing better to do than to defend the murderers of Oradour-sur-Glane.

JEAN MASSON: And where were you at that time, Monsieur Tillon?

TILLON: When?

MASSON: At the time of the Oradour massacre.

TILLON: I shall give you a very simple answer. *Vous êtes un imbécile.*[2]

The answer was no doubt justified, considering that Tillon had been the chief of the French Francs-Tireurs-Partisans guerillas; but all this did not heighten the tone of the debate. The Communists had nevertheless, scored a point in drawing attention to the presence of SS-men

[2] *Débats, Assemblée Nationale*, June 10, 1949, pp. 3303-7.

and former *miliciens* in Indo-China, which went counter to the official tricolour propaganda. The savagery and bestiality of the Indo-China war was a theme that was to recur over and over again in the years that followed. A whole literature grew up round this theme, such as the unforgettable *Opération gâchis* by an ex-soldier in Vietnam, Arnoux de Pirey, which *Temps Modernes* published in 1953.[3]

But all this was still small stuff, compared with what was to come early in 1950 when the *affaire des généraux* seemed on the point of developing into the biggest political row in France since the *affaire Stavisky* in 1934, and when, a few days later, the ratification of the Auriol-Bao Dai agreements came up for parliamentary discussion.

3. RIVALRY OVER THE INDO-CHINA FLESHPOTS

Bollaert, who had prepared these agreements, was a "Third Republic" Radical, with certain "Masonic" contacts among the Radicals and Socialists in Paris (hence perhaps the patronage he was giving to General Xuan, who was considered the chief Vietnamese contact of certain "Masonic" Socialist groups in France). Unlike d'Argenlieu, who made no bones about looking upon the war in Indo-China as a plain war of colonial reconquest, Bollaert preferred to camouflage his policy with sonorous (if deflated) words drawn from the vocabulary of the Third Republic, and liked to represent the Bao Dai régime as a triumph for Democracy. Léon Pignon, his successor, and a close associate of d'Argenlieu in 1945–6, did not even take the trouble to camouflage the real nature of the Vietnamese "operation". With Pignon as High Commissioner, and with Coste-Floret and, after him, Letourneau as Minister of Overseas France (or of "the Associated States"), Vietnam became a political stronghold of the MRP. As Bourdet wrote in *Temps Modernes* in September 1953:

By this time, the war itself became merely part of a vast racket. They now all talked of fighting the war "to a finish", partly because of the profits derived from it by all kinds of politicians and by all the various business sharks allowed to share in the cake; and partly because the MRP were now too deeply committed, knowing full well that any peace negotiations and even any change in personnel would show up certain of its most eminent members (p. 418).

The Pignon régime was marked not only by the re-emergence in Indo-China of some of the worst Vichyites, including two who had

---

[3] It should, all the same, be added that the presence of so many Germans in the Foreign Legion had another side to it. Thus, in March 1952, *Esprit* alleged that soon after the war many German war prisoners had been "bullied and starved" into joining the Legion.

served under Admiral Decoux, and who were responsible for the horrible concentration camp of Poulo-Condor, known as "the Auschwitz of Indo-China", but also by a spectacular development of corruption and of some of the more grandiose rackets: the racket in import and export licences, the opium racket and, above all, the piastre racket—on which immense fortunes were made at the expense of the French Treasury, and which was alleged to provide a constant flow of money into certain Party funds in France itself. The mechanism of this racket was particularly simple: the Indo-China piastre had one exchange rate in Indo-China, and another in France; and whoever could engineer "transfers" and (for a consideration) obtain "licences", pocketed the difference. The Parties that had taken an interest in these rackets—particularly the import-export licences and the piastre transfers—were said to be the MRP, the Socialists and de Gaulle's RPF, one of whose leading members was personally shown up in the sensational (if, at times, somewhat hysterical) book, *Le Trafic des Piastres*, published in 1953 by a former French official in Indo-China, M. Despuech, who, defying all threats, decided to "spill the beans".

4. POLITICIANS, CROOKS, AND GENERALS

The story of the *affaire des généraux*, which broke in Paris in January 1950, had, as its background, this rivalry between the MRP and the Socialists. It would take volumes to tell the story in full; but these appear to be the most salient facts:

An adventurer with a very murky past, named Roger Peyré, wormed himself into the confidence of certain Socialist and Radical circles to which he had been introduced by M. Bouzanquet, a leader of Force Ouvrière, the Socialist trade union federation. Their plan was to get Pignon, the protégé of the MRP, replaced as High Commissioner by General Mast, a protégé of the Socialists. General Revers, the French Chief of Staff, was drawn into the operation, and naïvely allowed himself to be dazzled by Peyré who claimed to exercise immense influence among the top-ranking political personnel of the Fourth Republic. Revers went to Indo-China and probably without any ulterior motives (though his conclusions no doubt played into the hands of Peyré and Mast) drew up a report in which, as already said, he favoured peace talks and, in any case, the limitation of France's military activity in Tongking to a well-fortified "redoubt" round the delta. He also commented on the weakness of the Bao Dai régime and, by implication, criticized Pignon and his group at Saigon for their determination to continue the war at any price.

If the Government had accepted the conclusions of the Revers report, it would probably have led precisely to the results Peyré and Mast had been hoping for: Mast would have been appointed High Commissioner; Peyré would have become No 1 racketeer in Indo-China; the Radicals and Socialists would have taken over from the MRP all the key positions these were now holding in the Administration, and with them, all the import-export and piastre fleshpots. Whether it would have meant the end of the war in Indo-China is much less certain: it would, after all, have been in Peyré's interests to see the war continue, together with all its bounties. Revers, though no doubt hoping that the "all-powerful" Peyré would help him along in his career, does not personally seem to have been financially compromised in the *affaire*, but he certainly behaved extraordinarily foolishly for a man in his position. For all that, he probably acted in good faith, believing that the "plot"—which, if successful, might end the war—was in France's interests.

A curious figure, working in contact with Peyré, was a Vietnamese, Nguyen Van Co, who, acting on behalf of Bao Dai and General Xuan —or, at any rate, of one of their cliques—was alleged to have distributed funds to numerous French politicians, and to have treated them to expensive lunches. This practice has been compared to the method used by Chiang Kai Shek's agents to subsidize members of the China Lobby out of funds paid by the US Government to "Nationalist" China.

What blew the whole Peyré-Van Co-Mast plan sky high was the leakage of the Revers Report. The version generally accepted in 1950 was that Revers had injudiciously communicated the text of his report to certain Vietnamese supporters of Bao Dai; and that these, playing a double game, had passed it on to Vietminh. Later, however, it was learned that what Revers had given his Vietnamese friends was only the political, but not the military part of the Report; and if Vietminh got hold of the military part as well, it was not from Revers but, on the contrary, through certain channels close to the MRP who could not afford to allow the Socialists and Radicals to capture their Indo-China *fief,* and had to wreck the Peyré-Van Co-Mast project at any price.[4]

After an article, containing many revelations and even more innuendoes had appeared in *Time* Magazine, the *Monde* published, on January 13, 1950, an unsigned article, entitled: "Is there a Revers-Mast Affair?" Four days later the National Assembly met in a feverish atmosphere to hear M. Bidault, the Premier, make a "Government communication" concerning what came to be known as the *affaire des généraux*. It was obvious that the whole *affaire* was a good deal more intricate than appeared from Bidault's relatively short statement, and,

[4] An article in *Temps Modernes* (September 1953, p. 420) makes very specific allegations on this point, but perhaps with not enough hard evidence to support them.

at the suggestion of M. Paul Rivet, the Assembly decided to set up a parliamentary Committee of Inquiry. The allegations already published in the press and partly confirmed by Bidault included some of the following:

(1) Both General Mast (former Resident-General in Tunisia) and General Revers (the French Chief-of-Staff) had been in close contact with Roger Peyré;

(2) Revers and Peyré had both visited Indo-China about the same time during the previous year and there existed between the two men a somewhat mysterious relationship of "mutual patronage";

(3) Peyré had been given the Legion of Honour for his allegedly admirable Resistance record by M. Teitgen, at that time MRP Minister of Justice; only unfortunately, it was learned that Peyré, far from being a hero of the Resistance, had, in reality, collaborated with the Germans, though, no doubt, to "cover" himself, he had also done a little espionage for the French as well. Teitgen while admitting that he had given the adventurer the Legion of Honour, declared that he had done so at the insistence of General Revers who had, moreover, he alleged, later recommended Peyré for promotion in the Legion from *chevalier* to *officier*.

(4) Before the scandal blew up Peyré had managed to escape to Brazil, with the obvious connivance of certain police authorities and possibly, it was alleged, with the connivance of the Ministry of the Interior itself, headed, as it happened, by a Socialist, M. Jules Moch.

(5) The news of the leakage of the Revers Report had been revealed by one of the French police services, which, it was alleged, had deliberately provoked a fight on a Paris bus, in the course of which a number of people were taken to a police station; when they were searched, one of them, a Vietnamese—presumably a Vietminh agent—was found in possession of a copy of the Revers Report.

(6) A few days later, on September 24, 1949, it was further alleged, M. Queuille, the Radical Premier, and two of his Socialist Ministers, M. Ramadier (War) and M. Moch (Interior) decided that this was not a matter for the Courts, but "a Government matter", and that no action was called for. There was a strong suspicion that MM. Queuille, Ramadier, and Moch thought it more expedient to hush up the matter. The first two later argued that, since the Report found on the Vietnamese contained no secret military information, there were no grounds for prosecution; moreover, they suggested that it was not in the interests of the country to implicate the French Chief-of-Staff and another prominent General.

(7) General Revers regarded as disastrous the *jusqu' aboutiste* war policy of Coste-Floret and of the High Commissioner, Léon Pignon, and he was anxious to have the latter replaced by a soldier, namely General Mast.

(8) Mast, who was working in close contact with Van Co (a Bao Dai representative in Paris, but also suspected of being in contact with Vietminh) was conducting a major campaign among politicians against Pignon and in favour of his own appointment to Saigon.

(9) Van Co had been spending money on various politicians and news-

papers, but many important records—such as the counterfoils of Van Co's cheque book—had mysteriously disappeared, and had not been photographed by the police even when these were available; moreover, certain documents had been burned at the Ministry of the Interior; although it was explained by M. Moch that only "redundant" papers had been destroyed, the haste shown in destroying these documents—even if they *were* only duplicates—seemed suspect.

4. MUDSLINGING

As already said before, it would take volumes to relate in detail all that happened on the Committee of Inquiry. What emerges most clearly of all is that the Communists were determined to use the *affaire des généraux* as a means of showing up all the dirt and corruption that were now an inseparable part of the war in Indo-China; and that the MRP thought the *affaire* an excellent opportunity for discrediting the Socialists, and for consolidating their own position both in Paris and Saigon (it is, for instance, certain that, thanks to the *affaire*, Pignon was maintained as High Commissioner at Saigon much longer than he would otherwise have been). The Gaullists, for their part, went a good deal further still. They knew, by the beginning of 1950, that their electoral chances had declined since their sweeping election victory in October 1947, and many of them thought that their best bet was to take advantage of the *affaire* to strike at the régime itself by discrediting not only the Socialists, but President Auriol. A violent campaign was started by the Gaullist press, notably by *Carrefour*, suggesting that the "mysterious powers" of Peyré, working hand-in-glove with certain important Socialists, emanated from his close contacts, if not with the President of the Republic personally, at any rate, with certain members of the President's family and immediate *entourage*. There were countless innuendoes against a certain "M. Paul"—Paul happening to be the Christian name of the President's son. The political nature of this campaign against the President of the Republic and his family was only too obvious, but, in the end, the Gaullists failed to prove anything.

To the Communists, the exploitation of the *affaire* was of great value, and their member on the Committee of Inquiry, M. Kriegel-Valrimont, did not hesitate, contrary to the rules of the game, to publish in *L'Humanité* detailed daily accounts of the Committee's proceedings. To show up the "corruption" of the régime (Socialists included) and the *pourriture* surrounding the war in Indo-China was particularly useful from the Communist point of view at a time when the CP had given orders to the working-class to sabotage armaments production and especially arms shipments for Indo-China, and when the Government was preparing to table a stiff anti-sabotage Bill before the

Assembly. It also generally helped the Communists' Peace Campaign (the Stockholm Appeal for the outlawing of the Atom Bomb was about to be launched) and, in particular, their campaign for terminating the war in Indo-China which could, more easily than ever, be shown up as an unclean colonialist racket.

When, on January 27, ten days after Bidault's first official statement on the *affaire des généraux*, the Auriol-Bao Dai agreements came up for ratification, the Communists let loose Mme Vermeersch, the wife of Maurice Thorez. In the midst of a two-hour uproar she showed up the evils of colonialism in Indo-China, the wickedness and hopelessness of France's war "against the people of Vietnam" and the "complete cynicism" of the Bao Dai "experiment". Coste-Floret angrily expostulated: "There is no Bao Dai experiment; there is a complete Bao Dai success." But Mme Vermeersch would have none of it.

The violence of the meeting is best rendered by a few quotations from the verbatim report, as published by the *Journal Officiel*:

MME VERMEERSCH: The people of Vietnam are not burning French villages; but you are burning down Vietnamese villages, following in the footsteps of the Nazis who burned Oradour and Ascq and massacred all its inhabitants. [*Loud protests on Right, Centre, and Left. Cheers on Extreme Left. Uproar.*]

M. JEAN CATRICE: You are unworthy of being a Frenchwoman. Get out!

VOICES ON RIGHT AND CENTRE: Get out, we tell you! No more of this! No more of this filth! Get out! [*Mme Jeannette Vermeersch, turning to her hecklers, cocks a snook at them. Laughter and cheers on Extreme Left. Protests on Right and Centre.*]

THE PRESIDENT OF THE ASSEMBLY: Madam, you have no right——

MME VERMEERSCH: I have been insulted——

SHOUTS ON RIGHT AND CENTRE: Get out! [*Cheers on Extreme Left. Prolonged uproar. The Ministers and numerous Deputies on Right and Centre leave the debating-hall.*]

VOICES ON EXTREME LEFT: Off to the banquet! Go and collect your cheques!

It went on like this for hours. At one point, a Centre Deputy, in interrupting André Marty, who had taken part in the French naval mutiny in the Black Sea in 1919, referred to him as "*le mutin*". The Communists thought he had said something else.

VOICES ON EXTREME LEFT: Who said "*putain*"?

MME VERMEERSCH: Who said that? Who has dared to insult me like this? Nobody answers! You cowards!

M. ANDRÉ NOEL: I said "*mutin*" in speaking of M. Marty. [*Loud protests on Extreme Left. Uproar.*]

THE PRESIDENT OF THE ASSEMBLY: You see how overexcited you all are. A word was uttered which, had it been the word which you thought you had heard, Madam, would, indeed, have been intolerable. I would have been the first to protest. But now, please let us be reasonable for a few minutes....

But that wasn't the end of it yet.

Suddenly the theme of Madagascar was introduced into this debate on Indo-China. M. Arthaud (Communist) referred to 80,000 natives having been massacred in March 1947, and he declared the former High Commissioner in Madagascar, M. de Chevigné, to have been responsible for it.

M. PIERRE DE CHEVIGNÉ (MRP): The majority of the victims, as you know, were killed ...

M. ANDRÉ MARTY: By you!

M. PIERRE DE CHEVIGNÉ: By the rebels [*Uproar on Extreme Left*] because they had remained faithful to France. [*Cheers on Right and Centre. Violent protests on Extreme Left.*]

M. ANDRÉ MARTY: You swine!

M. ANDRÉ ARNAUD: How dare you insult the corpses you yourself have piled up?

M. PIERRE DE CHEVIGNÉ: I am glad to have this opportunity of paying a tribute to these thousands of humble Madagascar officials, postmen, railwaymen, teachers who were massacred ...

VOICE ON EXTREME LEFT: By you!

M. PIERRE DE CHEVIGNÉ: ... because they did not want their school, their railway station, their hospital or their post office burnt down. That is why they died with thousands of others who did not wish to betray France.... And there were also those who died because they were dragged off to the forest against their will; and that is how thousands of women and children and old people died of misery and hunger.

M. ANDRÉ MARTY: And what about all the witnesses you shot?

M. MARCEL HAMON: M. de Chevigné, you are completely dishonourable. Will you shut up?

M. ANDRÉ MARTY: And what about the police tortures? ... You should be brought before the High Court. And what about the witnesses you shot before the opening of the trial of the Madagascar Deputies?

M. de Chevigné said that there was perfect peace in Madagascar now. "Yes—the peace of the cemetery!" several Communists cried. "*En Haute Cour! En Haute Cour!*"

Nobody took M. de Chevigné's story very seriously; there was an awkward silence on the Socialist benches, and the Government, indeed, was careful not to intervene in the debate at this stage, and changed the subject at the first opportunity. But it was noted that M. de Chevigné had not challenged the figure of 80,000 dead.[5] For all that, on

[5] The more or less "official" figure given some time later was "only" 20,000 dead.

January 29, after many more violent incidents at the Assembly, the Auriol-Bao Dai agreements were ratified by 401 votes to 193. The Socialists, before the final vote, tabled a motion in favour of a truce in Indo-China; but this was more in the nature of a platonic gesture.

5. WHAT THE INQUIRY SHOWED

The Committee of Inquiry into the *affaire des généraux* continued to sit for several months; it was a striking example of the mutual grave-digging that went on among the different Parties and among the various police forces; particularly blatant was the rivalry between the SDECE—a successor of the wartime BCRA—and the DST, the secret police under the authority of the Ministry of the Interior. At one of the more sensational meetings of the Committee, a Colonel Fourcaud, of the SDECE sharply attacked M. Jules Moch, who, together with the DST, he alleged, had deliberately tried to hush up the *affaire*.

It is unnecessary here to go into the details of the two Reports adopted by the Committee of Inquiry a few months later—the Duveau Report on the responsibilities incurred by Generals Revers and Mast, and the Delahoutre Report which emphasized the numerous irregularities committed by the police, the loss and disappearance of documents, the facilities given to valuable witnesses like Peyré to escape, etc. The Report, while admitting that M. Queuille and M. Ramadier had not acted regularly when they "dropped" the case in September 1949, rather suggested that they had done so for "respectable" reasons, not wishing to complicate the delicate military negotiations in progress in Washington at the time by casting aspersions on the French Chief-of-Staff. M. Moch, on the other hand, was not explicitly or even implicitly "cleared"—a fact which was to give rise to an extraordinary anti-Moch manœuvre at the National Assembly some months later.

Already on May 4, the National Assembly passed a motion in terms of which M. Ramadier had acted "in the national interest"; since M. Ramadier had acted on behalf of M. Queuille, the latter was also implicitly exonerated.

As for the two generals, they were sent before a disciplinary tribunal and pensioned off.

But the truth is that although the Committee of Inquiry washed a great deal of dirty linen in public, the results of its work were disappointing and inconclusive; and if, in January, it looked as if the *affaire* might develop into another *affaire Stavisky*, the general public seemed to lose interest in it remarkably quickly. It is also probable that the attempts on the part of the Gaullists to undermine the whole régime, notably by implicating the President of the Republic, encouraged the governments to push the whole *affaire* out of the limelight, and let it peter out as soon as possible—in the midst of a welcome general indifference.

The reason for this indifference was obvious: instead of concentrating on the misdeeds and rivalries of the "gangs", the Inquiry devoted most of its time to the minor question of the "leakage" of the Revers Report —a *secret de Polichinelle*, anyway.

What, in the last analysis, was the real significance of the *affaire des généraux*? Basically, it was a curious by-product of the rivalry between the MRP and the Socialists for the key posts in Indo-China—a rivalry which went parallel with the rivalry between two major clans of racketeers. One of these clans had tried to make use of Revers and Mast. Mast was ambitious; but, like Revers, he no doubt also sincerely desired the adoption of a policy that would eventually lead to a compromise peace. On October 5, 1949 Revers had written to M. Queuille: "I fear that the sacrifice of our soldiers may one day prove to have been completely useless." This more or less corresponded with the Socialist line, and was in conflict with the policy of the MRP. Was there much actual corruption of politicians in Paris by Van Co, with his famous cheque-book and his banquets? This is very hard to say; for it was never quite clear for what specific purpose Van Co could have distributed funds among the politicians. Van Co himself pleaded that the *affaire des généraux* was a "prefabricated scandal" calculated to camouflage "the failure of a policy"—the policy of the MRP.

Not that the Committee of Inquiry had wasted its time altogether. It revealed all kinds of strange things going on in the Fourth Republic —the rivalry of police forces (and no longer merely the old rivalry between the two traditional forces—the Sûreté and the Police Judiciaire —but also between them and that wartime creation, the SDECE); the interference of Parties in the promotion of generals and high officials, etc. It also illustrated in a striking manner the wholly disproportionate increase in France since the war of the so-called "sundry incomes" which had little or nothing to do with industry, agriculture or *bona fide* trade.

Wherever there were any restrictive regulations, e.g. in the case of the Indo-China piastre, export and import licences, etc., there were also "rackets". As François Goguel wrote in *Esprit* (April 1950, p. 684):

All these rackets give rise to the payment of innumerable and—economically—wholly sterile "brokerages" and "commissions" for the benefit of "well-placed" persons in possession of the necessary signature or rubber stamp.... This is the field in which business sharks, politicians and, sometimes high officials so often meet in the most suspect conditions.

If, thanks largely to Marshall Aid, and with the disappearance of the black market, there was no longer quite the same scope for "rackets" in France as before, Indo-China had become in 1949–50 the French racketeers' favourite hunting-ground.

6. INDO-CHINA, RACKETEERS, AND BIG BUSINESS

On the whole, it was not in the interests of the racketeers that the war should come to an end. As for the allegations that Big Business was trying to keep the war going, as well as all the special opportunities for making money that this war had created, there is a good deal of evidence to show that these allegations were not unfounded. The parliamentary committee specially set up in 1953 to inquire into the piastre racket was particularly interested in the part played by the powerful interests that had been active in Indo-China throughout the war years; and its conclusions were not complimentary. The question was also often debated at the National Assembly.

Thus, M. Georges Cogniot (Communist) made the following assertions at the National Assembly on May 18, 1953[6]:

The country would like to know why the exchange rate of the piastre was not changed before now, and what was the volume of transfers, year by year, since 1945 ... also whether there exists a register showing the persons and the amounts. The country feels more and more that this war means a shower of fire and steel for some, and a shower of gold for others. Let us just consider these figures:

The Banque d'Indochine admits a profit of 502 m. francs in 1951, as against one of 53 m. in 1947; the Cie. du Cambodge, 717 m. against 44 m., the Plantations des Terres Rouges 1070 m. against 100 m., etc.

Forty-five capitalist societies whose balance sheets I have before me admit to have pocketed 10,101 m. frs. in 1951 against 1,250 m. in 1947. And this is only a small proportion of the real profits.

The Institut National de la Statistique shows that on April 23, 1953 (1949 representing 100) the general index of shares quoted on the Paris Bourse was 149 but that the index of the shares of companies exploiting Indo-China was 197.

Big Business, in other words, wants the war to continue.

Later, even more specific charges were made about the part played in the piastre racket by Big Business, both by members of the Parliamentary Committee of Inquiry on the Piastre Racket and in a large number of French papers, notably *France-Observateur*, *Franc-Tireur*, *Temps Modernes*, *Esprit*, and, last but not least, the *Canard Enchaîné*.

But, apart from Big Business, there were also the gangs, and long after the *affaire des généraux* had been forgotten, these gangs continued to operate on a bigger scale than ever. It was not till 1953 that any steps

[6] *Débats, Assemblée Nationale*, 1953, pp. 2718–9.

were taken at all to put an end to the piastre racket, when the piastre rate was reduced from 17 to 10 francs, to the great dismay of all categories of racketeers.

There were very strong suspicions that the Piastre and Export Licence Kings stopped at nothing to save their "business" from extinction. The dual air disaster in the Persian Gulf in the summer of 1950 when, at a week's interval, two Saigon-Paris air liners crashed was more than suspect—all the more so as among the passengers killed were M. J. Rivet, the head of the Exchange Control Bureau at Saigon, who was an enemy of the "gangs", and Jean-François Almorin, the special correspondent of *Franc-Tireur*, who was going to show up the rackets— as was apparent from a private letter from him that the paper published, already after his death. Among other things, he was going to show that Saigon's Number 1 racketeer was an intimate friend of certain persons holding high positions in the Saigon administration. Many of Bao Dai's associates were also known to be deriving much benefit from the piastre racket.

7. RACKETS AND THE WAR CONTINUE...

This and other rackets were to go on for years; and meantime the French Army in Indo-China was to continue its thankless task in increasingly difficult conditions. In the summer of 1950 it firmly held part of the Tongking Delta and a small area round Saigon; the rest of the country was either "fluid", or simply under full Vietminh control. In these parts, Vietminh had by now embarked on major social and economic reforms, such as the anti-illiteracy campaign, land reform, the organization of health services, etc. The Vietminh forces, now helped by China, were growing in strength; whereas the equipment of the French Army was becoming increasingly obsolete and inadequate, particularly in the case of heavy equipment and aircraft. This army, called the "Army of the French Union" numbered in the summer of 1950 143,000 men, of whom 57,000 were French professional soldiers and volunteers, 16,000 men of the Foreign Legion (mostly Germans); 21,000 North Africans, 11,000 Senegalese and 36,000 men of various Indo-Chinese units, the least reliable part of this army. The war was now costing France about 150 milliard francs a year—an amount that was, from now on, going to increase very rapidly; and a high proportion of France's officers and nco's were bogged down in Indo-China, much to the detriment of France's military position in Europe.

The first clear signs that the United States was including Indo-China in its "strategic sphere" date back to this period. Soon after the outbreak of the Korean War President Truman announced that the USA would speed up the delivery of military aid to the French Forces and to the Associated States of Indo-China, and that an American Military Mission would soon be sent there. M. Maurice Duverger wrote a sensational article in the *Monde* in which he said: *"Les jeux sont faits"*... In it he discussed France's increasingly false position in Indo-China, and spoke with irony of the pointless Pau Conference at which the representatives of the Associated States were now going to meet to discuss a variety of "technical problems" with France, while the Emperor Bao Dai, no longer interested in anything, was having a good time on the Riviera, spending his ill-gotten gains on a new tennis court, on a yacht, and other amusements, much to the consternation of his subjects and much to the annoyance of the French, who had, somehow, expected him to treat the Triumph of Democracy in Vietnam in a more serious and solemn spirit.

CHAPTER THIRTEEN

THE IMPACT OF THE KOREAN WAR

THE war in Indo-China was so unpopular in France that the outbreak of the war in Korea—the news of which reached Paris on Sunday, June 25—was bound to be received with the greatest distaste, to say the least. That day nearly everybody was out of town—except those who were directly concerned with the French cabinet crisis resulting from the fall of the Bidault Government a few days before. The position of this Government had been weak ever since the Socialists had resigned from it in February for a number of reasons, among them the friction and unpleasantness that had been caused between the Socialists and the MRP over the *affaire des généraux*.

The first reaction to the Korean flare-up was that this was a local affair, and had better be treated as such. The Communist press hastened to describe it as "civil war in Korea", but the desire not to magnify it into a major international conflict was general. It was widely felt that the Korean war presented two major dangers: if it was not localized, it might spread all over the Far East and beyond; and even if it did not, but if the United States attached undue importance to it, it might greatly interfere with Europe's precarious economic and financial convalescence. Enthusiasts of the consolidation of Western Defence like Raymond Aron were aware of the danger of American attention being focused on the Far East and of being at least partly diverted from Europe, and the *Figaro*, for all its anti-Communism, published some extremely *nuancé* articles by Walter Lippmann, who warned the US Government against becoming too deeply involved in Korea—articles which confirmed the general impression in France that "*l'affaire a été mal engagée*", as a high official at the Quai d'Orsay remarked after Truman had stampeded UN into giving its blessing and patronage to the Korean War.

Except for the Communists, who took the line that Southern Korea had attacked Northern Korea, it was, nevertheless, generally assumed that the attack had come from the North, but, considering the behaviour of Syngman Rhee over a long period, most observers hesitated to speak of "unprovoked aggression". It was not, however, until some months later that the full extent of the Syngman Rhee provocations and the peculiar attitude of MacArthur were to be analysed outside the

Communist press, notably by an American writer like I. F. Stone, whose articles in *L'Observateur* aroused much attention, and especially by the *Monde* correspondent in Korea, Charles Favrel, whose "Letter to Mister Smith", published in *Esprit*, was the most savage French attack not only on American policy, but also on "the American character"; according to Favrel, this "character" was a compound of callousness, megalomania and anti-yellow racialism singularly reminiscent of the old Nazi mentality. It was an absurd over-generalization; but he had obviously returned from Korea deeply shattered by some of the things he had seen.

But even at the early stages of the war, many French observers felt that the whole thing wasn't quite above-board; Mr Dulles's visit to Korea and to the 38th parallel only a few days before the outbreak of war seemed a "curious coincidence"; and there was a tendency to agree with Mr Vyshinsky that it seemed unlikely that Mr Dulles had gone up to the 38th parallel merely to "smell the violets".

Probably the most widespread reaction was, at least at first: "A plague on both your houses." On June 26 the *Monde* wrote in its first editorial on the Korean War:

It may be too late to save Southern Korea; the unfortunate "democratic" republic of Seoul will have been the victim—let's be quite frank about it— of not only a Communist aggression encouraged by the Soviet Union, but also of the incoherence and the hesitations of American policy in the Far East.... In July 1948 it was decided to evacuate Southern Korea...on the ground that it was of doubtful strategic value to the USA.

After saying that the Syngman Rhee régime was rotten to the core, and could not expect to resist indefinitely against the Northern propaganda in favour of Unity—which was immensely popular in Southern Korea, despite the police terror, on which the Syngman Rhee régime was based—the *Monde* clearly suggested that America had better cut her losses in Korea:

No doubt France will unreservedly support the United States at UN. But have not the prestige of the United States and that of United Nations been engaged in a most unfortunate way?... We fear that the events of the next few days may show that the game has been lost in advance and that belated American help may make no difference; the same thing may well happen at Formosa before long.

And it concluded that the loss of Korea would at least have the advantage of teaching America a lesson—and of making her see that her Asian policy needed careful revision: America must see to it that the same thing didn't happen in South-East Asia.[1] Which meant that

[1] *Le Monde*, June 27, 1950.

America should cut her losses in Korea and Formosa, but help the French to hold Indo-China. It also meant that, from the French point of view, Indo-China was, by itself, causing quite enough trouble, and why add to the trouble by becoming involved in Korea as well?

Muddled thinking? Or different influences on the *Monde* pulling in different directions? For, curiously enough, two days before the outbreak of the Korean War, the very same *Monde* had come out with a sensational article in favour of ending the war in Indo-China—which, it said, was a terrible drain on her resources; and these, it said, would be much better employed in Europe. And now, scarcely a few days after the outbreak of the Korean War, Truman decided to send "massive help" to the French forces in Indo-China—which, with the opening of the anti-Communist Crusade in Korea, were now for the first time being officially recognized by the USA as valiant anti-Communist Crusaders.

It is scarcely an exaggeration to say, in the light of this new development, that it was Korea that gave the French war in Indo-China an "international standing"—and so gave it a new lease of life at a time when in France opinion was becoming increasingly vociferous in favour of winding it up. This new "international standing" of the Indo-China war acted as a great encouragement to all those financial and political interests in France which were in favour of continuing it. By the same process France became more and more dependent on the United States—even in a field where she had pursued a short-sighted but relatively "independent" policy of her own. As a result of this, the number of people in France who now acquired a financial interest in the continuation of the Indo-China war greatly increased.

Altogether, America's attitude showed almost from the start that the Korean War would lead to a hardening of US policy and probably to an all-out rearmament drive, with far-reaching economic and political repercussions among her allies. And there was a growing suspicion in France that not all was quite clear about the circumstances in which the Korean War had begun.

As for the Korean War itself, it caused two major scares in France: first, when the Fusan bridgehead was in danger of collapsing, and the American troops of being thrown into the sea; and, later, when MacArthur crossed the 38th parallel and drove ahead towards the Yalu River. In August, there was something resembling a minor panic in France; housewives could be observed laying in stores of provisions, and at the Quai d'Orsay officials were saying: "It will not matter if they manage to hold Fusan, but if they are pushed into the sea, then a major war will become inevitable." And French opinion was struck by the American refusal to consider any mediation offers coming from Nehru, let alone from the Russians.

Not that the panic in France ever reached anything like the proportions later depicted in the French film, *Avant le Déluge*. Nevertheless it seems to be true that, during the first few weeks of the Korean War, the number of signatures below the Stockholm Appeal for outlawing the atom bomb rose in France from 7 million to 11 million. MacArthur's Yalu Offensive, which was interpreted as a step towards a preventive war against China and Russia, caused even greater alarm; and it was generally agreed that Mr Attlee, who, under the pressure of a unanimous outcry in England, had flown to Washington on November 30, saved humanity from what would probably have developed into World War III. After Attlee's mission there were some melancholy reflections in France on the "gutlessness" of not only the Pleven Government, which did not dare say boo to Mr Truman, but of the National Assembly generally, where (apart from the Communists) only a handful of left-wing deputies had come out openly against "MacArthurism".[2] The Socialist Party in particular refrained from any kind of action, and M. Ramadier even regretted the failure of MacArthur's offensive, and argued that a crime was still a crime, even though justice had been helpless—which produced a sharp rejoinder from M. Albert Kahn, of the *Ligue des Droits de l'Homme*, that the "criminal" had never been given a hearing.

The attitude of the Communists lent itself no doubt to a good deal of ironical comment. During the early stages of the Korean War, when the North Koreans were sweeping victoriously across Southern Korea towards Fusan, the Communist press wallowed in the glories of *une juste guerre*;[3] after the Inchon landing and MacArthur's recapture of Seoul, the Communist press began to complain bitterly about the inhumanity of American war methods.

Not that America had made herself popular anywhere in France as a result of the Korean War. Far from it. Many found American self-righteousness over Korea particularly distasteful. As *Esprit* wrote in August 1950:

Although the USA is today clad in the garments of UN, let the Americans

[2] In all fairness it should be added that Pleven conferred with Attlee, and is not known to have discouraged him against going to Washington.

[3] Thus, night after night in June and early July the Communist *Ce Soir* would come out with banner headlines like "DEBACLE OF SYNGMAN RHEE'S FORCES", "AMERICAN CRUISER SUNK BY N. KOREANS", "US FLEE ABANDONING DEAD, WOUNDED AND TANKS", "LIGHTNING DRIVE TOWARDS FUSAN", etc., while editorials explained that even in the "police state" elections in South Korea Syngman Rhee had 80 per cent of the people against him, that that was why he *needed* the war, that the people of South Korea were overjoyed at their liberation by the Communists, and that American intervention was without the slightest reference to the wishes of the Koreans themselves.

not pretend that they never committed any of the crimes with which they now charge the Korean Communists. They have supported Fascism in Greece and Spain, the Nazi industrialists in Germany, and Chiang Kai Shek ... all of which is scarcely compatible with the edification of a new and democratic post-war world. And their colonization of Japan has done a good deal to poison the international atmosphere ...

The effect of this policy has been to maintain in power the most unpopular, the most corrupt governments, whom the American politicians imagine to be the safest instruments of a vast anti-Communist policy ... UN, which entrusted the United States with a military mission, is no longer in a position to speak of the name of the United Nations. UN was created by the Big Five. Since the USA refused to recognize the change of régime in China, and so, with France obediently following, provoked Russia's absence, the decisions of the Security Council inevitably became null and void.... With suspect haste, the United States used UN to legitimize a decision which corresponded rather too closely to its own selfish interests.... It thus gravely compromised an international agency whose weakness was only too apparent, but which, the peoples of the world still hoped, might act usefully as a mediator to avert a general conflagration....

And *Esprit* went on to say that those who had no enthusiasm for the war in Korea were treated as "Munichites":

Yet Munich was different. In 1938 we should have struck, because if we did not, Hitler was bound to strike at us before long. There was no other means of stopping him.... But the insidious "Munich" argument does not hold good in the case of Korea. For it can only drive Western soldiers into distant regions where they can figure merely as oppressors, as policemen in the service of a condemned order.... The invasion of Southern Korea was an act of violence. But to place "democracy" in the service of Bao Dai, Syngman Rhee and Chiang Kai Shek is another act of violence. (*Esprit*, 1950, No 8, pp. 182–5.)

And, three months later, in its November issue, *Esprit* printed an "anthology" of particularly ignominious and sadistic pieces of American war reporting from Korea which had been reproduced in the French press, such as a gloating UP account of a manhunt in the ricefields north of Seoul—real "horror comics" stuff. And, alongside this, there was the sanctimonious speech, followed by the Lord's Prayer, delivered by MacArthur in the presence of his friend Syngman Rhee at the ceremony celebrating the recapture of Seoul.

*   *   *   *

Never had anti-American feeling been so strong in France (and in England, for that matter) as in November and December 1950, i.e. at the very time when America was fighting her hardest battle in the name of the "Free World". The same words did not mean the same thing on the two sides of the Atlantic; Europe in 1950 was more scared of war than America, and Syngman Rhee made the whole thing stink.

Monde reports by Charles Favrel and Robert Guillain from Korea spoke of the "terrifying mentality" of the American GI's and especially of American airmen who cheerfully machine-gunned civilians in North Korea and wiped out village after village. It was the "Gook mentality" right enough. It is, however, only fair to add that, to many, it was ominously reminiscent of other reports from Indo-China of the *ratissage* of Vietnam villages by French troops and by the Foreign Legion.

The Korean War tended to heighten, especially among the French intellectuals, the feeling of guilt towards the "coloured people" generally. There was indignation over the American airmen's callousness towards the "Gooks"; but also over the treatment by the French and the Foreign Legion of the "Viets"; and in North Africa there were the "*bicots*" who also were getting a raw deal.

When MacArthur's troops were driven back from the Yalu by the North Koreans, now supported by the Chinese "volunteers", there was an unmistakable feeling of *Schadenfreude* in France—as there was, indeed, in England; and it was with a touch of sneaking admiration that the French press reported the proud and arrogant behaviour at Lake Success of General Wu—the lawful representative of 500 million Chinese. Gooks indeed!

By the end of 1950, after the fiasco of MacArthur's "Home by Christmas" offensive, the Korean War seemed for a time to settle down to a sort of "phoney war" along the old border, the 38th parallel, except for intense air activity. As the *Monde* wrote on December 27:

Despite the rejection of Peking's truce proposals, the "phoney war" that began four weeks ago is continuing. With the evacuation of Hungham not a single American soldier is left in North Korea and, apart from a few patrols, there seem to be no Chinese south of the 38th parallel.

Nevertheless, it did not think that this precarious stabilization of the Front could continue much longer, and since the initiative was now with the Chinese, it feared further complications, and urged the Americans either to negotiate on the basis of the Chinese terms or to pull out of Korea altogether—"as is suggested by the whole of the British Sunday press"—and, after that "reconsider the whole question of the Far East". The attempt to hang on to Southern Korea "can have only one certain result: it will prolong indefinitely the terrible sufferings of the Korean people."

This was to underrate the truculence of MacArthur, a truculence which was to be encouraged by what happened a few days later.

For on New Year's Day the long-expected Chinese offensive began, and Seoul was captured by the Chinese. A wretched Seoul citizen was shown in a *Franc-Tireur* cartoon saying to the Chinese: *"C'est pour la nuit, ou pour un petit moment?"* A good comment—for the war was becoming "phoney" in a different sort of way—a mere reflection of a hardboiled, diplomatic game on both sides. Thus, after the fall of Seoul, MacArthur seemed to be withdrawing at an abnormally fast speed, and it was strongly suspected that he was attempting to create the impression of an overwhelming Chinese superiority—which, in reality, did not exist—and so prepare the ground for a "tougher" American policy. Before very long the Chinese, more or less voluntarily, started withdrawing to the North, but their January offensive had been sufficient to create the atmosphere in which the US Government forced Britain and France and most of the other UN powers to join it in branding China as an "aggressor". Though more than doubtful about America's case against China, the French Government, like the British, nevertheless, agreed to demonstrate its "solidarity" with the USA.

Despite the Kaesong and Panmunjon talks, active war was to continue in Korea for two more years—though mostly in the air; it wasn't doing anybody much good, but, as the *Monde* had foretold, it "added enormously to the sufferings of the Korean people".

Despite ups and downs, the Korean War, with its periodic threat of "A-Bombs on Manchuria", encouraged the "roll-back" theorists in America in their fight against the "containment" theorists; the French and British appeals to America to "drop" Korea, while understandable from their point of view, did not take account of the mood in the United States at the end of 1950. It was a mood which scared Europe.

It was, indeed, in the next year that "roll-back" and "preventive war" propaganda was to reach its high-water mark, with the Eisenhower statement to *Paris-Match* in November 1951 foreshadowing a "showdown" in which the Western armies might have to march into Southern Russia or into "the area round Leningrad", and with the incredible special number of *Collier's* with its lyrical descriptions of a happy, though atomized Russia which had at last "found freedom".

Another consequence of the Korean War was to turn the war in Indo-China from a colonial war into a "Crusade against Communism", in which Asians were expected to fight Asians.

To Europe, and particularly to France, the economic and political consequences of the Korean War and the accompanying all-round rearmament drive of the "Free World" were very serious indeed. In the two years that followed, all French premiers and prospective premiers spoke nostalgically of the "stabilization" of 1949 and the early months of 1950 that had been so rudely interrupted by the Korean

War; it was followed by a rise in prices and the cost of living, in greatly increased budget deficits, etc. At the beginning of 1952 Edgar Faure referred to *le virage*—the sharp bend—of 1950, which cruelly upset the financial and economic balance that France was about to reach at the beginning of that year for the first time since the Liberation. The rise in commodity prices, the rearmament drive of the Free World, virtually dictated to it by Washington, the growing demands made on the French Treasury by an aggravation of the war in Indo-China and the pressing demand that Germany be rearmed—all these created new internal difficulties in France and increased her financial and political dependence on the United States and on the whims of Congress, the White House, the State Department, and the Pentagon.

CHAPTER FOURTEEN

SCHUMAN PLAN AND "EUROPEAN ARMY", THE TWO SHAKY PILLARS OF FEDERALISM

I. BIRTH OF THE SCHUMAN PLAN

THE greatest landmark in the story of France's "Federalist" ambitions was the birth of the Schuman Plan. It is extremely difficult to speak of it without, in the process, embarking on an endless technical discussion of its industrial and commercial aspects and of its highly intricate "supra-national" machinery. All this is outside the scope of the present book; and the most that can be done is to try to record public reactions inside France to the "general idea" of the Coal-Steel Pool. In view of the complexity of the subject, these reactions were seldom very coherent. Even so, it must be said that, from the very outset, an almost unprecedented effort was made to "sell" the somewhat indigestible idea to the French public.

The birth of the Plan on May 9, 1950, about six weeks before the outbreak of the Korean War, was celebrated by a tremendous display of fireworks from a part of the press, particularly in France and the USA. And the curious thing about it is that, at the time, literally nobody knew exactly what it was all about—neither Schuman himself, nor even the real inventor of the Plan, M. Jean Monnet. M. Monnet, the technocrat, who had been the *éminence grise* of one government after another under the Fourth Republic (Pleven was said to be particularly docile in his presence) was not really (as one of his close associates confessed) the "great technician" he was generally thought to be; but he had a "brains trust" of very able men under him. Monnet himself was largely a self-taught man, but one with a good deal of natural intelligence and financial acumen, ambition, a gambling spirit, important business contacts, especially in the USA, and a (somewhat naïve) breadth of vision. And the Schuman Plan was one of the most characteristic of Monnet's brainwaves. De Gaulle, who dubbed him "The Inspirer" had a hearty dislike (as will be seen from de Gaulle's later comment on Monnet) for his "cosmopolitanism", his "anti-national" instincts, and his everlasting desire to "mix the unmixables".

Having been disappointed (as we shall see presently) in the results of the Monnet Plan, Monnet began, in 1949, if not before, to think in terms of "Europe" and "Franco-German unity"—ideas in which he was greatly encouraged by M. Schuman. The "Schuman Plan" as such, which Schuman sprang on the world on May 9, 1950 was still at that time a very "general" idea,[1] none of the details of the plan having been worked out by either Monnet, or still less, by Schuman himself; and it was not until some months later that the experts, working under Monnet, elaborated the details of the Plan of which only a bare skeleton had been presented by Schuman to the Government, to Parliament and to the Press in May 1950. Monnet was not, apparently, primarily interested in coal and steel as such; to him (as to Schuman) the Schuman Plan was merely the foundation stone for European Federalism on a much wider scale; when, much later, in 1955, Monnet resigned from the chairmanship of the Coal-Steel Authority, it was not so much because it was working unsatisfactorily so far as coal and steel were concerned, as because, with the breakdown of EDC, the Coal-Steel Pool—which was to lay the foundations for a "federated" Europe—had failed in its ultimate object.

That the whole conception of the Schuman Plan when it was first launched upon the world was still an extremely vague one is confirmed, for example by M. Jacques Gascuel, who was closely associated with the original "launching" of the Plan, as well as by another authority on the subject, Professor Bernard Lavergne, who published a highly critical study, *Le Plan Schuman* in 1952, already after its ratification.

Lavergne condemned the Schuman Plan as a "forced Franco-German marriage" and as "a misapplication of the Federal Idea". Lavergne's argument ran as follows:

(1) There were many people in France who, since 1947, had been thinking in terms of building up a powerful industrial unit comprising all the countries of Western Europe, including Britain, which would, as it were, hold the balance between the United States and the Eastern bloc.

But these "neutralist" or "third force" plans soon took a very different turn; instead of being an independent edifice that could stand up to the United States, the project soon became one of the pet ideas of American diplomacy.

(2) The curious thing was that M. Bidault, the Premier was—at least at first—not at all favourable to the Plan which, early in May, was suddenly sprung on him by his Foreign Minister, M. Schuman. And oddly enough—though this was typical of M. Schuman's furtive statesmanship and diplomacy—neither M. François-Poncet, the French High Commissioner in Germany, nor the Quai d'Orsay, or even the French Government were properly informed of what was going on during the few days that preceded

---

[1] R. H. S. Crossman described it at the time as nothing but a metal spike of the supra-national autority, with a lot of froth round it.

the "Schuman bombshell" of May 9. It was true, however, that, during the previous week, M. Schuman had seen Mr Acheson. Whether the matter was discussed with him was never officially disclosed. But the British Government, at any rate, knew nothing.

(3) Here then was a case in which a "technocrat"—M. Jean Monnet—imposed on his country a Plan which, strictly speaking, was done without consultation with either Government or Parliament, and both of whom were eventually made to swallow the Plan because it was "awkward" by this time not to do so.

M. Monnet's new plan could at least partly be attributed to his frustrated ambition, as the initiator of the famous Monnet Plan, and partly to American encouragement. The Monnet Plan had, at least in part, been a failure. It had been over-optimistic, so much so that in some of its sectors it had been little short of autarkist in its targets. But the production of coal and lignite, for example, had not come up to the Plan's ambitious expectations: the output, in 1950, was not 65 million tons (i.e. 17 million tons more than in 1938) but only 53 million tons. The Plan had also provided for a large-scale mechanization of French agriculture—which did not meet with sufficient response from the peasantry.

(4) Since *dirigisme* had practically come to an end in France, men like Monnet now wondered whether it could not be taken up on an international level.... The old Stinnes conception of a *Konzern* having emigrated to the United States, M. Monnet was encouraged in 1949 by the Americans to study the idea . . . M. Monnet then suggested the idea to M. Schuman, who, fired by the desire to do great things, to bring about a decisive reconciliation between France and Germany, and anxious to give a material basis to the European Idea which was, until then, more dead than alive, as well as to please the Americans, accepted the whole idea with enthusiasm. Only three or four ministers were informed about it, and when, finally, on May 8, the Council of Ministers met, no serious discussion took place at all. Schuman gave them a rough sketch of the Plan, and, without really knowing what it was all about, they gave it their blessing.... They gave M. Schuman a free hand—all the more so as he enjoyed a reputation of high personal integrity, and as the greater part of Parliament had always had a soft spot for the "European idea".... This kind of irresponsibility [Lavergne concluded] would have been inconceivable under the Third Republic.

(5) The French public could not make head or tail of the subsequent negotiations. Parliament, for its part, was presented with the project only very late in the day, and apart from twenty or thirty deputies and senators with sufficient general knowledge to form an opinion on the Plan, few grasped its meaning.... In most cases the thing was looked at through the distorting prism of a few slogans or electoral prejudices; in many other cases, most of the deputies voted with their eyes shut, and simply obeying the decisions taken by their party. "That's what's called—to use a bold euphemism— 'parliamentary control'" [said M. Lavergne].... In short, but for M. Jean Monnet, there never would have been a Schuman Plan.[2]

[2] B. Lavergne, *Le Plan Schuman*. Paris 1952, pp. 14–15.

It was very much the case of a "technocrat" with a passion for supranational institutions confronting not only Parliament, the Government, and the press, but even the French steel industry with a *fait accompli*. Even Raymond Aron in the *Figaro* protested against the cavalier manner in which the French steel magnates were being treated and against the fact that "the experts had been allowed to embark freely on negotiations which were essentially political". It was not till December 1951 that the Schuman Plan was finally ratified in an atmosphere of doubt and resignation, and a good deal of indifference. Here it is sufficient to record that, in May–June 1950, the Socialists, at any rate, were still extremely worried about Britain's reluctance to adhere to the Schuman Plan, that the Communists were chiefly harping on the smothering of French industry by the Germans and the resultant unemployment in France, and that a common opinion, quoted by Lavergne, was that

from the moment Britain, with her 220 million tons of coal and her 16 million tons of steel was unwilling to join, it should have been a matter of the most elementary prudence for M. Schuman to abandon his Plan.

However, the Plan was not abandoned, for months the experts worked on it, finally producing a highly intricate document of thirty-four closely printed pages, while part of the public, vaguely reassured by the idea that the Plan had a sound "European basis", left it at that. In subsequent years the general public in France still found it hard to make up its mind about the Schuman Plan. Was it a good thing? Was it a bad thing?

One thing, however, was certain: in the Cold-War atmosphere of 1950–1 it had not increased trust and cordiality between France and Germany, and had not brought "Europe" any nearer. If only because, ironically enough, the Schuman Plan, that symbol of Franco-German friendship, was to be used, only a few months after its birth, as the peg on which to hang the supra-national "European Army", i.e. German rearmament. It was Pleven who was to do it less than six months later—again, it seems, largely at the instigation of the "great European", Jean Monnet.

2. THE CONFUSION OVER REARMAMENT

Less than a month after the outbreak of the Korean War a succession of "Atlantic" conferences began with a view to intensifying European armaments expenditure and armaments production; in the face of the "Communist Danger" the United States was expecting Europe to put her back into it.

A significant comment on all this coming and going is to be found in Jacques Armel's article, "The USA is Mobilizing Europe" in the *Observateur* of July 27, 1950:

All this is being done without faith; it is remarkable how deep the gulf is between the official policy and public opinion—i.e. those very people who are in danger of being conscripted in virtue of all these plans.... Among the widest sections of the public the dominant feelings are either resignation or hostility.... The importance of the new expenditure and the very vagueness of the American war objectives make it difficult for the ordinary people to subscribe to these sacrifices.... It may seem paradoxical, but it's a fact that what we are witnessing now is the organization of a Europe which is expected to be "military in spite of itself".

Below the surface, there was a good deal of comedy about it all. M. Pleven, the new Premier, who had succeeded M. Bidault at the end of June, was anxious to promise the Americans the moon, but was at the same time wringing his hands and pleading poverty. He was not the only one.

Altogether, the memoranda sent to Washington by America's European partners on what they could do by way of rearmament were not as satisfactory as the Pentagon and the State Department had hoped. The British and French memoranda made it clear that Europe could not defend herself unaided, and that military expenditure should not exceed 10 per cent of the national income; moreover, even M. Pleven argued that France would of course supply men, but it was important that Britain (and America) did likewise, and moreover, in proportions rather more favourable to France than in 1939–40. Altogether, it was no use expecting France to produce more than fifteen divisions, even though her soldiers and officers were available at bargain prices, compared with the cost of American or even British soldiers. As for Mr Attlee, he was not enchanted with the prospect of having a large British army on the Continent, and dwelt on the great part Britain could play in the production of armaments. And as for gallant little Norway, she merely agreed to spend an extra 3½ million dollars over a period of 2½ years, representing a 4 per cent increase on her existing defence budget. Hence (French commentators wrote) America's haste to turn to other places in search of soldiers. What about Turkey, or Greece, or maybe Spain, and—of course—Germany?

Among the French bourgeoisie[3]—apart from a few eccentrics who

[3] Here, as elsewhere, the word *bourgeoisie* is used in the French sense of "moneyed class" (which is not quite the same as the English phrase "middle class"). The term *bourgeoisie* comprises both the upper and middle class, but rather with an emphasis on the former. (Thus, the organ of the *bourgeoisie* is the *Figaro*, as distinct from *L'Aurore* and *Le Parisien Libéré* read chiefly by the *petite bourgeoisie*.) In French (and, for that matter, in Marxist) terminology *bourgeoisie* and "capitalism" are almost synonymous in most contexts.

wanted to arm five or six million "Europeans" for an anti-Bolshevik Crusade, or a few nervous people like M. Raymond Aron who thought Europe could be safe only if she had seventy fully-armed divisions (where from?) to defend her against Communism, there was no great eagerness either to raise large armies or to go to war. Nevertheless, it was necessary for the French bourgeoisie to "keep in with Washington", since Washington was the best guarantor of the capitalist order in France. It was therefore at least going to make a gesture, and show that "Communist saboteurs and Russian paratroops" would not be allowed to endanger France. The Socialist Minister of Defence in the Pleven Government, M. Jules Moch, hastened to declare, soon after the outbreak of the Korean War that the Government intended to increase four or five-fold the effectives of the gendarmerie and the garde républicaine by incorporating in them conscripts chosen *individually* who would, together with the police, be responsible for catching saboteurs (if any) and paratroopers (if any). It all savoured slightly of Darnand's anti-Communist police and *milice*.[4]

This was the essence of that *"défense en surface"* of which so much was talked in 1950 and which was, in reality, partly a panic measure, and, even more so, a gesture calculated to impress Washington. As for paying higher taxes, in the name of the defence of the Free World, the reluctance on the part of French big business was wholly undisguised—even among those who hoped to make big profits out of rearmament.

Anyway, the rest of the year was to be largely devoted to the discussion—both internationally and in France itself—of two major topics: the extent of France's rearmament and the necessity of German rearmament, on which the USA was now becoming categorically insistent.

On the eve of the Atlantic rearmament and German rearmament negotiations in the summer and autumn of 1950, the members of the French cabinet all seemed at sixes and sevens. Did anybody seriously believe in a Russian invasion of Western Europe? It seems highly unlikely, even though Queuille uttered one of his classical platitudes on one occasion, when he said: "It is better to be shorn than to be led to the slaughter"—which was not perhaps the best way of showing the American allies that France was wildly enthusiastic about the imminent new war expenditure. M. Moch was against German rearmament, and was trying to draw up a plan which would demonstrate to the Americans with mathematical precision that the Elbe Line could be held without German troops; M. Schuman, on the other hand, seems to have had some form of German rearmament at the back of his mind for quite a long time, though he swore to Parliament that he hadn't, notably when at the National Assembly on October 25 M. René Capi-

---

[4] *Cf.* Jacques Armel in *L'Observateur*, August 10, 1950.

tant, the Gaullist Deputy, openly charged him with having favourably considered the idea as early as 1947.[5]

M. Moch tried to send cold shivers down people's spines with his talk of Communist saboteurs and Soviet paratroops, while M. Pleven, apparently not very worried about these saboteurs and paratroops, said that measures should, of course, be taken against the Fifth Column, but that France didn't mean by that any "totalitarian" measures. Pleven was prepared to raise the term of conscription from twelve to eighteen months, and juggled with war expenditure figures which no one knew how seriously to take; while M. Petsche, the Minister of Finance, neutralist at heart, and not at all keen on a huge war budget (fully agreeing in this with French Big Business), liked to take the line with the Americans that the French would, of course, provide soldiers, but that it would be very hard to persuade "the French people" to pay more taxes.

Nevertheless, as early as August 5, the French Government committed itself *vis-à-vis* the USA to a major rearmament effort which in reality it proved unable to carry out. Some later suggested that it had never really meant its promises to be taken literally and "unconditionally"; as for the "conditions", these could give rise to a variety of interpretations. Thus, a delay in certain US arms shipments could, at a pinch, be interpreted as a reason for slowing down French rearmament. Altogether, there was a good deal of muddle, confusion, and incoherence in all this, as was to be pointed out some time later by M. Mendès-France, who said, among other things, that French ministers like M. Pleven went to international conferences not knowing what, if anything, they had to propose, not knowing what they could, or could not, agree to, and sometimes making promises which they just couldn't keep.

And then, in the middle of all these 1950 conferences, there came a day—it was September 11—when President Truman and Mr Acheson bluntly announced that Europe must have sixty divisions, ten of them German. In the days that followed, discussions continued, first among the "3", and then among the "12"—whom Mr Acheson found, on the whole, rather more amenable to German rearmament than the "3"; and it was on September 16 that Mr Bevin, much to the dismay of many of the Europeans, agreed to the "principle" of German rearmament. M. Schuman (though everything shows that he had already long before been prepared for it) later argued that he also had to subscribe—after a few more days' beating about the bush—to the "principle" (Mr Acheson was very emphatic about its being *only* a "principle"), as otherwise France would have found herself completely isolated. By this time, indeed, she was being supported in her opposition to

[5] *Débats, A.N.* 1950, p. 7223.

the "principle" by only Belgium and Luxemburg, and half-heartedly at that.

There were some who later argued that Ernest Bevin's sick and enfeebled state had played the part of Cleopatra's nose; in reality it was almost certainly only a question of time. The official policy in Britain was evolving in such a way that if German rearmament had not been agreed to in 1950, it would no doubt have been agreed to in 1951, and if not by Mr Bevin, then by Mr Morrison.

3. THE "PLEVEN PLAN"

It now fell to the French to try to limit the damage—or to play for time. Did Pleven's policy consist in trying both these methods? That was at any rate one of the views widely taken of the "Pleven Plan".

It would be neither instructive nor, still less, entertaining, to record in detail the endless discussions that went on, in the late summer and autumn of 1950, among the "3", "6", "12", etc, around the questions of Atlantic rearmament and German rearmament. But the full-dress debate at the National Assembly before which, on October 24, 1950, M. Pleven admitted for the first time the "principle" of what he euphemistically called "German participation in the defence of Europe" is unquestionably of the greatest interest. For this debate represents one of the major landmarks in post-war French history. It was here that EDC was, if not born, at any rate conceived. Trying to make the best of a bad job, Pleven hoped to establish a solid link between his plan and the Schuman Plan.[6]

[6] This debate, which opened on October 24, formed part of one of the most eventful parliamentary sessions since the war. Only a few days before, there had been a stormy debate on Indo-China, in connexion with the disaster of Caobang, a French stronghold in Northern Tongking, which, under Vietminh pressure, had had to be evacuated with the loss of 3,000 men; it was on this occasion that M. Mendès-France sounded more loudly than ever before his "*il faut choisir*" theme—meaning that France could not afford to "do everything", and that she had better try to wind up the war in Indo-China—which earned for him the comment in the *Année Politique*, edited by the *bien-pensant* M. André Siegfried, that it was "rather odd to hear a Radical use Communist arguments"!

The debate on German rearmament was followed by several others, notably one in December on the whole question of French rearmament and the financial complications that this involved. In the interval there had been another debate on Indo-China and also the extraordinary manœuvre by the Communists to implicate M. Moch in the *affaire des généraux* which led to a secret vote by no fewer than 235 deputies of different parties, including several MRP members (and, it was suspected, even a few Socialists) in favour of sending M. Moch for trial before the High Court. The manœuvre nearly brought down the Pleven Government. It was, above all, a demonstration of personal hostility towards M. Moch, and the incident was not closed until M. Pleven had first tendered his resignation (which the President refused) and had then extracted from the Assembly an *open* vote favourable to M. Moch.

This three-day debate began with a statement from M. Pleven, who outlined what came to be known as the "Pleven Plan", the original French version of EDC. He started with a phrase that was no doubt calculated to please the USA: *"Mesdames, messieurs,* the ideal of collective security has won a victory in Korea." However, what came next was more important—an outline of the "Pleven Plan" and its underlying principles.

At recent meetings in New York [Pleven said] the suggestions of the French Government, represented by MM. Schuman, Moch, and Petsche, were largely taken into consideration by our co-signatories of the Atlantic Pact. They recognized the necessity of defending the Atlantic Community against all eventual aggression and as far to the East as possible. They decided to increase the forces stationed in Europe for that purpose. They agreed that all these forces, whatever their nationality, be placed under the command of a single chief.

Pleven went on to say that, under special agreements, France would benefit from substantial financial and armaments aid. Like France, every nation would have to make sacrifices by increasing the term of conscription and by increasing their defence budgets.

After that Pleven came to the most awkward point of his *exposé*:

Germany is not a member of the Atlantic Pact; nevertheless she is to benefit from the system of collective security arising from it. It is therefore only fair that she should contribute to the organization of the defence of Western Europe.

Promptly Pleven rose to the lofty heights of "supra-nationality". He recalled the Council of Europe and the Schuman Plan.

The intra-European talks that followed our Schuman Plan proposal have been progressing favourably, and seem on the point of being concluded. The French Plan, as you know, provides for supra-national institutions: a High Authority, a Council of Ministers, an Assembly and a Court of Justice which should form the first political basis of a European Community.
In the opinion of the French Government, the creation of Europe will result in the adherence of other states to these institutions, and in the rapid and progressive establishment of similar institutions in different fields— agriculture, transport, price supervision, electric power, the distribution of raw materials, etc.
The French Government thought that the fulfilment of the Coal-Steel Plan would condition people's minds to the idea of a European Community before the awkward subject of common defence had to be considered. But world events have failed to give us a respite. . . .

Which was one way of saying that Korea had precipitated German rearmament. However, Pleven now assured the National Assembly that the French Government intended to stick to its supra-national schemes, because

any system that would lead, now or later, directly or indirectly, conditionally or unconditionally to the creation of a German army could only revive distrust and suspicion. There must be no formation of German divisions, of a German Defence Ministry, or the formation of a German national army, which would inevitably lead to a revival of German militarism. The prospect of this has been unanimously condemned by our allies, and would, indeed, constitute a danger to Germany herself.

Pleven therefore proposed that, once the Schuman Plan was signed, the French Government should ask that the question of Germany's contribution to European defence be "given a solution which would take account of the cruel lessons of the past".

The French Government proposes the creation of a European Army attached to the political institutions of Europe. [*Cheers on numerous benches on Left, Centre, and Right.*] This suggestion is directly inspired by the recommendations made on August 11, 1950 by the Assembly of the Council of Europe calling for the immediate creation of a united European Army which would co-operate, in the defence of peace, with the forces of the USA and Canada.

He went on to explain that the European Army could not be a mere assembly of national units; for, in that case, the European Army would look too much like an old-time coalition. He then dealt with the appointment by the member governments of a Minister of Defence who would be responsible "in conditions still to be determined" to a European Assembly; this might be the Strasbourg Assembly, or a specially elected Assembly.

The supra-national Minister of Defence [Pleven said] would receive his instructions from a supra-national Council of Ministers. The contingents provided by the member states would be incorporated in the European Army "at the level of the smallest possible unit". There would be a common defence budget; units required for overseas service, and not included in the European Army, would continue to exist as national units; the European Forces "placed at the disposal of the unified Atlantic command would operate in accordance with the obligations contracted under the Atlantic Pact both as regards general strategy and organization and equipment". There would, however, be a transition stage before the European Army assumed its "final" character. Also, the constitution of the European Army must in no way delay, or interfere with, the present rearmament drive or the organization of the Atlantic forces under unified command—a reference to SHAPE that was about to come into being.

This, said Pleven, was the basis on which the French Government would ask Britain and the free countries of Continental Europe to discuss the European Army; it would invite them, as soon as the Coal and Steel Plan had been adopted by the Six.

Pleven agreed that there were "great technical and psychological difficulties", but if there was enough will, faith, and imagination, and sufficient encouragement from the United States, these difficulties could be overcome. He added that he did not consider war inevitable, and said that France had joined those Powers which had urged the calling of a Big-Four meeting "to examine the causes of international tension".

4. WAS THE PLEVEN PLAN TRYING TO DECEIVE THE USA—OR FRANCE?

There was a strange feeling at the National Assembly that day—the feeling that France had fought in Washington with her back to the wall; and that she had had to give way under the combined pressure of America and Britain. Many thought that what Pleven was now attempting was a kind of *tour de force* —maintain the Atlantic Alliance but keep German rearmament within very narrow limits. Whether he, or anybody else, seriously believed in all the "supra-national" institutions of a "European Community", they seemed to many people like a clever device for trying to limit the damage. Only, there was a danger that the Americans would see that the device was a little too clever; and would they not, while paying lip-service to "supra-nationality", still do their best to prevent this from being used by the French as mere delaying tactics?

Or, on the other hand, as was suggested by M. Pierre Cot, was it not American but French opinion that M. Pleven was trying to bamboozle? Was the Pleven statement a polite No to America or was it, on the contrary, a timidly-whispered Yes?—"a Yes rolled in the honey and and syrup of Europeanism and supra-nationality so that it would not stick in the throats of the French?"

Finally, there were a few "Europe" enthusiasts who believed so firmly in "federalism" that they overlooked a major flaw in the Pleven Plan: which was that if some degree of federalism and "supra-nationality" was possible in the economic field (e.g. in coal and steel) Europe was very far from ripe for accepting the supra-national principle in so basically political a field as defence, and that the organic connexion M. Pleven was trying to establish between the Schuman Plan and the European Army was unnatural. Still, considering France's financial dependence on the USA, the Pleven scheme nevertheless seemed to the Government majority, for one reason or another, the least of all possible evils.

In the two-day debate that followed everybody was, broadly speaking, against German rearmament, except M. Paul Reynaud; but some were absolutely against it and refused to be deceived by Pleven's "syrup", while others—the "Europeans"—took the Pleven formulae (or pretended to take them) at their face value. Some right-wing speakers, like the veteran Louis Marin, took the traditionally anti-German line of the "old Lorrainer" and envisaged the possibility of a rearmed Germany ganging up with the Russians some day (altogether, there were numerous references to Rapallo and to the Soviet-German Pact of 1939), while the somewhat eccentric General Adolphe Aumeran bluntly declared that he was all in favour of an anti-Bolshevik Crusade, but that this would defeat its own ends if the foul Germans were allowed to take part in it! They had already once betrayed the Russian people when they invaded Russia and acted as butchers and not, as the Russian people had hoped, as liberators.

Left-wing speakers like Charles Serre, Pierre Cot, not to mention the Communists, indulged in the easy, but somewhat aimless game of quoting numerous passages from Schuman speeches about German rearmament being "out of the question", and even some less recent speeches to the same effect by Mr Byrnes and other American leaders. It was also argued that even if there was not yet a German army in existence, German rearmament in the industrial sense was already in full swing, with one Allied control after another in Germany coming into abeyance. Several speakers of different Parties also dwelt on the psychological aspects of German rearmament: they regretted that at a time when Germany was still pacifist in the main, her old warlike instincts should be aroused by the statesmen of Western Europe and America. As M. Charles Serre put it:

At present the Germans have a deep distaste for uniform. But it's a country rich in contradictions. We should encourage the present anti-militarism of Germany; instead, we are doing the very opposite.... In 1951 1½ million boys of the Hitler Jugend will reach the age of 21, and in the next two or three years 2 or 3 million more. Are you trying to revive the spirit in which they were brought up in their adolescence?

Moreover, he said, where was that International Authority that Pleven was talking about? Was it not a myth? It was difficult, he said, to "create juridical super-Fatherlands, except on paper". And where was that super-Government from which the super-Minister of Defence would emerge? Meantime the fact remained that German heavy industry was coming into its own again, the shares of Vereinigte Stahlwerke having risen between July 1948 and January 1950 from 11 to 55, and those of Siemens from 10 to 49.

M. Edouard Bonnefous (UDSR) took the line that, although there were strong pacifist influences in Germany—Heinemann, Niemöller, etc—militarism was by no means dead, and that it was better to accept the Pleven Plan than to allow Germany to rearm unilaterally.

M. Gilbert de Chambrun (Progressive), on the contrary, said that the French Government had accepted the principle of German rearmament without consulting the French people, the vast majority of whom would have said No. And he wanted to put two questions to the Government:

(1) If you get no European Council of Ministers, and no Common European defence budget, and no European Minister of Defence, and no British participation—if you get none of these things, will you reject German rearmament in any shape or form?; and (2) Since you speak of only small German units, will you reject German rearmament if you are offered German divisions?

It seemed, unfortunately, true (he continued) that men like M. Paul Reynaud, for example, were willing to accept German rearmament in any case, and on almost any terms. Also, there was a grave danger that, once armed, the Germans would themselves provoke a war; and he regretted to say that they had received some encouragement to do so, even from M. Schuman, who had refused to recognize the Oder-Neisse frontier.

M. ROBERT SCHUMAN: When did I say that?

M. GILBERT DE CHAMBRUN: You said it before the Foreign Affairs Committee one day. You actually said that France did not recognize the Eastern frontier of Germany. You caused great excitement on the Committee, as well as in the West-German and Polish press.

M. SCHUMAN: You are distorting my words. What I said was that France neither recognized, nor contested this frontier, because only the peace treaty could settle it.

M. DE CHAMBRUN: You said you did not recognize it.

M. SCHUMAN: I also said that I did not contest it. I said it was a matter for the peace treaty.

M. DE CHAMBRUN: The fact remains that your statement played into the hands of the German *revanchards* ... of those in favour of German rearmament, and of those very people who are likely to provoke incidents.

This little skirmish was significant of Schuman's policy of following a line that would not come into conflict with American policy. It was also in the pro-German "Locarno" tradition, which always implied the possibility of territorial change in the East and *status quo* in the West.

M. de Chambrun concluded by saying—again a classical argument that was to be repeated, in one form or another, a thousand times in the next few years—that *France should have had the courage to say No, because the American threat to rearm Germany without France's consent was a piece of bluff.* And this bluff should be called.

An entirely different line was taken by Paul Reynaud. First of all, he denied that German rearmament was a "new" question; it had been (he rightly remarked) at the back of people's minds for years, as a result of the unbalanced state of Europe.

If the French and British can defend the Elbe line, well and good. But what if they can't?

Reynaud then recalled that at Strasbourg Mr Churchill tabled a motion for the creation of a European Army. He (Reynaud), André Philip, and Georges Bidault tabled a similar motion, but complete with a European Authority controlling this army.

We pressed Mr Churchill to amend his own motion, and he agreed. And in his new version the European Authority took the concrete form of a European War Ministry controlled by a democratic Assembly.... The Conservatives, the Liberals and one Labour man voted for this motion; but, on instructions from Mr Dalton, the other Labourites abstained.

M. Reynaud then went hammer and tongs for the Labour Party. It was the Labour Party and not the British Conservatives, who were putting spokes in Europe's wheels. Labour was scared of Europe and its "liberalism". And he thought the Labour Party had behaved quite disgracefully at Margate; so much so that even M. André Philip, though a Socialist himself, was profoundly disgusted, and had said:

To read the Labour Manifesto, one would think that nothing had happened in the world at all since Ramsay MacDonald, and it is sickening to see them make the same old isolationist and nationalist statements which bear such a heavy share of responsibility for the disasters of the recent past....

At the same time Reynaud regretted that another Socialist, Guy Mollet, should have expressed the view that French opinion would not favour "Europe" if Britain refused to take part in it. Mollet had even said that he was just not interested in a "Europe" merely composed of France, Germany, and Italy—for what kind of basis was this for a Socialist Europe? M. Reynaud therefore wished to know whether M. Mollet, a member of M. Pleven's Government, was for or against the Pleven Plan? For his own part, Reynaud thought German rearmament completely inevitable; for, to avoid German rearmament, was France going to increase her term of conscription to three or four years?

Reynaud regretted that France should, in approaching the subject of German rearmament, embark on a orgy of self-pity. Yes—France had suffered; but then Holland had suffered more, yet the Dutch were favourable to German rearmament. And in conclusion he used the classical argument (the counterpart of the Gilbert de Chambrun argument) *that if France did not agree to German rearmament, America would go ahead with it all the same.*

Reynaud's attack on the Labour Party (even apart from the myth that he—together with Mr Churchill—was trying to build up of the "Europeanism" of the Tories) was typical of several things all at once: the hatred of the French Right for the Labour Party, their determination to go ahead with building up *their* version of "Europe" without England, and—in the last analysis—their preference for a Europe in which England would not be included, not even a Conservative England. For did M. Reynaud seriously believe that Mr Churchill was genuinely in favour of including England in the European Army and was not primarily aiming, with his Strasbourg motion, at bringing about a Franco-German alliance, so dear to his heart? M. Reynaud must have known that, once the Conservatives were back in office, they would be just as "nationalist", "insular", and anti-federalist as the Labourites—and as hostile as they to supra-national authorities. Already their hostility to the Schuman Plan had shown it.

For all that, Reynaud criticized the French Government for having "neglected" Churchill's Strasbourg motion which, he seemed to think, provided the basis for a more substantial "European Army" than what was provided in the Pleven Plan. Altogether, he thought the French Government insufficiently enthusiastic over the "revolutionary" decisions taken by the Pentagon to defend Europe in Europe itself—which, in the past, they had thought of doing from bases in North Africa. Now General Bradley had clearly stated that the USA "would lose the Third World War if Europe was lost to the Russians". Altogether, Reynaud talked of Russian invasion as if it were not only probable, but inevitable, and seemed distressed at the widespread French reluctance to take it seriously; and he commented on the widespread "neutralism" from which both France and Germany were suffering, a clear sign, in his opinion, of an "inferiority complex".

Other speakers, without actually using the word "neutralism", suggested, on the contrary, that this caution shown by French public opinion over becoming too deeply involved in the Pentagon's grand strategy pointed to a sound instinct of self-preservation. Altogether, the debate was on one of the most fundamental French issues.

It is not necessary to record in detail the other speeches that went on for two days, but a few points deserve to be noted.

The Communists (Bonte and Billoux) naturally denied that there was any Russian danger at all, and dwelt instead on the bellicose utterances of

General Guderian, General von Manteuffel and even some much more "moderate" Germans whose chief aim was to "reconquer" the lost Eastern provinces. And, recalling Hitler's New Order, Billoux exclaimed: "Making Europe—that was something Hitler invented!" And the Americans would play the same trick on Schuman as they had done before: while he was planning to chop up Germany into a mosaic of small states, they produced for him the Federal Republic; while he was planning small army units, they would create large army divisions.

Pierre Cot (Progressive) challenged the Government to produce any report from the French Ambassador or Military Attaché in Moscow to show that the Russians were preparing to attack Western Europe, and said that the only sound solution was to "neutralize" Germany. Altogether, he thought, there was something unhealthy about this debate; one only had to look at the Government bench; all the members of the Government were looking anxious and "hot and bothered" trying to defend something in which they didn't really believe.

Daladier (Radical) took the line that if Germany was to be integrated, it wasn't necessary for Germans to be actually soldiers; they could build fortifications, if necessary, or be made responsible for other parts of the European Army's "infrastructure"; the moral effect on the French of being mixed up with German soldiers would be very bad, he thought.

A good many other speakers agreed with this.

Perhaps the only real enthusiast of the European Army was the fiery MRP leader, P.-H. Teitgen, a great believer in "Europe", or rather, in a little and predominantly Catholic Europe.

What we are proposing to Germany is not at all a German army, or a revival of German militarism. What we are offering her is Europe—quite a different thing.

And Maurice Schumann echoed: "It's the very opposite of militarism"...

Speaking for the Socialists, Daniel Mayer was in a difficult spot. He was "against German rearmament"; he did not "particularly trust Adenauer"; he thought that if Germany had a strong German army, the old capitalist and militarist gang would run Germany, and if she had a weak army, "we might get a Korean situation" 100 miles from the French frontier. The *comité directeur* of the Socialist Party was against even the partial remilitarization of Germany. There was an amusing moment recorded in the *Journal Officiel* report:

DANIEL MAYER: To think that a Socialist, speaking against German rearmament...

JACQUES DUCLOS (Communist): ... before voting for it, as he will do...

DANIEL MAYER: ... would be heckled by the Right!

One could not deny M. Duclos a gift of quick repartee. For Daniel Mayer did, of course, vote for the Pleven Plan.

In answering the various questions raised, Pleven was categorical at one moment and evasive the next. He said the Schuman Plan must be signed before the European Army was agreed on; there would be no European Army without a European Defence Minister and a European Assembly controlling him; if these features of the French Plan were rejected, then France would not agree to any other form of German rearmament. In the same breath he said, however, that it would be Utopian to try to stop fifty million people from taking part in the defence of their own country. Also—though without producing any evidence other than that Eastern Germany had a large armed police force—he argued that the rearmament of Germany (implying the existence of an army) had been started by the Russians. As for whether France would still go ahead with the Plan even if Britain refused to adhere, Pleven said this was a hypothetical question; all he could say was that the French Government would do its utmost to bring Britain in. But on the size of the German units to be "integrated" Pleven was extremely vague—this was obviously the point on which the Americans were determined to be tough.

The motion of confidence in the Government, the text of which specified that there must be no German army and no German general staff, was passed by 343 votes to 225. The position of the Gaullists in relation to the European Army was "negative". Their spokesman, M. Capitant, strongly criticized the whole idea, attacked Schuman for having planned German rearmament on the quiet for a long time, and echoed de Gaulle's own press conference some months before, when the General, in one of his more grandiose moods, declared that the leader of Europe must be France, and no other country. What de Gaulle had said was this:

The present Council of Europe is incapable of assembling Europe.... The only working basis for Europe is a practical Franco-German *entente*, which alone provides, on this old Continent of ours, genuine economic and strategic possibilities.

There must also be European institutions directly elected by the citizens of Europe and enjoying, in economic and strategic matters, a part of the sovereign rights delegated to them by the member states.

There must also be a system of common defence, the plans of which should normally be drawn up by France, and whose chief should be appointed by France, just as in the Pacific this predominant rôle should be played by the United States and, in the East, by England, the whole under the general direction of a combined General Staff.... In this way alone can Europe grow strong and coherent again, and in this way alone can hope be revived from the Atlantic all the way to the Urals....[7]

[7] Press conference, August 17, 1950.

It was like a last flash in the pan of *grandeur française*, and de Gaulle's spokesman at the National Assembly was obviously handicapped by his leader's plans, which, earlier in the year had already taken the form of a revival of "Charlemagne's Empire".[8]

The general public were not at all enchanted with the American rearmament drive, with the pressure brought to bear on France that she intensify her own rearmament and subscribe to German rearmament; but the Third Force governments, unlike de Gaulle, at least had two great advantages: they appeared to enjoy the relative goodwill of the United States, and they left themselves plenty of room for muddling along and for resorting to delaying tactics.

5. US "REVISES" PLEVEN PLAN

The Pleven Plan having been approved by Parliament "in principle", it was now for the Government to see whether it could get it adopted by the Allies; and here difficulties arose almost immediately. There followed months, and indeed, years of haggling. It was a sort of three-cornered fight among *France* which wanted a minimum of German rearmament, surrounded by a variety of guarantees and precautions and supra-national controls, the *United States* (usually supported by Britain) which was in a hurry to get actual German military manpower with little more than nominal satisfaction (if that) being given to the French; and *Germany*, which was less interested in providing troops for the "European Army" than in securing sovereignty and equal rights.

Another object of hair-splitting discussions was the precise relationship that was to be established between the Atlantic Pact and the European Army. In the National Assembly Teitgen had exclaimed: "We are not giving Germany an army, we are giving her Europe!"—which sounded magnificent, but did not quite fit in with American intentions.

As regards the Atlantic Pact, there were no major technical difficulties in the way. Its Military Committee, composed of twelve Chiefs of Staff decided on October 27, 1950 to create a Supreme Command in Europe under General Eisenhower. The General Staff at Fontainebleau would be "gradually absorbed" in this new SHAPE organization. The French argued that, provided the European Army was given all the supra-national trappings of the Pleven Plan, there would be no harm in having it "integrated" as a "contingent" in the SHAPE forces, with the provision that no German officers be given any high commanding position.

The American and British attitude to the Pleven Plan was a rather

---

[8] De Gaulle's press conference, March 16, 1950.

mixed one. When, after the Assembly's vote, Moch, as Minister of Defence, travelled to Washington, he found that the Americans were already proposing the formation of two German divisions right away and the creation of recruiting offices in Germany, without anything being first done about the Pleven Plan at all.

Moch, not unnaturally, opposed this, saying that he had come solely to recommend the Pleven Plan. According to the French press, this greatly annoyed not only General Marshall, but also Mr Shinwell. But matters were further complicated by reactions in Germany. Here there were, broadly speaking, three currents: a "neutralist" current, represented by men like Niemöller and Heinemann, who had shortly before resigned from the Adenauer Government; the "equal-rights-first" current represented by the Social-Democrats and their leader, Kurt Schumacher, who went on saying that the Germans "were not an army of mercenaries", and finally Adenauer himself who, at that stage, was playing a waiting game, expecting before long to get much better terms than those provided in the Pleven Plan.

Nevertheless, the French Government decided that, in the course of its Washington talks, it could not very well adopt "a purely negative attitude". Already on November 2, Moch agreed that German batallions of 800 to 1,200 men be incorporated in the "European Army" and suggested that this army—complete with its supra-national machinery, of course—be composed of 100,000 men by the end of 1951, "by way of experiment". Mr Spofford, who did most of the negotiating on behalf of the US Government, thought M. Moch's proposals wholly inadequate, and proposed that there be fully equipped German "combat teams", the size of these teams to be settled later. He agreed that no senior German officers be allowed to take part in the organization or command of the European Army; in return for this "concession", he asked that the French stop pressing for the immediate formation of a European Defence Ministry.

By the middle of November Spofford, in the face of French resistance, nevertheless made some headway: he had managed to get the French to agree to the "principle" of "combat teams" of 5,000 or 6,000 men; the French, nevertheless, went on demanding that the principles of the Pleven Plan be accepted.

Meantime, on November 3, the Soviet Government had sent a Note to France, Britain and the USA proposing new talks on the demilitarization of Germany; although the Note was badly received in London and Washington, M. Schuman took a more "subtle" line: on the following day already he remarked that talks with the Russians were not necessarily useless: the talks in 1949 had, "after all", led to the termination of the Berlin Blockade. And M. Herriot, at the National Assembly on November 16, said that "when the lives of millions of people are involved, one ought to negotiate even with the Devil".

But while not rejecting the Soviet proposals outright, Schuman nevertheless went on boosting the "European Army", telling a German paper that it was "in Germany's interests" to join it; and he also pleaded at great length in its favour on November 24, before the Council of Europe. The German Socialists at Strasbourg were wholly hostile to the idea; but what could not help puzzling the French was the British attitude: whereas the Labourites at Strasbourg were frigid, to say the least, and abstained from voting on the motion in favour of the European Army, Mr Duncan Sandys and other Conservatives were among its most wholehearted supporters!

On the whole, however, the Strasbourg Assembly was far from making much headway; the General Affairs Committee, including M. André Philip, proposed the creation of a common Political Authority "competent in matters of security and foreign policy"; but this was rejected by 59 votes to 39 and 12 abstentions. The impression was growing at Strasbourg that Federalism as such was not making much progress and that the most that the Council of Europe could hope to achieve was the endorsement by at least some of the Powers of the "specialized agencies" such as the Coal and Steel Pool and—with luck —the European Army. But it was not until nearly a year later that M. Spaak, in resigning his presidency of the Strasbourg Assembly, gave vent to all the bitterness and frustration of the all-out "Europeans".

6. "EUROPE IS SCARED"

Altogether, the situation by the end of 1950 was a highly confused one. Britain was asking France to be less rigid in her defence of the "principles" of the Pleven Plan "in return for the reasonable attitude now adopted by the United States in Korea"(!), and adopt the Spofford Proposals for the immediate formation of large German combat teams —a plan the French Government was reluctant to agree to, since these combat teams might, before long, develop into regular and "unintegrated" divisions. The instructions sent to M. Alphand, the French representative at the London talks, as a result of the French cabinet meeting of December 7 were a strange hotch-potch of concessions, conditions and reservations, including the opinion that perhaps nothing had better be decided at all until some further talks with the Russians and Germans.[9]

If no appreciable progress was being made as a result of both French and German resistance, the negotiations concerning SHAPE were

[9] *Année Politique*, 1950, p. 272.

more successful, and on December 19, President Truman announced the appointment of General Eisenhower as head of this new organization which, before long, was to set up its provisional headquarters at the Hôtel Astoria in Paris. In the United States meantime a verbal duel had broken out between ex-President Hoover who came out in favour of abandoning Western Europe and of concentrating on the defence of the British Isles, and President Truman who assured his predecessor that Europe was taking its rearmament "seriously".

There were other developments: the United States was seriously considering bringing Spain into the defence of the "Free World", which met with much opposition in France, where it seemed somewhat incongruous that Franco should be asked to defend freedom and democracy—even though the cynics remarked: "If Syngman Rhee, why not Franco?" And then there was Indo-China, where the Americans were now beginning to patronize the Bao Dai régime.

On December 24, the *Monde* published the following slightly grotesque message from Saigon:

The agreement for military aid for the defence of Indo-China and the new Franco-Vietnamese economic conventions were signed at the Town Hall at Saigon today. The Emperor Bao Dai, M. Letourneau, General de Lattre de Tassigny, Mr Heath, the US Minister, Mr Tran Van Huu, Prime Minister of Vietnam, and the Defence Ministers of Laos and Cambodia were present.

Referring to US military aid, M. Letourneau paid a warm tribute to "noble America".

"The young Vietnamese Army," he said, "now being formed under the high authority of His Majesty Bao Dai...has already received great aid from the United States...while the Navy and Air Force of the French Union have been substantially re-equipped. But the brunt is borne by our land forces, and I am now assured that these forces will also shortly receive the indispensable equipment."

Mr Tran Van Huu said that this day of December 23 would be a great landmark in humanity's struggle for freedom and independence.... He stressed the similarity of the battle fought by the French in Indo-China and that fought by the Americans in Korea. Mr Heath then said:

"The agreement signed today is very similar to that signed by the United States with many other Asian, European, and American countries. It gives the Americans no right to establish bases in your country, to control your economy, to command your troops, or to enjoy other exceptional privileges. I say this to forestall the Communist screams...."

The French Government was no doubt pleased to have America take over some of the financial burdens of the Vietnam war. But the public was far from reassured; was not this aid going to perpetuate the war in Vietnam?

On December 28, the National Assembly discussed the 1951 budget, and particularly that French rearmament which had been decided upon soon after the outbreak of the Korean War.

The figures proposed by the Pleven Government were significant:

	1950	1951
	Milliard francs	
Civil expenditure	933	1039
Reconstruction and equipment	719	680
Military expenditure	449	780

The deficit was to be covered by 90 milliards of borrowed money and 255 milliards of US aid, of which 115 milliards was "civilian" and 140 milliard military aid.

M. Mendès-France was among the Government's severest critics:

In order to increase military expenditure to such an extent [he said] you must increase the national income, reduce consumption costs or, finally, cut down expenditure on capital investments.... These investments are already being severely cut down. For several years past, these items of productive expenditure have been continually cut. And now you are proposing another cut at a time when we are the only country in Europe whose production is below that of 1929. It's because you would not agree to the necessary sacrifices at the time of the Liberation. [An obvious reference to Mendès's defeat by Pleven in 1945.] The Monnet Plan was cut down to half. Genuine national defence comes from a country's industrial equipment, and what we need above all things is a powerful industrial potential.... We go on living from hand to mouth. Our military expenditure is already out of all proportion with our possibilities. Our social expenditure is greater than before the war and our reconstruction is far from completed.... Excessive rearmament will ruin our economy, and you've got to make the choice; if you try to do everything, all you will have is inflation.

M. Petsche, the Minister of Finance, tried to reassure M. Mendès-France that none of the major capital investment schemes would be affected: neither the coke-producing plants, nor the Donzère-Mondragon hydro-electric project; nor would the cuts affect any work already begun on the French railways, on Air-France, or in North Africa.

It was on these ominous notes of a new danger of inflation, of further cuts in public investments, of increased military expenditure, and of preparations for the arrival of General Eisenhower as the head of SHAPE at the Hôtel Astoria that the year 1950 came to an end.

Nineteen fifty-one was Election Year. But, except that it resulted in a farther swing to the Right in France, it did not substantially alter the problems foremost in France's mind. Except for the domestic probem of wages and prices, both of which, by 1952, became more or less stabilized, the three major external problems grew increasingly acute in the next three years: Germany, North Africa, and Indo-China.

Part V

BATTLES AGAINST ARABS, COMMUNISTS AND—AMERICANS
(1951-3)

CHAPTER ONE

THE MONTHS BEFORE THE 1951 ELECTION

WITH only one or two exceptions, every year in post-war France has tended to be a "year of transition". Transition towards what? That is what was usually hard to tell. But is not this more or less cautious groping in the dark typical of our "hideous epoch", as Sir Winston called it in February 1955? And, except for the General Election—which, in reality, changed very little internationally—1951 was just another of those "transition" years in France, in the course of which no clear decisions of any kind were taken in the international field, unless one regards as major decisions the ratification of the Schuman Plan and the French note to Tunisia of December 15 which opened an era of acute tension between France and North Africa. Early in 1952 that great champion of the Western Bloc, M. André Siegfried, examining the great "psychological problem" of Franco-German relations, admitted, in a tone of frustration, that "no fundamental decisions had been taken in 1951"; he felt, nevertheless, that things were going "the right way", and he tried to sound hopeful about "Europe, our Europe" becoming a reality. The Americans, he said, had had no experience of a German invasion, and were therefore in a greater hurry than France to see Germany "integrated" in the Western system, including its defence; having gone too far in their demands for German rearmament, they had now fallen back on the Pleven Plan as a basis of discussion; but the trouble now was that the Germans were beginning to lay down stiff conditions. And then there was Britain's reluctance to be associated with "Europe"; M. Siegfried thought the Americans were very upset about this, but were "grateful to France" for "the positive efforts" she was making.

The Pleven Plan and the Schuman Plan keep up among the Americans a spirit of co-operation, however precarious, because it is realized that but for the ratification of the Schuman Plan, American isolationism would again be strongly encouraged. Its rejection would have meant the withdrawal of a discouraged and disillusioned America, no longer believing that the Europeans were capable of making a Europe.

But, of course, the Americans could not quite see Germany in the same perspective as France was seeing her.... Only the crisis of

Europe was exceptionally tragic.... The destiny of a continent, the destiny of a whole civilization was at stake.... Perhaps French opinion wasn't realizing the terrible gravity of this European crisis.[1] And so on, and so on, all of it ending with a warning that if France did not show greater eagerness, the Americans might prefer to rearm the Germans, Turks, and Spaniards independently. It is remarkable how this little piece of *chantage* kept cropping up, year after year, both in American publications and in the writings of the French *bien-pensants*!

Perhaps M. Siegfried was right in saying "Europe" was "moving in the right direction"—but how slowly! The truth is that the announcement of the Pleven Plan at the end of 1950 was to open nearly a four years' period of *attentisme* and diplomatic ca' canny, in the course of which problem after problem was accumulated in France, in the "European" field, in the colonial field, and even in the realm of domestic reforms, without any clear solution being reached on any major issue. It is true that, in May 1952, the EDC Treaty was signed in Paris, but its subsequent ratification was to be postponed by one government after another, owing chiefly to the complete uncertainty whether there was a majority in the National Assembly to approve it. The EDC Treaty was not something France had devised or proposed spontaneously; it was the outcome of endless pressures to which France had been subjected in the course of nearly two years, especially on the part of the United States, and in its final form, its resemblance to the Pleven Plan was very remote indeed. Feeling against EDC in the country was so strong that it was not until M. Mendès-France, with his passion for "clear-cut decisions", became premier that Parliament was asked to make up its mind, one way or the other. Even the most ardent supporters of EDC like M. Schuman had until then been reluctant to take the grave risk of a fiasco, and preferred to play for time.

There were two other major external problems which kept, if not the country, at any rate the press busy throughout the 1951–4 period. One was Indo-China, the other North Africa. If, throughout 1951, General de Lattre de Tassigny succeeded, with American aid, in "stabilizing" the military situation for a time, both the military and political situation rapidly degenerated during the next two years, until the final disaster of Dien Bien Phu, after which the only alternatives were an all-out international war (if the USA so desired) or the negotiation of an armistice on terms which, obviously, could no longer be favourable. That was the task Mendès-France undertook at Geneva in June–July 1954.

The psychological effect of the growing realization that the war in Indo-China was becoming more and more hopeless (added to the psychological effect that, in Europe, France was being bullied into

---

[1] *Année Politique*, 1951, pp. xii–xiii.

"solutions" for which she had no liking) helps perhaps best to explain the innermost reasons for the incredible "toughening" of France's policy in relation to North Africa during the period of 1951–54. If it is true that, on the one hand, the capitalist governments throughout the world, alarmed by the growth of native African and Asian nationalisms, had become wholly hard-boiled and cynical (and this is just as true of France as it is of Belgium in the Congo, of Britain in Kenya and Malaya, of the United States in the Philippines and in the "independent" United Fruit republics of Central America, not to mention Malan in South Africa—whose example was *sub rosa* being more and more frequently invoked by all colonialists) it is probably also true to say that, in the case of North Africa, not only French capitalist interests, but public opinion generally were in favour of "hanging on". Instinctively, French opinion felt that if there were plenty of good reasons for writing off Indo-China, France should on no account abandon North Africa. For the last forty years it had been drummed into every school child that Lyautey and other great men had created a glorious French Empire in North Africa, that this was a "natural extension" of France, and that to lose it would merely mean handing it over to other capitalist powers, most likely to the USA, which was widely accused of giving every encouragement to the Istiqlal in Morocco and to the UGTT Trade Union Federation in Tunisia in their struggle against French domination.

The battle in France was, broadly speaking, between two conceptions—that of brute force on the one hand and that of conciliation, voluntary co-existence, and gradual emancipation and self-government on the other. Both schools accused each other of preaching policies that could only end in the loss of North Africa: the policy of brute force would lead to resistance and insurrection; the policy of self-government would lead to the rapid elimination of France from her North African empire.

In a later section of this book it will be shown how the policy of brute force was to gain the upper hand in Tunisia after the famous French Note of December 15, 1951 rejecting the Chenik Government's Internal Autonomy proposals, and how, in Morocco, the "tough" policy begun by General Juin ever since his appointment as Resident-General in 1948 was to reach its climax in the summer of 1953, when the Sultan was deposed by the French authorities at Rabat, with the tacit approval of the Quai d'Orsay.

But it should be said that if there was in France a violent conflict of ideas over North Africa between the intellectuals and the authorities, the general public in France tended to remain "neutral" with regard to the methods best employed for "preserving North Africa for France". The Right and the MRP were entirely in favour of a "tough" policy; the Socialists, while paying lip service to "emancipation" were, in reality, being restrained in their anti-colonialist ardour by the French Socialist organizations in North Africa (since these formed part of "white society", they were not sharply "anti-colonialist" by any means); as for the Communists, they were conscious of the unpopularity in France of any propaganda in favour of an all-out "liberation" of Morocco, Algeria or Tunisia, and preferred to concentrate on Indo-China instead; moreover, they were not in great sympathy with the "bourgeois nationalism" of either the Neo-Destour in Tunisia or the Istiqlal in Morocco, and knew only too well how these two parties persisted in proclaiming their anti-Communism. Their closest con-nexion with North Africa was through the MTLD, Messali Hadj's movement in Algeria, which had many supporters among the Algerian proletariat and sub-proletariat in France; and it was these Algerians in France who were always prominent in the predominantly Communist May-Day and *14-juillet* demonstrations in Paris and other French indus-trial centres. It was the presence of these Algerian elements in the May-Day parade of 1951, for instance, which caused the violent clash be-tween demonstrators and M. Baylot's police in the Faubourg Saint-Antoine—a clash in which several hundreds were injured.

But in the early part of 1951 North Africa had not yet become a major worry to France. In Morocco, it is true, General Juin, faced with the obstreperousness of the Sultan, Sidi-Mohammed Ben Yussef, organized a march on Rabat of the famous "Berber Horsemen", who threatened to depose the Sultan if he did not disavow the Istiqlal and sign a series of decrees submitted to him by the irate French Resident-General. A *Franc-Tireur* cartoon showed these "Berber horsemen" all wearing the classical garb of the Sûreté inspector—bowler hat, walrus moustache, hobnailed boots and umbrella. But after this little *coup de force* against the Sultan, little more was heard of North Africa for a while (except that the Sultan told an Egyptian paper soon afterwards that he had signed his disavowal of the Istiqlal under duress). It still seemed a sideshow.

The general public had plenty of other worries. The Korean War was still going on, with Seoul changing hands several times, and the air war becoming more savage every day. The dismissal of MacArthur in April no doubt caused great relief, and so did, two months later, the Russian offer of a cease-fire, which, in the end, led to the interminable Kaesong and Panmunjom talks.

But what happened during the few months that preceded the Elec-tion—that Election which was supposed to give France a "new start", but didn't? The year began, as already said, with the arrival of General Eisenhower as head of SHAPE; the Communists boasted that their threat to cause a riot had persuaded Eisenhower to "slink into Paris almost clandestinely", and had caused the French Government to cancel various military parades, receptions and banquets in his honour.[2] Some days later, the Communists organized a demonstration against Eisenhower—a relatively small affair, but one which was reported to have produced from "Ike" the melancholy reflection already quoted before. Around the Etoile there were more police than demonstrators, nearly all of whom were pushed into police-vans and driven off. Many were beaten up, among them (by mistake) a reporter from the *Figaro*.

The Pleven Government made Eisenhower's arrival in Europe coincide with a few anti-Communist measures: thus a decree was issued dissolving, as far as France was concerned, three Communist-dominated "world organizations", the WFTU, the International Democratic Women's Federation and the World Federation of Democratic Youth. The Government's critics challenged the legality of the dissolution of the WFTU at any rate, this organization figuring among the consultative bodies (category A) of UN. An anti-Communist purge was started about the same time in the upper strata of the French civil service.

Altogether, the Pleven-Moch Government was determined to be as popular as possible with the USA. It had got the National Assembly to vote the rearmament programme by a large majority "in order", as M. Moch put it, "to give America confidence in France", and in order, at the same time, to make sure that the flow of arms and money would continue. All the same, there was no enthusiasm at all for this rearmament; in the *Figaro* M. François Mauriac said that, for France, another war would mean death, and advocated talks with the Russians.

What particularly upset the French Government at that stage was Senator Taft's speech in favour of "peripheral strategy". Where in heaven had Taft got the idea that France was not keen on the Atlantic Pact or on the presence of an American Army in Europe? Clearly, it was these damned neutralists who were now actually *welcoming* the Taft speech! Coming on top of Eisenhower's arrival and Senator Taft's speech, the fight between the *Figaro* and the *Monde* early in January 1951 was particularly revealing. M. Pierre Brisson, editor of the *Figaro*, violently attacked the "neutralists" of the *Monde* as "sexless" people, to which M. Beuve-Méry, the editor of the *Monde*, replied in a little paragraph, marked by a Rabelaisian fruitiness unusual in the *Monde*, that it was all very well boasting about tremendous French virility— "but have you really *got* any . . . ?" And he added that there were only too many people in France who loved big words but who were meantime piling up their nest-eggs in some safe bank well beyond the ocean. Which, the next day, produced a yowl from M. Brisson, who said that, except for trifling sums, required for its office expenses abroad, the *Figaro* kept all its funds in France!

[2] *L'Humanité*, January 8, 1951.

It was in this atmosphere, and a few days before M. Pleven was due to visit President Truman, that Moch insisted on telling the Anglo-American press, in a carefully prepared roneoed script, that the "Neutralists" were traitors, no better than the Communists; that France believed in Collective Security; that she believed in Eisenhower "the Liberator of Europe", and that he, Jules Moch, a French Socialist, "had given body and soul to the task of reconstituting a mighty French Army". And this army, together with its allies (Germany was not mentioned) would "compel aggression to retreat". He assured his audience that the Communists were losing in influence, and that the French Government was being *very* tough with the Communists, [*loud cheers from most of the audience*] who were now being thrown out of all responsible jobs. And he also assured them that France was capable of the most wonderful *élans* and *redressements*: and he recalled the Convention which had introduced the Declaration of the Rights of Man and the metric system (*sic*), and had created revolutionary armies which were the terror of the crowned tyrants of the day; and there was the Paris Commune, and the Popular Front, and the glorious Resistance—(three achievements which, many in his audience thought, were all a little on the Red side, and perhaps rather unfortunate examples of France's reliability!). However, Moch obviously meant well, and he again assured his audience that there were only *three* Communist lieutenant-colonels in the French Army, and none above that rank, and they were being most *carefully* watched. And the talks with General Eisenhower were *most* satisfactory![3]

This Moch statement to the American press is not important in itself; but it shows to what lengths of humiliating buffoonery certain French Ministers went to make a good impression in the USA. Moch no doubt felt he had to reassure the Americans. Pleven was hoping to make a good impression in Washington, and to get more aid for Indo-China; Delattre was clamouring for it, and threatening that if the Americans did not send much help, it might be necessary to send *le contingent*, i.e. part of the French conscript army to Indo-China. Both Moch and Pleven made every effort to show that France was doing more than Britain. This was not always easy. And there were other difficulties. Thus, Moch and Pleven were fully conscious of the unpopularity of the American airfields that were about to be built in France, in accordance with the plans discussed with Eisenhower. At that time the shadow of Korea was haunting many people.

The Communists naturally made the most of it. Auguste Lecœur wrote in *L'Humanité* on April 10, under the title, *Les Américains en Amérique*:

[3] *Cf. New Statesman and Nation*, January 20, 1951.

The Marshall Plan no longer looks like Father Christmas. What is coming from America now is not cans of food, but guns and tanks.... It has all resulted in a sharp drop in our standard of living.... Eisenhower has been ordered to become the MacArthur of Europe. And the American soldiers now occupying France have been told that they are here to defend freedom and civilization. Just as in Korea. The Minister of the Interior has sent his cops all over the place with instructions dated 27-11-50, 24-1-51, and 8-2-51 to the following effect: (*a*) place the local services at the disposal of the occupation troops; (*b*) eliminate anything that might hamper the use of our railways by the American armed forces; (*c*) eliminate any opposition to the placing at the disposal of the Americans of the ports of Bordeaux and La Rochelle, of the railway connecting the two ports and of all installations and airfields in the region....

After which Lecœur quoted a confidential circular from M. Queuille, dated 28-2-51 asking his emissaries of the Ministry of the Interior "to do their utmost to create cordial contacts" between the Americans and the population. The note added that the Prefects should co-operate in this task.

This propaganda went on day after day. On April 26, Pierre Courtade wrote in *L'Humanité*:

Eddie Gilmore, Paris correspondent of A.P. has revealed that the French Government is postponing the publication of a communiqué announcing the establishment on French soil "of a large number of air bases for American fighters and bombers".... Eddie Gilmore thinks that this delay is due to the "delicate political problems now existing in France". He is too polite. It isn't a question of "delicate political problems"; the real problem is the growing anger of an entire nation which does not wish to be turned into a bomb-target.

M. Pleven and his Government were meantime doing their utmost to become the blue-eyed boys of America. At Washington, at the end of January, M. Pleven, in the words of the *Monde*, was given the most cordial reception, and had achieved the primary purpose of his journey: which was "to put an end to misunderstandings, and to strengthen Franco-American co-operation". What did this amount to? As the *Monde* said:

M. Pleven was most determined to secure American aid in Indo-China, and it is well known that this desire did not fail to have some influence on France's attitude at Lake Success.

In other words, France, in return for American aid in Indo-China, had agreed to support the motion proclaiming China the aggressor!

Mr Truman confirmed his promises concerning the dispatch of war material to the Franco-Vietnamese army now fighting in Tongking. It is reported that it will receive nine American squadrons.

For the rest, nothing very definite was decided. The *Monde* observed that the United States was favourable to the Schuman Plan, but not quite so favourable to the Pleven Plan, and that the talk in the American press about "the progressive integration of a democratic Germany in a vigorous West-European community" rather indicated that neither America nor France were considering any more the neutralization of Germany as the price that might be paid for an East-West agreement.[4] For one thing, Eisenhower had obviously been shaken by the state of mind in Europe, and was in no hurry to present his Report. In the circumstances, as the *Monde* editorialist put it, with his tongue in his cheek, one rather suspects:

M. Pleven could do no more than recall [to Mr Truman] the figures already published, and assure him of the good intentions of the French Government; but whether these were carried out completely depended, of course, on American aid.

As for the pleasant generalities about the problem of raw materials being "an object of international action" and about the two governments being aware of the importance of "the problem of inflation and the rise in prices", the *Monde* thought that there was still a lot to do before these "general formulae" had any chance of being applied. Even so, M. Pleven and certain Government supporters tried to persuade both themselves and the French public that France was America's blue-eyed boy, and M. Maurice Schumann even sounded slightly patronizing to Britain with its Labour Government (not very well looked upon in Washington at the time) when he declared at the National Assembly on February 7, *à propos* of M. Pleven's return from Washington, that French foreign policy now had acquired the "original and positive quality" of being "an irreplaceable link between the United States and Great Britain". Just like that.

Two observations are called for at this point. First, that the United States was in no hurry to take any particular action about inflation, which would stop the cost of living in France from rising very rapidly during this period; and secondly, that, perhaps with an eye on the French General Election, Eisenhower was urged by the French Government not to make a major issue of German rearmament just yet—lest it played straight into the hands of the Communist and other candidates opposed to this rearmament. Moreover, the Germans themselves were extremely divided on this issue.

[4] *Le Monde*, February 1, 1951.

Indo-China, North Africa, Germany—these were the three external issues which did so much to poison the political atmosphere in France in the next few years—until Mendès-France decided to find a solution to all three—only (as some of his critics said) to render at least two of them even more acute. Many, in later years, reflected that perhaps all these unimaginative, unenterprising Queuilles and Plevens and Pinays and Laniels were not so wrong after all to let sleeping dogs lie—at least the German dog! In reality, however, a decision in one way or another had become imminent; Britain and the USA were not prepared, in 1954, to wait any longer.

In the early months of 1951 France had, however, more immediate worries. The Korean War had sent up world commodity prices, and this rise was becoming increasingly reflected in the French cost of living. As *Franc-Tireur* put it, prices had taken the lift, and wages were walking up the stairs.

There had been relative stability of both prices and wages during 1949 and the first half of 1950; but since the outbreak of the Korean War, prices had risen in spectacular fashion. The following comparisons were quoted by *Franc-Tireur*:

Index of	1938 — 100 Hourly wage of unskilled worker (*manœuvre*)	Index of wholesale prices
April 1949	850	1847
December 1949	885	2001
June 1950	950	2085
October 1950	1082	2266
January 1951	1092	2460
February 1951	1095	2600
March 1951	1160	2680

It will be noted that there was a marked rise in wages between February and March; as a result of the wave of strikes that swept France during three weeks in March, the Government increased the guaranteed minimum wage (based on 200 hours' work a month) to 17,500 frs., but even this increase was very far from catching up with the cost of living. Thus, between March and June 1951 steak rose from 553 to 737 per kg., sugar from 93 to 107, etc.[5] By June 1951 no government had yet proved willing to consider the *échelle mobile*—the sliding-scale—which would tie wages to the cost-of-living index for which all the trade unions had been clamouring for years. The principle had, it is true, been accepted by the employers in a number of industries—

[5] *Franc-Tireur*, June 23, 1951.

notably the engineering and textile industries—but it had not yet been generalized by legislation, as it was to be a year later.

The great March strikes, supported by all the three major trade union federations, were, wholly unlike the strikes of 1947, strictly economic in character, and despite the great inconvenience they caused to the general public, they enjoyed great popular sympathy, and, in the end, the Queuille Government was obliged to agree to a number of concessions. For one thing, the General Election was approaching, and it was bad to antagonize the bulk of France's wage-earners more than necessary.

Queuille, who had succeeded Pleven only two months before the General Election in June (Pleven having resigned over the Electoral Reform issue), took a strictly *immobiliste* line, looked upon his Government as a caretaker government, was content to help the Assembly to pass the new Election Law after endless squabbles and discussions, to throw a small bone to the wage-earners, and let the post-Election government deal, as best it could, with the mounting budget deficit and the acute problem of rearmament.

Although the resignation from the British Government of Mr Bevan, Mr Harold Wilson, and Mr John Freeman in April 1951 caused some excitement in political and intellectual quarters in France, where this event was treated as the first major reaction against the ruinous rearmament policy the USA was trying to impose on Europe, it was obviously not the somnolent M. Queuille who was going to revise France's rearmament commitments at that stage and start a major row with Washington.

Queuille hoped that the Third Force would continue to rule France: "You are condemned to living together", he had once said to the Third Force parties—the Socialists, Radicals, and MRP; and the electoral law, with its completely cynical and hard-boiled system of *apparentements* was devised to help the Third Force parties to secure a working majority in the next parliament. Its purpose was to reduce to a minimum the representation of the Communists and the Gaullists.

The same line was taken by M. Herriot, the President of the National Assembly who, in his speech at its closing session, made some highly derogatory remarks about the two "anti-republican extremes". Obsessed by the "Gaullist menace" and the "Communist menace", both M. Queuille and M. Herriot did not seem to realize at the time that the social group that was in reality going to gain most from the Election was the "classical" Right. It scarcely occurred to them that this *also* represented a danger to "the Republic"—at least if the word was to be used in more than a purely formal sense.

The most notable result of the 1951 election was that it "debunked"

Gaullism as a vast political force in France; before long, as will be seen, a part of the Gaullists simply identified themselves with the "classical" Right—which was only to be expected, despite de Gaulle's own bitter outburst: "I did not save France to hand her over to Monsieur Pinay."

The Radicals gained in influence and importance; the Socialists and MRP both declined, and their "Third Force" alliance, which had been the cornerstone of the relative stability of the 1947–51 period, broke up soon after the Election over the seemingly moth-eaten issue of *laicité*; the Communists' voting-strength showed only a slight decline, compared with 1946, but, owing to the system of *apparentements*, their representation in Parliament was almost cut in half. As a result of the Election the political centre of gravity in Parliament shifted from the Left Centre to the Right Centre. But the pessimism and uncertainty that had marked the early months of 1951 did not come to an end as a result of the Election; if anything, the gloom deepened as the year proceeded. It is significant that it should have been not before, but some months after, the Election that Mendès-France came out, in December 1951, with the most devastating—nearly three-hour—criticism of the mismanagement of both home and foreign affairs.

But before proceeding with an account of the 1951 Election, it would seem useful, at this stage, to have a close look at the political parties as they looked at the time.

CHAPTER TWO

THE FRENCH POLITICAL PARTIES AND THE 1951 ELECTION

I T IS a truism to say that the Frenchman is an "individualist", and that the over-simple statement that any man who's born alive is "either a little Liberal or a little Conservative" applies much less to France than it does to England. It is true that during several years before 1914, France could be roughly divided into *la gauche* and *la droite*; though here too, there were numerous subdivisions and *nuances*. To take a simple example: was Péguy a man of the Right, or a man of the Left? Or Clemenceau? Or Caillaux? Or Briand? Or even Poincaré? Poincaré was a conservative, but not a "reactionary", and he himself admitted to have a soft spot for the Radicals because these seemed to him like "the flesh and blood of provincial France". The time factor also counts. The Caillaux who in 1907 proposed for the first time to introduce income-tax in France, seemed a man of the Left, almost a revolutionary; the Caillaux who, thirty years later, overthrew the Front Populaire Government at the Senate became for the Socialists a byword of "reaction". It was not that the man had changed, but that the political scene around him had shifted; he still stood where he had stood thirty years before, but now he was no longer on the "Left" of the political scene, but on the "Right". Today the Radicals are, on the whole, a Right, not a Left, or even a Centre party—or at least they were until they were "shaken up" by Mendès-France in 1955.

British and American newspaper readers lose patience when they read about French cabinet crises and French parliamentary parties; why, they ask, shouldn't two or three parties be enough for any country? They aren't enough in France, and the simple, perhaps over-simple answer is "individualism". But it is not only that; there are historical traditions which survive in some small party which is not quite the same as its neighbour; or there is some new mood or move-ment of opinion which does not quite fit the pattern of a party that is already in existence; thus, many Gaullists might not differ greatly, in the last analysis, from the conservative Right; still, they differed from them sufficiently, at least at one period, to start a "party" of their own. Or else, take the *progressistes*. Same as the Communists? Again, yes and no. The whole social background of a "progressive Christian" like Gilbert de Chambrun makes it difficult for him to be "simply" a Communist; similarly, it is both psychologically easier and tactically more advantageous for an ex-Radical like Pierre Cot not to have to submit to the rigid discipline of the CP, and to remain a mere "progressive".

There are, as will be shown, many subdivisions among the Radicals, the MRP, and, indeed, most other parties, not least on issues like German rearmament, colonial policy, etc.

Yet despite these numerous subdivisions, the 1951 Election showed that at that time, at any rate, France could, broadly speaking, be divided into six parts which, owing to the trickery of the *apparentements* system,[1] resulted in the election of a "hexagonal" Chamber with six almost equal sides: (1) the Communists, (2) the Socialists, (3) the MRP, (4) the Radicals, (5) the "classical" Right comprising the "Independents", the "Peasants", etc, and (6) the Gaullists, a part of whom, however, became virtually absorbed in the next couple of years in "group 5". But the number of voters behind these six groups was by no means identical. Each of these sides of the "hexagon" is worth at least a brief examination.

I. THE COMMUNISTS

These hold an exceptional place in the Fourth Republic. In much of the recent writing on France, especially in England and America, there has been a tendency to take it as an axiom that they are "evil", and to look upon them as a force which is responsible for France not being entirely "with" the West, and for her not being "entirely" democratic. The first argument is well founded; the Communists are the

---

[1] The main feature of the *apparentements* was the provision that if the "associated" parties polled more than half the votes cast, they divided among themselves all the seats of the constituency (a constituency being usually a *département* or part of a *département* with an average of about 5 seats). Otherwise the seats were allocated (roughly) on the basis of P.R. The *apparentements* system did not apply to the Paris area (Seine and Seine-et-Oise).

Here is one of many examples of how advantageous it was to be *apparenté*:

DORDOGNE (5 seats). Votes cast: 197,963.

Associated Parties:

Radical	40,918	2 *seats*
Socialist	36,033	2 *seats*
MRP	14,136	1 *seat*
"Peasant"	13,900	*nil*

Isolated Parties:

Communist . . .	61,517	*nil*
RPF (Gaullist) . . .	25,099	*nil*

With 14,000 votes the MRP got one seat, with 61,000 votes, the Communists got none.

loudest—though not necessarily the most effective—opponents of the Western Bloc in France. The second argument is much more dubious; and it has indeed been argued, with some reason, that the existence of a dynamic force on the Left, though by no means "democratic" in the bourgeois sense, and even anti-democratic, has tended to act as a protection of traditional bourgeois democracy against the stranglehold of the equally, or more anti-democratic extreme Right.

This is a point fully recognized by M. Jacques Fauvet, the *Monde*'s expert on home affairs, who, in his excellent book, *Les Forces Politiques de la France* (Paris, 1951), explains what he calls *la loi de la pesanteur*, the law of gravity. It is often argued, he says, that France would be a better place if the Communist Party were prohibited or otherwise eliminated.

Some say its elimination is essential to national defence.... Some even argue that the Communists are like Russian paratroops already on the spot. ... On the other hand, the argument of men like M. Moch is that nobody must be prosecuted for his opinions, and that the Communist Party cannot be prosecuted *as such*, but that any Communists who act in a manner contrary to law and order should be prosecuted.... Also, a clandestine Communist Party might be more dangerous than a CP existing openly....

What then, according to M. Fauvet, is the main objection to prohibiting the Communist Party? It is simply this: *One cannot fight the Extreme Left, except with the support of the Extreme Right. It is one of the laws of history and of gravity. Many anti-Communists are much too afraid of "being eaten up next"*. For negative anti-Communism, he says, is equally dangerous. The Centre may start wiping out the Communists, but in doing so, it would only play into the hands of the extreme Right, for the extreme Right alone would be wholehearted in its anti-Communism. That is what restrains the Centre, which does not want to play the part of the sorcerer's apprentice.

The fact that, ever since the Liberation, about five million Frenchmen have steadily voted Communist and that all attempts made by both the Socialists and the Gaullists to detach a large part of the electorate from the Communists have failed, shows that here must be some powerful psychological, social, and economic reasons why over 25 per cent of the French electorate vote for them.[2] It has often been argued that people vote for the Communists when they are "economically discontented". A Socialist Minister once even remarked in the National Assembly that poverty was Communism's best ally, to which Duclos aptly replied: "Well, what are you waiting for to fight this ally of ours?"

[2] Twenty-six per cent of the *votes* cast, but about 20 per cent of the *electorate*, including the abstentions. This difference has been a frequent object of quibbling.

But it isn't only that. Just as it is not true that the Communist Party is solely a working-class party, or that the entire working-class votes Communist, so it is also untrue that poverty is the only reason why Frenchmen vote for the Communists. Some of the best-paid French workers, notably in the Paris engineering industry (where there are men earning as much as 100,000 francs a month) are often found to be among the most ardent Communists, just as, at the other end of the scale, can be found poverty-stricken old women voting for the Right or the MRP.

Since 1947 the Communists have been the Opposition Party *par excellence*; and it is true that the malcontents tend to vote for the Communists; it is, however, also true that the greater part of the working-class vote Communist out of a sense of "class solidarity", much as the British working-class votes Labour.

As Fauvet says:

The Communists embody the traditional values of the Left. The CP produces almost invariably a number of traditional reflexes of great emotional power.... A very large number of Frenchmen tend to identify the Communist Party with freedom, peace, *la patrie*, and social justice.

And, above all, the Communist Party has largely succeeded in inheriting (or "usurping" or "annexing", as Socialists like Léon Blum have so often complained) the revolutionary temperament, the revolutionary tradition of France; for who except the Communists are in the tradition of the revolutionary struggle of the working-class, in the (albeit sentimentalized) tradition of 1848, with its barricades; of the Commune; or of the glorious days of the Popular Front of 1935–6?

It was not for nothing that, for years, the Communists exalted the part they had played in the Popular Front and in the Resistance, always with the innuendo that Blum had betrayed the Popular Front and the Spanish Republic, and that most of the Socialist Deputies had voted for Pétain, and so were "traitors" to their class. And even if, in 1947, the Communists made themselves extremely unpopular with their political strikes, there is little doubt that, after that, they at least partly made up for it with their peace propaganda.

There is another point that has helped the Communists. There are black sheep in the Communist Party as elsewhere; but in hardly any of the numerous pre-war and post-war scandals have any Communists been involved. No wonder that Thorez sang paeans of praise to the purity and almost monastic frugality of the Communists, in his Report at the Genevilliers Congress in April 1950.[3]

[3] It must be said that, coming from Thorez, this praise of Communist frugality was perhaps a little misplaced, and may have aroused a few ironical thoughts among the rank-and-file. For Thorez personally is by far the most

Also, a certain prestige, a "political sex appeal" attaches to the Communist leaders. I remember a Socialist Deputy at the Socialist Congress in 1950 saying: "*Thorez, ça a de la gueule*—and so have most of the other Communist leaders. Even Duclos; he's small and fat and ugly as a toad, but he's got personality, and a quick wit, and the cartoonists love him. Our Léon Blum—well, Blum was perhaps impressive in a literary *salon*; he was wholly out of his element in a working-class crowd; as for the others—Guy Mollet, or Moch, or Ramadier, or Daniel Mayer, and the rest—they couldn't arouse any popular enthusiasm. They just lack *something*. They are so nondescript, so 'ordinary'. There are 10,000 schoolmasters in France looking *exactly* like Guy Mollet."

Since then, it is true, Thorez has been a sick man and has lost most of the glamour he had acquired in the '30's with his official autobiography, *Fils du Peuple*, and with his dazzling oratory of 1936—when he looked like the Ideal Proletarian Hero, and was rapidly becoming the "beloved leader", second only to Stalin himself. Moreover, Marty, Lecœur, and Tillon have been eliminated from the Party; nevertheless, the rest have continued to cultivate, as much as ever, the pose of the tough, hard, and virtuous working-class leader.

And the Communists' "obedience to Moscow", and Russian concentration camps, and all that—the stock-in-trade of all anti-Communist propaganda? Why, in spite of it, why, in spite of the gigantic anti-Communist and anti-Soviet propaganda which, for several years, had

privileged person in the French CP. For years he had been built up as a kind of French sub-Stalin. Not only does he own a house at Choisy-le-Roi, outside Paris, but also a house near Rambouillet; while, in 1954, because of his severe illness, he was also given by the Party a villa on the Riviera. Compared with him, none of the other Communist leaders are materially well-off. A few, like Duclos, supplement their meagre net income as deputies by writing for Communist papers in France and in the People's Democracies or the USSR, thus earning perhaps an additional 50,000 or 60,000 francs, but the rank-and-file Communist deputy, with a bare 30,000 or 35,000 a month to live on often has nowhere to live in Paris, and "camps out" with fellow-Communists who have homes in the capital; wives of these rank-and-file deputies are sometimes reduced to supplementing the family income by doing various menial jobs like "charring". The Party funds do not, of course, depend entirely on the ruthless levies made on deputies' salaries. The Communist Party also owns a number of more or less profitable "businesses"—sixteen or seventeen in number, among them a chain of co-operative shops, a tourist bureau, a number of garages and cinemas, a filmmaking organization, etc. It is also believed that the CP receives some funds from abroad, though probably not very much. But these funds reach it by such devious means that they have been found to be as difficult to trace as other funds which are unquestionably paid from US sources to various French papers and propaganda organizations. What suggests that foreign funds received by the CP are not generous is, for example, the disappearance, in 1952, of the only Communist evening paper in Paris, *Ce Soir*. Useful pro-American Paris dailies, though run at a loss, are not generally allowed to close down.

preceded the 1951 Election, did five million Frenchmen still vote Communist? There are several reasons. As Fauvet says,

Soviet nationalism doesn't worry the greater part of the French workers, because in their view, the interests of Soviet nationalism coincide with those of real French nationalism.

Secondly, there is the simple argument, particularly "useful" in the present post-war world, that if the "capitalists" are working hand-in-hand with American imperialism, why shouldn't the French CP depend on its moral, political (and perhaps even financial) support on the Soviet Union? If one is not treason, why should the other be? And as for anti-Soviet propaganda, it just cuts very little ice with the habitual Communist voter. And even if there *are* concentration camps in Russia —then, there must be some good reason for it, the rank-and-file Communist argues. Is the ruling class in France, with its Indo-China war and its tortures in Algeria and Morocco in any position to be self-righteous?

The over-emphasis of anti-Communist and anti-Soviet themes in all American and "capitalist" propaganda also renders this propaganda suspect in the eyes of most French intellectuals—except for the "slave labour", which is always hard to swallow, even if the figures are greatly exaggerated.

How many of these intellectuals are wholly Communist? And what makes a French intellectual accept Communism? There are not many intellectuals who accept Communism wholeheartedly, or who acccept its discipline. No doubt it flatters the Communist Party to have Joliot-Curie or Picasso on its platform on festive occasions; but there is, naturally, something equivocal and paradoxical about Picasso's Communism; his art is seldom, if ever, Communist art, though it is, in a sense, great anti-capitalist art; his *Guernica* is a work of genius, but his imaginary portrait of Stalin was a dismal failure, and Aragon had to apologize for having published it in *Lettres Françaises*.

Aragon, despite his surrealist past, is the "perfect" Communist writer, a kind of Fadeyev of France, at least where his recent novels are concerned. Eluard was a greater poet than he, and it was this sensitive French poet, also a former surrealist, who wrote this astonishing piece of quasi-religious "symbolist" poetry to celebrate Stalin's seventieth birthday:

> ... Grâce à lui nous vivons sans connaître l'automne
> L'horizon de Staline est toujours renaissant
> Nous vivons sans douter et même au fond de l'ombre
> Nous produisons la vie et réglons l'avenir
> Il n'y a pas pour nous de jour sans lendemain
> D'aurore sans midi de fraîcheur sans chaleur

Staline dans le cœur des hommes est un homme
Sous sa forme mortelle avec des cheveux gris
Brûlant d'un feu sanguin dans la vigne des hommes
Staline récompense les meilleurs des hommes
Et rend à leurs travaux la vertu du plaisir
Car travailler pour vivre est agir sur la vie

Car la vie et les hommes ont élu Staline
Pour figurer sur terre leurs espoirs sans bornes.

Was this *outré*, absurd, unnatural? It would be unwise to say so.[4] As to many Russians, so to the French Communists, Stalin became, during and since the war, a symbol of great emotional power, and no one can doubt this who attended the vast memorial meeting at the Vélodrome d'Hiver the day after Stalin's death, when numerous French *metallos* and railwaymen and their women literally wept with emotion, even despite many months of bitter doubts and acute unpleasantness caused by the Slansky Trial, the "Jewish doctors' plot", the expulsion as a "police spy" of André Marty, and the like. And there is little doubt that the death of Stalin—as well as the illness of Thorez, a man who had symbolized proletarian youth and vigour so well at the height of the Front Populaire in 1936—robbed the French Communists of two valuable emotional assets, and rather "complicated life".

The French Communist leadership is distrustful of the unstable bourgeois intellectual, even if he is entirely pro-Communist. As Fauvet says:

The time has passed when the CP accepted and sought the appointment of "intellectuals" to responsible posts within the Party. People like teachers and journalists are suspect.... A thing like Titoism shook two categories of Communists—the intellectuals, and the newcomers.... The rest were easily convinced by the elementary argument that "if the Soviet régime were to disappear, the People's Democracies and the Communist parties in the capitalist countries would carry no weight and would be swept away." Every man's attitude to the Soviet Union is the real touchstone.... The Party now wants the *cadres* of the Party to be strictly proletarian, equally alien to opportunist deviations as to sectarian deviations.... In the cells and in the "sections" discussions can be as lively as you make them, but ... the general line must be above discussion....

It is, indeed, true that intellectuals (like the late Gabriel Péri or the late Paul Vaillant-Couturier), who were prominent in the front rank of the CP before the war, no longer hold in it the same position.

It must, however, be added that, in recent years, the Communist

---

[4] It would be unwise, in the case of the Eluard poem. On the other hand, some of the cruder Stalin propaganda of 1950, like the film, *L'homme que nous aimons le plus au monde* made even many a diehard *militant* squirm.

Party has sought to create a new type of intellectual—not a mere *sympathisant* or fellow-traveller, but the intellectual who is, at the same time, a hard-boiled Party member. This naturally raises the question whether, especially in France, this is not a contradiction in terms.

The "Communist intellectuals" now include not only literary theorists like Roger Garaudy, whose strictly Marxist analysis of modern literature (notably his *Littérature de Fossoyeurs*, with its "outrageous" essays on Malraux, Mauriac, Sartre, and Koestler) is interesting, if not always convincing; but also a whole galaxy of young novelists following more or less the principles of Socialist Realism, and a *pléiade* of Socialist-Realist painters, with Fougeron at their head. Some of the novels are good (such as Courtade's *Rivière Noire*, a novel on Indo-China), others much more pedestrian (such as the "anti-American" novels of André Stil), while the paintings and drawings also greatly vary in quality. Nevertheless, *Esprit,* for example, thought the Fougeron exhibition in the rue La Boëtie in the heart of the Paris "West End", a highly significant phenomenon, if only because for the first time within living memory had an art show been invaded by hundreds of working people, whose comments, the *Esprit* writer remarked, were, if not much more intelligent, at any rate, a good deal fresher and spontaneous than the comments made by the ordinary run of exhibition-goers. It should be added that if Communist journalism is on the monotonous side (hence the sharp drop in the Communist press since the Liberation) it can at least boast of three outstanding cartoonists, the late H. P. Gassier, the ferocious Mitelberg, and the equally incisive, but much "lighter" Jean Effel.

Laurent Casanova, recalling a speech by Maurice Thorez in 1948, in which he said that "a certain number of Communist intellectuals had not yet fully accepted the political and ideological positions of the working-class", made the following comments in his book, *Le Parti Communiste, les Intellectuels et la Nation*:

Thorez took the view that these faults arose from a certain self-satisfied feeling among Communist intellectuals who think they can give lessons of Marxism to the Party, and educate the Party, as it were.... There are, indeed, two ideas at the back of the mind of many intellectuals, even those with the very best intentions.... They want to give the people access to culture, and to become "the Prince's Counsellor".... The idea is, however, rather obsolete.... For today you cannot talk of "the people" without realizing that the existence of a modern proletariat amongst it is the determining factor.... And at the head of it stands a party with a complete doctrine of scientific socialism....

To Casanova, it is clearly a case of the Party having to educate the intellectuals and not *vice versa*:

Intellectuals who come to the proletariat often have to submit to a painful process of seeing certain previously accepted values criticized. They do not like it, and tend to seek ideological and political compromises.... The enemy, always on the watch-out, finds this playing into his hands.... Thorez is therefore quite right when he says: "When our young intellectual comrades make mistakes, they must be helped, and criticized in a fraternal spirit, just as Communists criticize other Communists, without any fundamental concessions but also without excessive outward violence.[5]

Clearly, the Party is not, as a rule, *flattered* any longer by the adherence of intellectuals; it rather looks upon them as a useful, but fundamentally vulnerable and unstable element whom only a long process of indoctrination can turn into real Communists.

It is outside the scope of this book to describe in detail the organization of the French Communist Party, but it may be said, that with its local cells and *sections*, its departmental federations, its national congress, its central committee, its political bureau and its secretariat, its youth movements, its machinery for controlling the *cadres* and its party schools, its almost organic link with the CGT, and its propaganda and intelligence services it has the most elaborate and closely co-ordinated of the French party machines.[6]

Its membership, too, is higher than that of any other party (with the exception of the RPF in its heyday), and at least half the members are *militants*; the membership figures quoted by Fauvet are:

1934	45,000	1946	906,000
1937	333,000	1947	894,000
1945	544,000	1949	762,000
		1950	850,000(?)[7]

In 1951, the great revolutionary days of the Resistance and the Liberation were a thing of the past; the rôle of the Communists as a government party had also come to an end in 1947; the prospect of a Communist revolution or even of a return to power, in any degree, was infinitely remote. The political strikes of 1947 had been a failure, and anti-Communist propaganda in the country was stronger than it had ever been; among the working-class there was a good deal of fatigue and disillusionment, and after the abortive attempt to organize sabotage against American arms shipments to France and against French

[5] L. Casanova, *op. cit.* (Paris, 1949), pp. 69–80.

[6] At the end of 1953 there were 2,562 *sections* and 19,219 cells, including over 5,000 *cellules d'entreprise*.

[7] Fauvet was right to query the last figure. Since 1947 there had, apart from an "artificial boosting" in 1952–3, been a steady decline in the number of Party members (partly because admission was made more difficult); in May 1954 the membership was 506,000. (Marcel Servin's Report, *Cahiers du Communisme*, 6–7, 1954, p. 732.) By 1955 there was a further drop.

arms shipments to Indo-China, the Communists were now encouraging only purely "economic" strikes.

It was in these highly unfavourable conditions that the Communists prepared for the 1951 Election. Their chief assets were that they were the "Leftest" of all the major parties and that, for years now, they had conducted a very effective anti-war campaign.

Personally, what is a Communist like? The answer is simple. Most workers in France are more or less pro-Communist (even though many of them would read a sports paper like *L'Equipe*, or an "entertaining" bourgeois paper like *France-Soir* rather than *L'Humanité*); it has often been said that if in England or America, there were as many Communists as in France, people would know that Communists were just "ordinary people", and that Communists "didn't eat babies". But, in reality, the matter is more complicated than that; a part of the French bourgeoisie, though without believing it, still like to think that the French Communists *do* "eat babies". In a later chapter, dealing with the first serious attempt made by the Government since the war to outlaw the Communist Party, many of the other aspects of the peculiar position of the French Communist Party and of the French working-class in France will be discussed. Here it is sufficient to say that if a large proportion of the French intellectuals was sharply anti-Communist in 1948–9, it became much less so in 1952–5. In this the influence of J.-P. Sartre was among the most important.

On the other hand, the international *détente*, improved economic conditions in France, and the extraordinary consolidation of capitalism by 1955 created for the French Communists a number of new political and doctrinal problems which were very different from those of 1951.

2. THE SOCIALISTS

They still call themselves officially SFIO—*Section Française de l'Internationale Ouvrière*, and are the only French Party to describe themselves as the "section" of any international organization. The late Louis Lévy, returning from a COMISCO Conference in 1951, liked to say that there were strong "emotional" links between the various "reformist" Socialist parties of the world, and especially of Europe, as well as many "pragmatic" and "practical" points of contact, even though the lack of a common doctrine was very striking; he claimed that the European Socialist parties fell into three groups—Marxist, non-Marxist, and anti-Marxist, and that, in spite of appearances, the French and Belgian Socialists could still, from the point of view of doctrine, be considered as "Marxist" parties. The same did not apply to either the Labour Party or the Socialists of Scandinavia. Marxists *en principe* —to use that wonderful French formula covering a multitude of sins.

We have seen in an earlier chapter Blum's somewhat tortuous reply to the question whether he was a Marxist, and his reference to the Party's Declaration of Principles. Doctrine is, however, the thing which, in practice, matters less to the French Socialists than to almost anybody else. What does matter, however, is this: if, in a sense, the Communists act as a powerful *corrective* in the Fourth Republic, so also do the Socialists; the former, it might be said, act as a corrective on the *national* plane, the latter on the *government* plane.

For the Socialists are essentially a government party, and even when they are not in the government, they try to act as a constructive opposition party.

Today [says Fauvet] they lack the method of Marx, the faith of Jaurès, the austerity of Guesde. Then what have they left? What they have left is governmental power. It is a lot and it is nothing. (*Op. cit.*, p. 67.)

He might also have said that they were an extremely bureaucratic party and had tended to become more and more so in recent years, with Guy Mollet becoming, as Bourdet put it, "as big a bully as Herbert Morrison".

The French Socialists are a party suffering from frustration. In what was probably the last public speech he made, at the Socialist Congress of 1949, Blum, throwing out his long arms in preparation for a sublime embrace, piped in his high-pitched voice: "*La classe ouvrière, la class ouvrière, elle est à nous, A NOUS!*" It was what one Socialist speaker at the same Congress called "the Coué Method" of French Socialism.

They suffer from an even greater number of contradictions than most other parties. Their Declaration of Principles says that "the Socialist Party is an essentially revolutionary Party . . . has always been and continues to be a party of the class struggle". It is, indeed, a party with a revolutionary tradition and a revolutionary vocabulary; yet in reality it is essentially a reformist party; also, it is a "working-class party" with only a small working-class following and a large *fonctionnaire*, *petit-bourgeois*, and peasant following. It has, under the Fourth Republic, largely taken over the old electoral clientèle of the Radicals, including the old-time anti-clerical elements.

There is something pathetically moth-eaten and down-at-heel about the "symbolism" displayed at Socialist Party congresses. If the Communists' hammer and sickle and the Gaullists' Cross of Lorraine are still symbols of some significance, the Three Arrows of the Socialists can do no more than arouse among older people distant and melancholy memories of the Weimar Republic; and the large enlarged photographs of Jaurès and Guesde also have very little connexion with the present problems of the SFIO. And perhaps most striking of all at Socialist congresses is the atmosphere of acute anti-Communism. The Socialists' attitude to the MRP, to the Radicals, and even to the Right is *nuancée*; for a short time Gaullism and Communism were equally great enemies; but the RPF did not last long as a major menace to the Republic, whereas Communism is, to the Socialists, the chronic and perpetual Enemy Number 1. At Socialist congresses all the literary or practically all the literature on the bookstalls, apart from a few dusty and faded copies of Jaurès and Guesde, is anti-Communist literature, ranging from Léon Blum pamphlets to the works of Dallin, Kravchenko and General Anders!

The whole post-war history of the Socialist Party is a story of good intentions and unfulfilled resolutions. All the talk of "united action" with the Communists, fashionable in 1944, came to nothing (through the fault, it is true, of not the Socialists only); in 1945 the SFIO-UDSR marriage was also soon dissolved: in 1946 there was a "palace revolution" inside the Party, when Guy Mollet took over the leadership from Daniel Mayer, but it did not substantially affect the policy of the Party; a year later a rigidly *dirigiste* policy was laid down which, only a few months afterwards, was swept away by the rising tide of American-inspired "economic liberalism". "Participation" and "non-participation" have been a constant dilemma with the Socialist Party, and the object of frequent conflicts between those who believed that the Republic could be best defended from inside the Government and those who thought it could be best defended from outside. Whether the motives of the "participationists" are always pure and unselfish is of secondary importance; what should, however, be emphasized is that, *in so far as the Socialist Party has played a salutary part in the life of the Fourth Republic, it has certainly been as a defender of this Republic, of this "bourgeois democracy", with all its faults.* In 1947–8 it was the Third Force, chiefly composed of the MRP and the Socialists, which succeeded in breaking the political strikes organized by the Communists and, at the same time, in building a powerful dam against the tidal wave of Gaullism which threatened at one moment to flood the whole country.

Probably it was only a false alarm; "Gaullism" was too mixed and incoherent a movement to "take over"; nevertheless, nearly 40 per cent of the people of France, had, in a moment of panic, voted for it. At the risk of making themselves—or at any rate, certain of their leaders like Jules Moch—detested by the working-class, the Socialists supported wholeheartedly, in the name of the Republic, the two-front battle against the Communists and Gaullists.

In this sense, the Socialists, like their MRP allies, have been given great credit for having "saved the Republic".

Only what kind of Republic? The Socialists have, naturally, no great illusions about the possibility of creating a "Socialist France". It might be possible if they could make a single front with the Communists, or if the entire working-class deserted the Communists and came over to them—but both eventualities were out of the question in 1951. The world is divided in two; and the Socialists have no choice other than being "with the West". There were, around 1950–1, some mildly "neutralist" currents among the SFIO, but they never came out into the open, and even Bevanism, with its implied "anti-Americanism", was always frowned upon by the Socialist leaders.

In Parliament, until 1951, the Socialists had always put up something of a fight in favour of social reform, higher wages, etc—though always within the limits of what they thought "possible" with a given government majority. Since the departure of the Communists from the Government, they had fought successfully, first for the "minimum wage", and then for the adoption of the sliding-scale principle. Except during a short spell, when they had quarrelled with M. Bidault over a question of wages and, at the same time, over the *affaire des généraux*, they had been in the Government right up to the 1951 Election. Their chief argument in 1951 was that if nothing had gone very well, everything might have gone much worse, but for their participation in the government and their "vigilant defence of the Republic".

The fact remains that the Socialists are a government party, and a government party in the Western world; hence their inevitable pro-Americanism and anti-Sovietism; hence also their often hesitant and ambiguous attitude to things like the war in Indo-China ("terrible war, but we mustn't play into the hands of the Communists"); hence also their doubts and hesitations over North Africa. They would like the Arabs to have a square deal but the French Socialist Federations in North Africa form, in spite of themselves, part of the *colon* society, and the Socialist leadership is conscious of the unpopularity of any propaganda in France in favour of excessive "generosity" *vis-à-vis* Moroccan and Tunisian (let alone Algerian) independence claims. At Algiers, to this day, the Algerians talk about the "impossible" régime of M. Naegelen, the Socialist Governor-General, who "cooked" elections even worse than any of his more right-wing successors and predecessors.

No doubt, there was "Europe". And in 1951 most of the Socialists liked the "European" jargon of Strasbourg. Although they (like the British Labour Party) had failed to promote a Socialist Germany, and had also failed to agree on any major international issue with the German Socialists, they still believed in "Europe". They more or less unanimously supported the Schuman Plan; they were less sure about the "European Army", but nevertheless supported the re-armament drive of 1950; anti-Communist sentiment had helped to kill what doubts they had on the subject. When, in 1952, it came to discussing German rearmament in all seriousness, they were much more divided; and yet the majority, wholly ignoring the pleadings of the German Social-Democrats and the warnings of Bevanism, were pro-EDC, M. Gouin, radiating anti-Communist hatred (he still hadn't quite got over Yves Farge and the *affaire du vin*) being among its most passionate supporters. In 1952, the bitterness of the discussions over EDC at the Socialist Congress at Montrouge was such that it even produced a little wave of anti-Semitism against the more determined opponents of EDC like Jules Moch, Daniel Mayer, and the late Salomon Grumbach.

No doubt, in 1951, the French Socialists still had a small working-class clientèle, especially in the Nord and the Pas-de-Calais, but nearly all their deputies looked "middle-class", and so was most of their electorate. They were not too happy about it; they knew that, since 1945, their support in the country had declined; if, on balance, they had not lost more votes, it was because middle-class votes had made up for the working-class votes they had lost. But they had the support of the bulk of the *instituteurs* and of the postmen, the latter very nearly a "proletarian" group, both economically and in their mental make-up. (It was, indeed, the Force Ouvrière postmen of Bordeaux, for instance, who were to start the great wave of strikes in the summer of 1953.)

Not only because the Communists (and the MRP for that matter) had a more impressive Resistance record than the Socialists, but also intellectually, these suffer from a marked inferiority-complex. The French intellectual with his non-conformism and his highly-developed critical sense, is repelled by the "mediocrity" and the "possibilism" of the French Socialists, this "possibilism" inevitably resulting in the absence of any ideological or intellectual basis, and in a frequent lack of intellectual integrity. If a very large part of the French intellectuals are "Left", they are definitely not "SFIO", a party of big and small bureaucrats, who publish the most unreadable of all French newspapers, *Le Populaire*. No doubt, there are a few successful Socialist papers in the provinces; but they are "good enough for a provincial public, not for Paris". It is also true that the Socialists are, indirectly, supported by a number of other papers, like *Franc-Tireur*, but this is "anarcho-trotskyist" in style and temperament, and is pro-SFIO only *faute de mieux*. But its anti-colonialism and anti-clericalism (which are like those of the *Canard Enchaîné*) go much further than any official SFIO utterances. There are also important Socialist influences on some other papers, notably *France-Soir*, Georges and Charles Gombault—both members of the SFIO—being among the most influential members of its staff.

There are no great names in art and literature that are specifically associated with the French Socialist Party; nor have the Socialists built up any "intellectual" group comparable with the Communist group comprising Picasso, Léger, Aragon, Eluard and all the younger Communist "intellectuals". The SFIO is supported by a certain élite among teachers, university professors, and lawyers, but creative artists have kept clear of it.

The two great assets of the SFIO in electoral terms are its *laïcité* and its anti-Communism; in all constituencies they tend to play on the republican traditionalism of a part of the electorate, and on the anti-Communist instincts of many traditionally-minded Frenchmen who, nevertheless, like to be *à gauche, mais jamais au-delà*. In this sense the SFIO is an "anti" rather than a "pro"-anything party. But when all is said and done, the SFIO is still, in a way "the last surviving heir of the idealist doctrines of the nineteenth century, of an idealism the optimism of which has survived so many violent shocks".[8] Hence the Socialists' Europeanism, despite all the heavy odds against it; hence also their half-hearted anti-colonialism and anti-militarism and anti-clericalism—all of which, however, would be much less half-hearted but for the existence of the Communists and the Soviet Union.

Above all, the Socialists in 1951 were, and still are, very conscious of being a government party; it was they who supplied the Fourth Republic with its first president, Vincent Auriol; it was they who had their men in the Government or at the head of the Government ever since 1944; it was they who steered the ship of state through the dangerous straits between Gaullism and Communism in 1947. Their people had been mixed up in the Wine Scandal and in the *affaire des généraux*, many of their people were involved in all the unsavoury intrigue of parliamentary and local politics and police scandals, all of which made them an easy butt for malicious columnists and cartoonists. All the same, if France was still shuffling along a narrow "democratic" path it was thanks to the SFIO. But as social reformers, and as promoters of a high standard of living for the working-class or of a great housing programme, they had not proved a success. Their achievements —such as they are—had been political, rather than economic. And as a Party, they lacked the "dynamism" of the CP. They had much fewer members, only a very small number of active *militants*, and no Youth Movement to speak of. They had shown little interest in the "family" (most "family" organizations in France were, and still are, either Communist or Catholic), and not only the Communists, but even the MRP (through the CFTC) had a wider working-class following than the Socialists.

[8] Fauvet, *op. cit.*, p. 91.

3. THE MRP

The MRP, like the Socialists, had been in office ever since the Liberation. Earlier chapters in this book will have shown how the MRP, "the child of a progressive Catholic tradition and of the Resistance" (Fauvet) became one of the three great "Resistance" parties of the "New France" that emerged at the time of the Liberation. Not only the "progressive" Catholic elements in France, but also all those who saw in de Gaulle the champion of law and order and who, in 1944–5 considered the MRP to be "de Gaulle's Party", supported the MRP as "the least of the three evils"—at least until further notice. By 1947 a very large part of the MRP vote went over to de Gaulle's RPF; but, as has been seen, the "Gaullist landslide" of October 1947 was something of an accident due to a combination of exceptional circumstances; and with more "normal" conditions setting in, especially after 1948, many of those who had voted first for the MRP, then for the RPF were now beginning to feel that the "Classical Right" and the Radicals were at last coming into their own again. *Both the MRP and the RPF were, as it were, the backwash of the War and the Resistance,* or, as one commentator unkindly put it, the "mumps and measles" of the Fourth Republic. Now that the Fourth Republic had grown up, it was beginning to look more and more like the Third. However, the MRP was not to disappear—though it became more and more identified with the Right.

The leading members of the MRP had been prominent in the Resistance; Bidault and others had talked a lot about a "New France", of "renovation", and *révolution par la loi.* For three years they had "co-operated" with the Socialists and Communists, and had taken responsibility for the "progressive" reforms of 1945–6. But by 1951 their position had become equivocal. They had completely broken with the Communists; as a government party they had become increasingly conservative; it is true that the Third Force—that *mariage de raison* between the MRP and the Socialists—had "saved the Republic"; but relations between the two parties had become strained over the question of schools; and in 1950 it had even come to a temporary breach with the Socialists, who, always with an eye on their deadly Communist rivals, were now insisting on a more generous wages policy than the MRP were willing to agree to. There had also been much unpleasantness between the two parties over the *affaire des généraux,* and the Gaullists had certainly done their best to detach the MRP from their Socialist partners.

There were, of course, "good MRP's" and "bad MRP's", but the "bad MRP's" had greatly gained in influence. At the Lyon Congress of the MRP in May 1951 one was struck by the idealism, the very "progressive" views of some of the younger people (for example, the small group that published a paper called *Positions*) who claimed to be "in the best Marc Sangnier tradition", who were "socially minded", attached the greatest importance to the Catholic trade union federation (the CFTC) co-operating as closely as possible with the Socialist FO and even with the Communist CGT, and who, in their paper, conducted an anti-colonialist campaign very similar to that of *Témoignage Chrétien* (another Catholic group not, however, affiliated in any way with the MRP). Yet the "socialism" of the MRP was clearly on the decline by this time. Shortly before, three deputies who were described by the leaders as "unrealistic sentimentalists" (if not "fellow-travellers"), among them the famous Abbé Pierre, the friend of the Paris down-and-outs, had resigned from the MRP in disgust. The Abbé Pierre had written in his letter of resignation:

In a few months it will be the end of all the hope with which we entered the political struggle. It was the hope that in the heart of the people there would be a full reconciliation between their Christian faith and the hunger and thirst for justice, social justice, as well as all other justice.

By a curious stroke of irony the abbé had used almost exactly the phrase used by M. Bidault only a few weeks before in his oration outside Notre-Dame at the funeral of Marc Sangnier, the "father" of Progressive Catholicism: "Marc Sangnier put an end to the centuries of incomprehension between Christian faith and the large part of our people."

Yet it was not M. Bidault, still less M. Paul Coste-Floret or the Vatican-sponsored M. Teitgen, with his dreams of a Little Catholic Europe who were going to accept such lofty sentiments as the basis for a practical day-to-day policy. They had budgets to balance, they had to see to it that the flow of dollars was maintained; they had to see that the war in Indo-China continued and that nothing of any vital importance was given away to the Neo-Destour or the Istiqlal. They were "building Europe", they were keeping the French Empire together; they had "saved the Republic"; and now they were going to "clericalize" it as far as possible. And it was not from *Positions*, or *Terre Humaine*, or *Témoignage Chrétien* that they were going to take their line. They were a government party, and if, after the Election, they could not go on co-operating with the Socialists, they might well co-operate with their right-wing neighbours. The *apparentements*, at any rate, would help them to keep their most dangerous rival, the RPF, in its place.

The next few years were to show how the MRP was to identify itself, more and more, with the Classical Right—with those conservative forces which for a time at any rate, were to gain virtual control of the

Government as a result of the 1951 Election. And it is significant that the famous strikes in the summer of 1953 were stopped in the end, with no great gain for the strikers, through the pressure brought to bear by the MRP ministers in the Laniel Government on the leaders of the CFTC, and through their successful effort to break the unity of action between them and the Communist CGT. It caused a good deal of bitterness among the rank and file of the Catholic trade unions.

4. THE GAULLIST RPF

Looking back to 1951, it is curious to recall how seriously de Gaulle and the RPF were still being taken at the time of the election campaign, even though there had already been a good deal of evidence that de Gaulle's influence had sharply declined since his triumph in the municipal elections of October 1947. It is true that shortly before the Election the Gaullists made a number of very bad mistakes. General Koenig was conducting a campaign for an enormous French Army, complete with a standing force of twenty divisions, and a possible extension of the military service to three years; while de Gaulle himself, in his May-Day speech at the Bois de Boulogne had spoken of a *"rendez-vous* in the Champs-Elysées" which evoked unhappy memories of the stormy days of the Croix de Feu in the middle 'thirties, and gave the more nervous people bad dreams of a "march on the Elysée" after de Gaulle's great election victory.

A nation-wide campaign had been organized, called the *campagne de la Carte Nationale*; for 100 francs you bought a card which you sent to de Gaulle.

On one half of the card the following text was printed:

De Gaulle wants that France should be—
(1) *Governed.* Liberate the Republic of the stranglehold of the parties and rule the country for the good of the Nation.
(2) *Well served.* Enforce order on finance, the public services and the administration.
(3) *Prosperous.* Bring about a massive increase in production through associating capital and labour in industry. Turn the country into the granary of Europe by equipping agriculture.
(4) *Defended.* Make an army that would be France's own army. Make a French Union which would be truly French. Lead Europe to Unity, and so increase the chances of peace in co-operation with the Atlantic States, which will be associated with France, but will not be her masters.
(5) *France should be France.* Liquidate the separatists [i.e. Communists]; do away with the Parties; make the French people unite under the aegis of a just and powerful State.

The other half of the card, with the question, *"Frenchmen, French-women, what do you think of this?"* was left blank for comments to be sent to de Gaulle.

Rassemblement, the official organ of the RPF, published photographs of numerous cards with the comments, all more or less on the same lines, approving the "programme", assuring de Gaulle of the writer's "devoted sympathy", and hoping that he would make France "clean".

It also printed photographs of bulging mailbags arriving at the rural post office of Colombey-les-Deux-Eglises, where de Gaulle lived.

It was believed at the time of the Election that de Gaulle had thus collected something like £40,000 or £50,000 for his "election fund". Whether, as an MRP leader told me, the RPF was also receiving funds from the American Republicans (while the Third Force were supposed to be subsidized by the Democrats) is difficult to ascertain. It seems improbable, since de Gaulle was not well looked upon by either Republicans or Democrats, who were both finding the Third Force parties much more amenable. His undertaking to liquidate the Communists may, however, have impressed certain elements in America. It was more than what the Third Force (or even the Classical Right) were officially promising, though one may well imagine that "Radicals" like J. P. David and Martinaud-Déplat were looked upon with high favour by the Republican Extremists in Washington.

What is much more important, however, is that de Gaulle received little financial support from the French *patronat*, which considered his plans for scrapping the trade unions as dangerous and amateurish. It was much less trouble to play off the trade union federations one against the other, as the MRP ministers, for instance, were doing. On the poor view big business and finance were taking of de Gaulle the *Canard Enchaîné* was highly informative. The RPF, it wrote on May 16, were trying to make friends at the Bourse. But the Bourse wouldn't hear of it.

If the RPF get away with it [these gentlemen say] stocks will go down the drain the very next week, and we'll fall back on gold. You'll see how it'll climb! You ask why? We'll tell you. At the Bourse we are convinced that the RPF in power will mean undiluted Communism in six months' time.

5. THE RIGHT AND THE RADICALS

Little need be said about them at this stage. Throughout the campaign so much attention was given to de Gaulle that most people scarcely realized that the real arbiters of the new National Assembly would be these dull, uninteresting, outmoded, old-fashioned groups, and that it was they who would, before long, bring about the disintegration of the RPF as a single political force.

Ever since the Liberation, these two groups had been under a cloud. Except for a few individuals, they had played no part in the Resistance. If the Right were wholly Vichyite, the Radicals had, in the main, condoned Vichy, and had, on the quiet, hankered for a return to the Third Republic.

The Socialists had stolen a large part of the Radicals' electorate, and the Radicals, who had received most of their support from the provincial *petite bourgeoisie* and part of the peasantry, were now chiefly dependent on the shopkeeper class and on the wealthier part of the peasantry; their electoral clientièle was in many cases much the same as that of the Right, except that they still appealed, to some extent, more than the Right did, to people with "Republican traditions", with a slight admixture of *laïcité*. However, the most outspoken champions of *laïcité* now were not the Radicals, but the Socialists.

There is no doubt that Radicals and especially the Right were the two groups who enjoyed the greatest financial support from the French *patronat*. They were also supported by a large part of the press, and on June 19, immediately after the election results were known, the *Figaro* triumphantly announced that the real victors in the Election were the "Fourth Force", an ephemeral name given to an electoral combination mainly composed of the "classical" Right and the Radicals.

It should, of course, be pointed out that the Radicals are one of the least homogeneous groups, and that it is impossible to generalize about them: they comprise many old-fashioned small-town politicians ("good republicans"); "Jacobins" like M. Daladier, with a strong authoritarian streak which he demonstrated in the past; old-fashioned bourgeois nationalists like M. Herriot; Big Business representatives and all-out colonialists like M. René Mayer; the "unclassifiable" Mendès-France; and, finally, a "McCarthyite" fringe composed of people like M. Martinaud-Déplat. As in all other groups, so among the Radicals, there were many different opinions on the crucial question of German rearmament.

6. UNORTHODOX CANDIDATES

Among unorthodox candidates who aroused the greatest interest in the 1951 election were the "neutralists", with Rivet and Bourdet at their head. Their meetings, supported by the non-conformist left-wing intelligentsia of Paris, were well-attended, but electorally it all proved a complete failure. This showed that only a very small proportion of the electorate go to meetings, and that the habit of voting for a big party, as well as the fear of playing into the hands of "the enemy" by voting for a small new party and so splitting the vote of a big party, are too strong.

Bourdet's failure (all he polled was 8,000 votes, whereas 25,000 was the minimum required in the Paris constituency he was contesting) illustrated the fact that even strong currents of ideas, without a strong organization behind them, usually find it impossible to fit into the electoral machinery which has rules of its own.

The following simple table (Fauvet, p. 264) shows the "general" attitude of the six main groups in the three essential fields of home affairs:

		Com.	Soc.	Rad.	MRP	Right	RPF
EDUCATION	MONOPOLY	X	X				
	NEITHER MONOPOLY NOR SUBSIDY				X		
	SUBSIDY					X	X	X
ECONOMIC POLICY	COLLECTIVIST	X					
	"DIRIGISTE"		X		X		
	LIBERAL			X		X	X
POLITICAL STRUCTURE	PEOPLE'S DEMOCRACY	X					
	PARLIAMENTARY DEMOCRACY		X	X	X	X	
	"AUTHORITARIAN DEMOCRACY"						X

Although this table cannot be taken too literally (thus the planned economy or *dirigisme* of the MRP is one of principle rather than of consistent practice) it still corresponds roughly to the actual position.

On the other hand, it would be almost impossible to draw up a similar table with reference to foreign policy unless one ignored in each case (except possibly in the case of the Communists—though even here there are conflicting currents) the almost countless subdivisions and *nuances*, not to mention the numerous variations caused by the changing international scene.

7. ELECTION CLOSE-UP

The General Election of June 17 went off very quietly, except for a few minor local incidents. The election meetings varied in interest, those of the Gaullists and Communists attracting rather more attention than the others.

The following notes, written at the time of the election campaign, provide a fair idea of some of its main features.

May 25

This is no routine election. As M. Herriot—now a man of nearly 80—exclaimed at the end of his emotional address to the Radical Congress on Friday:

"Never, on the eve of an election, have I felt such anguish as today; either the parliamentary republic will be saved, or else there will be violent clashes that may put an end to a régime which, since 1870, has given good results."

He described the new French electoral system as a "monster", but said that the Radicals must "accommodate themselves" to it in order to save the Republic from the double threat of Communism and Gaullism. Although he called the Communists all the names imaginable, it was clear that he considered Gaullism the greater and more immediate of the two dangers, and he begged the Radicals on no account to gang up with Gaullist candidates in any constituency.

It's all very curious. Herriot, the Radical chairman, calls the system with its *apparentements* a "monster"; the MRP and Socialists too, have been calling it a "regrettable" and "deplorable" system, all of them forgetting that they took months to put it into operation and that finally they all voted for it. And now, listening to them, one would think it had been imposed upon them by some supernatural power. What's the explanation for this lack of enthusiasm? It seems that all the Third Force parties have become conscious of an important fact since the electoral reform was voted: and that is that it has been very badly received in the country. Millions of prospective voters seem to have reacted with some distaste to the whole thing. The purpose of the electoral reform was to "keep the Communists and the Gaullists out" and to assure the success of the Third Force—*des vraies forces républicaines*. In other words, the Election results were being "legally cooked in advance", as somebody put it. One might dislike both Gaullists and Communists, but if one respected the Sacred Will of the Sovereign People, it didn't look nice.

And then there is the muddle over the *apparentements*. Take Brittany, for example. The question of religious schools is of the greatest importance here. If a clerical MRP candidate is "associated" with an anti-clerical Socialist or Radical, the Catholic voter will obviously say to himself that by voting for the MRP man he may get himself elected, but, in doing so, he will also help the anti-clerical to get elected; so why not simply vote for the Gaullist? In other constituencies the Communists may benefit from similar considerations.

May 27

The election hoardings are just beginning to go up, but most of the candidates' posters have not yet been printed. The delay is due to the fact that it wasn't until last Saturday that the *apparentements* in the various French constituencies were officially announced. They contain relatively few surprises. As was provided in the election law, the Paris area (i.e. the Seine and Seine-et-Oise *départements*) will vote on the basis of the PR; in the rest of France some 15 (out of the 90) *départements* will have no *apparentements*. The rest of the *départements* fall into three categories—in most either the Third Force parties proper (i.e. Socialists, MRP and Radicals) will be "associated", or there will be a larger "association" stretching all the way from the Socialists to the non-Gaullist Right; finally, there will be some fifteen constituencies where the Gaullists will be "associated" with either the so-called right-wing "Independents" or, in a few cases, with the MRP or the Radicals. In a number of cases the Gaullists rejected overtures from the others: the most notable case was that of M. Robert Schuman, the Foreign Minister who, in the Moselle, was flatly turned down by the Gaullists to whom he had offered an "anti-Red alliance". In other constituencies, however, it worked the other way: it was the Gaullists who were snubbed by the "moderate" candidates.

June 3

De Gaulle has so far played his hand very badly, and has also been very unlucky. First of all, especially after de Gaulle's famous May Day speech, Gaullism has come to mean Adventure and Revolutionary Change, and the mood for it just isn't there. No explaining-away has removed from the minds of millions of Frenchmen the distaste caused by the General's phrase about the "*rendezvous* in the Champs-Elysées". Secondly, the more the Gaullists talk, the clearer is it becoming to the electorate that they have no constructive financial and economic programme, and are simply asking to be taken on on trust. Further, there are three other extremely important factors playing against the Gaullists. (1) The Gaullist plan to dissolve the trade unions has made the big employers extremely nervous; although most of the workers are Communists, there have lately been few strikes and very little social unrest, and the Gaullist plan, if put into operation, might— indeed would—start no end of trouble. (2) The Vatican's *Osservatore Romano* recently came out with an article virtually calling on good Catholics in France to vote for the MRP, the "Third Force" Catholics, rather than for de Gaulle. (3) De Gaulle has hardly any press. Except for two weeklies, *Carrefour* and *Rassemblement*, and some local sheets, there is in fact no Gaullist national daily, even papers like *Aurore* and *Le Parisien Libéré*, which were unmistakably Gaullist in the past, now having become much more cautious, while *Figaro* has become outspokenly critical of de Gaulle. Have the publishers been influenced in this by Big Business, or by America, or are they simply concerned about their circulation? It might be a little of everything.

At a number of Gaullist election meetings I went to in Paris I was struck by the defensive tone of many of the speeches. It was as if Gaullist candidates felt obliged to spend a lot of time explaining away the *gaffes* of the General's May Day speech. They went out of their way to demonstrate that de Gaulle was *un bon républicain*; and at election meetings in the South de Gaulle himself has been proclaiming with a kind of petulant arrogance that it was he who, in 1945, "gave France the Republic".

All the same, the largest factor in the RPF's favour is that they have a Man, an impressive Figure, which is more than any Party, except the Communists, can boast of—and Thorez is, for the present, available only in effigy, his sick body still being in the care of Soviet physicians.

But, except for a small semi-hysterical minority of a kind one would find in all countries, it would be wrong to suppose that de Gaulle is "adored" in the manner of Hitler or Mussolini. His personality is cold and far from "magnetic". The fact that he surrounds himself with a certain aura of mystery, is seldom seen in public, and often speaks in riddles cuts both ways.

De Gaulle's following is an extremely mixed one. It includes millions of middle-class grousers; it includes people who will vote for de Gaulle rather than for any tricky *apparentement*; he also appeals to all that is "anti-parliamentary" in France—some (but not all) Vichyite elements among the middle class (the RPF is, among other things, the great Amnesty Party), the survivors and successors of the pre-war Leagues, and finally, the elements most acutely terrified of the Communists and of the Soviet Union.

On the whole one does not have the impression that France is on the eve of a *coup d'état* or that revolutionary passions, one way or the other, are acutely inflamed. The Communists have been sounding the alarm over the simple fact that the Election has been fixed for June 17, that is, the day before the Gaullist anniversary on June 18, and on that day, they say, the more or less victorious Gaullists will hold their victory parade in the Champs-Elysées and carry out their *coup d'état*. This is only conceivable if they won an overwhelming victory (which is most unlikely).

The parliamentary parties are de Gaulle's bugbear. This does not, however, mean that he intends, as has been suggested by Herriot, to bring about a One-Party system in France. What is more likely is that he will try (provided there are enough Gaullists in the new Assembly) to dominate the whole Right and Centre, including the MRP, turn them into obedient tools of the RPF, and through eventually eliminating (i.e. outlawing) the Communists, to acquire a complete "legal" hold over an obedient Parliament. He wants to change the Constitution to one providing for some of the following measures:

The President will be elected by a vast "national college" comprising, in addition to Parliament, "the representatives of local assemblies and of the country's intellectual and economic activities". The President will appoint the Cabinet. On major questions he will have the right to call for a nation-wide referendum. He will personally negotiate and ratify treaties, and merely "inform" Parliament of them. In the event of a conflict arising between the President and Parliament, he will have the right to dissolve the Assembly, or submit the cause of conflict to a referendum. The trade unions, in de Gaulle's view, undermine the authority of the State, and national trade unions will be prohibited, to be replaced by "capital-labour associations" functioning only within the framework of each particular concern; these "associations" would "tend to safeguard the workers' welfare".

Such a system would, in fact, amount to a thinly disguised personal dictatorship; as M. Georges Izard recently wrote in an article which was mainly favourable to de Gaulle: "He is a kind of MacArthur of our democratic institutions." It was meant as a compliment.

If de Gaulle's home programme abounds in obscurities—he says, notably, very little about the all-important financial and economic nightmares besetting France, his international programme is equally obscure. But a few points emerge: he is against the Communists because they are "inviting a Russian invasion": he is also against "the Parties" because they are allowing France to be enslaved by the United States.

It is certain that there are, among the top Gaullists, numerous generals who, like de Gaulle himself, like to talk in terms of building a mighty French Army which will help to safeguard "French Independence" in international affairs; it is also known that, on a purely sentimental plane, many young Gaullist officers have been offended by the bossy ways of the American Army authorities in France. The idea of a semi-Fascist Europe, with France as its nucleus, and with a "strong Germany" as its chief partner, also enters into the Gaullist conception of a happy future.

But the strongest views of all, perhaps, are those held by the Gaullists about the French "Empire". They are opposed to any outside interference with this. The suggestions made, at the time of the Singapore Conference, about the RAF's eventual participation in the war in Indo-China produced violent resentment in the Gaullist press; and, in North Africa, the Gaullists are known to have thousands of their "own men" in key positions. It is believed that de Gaulle is extremely hostile to allowing the Americans to establish themselves firmly in their air bases in North Africa.

June 9

Nobody believes any longer that the Gaullists will get 200 seats. About 6 × 100, i.e. about 100 apiece seems the most reliable forecast.

How have the Third Force parties, and particularly the Socialists, been faring? Thanks to the *apparentements,* and with the encouraging example of Italy before them, they are fairly confident of not doing too badly.

A typical Socialist meeting was held in the Latin Quarter by M. Verdier, editor of the *Populaire* and head of the Socialist list in Paris-South. It is curious that, except for the Communists, no party in France really "talks big", each rather boosting itself as a lesser evil. The Socialists, too, were constantly apologizing; of course, they had done their best, but allowances had to be made for the fact that they were in a Coalition Government, and that, in all matters, they had had to fight against their more conservative partners. If only they had been in the position of the glorious Labour Government! But, alas, they weren't! Still, *apparentement* even with people many of whom they could not trust, meant a minimum safeguard of Personal Liberty in France.

Here were some of the main points M. Verdier and the other speakers made:

The Socialists were not exactly planners, but they believed in "a modest form of *dirigisme.* In the matter of wages, they were in favour of the sliding scale, which their Radical and MRP partners had always opposed, and in favour of a stricter control of capitalist profits. The radiant model of Britain should be followed.

Peace had to be conquered, but not by the methods advocated by the Communists. Soviet imperialism was the greatest menace to peace, and the Stockholm Appeal which, by prohibiting the atom bomb, was only going to facilitate "small wars of liberation", was a swindle. Even so, the division of the world into two blocs must not be accepted; European Union must be the first stage in an all-round unification of the world. (All this was a little on the glib side.)

Gaullism had nothing to recommend it except the personal prestige of de Gaulle, and as Raymond Aron, Gaullism's "philosopher" had himself admitted, nothing would be left of the RPF if de Gaulle suddenly disappeared. Besides, there were dangerous people in the RPF, men who had led the anti-parliamentary revolt of February 6, 1934. The Socialists had to fight on two fronts—against the Communists, who, as the People's Democracies showed, were the deadly enemies of all self-respecting Socialists and of personal freedom; and against the Gaullists, who were Fascists in disguise. If the French people were not entirely satisfied with the Socialists' record, it was because they were not strong enough in the last Assembly; only a large Socialist Party could effectively increase the welfare of the working-class, and so reduce Communist influence, as could be seen from the glorious example of Britain.

Finally, there was a kick at the "neutralists", with the usual, somewhat superficial "Belgium and Holland in 1940" argument.

In virtue of their "democratic tradition", the Socialists allowed hecklers five minutes each at the close of the meeting. The audience was almost entirely a middle-class one, with some Gaullist students amongst them, who made a lot of incoherent noises during the speeches. But when called upon to speak, they had little to say, except that the Socialists had "neglected the French Army"—which produced the reply that M. Moch was, on the contrary, "a great Minister of Defence". Much more embarrassing to the Socialists were a couple of Communists and also a Trotskyist, all of whom accused the Socialists of "condoning colonialism" and of "encouraging the war in Indo-China". One Communist screamed: "Are you or not for the self-determination of peoples?" to which he got no reply; and another asked what the Socialists thought of "their British colleague, Mr Bevan, who knew you couldn't have both rearmament and social welfare"—to which there was no reply either. Instead, M. Verdier again said that the Socialists, as mere members of a Coalition, could not be held responsible for all that had happened in Indo-China; great mistakes had been made in the past; but although the war had "undoubtedly" been started by Ho Chi Minh, some good chances of negotiating a peace settlement had, nevertheless, been missed; but now it was very difficult, as the other Coalition parties had different views on the subject. If only the Socialists were stronger, and so on. It was all a little embarrassing; the hecklers had certainly touched on the French Socialists' sorest spot. However, thanks to the *apparentements*, they expect not to do too badly.

June 12

The anxiety over the Atlantic Pact, at least in its present state, is loudly voiced at Gaullist meetings. De Gaulle's phrase: "We want the other Western Powers to be our allies, not our masters" was the one phrase, throughout his otherwise rather woolly speech at the mass meeting at the Vélodrome d'Hiver on Friday, which brought the house down.

Perhaps it is best for the Gaullists to remain vague, for when they become precise, the result is often disastrous: nothing has scared people more in the past week than the indiscretions of General Koenig, one of the leading Gaullist candidates, who announced that it might be necessary to increase the term of military service to two or even three years if France was to be endowed with a mighty army; that 10,000 reserve officers and 20,000 reserve NCO's would have to be called up; and that large numbers of French troops would have to be sent to Indo-China.

All this was different from the generalities of General de Gaulle himself or of his propaganda chief, André Malraux, who made a striking speech at the Cirque d'Hiver. He is not standing as a candidate, but his great literary gifts are being used to give the Gaullist movement a romantic aura and "intellectual prestige". Malraux's speech was a literary masterpiece; he sounded as if he and the Gaullists were the legitimate heirs of the Great French Revolution! "Think," he cried, "of the soldiers of Valmy and Jemmapes. Those were the days when the whole world gave itself to France! Those were Republicans indeed; And now, look at them—Herriot, Pleven, André Marie—bah!" All this had no connexion at all with much more serious matters like the Gaullist plan to disband the trade unions— but it sounded good. And, of course, there was nothing so prosaic in Malraux's great harangue as the price of steak. For catching votes, it was utterly useless.

In the villages and smaller provincial towns where life is slower and easier, and where there is not the same awareness as in Paris and in the large industrial centres of the grim international situation, the government parties appear to be doing rather better than the two extremes. But in Paris there is no inclination to take the MRP, the Socialists or the Radicals seriously, and of the "republican parties", the plain conservatives alone seem to have a substantial following. A small, but nevertheless significant phenomenon in Paris are the rather stormy meetings held by M. Isorni, Pétain's counsel, which are outspokenly Vichyite and "guarded" by young thugs very reminiscent of the Vichy *milice*.

The big draw in the working-class quarters are the Communists' meetings. The humour at these is sardonic, and the general mood grim. Much is said about the achievements and peaceful intentions of the Soviet Union, but even more is said about the price of meat or about the slum children who are, more and more frequently, bitten by rats since the Paris town council decided, in its recent economy drive, to cut down on rat poison.

It is this intimate knowledge of all working-class grievances that gives strength to the French CP. They also strongly feel that a big police action against them may be close at hand, and they are in a defiant mood.

The grouping, calling itself the "Fourth Force", and consisting of all the extreme Right parties (other than the RPF) and at least part of the Radicals seem to have high hopes of gaining a controlling interest in the new Assembly.

In provincial France the elections passed off quietly. A striking phenomenon I observed, particularly in Normandy, was a certain incoherence of the Gaullist election meetings. Neither the hero-worship of the General, nor the purely negative anti-Communism of the RPF were making sufficient impression, and the electorate were much more interested in local problems—like the eternal question of the *bouilleur de crû* (the small tax-free distiller)—to which some of the RPF candidates could find no clear answer in their "book of words". Other Gaullist meetings in the countryside were scarcely distinguish-able from plain conservative meetings, and the candidates clearly thought it wiser not to talk in "revolutionary" or unduly anti-parliamentary terms. Among the *apparenté* parties a certain reluctance could be observed to discuss the school problem—the "association" of clericals and anti-clericals making this an awkward subject.

Questions like the cost of living were of the greatest interest to the electorate, and on this point every candidate felt bound to make promises. Most striking of all, perhaps, was the almost total neglect of international questions at a very large number of election meetings, the rearmament of Germany, in particular, having been deliberately kept in the background before the election by both the French Government and the Americans, so as not to make it a major issue. The Communists talked more than the others of peace, though they also concentrated chiefly on domestic problems.

8. THE HEXAGONAL ASSEMBLY

The most important immediate result of the election was the failure of the Gaullists to sweep the country. The most important long-term result—which became quite obvious only a few months later when a part of the Gaullists supported the formation of the Pinay Government, was the shifting of the political centre of gravity a good way towards the Right.

There were fewer abstentions than had been expected; probably the eve-of-the-poll propaganda about "no vote" being "a vote for Stalin" had something to do with it. The abstentions amounted to just under 20 per cent, as against nearly 22 per cent in November 1946. The Communists and *progressistes* polled just over 5 million votes, a loss of some 9 per cent, compared with 1946; their poll dropped from 28 to about 26 per cent; the Socialist poll dropped from some 15 to 14 per cent; the MRP poll from 17 to 12 per cent; the Radicals with

8 per cent and the Right with 9 per cent of the poll suffered some losses and the Gaullists scored over 4·2 million votes, or some 21 per cent. (Owing to the *apparentements*, only an approximate percentage can be given in most cases.)

As M. François Goguel noted in his study, *Géographie des Elections* (*Esprit*, September 1951), the result still showed a small *laïque* majority, and did not show a majority disavowing the post-Liberation reforms; nor did it, in theory, produce a pro-free-enterprise and anti-*dirigiste* majority. But whereas there was a majority for the "democratic republic" (i.e. for the *status quo*) against the two extremes, it was a small one, and there was no coherent majority for anything else: what there was, instead, were three "possible" majorities: a "Third Force" majority, based on the Socialists, MRP and Radicals, more or less supported by certain elements on the Right; a Centre majority of MRP-Radicals-Right, more or less supported by the Socialists, and a Right majority, including the "classical" Right, the Radicals, and the MRP, more or less supported by the Gaullists.[9]

The distribution of seats at the National Assembly, compared with the previous one, was as follows:

	Old Assembly (January 1951)	New Assembly (January 1952)
Communists, *Progressistes*, etc	179	101
Algerian and African Nationalists, etc	24	12
Socialists	99	106
MRP	145	88
UDSR	15	23
Radicals	46	76
RPF (Gaullists)	23	117
Right	81	99
Others	9	5
	621	627

The "electoral" map of France had not greatly changed since 1946, except that the RPF had taken over a large number of MRP votes (though it was nothing like the "landslide" of 1947) and some Radical and Right votes. Oddly enough, the RPF also seemed to have gained a certain number of Communist votes in the Paris area—though not very many. The principal Communist losses were in some rural areas

---

[9] The successful (ostensibly "republican") candidates of the "classical" Right included such freaks as Maître Isorni and other avowed Pétainists.

like the Aveyron, Cantal, and Haute-Loire where, in 1946, they still enjoyed the prestige of the great "Maquis" Party and of a major government party. This glamour had now worn off.

The RPF were strongest in Paris and other urban centres, especially north of the Loire, and much weaker in the rural areas, except in the traditionally conservative constituencies of Brittany, Normandy and Alsace-Lorraine. Practically everywhere south of the Loire the country was "republican", though with a strong Communist admixture, notably in the Haute-Vienne (Limoges), the Corrèze and most of the Rhône Valley, where the Communist poll was often between 35 and 40 per cent.

There is a point that should be emphasized. If the election had not been held under the strictly dishonest system of *apparentements*, but under the proportional system of 1946, the results would have been: Communists 150, Socialists 91, MRP 66, Radicals 65, Right 77, Gaullists 143, others 7 instead of, respectively: 101, 106, 88, 76, 99, 117, 5.[10]

In the course of the next few years, when the National Assembly resorted to delaying tactics over the ratification of EDC or other forms of German rearmament, it became almost a daily habit of the British (and, to a lesser extent of the American) press and even of some leaders to abuse the "frivolousness" of the French Parliament (viz. Mr Attlee's attack in the Commons on March 14, 1955) and to say that the National Assembly was "unrepresentative" of the French people. In reality, if it was at all "unrepresentative", it was in the *opposite* sense: with a larger Communist and Gaullist representation in the Assembly, the opposition to German rearmament, as proposed by Britain and the USA, would have been even greater. If, in the end, the Paris Agreements were ratified, it was under British and American pressure, and against the true will of Parliament, and, even more so, against the will of the French people. But, on the other hand, it is equally true that the electorate did not in 1951 give nearly enough attention to foreign affairs: in particular, did not feel sufficiently strongly on a question like Indo-China; and it did not explicitly disavow the men who had been most responsible for the perpetuation of the war.

[10] A few small groups are not included in this calculation, substantially correct, given by *Carrefour*, June 20, 1951.

CHAPTER THREE

GLOOM AND THE "ATOMIC" JITTERS

T HERE are certain periods in the post-war history of France when a consecutive, chronological account of what happened would be as good as meaningless. Looking back on the six months that followed the General Election of June 1951, the obvious "events" are the passing of the Barangé Act, with its subsidies to all primary education, including the "free" schools; the acceptance by the National Assembly of the principle of the sliding-scale for wages (this acceptance of the principle did not, however, produce any actual legislation until nearly a year later, when prices and wages had become, more or less, stabilized, anyway), and the meeting of the UN Assembly in Paris at the end of 1951—where North Africa suddenly came before the international forum.

Each of these events was, in its own way, important. But they were (except North Africa) somehow irrelevant to the international atmosphere in which France was living during those months. More significant was the pessimism that marked this period—a pessimism that was reflected in the more-than-two-hour speech of M. Mendès-France at the very end of the year diagnosing all the ailments from which France was suffering, both internally and internationally; in the widespread feeling of "*pourissement*" among the intellectual groups; and in the sharp French reactions to the various manifestations of the roll-back and preventive war policy in which the international press abounded at the time of the UN Assembly at the Palais Chaillot. Typical of this period were also the cheerless results of the inquiry made by *NEF* into the state of mind of the young French generation. Altogether the feeling of aimless drifting to some unknown catastrophe was perhaps stronger at the end of 1951 than either before, or later—in the seemingly more stable world of Atomic Equilibrium a few years later.

I. THE SCHOOL QUARREL: "BACK TO VICHY"

Little need be said about events like the reassembly of Parliament after the General Election or the Barangé Law. The composition of the 1951 Chamber was unlike that of its 1946 predecessor; the centre of gravity had moved substantially to the Right, and the MRP hastened to introduce new school legislation which would have had no chance of being passed by the old Assembly. In doing so, they showed that they were prepared to break with the Socialists. However, before they did so, it was necessary to wait until a new government was formed; and this was a difficult and laborious process, since there were three possible majorities, but none of them very obvious. For the "classical" Right were not yet fully prepared to take over, in the absence of sufficient Gaullist support; a left-centre coalition was also difficult to bring about, owing to the fundamental disagreement between the Socialists and the MRP on the school issue; and, after a month's "cabinet crisis", it was finally the pale M. Pleven who succeeded in forming a government, after M. René Mayer and M. Petsche had failed.

His government was a coalition of UDSR's, Radicals, MRP's and members of the Right—i.e. men who were either favourable to the school reform sponsored by the MRP or did not have such strong views on the subject as the Socialists had. The Radicals were no longer the great *laïque* party they had been before the war. As for the Socialists, *laïcité* was now one of the few things on which they held very strong and almost doctrinaire views, and when, in the end, on September 10, the Barangé Act was passed, M. Charles Lussy, the Socialist spokesman, saying farewell to the Third Force and the Socialists' MRP partners of the last few years, exclaimed: "The Socialists will not forget. They will not forget that the MRP were willing to risk the very existence of the régime. You must bear this responsibility."

Was it much ado about nothing? So it would seem to outsiders not aware of the fundamental quarrel that had—off and on—gone on in France for over half a century. Even so, the fact that public funds should be used to pay parents' associations 1,000 frs. per term for each child going to a first-degree religious school seemed to the Socialists like a major violation of the *laïcité* principle, like a subsidy to religious teaching and a partial return to "Vichy".[1] Anyone unacquainted with the kind of textbooks used in some of the religious schools—notably on French history—would scarcely realize the importance of the *laïcité* principle; in these textbooks the Third Republic, for example, is treated in a highly critical manner because of its "un-Christian" spirit.[2]

[1] The same subsidy, it is true, was payable through a local authority for children attending state schools, but in this case the money was principally devoted to improving equipment and the actual school buildings, and not for paying the teachers.

[2] A striking example of this kind of history is the *HISTOIRE DE FRANCE du cours moyen au certificat d'études*, by H. Guillemain and F. Le Ster, published in 1946 for use in the *écoles libres*. Thus we read in the chapter on the Third Republic: "Jules Ferry, a very patriotic Lorrainer, exercised great influence between 1880 and 1886. Outside France he successfully prepared the conquest

The Barangé Act was voted by the Gaullists, the whole Right, nearly half the Radicals and, of course, the whole MRP; the Socialists and Communists and 46 Radicals voted against. The heated discussions, which lasted for several days at the National Assembly, and in which different deputies surveyed the State-and-Church issue almost since the dawn of history provided a fascinating insight into the workings of French minds in connexion with this fundamental problem of French political philosophy. There was, needless to say, an uproar over the vote. The Comité de Défense Laïque announced that, as a result of it, "the Republic was now irretrievably divided"; and, in surveying the year 1951, M. André Siegfried considered the "reappearance of the school issue" (which, he said, "had sounded the death knell of the Third Force"), as being by far the most important internal development in France.[3]

Although, in the months that followed, the Socialists began to feel that the issue that had been raised was "philosophical" rather than one of major practical politics, the Loi Barangé which gave financial help (though in greatly varying degrees) to the religious schools, certainly contributed to a consolidation of the forces of the Right, and prepared the way for the "Pinay majority", which finally emerged at the National Assembly in the following March.

of several colonies. But inside France, he conducted an anti-clerical policy. . . ." "The Third Republic accomplished many important educational reforms. Unfortunately this work was often anti-religious. . . ." "It is too often repeated that the Socialists were alone in demanding social improvements. Nothing could be more untrue. The Church has never been indifferent to the welfare of the workers. The great Pope, Leo XIII wrote in 1891," etc. "At the Chamber, a Catholic deputy like de Mun. . . .", etc. The chapter on the great inventions during the early twentieth century concludes as follows: "And yet the people were not happy; there was great discontent in the world. Too often had the governments neglected to build education on the solid foundations of Christian faith." In earlier chapters we find: "Napoleon III sincerely loved the people. . . . No monarch gave as much care as he to the welfare of the workers. . . . He governed France as an absolute monarch during the first half of his reign; freedoms . . . were practically suppressed, but the French easily consoled themselves because the country was enjoying unusual prosperity." ". . . Nearly everybody approved of the *coup d'état* of December 2, 1851, because people were tired of disorder. . . ." "Danton was very ugly. He looked like a furious bulldog. He was very violent. . . . He was dishonest. . . ." "Marat was a horrible creature. It is said that he looked like a toad. . . ." "Robespierre spoke in a polite and gentle voice. But he suffered from insane pride. He thought he was always right. He wanted to put to death all those who did not think like him. . . ." The whole tone of the book tends to be monarchist and anti-republican.

[3] "The reappearance, with all their old virulence, of all these passions which shook the 3rd Republic, shows to what extent certain problems which seemed long solved and out-of-date, can still remain explosive even after two world wars." (*Année Politique*, 1951, p. vii.)

2. FRANCE "THE WORST STRAGGLER"

Internationally, France was faced during this period with almost precisely the same problems as before the Election, except that, with the Election over, both the Americans and the French Government began to discuss more openly than before the "European Army" project, which had been left dormant during the pre-election months.

From the French point of view, everything in world affairs seemed to be going wrong. In September, at the Three-Power Conference in Washington, Mr Acheson said that, before the end of the year, Western Germany should be "integrated in Europe". Already in the two previous months the French Ministers had made important concessions on what was euphemistically called "the technical plane"; they had, in fact, agreed to the integration of German forces, "on a level", as the *Monde* put it, "that was nearer to the classical division than to the 'combat team' envisaged by the Pleven Plan". No doubt, the French ministers did not like it; and were fully aware of public opinion in France growing restive; in the USA, on the other hand, France was having a rather shabby press, the *New York Times* of December 10 calling France "the worst straggler" of the lot, even when allowance was made for her war-effort in Indo-China. No doubt the *New York Times* knew that the *Monde* of September 29 must have been at least partly right when it suggested that the French Government, increasingly weary of American prodding, were at heart much keener on a unified and disarmed Germany than on the kind of "European army" that was threatening to emerge from all these talks.

M. Moch, now no longer in the Government, was now denying his "paternity" of the European Army—the child had become totally unrecognizable. Except for M. Reynaud (who was now paying warm tributes to Eisenhower who, he said, had defeated the Pentagon doctrine of peripheral defence based on the Pyrénées, few people were pleased with the way things were going.

The Ottawa Conference in September produced the news that eleven new American air bases were to be built in Europe, eight of them in France.

All over France the Communists were now redoubling their efforts to plaster walls, bridges, and quaysides with inscriptions of *US GO HOME*. Along with this campaign went several others—for instance, that for the release of Henri Martin, a young French sailor who, revolted by what he had seen in Indo-China (he had witnessed the famous shelling of Haiphong in December 1946) had joined the Communists, and was now sentenced to five years' solitary confinement for distributing propaganda leaflets against *la sale guerre*. His case of "conscientious objection" was taken up by numerous non-Communist intellectual groups.

A campaign was also started by the Communists against *Paix et Liberté*, a propaganda organization which was spending enormous sums on anti-Communist and anti-Soviet posters and which, M. Fernand Grenier, the Communist Deputy, claimed, was receiving a subsidy of two milliard francs a year from the Government.[4] He also objected to the head of this organization, M. Jean-Paul David, being allowed to "treat the Communists as a Fifth Column" on the official French radio twice a week, while they (the Communists), though representing five million Frenchmen, were not allowed to answer him.

It was a point on which the Communists felt very strongly.

De Gaulle, though already a little subdued as a result of the RPF's relative failure in the Election, nevertheless severely criticized the Government at the Congress of the RPF at Nancy in November. He disapproved of the Schuman Plan and of the European Army which, he said, meant the creation of a German army and the absorption of the French Army, and, generally, disliked the Government's "slavish" foreign policy *vis-à-vis* the USA. The General still made some proud claims: "We were the spirit of France; we are now her strength and her organization; we shall be her victory."

He planned to set up a *comité d'action ouvrière*, so as to secure some support from the working-class; but it was obvious that he no longer felt quite as confident as before; and he suggested that the RPF should be ready to talk to other parties. Did he already feel that some of his *compagnons* in the National Assembly were soon going to desert him?

But with his views on the European Army there was now widespread agreement. "If our Allies", he said, "now want the European Army, it is because its whole character has changed since last year." Like the Communists, like many others, the Gaullists protested against the establishment of American air bases, especially in Morocco, "without a counterpart".

There had, of course, been a "counterpart": for four years France had been getting Marshall Aid; the amounts received between April 1948 and November 1951 had amounted to some 2½ billion dollars, of which the following were the principal items (in million dollars): coal and oil, 561; cotton, 366; machinery and equipment, 411; non-ferrous metals, 151; cereals, 79; fats, 65; technical services, 15.

But now Marshall Aid was coming to an end and Congress was now

---

[4] *Débats, A.N.*, 1951, November 8, 1951, p. 7732.

thinking almost exclusively in terms of military, and no longer economic aid.

And meantime, the Indo-China war was going on and on; General de Lattre de Tassigny was pleading with the Americans in Washington, and explaining to them, that with the setting-up of the "Associated States", the war was in no way a "colonial war" any longer; and he asked that the USA give all the necessary aid, so that the war could be fought to its victorious conclusion. He also argued in favour of organizing a mighty Vietnam (Bao Dai) army.

De Lattre, who, in 1945, had hobnobbed with the Communists in Paris and with Marshal Zhukov in Berlin, was now trying to give Washington its money's worth. On September 20 he declared in Washington:

Today there is a city in the world which is of immense importance; and that is Hanoi, the capital of Tongking.... If Hanoi is lost, the road will be clear for the Communists all the way to Suez.

Four thousand officers, he said, were needed for the Vietnamese Army; 700 had been trained, and 300 more were training; but a lot of money and equipment was needed before the remaining 3,000 were trained, and the army was properly equipped and organized. With or without conviction he was subscribing to the principle of "Asians fighting Asians".

During the same month, Tran Van Huu, Bao Dai's premier, had numerous talks with Acheson at San Francisco and with President Truman in Washington, and there were discussions about a "Pacific Pact", rather on the lines of the future SEATO.

Clearly, the USA was taking an increasing interest in the Vietnam war; this was, no doubt, at least until further notice, a financial asset for France—in the sense that the USA was now paying part of the bill; only the fact remained that, also until further notice, it was the French who would have to do most of the fighting in the name of the Free World . . .

Nevertheless, certain French politicians and diplomats now began to take the view that the Indo-China war was also a diplomatic asset for France; so long as she was fighting there, she would have to be treated with some regard in all international discussions. It is, indeed, significant—if one looks a few years ahead—that the threat of the "empty chair" should not have been uttered until after the Geneva conference of 1954, which put an end to the fighting in Indo-China.

In 1951, for this reason, the French could still afford, to some extent, to ignore excessive American pressure. Mr Hanson Baldwin, believed to voice the views of the Pentagon, was saying in the *New York Times* of December 4 that if there was no European Army in the next few months, it would be necessary to build up a German national army; but at that time the French Government, with its "great war record in Indo-China", could still play for time.

All the same, the general mood in France was one of weariness and disgust. Not without a touch of weariness, the National Assembly ratified in December the Schuman Plan. M. Maurice Faure (Radical) was among those who supported the ratification on the ground that "its rejection would mean that the realization of Europe would be delayed by twenty-five years". But who seriously believed any longer in Europe?—or who seriously thought that the Schuman Plan could (at its best) do much more than rationalize coal and steel production and marketing? M. Jacques Soustelle (Gaullist) acutely distrustful (like de Gaulle himself) of M. Jean Monnet, the "power behind the throne", went even further—he thought the Schuman Plan was not European, but anti-European:

We are all in favour of a European confederation, comprising Germany. . . . But what worries us about the Coal-Steel pool is that instead of bringing us nearer to "Europe", it is taking us away from it. Instead of delegating our powers to a democratic Assembly, we are asked to abandon an important sector of our economy to a stateless and uncontrolled autocracy of experts.[5]

Nevertheless, though often without much faith, the "Europeans" won. A few French European enthusiasts welcomed the Conservative victory in Britain that autumn

because, while in opposition, Mr Churchill had done more than anyone else, to launch the European Idea. . . .[6]

But it was mere wishful thinking. As was recorded by *Année Politique*:

Sir David Maxwell-Fyfe, speaking at Strasbourg on November 28, soon made it clear that Britain was not interested in abandoning any fraction of its national sovereignty in the name of "Europe".[7]

The French never quite forgave Churchill for leading them badly astray in this matter.

Apart from "Europe", what else was there to believe in? Prosperity at home? Since the Korean War, living conditions in France had been

---

[5] *Débats, A.N.*, December 6, 1951, p. 8881.
[6] *Cf. Année Politique*, 1951, p. 343.   [7] *Ibid.*, p. 345.

deteriorating. The foreign trade gap was widening; inflation was again in full swing; wholesale prices had risen from the 1950 average of 108 to 137 in July 1951 (1949 = 100); at last, in September, the minimum wage was belatedly raised from 87 fr. an hour to 100. There were immense difficulties over the budget, and military expenditure could not be decided upon by the French Assembly without NATO coming to a decision first. All this was depressing and a little humiliating.

It was this general depression over the state of affairs in France that psychologically prepared the country for the (at least temporary) acceptance of the "Pinay experiment" a few months later.

3. MENDÈS-FRANCE AS CASSANDRA

Altogether, the atmosphere was unhealthy. And it was in this atmosphere that Mendès-France made his famous speech of December 30, which was perhaps the first of his speeches to receive truly nation-wide attention. These were the main points he made:

French production in 1951 was no higher than it had been in 1929.

All other European countries showed a substantial increase over the 1929 level.

Yet France's needs in 1951 were far greater than in 1929. France had not the means to pay for everything; it was better to make the choice than to let circumstances make the choice.

Ten times since the Liberation had wages been "adjusted" to prices, but the balance had never been maintained. Naturally, there was no question of scrapping any one of the major items of expenditure: social services, military budget, the standard of living, or reconstruction. But priorities should be set up in each category of expenses, and the working-class, to improve its standard of living, should work longer hours.

A proper income-tax system should be enforced as in England. There was a greater inequality of income in England than in France, but not such great inequality of private spending.

Indirect taxation now represented 69 per cent of France's revenue, as against 55 per cent before the war.

The total deficit for 1952 could be estimated at about 1,000 milliard francs, and large-scale inflation, which had been the rule in France for over thirty years, was continuing. There was much wasteful spending, which must be cut, some of it "fancy spending", like the costly Paris–Lyon or Paris–Lille night airmail or the ornate equipment of certain fashionable motor-roads, at a time when people who had lost their homes in the war still had nowhere decent to live.

Subsidies, like that of coal, by being wholly indiscriminate, were wasteful. Coal that went into important industries was being subsidized in the same way as coal used for heating night-clubs.

The nationalization of the principal banks had not produced the necessary economies; it would have been rational to scrap some of several branch offices in the same street, since they all belonged to the State, and were no longer competing.

The French railways were running at a heavy loss, because motor transport, represented by powerful pressure-groups, was opposed to a rational co-ordination of the two forms of transport.

The Monnet Plan had not come up to expectations. Neither the coal production target, nor the electricity target had been reached; and the same was true of practically all other branches. The chief reason for this was that, since the Liberation, not nearly enough had been spent on capital investments. And things had gone from bad to worse. If, in 1949, these investments were still twice as large as military expenditure, investments in 1952 would be equal to less than half the military expenditure. Yet capital investment represented military power, security and national independence, and all cuts in these investments were an extremely grave matter.

The successive Governments had been relying too much on American aid, *espoir suprême et suprême pensée*. M. Pleven's and M. René Mayer's speeches in Parliament all seemed to be addressed to America, and not to France. No doubt, the Marshall Plan had been a godsend to France; she had received under it food and masses of raw materials, and some equipment; but during the Marshall Aid euphoria, she had failed to prepare herself industrially for the future—which she should have done; and now Marshall Aid was at an end, and all that could be expected in future was military aid. And it was shocking to see the Governments letting the Americans take all the decision in matters of military expenditure. The Governments of the last two years had a bad habit of assuring the Americans that France would do this and that, and of telling the French that the Americans would pay. Since neither was quite true, there was grumbling and discontent on all sides; and France was making heavy sacrifices without earning for it any political credit. France was spending much, but for a number of reasons, chief of which was inflation, was not producing all the required results. Her undertaking to have 10 fully equipped divisions by the end of 1951 had not been fulfilled. There were only 6 divisions with a 70 per cent complement, and 4 divisions with a 25 or 35 per cent complement. (At this point the Minister of Defence, M. Bidault, intervened and said that the first 5 divisions were "*à peu près*" complete—this "*à peu près*" provoking some ironical remarks from Mendès-France.)

Moreover, 5 additional divisions had been promised, where were they? M. Moch himself had privately remarked that the promises made by the French Government at the beginning of the Korean War had been simply "lunatic".

It was these irresponsible promises made at international conferences which were undermining France's credit abroad. French ministers went to these conferences now never knowing exactly what they wanted, or what they could, or could not, promise. It was largely due to inflation which he (Mendès-France) had tried to prevent in 1945. Now, in 1951, prices had risen 30 per cent, though the Government had forecast only a 5 per cent rise; what kind of healthy budgeting was possible in such conditions?

Britain was also threatened with inflation, and it was notable that one of the first things to be said by the new Conservative Government was that war expenditure must not exceed the country's material possibilities; the defence budget had already been cut by £250 millions.

There was only one obvious thing that France could do: and that was to change her Indo-China policy. It was not a question of abandoning Indo-China, or capitulating. It was a case of negotiating with Vietminh; some thought it was wicked to negotiate with Communists; but what were the Americans themselves doing in Korea? French Governments were, instead, talking in terms of "internationalizing the war", or embarking on multi-lateral talks, in which France could only be the loser.

And he concluded:

You will never organize national defence in Europe so long as you leave your *cadres* in Indo-China, as long as you lose a large number of officers every year, so long as you spend 500 milliards a year—which ... only add to the inflation in France, to poverty, higher prices and internal quarrels, on which Communist propaganda alone can thrive.... By some incredible parodox we have given priority to Asia, thus siding with MacArthur and the American anti-Europeans.... In such conditions the Germans are bound to gain crushing superiority in the European Army in a very short time.... Courage, order and lucidity in the conduct of both our military affairs and our industrial organization alone can persuade Mr Vyshinsky that we are not losing the Cold War.

In the course of his two-and-a-half-hour speech Mendès-France had touched on many other topics—housing, in which France was lagging behind all other countries in Europe, and much else. But what impressed itself most on public opinion was his demonstration that "a choice was necessary", and that if anything had to be discarded, the obvious thing to discard was the Indo-China war. Yet M. Bidault had simply uttered an angry, defiant: "*Non!*"

Although by this time Mendès-France was no longer being accused of talking like a Communist (not even by M. Siegfried's publication) the French Governments preferred to continue the hopeless adventure.

Nevertheless, the feeling had been created that here was a man who might be able, some day, perhaps before it was too late, to drag France out of the bog.

4. FRENCH JITTERS OVER "PREVENTIVE WAR" TALK

The feeling of being in a bog was a very strong one at the end of 1951. What was there to hope for? A great reorganization and austerity drive, as recommended by Mendès-France? Not enough people were in a mood for it. Start talks with Ho Chi Minh? This would be playing into the hands of the Communists and might incommodate the USA. For, by this time, the USA was all in favour of the French carrying the Indo-China baby.

Altogether, at the end of 1951, France was in a curious and almost exceptional state of demoralization, which was attributed to all kinds of factors in a remarkable study in *Esprit* in November 1951:

A sort of heavy sadness is overhanging the country, paralysing people's brains and drying up their courage.... Meantime Asia has come into the limelight of history and Islam is stirring. Russia and America have monopolized world diplomacy and world strategy.... One wishes that a healthy France could carry some weight in this trial of strength.... Instead, she is like an old lady asked to important meetings merely out of respect for her age.... Curious how in the last election they said scarcely anything about Germany, or Vietnam or our desperate housing problems.... But once you start a fight between the *instituteur* and the *curé*, then at last you feel at home, in eternal France, Mother of Revolutions and Elder Daughter of the Church.... Inflation has become a means of governing.... Our statesmen have no courage: no Morrison to say that he prefers the humiliation of Abadan to war; and no Bevan among our Socialists. The last newspapers that have the courage to speak up are being strangled.... "Party discipline" and "solidarity" have become the substitute for telling the truth.[8] Everywhere fear is exploited, and fear breeds conformism.... The press, the wireless, the cinema, all try to frighten the ordinary citizen with the terrors of tomorrow—atom bombs or Siberian camps.... In all this agitation anti-Communism holds an important place. It crushes all independent thought. ... A country that was recently anti-Fascist is now being advised to have Franco as an ally and to trust German divisions to save it from Bolshevism. The Atlantic policy, with all its contradictions, is bewildering to the French. How, in such a falsified world, can you blame the French for being sick and tired of it all, and for seeking refuge in irony and indifference? And if they are indifferent, is it not because... they feel helpless, since everything is decided in Washington?... A nation cannot really live without a minimum of common values. Those of the Resistance were destroyed once again by the Great Lie of bourgeois democracy. In the name of what ideal could a people rise today in the midst of economic oppression, political corruption and the cynical lies told to the coloured people under our rule? This squandering of national values has had the worst effect among the young people.... The result is a nation without faith and cohesion, qualities which will not be restored by the recruiting sergeants of the European Army....

This "lack of prospect", this indifference or fatalism were, naturally, encouraged by many things.

In October 1951 General Eisenhower was saying in the same breath, in an interview with *Paris-Match* that a showdown might be close at

[8] It is curious that the French should not have realized how much truer still this was of the British press!

hand; the Russians' "noses would bleed"; that perhaps the armies of the West would, before long, be fighting in the Ukraine or "in the neighbourhood of Leningrad"; and that it was such a pity that the French seemed to lack the old virtues of Verdun! "We should like to rediscover in France the spirit of 1792, the spirit of *la patrie en danger*, or the 1916 spirit of Verdun",[9] said the head of SHAPE.

Verdun, where 300,000 Frenchmen lost their lives in one of the most horrible slaughters of World War I, was the last thing in the world to arouse enthusiasm in France, and the remark showed a singular *manque de psychologie* on Eisenhower's part. Similarly, there was no eagerness for fighting "in the neighbourhood of Leningrad". However, Eisenhower was fairly complimentary about France, said she was doing, by way of rearmament, "as much as anybody else", and took at their face value the French Government's promises to have 10 fully equipped divisions in Europe by the end of 1951, 15 in 1952, and 20 in 1953. But he felt she had lost her sense of "leadership" and "mission". Of the *US GO HOME* scribbles Eisenhower spoke more in sorrow than in anger. The French people should understand that the Americans were in Europe to protect France, and would gladly go home once Europe was capable of looking after her own defence.

All this talk of "roll-back" and of a "victorious" World War III was nerve-racking; and there was any amount of it at the end of 1951.

Thus, in the London *Observer*, Mr Sebastian Haffner was preaching week after week the "isolation" of Russia through the creation of "overwhelming" strength by the Free World:

To achieve this super-state demands the permanent mobilization of Western power and the equally permanent integration of all the developed countries in the world—except Russia herself—into one system which must in time acquire the attributes of a super-state. Such a super-state will be powerful enough ... to deter Russian aggression, *to enforce a territorial settlement in Europe and Asia, and to tolerate Russian independence*. These are the minimum requirements of peace.[10]

This was "Roll-Back" with a vengeance. The person who interviewed Eisenhower for *Paris-Match*, whom I saw a few days later, also expressed the view (no doubt derived from Eisenhower) that the Russians were "scared stiff" and would be "only too glad to withdraw to their 1938 frontier, if they could limit the damage to that"!

All this was being received with great distaste in France.

[9] *Paris-Match*, October 27, 1951.   [10] *The Observer*, November 11, 1951.

5. COLLIER'S JOLLY ATOM WAR

But the best was yet to come. To coincide with the opening of the UN Assembly in Paris, *Collier's Weekly* produced its famous number purporting to be a *reportage* of 1960, "five years after the end of the Atomic War", with its lyrical accounts of delighted Russian crowds flocking to an American fashion parade, in the midst of the atomic ruins of Moscow, and with similar inanities and insanities by well-paid writers. The French press—even the *bien-pensant* press—reacted angrily to this publication which was clearly trying to "condition" the "Free World" for a preventive atomic war. It created greater anti-American feeling than anything had done for a long time. Perhaps the best comment on it was the skit published in the *Canard Enchaîné*, which wrote a *reportage* on America and Russia after both countries had been almost simultaneously blown up.

It was a very short war, as you know.... There was a Russian bang and an American bang almost at the very same moment. In the rue des Petit-Pères we neither felt nor heard anything. One of our friends thought his glass gave a sudden shiver, but, since he was at his twelfth *pastis*, we didn't take any notice.... The papers did not begin to suspect anything until forty-eight hours later. It was odd not to have had any news for so long of either Truman or Stalin. Then the rumour started: "The war has broken out", but followed immediately by the rumour: "The war is over ..."

Certainly, it was a sensational bit of news: no more Russia! No more America!.... There was panic at the Ministry of Finance: "What about the next Marshall Aid instalment?" In the Grands Boulevards Communist demonstrators were shouting: "*A New York!*" and in the Champs-Elysées, anti-Communists were yelling: "*A Moscou!*" When they were told that neither place existed any more, they joined in a single parade in the place de la Concorde, sang the *Marseillaise*, and then dispersed in various bistros.

Then some months passed, and suddenly came the startling news that some heroic explorers had (unwisely) rediscovered America, and that some Americans were still alive. And some others who had parachuted into Russia, found that there were also some Russians in existence. The French Communists got alarmed at having turned the *Humanité* into an anarcho-syndicalist paper; but they were wrong to worry.

At this point the *Canard* launched its "world-shaking appeal":

These poor people must be re-educated, they must be taught real civilization. They must learn to live, which they had never learned in the days of their splendour.

And then, *à la Collier's* came the first *reportage* on post-atomic America:

New York, November 5, 1955

Our first contacts with the tribes of North America warrant high hopes. Ten Angling Clubs have already been set up. This peaceful sport has become very popular with the natives, who wish to have nothing further to do with baseball or TV.

French cooking has swept the country.... The Brillat-Savarin Club has already a million members.... An Anti-Robot League has been created. Its members have been destroying all mechanical devices that can still be found among the ruins. No more automobiles, no more airplanes, no more radio or TV sets, no more refrigerators, washing, eating, drinking, or love-making machines. The use of slogans is strictly prohibited. People are learning to think for themselves. Charlie Chaplin has been proclaimed President of the United States.... We are on our way to Hollywood, where we are starting a new magic-lantern industry....

The report from Moscow said:

Moscow, November 5, 1955

We got here just in time.... The Russians were returning to their old habit of eating new-born babies. After we had distributed among them several million tins of *cassoulet* they left the babies alone. Since being freed of their rulers, these people have been obsessed with the idea of setting up Communism. "We now want to know what it really is", a good Russian told me. "We want it for ourselves, not for future generations," he explained.... They have started by locking up all generals and all policemen and by prohibiting the use of ikons.

The sales of the *Canard Enchaîné* that week were said to have increased by over 100,000 copies! It was a typical French reaction to the Preventive War propaganda which was in full swing at the time.

The Old World was cocking a snook at the Brave New Worlds, East and West.

6. "this is the era of total anguish"

And, to dwell a little longer on the *Stimmung* in France, so typical of the 1951 period (but by no means confined to this particular time), there was the remarkable inquiry, made by the magazine *NEF* into the state of mind of the young generation.[11]

Perhaps the title of the symposium was not a very happy one. It was called *Mal du Siècle*—and its avowed purpose was to inquire whether there was in France an equivalent of that alleged malady from which frustrated and long-haired young men suffered in the days of Alfred

---

[11] It may be of some interest that the editor of this review was Mme Lucie Faure, the wife of M. Edgar Faure, the Radical leader, who became Premier early in 1952, and again in 1955.

de Musset. The same complaint was called *Weltschmerz* by the German Romantics, and later degenerated into the Baudelairian *spleen*. Most contributors to the special *NEF* number seemed to think there was no such thing as a *mal du siècle* of the old introspective kind, if only because most people couldn't afford it financially these days! In any case, if there was any such thing, it could only be limited to "intellectuals". To quote a significant entry, that of a Paris third-year student:

I only want to write about students, and even so nothing proves that I am typical, because each man has his own problems. Are not the main problems for students the choice of a career, and all that? And yet, there is something common to all young students these days; it is impossible for a young man today not to be in a state of anguish. Will we all be Russians tomorrow, or Americans, or will we still be allowed to remain French? We don't know whom to believe. We hear of heroic deeds, and we see all sorts of crooks being glorified. But I'm wrong to talk about all this, or about the Marxist-Existentialist-Christian triptych. That's a lot of blah. All this blah is drowned by a much louder clamour—the clamour for bread-and-butter. Everyday life is much too hard for analysing one's state of mind.

There was, amongst the young, a good deal of intellectual anarchism, or nihilism—the kind of nihilism, as one writer put it, that swept France during the Hundred Years War and the Great Plague, when death seemed to dominate all thoughts. Another young writer put it slightly differently:

Our era is an era of Total Anguish. At a time when all that the future seems to hold in store is atomic and other catastrophes, a deep gloom pervades our thinking, and the existentialist doctrines are no mere accident.

This was, no doubt, an extreme case; and, amongst the young, one found a sharp reaction against this existentialist catastrophism, especially from two groups—the Catholics and the Communists. The Communists in France, curiously enough, were about the only young people still actively interested in politics.
As M. Michel Delsol wrote:

Outside the Communists, French youth is almost totally uninterested in politics today. The great political parties have very few young *militants*, and their only common ground is really their anti-Communism.

There was much disillusionment among the young: those who fought in the Resistance were disillusioned to find that "the Republic is back in the hands of the old Radical fogeys"; young Socialists saw no Socialist Party in France worth speaking of—for it was only a bureaucratic machine, without any *mystique*. The young Communists, though still believing in something, if only out of a spirit of contradiction, were increasingly feeling on the brink of persecution and saw little chance of a Communist triumph in France; but although, in the main, democratic liberties still existed in France more than they did in other countries, the word "democracy" was acquiring a more and more hollow sound.

Everybody knew at heart that "democracy" was meaningless in the overseas territories, and that the Nazi and totalitarian régimes in Europe had all left an ugly mark on France, as on so many other countries.

A famous lawyer, Maurice Garçon was also quoted:

In matters of liberty, the Frenchman is still a privileged person, but this liberty is threatened.... In freedom of expression an ominous tendency towards censorship can be observed.... The "pre-investigation" in criminal cases, though illegal, is an old, long-standing complaint; but today these ills go a good deal further.

And he quoted in support of his view, a pretty hair-raising passage from a manual by a M. Lambert, a teacher at the High School of Police on the legitimacy and effectiveness of third-degree methods—such as making a prisoner sit erect on a chair for forty-eight hours, refusing him food, water, and sleep.

It all contributed to a mood of nihilism and cynicism; and other values too, had been upset. The progress of science has not contributed to happiness. There was an uneasy feeling that the progress of human society and the human personality had not kept pace with the progress of science in any field. Political values, too, were uncertain. The unenthusiastic acceptance of parliamentary democracy as a lesser evil went, somehow, with a sneaking admiration for Soviet society in some cases—it had, for instance, solved the "slave or Amazon" dilemma of French women—or with a secret hankering for Führerdom in others.

As one young student wrote:

We don't mind belonging to sports and tourist associations, but we have no use for political groupings.... As for the *Mal du Siècle* you talk about, there's really no such thing. But there is a lot of anxiety—over the meaning of life, material progress and spiritual decline, and the future of France. Amongst many of us, the future of France is the chief worry. It is a burning subject; and we've lost our heads, and we want guidance. Earlier generations had their masters—Maurras, and Gide, Alain, Barrès, or Péguy. We have nobody. We are being offered Sartre, which is just ridiculous....

Despite the ignominious end of the *Action Française* there was again a vague hankering for Maurrasism and other dictatorial doctrines; but, in practice, there was little action on these lines, as could be seen from the half-heartedness and mental reservations with which de Gaulle, the only serious candidate for Führerdom, was surrounded. Because even the belief in Fascism implies some degree of optimism. And as, for instance, Henry Bernstein the playwright put it in one of the interviews published in *NEF*:

Pessimism and anguish existed in the nineteenth century, but not this almost unanimous feeling of insecurity and of grave peril, the chief element of our moral climate. The notion of *duration* has been lost, nobody believes in the future, and the young have lost hope. . . .

Or as M. J. M. Domenach, of *Esprit*, put it:

We men of the Resistance are disillusioned. . . . But not everybody knew the Resistance. And now there is the atom bomb. And atom bombs leave no room for heroism, and no one dares hope for the return of Napoleon. The *mal du siècle* today is not a malady of the idle, but a malady of the active, and the proletariat, the most active element, has abandoned the Republic. . . .

Every utterance published in *NEF* was tinged by this feeling of "not being able to look ahead", by "the myopia with which we all now look at life", as Henry Troyat said. Others simply accepted decay almost as a "way of life"—notably the riff-raff of Saint-Germain-des-Prés, with their tartan shirts and their "existentialist" poses, the more literate of whom wrote third-rate imitations of Villon, while others merely sponged on American tourists. Other young people of the bourgeoisie closed their minds to the future and merely sought worldly success above all things. Money, money! *Arriver!* Others still admired men of action—witness the enormous fan-mail received from young people by Maurice Herzog, hero and martyr of the French Himalaya expedition. Here were some of the sentiments expressed:

I have two passions—Music, with Bach, Beethoven, and Mozart above all others, and Mountains. . . . But who cares? Love of what is Pure and Beautiful is so rare these days. . . . When so many young men only think of pleasure and money, a man like you is all the more admired. . . . We lack purity. . . .

Others took to religion; a larger number than before the war took religious orders, and the missionary societies had long waiting lists.

All this perhaps belonged to the realm of "intellectualism", with little effect on the broader masses of the population—the peasants, the workers, the *fonctionnaires*—who went on living from day to day, and who, unlike the more sophisticated people, had a curious faith that, whatever might befall them, France would, somehow, go on for ever.

Yet even amongst these people, not all was well. Economic discontent and bad housing had bred a sordid "sub-existentialism" of sorts. And this discontent, combined with a sense of insecurity, was producing anti-Americanism and a large Communist vote.

All these different symptoms and manifestations of "catastrophism" in France coming all at once at the end of 1951 were not perhaps quite accidental. The Russians had exploded their third atom bomb; on the other side, there was more and more talk of "preventive war" and "Roll-Back", before it was "too late". The atmosphere at the UN Assembly in Paris that winter with Acheson and Vyshinsky snarling at each other, was particularly poisonous; the cost of living in France was still rising and a financial catastrophe seemed close at hand, with the $ fetching 500 francs on the black bourse. The Indo-China war and even the Korean War—despite the futile cease-fire talks—seemed to be going on for ever, and now major trouble was also beginning to pile up sky-high in North Africa.

In 1952 North Africa—first Tunisia, and then Morocco—seemed at times to eclipse all other problems. Germany, "Europe", the European Army were no doubt more important in the long run, but in their case, France could still afford to play for time. But North Africa acquired an unexpected acuteness at the end of 1951 when M. Pleven's Government put the clock back with its ruthless Note of December 15 rejecting in effect that internal autonomy—or home rule—for which the Chenik Government had been politely asking for many months past.

LIST OF GOVERNMENTS SINCE THE LIBERATION
WITH SOME OF THE PRINCIPAL POSTS

Date	Prime Minister	Foreign Affairs	Defence	Finance	Economy	Justice	Interior	Colonies or "Overseas France"
9-9-44	De Gaulle	Bidault	Diethelm	Lepercq Pleven (14-11-44)	Mendès-France Pleven (7-4-45)	de Menthon Teitgen (31-5-45)	Tixier	Pleven Giaccobbi (14-11-44)
25-11-45	De Gaulle	Bidault	De Gaulle Michelet (Army)	Pleven	Billoux	Teitgen	Tixier	Soustelle
21-1-46	F. Gouin	Bidault	Gouin Michelet (Army)	Philip	Philip	Teitgen	Le Troquer	Moutet
23-6-46	Bidault	Bidault	Michelet	R. Schuman	de Menthon	Teitgen	Depreux	Moutet
16-12-46	Blum	Blum	Le Troquer	Philip	Philip	Ramadier	Depreux	Moutet
22-1-47	Ramadier	Bidault	Billoux Delbos (7-5-47)	R. Schuman	Philip	A. Marie	Depreux	Moutet
24-11-47	Schuman	Bidault	Teitgen	R. Mayer	R. Mayer	A. Marie	Moch	P. Coste-Floret
27-7-48	A. Marie	R. Schuman	R. Mayer	Reynaud	Reynaud	Lecourt	Moch	P. Coste-Floret
11-9-48	Queuille	R. Schuman	Ramadier	Queuille	Queuille	A. Marie	Moch	P. Coste-Floret
28-10-49	Bidault	Schuman	Pleven	Petsche	Petsche	R. Mayer	Moch Queuille (6-2-50)	Letourneau

Date	Prime Minister	Foreign Affairs	Defence	Finance	Economy	Justice	Interior	Colonies or "Overseas France"
12-7-50	Pleven[1]	R. Schuman	Moch	Petsche	Petsche	R. Mayer	Queuille	Letourneau[2] Mitterrand
13-3-51	Queuille	R. Schuman	Moch	Petsche	Faure (budget)	R. Mayer	Queuille	Letourneau[2] Mitterrand
3-8-51	Pleven	R. Schuman	Bidault	R. Mayer	R. Mayer	E. Faure	C. Brune	Letourneau[2] Jacquinot
20-1-52	E. Faure	R. Schuman	Bidault	Faure	R. Buron	Mart.-Déplat	Brune	Letourneau[2] Jacquinot
8-3-52	Pinay	R. Schuman	Pleven	Pinay		Mart.-Déplat	Brune	Letourneau[2] Pflimlin
8-1-53	R. Mayer	Bidault	Pleven	Bourgès-Maunoury	R. Buron	Mart.-Déplat	Brune	Letourneau[2]
28-6-53	Laniel	Bidault	Pleven	Faure	Faure	Ribeyre	Mart.-Déplat	Jacquet[2] Fréd.-Dupont[2] (1-6-54) Jacquinot
18-6-54	Mendès-France	Mendès-France	Koenig Temple (3-9-54) Koenig	Faure	(Faure)	E. Hugues G. de Beaumont (3-9-54)	Mitterrand	G. La Chambre[2] Buron
20-2-55	E. Faure	Pinay	Koenig	Pflimlin	Pflimlin	R. Schuman	Bourgès-Maunoury	Teitgen

[1] Preceded by a "still-born" government under M. Queuille.

[2] These, as distinct from the Minister of Colonies or Overseas France were Minister or Secretary of State for Indo-China.

It will be observed that Foreign Affairs and Indo-China were, until 1954, strongholds of the MRP, and the Interior, first a Socialist and since 1949, a Radical stronghold.

THE YEAR OF MONSIEUR PINAY

1. "I AM MR CONSUMER"

THERE are certain historical events which, when they occur, cause the greatest surprise; but, looked at a few months later, they seem not only perfectly logical, but historically inevitable. To such events belongs the investiture, on March 6, 1952, of M. Antoine Pinay, a little-known member of the classical Right and a former member of Pétain's National Council who had, unostentatiously, held a number of economic posts in previous governments, but who seemed more interested in his *mairie* of Saint-Chamond, in the Loire, than in a government career.

M. Pinay, who was in the hides and leather business, was a small industrialist, and very much the average Frenchman of popular imagination; and he made the most of being just "an ordinary chap", and not a cunning politician or brilliant intellectual. His speeches, notably to rural audiences, were marked by a platitudinous, paternalist, *père-de-famille* type of moralizing which often sounded like a humble imitation of Pétain's talks to his "children". Only a few weeks after his investiture, he declared in a press interview: "I am Mr Consumer, and I stand at the head of a league of 43 million Frenchmen."[1]

Among the various measures he proposed (and, in some cases, carried out) were a "fiscal amnesty"; the cultivation of "confidence"; the floating of a "gold" loan; a nationwide campaign for lower prices, etc; and his utterances included a certain amount of demagogy directed against Big Business, such as his proposal to prohibit price rings, i.e. the fixing of minimum prices by trade groups (*ententes profesionnelles*). The main features of his budget were a reduction in capital investments, the maintenance of military expenditure and—no new taxation, always a popular slogan in France—and, indeed, anywhere.

Pinay was lucky in more ways than one. He was invested by the National Assembly as a result of a highly significant development: the desertion from the Gaullist RPF of 27 members, who rallied to the support of plain Monsieur Pinay, the "common-sense Frenchman", and former Vichyite. It was on that occasion, as already said, that the

[1] *Paris Presse*, April 18, 1952.

General grimly remarked: "I did not save France in order to hand her over to Monsieur Pinay."

As we have seen, the RPF had not done very well in the General Election; and, what is more, the election campaign had shown that, far from being a homogeneous totalitarian movement or a romantic movement that had originated in the Resistance, both its candidates and its voters were a very mixed crew, many of them much more in sympathy with plain "conservatism" and even Vichyism than with anything de Gaulle, the "socially minded" Soustelle or the "romantic" André Malraux, with his love of "action for action's sake", stood for. To many of these people the sensible and unexciting M. Pinay appealed far more than the General. So twenty-seven "Gaullists" deserted the RPF fold in Pinay's investiture vote, and it was during the following months that the RPF largely disintegrated, with their vote in local elections and by-elections declining from over 20 per cent to a mere 10 per cent or less.

There were two things that greatly favoured Pinay. One was the simple fact that there was in reality a Right-Centre majority in the 1951 Assembly which had not yet manifested itself. Neither the Pleven Government of August 1951 to January 1952, nor the unfortunate Edgar Faure Government, which had, after that, lasted for forty days,[2] reflected yet sufficiently the swing to the Right in the country that the Election had revealed. Pinay, supported by part of the Gaullists who had lost faith in any special "mission" of the RPF—as well as by the whole "classical" Right and most of the MRP—produced (if only for a time) that Right-wing majority which was in the logic of things. (The non-Pinay RPF members mostly abstained.)

The very fact that he concentrated on home affairs made it particularly easy to form such a majority. Had Pinay made questions like German rearmament his principal platform, the formation of a right-wing majority would have been more difficult; but on a number of top-priority home problems it was feasible. It is true that in May 1952 the European Army Treaty was signed in Paris by the "6", but ratification still seemed far off, and meantime there were other ways of keeping the USA in good humour, for instance by starting an anti-Communist drive in France.

The new Premier succeeded in creating a "Pinay legend" during

[2] Its brief existence was marked by the Lisbon Conference, so humiliating to France; by a serious military setback in Indo-China, the loss of Hoa-Binh (captured in the previous November and then described as "the key to Vietminh's whole system of communications"); by the flare-up of serious trouble in Tunisia; and by a financial panic which sent the black-market rate of the dollar to over 500 francs. This panic had been substantially strengthened by an open attack on the Government's financial policy by M. Baumgartner, Governor of the Bank of France.

his eight months in office in 1952, and there is no doubt that Pinay is one of the very rare French politicians of the Fourth Republic who managed to acquire genuine popularity with wide sections of the public. His name was to be associated for years afterwards with a fundamental fact in French post-war history: the virtual stabilization of prices and of the cost of living. The whole period of 1944–51 had been marked by a virtually continuous inflation and rise in prices, and it was under the Pinay Government that prices at last came, more or less, to a standstill. The chief reason for this was a simple one.

Since the middle of 1951 there had been a marked drop in world prices, and it was Pinay who was lucky enough to reap the benefits of this inside France.

As the *Monde* wrote shortly after he had formed his government:

The boom in raw materials, due to the Korean War, caused in France, as elsewhere, a rise in prices. . . . Recently, after a sharp drop, raw materials have become stabilized, some prices having returned to their pre-Korean level. . . . The slowing-down of stockpiling and of rearmament has had a salutary effect. . . . The slight decline in French prices last month [February 1952] had foreign as well as domestic reasons. Throughout 1951, despite the fall in raw materials, our prices continued to increase. Numerous factors maintained a belief in an indefinite inflation process. . . . M. Pinay's chief target is to destroy this collective inflation psychosis. (*Le Monde*, March 21, 1952.)

The article enumerated various factors in favour of stabilization and even of a certain drop in prices: the slump in consumer goods, a good harvest, and the desire on the part of M. Pinay to avoid new taxes, and to raise loans on the strength of renewed confidence in the franc. That some of M. Pinay's financial methods were extremely dubious is certain (not only British taxation experts but even some high officials in the French Ministry of Finance were outraged by his "fiscal amnesty" for instance); also, after the sliding scale had at long last been introduced, all kinds of subterfuges were resorted to to prevent the cost-of-living index from going beyond a point when a wage increase became necessary: thus, to maintain their profits without a price increase, dairies were allowed to sell poor-quality milk! The fact nevertheless remains that numerous prices and standard charges (e.g. fares on Paris buses and the Métro) in 1955 were still those which had "found their level" under the Pinay Government in 1952. The legend of the *"Baisse Pinay"*—even though, in March 1952, it did little more than help shopkeepers to get rid of their surplus stocks with a great display of civic-mindedness—has, nevertheless, not been forgotten. For the first time since the war prices had (broadly speaking) stopped going up. Provincial France showed its appreciation for Pinay when in the

Senate elections in May the Right made some substantial gains. (The voters, however, drew the line at making M. Flandin, Pinay's *protégé*, and an old Vichy crony, a Senator.)

But the Pinay period is significant in some other respects as well. It was the period when France became particularly tough in two directions: against the North Africans beyond the Mediterranean and against the Communists at home.

Was there a connexion between the two? Not perhaps on the face of it. The two problems—Arab nationalism in Tunisia (which was the first to flare up) and Communism inside France—were practically unconnected; yet the treatment given to both problems under the Pinay Government was significant of the political "climate" in which France was now living, and often the same people were involved in the two "hunts"—for example M. Martinaud-Déplat, who was not only the "anti-Red" Minister of Justice, but also a pillar of the North Africa Lobby. The swing to the Right in the 1951 election had encouraged several groups of people. The North African Lobby felt that the time had come to drop all the "democratic blah" concerning France's Arab subjects and protégés overseas in favour of a tougher "Empire" policy.

Already at the end of 1951 this Lobby had scored its first great success by getting the Quai d'Orsay to reject, in its Note of December 15, the Chenik Government's proposals for internal autonomy for Tunisia. That was the real beginning of the great Battle for North Africa.

Secondly, it was under the Pinay Government that its Minister of Justice, M. Martinaud-Déplat, popularly known as "France's McCarthy", and its Minister of the Interior, M. Brune, did something which looked singularly like an attempt to outlaw the French Communist Party.

Both these episodes with their far-reaching consequences deserve to be closely examined.

2. THE TUNISIAN FLARE-UP

Without looking too far back into the history of Franco-Tunisian relations, it is sufficient to recall here that under the pressure of a powerful nationalist movement, the Neo-Destour, led by Habib Bourguiba and supported by the UGTT, the Tunisian Trade Union Federation, headed by Ferhat Hashed, the French Governments of 1950, and particularly M. Robert Schuman, the Foreign Minister, embarked on what came to be known as the "Tunisian experiment"—which was an attempt to arrive at a *modus vivendi* with the Tunisians by discussing with them at least some of the demands put forward by Bourguiba in April 1950.

These seven demands, which in reality aimed at establishing at least "internal autonomy" in Tunisia (i.e. home rule in all matters other than the armed forces and diplomacy) were the following:

(1) Revival of a Tunisian executive, holder of national sovereignty;
(2) Formation of a Tunisian Government responsible for public order and appointed by the Bey;
(3) Abolition of the post of French Secretary-General, now virtually wielding sole administrative authority in the country;
(4) Abolition of the *contrôleurs civils*, who are the agents of that "direct administration" which is incompatible with Tunisian sovereignty;
(5) Abolition of the French gendarmerie;
(6) Establishment of elected municipalities including French representatives in all localities having a French minority;
(7) Creation of a national assembly, elected by universal suffrage, and which would elaborate a democratic constitution. This, in turn, would settle the future relations between France and Tunisia, full account being taken of the legitimate rights of France within the framework of Tunisian sovereignty.

This was asking for far too much; but the mood of the French governments in 1950 was still on the "liberal" side; thus M. Robert Schuman, speaking at Thionville in 1950, went so far as to say that France's "final objective" was to lead towards independence all territories within the French Union. And at the Senate he announced on July 19, 1950: "We cannot maintain indefinitely direct administration by the French; that is precisely the object of the reforms we have in mind."

It was in August 1950 that the Bey and the French Resident-General agreed on the formation of a government under M. Chenik, comprising, apart from the usual French ministers, six Tunisian ministers, among them Salah Ben Yussef, representing the Neo-Destour, and Dr Ben Salem. The purpose of this government "formed within the framework of the Protectorate treaties", was "to negotiate . . . institutional modifications which would lead Tunisia by stages to internal autonomy."

It must be said that since the moment that the Chenik Government was formed, it met with nothing but delaying tactics on the part of the French authorities in both Tunis and Paris, and with the most violent hostility from the Rassemblement Français in Tunisia, which also had its spokesmen and supporters in the French National Assembly, notably M. Quilici, M. René Mayer, and a number of other influential deputies and senators, some inside the Government.

In October 1951, after numerous fruitless negotiations, M. Chenik presented the French Government with a memorandum in which he made three proposals:

(1) The Government should be all-Tunisian;

(2) There should be a representative assembly, but during the transition period the Government would legislate, subject to parliamentary amendment;

(3) Officials must be Tunisian, but the French officials now serving in Tunisia will be maintained, and French technicians will be specially recruited for Tunisia.

Chenik also proposed a series of special agreements safeguarding France's strategic, military, economic, and cultural interests.

Senator Colonna, representing the French in Tunisia, and regarded as one of the heads of the "North Africa Lobby", sent a memorandum to the French Government on October 26 recommending the rejection of all the Tunisian demands. He wrote:

The Tunisians cannot be much trusted and they are incapable of either administering or governing their country. We must continue to hold all the command posts, both in our own interests and in the interests of France; for once Tunisia is free, she will, whatever her promises, join the other camp—maybe the Arab League, or the USA or the USSR.[3]

And Senator Colonna urged the French Government to dismiss the Chenik Government and to appoint a new government under the "trustworthy" M. Baccouche. (It was precisely M. Baccouche whom, a few months later, in March 1952, M. de Hautecloque, the "tough" new Resident-General, *did* inflict on the Bey, after duly deporting to the Far South the members of the Chenik Government.)

The final reply, much on the lines of the Colonna recommendations, was drafted at the Quai d'Orsay (according to press reports) by M. Maurice Schumann (Secretary of State and M. Robert Schuman's right-hand man), and a permanent official of the Quai, M. Puaux, son of Senator Puaux, another leading member of the North Africa Lobby. The Note—or rather, Letter—was, however, signed by M. Robert Schuman himself, despite all the good intentions he had expressed to the Tunisians. After speaking at great length about all the good done to Tunisia by France since the establishment of the Protectorate in 1881, the Letter clearly rejected the proposal for a "homogeneous" government, and the French press in Tunisia loudly rejoiced over the affirmation of "the co-sovereignty principle".

It is true that although M. Robert Schuman tried to argue a few days later that there had been a "misunderstanding", he nevertheless refused to see Chenik again, and declared that the Letter of December 15 was his "final word". At the same time the conciliatory Resident-General,

<hr />

[3] *Cf.* Jean Rous, *Tunisie, Attention!* (Paris, 1952).

M. Périllier was replaced by a diehard, M. de Hauteclocque, the French Ambassador in Brussels.

Chenik returned to Tunis empty-handed, followed soon afterwards by Bourguiba, who proceeded to harangue his fellow-countrymen, telling them to prepare for bloodshed, but, at the same time, warning France that Tunisia would appeal to UN.

The day M. de Hauteclocque arrived in Tunis in the midst of a great military and naval display, two members of the Tunisian Government, Salah Ben Youssef and Badra suddenly turned up at the Palais Chaillot in Paris, where the UN Assembly was still sitting, causing great bewilderment among the UN officials. M. Trygve Lie, Secretary-General of UN, finally decided that the Tunisians' appeal to the Security Council against their "Protector" was irregular. Technically, France alone could, on Tunisia's behalf, present this complaint "against France" to UN. As this was obviously out of the question, it was the group of fifteen Afro-Asian countries which finally came to the support of the Tunisians. The question was brought before the Security Council on April 1, when the question arose of placing Tunisia on the agenda; Pakistan, Chili, Brazil, Poland, and the Soviet Union voted in favour; the USA, Greece, and Turkey abstained; France and Britain voted against. The American vote was the most interesting, and one that disturbed the French most. For not only were the CIO and the AF of L strongly supporting the Tunisian trade unions, but the Truman administration itself was still pursuing an "anti-colonialist" policy in respect of North Africa.

There is no doubt that in 1952 the Tunisians (and Moroccans, for that matter) looked upon the United States as their protector against the French, while the French *colons* looked upon the USA as Enemy No 1. The fear of being ousted by the Americans from North Africa (and, in one way or another, replaced by them) seems to have been quite genuine at the time. As *Combat* wrote on January 23, 1952:

Blood is running down the streets of Tunis. . . . We are pursuing a policy of "firmness", without remembering that we haven't the means of pursuing such a policy. . . . Are the Moslems so ill-informed that they don't know that our foreign policy is increasingly influenced from outside? . . . In Tunisia, as in Morocco, they know that Washington is the real boss who merely tolerates—for how long? our presence in Casablanca and Bizerta. . . . Six years ago a "tough" general bombed Damascus in revolt. A few days later, we were chucked out of Syria on orders from Churchill. . . .

So wrote a paper that was favourable to Franco-Tunisian conciliation. But the same apprehensions were felt by the *colons*; and one of the strangest features of the Pinay epoch was this fear of American interference in North Africa, and the threat made by spokesmen of the

North-African Lobby that if America supported any Tunisian or Moroccan complaints against France before UN, it would be powerful enough to "start an anti-American campaign throughout the entire French press". (No doubt with the unsolicited, but welcome co-operation of the Communists!) And if, at the end of 1952, Ferhat Hashed was murdered by the French colons, it was because he was considered an American stooge.

What is interesting is that these apprehensions lasted so long as the Truman Administration was still in office, and the CIO and AF of L were powerful enough to support the labour movements in Tunisia and Morocco; after the Republican victory in the USA at the end of 1952, the French were allowed a free hand in North Africa--no doubt in return for certain assurances concerning Europe and Indo-China. It was then, indeed, that their toughness spread from Tunisia to Morocco, as will be seen.

It is impossible here to recount in detail the stormy events which marked the beginning of the great North African crisis, from which France has suffered ever since the beginning of 1952. The principal landmarks, during this first stage in Tunisia (i.e. after the abortive Tunisian appeal to UN in January) were the following:

On January 15 M. de Hauteclocque summoned the Bey to dismiss the Tunisian members of the Chenik Cabinet. The Bey did not answer the summons.

On the following day, having prohibited the meeting of the Neo-Destour Congress, which was to be held two days later, the Resident-General ordered the arrest of 150 Neo-Destour members.

On the 17th, rioting broke out in Bizerta and other towns.

On the 18th, Bourguiba and a number of other Neo-Destour leaders were arrested. To protest against these arrests, shops closed in the *medinas* and the UGGT called a general strike. Riots broke out in the countryside, followed by the famous *ratissage* in the Cap Bon area. The killing, raping, and looting of which the Foreign Legion in particular was guilty, produced a wave of protests in Paris, though General Garbay, the French C.-in-C. in Tunisia (who had already distinguished himself in the Madagascar massacres in 1947) treated the outcry with remarkable cynicism.

It should be recalled that all this happened still under the Edgar Faure Government; and while M. Faure was not at all in favour of these methods, he found it hard to cope with the *colon* influences at the Quai d'Orsay, or with the independent behaviour of the French officials and military in Tunisia itself. Nevertheless, he refused to reiterate Hauteclocque's demand that the Bey dismiss the Tunisian ministers, and merely asked that the complaint to UN be withdrawn. At the same time he got M. François Mitterrand, his young Minister of State in charge of Tunisian affairs, to draw up new French proposals which would have a good chance of being accepted by the Tunisians as the basis for a settlement. This Mitterrand Plan—the main purpose of which was to grant the Tunisians a considerable degree of internal autonomy, while safeguarding France's rights in Tunisia would (as Bourguiba himself was to say a few months later), have been enthusiastically accepted by the "moderate" Chenik Government, and could still be accepted as a "basis of discussion". When I was in Tunis in July 1952, I found among the Tunisian nationalists, such as Dr Sadok Moqqadem, general agreement that the Mitterrand Plan was "acceptable."⁴

But by this time M. Pinay was already in office, and, not being deeply interested himself in the Tunisian problem, he surrendered it to the tender mercies of the Quai d'Orsay and of M. de Hautecloque.

The latter did not wait long to act. On March 25 he demanded again that the Bey dismiss the Tunisian ministers; since this demand produced no reaction other than a telegram to President Auriol, in which the Bey complained of the Resident's "truculent manner", M. de Hauteclocque had Chenik and three other ministers arrested the next day, and deported by plane to the Far South. Bourguiba, for his part, was transferred from the mainland to the island of La Galite. If Ferhat Hashed was not arrested, it was only because of the outcry such an arrest would have caused in the USA. Martial law was proclaimed in Tunis, complete with an 8 o'clock curfew, thousands of arrests were made, and a police terror, complete with beatings-up and tortures set in on a large scale. At the same time, Hauteclocque forced the Bey to appoint M. Baccouche to succeed Chenik as Prime Minister. Baccouche was a typical *beni-oui-oui*, a wealthy landlord, and principal shareholder of the Tunisian branch of Coca Cola.⁵

It took him a fortnight to find any Tunisians willing to enter his

⁴ For full details of this plan see Jean Rous, *Tunisie, Attention!* pp. 74–5 (Paris, 1952).

⁵ Baccouche's line was that the very inadequate French proposals were "better than nothing" and that once these "reforms" had been accepted, Tunisia could eventually "ask for more", whereas if nothing was agreed upon things would go from bad to worse. The pomp which surrounded the *beni-oui-oui* premier was described by the author in the following passage:

"Oh, that office of M. Baccouche's! It wasn't an office—it was the Arabian Nights with a vengeance, in Technicolor. He received me in the 18th-century Palace of Dar El Bey; in the Moorish 'waiting-room' fezzed gentlemen were not sitting or standing, but reclining on couches; one almost expected a gong to be struck, and the magic doors to fly open and to let in a swarm of Matisse-like odalisques.

M. Baccouche, wearing a gorgeous white robe, to which was pinned the rosette of the Legion of Honour, addressed me in almost perfect English. One of the richest men in Tunisia, and said to be the chief shareholder of the Tunisian branch of Coca Cola, M. Baccouche was extremely charming. He talked about London, which he had first visited as a youngster in 1906; he said he government. According to Tunisian sources, 20,000 people were arrested in March and April. It is true that in May many of these were released, including Chenik and two of his ministers, but there were still, acccording to estimates of the US Consulate, 6,000 or 7,000 persons in prisons, camps and police stations, though officially the French admitted "only" 1,900.

During the summer, there was something of a lull; the curfew was abolished, and although there was still some terrorism and counter-terrorism in the form of a few "sardine-tin" bombs being thrown every day, it did not amount to much. It looked as if the Tunisians were waiting for a new Franco-Tunisian agreement—not that the seven-point proposal now made by the French was considered acceptable by either the Tunisians or the die-hard *colons*.

But one could not help feeling that more trouble was in store. When I saw Ferhat Hashed, the head of the Tunisian trade unions in June 1952, he looked uneasy, and showed me several letters of threats, among them a leaflet from the "Red Hand", marked with the rubber-stamped picture of a hand in red ink, and saying that the hand was "red with the blood of the enemies of France".[6] At the Residence, the young noblemen in M. de Hauteclocque's entourage, commented viciously on Ferhat Hashed and on his "constant hobnobbing" with the US Consulate.

What brought the Tunisian crisis to a head was the decision by the Bey, finally disillusioned in the half-promises coming from the French, to form, in August, a sort of "Crown Council", composed of forty prominent Tunisian personalities. The French took this establishment of an unofficial all-Tunisian parliament very badly, all the more so as it encouraged the Bey to assume a much more independent tone *vis-à-vis* the French.[7] What is more, American opinion was becoming increasingly favourable to the Tunisians, and the Bey publicly repudiated the two Tunisian "spokesmen" who went as members of the French delegation to the UN Assembly in October when, whether the French liked it or not, Tunisia was about to be included in the agenda.

loved hansom cabs, and asked if the Cecil Hotel was still standing; and he told me all about Miss Gandon, the governess who had been in his family for years and had taught him and his sisters English. And he said how greatly he admired Mr Churchill, and also General de Gaulle, and how marvellous the British were during the war. . . . Throughout, there was an amused twinkle in his eye, which suggested that he was rather inclined to treat the magic setting of the Dar El Bey, and British correspondents, and his French masters, and even himself, as being all part of one rich, huge joke." (*New Statesman and Nation*, July 19, 1952.)

[6] Ferhat Hashed, fair and blue-eyed, who received me at the very humble headquarters of the UGTT could have passed off as a French trade union official. He had a charming personality and spoke perfect French with a strong *Midi* accent.

[7] *Cf.* C. A. Julien, *L'Afrique du Nord en Marche* (Paris, 1952), pp. 263–4.

But the Republican victory in the Presidential Election in the USA drastically altered the situation in the French die-hards' favour. One of the first things the French Government secured from the new Administration was a "neutral" American attitude *vis-à-vis* North Africa. On December 4 the detested Ferhat Hashed was assassinated by the "Red Hand"—or some similar *colon* organization (although the identity of the assassins was known to the Résidence, no one was arrested—much to the disgust of M. Mèndes-France who had gone to Tunis to act as legal counsel to Ferhat Hashed's widow).

The murder of Ferhat Hashed had innumerable repercussions in the rest of North Africa, the most important of which was the protest strike at Casablanca. This gave the dynamic M. Boniface, the "Prefect" of Casablanca, the long-desired opportunity to stamp out the Moroccan Trade Union Movement in a massacre in which several hundred Moroccan workers were killed.

Later, the full story of this episode, which led to one thing after another, and finally to the deposition and deportation of the Sultan, will be told. Here it is sufficient to say that by the end of 1952 the French Government entered upon a period of ruthless repression in North Africa, hoping—now that they had been given a free hand by the USA—to intimidate the Arabs into complete submission.

While on the subject of Tunisia, a few general reflections should be added. As distinct from Algeria, Tunisia has only a relatively small European population (250,000 including 150,000 French) out of a total population of over three millions. The Tunisian Nationalist Movement is run mostly by French-trained intellectuals, and professional men not fundamentally hostile to France. The UGTT, the Tunisian Trade Union Federation, a member of the International Confederation of Free Trade Unions had in 1952 a membership of 100,000 and its leader, Ferhat Hashed enjoyed great personal authority. He also was a man of French culture, and nationalist first and Socialist only second; and while admitting that native employers were often worse than French employers, he declared the primary objective of the Trade Union Movement to be national liberation; only after that would the trade unions tackle the relationship between native labour and native capital. He declared himself violently anti-Communist. Even so, it was curious to hear one of M. Baccouche's ministers—a big landlord—declare that if ever the French handed Tunisia over to the Tunisians, the Tunisian bourgeoisie would not thank the French for the "troublesome heritage" they were leaving them—a Nationalist Trade Union Movement they had foolishly allowed to be set up!

It is important to emphasize this point: the Nationalist Movement in

Tunisia, while progressive in many ways, and anxious to improve the health and education services (in 1952 only 15 per cent of the native children of school age were able to go to school, as against about 100 per cent of the European children) would not necessarily improve the economic condition of the Tunisian people if the French went. There was, and still is, almost general agreement among Tunisians that, at least for a long time, the presence of the French will be indispensable.

Whether Tunisia should remain indefinitely a "protectorate" was, however, another matter. Many Tunisians in 1952 often liked to refer to Libya, which though a far more backward country than Tunisia, was nominally, at any rate, independent. Why?

Much of the anti-French feeling in Tunisia, and, even more so, in Morocco was caused by personal or "sentimental" factors—the overbearing behaviour of many of the French authorities, and particularly the "*Herrenvolk*" attitude assumed by the women-folk, particularly of the small French business man or *fonctionnaire*. This, to many, was even more important than the fact that the French were reluctant to abandon too many of the *fonctionnaire* jobs to Tunisians, or that, in their capitalist exploitation of Tunisia, they were paying farm labour four or five times less than they were paying similar labour in France.[8]

3. ATTEMPT TO SUPPRESS THE CP—DUCLOS AND THE CARRIER PIGEONS

The strange happenings in Paris in May 1952, in the course of which the French Communists suddenly burst into action, after lying low for a long time, whereas the Pinay Government—or rather, some of its members—made the first major attempt under the Fourth Republic to outlaw the Communist Party, deserve to be closely examined. Not only are they a major landmark in French Government policy *vis-à-vis* the Communists, as well as something of a turning-point in the history of the French Communist Party, but seldom, if ever, in the whole story of the Fourth Republic were any events so deliberately and systematically misrepresented in the greater part of the French press and, above all, in the World press. Even the most reputable papers in England and America swallowed uncritically the extravagant official French story of Duclos's "wireless transmitter" and his two "carrier pigeons".

The occasion which gave rise to all these happenings was the arrival in Paris of General Ridgway, who, after commanding the UN forces in Korea for some time, had been appointed to succeed General Eisenhower as head of SHAPE. For several months Communist propaganda

[8] For what followed in Tunisia see Part V, Chapter IV, 5 and Book VI, Chapter II, 3.

had concentrated on denouncing the bacteriological warfare on which, it alleged, the Americans had embarked in Korea; and Ridgway was constantly referred to in the Communist press as the "Bacterial General" or as "General Plague". His arrival in Paris seemed to call for some kind of protest. There had been a number of similar protest demonstrations in the past, notably against the arrival of Eisenhower in January 1951; but they had not been a great success, and the ruthlessness shown by the police did not encourage the rank-and-file Communist workman to stick out his neck unduly—all the more so as, apart from the dubious privilege of being beaten-up by the police, there was also the serious danger, in the case of a probable arrest, of losing one's job. The Communist leadership were quite conscious of the drawbacks that these demonstrations presented. Nevertheless, they were determined to make the most of "General Plague's" arrival in Paris. There seem to have been some important "general policy" reasons for this.

It will be remembered that Maurice Thorez, who was struck down by partial paralysis in 1950 was sent, at the end of the year, to Moscow, where famous Soviet specialists were expected to cure him completely. Although over eighteen months had passed since Thorez's departure for Moscow, his health was still far from perfect, and, in his absence, there appears to have been a good deal of confusion and uncertainty among the Communist leaders in France on what policy to follow. There was much talk of the rivalries and conflicts at "the top"—among Duclos, Marty, Billoux, Lecœur, and others. Duclos was reputed to be the leader of the "moderate" wing opposed to any rash action. Finally, it seems, it was decided to send Billoux to Moscow to discuss the position of the French CP with the convalescing Thorez and, possibly, with some of the Soviet leaders. As a result of this visit to Moscow, Billoux published in the May issue of the *Cahiers du Communisme* an article which called for a much "harder" Communist line than in the past two years, warned the Communist Party against dubious alliances— which could only be alliances between "traitors and the betrayed"— and called for "direct action" against all "warlike enterprises".

The action of the masses [Billoux wrote] has been insufficient to bring about a change in French policy. It has gone from bad to worse. The Pinay Government must indeed, be considered the most reactionary government we have had since the end of the war.... Conditions today are favourable for a radical change in France's political situation. But the action undertaken so far has proved insufficient, and what we need is that this action should improve both in quantity and quality.

National independence, Billoux continued, could only be reconquered through the defeat of the French bourgeoisie, which was guilty of "national treason", since it was abandoning France to

"American occupation". Far from being a "victim" of American Imperialism, the French bourgeoisie was its accomplice. In the circumstances, there could be no "national union" between the working-class, the middle class, and the capitalists. And, after a particularly virulent attack on the Socialist leaders, Billoux urged mass action against the "installation of American bases in France, against the transport of American war material, against the war in Vietnam and Korea", etc. He also insisted on the support to be given to the colonial peoples in their struggles for independence, and even to "the national claims of the people of Alsace-Lorraine".

What did all this mean? Various interpretations were given to the Billoux article; but it seems probable that it was prompted by the following considerations:

(*a*) a loss of "dynamism" among the Communist rank and file, as revealed by Communist losses in staff elections in the mines, at Renault's and among postal workers, losses attributed to an excessive tendency to "compromise" with non-Communists;

(*b*) a general "softening-up" among the rank and file, and the decline of the "revolutionary temperament", due to fatigue, disillusionment, and seemingly more normal economic conditions;

(*c*) the need to re-create a certain "sectarian" spirit among the Communist rank and file, different, for example, from the non-sectarian and "intellectual" spirit of that "broadminded" Communist weekly, *Action*, which had, somewhat mysteriously, closed down only a few weeks before, even though its survival could have been secured by the Party at only small expense;

(*d*) the need to "activize" the campaign against German rearmament and the war in Vietnam and Korea.

But all this belongs, as it were, to the "theoretical" background of the famous anti-Ridgway demonstration of May 28, which resulted in the fantastic "pigeon" episode.

No one who lived in Paris during those days could have failed to observe that, for some weeks past, there was something "in the air"; that the Pinay Government or rather its two "McCarthyite" members, M. Brune and M. Martinaud-Déplat, assisted by M. Baylot, the Prefect of Police, were preparing for some kind of show-down. There were straws in the wind. An anti-American play on Korea by M. Roger Vailland gave rise to some police-organized rioting inside the theatre, and after one performance, the play was arbitrarily prohibited by the Prefect of Police. Then, on Sunday, May 25, M. André Stil, the editor of the *Humanité* was arrested and taken handcuffed to prison for having written an anti-Ridgway article in which he had called on the people of Paris to demonstrate against the "Bacteriological General".

This arrest was completely arbitrary, as the offence did not in any way fit the Law of July 7, 1848, under which M. Stil was arrested.[9]

But this was only a beginning, though a significant beginning. Three days later, on May 28, the "anti-Ridgway" riots started about 7 p.m., chiefly around the place de la République, but also in some other parts of Paris, notably in the Latin quarter.

As I wrote at the time:

The place de la République and other "strategic" points were black with police and *gardes mobiles*, heavily armed with truncheons, pistols, tear-gas bombs and whatnot; and it required a good deal of physical courage to "demonstrate" in such conditions. That explains why only the most determined and fanatical *militants*, many of them carrying "*Ridgway Assassin*" "GO HOME" and "Vive la Paix" banners attached to crossbars, instead of ordinary pieces of wood, ventured to challenge the police at all. Hence, on the one hand, the official theory of the Communist "commandos" who, it was said, had alone taken part in the riots and, on the other hand, the theory, widely current abroad, of the "total indifference of the population". In reality there are many degrees between "total indifference" and the willingness to take the serious risk of having one's skull cracked by the police.

After describing a particular incident, I continued:

Yet there was nothing particularly new about the riots. . . . In the middle 'Thirties such riots were a frequent occurrence. If, as the Government said, Ridgway was only a pretext for the riots, then it might be said with equal justice that the riots were only a pretext for the arrest of Duclos and the charge that all this was "a plot against the safety of the State". . . . The famous Concorde riots of February 6, 1934, when the rioters did try to break into the Chamber of Deputies were a much more obvious "plot against the State", yet none of the leaders was charged with plotting. Wednesday's riot, on the contrary, had no particular objective; there was no storming of any public building; its only obvious purpose was to "protest".

There is not the slightest doubt that the arrest of Duclos was a very deliberate police frame-up.

The first official news [I wrote at the time] was that he had been arrested "red-handed" on the scene of the riots, and that in his car were found a loaded pistol, a truncheon, a wireless transmitter, and two carrier pigeons.

---

[9] Cf. *L'Observateur*, May 29, 1952, which recalls that, at the time of M. Stil's arrest, the anti-Ridgway demonstration had not yet been prohibited by the Government, and that, moreover, Stil could not be arrested, under the law of 1848 for his *provocation à l'attroupement* before this *attroupement* had actually taken place.

The wireless was intended to "intercept police messages" and to send out instructions to the "commandos", and the carrier pigeons, no doubt, to carry the communiqués of the fighting to Stalin. Later news said that the pigeons had been found dead, smothered in a blanket, but "still warm". Later still, it was learned, but this time not officially, that they were not carrier pigeons at all, but ordinary pigeons, and Duclos explained that he had got them from a farmer friend the same day, and that he and his wife were going to eat them *aux petits pois.*[10]

The loaded pistol and the truncheon belonged, true enough, to the driver, who was also Duclos's bodyguard; as for the wireless "transmitter", it turned out to be an ordinary receiving set with which about half the cars of the world are equipped; and the pigeons were ordinary pigeons (dead ones, and not even "still warm") ready for the casserole.

The story of the carrier pigeons, though reported in all seriousness by numerous papers, like *Paris-Presse*, the *Figaro*, and the *New York Herald-Tribune*, was, in fact, the thing that made the arrest of Duclos not only extremely grotesque, but also highly suspect in the eyes of practically everybody in France. It was clearly a police frame-up; and this became even more obvious as other circumstances of Duclos's arrest came to be known. He had, it was at first reported, been caught "red-handed", *en flagrant délit*—that is, in the only way in which a Deputy can be arrested without his parliamentary immunity having first been raised by the National Assembly.

In reality, the *flagrant délit* was another invention by the police, since Duclos had been arrested not *during* the rioting, but at least half an hour after all the rioting had stopped.

Since this was clearly established, Duclos should have been immediately released; instead he was locked up at the Santé Prison and charged with "conspiracy against the safety of the State".

Despite the greatest scepticism that the "carrier pigeons" and the rest of the incident had aroused everywhere, a large part of the French press (especially the *Figaro*, *France-Soir* and *Paris-Presse*) proceeded, during the next few days, to build up a tremendous Communist scare. The Police did all it could to encourage this campaign. Communist headquarters were raided and searched all over the place by spectacularly large police forces and with a total disregard for all the legal rules attached to such searches; a "gigantic Communist espionage organization" was discovered at Toulon, and so on. Apart from the 718 persons arrested on the night of the riots, there was a further wave of arrests among Communist officials and *militants*; Communist papers were seized by the police; and for a time a large number of Communists avoided spending the night in their own homes. Then there was the

[10] *New Statesman and Nation*, June 7, 1952.

story of the Duclos Notebooks which, together with 30,000 francs and some other papers were seized by the police at the time of his arrest. The 30,000 francs vanished, but the notebooks, singularly enough, were sold by the police to an American news agency. Soon afterwards an "edited" version of these notebooks appeared in a right-wing French paper, which had, throughout, been working in close co-operation with the police.

The arrest of Duclos caused the CGT and the Communist Party to call a general protest strike for June 4. This strike was largely a failure —not, as was claimed by the *Figaro*, because the working-class were "indifferent" to Duclos, but because they did not think the strike could be effective; moreover, the risk of being dismissed so soon before the *congés payés* was too great.

What began to worry more and more people in France, in the midst of the police raids on Communist headquarters, the hysterical campaign conducted by the right-wing press, and the systematic faking of news, was how far the Government intended to go. Would it try to outlaw the Communist Party as such? The *Monde*, unwilling to join in the anti-Communist hysteria of the *Figaro*, the *Aurore* and *France-Soir*, warned the Government against going "too far". The Socialists, though generally hostile to the Communists, began to remember the Reichstag Fire, and felt uneasy. M. Moch solemnly declared to the American press that the Communist Party would not be prohibited. Among the intellectuals the uproar was greatest. Mauriac expressed his thorough dislike for M. Brune's and M. Martinaud-Déplat's methods, and finally, inside the Pinay Government itself, a sharp reaction, led by M. Pleven, set in.

For one thing, the faking of news by certain members of the Government, the police, and the press had gone too far. It was, after all, M. Brune, the Minister of the Interior (and Martinaud-Déplat's closest crony), who had covered himself with ridicule with his "carrier pigeon" story. And then there were the screaming banner headlines of *France-Soir*:

P.C.: GRAVE AFFAIRE D'ESPIONNAGE DECOUVERTE
A TOULON

Importants documents saisis chez un militant: plan de sabotage des arsénaux, carte ultra-secrète du port militaire (June 8),

or else:

LE 2ᵉ BUREAU DU P.C. DEMASQUE (June 10)

Much to the fury of *L'Aurore* and the *Figaro* M. Pleven, the Minister of Defence, issued a communiqué saying that the documents so far seized at Toulon contained nothing secret.

The whole anti-Communist Operation with its police frame-ups and its trumped-up charges and faked news practically petered out by the beginning of July, after the Court in charge of prosecutions (*Chambre des mises en accusation*) dismissed the charge of "conspiracy" against M. Duclos and ordered his immediate release. So annoyed were certain people that a bomb was actually thrown into the house of M. Didier, the magistrate who had ordered this release. (Didier was, by a curious coincidence, the only judge in France who had refused an oath of allegiance to Pétain.)

But the general public were, on the whole, relieved; even among those most hostile to the Communists there were many who felt that the affair had been badly mishandled; that too many of the things that M. Brune, M. Baylot, and M. Martinaud-Déplat had done were wholly arbitrary and illegal, that they had aroused (which was worse) a great deal of angry laughter, that the whole operation stank of McCarthyism and evoked unpleasant memories of the Reichstag Fire technique. The reaction (and this was important in France) was strongest among the intellectuals, who saw in the arbitrary actions of the police against the Communists a serious menace against many freedoms, particularly the freedom of the press. "It's the Communists today; it'll be us next", was a most widespread reaction.

Many of the most prominent intellectuals saw in the "operation" a very ominous danger signal. In particular, it started Jean-Paul Sartre on a new line of thought which produced, before long, his two remarkable essays, *Les Communistes et la Paix* (followed by a third one two years later), which deeply affected much of the thinking on the non-Communist Left, and greatly modified the previous prevalent attitude to the CP. Sartre, who in 1948 had himself advocated the constitution of a "non-Communist Left" now proceeded to ridicule the "anti-Stalinites" on the Left, like the *Franc-Tireur* group with their impotent conception of what he called, sarcastically, *le Parti Démocratique, Social, Hardi*, and whose anti-Communism was inevitably leading them straight into the McCarthyite fold. He savagely ridiculed the ex-Communists in particular, the various sub-Koestlers of *Franc-Tireur* who, he said, went through four "classical" stages:

I sometimes come across them, these excluded Communists; they have still kept something of a tender smile, but there is something slightly haggard in their eyes; the contradiction of our epoch lies within them. For how can you believe *all at once* in the historic mission of the Proletariat and in the treason of the Communist Party, once you have realized that the one keeps on voting for the other? They wriggle out of it, all the same, but painfully, and within a short or a long period they all pass through these four fatal stages.

First stage: "The PC is wrong, but *all the same*, we cannot go against the Proletariat."

Second stage: "The working-class, I shall always love it; but one must, *all the same* recognize that it hasn't proved very far-sighted. See how the German workers allowed themselves to be bamboozled by Hitler."

Third stage: "I have lost interest in the working-class since they are cheerfully tolerating Soviet concentration camps."

Fourth and final stage: the Apocalypse: "JOINING ALLIANCE WITH USA STOP DROPPING ATOMBOMBS ON RUSSIA STOP HANGING ALL COMMUNISTS STOP REBUILD-ING ON RUINS TRUE INTERNATIONALIST DEMOCRATIC REFORMIST SOCIALISM."[11]

Sartre then argued why, in his view, the French Communists con-tinued to have the support of the French working-class, why the French intellectual—who saw eye-to-eye with the Communists on questions of war and peace, on Indo-China and colonialism, and who felt as deeply as they did about the social injustice of the Capitalist system, and loathed as deeply as they, all that Baylot and Martinaud-Déplat stood for—was inevitably drawn towards them. And Sartre argued against the pet theory of the *Figaro*, as well as of *Franc-Tireur* that the "Stalinite" was the "French working-man's evil genius"; and he also explained why, in his view, the "demonstration" against Ridgway of May 29—and it *was* nothing other than a demonstration—could not physically have been anything *but* a failure; why the general strike of June 4 had also been a failure: people did not want to have their skulls cracked, and they did not want to lose their jobs; but it did *not* mean, as *Figaro* and *Franc-Tireur* were trying to prove, that the working-class were *against* the Communists. Some had talked of "fatigue", and "indifference" on the part of the working-class; by failing to support the general strike—which was to be a mass protest against the arrest of Duclos—they had, the *Figaro* argued, disavowed the Communist Party. In Sartre's view, it was not as simple as that: politically and emotionally they were not against the strike; but practically and individually they were, for a hundred and one reasons, because the revolutionary temper was lacking in the conditions of the given moment, and because the era was an era of pessimism. The working-class had helped the bourgeoisie to build up the Fourth Republic, and had received no thanks; and it had protested in vain against the war in Vietnam, and the Atlantic Pact and German rearmament; a protest against Duclos's incarceration could serve no immediate purpose and could only harm the worker *individually*; but it did not mean he had lost his class-consciousness, that he trusted the bourgeoisie one whit more than before; "and he went home that night with a sense of uncertainty, feeling neither very proud, nor very happy".

In that essay, written in 1952, Sartre already foreshadowed the state of mind of the French working-class which became even more pro-nounced two or three years later—a strong class-consciousness, but, at

[11] *Temps Modernes*, July 1952, p. 2.

the same time, a feeling of helplessness; a realization that capitalism had come into its own again for many years to come, and that Lecœur was wrong to have said at the Soviet Party Congress in Moscow in October 1952 that Socialism "was something that not only our children, but we too would enjoy". If in 1952 the working-class failed to strike, as it had struck in 1920, 1936 and 1947 was it, Sartre asked, because it had lost its class-consciousness?

Does the worker think capitalist exploitation today fairer and more humane? Does he accept colonialism and imperialist wars and police repression more cheerfully? Will he throw his leaders overboard and fraternize with the boss? Just try out this experiment: talk to any one of those who failed to strike on June 4: speak to him like a friend, and then gently try to shoot a few little poisoned darts at Communist policy; for all you know, he may agree with you, but whether he does or not, he will break off the conversation, because he will have seen at once that you are a class enemy.[12]

And because the French employers were proud to be "the most backward employer class in the world", and had pursued a policy of small expenditure and high prices, and had failed to do what had been done in the USA and in Scandinavia, the French worker felt "doubly robbed".

For these, and many other reasons (Sartre argued) the French worker continued to be uncompromising to a pretty exceptional extent. Perhaps he knew no longer what Revolution meant; and yet, how was one to describe that uncompromising violence, that contempt for opportunism, that Jacobin tradition, that catastrophism which placed its hopes on some cataclysm rather than on the prospect of indefinite progress?

In this I see a revolutionary *attitude*.
... Only an *attitude* is not enough; it means that the French worker is a revolutionary without Revolution; because the future is blocked by a blood-stained wall; nevertheless the worker remains faithful to his beliefs and traditions.

However, that is another matter; and, to return to the Communist "conspiracy" of 1952—what happened after the liberation of Duclos?
While, as we have seen, M. Pleven opposed the wholly irregular methods employed in the Duclos affair by Brune and Baylot, it was he who, as Minister of Defence, instituted in the months that followed, a variety of legal proceedings against Communist trade unionists and against Communist Deputies with the help of some highly controver-

12 *Temps Modernes*, October–November 1952, p. 716.

sial legislation concerning the "demoralization of Army and Nation".[13] Non-Deputies like the CGT leader, Alain Le Léap, and others were arrested in October 1952, and Pleven also demanded that the parliamentary immunity be raised in the case of several Communist Deputies who had written "seditious" articles against the Indo-China war. However, with this war becoming increasingly hopeless and discredited, all this legal action was eventually abandoned; and, paradoxically enough, it was not until *after* the armistice in Vietnam that new legal proceedings were taken—but this time against non-Communists like Martinet and Roger Stéphane of *France-Observateur*—for the purpose of proving, as it were, that the French Army had not lost the war in Indo-China, but had been stabbed in the back by the left-wing press in France! It was an attitude strangely reminiscent of the Nazi myth that the German Army had not been defeated in 1918 but been "stabbed in the back" by the German Social-Democrats.

But it deserves to be noted that all these "Reichstag Fire" and "McCarthyite" tendencies began to manifest themselves very clearly for the first time in 1952, and became crystallized, as it were, round the seemingly ludicrous *affaire Duclos* with its carrier pigeons. It was the sharp reaction to these methods on the part of the French intellectuals which discouraged M. Pinay against going on with them; subsequent events—especially at the time of the *affaire Dides* in 1954—were, however, going to show that French "McCarthyism" had by no means abandoned the struggle. And again the battle was to be waged on two fronts—on the one hand, against North African nationalism, on the other, against the Communists and (this time even more so) against the non-Communist intellectuals.

The historical significance of the *affaire Duclos* naturally did not escape the attention of the Communists either. Duclos, while imprisoned at the Santé, made the most of it, particularly by writing a scathingly ironical letter to Vincent Auriol, the President of the Republic, in which he quoted with great gusto various "seditious" utterances made by Auriol at the time when he was still a militant Socialist, and warning him that if Brune and Martinaud-Déplat were allowed to get away with it, there would be no limit to their "McCarthyist" witch-hunt in future.

Both Aragon and Eluard broke into verse, Aragon writing some pungent lines in the manner of Victor Hugo's *Châtiments*:

> Si Louis-Napoléon disait le Deux Décembre
> Je suis le Président légalement élu

[13] The doubtful validity of this legislation is discussed at length by that prominent jurist, M. André Blumel in *Temps Modernes*, April 1953.

Le Traître-Maréchal communistes exclu
Avait aussi reçu l'assentiment des Chambres

Admirez leur amour de la légalité
Quand le Reichstag brûla Goering était ministre
Les Nazis CRS et sur un beau régistre
Le greffier inscrivit Dimitrov arrêté

Il faut bien ménager l'opinion publique
A défaut d'incendie on invente un complot
Et qu'il fasse enlever le Député Duclos
Monsieur Brune à son tour défend la République.

On a much higher level was the poem of Eluard, *A Jacques Duclos*, rendering something of the nightmarish atmosphere of the night of May 28, with the blood and violence at one end of Paris and the great Free-world "cultural" fêtes of the *Œuvre du XXᵉ Siècle* at the other end, complete with Stravinsky, the galas of the Quinzaine de la Rose, and the Nuit d'Elégance at Versailles:

Nos maîtres sont cachés dans la gueule des bêtes
Et le venin guette le sang
La misère et la guerre sont en plein soleil
Nos maîtres fêtent le printemps. . . .

Nos maîtres leur esprit s'envole vers les guerres
Folles de plus en plus abstraites
Où l'homme connaîtra qu'il n'est rien sur la terre
Que pourriture et que squelette. . . .

And, on the other hand, the Oppressed:

Ils savent qu'en Corée au Vietnam à Tunis
Leur semblables lèvent la tête
Ils se savent majeurs dans la famille humaine
Ils rient comme Beloyannis. . . .

And then this nostalgic, verbally exquisite ending:

Et ce printemps de lutte où la moitié du monde
Illumine l'autre moitié
Nous mène aux bords rêvés de notre éternité
Sans rien attendre que l'été
L'été comme un baiser à la clarté profonde.

This was almost Eluard's last poem; he died a few months later; its undertones of gloom and foreboding are unmistakable—despite the triumphant laugh of Beloyannis, the Greek Communist who had been executed at Athens two months before.

It was Picasso who, about the time of his execution, had drawn a striking picture of the laughing Beloyannis with a carnation in his hand.

4. THE IMPACT OF THE SLANSKY TRIAL AND THE MARTY-TILLON PURGE

So much for the "revolutionary romanticism" that burst into flower for a short time at the time of the Duclos Affair. One of the curious sequels of this was a return, by the French Communists, soon afterwards, to a more "moderate" line. Now suddenly they no longer identified the *whole* of the French bourgeoisie with American imperialism. This line, in contradiction with the famous Billoux article of the previous May, was put forward by Etienne Fajon.

Independently of this, however, the Communists' stock slumped heavily towards the end of 1952. There were many reasons for this. A serious crisis broke out inside the French CP, partly as a result of the Duclos Affair; and this crisis resulted in a "purge", of which two of the leading Communists, Marty and Tillon, were the victims. But, worse still for the French Communists were first, the Slansky Trial in Prague and secondly, soon afterwards, the hair-raising story of the "Jewish doctors" in Moscow.

In the anti-Communist press the old Koestlerian "Darkness at Noon" themes were taken up with great gusto; to these was now added the new theme of "Communist anti-semitism", which produced hoots of joy even from French quarters themselves notorious for their anti-semitism. The French Communists' attempt to argue that anti-Zionism and anti-Semitism were not the same thing did not fit all cases by any means. Intellectuals, who had staunchly defended the Communists at the time of the Duclos affair, were once again, as in 1948–9, perturbed by the purge inside the French CP, and the lurid developments in Prague and Moscow.

The Prague Affair was made particularly tangible by the fact that the wife of London, one of the men condemned to be hanged, had publicly asked that her husband be punished as a traitor; and she happened to be the sister-in-law of Raymond Guyot, one of the French Communist leaders. In the National Assembly on December 13, 1952, all hell broke loose when, challenged on this score, Guyot proceeded to defend his sister-in-law's behaviour, and read out the letter she had addressed to the Court:

After the arrest of my husband ... I believed that he was the victim of traitors trying to use him as a screen.... Alas, after the reading of the indictment at the [Slansky] trial, my hopes were shattered. My husband was not a victim, but a traitor to his Party and his country.

M. F. DE VILLENEUVE: Your conception of "country" is quite different from ours.

M. J. FONLUPT-ESPÉRABER: Really, we haven't got the same civilization.

M. FRÉDÉRIC-DUPONT: You had better send a copy to Mme Marty for her guidance. . . .

M. RAYMOND GUYOT: The letter then says: "It is a hard blow. A traitor lived in the midst of our family. . . . During the Occupation my father used to say: 'I am proud to think that my children are in prison for having been faithful to the Communist Party. . . . I would rather know they were dead than that they were traitors.' And now we see the father of my three children being tried by the People's Court as a traitor. I had to tell the two elder ones . . . I cannot, as a Communist and a mother but rejoice that, in the interests of the Czechoslovak people and of world peace, this group of traitors should have been caught, and with all other decent people, I say that the traitors you are trying should receive the punishment they deserve." (*Cheers on extreme Left; uproar on Left, Centre and Right.*)

M. ROBERT MONTILLOT: Magnificent!

M. R. GUYOT: And now you can have your spies and your traitors, and long live the Communist Party and the Communists of all countries! (*Uproar.*)

M. FRÉDÉRIC-DUPONT: You swine!

M. E. CHARRET: You should be ashamed of yourself, Monsieur Guyot.

M. J. FONLUPT-ESPÉRABER: Aren't you afraid of your wife?

M. DE VILLENEUVE: Don't you even realize what you are doing? You are a poor fish.

M. F. SAMSON: You are a bunch of slaves.

M. L. DELBEZ: We've never seen anyone sink so low.

M. DANIEL MAYER: Leave them; they are more to be pitied than to be blamed. . . .[14]

The Communists were acutely conscious of being fair game in the circumstances; as had happened so often before, they had to suffer for certain things that were happening outside France and outside their control; it was heavily taxing their party discipline. The contrast was too striking between Eluard's "*une moitié du monde qui illumine l'autre moitié*" and the sinister atmosphere of the Prague trial. But, if anything, it increased the spirit of defiance among the hard core of the Party; there were, soon afterwards, a number of French doctors (including a few Jews) who demanded the severest punishment for the Moscow doctors who had "murdered Zhdanov"; when later, after Stalin's death, the Moscow doctors were cleared, the French doctors, as consistent Party members, declared that "*at that time* we were right to demand their punishment".

It was always this aspect of the French Communists that made so

[14] *Débats, A.N.*, 1952, p. 6314.

many French intellectuals squirm. The Communist press, it must be said, was conscious of the distaste aroused by the Prague trial, and tended, if anything, to play it down.

The "purge" in the French CP in December 1952 can only be briefly discussed here. The indictment against André Marty and Charles Tillon by Léon Mauvais before the Central Committee of the CP on December 5, 6 and 7 runs into 60 closely printed pages; and it is impossible to discuss in detail all the charges of "fractionalism", opportunism, indiscipline, and *blanquisme* that were brought against Marty, the famous rebel of the Black Sea and chief organizer of the International Brigade in Spain, and Tillon, the Leader of the Francs-Tireurs-Partisans in the Resistance and later a minister in the de Gaulle Government. These two were, or had been, men of action who had dealt with revolutionary situations and revolutionary human material, and were temperamentally very unlike the Party bureaucrats. But a few points of the charges against them stand out very clearly:

Tillon and Marty were both guilty of "nationalist deviations", which had found expression in their critical attitude to Thorez and others who were in Moscow during the war. Tillon, in particular, had tended after the liberation to treat the Communists in the Resistance as the élite of the Party.

They had systematically underrated the decisive rôle played by the Red Army in the Liberation of France.

They had both toyed with the idea that in 1944 the Communists could seize power in France, ignoring the fatal effect this would have on inter-allied relations. Marty had also been severely opposed to the dissolution of the *milices patriotiques* in 1945, and had criticized the participation of the CP in the governments of 1944–7, thus displaying an irresponsibly romantic Blanqui spirit, which had been severely condemned by both Marx and Lenin as something alien to the class struggle; the line they had taken resembled that of "the traitor Tito", who also had blamed the French Communists for not having attempted to seize power in 1944.

Marty had also condemned the Soviet-German Pact of 1939 (though this was not discovered until later), and had been sceptical about the Soviet Union's chances of defeating Germany.

More recently, Marty had opposed to the World Peace Movement's campaign in favour of a Big-Five Pact his own "nationalist" campaign, merely against West-German rearmament; and had been guilty of allowing the leadership of the Movement (which was originally Communist) to become "diluted".

Marty and Tillon had undermined the principles of democratic centralism, the principle of "same discipline for all Party members", and had attempted to seize the leadership of the Party.

Marty's attitude at the time of "anti-Ridgway riots" of May 28 had been particularly suspect, not least because of his contact with Baylot, the Prefect of Police, who was a close friend of André Marty's brother, Jean

Marty; while Duclos was in prison, Marty had hoped to become the leader of the Party, and had sharply attacked Duclos for falling into a police trap.

The Central Committee (Mauvais declared) had shown a lamentable lack of vigilance *vis-à-vis* Marty's and Tillon's "fractionalist activities" during several years and the elimination of their nefarious influence was long overdue.[15]

It was well known that there had been disagreements between Thorez and Duclos, on the one hand, and Marty and Tillon on the other on a number of issues for many years past; why was all this being raked up now? And was not the story of Marty's "contacts with the police" a somewhat trumped-up charge which, however, strangely fitted into the atmosphere of crisis and suspicion in which the Communist parties of the world were living during those few months before Stalin's death, complete with Slansky Trial, Jewish doctors, and the rest? It is true that Marty was a particularly unsympathetic character, disliked inside the Party as a bully and disliked, more perhaps than any other Communist leader, outside, where many saw him through the eyes of Ernest Hemingway, who had (probably unjustly) depicted him as "the butcher of Albacete" in *For Whom the Bell Tolls*.

But all that can be said with any certainty is that the reasons for the elimination of Marty and Tillon from the CP were very numerous, confused, and even contradictory; and that what precipitated the crisis in 1952 were two things—the Duclos Affair and the worldwide "vigilance" campaign started by the Kremlin.[16]

In a book *L'Affaire Marty* that Marty published in 1955, after a three years' silence, he explained many of the fundamental disagreements that had existed for years between him and other Communist leaders. He denied ever to have favoured the "seizure of power" by the Communists in 1944; but admitted to have been profoundly disappointed by the line taken by Thorez in November 1944 when he placed the working-class in the service of de Gaulle, thus going contrary to the revolutionary spirit of the French workers. In the end, as was to be expected, the French workers were "duped". Similarly, he considered it a fatal mistake to have dissolved the *milices patriotiques*, the Liberation Committees, and all the other sources of "revolutionary energy" that the Resistance had created. Marty also criticized the

[15] Leon Mauvais, *L'Unite du Parti: rapport présenté au Comite Central du PCF, Dec. 1952*; also Leon Mauvais' article in *Pravda*, January 18, 1953: *Borba Fran. Kom. Partii za yedinstvo svoikh riadov.*

[16] The zigzags of Communist policy during that period were particularly baffling. One explanation given for the reaction against the Billoux line and a partial return to the *main tendue* policy was the new Stalin thesis of September 1952 on the imminent conflicts inside the Capitalist world and especially between the USA and its European allies, which made the "National Front" idea (in total opposition to the Billoux article) desirable.

"peace movement" for having neglected all serious "direct action", and for having salved its conscience by "collecting signatures", including "distinguished" signatures like J.-P. Sartre's—which, however, meant little to the working-class *militant* and had nothing in common with organizing an effective mass movement. He thought that the great strikes of the summer of 1953 provided the CP with a unique opportunity for exercising tremendous pressure on the Laniel Government, and for forcing it to accept many major political demands (such as the abandonment of the "monstrous" electoral system, with its *apparentements*) but that in this case, as in so many others, the French Communists had pursued a timid policy and had shown a deplorable misunderstanding of revolutionary tactics. Indeed, he suggested that they weren't really a revolutionary party at all.

In the light of Marty's book, the charge of *blanquisme* brought against him becomes more understandable than ever!

5. THE DECLINE AND FALL OF PINAY. RIGHT-WING ANTI-AMERICANISM

The Pinay "experiment" started well; but its premises were over-simple, and it was bound to fail. The biggest pillar on which it rested —the "gold loan"—was a failure, rather than a success, whatever some papers said to the contrary. Pinay had hoped that borrowed money could "replace" taxation to the tune of 650 milliard francs; although over 400 milliards were subscribed, the greater part of these subscriptions were made with "old" bonds, and only 195 milliards of "fresh" money entered the coffers of the State. Worse still, Pinay had hoped, by his spectacular "confidence" drive to unfreeze a large proportion of the hoarded gold, estimated at the colossal figure of 2,500 to 3,000 tons. All the gold that came out of hiding was—35 tons!

Thus the "amnesty" to illicit hoarding and tax evasion had been in vain, and three or four months after the beginning of the "experiment", it was obvious that the budget deficit had by no means been absorbed.[17] In the end, M. Pinay felt obliged to consider new forms of taxation, and at this stage his precarious majority disintegrated; after this had fallen to a mere handful of votes Pinay, without waiting to be overthrown, flew into a temper and resigned on Christmas Eve.

As Fabiani wrote in *Combat* as early as November 12:

The euphoria of the first months has vanished.... It is true that, up till

[17] The anti-Communist operation in May was expected to encourage subscribers to the loan; but in reality, it cut both ways; a fairly common reaction was to recall 1939 and to say: "If they have started locking up Communists, then they must think war is round the corner, and we'd better hang on to our gold."

now, the Assembly has supported Pinay for more or less dubious electoral reasons and under pressure of a public opinion which likes any man who promises it a golden age, with few taxes to pay. . . . But now even Pinay has let the cat out of the bag; his fiscal reform implies 200 milliards of new taxation. . . . The loan was *the* great remedy—but provided there were enough subscribers. The slowing-down in capital investments has created a slump in both home trade and foreign trade. Credit is tight and unemployment is rearing its ugly head in the engineering industry. . . . The book-keeping methods of a *petit bourgeois* of the reign of Louis-Philippe are useless in a changing world requiring much more complex methods.

The following may be said to have been the chief reasons for Pinay's downfall:

(1) Disagreement on the new taxation;
(2) a rapprochement between the "orthodox" Gaullists and the MRP, both critical of the economic stagnation the Pinay "experiment" had produced;
(3) the doubtful support he was receiving from the Radicals, and even the "Peasants" and "Independents" on the Right. The reason for this was that Pinay's drive for "lower prices" seemed to endanger certain agricultural interests, all the more so as his "liberalism", though welcomed for its "non-interference" in their own affairs, was reluctant, when necessary, to provide subsidies, price-fixing and customs protection.
(4) Pinay's tendency to talk to "the people" over the heads of Parliament; this was never popular at the National Assembly. (Doumergue had discovered this in 1934, and Mendès-France was to discover it again in 1954–5.)
(5) Conflicts inside the Pinay Government over foreign policy. The enthusiasm of M. Schuman, the Foreign Minister, for the European Army was very far from being shared by all his colleagues. Pinay himself seemed to have serious doubts on the subject, and the relations between him and his Foreign Minister, whom the MRP had "inflicted" on him, were known to be strained;
(6) last but not least, the growing scepticism of Big Business and the Inspection des Finances *vis-à-vis* Pinay's financial methods.

The international position of France in 1952 was a very curious one in many ways. In February, before the Lisbon Conference (while M. Edgar Faure was still Premier) there was a full-dress debate on re-armament and on the eventual "integration" of Germany in the European Army. The interminable motion passed at the end of the debate was a "white-nigger" masterpiece, full of provisos, conditions and reservations concerning the integration of Germany, which, nevertheless implicitly authorized the Government to sign the Paris-Bonn agreements subject to subsequent ratification. Although, in May, the "6" signed in Paris the European Army treaty, it was only too well realized that this treaty went far beyond the seemingly innocuous "Pleven Plan", and that a number of amendments and addenda would have to be agreed to before the ratification of the Treaty could even be considered by France.

Very striking at that stage was the contrast between the extreme "poverty" of the French Army in Europe and the big ambitions that Herr Blank and other Germans were already expressing. On June 12, Pleven announced that there were only 5 "full-strength" French divisions in existence, 5 in process of formation, and 2 "still to be created"; while the position of the Navy and the Air Force was even worse; it was clear that France could have no adequate armed forces in Europe, so long as the Indo-China war continued. This was strongly stressed in the same debate by M. Max Lejeune (Socialist) who said that at least one quarter of France's officers and NCO's were bogged down in Indo-China.[18] General Koenig (Gaullist) said that France had only "the shadow of an army in Europe", and that its drive and morale were very poor.

As against this, the West-German leaders were becoming extremely arrogant. Thus on June 18, almost immediately after Pleven's "confessions" on the wretched state of the French Army, Adenauer took a much tougher line on the Saar than he had promised Schuman to take; while Herr Blank, described in the French Press as "the future German Minister of War" gave a lecture to the students of the University of Bonn in which he said that Germany should have an army of 520,000 before long, and announced further plans for having 60 German divisions by 1960, with a budget of 20 milliard marks (i.e. a far bigger war budget than anything ever contemplated by France).

All this upset the French greatly. At the Radical Congress in October, M. Herriot reacted violently against German rearmament and solemnly warned France against "thoughtless negotiations" on the subject and against an attitude of fatalism or indifference.

The situation abounded in curious contradictions. On the one hand, there were "Europeans" like M. Schuman who still seemed to believe in "Europe"; but it always felt as if, on this question of "Europe", France and the USA were talking at cross-purposes. European federalism, of which the Coal-Steel pool was the first concrete expression, was what interested the French "Europeans" most; to the USA the primary aim of "Europe" was the constitution of a reliable land army within a short time, with the Coal-Steel pool as a useful appendix. If for at least two years this fundamental contradiction was covered up by words of Atlantic conformism by men like M. Pleven and even M. Schuman, something like a European rebellion broke out against this in 1952. As

---

[18] Not that this prevented M. Letourneau, on a visit to the USA at that time, from declaring that "any government that proposed pulling out of Indo-China would be overthrown immediately". It was also he who declared, some time later, that on no account would he ever negotiate with Ho Chi Minh.

Combat wrote on October 20, in connexion with the Radical Congress, where the European Army Treaty in its existing form was condemned:

The old Radical Party had clearly announced its refusal to accept German rearmament under the guise of a European Army which, after endless surrenders, was finally accepted by MM. Pleven and Schuman. It is doubtful whether the Bonn and Paris agreements will be accepted ... and one can only wonder how many months and years it will take before any agreement can be reached.

No wonder Washington is upset. The long-contained European rebellion has at last broken out against a revival of the Wehrmacht and its general staff. The trouble all along has been that instead of concentrating on a purely "European" Europe, we should have resigned ourselves to a Crusading Europe. ...

In this atmosphere M. Pinay decided to play for time. On October 22 he undertook, before submitting the Bonn and Paris Agreements for ratification, to try to secure an American guarantee, direct British participation in the European Army and the setting-up of a "political organization" of Europe—all of which obviously was a very long-term affair. Like the greater part of the country and unlike M. Schuman (against whom a strong campaign had been launched about that time both in Parliament and in the Press) M. Pinay was not in a hurry to see the European Army ratified.

There was something else. Aware of a strong wave of anti-American sentiment in France, Pinay made some political capital out of it (just as, for a time, he did out of the anti-Schuman agitation). We shall see presently how. For what were the chief causes of this anti-American feeling?

(1) The constant American pressure in favour of German rearmament;

(2) the support given by the Truman administration to Tunisia and Morocco at UN;

(3) American "recklessness" in Korea, where, more than a year after the opening of cease-fire talks, the American command thought fit to organize raids by 500 Superforts on the Yalu installations, thus not increasing, but reducing the chances of an early settlement;

(4) the "petulant" tone often adopted by the US Government in its dealings with the French Government, and the numerous "misunderstandings" over "off-shore" and other American aid to France;

(5) the implantation of American bases in France;

(6) the American way of looking upon France as a mere instrument in the hands of Washington in its cold war against Moscow.

But, as *Combat* rightly pointed out, "you cannot combine a hat-in-hand attitude with national dignity".

... and therefore, as was to be expected, American financial aid, though seemingly disinterested at first, has become for us an ever-growing burden. ... Our commitments have grown at the same time as American aid has shrunk. Our protests over the slowness of the "off-shore" orders, followed by an American Note which M. Pinay rejected as "inadmissible" merely puts a final touch to the picture. We have been reduced to the state of a satellite ... and all that certain people deduct from this is that we should ask for more and more "off-shore" orders, not realizing that this can only increase our dependence on the USA. (*Combat*, October 12, 1952.)

It is quite true that M. Pinay had "blown up" a few days before when an American Note was presented to him, not only discussing "off-shore" credits in a somewhat acid tone, but actually criticizing France's financial policy for its incapacity of making French multi-millionaires pay proper income tax, and also fixing the amount of money the USA was expecting France to spend under her war budget in 1953. Pinay "rejected" the Note as a piece of "inadmissible" inter-ference in France's home affairs, and—made himself remarkably popular in France, if only for a few days.

This sudden truculence was no doubt calculated. The North African Lobby, as ʾalready said, was up in arms against American "inter-ference" in Tunisia and Morocco, and practically the whole of the French press was ready to start off on an anti-American campaign if the encouragement given to the Tunisian Nationalists at UN by Mr Gross, the US spokesman was allowed to continue. Already right-wing papers like *L'Aurore* were asking who the Americans were to teach France how to treat the Arabs. "They exterminated the Red Indians, and look how they treat their negroes!"

For a time, this "rightist" anti-Americanism supplemented the more permanent "leftist" anti-Americanism which, in 1952, took the form of Bevanism (this aroused particular interest among the French left-wing intellectuals), and produced a revolt against excessive rearmament, which in Belgium actually forced the Government to reduce the term of conscription from 24 to 20 months.

J. M. Domenach in *Esprit* (December 1952) commented on these two brands of anti-Americanism, saying that the revolt against satelliza-tion and against the anti-Soviet Crusade was perfectly respectable, as was also the movement against the intellectual intoxication of France by American films, books, horror comics, and *Digests*. It was legitimate for France to feel that America was robbing Europe of her chance of acting as a mediating Third Force in the world.

But there was (he argued) a disreputable form of anti-Americanism, which screamed "What about the Negro problem?" simply so that no one should interfere with the ill-treatment of North Africans by the French themselves.

He also deplored the tendency among official persons like President Auriol and M. Herriot to embark on the slightest occasion on a song of self-pity, with hints to the effect that the Americans were not realizing France's past greatness and all her sacrifices in the two World Wars.... All this did not excuse sufficiently her industrial backwardness and her out-moded financial system, and it was only as a well-ordered modern indus-trial state that she could hope to keep a worthy place in the world....

Then a funny thing happened. Some people seem to have got scared by Pinay's anti-American outburst; and were determined to reassure the public that America still loved France. In the course of the Presi-dential Campaign a French radio correspondent was instructed to ask General Eisenhower to say a few nice words about the French. Which he did (Presidential candidates being always very voluble). But no sooner was Eisenhower's election victory proclaimed, than the record with his "pro-French" remarks was broadcast, with the clear indication that Eisenhower's very first thought, on being elected was to send a message to France!

This was a remarkably childish stunt, which was immediately shown up as a fake by the left-wing press.

Eisenhower's election victory was an important landmark in French post-war history. For one thing, throughout 1952 the French Govern-ments had played a waiting game over German rearmament, Indo-China and much else, on the ground that major decisions might just as well be postponed until after the Presidential Election. New policies would soon have to be shaped and even decisions taken more or less in accordance with the policy of the new American administration.

As already said, the very first result of Eisenhower's victory was one which the Right parties in France cordially welcomed: it was the end of Truman's "anti-colonialist" policy. Almost immediately after Eisenhower's victory, the North African French got tough. Ferhat Hashed, the Tunisian trade union leader, was murdered on December 4, and a few days later M. Boniface, the Strong Man of Morocco, delivered a crushing blow at the Moroccan labour movement at Casa-blanca. Meantime at UN France has refused to attend the discussion on Tunisia which opened before the Political Committee on December 4 on the ground that Tunisia was "outside the competence" of UN. The Arab-Asian complaint, tabled by the Pakistan delegate and favour-ing the termination of the Protectorate treaty, was defeated by 27 votes against 24 and 7 abstentions—hardly a smashing victory for France; but Mr Jessup, the US delegate had at least taken a more "pro-French" line than Mr Gross two months before; and this was important. In the end, merely a platonic expression of "confidence" was voted by the Assembly in France's efforts to "favour the effective development of the free institutions of the Tunisian people"; which really committed nobody to anything. A similar resolution was finally passed, a few days later, on Morocco. Britain and Belgium had been France's staunchest supporters throughout these discussions. M. de Hauteclocque (after a first abortive attempt a week earlier) extracted from the aged Bey on December 21 the signature of two decrees reforming the municipal and caidal system in a manner acceptable to the French. The Bey was threatened with deposition, and was told that his son, Prince Chedly, his daughter Princess Zakia and her husband, Dr Ben Salem (the three of them considered by the French as the "Resistance clique" at the Palace), would be immediately deported. The plane was ready to take off. The Bey submitted.

This "victory" in Tunisia really settled nothing; for the municipal elections a few months later were largely boycotted by the Tunisians; but it was treated at the time as a French *revanche* against the Bey, who had behaved in an "impudent" manner on many occasions throughout the year. It was high time he was put in his place.

It was the last victory of M. Pinay, or rather of the North African diehards in his Cabinet, MM. Martinaud-Déplat, Brune, Pleven, and de Chévigné.

A few days later M. Pinay resigned and was succeeded by a slightly less right-wing government under M. René Mayer. Tension did not relax in North Africa, but throughout 1953 attention became focused no longer on Tunisia, but on Morocco.

CHAPTER FIVE

THE BATTLE OVER EDC BEGINS

I. ORADOUR *versus* WASHINGTON

O N JANUARY 12, 1953, Adenauer said at a press conference:

The great factor in the present-day situation is the Oradour Trial. This trial will reveal all the details of this horrible business in the eyes of the whole world. We shall be told that the Waffen-SS, who merely obeyed orders, were responsible. But, believe me, this trial will revive in the eyes of foreign opinion the picture of a savage and bloodthirsty Germany. Unfortunately we Germans do not fully realize it.

It *was* a "great factor". Now that France's allies were preparing in all seriousness to tell the French to hurry with the ratification of EDC, there was in France a succession of trials and other incidents like the Finaly Case, which reminded anybody, who might have forgotten, of all the most bestial sides of the German occupation. And all this, in the eyes of the majority of French opinion, made the rearmament of Germany in any shape or form look untimely and incongruous, to say the least. It might be argued that it was only a "sentimental" and "emotional" reaction; but it was one which undoubtedly counted throughout, and especially in 1953. It was not perhaps a mere coincidence that the war criminals involved in these trials, and who had been in prison for several years, should have been brought up for trial just at this time.

There had already been two horrible trials at the end of 1952—that of the French Gestapo men who had worked in the torture chambers of the rue de La Pompe in Paris; and that of the two German professors who, in the camp of Struthof, had conducted experiments in human vivisection.

And then, on January 13, the trial opened at Bordeaux of the twenty-one members of the SS Reich Division who, on June 10, 1944, had taken part in the massacre of the 642 men, women, and children of the village of Oradour, near Limoges. It is unnecessary here to record the harrowing stories that the accused, more or less calmly told the Court—stories of how the village was surrounded by the SS; how the people were either massacred in their own homes, or machine-gunned *en masse* in the market-place, and how over two hundred women and children were driven into the church, where the massacre continued with the help of hand-grenades, and how straw and firewood were thrown over the bodies—many of them still alive—and how the church was then set on fire. The indictment, the admissions of the accused, and especially the evidence given by the handful of survivors who had miraculously escaped the massacre, but had seen and heard it from their hiding-places, certainly aroused a wave of anti-German feeling in France, the like of which had not been seen for some years.

And in the Limoges area there was intense feeling against the wave of protests coming from Alsace, where it was thought "intolerable" that the fourteen Alsatians (among the twenty-one) should be tried on the same basis as the Germans. The argument was that they were "*malgré moi*" SS-men, who had been "forcibly" incorporated in the Waffen-SS—only one was actually known to have joined the SS voluntarily—and as SS-men they "naturally" had to obey orders. There was very little sympathy in France with these arguments; none of the Alsatians at Oradour had shown any signs of shirking his "duties", and it seemed, to say the least, improbable that any Alsatians, unreliable from the Nazi point of view, would be allowed the privilege of joining this super-élite of the German Army. Yet this was precisely what opinion in Alsace would not allow to be assumed; and the danger of an Alsatian revolt, not so much in defence of the Alsatian SS-men, as against the assumption that they were no better than the German SS-men, was so great that the French National Assembly hastened to revise the 1948 law establishing "collective responsibility" in war crimes.

This did not, however, settle the matter. Although they were now being tried for their "individual" and no longer their "collective" actions, the Bordeaux Court still found it impossible to acquit the Alsatian SS-men. The only official volunteer among them, Boos, was sentenced to death, but of the "*malgré moi*" men, nine were sentenced to several years' hard labour, and four to several years' imprisonment. One of the Germans was sentenced to death, the rest to terms of imprisonment or hard labour.

The verdict certainly reflected the state of feeling at Bordeaux; but in Alsace it only produced a further uproar, and, on February 18, the National Assembly—though with nearly all parties sharply divided on the issue—hastened to pass an Amnesty Bill, which was (very reluctantly) endorsed by the Senate, in favour of the Alsatians (except Boos); at 3.30 a.m., immediately after the vote was known, the Alsatian SS-men were allowed to slink out of Bordeaux prison. In broad daylight they might have been lynched.

The municipality of Oradour refused the "*citation à l'ordre de la*

Nation", an honour which was included for it in the Amnesty Law as a consolation prize. And then there followed protests from Bonn against the "discrimination" against the German SS-men—which rather undermined the Alsatian argument.

All these complications over Alsace gave only additional publicity to Oradour and did not increase the desire to "forgive and forget"—and let Frenchmen and Germans rub shoulders in the same army. There was, indeed, a strong feeling in France at the time that the European Army project was as good as dead, that the mood in the country was overwhelmingly against it, and that there was no majority for it in Parliament, all the Communists, nearly all the Gaullists, most of the Radicals and many Socialists and right-wingers being against it.

After the Assembly debate on January 6 that had followed the investiture of M. René Mayer, the new Premier, the *Monde* published an editorial, entitled "Is the European Army Buried?", in which it concluded that it certainly was, as far as French parliamentary opinion was concerned. Only there was this snag: if France were to say so, there would be "a serious crisis in Franco-American relations".

The paradoxical aspect of the whole thing is that if, for a long time, the United States was opposed to an integrated army, it is now all in favour of it, with nothing to propose as an alternative.... This whole business of German rearmament, which was badly started off by Mr Acheson thirty months ago, seems to have reached a dead end. (*Le Monde*, January 8, 1953.)

The Mayer Government, it is true, went through the formality a few days later of "tabling" the Bonn and Paris agreements at the National Assembly, but with assurances to the effect that they would try to secure further guarantees from Britain and America, so that the European Army could be ratified by "the largest possible majority". It was quite clear that for the treaties, in their existing form, there was no majority at all; a point that was made doubly obvious on February 3 when both the Foreign Affairs Committee and the Defence Committee appointed two determined opponents of the European Army as *rapporteurs* of the ‍raft treaty—Jules Moch (Socialist) and General Koenig (Gaullist) respectively.

It was clear, all the same, that the new American Administration was in a hurry for its "European Army", and that it was going to get tough before long. Already at the end of January *Life* Magazine published a particularly vicious editorial, in which it treated the French National Assembly as "a bedroom farce", in which "Marianne—Zsa-Zsa Gabor" expects her American sugar daddy to slip another billion-dollar note down her stocking; but this jovial article ended on a menacing note: *Life* was calling on the French to remove that "Number 1 Obstacle"—their "political system"—which was standing in the way of the "unification of Europe". Just like that.

The fact that, in this matter, at any rate, the "obstacle" was reflecting the will of the French people was conveniently overlooked.[1]

The *Life* editorial rankled with M. René Mayer; for the first thing he said, on arriving in Washington nearly two months later was that "he had not come to ask for a billion dollars, but only to establish contact."

A few days after the *Life* editorial Mr Dulles, the new Secretary of State started on his career as "Europe's Bully No 1". He recalled that the USA had already spent thirty billion dollars in Europe since the war, and this money had been "invested" in the hope that Europe would achieve unity. But if it was found that France, Britain, and Germany were each to go their own way, it would be necessary to "give a little re-thinking" to America's policy in Europe.

In Paris this was interpreted as a threat either to build up the Wehrmacht again, regardless of France's desires, or (what was less likely) to adopt "peripheral strategy". It was also an admission on the part of the USA that it did not consider the European Army as being "in the bag".

The *Monde* urged M. René Mayer not to get flustered, and to keep to his promise not to consider the ratification of EDC until the Saar problem had been settled satisfactorily.

Looking over this and the subsequent period, until the final French surrender in 1955, we find that French foreign policy, with its rather tortuous line, can be roughly divided into the following stages:

First Stage. Modifying EDC

In February and March 1953 René Mayer and Bidault, both of them eager "Europeans", and apparently anxious to get EDC ratified in the end, considered that there was no chance at all of this unless the Treaty was substantially modified.

Hence the Mayer-Bidault visit to London in February (significantly enough, the first official French visit to London in the past three years), in the course of which they "submitted to Her Majesty's Government a certain number of ideas", including British technical co-operation with the European Army, the maintenance of British Forces on the Continent, etc, and some other measures that did not meet with much response from the British.

---

[1] To attacks of this kind there are invariably two sets of French reactions: on the one hand, the *Canard Enchaîné* type of retort, which is to embroider on the "bedroom farce" theme to the point of making the whole thing, and its original author, doubly ridiculous; and the—less usual—chestbeating reaction like Maurice Ferro's absurd "Open Letter" in the *Monde* (January 26, 1953) on the lines of "Oh, how can you forget what we did for you in your War of Independence! We gave you more than you have given us in Marshall Aid. We are fighting Communism, our common enemy, in Indo-China, etc, etc."

Hence also the French drafting of a number of "additional protocols" which were submitted to the other signatories of the EDC Treaty during the Rome Conference on February 20–1. M. Bidault explained that without the adoption of these "interpretive protocols", as he described them, the National Assembly would not ratify. After laborious negotiations, France received partial satisfaction on March 24, when a number of protocols (most of them were called "agreements") were initialled by the "6". On the Saar, however, very little progress had been made, and the National Assembly was scarcely more favourable to the ratification of EDC than it had been in January.

Moreover, what made this ratification even less likely now was the Russian "peace offensive" that had followed the death of Stalin on March 5,[2] and the possibility of an understanding with Russia on some new basis tended to put an additional brake on Ratification.

Second Stage. Linking EDC and Indo-China

To keep Washington in good humour (if possible) the French Government did not merely (as Belgium and Britain had just done) send its Foreign Minister there at the end of March, but decided that the Premier would go there himself, accompanied by Bidault (Foreign Minister), Bourgès-Maunoury (Finance) and Letourneau (Indo-China). The Government-inspired press said that Washington was "surprised but flattered" at the arrival of such a large French party.

Not that they had a good press in America; far from it. For one thing, the Government had just had to ask the Bank of France for a short-term loan of 80 milliard francs—a piece of pure inflation, which contrasted oddly with the Pinay myth of only a few months before.

But the importance of the Washington talks is unquestionable. The new US Administration now recognized more openly than before that the war in Indo-China was not a "colonialist" war, but part of the general war, "against World Communism". Whereupon M. Mayer pointed out to President Eisenhower that "additional aid to Indo-China would kill two birds with one stone: increase the number of Bao Dai troops in Vietnam ["Asians fighting Asians"] and strengthen France's land forces in Europe".

Eisenhower could not, at that stage, commit himself; Congress would have to be consulted. But the French Ministers left Washington with the pleasant illusion that the *guerre incomprise* (as Mayer had called it) was beginning to be "understood" by the United States, and that if

---

[2] The French Communists reacted to this with genuine emotion, which expressed itself at numerous mass meetings held throughout the country. In view of the more restrained mourning in Moscow, François Mauriac ironically compared the French Communists to mere acquaintances who go to a funeral, and weep more than the bereaved family.

As distinct from Britain, French public buildings flew flags at half-mast the day after Stalin's death. There were some protests from Right-wing deputies, but M. Herriot explained that this was a fitting tribute to an allied war chief who had greatly contributed to the liberation of France.

was financially advantageous for France, in the long run, to let this war continue. And throughout 1953, and almost until the final disaster of Dien Bien Phu, Letourneau and Dejean and General Navarre, and the rest of them continued to express their "confidence" in final victory "with American help". The Mayer-Bidault-Letourneau visit to Washington in March 1953 marked, as it were, the official beginning of this policy—and at a time when in France the outcry for ending the war was louder than ever.

Third Stage: Looking to Russia

During the NATO session in Paris at the end of April something very curious happened. Bidault, in a speech made at a luncheon on the first floor of the Eiffel Tower, talked about the blessings of disarmament and the need for German unity, but opposed the idea of an "armed but neutral Germany" (which Moscow had suggested in 1952). He also dealt with various other topics, but, oddly enough, did not breathe a word about the European Army.

Dulles, obviously dismayed, received the press the same evening, and exalted the virtues of the European Army, and again threatened Europe with a "re-appraisal" of US policy if there was no EDC. Bidault, a less fanatical "European" than Schuman and some other MRP's, apparently decided on that occasion, to play for time, and wait for the next Russian (or British) move.

His instinct proved right in this case: for a fortnight later came the famous Churchill speech of May 11 in favour of top-level talks with Russia.

The Foreign Affairs Committee of the National Assembly obviously welcomed Churchill's speech (apart from his advice that France increase her term of military service from eighteen months to two years), and passed a unanimous resolution in favour of top-level Four-Power talks, recalling that President Auriol had already proposed this at the UN session in 1951.

René Mayer, on the other hand, reflecting the cool reception given to the Churchill speech in America, made no reference to it at all in the long speech he delivered before the National Assembly on the following day. The Churchill proposal was, before long "diverted" by Eisenhower's proposal, on May 21, of a "preliminary" Three-Power conference at Bermuda, between him, Churchill and René Mayer. But alas! that was the very day on which René Mayer was defeated on a financial issue by the National Assembly, and resigned. The Russians, fearing a preliminary "gang-up" against them, took Eisenhower's plan for a Three-Power meeting very badly.

Fourth Stage. Interval

Between May 21 and June 28 France was without a government. The highlight of this crisis was the investiture speech of M. Mendès-France on June 4 implying drastic innovations in France's foreign policy. By a handful of votes he missed being appointed Premier.

Fifth Stage. The Ultimatum Stage

France was now back in the bog, with M. Laniel as Head of the new Government. In the main, Laniel pursued the old René Mayer policy, promising ratification of EDC as soon as humanly possible, and hoping for substantial help in Indo-China. At the long-delayed Bermuda Conference in December, the era of what might be called Anglo-American ultimatums to France was opened. The demand that EDC be ratified without delay became increasingly peremptory. The agitation against EDC in France became correspondingly more violent.

This stage included as an interlude the abortive Berlin Conference with Molotov in February 1954.

Sixth and Final Stage. The Cutting of the Gordian Knots

This was the Mendès-France era, in which decisions were at last taken on Indo-China, EDC and German rearmament. The decisions on Germany were taken in a spirit of fatalism and resignation.

The fundamental fact of all these tortuous negotiations spreading over nearly four years is that, despite assurances, promises and other ways of keeping the United States in an at least relatively good humour, all the French governments from the end of 1950 (Pleven Plan) till the actual rejection of EDC in 1954, knew that *at no time* was there a majority in the National Assembly or in the country, to sanction EDC.

If finally, in 1955, German rearmament was agreed to in a different form, it was only because of two years of ever-growing American and especially British pressure and threats, which, it was thought, could no longer be ignored. The heavy guns were first turned on France at the Bermuda Conference in December 1953.

Moreover, with H-bombs on both sides, the problem, as we shall see, was no longer quite the same.

2. TANGLE OF GRIEVANCES AND THE FALL OF THE RENÉ MAYER GOVERNMENT. THE DECAY OF GAULLISM

The fall of the René Mayer Government on May 21 was one of those things which are only too readily attributed in Britain and America to the "frivolousness" and "fatuousness" of the "French political system" or even of "the French character", and provoke remarks on the lines of "why can't they, like other countries, have a sensible two-party system?"

Yet seldom was there, in the whole history of the Fourth Republic, such a strong coalition of grievances which made the fall of the René Mayer Government inevitable.

It reminded one of Rochefort's famous gibe at Napoleon III: *La France a 36 millions de sujets, sans compter ceux de mécontentement.*

A few words should first be said on some of the outstanding events of the four and a half months of the Mayer Government—though not all had a direct bearing on its final downfall. First, there was the uproar in January over the Boutemy case, which continued to rankle with the Left and even with some of the MRP. M. Mayer had included in his Government a right-wing Senator, M. Boutemy, who was not only shown up as a man who had been a Prefect under Vichy, and one who had been closely associated with Pucheu, the ruthless Minister of the Interior, but who was also the *homme de confiance* of the Employers' Federation, and was known to have much to do with the distribution of funds and subsidies to certain right-wing parties. As "Pucheu's assistant" he was howled down in the National Assembly, called an *assassin* and finally forced to resign. The communists were the most abusive in their language; but their campaign against Boutemy was more or less openly supported by the Socialists, the MRP and others who had been associated with the Resistance. It was the first major revolt by the "Resistance" against "Vichy" that France had seen for a long time, and seemed like a belated reaction against Pinay, the first Vichyite premier of the Fourth Republic. Boutemy, coming on top of Pinay, was too much to swallow, "*Les Vichystes commencement à exagérer.*"

Without having any direct bearing on the fate of the Mayer Government, the famous *affaire Finaly* which continued throughout this period, and which created a particularly dramatic "anti-clerical" outburst of feeling, especially in some parts of provincial France, nevertheless also contributed to the general *malaise*. The case concerned two Jewish children, sons of Austrian refugees, who after the deportation of their parents by the Nazis in 1943, were saved and brought up by a Mlle Brun of Grenoble. In the ten years that followed, the boys grew up to be Frenchmen and devout Catholics. But meantime legal proceedings had been taken by the boys' Jewish relatives in Israel, who claimed to be their legal guardians; and their claim was confirmed by the French Courts. There followed what the anti-clericals called a "*curés'* conspiracy", complete with the defiance of the French Courts. The boys were smuggled out of France into Franco Spain, where they remained in hiding for several weeks.

Some particularly die-hard Basque priests had played a leading part in the "operation", and the Hierarchy of the French Church was placed in a very awkward position; for although many non-Catholics' sympathies went to the people who, at the risk of their lives, had saved the Finaly boys from being murdered at Auschwitz, and to the boys themselves, who clearly preferred to remain Frenchmen and Catholics, the case, nevertheless, developed into a trial of strength between the Republican Law and the *curés*. In the end, the hierarchy was obliged to intervene and propose a face-saving compromise, which nevertheless resulted in the boys being taken away to Israel. This painful affair created two simultaneous undercurrents of anti-clericalism and anti-Semitism in the country, and also added fuel to the blaze of anti-German feeling that the Oradour Trial had already caused. Indirectly, at any rate, it thus contributed to the anti-EDC feeling in the country.

The Mayer Government was considered to be in favour of EDC; Mr Dulles, on his return from his European trip, had expressed confidence in "Europe's" sincere desire to go ahead with it. Together with this EDC policy, there went the Mayer Government's undignified courting of "American goodwill", which assumed numerous forms, including another arbitrary and "well-timed" drive against the Communists. To coincide with the Mayer-Bidault-Letourneau visit to Washington, the well-known M. Duval, a judge at the Paris Military Tribunal (who had already distinguished himself in the case of Duclos and his "carrier pigeons", and who was again to distinguish himself in his handling of the *Observateur* affair in 1954–55) issued warrants for the arrest of André Stil, editor of the *Humanité*, Benoit Frachon, secretary-general of the CGT Trade Union Federation and several other Communists and CGT officials on charges of endangering the "external security of the State". (This, in most cases, again meant speeches or articles against the war in Indo-China.) As in the Pinay Government, so in the Mayer Government, M. Brune was Minister of the Interior and M. Martinaud-Déplat Minister of Justice.

At the National Assembly on May 13, M. Christian Pineau (Socialist), though by no means pro-Communist, protested against the kind of anti-Communism "which has no basis other than hatred, and the desire to curry favour with certain home and foreign interests". Among the Socialists, there was also a strong feeling after Mayer's Washington visit that he was dragging France deeper and deeper into the Indo-China bog. Also, there was some uneasiness over his handling of the explosive situation in North Africa.

But there were more direct reasons for the overthrow of the Mayer Government.

One was the serious crisis in the RPF. The split in the RPF at the time of Pinay's investiture a year before had already badly shaken the Gaullist Movement. The ordinary "conservative" elements in the country (the "classical Right"), who had rushed to de Gaulle for shelter in 1947, and a part of whom had still supported the RPF in the General Election of 1951, had since been largely won over by M. Pinay—or else simply did not see clearly any longer what de Gaulle was supposed to represent, positively or even negatively.

The municipal elections of April 1953 were as great a defeat for the

RPF as those of October 1947 had been a victory. While comparisons with 1947 are almost impossible to make (since, at that time, the "classical Right" was closely allied to the Gaullists), it may be said that, broadly speaking, the Gaullist vote dropped from over 30 per cent in 1947 and over 20 per cent in 1951 to a mere 10 per cent in 1953. In Paris only 10 Gaullist town councillors were returned, as against 52 in 1947; at Versailles, 2 instead of 18; at Marseilles, 4 instead of 25; at Lyon, 7 instead of 23, etc. Only at Lille and Strasbourg were their losses insignificant. All the other parties (except the Communists) gained at their expense, especially the "classical Right" and the Radicals. The Communists lost some seats, but very few votes. In industrial areas they were as strong as ever, though they lost some ground in rural areas.

De Gaulle, shaken by the *débâcle* of the RPF in the elections, thereupon washed his hands of the Gaullist deputies (who still represented a factor of considerable strength in the National Assembly), gave them "a free hand" in their future activities, and withdrew from them the RPF label. The RPF, he said, could no longer be associated with the "sterile régime" of the Fourth Republic.

M. Diethelm and M. Gaston Palewski, two of the leading Gaullists in Parliament took the line that, despite the "freedom" de Gaulle had "found it necessary to give them, at least for the time being", they should try to preserve "internal cohesion", and should do what they could to prevent the Assembly from being split into two blocs of Left and Right. Which meant, in effect, that they should make use of their peculiar tactical position for defending the country against the "social reaction" of the "classical Right," and throw in their weight, wherever necessary, to defend "the national interests of France". Although this position lacked precision, the URAS (*Union des Républicains d'Action Sociale*) as the RPF group now came to call itself, decided in effect not to identify itself automatically with any other party or any particular majority, and to treat problems like the EDC from a "national", and not any "party" point of view. On a number of points they saw eye-to-eye with the Socialists, as could, for instance, be seen from the applause they gave M. Daniel Mayer when, on May 12, he launched a general attack on the "reactionary" policy of the Mayer Government, which, he said, was "ruling not only without, but against the working-class".

M. Vallon, another Gaullist (who was soon afterwards to leave the RPF), attacked the Mayer Government a few days later for quite a different reason, after this Government had asked for extensive plenary powers in numerous fields: "We cannot give you these powers; for it means that the present policy will continue; and the final aim of this policy is the European Army".

But this was only one reason for the Gaullists' hatred of Mayer; they also resented the hostility shown to the RPF candidates by the Government parties in the municipal elections.

Paradoxically enough, Mayer had also made himself unpopular with his own supporters, who included elements in Parliament closely associated with important pressure-groups; for among the various financial proposals Mayer had put forward were new taxes on alcohol; a restriction of the privileges of the *bouilleurs de crû* (the four million tax-free home distillers); a new tax on road transport; an increase in the taxation of oil refining, etc. It was this extraordinary and often wholly incoherent coalition of grievances and criticisms that brought the Government down on May 21 by 328 votes to a mere 244. Apart from the Communists and Socialists, nearly all the Gaullists, as well as an appreciable number of "Peasants" on the Right, and even some right-wing "Independents", MRP's and Radicals voted against. Seldom had a Government been brought down for such a variety of general and specific, direct and indirect reasons. The country seemed ripe for some kind of New Deal; there was discontent over internal conditions and anxiety over all the pressures from outside, to which the Mayer Government was only too readily submitting.

The Cabinet crisis of May–June 1953 that followed lasted for over a month. Its highlight was the attempt by Mendès-France to be appointed Premier. He failed; and it is perhaps idle to speculate on what would have happened had he succeeded. Would the war in Indo-China have ended a year earlier than it did, and in much more favourable conditions? Would EDC have been rejected a year sooner? And if so, what would have been the sequel?

But apart from *the German problem which, in the end, proved in reality to be outside France's control*, it is probable that the great disasters that befell France in the next twelve months in Indo-China would have been avoided. And it is practically certain that the terrible blunders made in North Africa under the Laniel Government—notably the *coup de force* in Morocco against the Sultan in August 1953—would not have been made.

CHAPTER SIX

WHY MENDES-FRANCE FAILED IN 1953

T HE Cabinet crisis which lasted from May 21 to June 28, 1953 was unlike any other cabinet crisis in the history of the Fourth Republic. It is true that, at the end of it, France "slipped back into the bog again"—to quote a cliché used by a very large part of the press—and, indeed, by the man-in-the-street. But the impact of this crisis—or rather of its principal episode, the investiture speech of Mendès-France, the second of the candidates to stand for "election" to the Premiership —on the subsequent course of events in France is unmistakable. "Something new at last"; "at last an attempt to get us out of the rut", "a breath of fresn air"—these were phrases used, both at the time and afterwards, by editorial writers, by speakers in parliament, and so on. It was unfortunate for Mendès-France that the clause in the 1946 Constitution under which the "sovereign Assembly" appointed a new premier only if he was "invested" by a "constitutional majority" (of 314 votes, as it was in 1953) should have proved such an obstacle. This meant that the absolute majority of Deputies actually had to vote *for* him; and to be approved by 301 votes to 119, the rest of the Deputies abstaining (as happened in the vote of June 3) was insufficient. As a result of this seemingly absurd minor technicality, the Mendès-France "experiment" had to be postponed for a year. It is worth noting that even if the 100 Communists had abstained (which was the solution recommended at first by the progressistes, the small "fellow-travelling" group allied to the CP), Mendès-France would still have been thirteen votes short of the "constitutional majority".

It must, however, be added, that apart from that, the majority of the Assembly was not yet prepared to face the "era of decisions", which is what Mendès-France was proposing.

Mendès-France is one of the few outstanding statesmen whom France has produced in the last twenty years, and one who has shown greater technical qualifications, a higher all-round "culture" and a better mental grip of the economic and other realities of the moment than most; nevertheless, he has his weaknesses. Even in the remarkable investiture speech of 1953 he made, in the opinion of many observers, a number of psychological mistakes. For instance, he was much too vague on the crucial question of Indo-China, while on the equally crucial question of the European Army he adopted a "philosophical", middle-of-the-road attitude which both those favourable and those unfavourable to the European Army found somewhat disquieting. His ambiguous position made both sides hesitate.

The part of his speech devoted to France's economic problems was gloomy. He spoke of the "decline of France". The budget deficit in 1953 would amount to 1,000 milliard francs. Since 1929 production in the USA had doubled; in Britain and Western Germany it had increased by 50 per cent, and in France by only 8 per cent. In one year Western Germany had built 437,000 new houses, and France only 80,000.

Again he sounded the *leitmotif* of his speeches of several years past: "to govern is to choose". One couldn't do and have everything all at once. He hinted that social security charges would have to be adjusted, even though he emphasized that social security was "an essential element of progress"; military expenditure also was too high in relation to the national income, higher than in the other "Atlantic" countries.

Then came the vital passage on Indo-China. It was not like the spectacular offer Mendès-France was to make a year later, fixing a deadline for an armistice:

France [he said] is today using up in the Far East a large part of its human, material, and military resources. It means that we have correspondingly less in Europe.... At Bermuda we must impress upon our allies the fact that the Indo-China war is a crushing burden, which is sapping the strength of France. In the light of the general evolution of events in Asia, we shall submit to them a precise plan with a view to solving this painful conflict.

He added that he could not at that stage say more.

This was a mistake; his phrase was not a sufficiently clear repudiation of the policy (supported at that time by the MRP) in favour of "internationalizing" the war. After returning to economic problems, and saying that French economy must be "relaunched", through the development of the export industries and a large building programme, as well as through a general programme of capital investments, he turned to North Africa. This should receive a fair share of these investments; the problems there were economic, as well as political. While saying puzzlingly little about Morocco, Mendès-France foreshadowed reasonable negotiations with Tunisia on the basis of the "internal autonomy" principle, and a departure from the disastrous policy pursued since December 1951.

But the most important part of Mendès-France's proposals concerned foreign policy:

> Even if our allies are tactful enough not to stress it, we must realize that so long as France must count on foreign aid to meet her commitments, so long as two-thirds of the cost of her Army is paid for out of gifts from abroad; and so long as she wages a war in the Far East, half the cost of which is borne by the USA, she cannot properly pull her international weight. France's foreign policy will, in the last analysis, be determined by her internal reorganization. Secondly, we must, together with the other nations of Europe, which are faced with identical problems, look for common solutions.

He argued for the "closest possible association" in all matters between France and Britain, as regards both the organization of Europe and the establishment of close links between Europe and Britain's and France's "enormous overseas possessions".

And then came this brilliant, but somewhat ambiguous analysis of France's attitude to Germany and the European Army. It was like a philosophical analysis of a few fundamental features of France's position in the world, and of the French character, as it were. *Zwei Seelen wohnen ach! in meiner Brust....* The eternal conflict between international acquiescence and conformism on the one hand, and resistance to such conformism, resistance against German rearmament and the *pax americana* on the other.

Mendès-France did not put it quite that way.

> The European Army [he said] is one of the gravest present-day problems. ... But we cannot treat it merely on the strength of our preferences and our anxieties; we must treat it on the basis of facts which it is no longer in our power to change.
>
> There is in Eastern Europe today an important military force. It is also true that the rearmament of Western Europe is today in the interests of peace. One can argue about its extent... but no one among the National parties [i.e. outside the Communists] will deny that we must have the means of defending and consolidating peace.... It is also a fact that, in these conditions, the question of German rearmament, and of its nature and limits has arisen....

On this question, Mendès-France argued—a question which, he said, was a "painful" one for every Frenchman—the French Parliament had expressed its preference: rather than see a German national army revive, it preferred the creation of an international force including German units.

The trouble was, however, that once this principle of the thing had been repeatedly accepted by the French Assembly, the Allies had gone far beyond what France was willing to agree to.

As a result of long and complex negotiations, the treaties had now taken a form that had "little in common with what the French Parliament had considered as possible in the first place".

The next phrase suggested that the French Ministers who had taken part in these negotiations had been bamboozled and bullied into accepting far more than they had originally been authorized by Parliament to accept:

> That is the kind of thing that often happens in the course of international negotiations. . . . It would be dishonest on our part if we did not explain to our allies the grave apprehensions which the French feel about it. . . . The truth is that there isn't a single one amongst us who does not feel strongly divided on the subject. The division is not so much between Frenchmen, as in the mind and heart of each one of them. . . .

The programme Mendès-France was proposing fell into two parts: first, try to secure a variety of new guarantees from the Allies at the Bermuda Conference; and then let Parliament freely decide on whether these guarantees were sufficient. He undertook not to exercise any pressure on Parliament on that occasion, and promised that if the Government were defeated on the EDC issue, it would not resort to the dissolution of the Assembly.

The only party to support Mendès-France unanimously were the Socialists; on their behalf M. Dépreux declared that the Mendès-France speech was a "document of historical importance" which would always have to be consulted by any future candidates for the Premiership; it was also "like a breath of fresh air sweeping across our republican country"; he particularly welcomed Mendès's intention to resume reasonable negotiations with Tunisia.

Suddenly the Right began to fear that a left-wing majority might unexpectedly emerge: there was great anger and nervousness among the MRP diehards over Mendès's plans or potential plans for North Africa and Indo-China; de Gaulle, who—though no longer officially connected with the parliamentary Gaullists—was phoned up by one of these, General de Bénouville, at his home at Colombey-les-Deux-Eglises, and agreed that Mendès-France was personally "unsuitable", and that his views on North Africa and Indo-China were "disquieting".[1]

---

[1] *Le Monde*, June 6, 1953. It was later explained by Gaullists that if de Gaulle thought Mendès "unsuitable", it was chiefly because "he did not think Mendès had the guts to stand up to the Americans over EDC".

Most curious of all was the conflict among the MRP. On the one hand, M. Teitgen expressed his "intuitive anxiety"(!) over many of the things Mendès had said; M. Schuman was, in the main, hostile, though he agreed with Mendès about Tunisia; M. Letourneau "of Indo-China" was even more hostile, and so was M. Bidault, though he refused to say anything at the MRP meeting. In short, the men responsible for the pursuit of the Indo-China war and for the tough North Africa policy of the last two years were dead against Mendès; on the other hand, the left-wing of the MRP, which was in contact with the Catholic trade unions and favoured the re-entry of the Socialists into the Government, were pro-Mendès.

The final vote of the principal parties was significant:

	For	Against	Abstained
Communists and Progressistes	—	101	—
Socialists	105	—	—
MRP	52	2	29
UDSR	19	—	3
Radicals	68	—	6
Right (ARS—i.e. dissident Gaullists—"Peasants" and "Independents")	16	14	99
URAS (Gaullists)	25	2	52

Including the various splinter groups and *non-inscrits* the total of votes cast for Mendès-France was 301, and against him, 119; there were 191 abstentions, or rather 202 if one adds to the abstentions those who officially (like M. Schuman) "did not take part in the vote", a subtle distinction in French parliamentary procedure on which we need not dwell.

Strangely enough, as one looks closely at this vote, there was a kind of crazy logic about it; there were, in 1953, sharp divisions in Parliament over Indo-China and North Africa—and, apart from that, a vast amount of indecision and hesitation. Paradoxically, Mendès-France's own indecision on German rearmament seemed to be reflected in the large number of people who could not decide whether to vote for or against him. One widespread view was that even if he had been "invested", he would not have been able to form a government, and would (even if he had formed one) not have had a lasting majority, and that the purpose of his 1953 "entry" was merely for future uses and for future reference. This is not necessarily true.

Little need be said about the other abortive investitures during the five weeks when France was without a government. Before Mendès-France's attempt, Paul Reynaud had tried to be "invested", was flatly turned down by 295 votes against 274; after Mendès, Bidault tried, and failed by only one vote; the worst of the "also-rans" was André Marie, who collected only 272 votes; finally, out of sheer exhaustion, the Assembly "invested" a little-known right-wing politician, M. Joseph Laniel. He was a godsend to the caricaturists; he was heavy, slow and bovine to look at; he had the virtue of having been, as one of the less active members of the CNR, at least nominally associated with the Resistance. He was a Norman industrialist, who was said to be the third-wealthiest man in Parliament.

Quite wrongly M. Laniel was at first credited with being a very cunning Norman whose *peut-et' ben qu' oui, peut-et' ben qu' non* approach to negotiations might prove a great asset. In reality, he played his hand remarkably badly throughout his relatively long term of office; also, he was very unlucky. At the Bermuda Conference, which, after many delays, finally took place in December, Laniel was treated like dirt by both Churchill and Eisenhower; and by allowing his brother, an altogether absurd character, to be his principal canvassing agent when he decided to run for President of the Republic at the end of the year, he made himself and his whole family a laughing-stock. Earlier, in the summer of 1953, he had to deal as best he could with the interminable postal and railway strike that broke out at the height of the holiday season; and later in his career he had to face the infernal music of Dien Bien Phu; the terms of virtual capitulation he "dictated" at that time to Ho Chi Minh are sure to be included in any anthology of political cretinisms, of which a fairly good supply is provided by the leaders of the Fourth Republic.

In reality the bovine M. Laniel was, politically, an ox rather than a bull, and the men in his Government who called the tune were Bidault (Foreign Affairs), Pleven (Defence), Reynaud and Teitgen (Vice-Premiers), and Martinaud-Déplat (Interior)—the Old Gang with a vengeance. Their presence in the Laniel Government was like a very deliberate defiance of all the hopes and illusions created in the country by the sudden emergence of the Mendès-France phenomenon. The only prominent members of the "other" school were (more or less) Edgar Faure, the Minister of Finance, and (more definitely) M. Mitterrand (officially "Minister-delegate to the Council of Europe"). It was Mitterrand who rebelled against the policy pursued by the Old Gang in North Africa, and resigned from the Government on September 2, a fortnight after the overthrow of the Sultan of Morocco. Mitterrand had published, only a few months before, his book, *Aux frontières de l'Union Française* with a preface by Mendès-France, in favour of winding up the war in Indo-China and of adopting a politically liberal and economically constructive policy in North Africa, which, he argued, could by now have become "France's California" if only all the money hadn't been wasted in Indo-China. The Government, of which he was a member, was pursuing the diametrically opposite policy.

Perhaps the only positive achievement of the Laniel Government was the relatively skilful handling of its financial and economic problems by its Finance Minister, M. Edgar Faure, who consolidated, as it were, the stability of the franc and the cost of living—a stability which had become seriously endangered in the last days of the Pinay Government in 1952 and under the René Mayer Government in the earlier part of 1953. The capitalist system itself had become more self-confident than it had ever been since the Liberation. As in England and America, so in France there was in 1953 and 1954 a boom in stocks and shares; and a curious phenomenon of this period was the "catastrophic" fall in the value of gold, that peaceful haven to which investors would flee in days of uncertainty. Though due to a large number of internal and international factors for which Edgar Faure was by no means solely responsible, this phenomenon created for the first time since the war a situation in which industrial shares became unquestionably more attractive even to the most cautious than the unproductive hoarding of gold. Gold, for which fabulous prices (over 6,000 frs. per *louis*, i.e. nominally the equivalent of £15 or £20 for a gold sovereign) used to be paid in the years just after the war was now badly letting the hoarders down. Between June 1953 and December 1953 alone the gold *louis* lost a quarter of its value, depreciating from 3,900 to just over 3,000 francs. What facilitated M. Faure's task and stimulated "prosperity" was the prospect of ever-increasing American help to keep the Indo-China pot boiling.

CHAPTER SEVEN

MOROCCO IN THE HANDS OF THE HE-MEN

"I F ONLY..." is always a futile phrase in any historical narrative. Yet the temptation is great to say that *if only* Mendès-France had received those extra thirteen votes, the Sultan of Morocco might not have been deposed two months later. Perhaps those thirteen votes really were the "Cleopatra's nose" of Morocco.

Although Mendès-France was fairly precise about Tunisia, and extremely vague about Morocco, it is still scarcely conceivable, had he been able to form a government in June 1953, that he and his ministers would have allowed M. Boniface, the Strong Man of Casablanca, and El Glaoui, the Pasha of Marrakesh all the facilities that they were given by M. Bidault for fulfilling their long-cherished ambition of getting rid of the Sultan.

It is unnecessary here to discuss the establishment of the French Protectorate over Morocco in 1912, or the highly intricate international negotiations that preceded it, notably at the Conference of Algeciras; or the Agadir crisis of 1911, which nearly precipitated World War I. But it is useful to remember that if the outbreak of this war three years later cannot be regarded as anything other than a major disaster for France, it at least had the virtue of "confirming" France's sole mastery over Morocco (except for Tangier and the Spanish Zone in the North). Under the general leadership of Lyautey, the French rapidly gained control of what was then called *le Maroc utile*; and by 1924 they had (except for a few "unpacified pockets") also "pacified" the South and East. There followed, it is true, the Riff war of 1925–6 which, for a time, endangered France's position, but when this was over, France's control of Morocco became absolute and unchallenged—until the later stages of World War II.

To this day French school-books say that Lyautey was the great man who "made Morocco". But in the last few years, Lyautey had somehow lost his glamour in the eyes of the French settlers in Morocco and of the "hard" men in the French administration. For if the Left in France often criticized Lyautey in the past for always having sought the co-operation and support of all that was most conservative and traditionalist in the country, the French He-men in Morocco have lately tended to criticize Lyautey for having taken much too "generous" a view of the Protectorate Treaty, for having spoken against *administration directe*, for not having made it clear to the Moroccans that not they, but the French would run Morocco till the end of Time, and, above all, for having made the Sultan the centre and the rallying-point for a heavily-centralized country.

In April 1953 the quarrel round the name of Lyautey took on quite alarming proportions in Morocco. General Catroux, a man "reared in the Lyautey tradition", was going to give a lecture at Casablanca on —Lyautey, of all subjects! The He-men of Casablanca, led by the dynamic M. Boniface, the *Chef de Région* (i.e. Prefect) threatened to make things so hot for Catroux that General Guillaume, the Resident-General urgently cabled to Catroux firmly requesting him to cancel his visit. Catroux had shortly before written a number of articles in the *Figaro* in which he had argued that the policy pursued by the French in Morocco for some time (especially since 1948 when General Juin became Resident-General) was wholly out of keeping with "the Lyautey doctrine", and that since the Casablanca massacres of December 1952 France was heading for disaster. He emphasized the importance for France to come to terms with the Sultan, the temporal and spiritual head of Morocco. This kind of advice was the last thing the He-men of Casablanca wanted at a time when they were almost openly plotting to overthrow the Sultan.

What then were the conflicting forces in Morocco before the *coup de force* of August 1953?

As in the rest of the Moslem world, nationalism had made great strides in Morocco since the end of the war, or rather, since 1943. The influence of the Arab League was considerable (greater, indeed, in Morocco than in more "European" Tunisia); but what had perhaps encouraged Moroccan nationalism most of all were things like the Atlantic Charter and especially the assurances the Sultan had personally received from President Roosevelt in 1943. This meeting between Roosevelt and the Sultan had been arranged over the heads of the French, and Roosevelt had told the Sultan that the USA had every intention of encouraging the Moslem countries' progress towards *independence*—the most explosive word, the French thought, that could possibly have been used. To the French settlers and officials Roosevelt became Enemy No 1.

Until the landing of the Allies in North Africa, the French had indeed, "sat pretty" in Morocco. General Noguès, the "uncrowned king of Morocco" worthily represented Marshal Pétain.

If, after the war, the leading French personnel in Tunisia was predominantly "Gaullist", and in Algeria Radical-Socialist, in Morocco it remained essentially Vichyite. The authoritarian, "paternalist" attitude of Vichy suited the French settlers, officials and business interests best. And nothing suited them less than the encouragement given by Roosevelt to the Sultan and to the then still embryonic Moroccan nationalist movements.

The first important nationalist movement, which came into existence around 1943, was the Istiqlal, originally middle-class in composition, and with its biggest support coming from the shopkeepers of Fez, a centre of Moslem culture. But one cannot deal with Moroccan nationalism without taking into account a very important factor, peculiar to Morocco.

The country was in a state of economic boom ever since the end of the war. In 1945–7 important elements in the French business world, afraid of both home and Russian Communism, tended to look upon Morocco as a peaceful haven for private investments. There was a substantial flow into Morocco of both French and foreign investments, and a considerable number of Frenchmen went to Morocco during those years to get rich in a short time.

Hence, among other things, the "miracle" of Casablanca, which in 1953 already had a population of over 700,000, with magnificent parks and public buildings, still rather in the "African" tradition of Lyautey, and those dozens of skyscrapers, office-blocks and vast blocks of luxury flats, with rents higher than in the Champs-Elysées, which already belonged to a different stage of development. All this building in Casablanca, that capitalist Eldorado in its purest form, the opening of numerous factories, the development of mining in Eastern Morocco, and so on, all created a large demand for cheap labour. Hundreds of thousands of Moroccans, driven to Casablanca by hunger, but partly also by the glamour of this monstrous new city, lived there, in 1952–3, in appalling conditions of squalor, a large proportion of them in the *bidonvilles*, those thousands of hovels built out of tin cans (hence the name) and odd pieces of wood and corrugated iron.

The emergence of an industrial proletariat in Morocco marked the second stage of Moroccan nationalism, and it was the first attempts of this Moroccan proletariat to organize itself on trade union lines—with the help of some of the more "Europeanized" and progressive elements of the "older" nationalism of the Istiqlal, which in 1952 aroused the greatest anxiety among the French administration.

The French He-men of Casablanca had been hoping for a showdown for some time; and the "protest strike", called by the Moroccan trade union federation after the murder of Ferhat Hashed in Tunis on December 4, 1952, gave them the opportunity they had been waiting for.

The documentation and evidence assembled by the Paris Catholic weekly, *Témoignage Chrétien*, by *Franc-Tireur*, *l'Observateur*, *Esprit*, and authorities on the subject like Professor C. A. Julien of the Sorbonne and many others shows that if the "protest strike" developed into rioting, it was because this rioting was deliberately provoked by the French police. From the number of casualties it is indeed quite clear who wanted a showdown: four or five Frenchmen were killed and at least 400 or 500 Moroccans (some estimates at first put the figure as high as 1,200). The He-men of Casablanca had some good reasons of their own for wanting this bloodshed: it was necessary to nip in the bud not only an aggressive sort of proletarian Moroccan nationalism, but, above all, the development of a proper Moroccan trade unionism, which, like its opposite number in Tunisia, was beginning to receive every encouragement from the ICFTU.

The following notes[1] were written during a visit to Morocco in the spring and early summer of 1953, in the course of which I was able to see, among others, General Guillaume, the Resident-General (who was almost ferociously silent on the great political crisis that was then brewing, but was good enough to devote the *whole* 35 minutes of our meeting to explaining to me, with the help of an atlas, the latest irrigation schemes throughout Morocco!) and the top He-man of Casablanca, M. Boniface, who, on the contrary, was perfectly candid on how to keep the Moroccans in order, and on how desirable he considered the elimination of the Sultan.

When he referred to His Majesty as *un emmerdeur*, it was clear that Sidi Mohammed Ben Yussef's chances of a long and prosperous reign were very slender indeed.

It should be recalled here that Morocco had been, ever since the December riots, the subject of violent controversies in France, and that the supporters of a "liberal" policy—among them the *France-Maghreb* Committee which included M. Mauriac (who was the biggest thorn in the side of the French He-men in Morocco) were drowning by their loud protests the clumsy press campaigns orchestrated by the North-African Lobby. The French He-men in Morocco were becoming not only furious, but alarmed by the outcry among the French intellectuals, by the fact that Parliament was becoming more and more Morocco-conscious, and—worst of all—by the fact that Mauriac was "inflicting" his articles even on the usually so well-behaved *Figaro*.

Casablanca, April 1953

... M. Boniface, the "Prefect" of Casablanca makes no bones about having been tough with them in December. In fact he proudly claims full responsibility for having suppressed "the Communist-Nationalist riots".

I would not deny for a moment that I was impressed by M. Boniface. He looks remarkably like Marshal Juin. Like the Marshal, *il a de la gueule*,

[1] Some of this material was used in the author's articles that appeared in 1953 in *L'Observateur*, the *New Statesman and Nation*, and *The Nation* (New York).

as they say in French—a terrific personality, full of boisterous *bonhomie*, and superbly conscious of being invulnerable—whatever Paris had to say.... Was it not, indeed, to him that M. Robert Schuman recently alluded when he wrote in the special Tunisia-Morocco number of *NEF* that there were certain officials in key positions in Morocco who were so thoroughly backed by the vast financial interests on the spot that no French government could possibly get rid of them?

He started right away with an attack on Mauriac—who worries the die-hard *Français du Maroc* probably more than anybody else. "Very un-Cartesian", he said, "for a French writer to write on things he knows nothing about. Morocco, mind you, is a very complicated country. Damn it, I ought to know! I've lived here since the age of six. I speak Arab, I speak Berber. *I* know what I'm talking about.... They call us 'colonialists' —well, let them. But the fact is that the Moroccan people admire us and love us—yes, *love* us."

He went on in his exuberant way:

"We've done wonders here. It was quite a medieval country when we first came. Morocco in 1912—of course, it had its charm. People were friendlier in a way; but they fired guns at you.... Now Morocco has been surrendered to civilization. We've stamped out banditry and malaria, and people have started thinking for themselves. We don't mind that; it was part of the programme. But it's still a very backward country, and one can't go too fast—least of all with Moslems. Of course, we'd like to send a million Moroccan children to school, and not just 200,000. But one needs time and money. Even so, in 1912 they had *nothing*—no schools, no hospitals, no roads, no telephones—not a damned thing, and we've managed all this despite two wars we've had to fight ..."

"And the Sultan?" I ventured to interrupt.

"*Ah, celui-là, c'est un emmerdeur!*" said M. Boniface quite bluntly. "He ought to stick to his women and his menagerie and his monkeys and things; that's much more in his line than mucking about with politics and fancying himself a sort of Führer! He's ambitious, and keeps pestering us with his so-called reforms; in reality his prestige in the country is very doubtful...."

And then came the favourite divide-and-rule argument:

"The Berber South doesn't think much of him. The religious Fraternities throughout the country think him a bad *chérif*. Large sections of the population in Morocco are opposed to 'totalitarian Moslemism' and prefer to worship their local saints. It was we who created the central authority of the Sultan; but Morocco is still deeply divided; we don't have to 'divide and rule'; the country *is* divided—quite unlike Tunisia in this respect."

"And the Istiqlal, *Monsieur le Préfet*?"

"*C'est rien. C'est zéro.* A few half-baked intellectuals with wishy-washy ideas about Western democracy and the French Revolution. The Moroccan people despise them—yes, *despise* them. They picked up a few ideas from the Communists, and off they went trying to cause trouble among the proletariat of Casablanca. Also tried to set up Istiqlal cells all over the place; didn't amount to much. Of course they were encouraged by the Sultan. Young people spouting slogans, waving flags—a lot of nonsense. A crazy press, too, going in for blackmail and intimidation. When they started their nonsense in Casablanca we had to put our foot down firmly—very firmly. We had no right to be weak. We've got to defend ourselves."

The country was full of immense possibilities, M. Boniface concluded, and it wasn't the Istiqlal who were going to interfere with the great work that was being done.

It was a revealing talk. Play off the Berbers against the Arabs; encourage the feudal lords of the South and the reactionary and most obscurantist religious "fraternities" to gang up against the Sultan—and depose him, if possible—was not this M. Boniface's—and not only M. Boniface's—major ambition? And so preserve the *status quo*—at least for as long as possible.

... A very pleasant young man of M. Boniface's staff took me in his car round the *bidonvilles* to show me where and how the Riots had started. He agreed that the *bidonvilles* were "pretty horrible". We then looked at some of the new "garden cities" which will eventually absorb the whole of the *bidonville* population. "We are certain that in three or four years' time there will not be a single *bidonville* left in Casa," he said.

... Mauriac rankled with him, too; but he spoke of him more in sorrow than in anger.

"Now," he said, "if Mauriac had published his reflections in some philosophical review—well, it wouldn't have been so bad—but to publish them in the *Figaro*—*which everybody in Casa reads*—no really! Why, doesn't he realize that there are many good Catholics in Morocco, and that they might get *demoralized* by his sob stuff about our 'Christian duties' to the natives! It's really a form of sabotage!"

*   *   *   *

Rabat, April 1953

The more I see of the French in Morocco, the more do I feel that they are like a different race. "We are dynamic here," they will say, "we are no sticks-in-the-mud as they are *dans la Métropole*...."

In France, especially in provincial France, where life is slow, people will sometimes wistfully say that France is an old and tired country, and not a great power any more. No such feelings of humility and resignation among the French in Morocco. They are buccaneers, they are thugs—but many who are not mere speculators and profiteers are conscious of being Empire-builders, and of having "made Morocco"—with French brains, French money, French technicians.... "Why! the French are quite unrecognizable —nothing *vernegert* about them here," said a German visitor—obviously an ex-Nazi—to a French official at Rabat recently; and this official repeated the remark to me with a smirk of satisfaction.

The Frenchmen in Morocco most hated by the *indigènes* and despised by the *fonctionnaires* with a sense of "mission" and by the efficient French technicians (these are, if not liked, at any rate respected by the Moroccans) are the "spivs", the real-estate speculators and boom profiteers who came here in large numbers after the war. They behave disgustingly to the natives, and their women-folk even more so. In general, French women behave much more objectionably to the natives than do the more responsible of the men....

*   *   *   *

Up on the hill, in the beautiful *Résidence* quarter of Rabat—a whole city of sumptuous white villas, which is the administrative centre of Morocco—I have had numerous talks with French officials; and I found that most of them were—or at least sounded—a good deal more "reasonable" than the fire-eating Boniface. They readily admitted shortcomings; they thought "native" wages were too low, and said the Residence was having to fight a stiff battle against the reticence (a nice euphemism!) of certain employers! Of course, there were only 200,000 Moroccan children at school, instead of 1,500,000—but it took time to train teachers. In time *all* children would go to school; the situation, with all due respect to the Arab League, was much less bad than in Pakistan or Egypt or Iraq. "Quite a number" of young Moroccans went to French *lycées,* and there were 350 Moroccan students in France.... It wasn't true that the French settlers had taken *all* the good land—they had taken just "ordinary" land—and improved it; not more than 20 per cent of the arable land, anyway.... The hardest of all problems was to get the small peasant to improve the methods of cultivation and to increase his output per acre; the peasants tended to breed too many bad-quality animals which ate up everything, including young trees, but not strong enough to pull a metal plough; hence the tendency to stick to the old wooden plough which tended to cut the harvest in half; it was a vicious circle.... But gradually they were learning and irrigation was making rapid progress. Only the Moroccans weren't in the habit of administering *any-thing*; "We asked a year or two ago the local Moroccan authorities to organize the proper registration of births and deaths; after several months of complete confusion we had to take over, using the Moroccans merely as a screen.... What added to the muddle in the towns was that about half the parents of new-born infants wanted them named after the two most popular Egyptian film stars!"

*   *   *   *

Since Eisenhower's victory the USA has no longer been giving any encouragement to Arab nationalism; one theory is that the Casablanca riots played into the hands of the French, who screamed as loud as they could about the menace of Communism which they (the French) were alone capable of checking.... Washington was impressed.

The Americans (officially only 17,500) at the four huge American bases in Morocco lead an isolated kind of existence—except for trips to the bars and *dancings* of Casablanca. Only they are very cagey; all that goes on at Nouasseur and elsewhere is highly secret, and French airmen I met told me that contacts with the Americans were practically nil. "They are believed to have an atom bomb at Port-Lyautey, but nobody's seen it!" And these airmen rather took the de Gaulle line that, with these Moroccan air bases, France had given away far too much for nothing.

*   *   *   *

The Sultan had not been receiving any visitors, since his mysterious "accident" some days ago. But his proposals, as outlined to me by Prince Moulay Hassan, are on the following lines:

It would be disastrous if the French suddenly left, leaving the country without technicians, police, or administrative *cadres*. But time limits should be fixed: what about say, 25 years for the progressive introduction of Home Rule? Steps should meantime be taken to train Moroccan *cadres*.

French economic interests could be fully guaranteed. Meantime, however, the French had proposed nothing except a few "fragmentary" reforms. A beginning was required, with the recognition of the principle of free elections, freedom of assembly, association and the press, to begin with. After that the Elected Municipalities Reform should be brought about.

In the French towns, where the French have special economic interests, the municipalities could, *during a certain period*, be elected on a parity basis (50 per cent Moroccans, 50 per cent French); but not, as the French would have it, in all localities. The French should abandon their practice of appointing their stooges everywhere. The Sultan also had plans for recasting the whole legal system on more "European" lines, which would take legal power out of the hands of the *caids*, now nearly all French stooges.

The Sultan's greatest nightmare was co-sovereignty—the root of the trouble in Tunisia; he was against Frenchmen—except as Moroccan citizens —sitting in any future Parliament; nor was he favourable to a half-French, half-Moroccan government (Tunisian model). He was in favour of an all-Moroccan Government, assisted by French technicians. (In fact, the very opposite of the present purely ornamental Maghzen, with its grand Vizir, etc, subscribing to the decisions of the Resident-General.

Similarly, the Sultan is in favour of "complete trade union freedom"; but the French will only consider trade unions with a half-French, half-Moroccan governing body.

On these and other points there has been a long conflict between the Sultan and the French. At present the French are monopolizing practically all the key positions in Morocco; but, more important, *they are also aiming to perpetuate their presence in any "new" Moroccan institutions that may be created.* The Sultan, on the other hand, while trying to "colonize" the present institutions with Moroccans, is endeavouring, at the same time to agree only to the formation of new institutions from which, within a "reasonable" time, the French could be eliminated altogether.

Needless to say, the French don't like it, and Prince Moulay Hassan thought it quite possible that his father would be deposed, not officially by the French, but ostensibly by the good "Old-time Conservatives" like El Glaoui, El Kittani, "the grand old man" of the Karayouine University at Fez, assisted by all the more obedient Pashas, caids, and other French stooges. These "saintly" and "conservative" elements disapprove (or so the French say) of the Sultan's "unorthodoxy" and "modernism" and of his daughters having discarded the veil.

*   *   *   *

Marrakesh, May 1953

There is no place in Morocco tourists love so much as the Djemman-El-Fna, the great square in front of the native city of Marrakesh. At nightfall the square is crowded with story-tellers, beggars, snake-charmers, acrobats, jugglers, pimps, open-air barbers, and pastry cooks; what a symphony of screeching, guttural noises and colours and stinks! The "native" quarter, with its labyrinth of narrow lanes and thousands of miserable little shops and crowds of veiled women, and its donkeys (the shrill bicycle bells alone add a modern touch to the scene), is filthy and sordid in the extreme; and the large Jewish part of Marrakesh is filthier still. "How do all these shop-keepers manage to live?" I asked one of the few "progressive" Moroccans I could find at Marrakesh. He told me a long story of almost unbelievable misery and disease and human degradation. French doctors were doing their little bit to help; but not nearly as much as in the "Sultan's part of Morocco". Here they did not have to bother. The people were backward, ignorant, and passive. The caids and the sheiks (local officials) were levying pretty well whatever they felt like levying on the peasantry ("no wonder a lot of them try to escape to Casablanca—even to the *bidonvilles*—where they are not much worse off than at home"); but so long as there was no active opposition to the feudal order in the South, and so long as El Glaoui, the aged Pasha of Marrakesh continued to rank as "France's best friend", there would be little hope of improved conditions in the South. Already, in Casablanca, I had heard from a prominent Moroccan lawyer the story of how he had been literally driven out of Marrakesh on direct orders from the Pasha's palace, because he was going to get married in Marrakesh—with the bride not wearing the veil. It was an intolerable provocation to "all the traditions of the Berber country". The Pasha, he said, could, at his own exclusive discretion, lock anybody up for three months—without any right of appeal.

This is the kind of thing against which the Moroccan nationalists have been rebelling. Lyautey's policy was, indeed, to unify the country under the authority of the Sultan; the present French tendency is to stress the differences between the Arab part loyal to the Sultan and the Berber part where the Sultan "is not really recognized". The display of the Sultan's portrait in shops is virtually prohibited at Marrakesh. It has, indeed, been part of the French colonialists' policy to seek the support of all that is most reactionary, obscurantist and "veiled" in the country.

*   *   *   *

Casablanca, June

The Istiqlal has, more or less, gone underground. It is not allowed to publish any papers, and of its six principal leaders three are in prison, one has been deported (*"éloigné"*) and two are abroad—one in Egypt and one in New York. The French say that 400 people are in prison; the Moroccans say 4,000. Nevertheless, at Fez, which is the "middle-class" stronghold of the Istiqlal, I found people extremely agitated. There were sporadic pro-Sultan demonstrations; there was the Sultan's picture in most shop windows, and all over the place his portraits were being sold.

*   *   *   *

Casablanca is still haunted by memories of the December "riots". *La Vigie Marocaine* and other *colon* papers worked the Europeans up into such a panic that these lost their heads completely, and after the trade union meeting of December 8 proceeded to beat up and lynch any Moroccans they could see coming from the meeting. A particularly ugly story, which has not yet been fully told.

*   *   *   *

Trade unionism is in fact right in the centre of the Moroccan conflict. What the French authorities fear most is the creation in Morocco of a *native* trade union organization, on the lines of the Tunisian UGTT—all the more serious in Morocco where industrialization is making much more rapid progress than anywhere else in North Africa. It was no accident that the people who had gone to the trade union meeting on December 8 should have been treated with particular savagery.

What are the French afraid of? The Moroccan trade union federation is a branch of the CGT, controlled in France chiefly by the Communists. In Morocco, however, the Istiqlal were gaining more and more control of the trade union movement; and, according to Moroccans well inside the movement, the Istiqlal were planning, at the proposed meeting in February 1953 (this, in view of what had happened, never took place) to eliminate the French and Moroccan Communists from the governing body of the trade union federation and to give it an exclusively Istiqlal board. Not only that—but to apply for membership in the ICFTU (International Confederation of Free Trade Unions), which is eminently "respectable" from the American point of view. The CIO and AF of L belong to it; and so does the Tunisian federation.

This was obviously the last thing the French authorities wanted, and not only have they denounced the Istiqlal for its "collusion" with the Communists, but, in demanding that there should be no trade union federation in

Morocco without a 50 per cent French membership on the board, they are in fact, demanding that there *should* be French Communists at the head of any Moroccan trade union, so that the "collusion" between Communists and Istiqlal may, willy-nilly, be perpetuated! Anything, in short, to prevent the Moroccan trade unions from becoming "respectable" in American and Social-Democrat eyes.

Alternatively, other French interests simply prefer to authorize something in the lines of Vichy's *syndicats d'entreprise*, incapable of any sort of policy or mass action whatsoever.[2]

*   *   *   *

These notes, written two or three months before the overthrow of the Sultan, explain the background of this extraordinary operation. What then were the next steps taken by El Glaoui and his French friends—the most powerful among them being Marshal Juin, M. Boniface, and the big men of the North Africa Lobby, among them M. Martinaud-Déplat, the Minister of the Interior in the Laniel Government?

First, the people on the spot organized the collection of Pashas' and Caids' signatures for a Petition demanding that the Sultan be deposed. This operation was not entirely successful. Several of the Pashas declared their loyalty to the Sultan, while numerous Caids wrote to the Sultan to explain that they had signed the petition under very heavy pressure from the French authorities.[3]

Actually the names of these signatories were not published at the time. Moreover, the Oulemas—i.e. the "learned men" who elect the Sultan—in July almost unanimously supported Sidi Mohammed Ben Yussef.

But El Glaoui and the He-men were not to be discouraged. The Pasha of Marrakesh, who had attended the Coronation in London as a guest of Mr Churchill's, went to Paris in July, where he received further encouragement from Marshal Juin who, in his speech before the French Academy, said that El Glaoui "personified loyalty to France in Morocco".

Meantime the ground for a final showdown had been carefully prepared in Morocco, and on his return there on August 6, El Glaoui

[2] These notes do not make it quite clear that there are also some genuinely liberal Frenchmen in Morocco who have maintained friendly relations with Moroccans, particularly with the intellectuals amongst them. Such liberal Frenchmen constitute, however, only a minority, and are *mal vus* by the authorities.

[3] These letters were to be shown by the Sultan to the French deputy, Pierre Clostermann on August 11. It was he who on that day carried the Sultan's last letter to President Auriol, in which, in a final attempt to save his throne, he not only condemned the "reactionary extremism" of the Glaoui, but also "the revolutionary formulae of the Istiqlal". (*Cf. L'Observateur*, August 27, 1953.)

issued a proclamation against the Sultan. Two days later, in General Guillaume's absence, the Résidence published a statement declaring its "neutrality" in the conflict between the Sultan and El Glaoui.

Encouraged by this, El Glaoui, back at Marrakesh on August 12, called a "supreme council of Pashas and Caids", and summoned from Fez his candidate for the Throne, the aged Sidi Mohammed Ouled Moulay Arafa, whom he was proposing to "nominate" Sultan on the following day.

On August 13, General Guillaume returned to Morocco, with instructions from the French Government to "put a brake" on the Glaoui's ardour—but "without using violence against him". The Resident phoned El Glaoui, asking him to "postpone" the nomination of the new Sultan; he next went to Rabat where he presented the ruling Sultan with a sheaf of decrees, typed on Résidence notepaper. The Sultan observed that this was quite out of order; General Guillaume replied that it was no longer any use being fussy about little things like that; there was no time to lose. He promised, however, that if the Sultan signed, the Glaoui would be "kept in order". After thinking it over, in what appears to have been a very emotional atmosphere, the Sultan signed the decrees, "for the ultimate good of his people"— even though he was now signing reforms which he had always refused to sign before. The seals were to be affixed on the following day.

Now, the Sultan's surrender was what suited El Glaoui least of all. Guillaume knew this, and hastened to Marrakesh to ask El Glaoui for a further delay. He was joined there on the following day (August 14) by a representative of M. Bidault, M. Vimont, a Quai d'Orsay official. The question that was discussed for several hours by El Glaoui, Guillaume and M. Vimont was no longer whether Sidi Mohammed Ben Yussef was to remain Sultan, but whether he was to be succeeded by his second son, the eighteen-year-old Moulay Abdullah, or by the Glaoui's candidate.

At this stage a new trick was resorted to; a motley collection of "caids and notables" assembled at Marrakesh, issued a proclamation saying that the Sultan could remain the temporal head of Morocco, but, since he was unfit to remain its spiritual head, they appointed Arafa the new "Imam", or spiritual head.

Hearing of this, the Sultan refused to affix his seals to the decrees he had signed the day before. At Casablanca the news of the "Imam operation" provoked serious rioting; and the even more severe rioting at Oujda that night caused twenty-six deaths.

The Glaoui, made impatient by the signs of hesitation the French Government was showing, now decided to force the pace. He threatened the French that if they allowed Morocco to fall into a "state of anarchy", they would be the first to be eliminated. How close the collusion was between El Glaoui and big French capitalist interests may be seen from the fact that this "anti-French" statement was made to the diehard *colon* paper, *Le Petit Marocain*. This "warning" was followed up by an old trick, already used in 1951 by General Juin; the famous "Berber horsemen" appeared in the neighbourhood of Rabat.

General Guillaume, who had gone to Paris to receive instructions from the Government, landed in Casablanca early in the morning of the 20th. His instructions were to secure the abdication of the Sultan and his replacement "either by his younger son or by Arafa, the Glaoui's candidate". The Glaoui, who was waiting for General Guillaume at Casablanca, naturally pressed Arafa's claims, and after the meeting, declared himself "fully confident" in the Resident-General. At noon Guillaume phoned Bidault, and three hours later, several cars, preceded by a tank, emerged from the Imperial Palace of Rabat on their way to the airfield. In the last car sat the Sultan and his two sons. A Dakota flew them to Corsica where they arrived as "guests of the French Government".

At Fez, surrounded by troops and police, an assembly of "oulemas and notables" elected the new Sultan on August 21.[4]

It is obvious from the above brief summary of the main stages of the Anti-Sultan Operation that the French Government had, by and large, given a free hand to El Glaoui and the He-men. It is true that M. Faure and M. Mitterrand protested from time to time against the way the whole Moroccan affair was being handled; but the He-men had M. Laniel (with business interests in North Africa), M. Pleven, M. Martinaud-Déplat, and M. Bidault (who, as Foreign Minister, was directly responsible for Morocco) on their side, even though at first Bidault was nominally opposed to what he called a "pronunci-amento" and had even sent instructions to Rabat to that effect. But it is obvious that he did not seriously expect his instructions to be followed.

What helped the He-men was (*a*) that the summer holidays were in full swing in France and (*b*) that the great postal and railway strike was at its height; everybody, including the members of the Government, had other fish to fry. When the *Comité France-Maghreb*, with M. Mauriac at their head, called on M. Laniel to warn him against the dangers of El Glaoui's machinations, they were given a cool and non-committal reception.

---

[4] This day-to-day account of the "operation" is based on the information published in the papers known for their good sources in North Africa, particularly *Le Monde*, *L'Express*, *L'Observateur*, *Témoignage Chrétien* and *Esprit*. Most of these are "anti-colonialist"; but the "colonialist" papers merely suppressed all unpleasant facts, and are therefore worthless as sources of information. An excellent sample of the "colonialist" point of view is provided by the above statements made to the author by M. Boniface.

No doubt the Quai d'Orsay had some qualms about the whole thing; what was being done at Marrakesh was thoroughly irregular in the light of France's precise obligations to the Sultan; hence Guillaume's half-hearted attempts at a "compromise" solution. But Bidault had in reality been won over by the He-men, and seems at one stage to have got himself into a "mystical" frame of mind, if one is to judge from the remark he is said to have made in a dreamy tone of voice to M. Clostermann, the Gaullist Deputy, who had just brought a letter from the Sultan to President Auriol: "No, I cannot allow the Cross to be defeated by the Crescent." It did not matter if the Cross was represented by M. Boniface, Big Business and the Glaoui! And later, when it was all over, Bidault is reported to have said: "How can we punish people who have succeeded so brilliantly?"

Of course, they succeeded "brilliantly". In an atmosphere of police terror, the "oulemas and notables" elected the new Sultan: the vague term "notables" obviously covered numerous people who had no business to be there at all, since the oulemas alone normally elect the Sultan.

There is no doubt that the Operation, which finally resulted in the overthrow of the Sultan, had received the fullest support from the greater part of the French business interests in Morocco, as well as from many influential groups in Paris. Among the strongest supporters of the "firm hand" in Morocco was Marshal Juin, who was widely believed to have done most of the wire-pulling, and to have been the real power behind the *coup*. It is significant that in a speech delivered at the French Academy only a few weeks before the Sultan's overthrow, Marshal Juin should have gone out of his way to praise the Glaoui and to launch a particularly vicious attack on his own fellow-Academician, M. François Mauriac. As the developments of the next few weeks were to show, the sword proved mightier than the pen.

No sooner had the new but senile Sultan been enthroned than he proceeded to sign away everything. Thus, on October 15, the docile old man affixed his seal to a decree reforming the old Council of Government, making it entirely elective instead of partly nominated; its two equal sections, one French, the other Moroccan, were henceforth to sit together.

This was precisely the type of reform, perpetuating the presence of the French in Moroccan institutions, which the deposed Sultan refused to sign on the ground that he could not buy elective institutions at the price of destroying the principle of Moroccan sovereignty, i.e. by allowing French citizens to participate in Moroccan parliamentary life.

The Council of Government, it is true, was no more than a consultative body, but the same principle was involved.

As the *Manchester Guardian* put it, with a nice touch of irony:

In the new Council of Government it seems probable that the French will generally be able to dispose a majority since some at least of the Moroccan delegates will be elected in part of the country where the Administration can, as is the practice in Algeria, dispose the seats. (*MG*, October 16, 1953.)

Several other reforms, consecrating the principle of co-sovereignty (such as the creation of a Council of Vizirs and Administrative Directors, another half-French, half-Moroccan body) were passed.

For a time it looked as if the He-men had successfully pulled off a brilliant operation, by turning Morocco into a plain Colony—with nothing more to worry about—at least not for a long time. In Paris, to discredit Mauriac and his *Comité France-Maghreb*, which had so staunchly backed the ex-Sultan, a major smear campaign was organized against the latter. Far from being a great progressive and liberal, or a sort of Moroccan Kemal Pasha, he was represented as a sadist and sex pervert of the worst sort, who had tortured many people to death in the horrible "dungeons" of his Palace. Even the near-Communist *Libération* came out with all kinds of funny stories about the Sultan's 75 concubines, 25 of whom had decided to "choose freedom" after the Sultan's deportation, while the rest were left on the hands of the unfortunate French officials, who didn't know what the devil to do with them.

As for Morocco, the reaction to the overthrow of the Sultan was violent at first only in spots—notably at Oujda. A wave of arrests throughout Morocco accompanied the enthronement of the new Sultan; and, for a short time, all seemed "peaceful" as often happens after a stunning defeat.

But already some weeks later, warehouses in Casablanca began mysteriously to burst into flames, and "collaborators" were being stabbed in the street; a bomb was thrown at the new Sultan himself, and during the two years that followed, a minor civil war was waged between French and Moroccan "terrorists". The editor of the diehard *Vigie Marocaine* was murdered; an attempt was made to assassinate M. Boniface; Moulay Idriss, one of his stooges, was murdered; similarly, the French extremists murdered not only many prominent Moroccans, but also some Frenchmen who were too "liberal", and tended to fraternize with "the enemy". In June 1955 French terrorists assassinated M. Lemaigre-Dubreuil, the owner of *Maroc-Presse*, an adventurous and legendary figure in the history of French North Africa,[5] who had,

---

[5] Lemaigre-Dubreuil, representing a big capitalist interest like the *Huiles Lesueur*, had played a leading part at Algiers in 1942 as a member of the "Weygandist" resistance against the Germans. He had taken part in "preparing" the US landing. He tells his story, under the pen-name of "Crusoe" in *Vicissitudes d'une victoire* (1945).

however, in the last few years, conducted, both in France and Morocco, a vigorous campaign for a more humane and liberal policy.

POSTSCRIPT: DECEMBER 1955

The amazing *dénouement* of the Moroccan drama already belongs to a new era, and the story can only be briefly told here. In July, 1955, M. Edgar Faure, determined to put an end to the growing chaos and bloodshed, appointed M. Gilbert Grandval, the former French High Commissioner in the Saar, Resident-General in Morocco. Grandval drew up a programme of liberal reforms, and advocated the abdication of the Sultan Arafa and his replacement by a representative Regency Council which would, in due course, settle the problem of the Throne. Grandval, treated as a "Mendès-France nominee", met with ferocious hostility from the He-men, who, on two occasions, all but lynched him.

Then came the terrible August massacre of dozens of French civilians (children included) by Moroccan tribesmen, and "counter-massacres" of Moroccans by French troops and the Foreign Legion. The situation got completely out of hand, and, under the pressure of General Koenig and other Right-wing members of his Cabinet (working in close agreement with the French generals on the spot), M. Faure recalled Grandval, and appointed General Boyer de Latour (former Resident-General in Tunisia) in his place.

At this point the "generals' rebellion" became even more apparent. Encouraged by the North Africa Lobby and by the French settlers' association, *Présence Française*, they continued to ignore the orders coming from Paris ("only the political orders, not the military orders", Marshal Juin was later to argue); and they also won over the new Resident-General who, instead of deposing Arafa and creating a Regency Council, merely arranged for Arafa to leave "provisionally" for Tangier, without abdicating or even handing over his seals to anyone except a vague cousin.

With an ominous armed rising having by this time started in the Riff, the danger of the whole of Morocco becoming a scene of carnage and civil war (with even the "faithful" Berbers suddenly also beginning to clamour for Ben Yussef) was immense.

It was then that the most spectacular *coup de théâtre* took place. A Regency Council of sorts had by this time been set up, but one that satisfied nobody. Suddenly it received the visit from El Glaoui, who announced that he did not recognize this Council, but that he now wished to submit to "the will of the Moroccan people", and desired the exiled Sultan Sidi Mohammed Ben Yussef, to return to his Throne. To this day there is some doubt as to El Glaoui's real motives in this spectacular *volte-face*: had he lost confidence in the French being able to hold Morocco? Had he been influenced by the Americans who, with their important bases in Morocco, did not want to see the country go to rack and ruin? Or finally, did he think that the alliance of the "two richest men in Morocco" (he and the Sultan) could counteract the revolutionary forces that were gaining in strength and momentum?

Ben Yussef (who, in the "liberal" days of Grandval, had already been consulted by General Catroux, on behalf of the French Government, about the Regency Council) was promptly brought back to France from Madagascar—where he had lived in exile for two years. Here M. Pinay, the Foreign Minister, literally *begged* him to return quickly to Rabat, especially now that Arafa (taking the Glaoui's lead) had, by this time, duly abdicated. The Glaoui himself was received by Ben Yussef (now proclaimed Sultan once again), and, lying flat on the ground and kissing his feet, the 87-year-old Pasha of Marrakesh begged his master's forgiveness, and said that "he prayed to the Almighty that He punish

CHAPTER EIGHT

A SMALL WORKING-CLASS VICTORY—WITH
LASTING RESULTS. HOW HIGH ARE
FRENCH WAGES?

Many British holiday-makers who went to France in the summer of 1953 will remember how they were stranded there without mail, without money, without means of transport. For suddenly, in the first week in August, at the height of the holiday season and of the *congés payés* a strike broke out which, with its snow-ball effect, practically paralysed the country within a few days. It all started among the Force Ouvrière postmen at Bordeaux, who decided to protest against some of the "economy" decrees prepared, almost surreptitiously, by the Laniel Government at the height of the summer holidays, and no doubt in the hope that nobody, at that time, would make a fuss. The decrees, calculated to save a few milliard francs, "reclassified" certain categories of postal workers, slowed down their promotion, delayed their retiring age, and showed, altogether, a re-markable disregard for the wretched condition of the lower ranks of the postal service. The fact that nearly two milliard francs a day were now being spent on the *sale guerre* in Indo-China made it even worse.

It was a spontaneous strike movement, that had started among the rank and file; and it spread from Bordeaux to other big cities, and, within a few days, the whole postal, telegraph and telephone service in the country came to a standstill. The Force Ouvrière leaders, impressed by the vigour of the strike movement, as well as the Catholic CFTC Federation, and the Communist CGT thereupon all gave the strike their blessing. The strike spread to the railways and to a large number of other public services, as well as to many private and nationalized industries. By August 12 nearly three million workers were on strike.

The strike had started essentially as an economic strike; but, before long, it acquired a political aspect. The Socialist and Communist Deputies, joined by a small number of MRP members, demanded that

---

all those who had deceived him". Who were they—Juin, Bidault, Boniface?

This concluded the insane "operation" of August 1953. Hundreds of French lives and thousands of Moroccan lives had been lost in vain. Whether the Glaoui-Sultan alliance will help the French to maintain themselves in Morocco, at least in some minor capacity and will also act as a brake on the revolutionary forces in the country, remains to be seen. But it may already be said that the "operation" of August 1953, which was to make the French sole masters of the country, has proved a short cut to that independence of Morocco which, in 1953, the Sultan was still willing to achieve "by stages" over a period of twenty-five years.

(See pp. 622–3 and Postscript, pp. 726–30 on the complications that followed Ben Yussef's triumphal return to Rabat.)

the National Assembly be called, expecting that, with the strikes continuing, the Laniel Government would either capitulate to the strikers or be overthrown.

It was at this point that one of the strangest bits of parliamentary hanky-panky was started. Since M. Herriot, the President of the Assembly, was unwilling to take any steps to call an extra-sessional meeting, it was for one-third of the Deputies—i.e. for not fewer than 209—to demand this reassembly in the midst of the summer recess. But how were they to communicate with the President of the Assembly, in the absence of a regular postal service? Those opposed to the re-assembly argued that telegrams (which, in exceptional cases like this, *were* transmitted) could not be taken into consideration, since they did not bear the sender's manuscript signature. In short, all kinds of subter-fuges were resorted to in order to prevent the fatal number of 209 written demands from being reached. Nevertheless, it looked at one moment, when the strikes were at their height, and when M. Laniel could already see himself surrendering to the strikers all along the line, that the figure of 209 "regular" demands was about to be attained. It was then that the MRP came to the rescue of M. Laniel: two of their leaders, M. Lecourt and M. Colin proposed to M. Laniel the following deal: in return for some assurances to be given to the non-Communist trade unions, they would persuade several MRP members to withdraw their demands for the reassembly of Parliament. This operation suc-ceeded in a few cases, but not in others, some of the more "socially-minded" MRP members, notably M. André Denis, flatly refusing to withdraw their signatures. By this time the calling of the Assembly seemed inevitable: 212 demands had already reached the President; but no! the majority of the *bureau* that examined them decided that four of the letters received from Communists had not been signed by them-selves. By 10 votes to 8 and 3 abstentions (including M. Herriot's) the *bureau* decided to invalidate the 4 letters, thus reducing the number of demands from 212 to 208—just *one* short! (As if the 4 Communists, even if they had, for some purely extraneous reason, been unable to sign the letters themselves, would have repudiated their Party's decision!)

It was by methods like these that the Laniel Government spared itself the unpleasant task, in August 1953, of having to answer awkward questions about the strikes which it had provoked, and—worse still—about the exceedingly strange things that were happening at that very moment in Morocco!

To keep the "comfortable" Laniel Government in office, and to be able to complete their Moroccan operation (as described in the last chapter), the MRP leaders assumed the rôle of strike-breakers. With a few concessions and by means of political pressure, they persuaded the leaders of the CFTC to break the unity of action among the three federations (Catholic, Communist, and Socialist) which had been so characteristic of the August strikes. Later, the FO were also admitted to the negotiations between the Government and the Catholic trade union leaders; but not the CGT.

The position taken up by the CGT leadership was very curious in these strikes of August 1953. While encouraging the rank and file to strike, the CGT leaders remained in the background, so much so that it was, at one stage, almost possible to speak of "a predominantly Communist army led by Socialist and Catholic generals". But after these "generals" had more or less surrendered to the Government, the CGT leaders saw no alternative to calling off the strike, if only in the name of "rank-and-file unity". As shown in a previous chapter, Marty was later to criticize the Communist and CGT leadership for having sacrificed a first-class opportunity for political action to the myth of rank-and-file unity; he argued that, with a little more dynamism shown by the Communists, the others would not have dared to call off the strike, and the Laniel Government might have been compelled by the strikers to agree to major reforms, including a revision of the electoral system and the abandonment of the *apparentements* (which, in itself, would have implied that the strike had become Communist-dominated). But it seems clear that, whatever the "Blanquiste" Marty thought, the Communist leadership in 1953 were not in a mood for embarking on a major political strike—not after their unhappy experiences of 1947 and 1952, and not with Russia depending primarily on France to hold up EDC. To the Communist leaders this was not the time for a major showdown on domestic issues.

Besides, is it possible to speak of the strikers' "capitulation" to the Government? It is true that if the strike had lasted longer, and the chiefs of the CFTC had not allowed themselves to be influenced by the MRP leaders, the strikers would probably have received much better terms than they did. But the wage increases during the next few months —some of these could be attributed directly, others indirectly to the strikes—show that the strikes of August 1953 were not a defeat for the strikers—though they could scarcely be called a major victory.

Without going into the details of the numerous wage agreements that were negotiated during the months that followed the August 1953 strikes, it is sufficient to say here that there was undoubtedly an improvement—though not a spectacular one—in working-class conditions during the latter half of 1953 and 1954.

Thus, according to the tables drawn up by the *Comptes Economiques de la Nation*, and published by the Conseil Economique on December 22, 1954, there was, as a result of the 1953 strikes, a certain increase not merely in wages, but also in *real* wages.

	Average money wages	Average real wages	Minimum real wages
1949	100	100	100
1950	106	95	99
1951	137	105	114·4
1952	161	112	115·3
1953	164	114	116·6
1954	174	121	135·0[1]

Estimates made by groups of employers, the Ministry of Labour, and the CGT do not seriously challenge these calculations. But, in the opinion of the CGT, the basis of the whole calculation is misleading, since 1949 was a year in which wages were lagging particularly far behind prices. Nor, as we shall see, does the CGT accept the inclusion in any estimate of the working-class's "wage level" the benefits derived under social security.

By and large the August strikes proved to be an at least partially successful reaction against the tendency to keep wages frozen at the 1952 level, whereas production and profits had not been frozen at that level by any means.

Politically, one of the results of the partial victory of August 1953 was greatly to reduce labour unrest during the next two years, when, among certain categories of wage-earners a certain material (though not necessarily political) *embourgeoisement*—complete with TV sets and Vespas —could be observed on an appreciable scale in France for the first time since the war.

Whether this relative prosperity will, in the long run, weaken the Communists is another matter. Mendès-France tends to look upon economic prosperity as the best remedy against Communism; but other factors also count: class-consciousness, the revolutionary tradition, and the ability—and the desire—of post-Stalin Russia to maintain among the French Communists an interest and belief in world Communism.[2]

---

[1] These overall figures, it is true, do not demonstrate numerous anomalies—such as certain exceptionally high wages in the engineering industries, sometimes as high as 100,000 frs. a month, or, at the other extreme, the fact that an unmarried *fonctionnaire* in Paris was paid in January 1955 only seventeen to twenty-one times as much as in 1938, whereas the franc had depreciated to nearly one-thirtieth of its pre-war value. Nor do the above figures demonstrate another phenomenon: the more rapid increase of women's wages than of men's wages; ever since the Liberation, there had been a growing tendency towards equalization, and if, in 1946, the discrepancy between men's and women's wages was 15 per cent, it was only 6·2 per cent in January 1955.

[2] The spectacular apologies made by Khrushchev to Tito and Titoism in May 1955 shook many French Communist intellectuals at first almost as much as the German-Soviet Pact of 1939 had done. It looked to many (at least for a few days) as though Stalinism was being replaced by something the contours of

All the same, was the working-class as a whole becoming noticeably more prosperous?

It will be remembered that, in the earlier parts of this book, dealing with the inflationary period of 1944 to 1951, there were frequent references to the constant race between prices and wages, with wages always lagging far behind, despite the periodic readjustments of the minimum wage and the wage level generally.

What, in reality, was the French level of wages in 1955, compared not with 1949, but with 1938?

An important all-round discussion on the subject was opened by the French Communists and the CGT in the first half of 1955, and numerous non-Communist experts joined in this discussion. What started the ball rolling was an article by Maurice Thorez in the March 1955 issue of the *Cahiers du Communisme*, in which he tried to show that the Marxist rule of "growing pauperization" fully applied to the French working-class—"not only", he said, "is there a relative impoverishment in relation to the national income, but an absolute impoverishment, i.e. a real decline in their standard of living".

In present-day France [Thorez wrote] *hourly wages*, generally speaking, are equal to only half their pre-war purchasing power. If the total volume of the proletariat's purchasing power is somewhat higher than one-half, it is because of the more extensive use made of labour. . . . But wages represent only 30 per cent of the national income today, as against 45 per cent before the war.

Even allowing for longer hours worked in the Paris engineering industry (45 hours a week instead of 39 in 1938) Thorez argued that the workers' real incomes had fallen by 38 per cent. This calculation

which were still hard to distinguish. If the German-Soviet pact was an understandable tactical move, did not Moscow's praise of the Yugoslav leaders go beyond mere tactics? How could it be reconciled with the seven-years' opera, *Tito the Bandit*, in which the French CP had conscientiously sung so many of the grand arias? No one was taken in by the clumsy excuse that "it was all Beria's fault".

If, on the other hand, it was a piece of "cold realism" in the international setting of 1955, then it was presented in a manner that was cruder than anything that had been done in the Stalin era.

And yet, many French Communists, while feeling that the "all-Beria's-fault" formula was a remarkably unfortunate way of turning the Tito-Stalin conflict into a love-all match, nevertheless reflected that it was, perhaps, after all, only a "convention" which nobody was expected to take literally, and that the end justified the highly surprising means. "If the bourgeoisie sniggers, let it snigger; on balance, it's Russia—and Communism—that gain." A number of local by-elections which took place after Khrushchev's Belgrade performance in June 1955 at any rate did not show any decline in the French Communist vote.

was based on the assertion that hourly wages had multiplied only 20·5 times, and prices 32·5 times.

The weak point of this argument was the figure of 32·5. Even the CGT had, in various documents, put the increase in prices not at 32·5 but at 30 times, while the Institut National de Statistique (though working on a somewhat doubtful basis, since the cost-of-living-index was calculated differently in 1938 and since 1949) put it at 25 times. The Comptes de la Nation, on the other hand, accepted the figure of 27. If one accepts this—more probable—figure, then the real income of a Paris *métallo* would not be 38 per cent but only 20 per cent below pre-war.

But overall statistics published by the Ministry of Labour showed that if the 20 per cent decrease in the real weekly wage income of the Paris *métallos* was probably correct, the overall decrease in the real wages paid throughout the country was only 13·5 per cent.

These figures, however, concern only actual wages; but what about social security? According to an inquiry by the Institut National de la Statistique in October 1953, an unmarried worker was earning only 18·4 times as many francs as before the war, while a married worker with five children was earning 36 times more; which meant that the one was much worse, and the other much better off. But the CGT has consistently refused to treat social security benefits as part of the wage-income.

Even wider than the disagreement in France on the cost-of-living index is that on the share represented by wages in the national income. Thus, a report presented by M. Georges Delamarre to the Conseil Economique in 1954 claimed that wages *plus* social security benefits showed an increase from 51 to 55 per cent of the national income between 1938 and 1954; he admitted, however, that "direct" wages had shown a drop from 48 to 43 per cent in the national income, but claimed that social security benefits, old age pensions, etc, had risen from 3 to 12 per cent.

A weighty argument used by the CGT against this calculation is that while the total amount of direct wages and social benefits paid is known almost to the last franc, the incomes of practically all other groups in France are much less well-known; this is true of shopkeepers, professional people, the peasantry and also of joint-stock companies, whose share in the national income is often calculated merely on the basis of declared profits, and not on the reserves put aside, the amounts going into *auto-financement*, not to mention concealed profits.

The question, therefore, whether the process of not only the relative, but also the absolute "pauperization" of the working-class in France could still be observed in 1954–5 is not an easy one to answer; and even inside the CGT a minority, led by M. Le Brun, and including a number of Communists, was not in entire agreement with the Thorez view that there was not only relative, but also absolute "pauperization" among the French working-class.

In their attempts to estimate the actual standard of living, observers have come across various favourable and various unfavourable symptoms: in the case of some working-class groups a tendency to spend more on luxuries like TV sets, Vespa scooters, etc, and to eat more expensive food (more meat and dairy produce and less bread); or, in the case of other groups (or sometimes even of the same groups), the tendency to spend less than before the war on clothes and, in view of the housing shortage, to put up with extremely bad (and sometimes, though by no means always) very cheap housing.[3]

Housing is a particularly sore point, at any rate with a minority of the working-class (and particularly with the Algerian proletariat and "sub-proletariat", now numbering nearly half a million in France) who, without the advantages of a pre-war house with a controlled rent, have sometimes to pay exorbitant prices for hotel rooms, often representing one-quarter or even one-third of the worker's income.[4] The French housing shortage, particularly in the Paris area, has hit the working-class more severely than any other category. According to official estimates some 400,000 people in the Paris area (or nearly 10 per cent of the population) are reduced to living in more or less squalid hotel rooms, with often as many as four, five, six, and even more people to a room.

What is certain, however, is that if, in 1954–5 there is "pauperization" in relation to 1938, there is, if anything, an improvement in living conditions, as compared with the 1949–53 period. This does not, however, mean that there is no *relative* pauperization, and that the *share* of the working-class in the national income cake has grown; although the statistics are very confusing, it is obvious that, with the impressive consolidation of capitalism in France in 1954–5, the capitalist bourgeoisie, on the whole, is richer than ever, while the standard of living of the working-class, though better than in 1951 (and in some cases a little better, and in other cases, less good than in 1938), is still, as the *Monde* put it, *plutôt médiocre*. It recalled that 1,200,000 working-class homes still had to live on less than 25,000 francs a month.

[3] What handicaps any exhaustive study of the problem is, in the view of the *Monde* (June 10, 1955), the absence of any sociological study of consumption and expenditure by the various income groups.
[4] Numerous studies have been published on the housing shortage in France: one of the most important—with many shocking "human documents"—is the special number of *Esprit*, Nos. 10–11, 1953.

CHAPTER NINE

TOWARDS BERMUDA

I. FRANCE AND THE ROSENBERG CASE

UROPE'S REVOLT" of 1952 had not subsided in 1953. The feeling
in France against EDC and against "American pressures" was
stronger than ever, and the New Look that Russia had assumed
after Stalin's death made French opinion even more reluctant than
before to surrender on the question of German rearmament. Whatever
the arguments in its favour in 1950 and 1951, these arguments no longer
sounded convincing. The danger of a Russian invasion, unlikely
enough before, seemed altogether impossible now. France was not alone
in her opposition. In Italy, de Gasperi, the most determined supporter
of a "Little Europe" suffered a setback in the 1953 election, losing his
absolute majority in the Chamber of Deputies; although, in Germany,
Adenauer had secured the ratification of the EDC by the Bundestag,
opposition to his policy was visibly growing in the face of the Soviet
peace offensive. The *rapprochement* between Russia and Yugoslavia
was a particularly striking example of Moscow's more conciliatory
frame of mind.

In France, the irritation at the thought that the USA (and later, in
October, Churchill) were trying to stampede her into the ratification of
EDC assumed a variety of forms—some of them rather surprising. On
the one hand, there were the careful and reasoned articles in the *Monde*
and other papers against the "time limit"; there were "white-nigger"
votes like that of the Radical Congress at Aix-les-Bains in October 1953
welcoming the "European Community", as a whole, but declaring
the "military community" to be *premature*; or the extremely non-
committal motion passed by the National Assembly after the six-days'
foreign debate in November, on the eve of the Bermuda Conference, a
debate the whole tone of which obviously infuriated both Churchill and
Eisenhower.

On the other hand, there were explosions of anti-American sentiment
in France with nothing quite to equal it anywhere else. The most
striking example of this was the almost nation-wide campaign in
favour of the Rosenbergs. The campaign proclaiming the Rosenbergs
to be innocent was originally started as an anti-American stunt by the

Communists; but, as time went on, more and more people joined in the outcry against the miscarriage of justice that was going to be perpetrated. Eminent French jurists argued that the evidence against the Rosenbergs was highly suspect, since they had been convicted on the evidence of witnesses like David Greenglass. Others, without going into all these details, felt that, whatever the case against the Rosenbergs, it was monstrous to have "tortured them with hope" for two years, and that their sentence should at least be commuted.

A large part of Parliament, including M. Herriot, numerous groups of intellectuals and others either pleaded for mercy or in favour of a retrial. The matter was taken so seriously in the press that on the *Monde* its Washington correspondent, Maurice Ferro, who had more or less followed the official American line on the Rosenbergs, resigned and was replaced by Henri Pierre, who had written several articles on the "McCarthyite" aspect of the Rosenberg case. Not only the Communist press, but the whole left-wing press, including the violently anti-Communist *Franc-Tireur*, pleaded passionately for "Julius and Ethel". In *L'Humanité* Mitelberg published one of his most ferocious cartoons showing a grinning Eisenhower, all his teeth made to look like little electric chairs.

The French Church leaders pleaded for mercy, and, altogether, the campaign for the Rosenbergs became almost a nation-wide movement the like of which had not been seen in France for a long time.

On the night of the execution there was rioting outside the US Embassy, and on the following morning *L'Humanité* brought out a special edition with the huge headline THEY HAVE MURDERED THEM.

The *Monde*, the same afternoon, tried to rationalize this mass protest, which was much more widespread than the uproar over Sacco and Vanzetti in 1928.

It is true [wrote Beuve-Méry] that other, even more horrible murders are committed every day throughout the world. It is also true that in many cases much less fuss is made over the formal side of things before sacrificing suspects and undesirables on the altar of Moloch the State. Nor are the French particularly well qualified to preach justice and equity to others.

How then explain that this sentence passed on a completely unknown young couple on the other side of the ocean should have created in our country a unanimity the like of which we had not known for a long time?

Is it not that the circumstances surrounding the killing of the Rosenbergs raised this brief news-item to the height of a symbol, the symbol of those essential values which alone justify all that the West stands for? In this sense, the execution of the Rosenbergs must be considered as a grave setback to the Atlantic coalition and a victory for its enemies.

The padlocked Soviet world, tired of its own tyranny, seems at last to be opening it doors. . . . Our world, which is still free, seems to be becoming harder and harder ... and more and more closed up. Free men are increasingly frightened of the growing shadows of gigantic idols, fed on lies and terror.... They are afraid of the time when they may be forced to choose between the rôles of hangman and martyr.... (*Le Monde*, June 21, 1953.)

Beuve-Méry hit the nail on the head: the campaign over the Rosenbergs was essentially an outburst against McCarthyism and—at the same time—against American foreign policy. It was a sequel, as it were, to the intellectuals' protest against the *affaire Duclos* a year before, it also played upon the feelings of French public opinion, exasperated as it was by the high moral tone of the Free World Leadership assumed by Mr Dulles, especially at a time when the French were less willing than ever to join in any sort of Crusade.

Whether the Rosenbergs were guilty or not was of secondary importance; it was, in any case, a good anti-American stunt to many. An amusing, though strictly non-conformist reaction to the whole affair was that of a charming old Frenchman I know, a veteran of Verdun who thought it "ignoble" to have murdered such a fine couple as the Rosenbergs—"people," he said, "who must have saved millions and *millions* of lives—by giving the atom bomb to the Russians...."

2. DULLES TAKES A WILLING BIDAULT FOR A RIDE

On May 11, 1953, Churchill had made his famous speech in favour of top-level talks with the Russians, but had received little applause from either America or the Foreign Office. The French, on the other hand, were favourable to the scheme—and so, oddly enough, was Adenauer, especially after the "East-Berlin Insurrection" of June 17, which, he thought, had created terrible difficulties for the Russians, and would make them more willing to abandon Eastern Germany.

The first American reaction to the Churchill speech, as said before, had been to propose a preliminary Three-Power meeting at Bermuda; but this, for a number of reasons, was postponed, not to take place until the following December. By that time it was decided that a Foreign Ministers' conference with the Russians would take place in the following February.

In the meantime, however, a three-power meeting was held in Washington, in July 1953, at which M. Bidault conferred with Mr Dulles and Lord Salisbury, who had temporarily come to replace Mr Eden, and who was even more lukewarm about the "old man's brainwave" than the Foreign Office. Nevertheless, it was decided in Washington to invite the Russians to a conference in Switzerland in September; but since, of the Four, France alone was, at that time, favourable to the meeting, it did not materialize.

At Washington, heavy pressure was brought to bear on Bidault, who was told that it was high time France pulled her socks up and ratified EDC. Though personally favourable to EDC,[1] Bidault argued that he did not think it would be ratified by the Assembly "in its present form", and, in any case, he rejected the American demand that it be ratified before the Four-Power meeting with the Russians. As against this, he agreed to the inclusion in the final communiqué of a warm reference to the EDC as "an essential stage" in the organization of European unity. In his private talks with Mr Dulles and Lord Salisbury he, however, made it clear that France would require some further British and American guarantees, before the ratification of EDC could be considered "in the bag".

Altogether, there were, behind the façade of unanimity in Washington, a good many differences among all three—over Chinese policy between Britain and the USA, over the EDC between France and the other two.

But if, in the matter of EDC, Bidault was obviously still playing for time, he was certainly anxious to know what America's intentions were in respect of Indo-China. The matter was becoming more urgent than ever. The Korean Armistice was about to be concluded, and it was hard to say what the repercussions of this would be in Vietnam.

General Navarre, the newly-appointed Commander-in-Chief in Indo-China was "talking big" and was proposing with the help of a dynamic "commando technique" to "activize" the war, and so restore faith in its ultimate purpose among the 200,000 men of the Expeditionary Force and among the 150,000 men of the Vietnamese (Bao Dai) Army. He was also proposing to draft more and more men into the Vietnamese Army on the "Asians fighting Asians" principle, so dear to Mr Dulles.

The Laniel Government was obviously divided about the whole thing. There were some, like M. Mitterrand, who were in favour of direct negotiations with Ho Chi Minh—a point of view which received unexpected support from the veteran President of the Assembly of the French Union, M. Albert Sarraut. But most of the members of the Laniel Government were in the unfortunate position of wanting a lot of American aid, and yet of wanting the war to "remain French". As Jacques Fauvet wrote in the *Monde* on July 10, 1953, just before M. Bidault flew to Washington:

Those who are particularly in favour of heavy American aid are, at the same time, opposed to American intrusion in the conduct of both military

[1] There was a difference between Bidault's attitude to EDC and that of Robert Schuman and P. H. Teitgen. Of the three MRP leaders, he was the least fanatical "European".

and political affairs by France and the Associated States.... They hold that if this war is still a little bit a French war, it should remain so.... Hence their rejection of the "internationalization" theory. It would deprive the war of its present character: that of a revolt against *la présence française*. Also, it might provoke Chinese intervention, and so prolong the war in Indo-China at a time when the war in Korea is coming to an end. M. Pleven, on the other hand, holds that since the war in Vietnam has, in any case, acquired a different character owing to the war in Korea, it might be best to look for a peaceful solution throughout the whole of South-East Asia.

Unfortunately, M. Pleven, the Minister of Defence, was seeing eye-to-eye with General Navarre, the new Commander-in-Chief; and Navarre's line was that there could be no peaceful settlement until "the military situation had been restored". In other words, Navarre was willing to negotiate—but only from "positions of strength". Fauvet, in the *Monde*, referred with some alarm to the "Navarre Plan" which implied an attempt, at some stage, to ask for reinforcements to be sent from France—at the expense of France's forces in Europe. He did not think Parliament would ever agree to it; nevertheless, the very possibility of such a question being raised seemed disquieting.

In Washington, Bidault talked a lot to Dulles about Indo-China, and impressed upon him the significance of the Navarre Plan—and also the great need for increased American aid. Although the French Foreign Minister mentioned the strong movement in France in favour of ending the war, Dulles clearly did not encourage such moods. On the contrary, he greatly welcomed the Navarre Plan, which would keep the pot boiling, and promised to do his best about the money.

Although, as we have seen, most of the members of the Laniel Government wanted the war to remain "as French as possible", Bidault, like Pleven, had already come fairly close to accepting the principle of "internationalization", and was determined that Britain and the USA assume at least the maximum "moral responsibility" for it, and the USA an ever-increasing financial responsibility. Hence the communiqué at the end of the Washington meeting in which Britain and America recognized that the war waged by France in Indo-China "against Communist aggression" was "essential to the Free World".

The Three (the communiqué continued) had examined the measures that would "hasten the outcome of the war in satisfactory conditions" and speed up "the re-establishment of peace in Indo-China" [from Navarre's "positions of strength", they might have added]. On the other hand (said the communiqué), Britain and the USA had noted with satisfaction the proposal of the French Government "to open conversations with the governments of Cambodia, Laos, and Vietnam" with a view to achieving their "independence and sovereignty"—a step in the right direction towards the establishment of a "free association" between these three countries and France.

It would be hard to find, in all the diplomatic annals of three responsible governments a greater. tangle of deliberate obscurities, contradictions, and equivocal statements than in this Washington communiqué on Indo-China. Did the Three want peace in Indo-China, or did they want the war to continue? Was not the reference to peace merely a sop to French opinion? Was it still a French war, or was it "morally" an international war "against Communist aggression"? What responsibility, if any, were Britain and the USA taking for its pursuit and outcome? And what, in the last analysis, did the mumbojumbo mean about the "sovereignty and independence" of Vietnam, Laos, and Cambodia, and their "free association" with France—unless it meant that the USA wished to deal with these Indo-China States independently of the French? There was a growing suspicion in Paris soon afterwards that Bidault had been saying one thing in Washington, and another thing to his colleagues in the Laniel Government—at least to those who either wished to end the war or who wanted it to "remain as French as possible".

Indeed, a few days after Bidault's return from Washington, a furious press controversy broke out in Paris. In the *Monde* of July 21, J.-J. Servan-Schreiber accused Bidault of having given Dulles a "blank cheque" on France.

He drew attention to the fact that Van Tam, the Vietnamese Premier, had been invited on an official visit to Washington and alleged that the USA had decided to deal direct with the Vietnamese Government and, if it so desired, over the heads of the French. Altogether, he said, the USA was preparing to become the "third partner" in the "co-sovereignty" of Vietnam, and suggested that *that* was, in fact, the real significance of the phrase in the Washington communiqué about the "sovereignty and independence" of the three Indo-Chinese States. For the rest, he argued that Bidault had boosted the Navarre Plan to Dulles and had asked for more money in return for this increased military effort on France's part—"blood for dollars".

In support of his allegations he quoted an unpublished confidential report of the Bidault-Dulles talk on July 12.

The *démenti* published by the Quai d'Orsay was more furious in tone than convincing.

Whether Servan-Schreiber's allegations were accurate in every detail or not, the fact remains that there had been too much talk in Washington of one kind or another, and that much that had been said gave rise, in the following months, to no end of misunderstandings and misinterpretations.

It was indeed, on *équivoques* like the Washington communiqué (which, one strongly suspects, was intended to keep French opinion quiet) and the Bidault-Dulles talks at Georgetown on July 12 that the

Laniel Government was going to "construct" its Indo-China policy during the next ten months—until the final catastrophe of Dien Bien Phu.

If M. Bidault had deliberately implored Mr Dulles to take him for a ride, he could scarcely have done better. In fact, he probably did. As for Mr Dulles, there is today no doubt at all in French minds that he encouraged the French to go on with the war, was delighted with the Navarre Plan, discouraged any attempt to talk to Ho Chi Minh, and made a lot of half-promises to Bidault (which Bidault was only too glad to record) but which Dulles had no certainty at all of being able to keep.

The Washington talks of July 1953 help to explain the persistence with which Bidault and Pleven[2] continued their disastrous Indo-China policy till the final crash. If Bidault's responsibility was great, that of Dulles, with his determination to keep a foothold in Indo-China, was even greater. But if, meantime, there was greater acquiescence in France than might have been expected, it was because the dollars, though earmarked "Indo-China", could, in agreement with the USA, be transferred to France's account with the European Payments Union.[3]

3. CHURCHILL'S "YOU RATIFY OR——"

The next few months in France were taken up—apart from some heavily written-up commando raids such as the famous Opération Hirondelle under General Navarre's new scheme in Indo-China[4]—by the strikes and by Morocco; and it was not until October that EDC came to the forefront again. The first stern warning that Britain (and America) were not going to stand any further nonsense from France came from Sir Winston Churchill, who in his speech at Margate, came down on France like a ton of bricks.

Only five months had passed since Churchill's famous speech of May 11 in favour of "top-level" talks with the Russians. Before Margate, it was rumoured that his speech to the Conservatives would make an even bigger bang.

[2] Pleven actually began to change his mind after his visit to Indo-China in February 1954, where he had talked to the generals on the spot. The *Canard Enchaîné* published a cartoon of Pleven in April 1954 in the rôle of Pontius Pilate washing his hands in the "basin" of Dien Bien Phu.

[3] *Le Monde*, June 10, 1953.

[4] A characteristic comment on this operation was made by *Combat* (July 22, 1953): "At the very moment M. Bidault was begging for another 100 million dollars, Opération Hirondelle was launched. This paratroop raid on Langson was a complete success, but even if it had involved great loss of life, it would still have served the purpose of showing that our soldiers deserved to be 'encouraged' to the tune of 280 million dollars. Their courage and sacrifice would have acted as good 'publicity' for a new appeal for funds. It is hard to think of a more cynical way of trading the country's dignity and national sovereignty."

Instead, [wrote the *Monde* of October 13] "the mountain has given birth to a mouse.... It was said that he was going to announce his visit to Moscow, where he would have a *tête-à-tête* with Malenkov. But nothing of the kind happened. His reference to Four-Power talks was platitudinous.... Where are the old fireworks? Apart from the Four-Power Conference, Churchill talked just like Mr Dulles. However, let's be fair: like Mr Dulles in his better moments. But all things considered, there is only one solid piece of substance in the whole speech; and that is that Germany must be rearmed—with or without EDC.

The Churchill speech annoyed the French. Bourdet wrote an article entitled: "Churchill Chooses Germany." Even supporters of the EDC were not at all sure that such truculence would help their cause. Everybody felt that Churchill's way of talking to France was "most unpleasant", as the *Monde* remarked, and it added a few acid reflections on Churchill's general attitude to France, even recalling in the process Mers-el-Kébir, where, largely through Churchill's fault, 1,500 French sailors had been massacred by the British Navy!

It is no use being surprised by the unpleasant tone in which Churchill summoned the French Parliament to choose between the ratification of EDC and the creation of a German national army. Even in his most francophil moments the Prime Minister has never failed to slip in a few bits of admonishment, in the manner of a stern father talking to a slightly crazy daughter. We doubt whether this is a good way of talking to us.... If he wants us to ratify the European Army, he only has to ... agree to Britain's entry into the European system of integration.... "Impossible", says London, "we've got the Commonwealth". Quite. But France has the French Union —and the problem is precisely the same.

Sir Winston, however, will not see it.... He considers it more politic to try to bully us with the Wehrmacht—an operation which everybody in France, whether pro-EDC or anti-EDC, will find distasteful. Moreover, our diplomats have plenty of juridical arguments to knock the scheme on the head....

"Juridical arguments"—how very French! As if the cemetery of the Treaties, Pacts and Agreements which were signed between the two wars and nearly all of which had died in their infancy—was not enough to remind the French of the simple fact that British "common sense" did not much believe in the lasting virtues of Treaties in a "changing world".

The Margate speech caused one of those periodic explosions of mutual antipathy between France and Britain; the French remembered that, after 1918, Britain had stupidly screamed about "French hegemony", and had done its best for years afterwards to restore a mighty Germany; that she had condoned all Hitler's treaty violations; that, in the end, she had left France in the lurch, and had, in a moment of panic, sunk a large part of the French Navy. That a corner of Vichy's highest anti-British card, the sinking of the Navy should have been shown at that stage even by Frenchmen traditionally "pro-British", pointed to a degree of French exasperation at which distinctions between Chamberlain and Churchill and between Vichy and anti-Vichy are eclipsed by the ancient conflicts between France and Albion. Again it looked as though History was repeating itself: again, as in the 1920's, Britain was backing Germany against France.

The Churchill speech at Margate was a landmark in more ways than one. For the first time had any leader of the Atlantic Alliance openly considered the possibility that France would *not* ratify EDC; until then it was somehow assumed that, sooner or later, she would. But since 1952 the signs that she would not do so had grown steadily; and, from now on, the British and American Governments were determined to bully France into this ratification. Only, to bully governments was easier than to bully a parliament; and the abuse systematically showered on the French National Assembly during the next twelve months in the British and American press was not certain to work the trick.

For one thing, on this issue of EDC, the National Assembly was not "unrepresentative" of French public opinion in the sense given to the word in numerous sweeping and remarkably rash assertions in the British and American press.[5] For one thing, the two most under-represented parties, the Gaullists and the Communists were anti-EDC, and even among the deputies who had been elected in 1951 under the *apparentements* system a high proportion were against EDC. That was the real reason why the advocates of EDC, like Pleven, René Mayer, Schuman, and Bidault never put EDC to the test at the National Assembly. When, finally, Mendès-France did it, the answer, as was to be expected, was a clear No.

4. DE GAULLE THINKS BRITAIN MAY STEAL THE FRENCH EMPIRE AND—LOOKS EAST

Outside Parliament, the opposition to EDC was at least as strong: the Army leaders, with Marshal Juin at their head, were more or less openly against it; the intellectual groups, with few exceptions, were opposed to EDC; and de Gaulle, in November 1953, made a point of declaring himself uncompromisingly hostile to it. He spoke on the eve of the big foreign debate at the National Assembly, and only a few weeks before Bermuda.

[5] One of the oddest demonstrations that "the French people" were pro-EDC was the "poll" published in one paper according to which, in the summer of 1953, 46 per cent were in favour of the ratification of EDC and only 22 per cent against—i.e. not even all the Communists—and nobody else!

At this press conference he again referred to "this monstrous treaty" which, he said, would rob the French Army of its sovereignty, separate the defence of France from the defence of the French Union, would go against all her traditions and institutions, and make her deliver her soldiers to an organism over which she would have no control. He blamed this and other "supra-national monstrosities" on "the Inspirer", M. Jean Monnet. It was he who, in 1940, had wanted to "integrate King George VI with President Lebrun"; in 1943 he wanted to "integrate de Gaulle with Giraud", and now he was trying to do the same with France and Germany.

Since victorious France has an army and defeated Germany has none [he parodied Monnet] let us suppress the French Army. After that we shall make a stateless army of Frenchmen and Germans, and since there must be a government above this army, we shall make a stateless government, a technocracy. As this may not please everybody, we'll paint a new shop sign and call it "community"; it won't matter, anyway, because the "European Army" will be placed at the entire disposal of the American Commander-in-Chief.

Instead, de Gaulle spoke of a Confederation of national armies among which Germany could hold a place, though at first only a minor and well-controlled place: but it must be a Grand Alliance, comprising Britain. However, he did not dwell on this "alternative" to EDC, and instead proposed something quite different: which was that an attempt should be made to explore the possibility of reviving the Franco-Russian alliance. France, he said, was still an ally of Russia against any revival of the German menace.

He was obviously more than fed-up with the West, and went out of his way to speak of America and Britain with sardonic humour. America, he suggested, liked to keep all her friends in watertight compartments, and liked, in particular, to have tête-à-tête talks with the Germans.

It is curious, very curious how the Americans are using open and secret pressure to compel France to accept the EDC which can only condemn her to decay.... The encouragement they are giving to Germany to become again the most powerful country in Europe can only lead to war sooner or later.

As for England, his remarks were even angrier:

Yes, Britain, too, though for different reasons, is demanding that we ratify the so-called European Army, though nothing in the world would induce her to join it herself. Abandon your soldiers to others, lose your sovereignty, lose your Dominions—that's fine for Paris, but not for London.... And why?

may I ask.... It's because we are on the Continent, "the unhappy Continent" as Churchill has already called it in anticipation.... No doubt, there will be a few British soldiers in Germany, and a few attentive British observers attached to the EDC.... Indeed, it's very pleasant to be the guest of honour at the banquet of a society to which you pay no dues.

De Gaulle was now getting vicious; it was as if the memory of Syria was still rankling. If it came to the worst, he now suggested, the British might, after all, help themselves to the French Empire—why not?

For if France, for the sake of EDC, is so determined to separate herself from her overseas territories, well, after all, where is the harm? In case of a world crisis, there might be a situation in which all kinds of new possibilities might present themselves to Lord Louis Mountbatten, C.-in-C. in the Western Mediterranean, or to Lord Alexander (*snarl*) *Vicomte de Tunis*, or to the King of Libya, who is just now, as it happens, paying a visit to Morocco....

Shades of Fashoda! Shades of Mers-el-Kébir!

5. THE ASSEMBLY REFUSES TO BE RUSHED INTO EDC

In the midst of the five days' foreign debate at the National Assembly at the end of November, the Russians suddenly agreed that a meeting of the four Foreign Ministers be held in Berlin early in the new year. No longer insisting, as before, on a Five-Power Conference, the Russians now agreed to discuss the re-establishment of a united, independent, peaceful and democratic Germany. They added, however, that they would ask that the Four-Power meeting be followed, soon afterwards, by a Five-Power meeting including China.

This Note, if anything, increased the uncertainty among many French deputies on what to do next, and the reluctance to commit France finally to EDC, despite the threatening tone adopted towards France during the past few weeks by the greater part of the British and American press. The real problem was put in a nutshell by M. Laniel himself, when he said that "we must have a foreign policy which would have the widest possible support". That is precisely what was lacking. Everything suggested that the Assembly was divided into a small majority hostile to EDC and a large minority more or less willing to support EDC, not so much, it is true (apart from a small number of EDC fanatics) for its own sake, as in the name of "Western solidarity".

M. Laniel himself was not unconditionally in favour of ratification. He recalled that, in his investiture speech, he had undertaken not to submit the EDC Treaty for ratification

until we are certain of having acquired a settlement of the Saar problem, after the signing of the interpretive protocols and after the conclusion of agreements with Great Britain.

None of these "conditions" had yet been fulfilled. No agreement had yet been reached on the conditions laid down on April 1, 1952, by M. Schuman concerning the Saar: (1) the maintenance of the economic union [with France] and of the conventions on which this union was based; and (2) the political autonomy of the Saar. As for agreement on the interpretive protocols and the agreement with Britain, the negotiations on these, said M. Laniel, were "proceeding satisfactorily".[6] But that was all. M. Laniel added that all these points would be "forcibly" presented to the Bermuda Conference. He little knew what was in store for him there.

It is interesting to note that, on one of his main points, M. Laniel was fully supported by M. Mendès-France. The latter said that, for nearly a week, he had followed the debate on EDC and had felt, in the course of it, a growing *malaise*. He was sure that many of his colleagues had the same feeling of discomfort. He did not think anything of any lasting value could come out of this discussion on EDC in the absence of a compromise on which practically everybody could agree.

He thought the supporters of EDC had drawn far too idyllic a picture of the whole thing; its opponents, on the other hand, had taken a wholly negative attitude, and had not taken sufficient account of the international consequences of a pure and simple rejection of EDC, which could only lead to the isolation of France.[7]

Many of Mendès-France's other arguments—on the economic aspects of European unity, on Britain's share in its defence, on the paralysing effect on France of the war in Indo-China already foreshadowed the policy he was to pursue six months later, as head of the Government, in the midst of the spectacular events of the summer of 1954.

As already said, the motion passed at the end of the debate on November 27, after much squabbling over its exact wording, was a real "time-marker". Drawn up by M. Garet, a right-wing Independent, it merely said that the Assembly approved the Government's statements and asked that "the continuity of the policy of building a united Europe be assured". Finally the motion was carried by 275 to 244 votes and 103 abstentions. The voting was partly determined by internal considerations: thus, the Socialists voted against the Laniel Government, though some were pro-EDC; most of the Gaullists, not satisfied with the wording of the motion, with its pro-EDC implications, abstained. It was agreed by all observers and practically the

[6] *Debats*, *A.N.*, November 24, 1953. pp. 5485-6.
[7] *Ibid.*, p. 5513.

entire press that, in the words of *L'Année Politique*, "the whole tone of the debate had revealed a growing opposition to the European Army and to the European Political Community"[8]—which, at that very moment was being discussed (quite aimlessly), at The Hague.

This was the atmosphere in which M. Bidault and the unfortunate M. Laniel set off for Bermuda a few days later.

6. AT BERMUDA CHURCHILL PREFERS A GOAT TO THE FRENCH PRIME MINISTER

M. Laniel was not exactly popular in France; but the way in which he was treated at Bermuda, especially by Sir Winston Churchill—acutely irritated by the French for several months past—caused, on balance, a good deal more annoyance than laughter in France—even among people who had little use for M. Laniel. When the plane carrying M. Laniel and M. Bidault landed at the Bermuda airfield, there was no band there to play the *Marseillaise*, and various other "protocol" bloomers were committed, for instance when M. Laniel, the *Premier*, was put in the same car as the *Foreign Ministers*, Number One car being reserved for Churchill and Eisenhower. Worse still, when, before that, Laniel and Churchill waited at the airfield for Eisenhower's arrival, Churchill—the French press reported—turned his back on the "unknown" French Premier, and instead stroked the beard of the regimental mascot goat of the Welsh Fusiliers—"*un animal sympathique*", AFP reported the next day, in connexion with a banquet at which the goat was present, "but one which has already been a little too prominent at this Conference."

"A bad-luck Conference", the *Monde* described it. The whole atmosphere was bad; both the British and the Americans were clearly showing all the time that they had "no patience" with the French; that they were sick and tired of their shilly-shallying over EDC, and that Congress must be told without delay whether or not France intended to go ahead with it before there were any more appropriations for Europe.

And then, a day after the Conference had started, M. Laniel had to go to bed with 'flu and a high temperature, so that Indo-China, in particular, was discussed, on behalf of the French Government, by M. Bidault, who was a notorious diehard in the matter.

For France, the Bermuda Conference was both annoying and disappointing in more ways than one. Churchill and Eisenhower wholly ignored the vote of the French National Assembly which had implied, among other things, that the conditions laid down by Laniel—Saar

[8] *L'Année Politique*, 1953, p. 436.

settlement, British participation, etc—be fulfilled before EDC could be ratified. Without giving the French any precise assurances on anything, Eisenhower, peremptorily demanded that EDC be ratified by March 15; and although Churchill—either deliberately or by a slip of the tongue —once sarcastically referred to the European Army as "the polyglot army"—he was no kinder to the French than were the Americans. Eden, according to the French press, had to "come to the rescue", and explain away Churchill's surprising wisecrack; some French observers wondered nevertheless whether Churchill was not already thinking of a national German army as a welcome alternative. The bullying of Laniel—a sick man—and of Bidault—not in very good form either[9] —nevertheless went on, day after day, till finally the French agreed, regardless of the implications of the Assembly's vote to sign the communiqué which said that EDC was "a necessity".

In Paris the prevalent feeling was that at Bermuda the French had been treated with deliberate shabbiness, and that "the era of ultimatums" had opened. One of the sharpest reactions to all this came from Claude Bourdet who in an editorial in *France-Observateur*, entitled C'EST CAMBRONNE QU'IL NOUS FAUT regretted that France was not represented at Bermuda by somebody like the Napoleonic general at Waterloo who said *merde* to Wellington's forces who were summoning him to surrender.

Worse still, the Americans made it clear at Bermuda that they were not interested in the French hankering for peace in Indo-China, and that they intended to ignore the proposal for armistice talks made by Ho Chi Minh only a week before in his statement to the Swedish paper, *Expressen*.

The plan brought by the American delegation [H. de Galard wrote in *France-Observateur* on December 10] contained no reference whatsoever to a possible armistice; it implied, on the contrary, that the war should be intensified; American instructors, with experience of Korea, would be sent to Indo-China, Vietnamese officers would be trained by the US Army; and a US Military Mission would take part in the organization of Vietnamese units. Also, American officers from Tokyo would be attached to the French High Command in Indo-China—something which, a year before, Delattre had firmly opposed. . . . And, last but not least, the supply of dollars and war material would be increased and speeded up.

In short, now that the French are anxious to end the war, the Americans are giving them all the things they had denied them for the last seven years.

All this can only lead to a hardening of the war, and it is only too obvious that Washington is determined to keep up its pressure in the Far East, and that since the end of the war in Korea, it intends to concentrate this pressure

[9] Only shortly before, he had fainted while making a speech at the National Assembly.

on Indo-China.... In the circumstances, the French Delegation had no difficulty in having the "vital importance" of the war in Indo-China referred to in the final communiqué—an adjective which, two years ago, Delattre de Tassigny had tried in vain for two whole days to extract from them.... In short, we are now being driven into continuing the war in Indo-China, whether we want to or not....

The war in Indo-China was indeed continuing, complete with Navarre's "dynamic" new technique and with the blessing of Bidault and the MRP.

On November 20, six battalions of paratroops had been dropped on Dien Bien Phu, "the key of the Thai country", the French Command explained. The capture of this isolated spot inside enemy country and nearly 200 miles from the Red River Delta, where the main French forces were concentrated, was hailed as a great success, and was calculated to tie up large Vietminh forces in the Thai country. In the weeks that followed, it was to be turned into a French "fortress".

The indications in December 1953 were, however, that the Vietminh Command were not taking Dien Bien Phu very seriously yet, and were, instead, preparing to attack Lai Chu, another newly-captured French stronghold in the Thai country. This the French found necessary to evacuate on December 11.

As a French military commentator, with greater foresight than General Navarre, wrote at the time:

Let us now suppose that what the French Command say is correct: that the situation at Lai Chu was disastrous and that it was absurd to tie up a large garrison in a spot completely isolated from the main theatre of operations. *But then, surely, the same is true of Dien Bien Phu....* There are only two ways: either we bring back to the Delta all the forces of the Expeditionary Corps and abandon nearly the whole country to Vietminh; or else we go out of our way to maintain garrisons in various places with the help of airlifts—garrisons which will not even be able to interfere with the enemy's movements. Whatever we do, General Giap [the Vietminh C.-in-C.] wins in either case.[10]

Giap was in no hurry to attack Dien Bien Phu; this, in the following weeks, encouraged the French Command to put more and more men and equipment into the "fortress". Yet the larger the French forces there, the more worthwhile was it for Giap to attack and destroy them.... However, that is another story, which will be told in due course.

But there is something ironical in this coincidence: while at Bermuda the USA was promising to help France to organize a bigger and better

[10] Roger Paret in *France-Observateur*, December 17, 1953.

war in Vietnam, the first act of the tragedy of Dien Bien Phu was already being played. Did Ho Chi Minh already know that, short of an early spectacular victory over the French, these would not be allowed by Washington to abandon the fight, or even to try to come to terms with Vietminh? By this time Vietminh had, with Chinese help, already built up a well-trained and relatively well-equipped modern army, a point which Navarre later admitted to have under-rated. At any rate, he was to claim that Vietminh's 105 mm. guns (made in USA) outside Dien Bien Phu had come to the French Command in Indo-China as a "surprise".

Part VI

THE END OF AN EPOCH

CHAPTER ONE

DISASTER IN INDO-CHINA

I. A TURNING-POINT

A T LAST came the time for great decisions—on Indo-China, North Africa, and Germany.

The year 1954 falls into two almost equal parts: the period before Mendès-France, and the time of the Mendès-France Government—which lasted till February 4, 1955.

It is perhaps still too early to see this period in clear historical perspective; but a few facts stand out clearly.

1. The first half of 1954 was one of great anxiety and pessimism, and, as the disaster of Dien Bien Phu was moving towards a climax, it looked for several days as though the danger of a Third World War breaking out was greater than it had been for years—greater, indeed, than at the time of the Berlin Blockade in 1948–9 or even at the time of MacArthur's Yalu offensive in November 1950.

The Four-Power Conference in Berlin earlier in the year had been a failure, and by refusing both free elections in Germany and an Austrian settlement, Molotov had been wholly unhelpful. On the other hand, the persistence with which Bidault, Dulles, and Eden had refused to discuss EDC with the Russians had not helped either.

2. Finally, in June, the catastrophic situation in Indo-China called for drastic remedies; and the obvious man to deal with this was Mendès-France, a man who in the course of the last few years had come to be regarded as the most coherent and constructive "leader of the Opposition". He tackled the Indo-China crisis with consummate skill, and with a new "style" of governing France which made him popular overnight not only throughout France, but stirred up interest in France and its new leader throughout the world. Whatever the mental reservations *vis-à-vis* Mendès-France among the French political parties, the popularity in the country of the man who was "finishing" the war in Indo-China was such that for two months no one dared openly attack him. With British help, and despite American bad humour, he negotiated his Indo-China armistice, and, only a few days later, taking Juin with him, he flew to Tunis and announced a new era in Franco-North-African relations. Was it a stroke of genius to

take Juin, the hero of the *colons*, with him? So it looked at the time; but was not Mendès-France being just a little *too* clever? The thought crossed a few people's minds. But Mendès-France felt that he must succeed quickly—as he had succeeded over Indo-China; or he would not succeed at all, and he could do this only by compromising with enemies. He did not have enough political friends to be able to go slow. The slightest mistake, or even a pause in his series of spectacular successes might prove fatal.

3. His prestige in the country was still at its zenith when he undertook the most daring operation of all: the Brussels Conference. This marked the beginning of his decline. By trying to "compromise" on EDC, instead of having it rejected outright, as it would have been, he upset most of the anti-EDC people; when finally, after the failure of Brussels, EDC was rejected, France suddenly became unpopular again with the British and American Governments, and the enemies of Mendès-France rejoiced. The British and American press now clamoured that he had "isolated" France; the campaign against him grew in intensity, and, dreading this "isolation"—for Mendès-France had always been afraid of being called a "neutralist", let alone a "fellow traveller"—he finally yielded to the peremptory Anglo-American clamour for German rearmament on a different basis. Having lost much of the support he had enjoyed among the people opposed to German rearmament, Mendès-France now became vulnerable in a very short time.

4. The glowing embers of envy and resentment on the part of the Right and the MRP burst into a blinding flame of hatred. Mendès-France was hated not only for what he had done, but also for what he might do before long, if he were given enough time. He became *un homme à abattre* to the men of the alcohol lobby, who had already witnessed his first skirmish with the Monster Booze, and who feared that worse trouble would come to them; he became *un homme à abattre* to the North Africa lobby, who were not at all reassured by his spectacular trip to Tunis, and were now screaming that it had only encouraged the Aurès rebellion in Algeria and the growing terrorism in Morocco.

Joining forces, Bidault with his MRP, the North African *colons*, and the alcohol and *betteravier* lobby, whose spokesman at the National Assembly was a M. Legendre, tried to blow up the Government from inside with their *affaire Dides*, with its cloak-and-dagger stories, its double and triple agents, its leakages of military secrets, its innuendoes against M. Mitterrand the Minister of the Interior, and its attempt to show that the war in Indo-China had not been lost, but that France had been stabbed in the back by a gang of traitors who were in close contact not only with certain members of the Government, but perhaps even with Mendès-France himself. People with long memories remembered ugly operations of the same kind in the past—such as the Salengro case in 1936, when Blum's Minister of the Interior was driven to suicide by *Gringoire's* press campaign. The operation against Mitterrand, despite Bidault's innuendoes, failed, but the military authorities picked on two whipping-boys, Gilles Martinet and Roger Stéphane of *France-Observateur*, who had "leaked" military secrets and so had helped to lose the war in Indo-China!

It was in this poisonous atmosphere that the Paris Agreements were ratified at the National Assembly by a small majority at the end of the year. Mendès-France pleaded for German rearmament; not because he wanted it, but because he dreaded that France would be isolated. Churchill and Eden, even more than the Americans, had threatened France with "the empty chair". Now that Mendès-France had done what so many of his friends on the Left had begged him not to do, the time was ripe for his enemies to turn him out; early in February before he had been given time to embark on his far-reaching programme of reorganizing France in a big way, he was overthrown, and amidst howls of angry abuse coming not only from the MRP, but also from others whose support Mendès-France, with his frail parliamentary basis, had sought in the past, even though he knew them at heart to be enemies.

What lessons are to be learned from this strange experience, almost, though not quite unique in the history of France—an experience in which an outstanding individual clashed with "the system" (as de Gaulle called it) almost as soon as the immediate danger was over? In what respects was Mendès-France's technique of Government different from that of his predecessors? How large a part in his spectacular success in the summer of 1954 did the support of public opinion play? Was there an alternative to surrendering on the question of German rearmament? The atmosphere of bitter resignation in which this rearmament was finally accepted by the country—did the country blame Mendès-France for it? Finally, will Mendès-France be merely remembered as an "accident" or will "Mendèsisme" continue either with, or without Mendès? Only a close examination of the clash of interests and political forces in France during those few months when "PMF" and "Mr France"—and, indeed, France herself—captured the headlines of the world press can answer some of these questions.

2. THE PRESIDENTIAL ELECTION

The "bad luck" Conference of Bermuda was the last major international event at the end of 1953, and M. Laniel returned to Paris feeling that both he and his country had been treated shabbily—just because Parliament was still reluctant to endorse EDC and German rearmament.

Personally he tried to make up for it by standing for President of the Republic, and failed again. The presidential election, in which the respective candidates' attitude to EDC was of the greatest importance, played into the hands of the foreign press which had already sharply attacked France at the time of Bermuda. "The Versailles Circus"—or some similar phrase—became the standard *cliché* in the Anglo-American press—merely because it took not (as usual) two or three, but thirteen rounds—and six days—to get a new President elected; and the election gave rise to an outburst of insulting remarks about French institutions and the French generally.

No doubt, the noisy canvassing done on behalf of the Premier by his brother, Senator René Laniel ("Monsieur Frère" as he was soon nick-named)[1] was absurd enough; but the election had a serious side to it— namely, the fundamental quarrel over EDC. Constitutionally, there was nothing wrong with thirteen rounds, though towards the tenth round, both candidates and voters began to be rattled and wondered how long the *impasse* could continue. It is significant that the two most outspoken "Europeans", M. Bidault and M. Delbos, dropped out almost immediately, one after the second, the other after the third round, and that if, in the end, Senator René Coty was elected by 477 votes to the 329 votes of M. Naegelen (the anti-EDC Socialist candidate, who was supported by the Communists)[2] it was largely because M. Coty had not taken any clear line on EDC. A strong supporter of EDC —or a passionate opponent, for that matter—would have stood no chance.

However, once the Presidential Election was over, few people gave it another thought. M. Coty—though, in the eyes of many, perhaps a little too far to the Right—seemed a particularly worthy man for the post. He had had an honourable, though unspectacular parliamentary and government career, and was personally *sympathique*, and the comic "Edwardian" photographs that the press published of the whole Coty family on the beach at Etretat in 1902, with the future President of the Republic wearing a striped bathing-suit and a boater, as well as the scurrilous (and not wildly funny) songs composed by the Montmartre *chansonniers*[3] about the out-size dimensions of *la Présidente*— a very worthy lady, for all that—did not do any harm. It was, if any-

---

[1] Soon afterwards M. René Laniel found himself in serious financial difficulties and was not allowed by the French police at Orly Airport to leave for South America. This extravagant episode, complete with "Monsieur Frère's" search by the Customs, did not enhance M. Joseph Laniel's prestige either.

[2] There were, moreover, sixty-five "other" votes.

[3] The Montmartre *chansonniers* (e.g. at the *Deux Anes*) often produced significant political satire under the Third Republic, but they hardly ever do under the Fourth. A badly-decayed profession.

thing, a tribute to a man's integrity if all one found to say against him was that his wife was fat.

It wasn't such a bad note, after all, on which to end the year of 1953. The new President seemed to symbolize republican respectability and continuity, and a nice little democratic touch was provided by the story in the press on how Mme Coty, on hearing that her husband had been elected President of the Republic late on the night of December 23 rushed downstairs and embraced her *concierge*.

3. BERLIN AND THE ODD BEHAVIOUR OF M. BIDAULT

Looking back on 1953 in their end-of-the-year editorials, most of the press agreed that it hadn't been such a bad year. Economic conditions were fairly satisfactory; and, internationally, there had unquestionably been an improvement. The *Monde*, in its editorial on New Year's day, thought things had looked much grimmer twelve months before. Eastern Europe, with its Slansky Trial and its "Doctors' Plot" seemed like a madhouse; in the USA the victory of the Republicans looked at first like a victory of the Roll-Back policy, with all the terrible dangers that this involved. In the East, Stalin's death had, if not caused, at any rate precipitated a return to sanity, while in the USA Russia's growing strength as a "nuclear" Power had had a salutary effect. Soviet atom bombs had discouraged preventive war talk in the USA and American fear of Russian atom bombs (the same *Monde* wrote a few days later) was perhaps *un commencement de sagesse*.[4] This "return to sanity" had been demonstrated by the Korean Armistice; between an extension of the war and a return to *status quo* both sides had, in the end, preferred the latter as a lesser evil. The Monde expressed the hope that at the Berlin Conference—the first conference of the Big Four Foreign Ministers since 1949—a serious attempt would be made to reach a general settlement on Germany and Austria. As for Indo-China, it thought it was high time that France came out with an independent policy—obviously an allusion to the fact that France was now being bribed and flattered by the USA into continuing the war, despite the extreme distaste for it in France itself. The fact remained, as was to be revealed soon afterwards, that the USA was now paying more than two-thirds of the cost of the war in Indo-China.

Germany and Indo-China: there was good reason in France to be apprehensive on both scores. As early as January 7 the *Monde* put the question bluntly. The whole conduct of the war was now dependent on American support, both political and financial:

If a military defeat and an American decision not to intervene compel

[4] *Le Monde*, January 6, 1954.

us in Indo-China to negotiate, it will perhaps be too late to do so in honourable conditions. Just because we refrained from negotiating on our *own* terms, any accident may now place us in a highly unfavourable position *vis-à-vis* Ho Chi Minh.

A prophetic remark, if ever there was one. It will be remembered that, shortly before the Bermuda Conference, Ho Chi Minh had, through his statement to *Expressen*, made a reasonable offer for negotiations, but although the Laniel Government was divided on the issue, those who, like M. Jacquet, were in favour of responding to it, were forced to submit to the "diehard" majority which decided to ignore Ho's overtures.

By the time the Berlin Conference was about to open, the "accident" which was to lead to the "unfavourable" position in which France would soon find herself (as the *Monde* had prophesied) was already figuring prominently in the news pages of the French press. Dien Bien Phu, a village on the border of the Thai country and Laos, 200 miles south-west of Hanoi, which was captured by French paratroops on November 20, had now been turned into a stronghold far in the enemy's rear, and was being treated more and more in the pro-Government press as the jewel in the crown of the Navarre Plan. It was looked upon as the gigantic trap into which Vietminh would fall, and the scepticism of a real Indo-China expert like Robert Guillain, the *Monde* correspondent, was ignored by the Laniel Government. It was this absurd self-confidence over Dien Bien Phu that partly accounts for the defiant behaviour of M. Bidault at the Berlin Conference. But that was not the only reason. He was being deliberately "built up" by Mr Dulles and Mr Eden as "the spokesman of the West", as The Man Who Would Not Compromise on EDC, and who would not allow Molotov to get away with his all-too obvious game of trying to create a split between France and her British and American allies.

Bidault came to symbolize at Berlin two things—the determination to have EDC ratified, and the determination to go on with the war in Indo-China at any price, despite the lip-service he paid, from time to time, to "peace".

What were the strange and tortuous workings of the mind of Bidault, the leader of that MRP which (together with a few other men like Pleven) was more responsible than any other Party for the useless seven years' war in Indo-China?

As one of his comrades in the Resistance, Claude Bourdet, bitterly wrote towards the end of the Berlin Conference:

What, after all, does M. Bidault want, what does the MRP, whose policy he personifies, want? Is it the "European myth" to which everything must be sacrificed, both in Europe and Asia, even though France would instantly throw off the "Carolingian" yoke if only she did not need the dollars for continuing the war in Indo-China? Or is it that terrible machinery that was set in motion by the bombing of Haiphong—a machinery which they no longer dare to stop, in case too many horrors and too many scandals are revealed? Is it the policy of the Vatican ... which aims at creating a little clerical Europe? Or are these people scared of John Foster Dulles who himself is being terrorized by McCarthy, who takes his lead from the most reactionary Catholic elements in America? (These last two questions go together.) Or, finally, is it not the terrifying vanity of Bidault which makes him so untractable, so prolific in the production of categorical statements and general definitions which are both woolly and peremptory—so peremptory that it never even occurs to him to wonder whether he is not following the road of madness? Or, on the other hand, does he regret all the things that he stood for in the past, and is he not so peremptory simply because he wants to camouflage the fearful confusion within him? Weak men are known to crash ahead in such "forward escapes".[5]

Naturally, no progress was made in Berlin on the German problem. This was to be expected. Duverger put the matter in a nutshell before the Conference opened, when he wrote in the *Monde*:

We are told that EDC must not be the object of any negotiations in Berlin. That is Robert Schuman's point of view. It is also the point of view of Adenauer, of nearly all the Americans, and many of the British. Which means precisely one thing: the German problem must not be discussed in Berlin. In that case the failure of the Conference is certain. That is what the supporters of EDC want to happen. And once Berlin has failed they will say: "You see, there's no alternative to EDC."

The "German problem" was, of course, discussed. There was the Eden Plan—which Molotov rejected. Various other proposals were discussed—including the Soviet Plan for a Twenty-five Power Europe, but with no result. The Eden Plan provided no guarantee against the whole of Germany being rearmed and "integrated" in the West, and the Russian Plan looked to many like a "European Monroe Doctrine" under which the USA would be told to "go home". Molotov, who might have upset the whole applecart had he proposed the neutralization of Austria, as the Soviet Government was to do a year later—when it was probably already too late to prevent German rearmament—did not think fit to propose anything of the sort in 1954. So the deadlock on Germany was allowed to continue—Molotov merely hoping that, in the end, France would reject EDC, whatever Bidault said to the contrary. Nothing on the lines of various "plans" put forward in France was even considered: such as the abandonment of EDC in return for the political liberation of Eastern Germany by the Russians, the

[5] *France-Observateur*, February 25, 1954.

"neutral Germany" resulting therefrom being jointly guaranteed by the USA and the USSR; or else the "improved version" of this old plan: the "integration" of a *neutral* Germany in the West. (Maurice Duverger in *Le Monde*, January 20, 1954.)

Bidault's part in Berlin was both active and passive. In embarking on what came to be known as the "Bidault Operation", Dulles apparently imagined that French vanity would be flattered; Bidault's prestige at home would be enhanced, and the chances of EDC vastly improved. As Henri Pierre wrote in a Washington dispatch in the *Monde* on February 6:

> Quite ingenuously the USA imagines that because the British and Americans have pushed Bidault into the limelight in Berlin, they will cure France of her inferiority complex which is responsible for those outbursts of ultra-nationalist sentiment, with its clamour for an independent French policy.... Not following, like the rest of the press, the official propaganda line, Shackford of Scripps-Howard alone pointed out that Bidault was not popular in France; that the French distrusted ministers over whom foreigners made an unusual fuss; and he wondered whether this Anglo-American love for Bidault would not be for him the kiss of death....

4. THE "MARKOS" MYTH AND LANIEL'S "CEASE-FIRE CONDITIONS"

The Berlin Conference would have been a complete failure but for one thing: the decision to hold the Korea-Indo-China Conference at Geneva in April. How had this come about? Molotov, in his private talks with Bidault, had proposed that Russia act as an intermediary in arranging direct talks between France and Vietminh. This Bidault rejected, but, under the pressure of French public and parliamentary opinion, and despite great reticence on the part of Dulles, he agreed to the Geneva Conference—though with what mental reservations may be guessed from the subsequent course of events.[6]

One of the most unsavoury aspects of the Berlin Conference was provided by the attempt made by Bidault to convince the French public that he had persuaded Russia (and China) to "abandon" Ho Chi Minh —presumably in return for the recogniton of the Peking Government by France and the USA and its admission to UN—though even a child would have known that Bidault had no authority to commit the USA on either of these points. Nevertheless, the story that China and Russia were going to "drop" Vietminh was made out to be Bidault's great achievement in Berlin: it implied an early French victory over Viet-

---

[6] He is also said to have "promised" Dulles the ratification of EDC in return for Dulles's reluctant acceptance of the Geneva meeting.

minh. The *Monde* and *Figaro* correspondents in Berlin were "briefed" by Bidault to play up the story; the vision of Ho Chi Minh in the rôle of Markos, the Greek guerilla leader who, in 1948, *was* abandoned by Stalin (though in a completely different context), also made its appearance, soon afterwards, in the British and American press—though what exactly the French were able to give Moscow and Peking in return was still far from clear. To add weight to the story, the official French news agency, on the eve of the debate on Indo-China at the National Assembly on March 9, came out with a remarkably garbled version (to put it mildly) of a speech made in Peking by Chen Yun, one of the Chinese Communist leaders. This "revised" version of his speech—which had only the remotest connexion with what he had actually said—"suggested" that China was willing to "drop" Ho Chi Minh, in order to consolidate world peace and internal Chinese stability. The full text of the speech, published in the *New China News Agency* bulletin of March 6 showed that the AFP version was a remarkably "free" rendering of what Chen Yun had said.

The publication of this strange "document" was intended to show what great things M. Bidault had achieved in Berlin—and also to sabotage in advance any serious negotiations at Geneva, or perhaps even to suggest that there was no need for any such Conference at all, since Vietminh was down the drain, anyway. However, one only had to study the Soviet press to see that there was not a word of truth in the "Markos" theory. This press played up Vietminh as it had never yet done before—a highly improbable prelude to "dropping" the Democratic Republic of Vietnam, as the Russians called it. Before Markos was dropped, there hadn't been a word about him in the Russian papers for months. *Pravda* treated with ridicule both Laniel's "conditions" for a cease-fire which he addressed to Vietminh in his speech of March 5, and Bidault's statement to the Foreign Affairs Committee of the Assembly whom he informed that he saw "no necessity to invite the representatives of Vietminh to Geneva", since he did not recognize the rebels as a "government".

Laniel's "conditions" for a cease-fire had been elaborated by M. Pleven, during the latter's visit to Indo-China in February, and by General Navarre. The conditions were so unrealistic that the American press, according to the Washington correspondent of the *Monde*, commented on them by saying that "fortunately" they had no chance at all of being accepted by Vietminh.

Laniel had demanded, among other things:

(1) the evacuation of all Vietminh troops from Laos;
(2) the creation of a no-man's land round the Tongking delta and a controlled withdrawal from it of all Vietminh troops (i.e. something the French had tried in vain to achieve by force of arms);

(3) the concentration of all the Vietminh troops within a specified area of Central Annam; and

(4) the disarming or evacuation of all such troops in South Vietnam.

No mention was made of Dien Bien Phu and other strongpoints in Vietminh areas held by the French; presumably Navarre intended to keep them. It all meant that Navarre was proposing the creation of a "continuous front" in Central Annam, and a total surrender to the French of the two most vital areas—Cochin-China and the Tongking Delta; the acceptance of these proposals by Vietminh would have meant a great strategic victory for France without a shot being fired.

Meantime, the London *Observer* had reported from Delhi counter-proposals which, it said, had been transmitted by Ho Chi Minh to India: their principal features were the creation of a 100-mile front just North of the 16th parallel; the surrender of Tongking to Vietminh and their evacuation of Cochin-China. These proposals broadly speaking, foreshadowed the terms of the Armistice that was finally negotiated in July. If they were contrary to Ho Chi Minh's constant insistence on the inseparability of the 3 Kys, it was, obviously, because he wanted to make their acceptance by France as easy as possible and so to avoid the risk of the war becoming "internationalized". These cease-fire proposals were made, however, without prejudice to any simultaneous or subsequent political settlement.

5. DIEN BIEN PHU

We now come to the most dramatic episode in the Indo-China War —the battle of Dien Bien Phu.

Dien Bien Phu was a stronghold which, under the "dynamic" Navarre Plan, had been artificially created for the purpose of disorganizing the enemy rear.

But the miscalculation was blatant. To quote a French military commentator:[7]

Paratroops had created on the frontier of the Thai country and Laos a "fixation point" for the regular units of the Vietminh Army. Experience had, however, shown that this "fortress", which was wholly dependent on an air-lift, had not prevented Vietminh troops from penetrating into the whole of Northern Laos.... The Navarre Plan expected Dien Bien Phu to attract towards it the enemy for "secondary operations", and provided for minor offensive operations against the enemy rear, complete with scattered tactical attacks. Instead, Dien Bien Phu became a besieged fortress, where only a major battle could be fought. As the weeks passed, the garrison had become more and more numerous, and, instead of being a "fixation point"

[7] Paul Rossel in *France-Observateur*, March 18, 1954.

for the enemy, it had become the "fixation centre" for the Expeditionary Corps. It was the French, and not Vietminh who were "bogged down" at Dien Bien Phu; and if Vietminh captured the place, the result would be a terrible weakening of the whole French position in the delta.

In November and December, soon after the first six battalions of paratroops had been dropped at Dien Bien Phu, the French forces could still embark on commando raids against the enemy rear; by February, Dien Bien Phu was already firmly encircled by Vietminh forces, though they were still careful not to attack.

An amazing first-hand account, relating to this period, was written by Robert Guillain in the *Monde*, describing the "peaceful week-end" he had spent at Dien Bien Phu at the beginning of February.

It was not a fortress in the ordinary sense; it was an "inverted" fortress—Dien Bien Phu was at the bottom of a "basin", and it was the jungle-covered hills around it that were occupied by the enemy. His first impression was one of being trapped, with invisible enemies watching him all the time; then, when he saw the labyrinth of underground passages—the "ant-heap"—complete with a forest of barbed-wire defences—that had been built in the last three months—he felt more reassured. The heart of the whole system was the airfield, with sometimes as many as 200 flights a day. Dien Bien Phu depended entirely on the airlift.

And what a strange army!—white, black, brown, and yellow.

When in Paris they talk about the army in Indo-China, they think of an army of Frenchmen, an army of white men fighting a yellow enemy. That was true in 1947. It was no longer true in 1951.... Today, at Dien Bien Phu you have before you a most extraordinary mixture of colours and races: Moroccans, Annamites, Algerians, Senegalese, Legionaries, Meos, Tonkinese, Thais, and Muongs.... So "yellow" has the expeditionary force become that the Frenchman has become almost a rarity.... Moreover, few Frenchmen have remained ordinary soldiers; nearly all are officers or nco's.

"Get the Viet down into the basin"—that (Guillain wrote) was the great dream of Colonel de Castries and of his whole staff. "Once he's come down, we'll catch him."[8]

But the trouble, in February, was that the "Viet" was not attacking. Giap was marking time, because he had great experience himself, and had also learned many tricks from Mao Tse Tung, among them the lesson that one did not attack an enemy stronghold without being sure of capturing it—without excessive losses.

Between the lines of Guillain's story one could read grave doubts

---

[8] *Le Monde*, February 14, 1954.

about the whole thing. Later, on May 10, when all was over, he wrote, looking back on it:

A visiting journalist allowed himself in the end to be convinced. And yet—plain common sense left a shadow of doubt in the visitor's mind. Before going to sleep that night, on my camp bed, deep down in the dugout, I wrote down in my notebook: "The first impression was one of being trapped and surrounded. That the enemy knew all about us, and that we knew nothing about him. A feeling of being in the lion's mouth. . . ."[9]

On March 16 the first details were published of Vietminh's long-overdue attack on Dien Bien Phu; they *had* "come down into the basin"; Colonel de Castries' dream had come true; but the awakening was not quite as happy as the dream.

Guillain wrote, no longer from Dien Bien Phu, but from Saigon:

One stronghold was captured by Vietminh after heavy hand-to-hand fighting; two other strongholds were attacked but not captured, despite the fury of the attack. . . . The French Command assure me that the situation is well in hand (*seventeen words cut by censor*). . . .
It started on Saturday afternoon with a powerful artillery barrage: note this: a great bombardment by *Vietminh's artillery*. For the first time Giap's famous artillery, which had never yet been in action, uncovered itself and fired at us. It is composed of 105 mm. guns, of American make. It was brought from the delta, along the RP41 highroad in Molotov trucks. . . .

And after the artillery barrage came Vietminh's suicide units who, armed with high explosive, often tied to their bodies, attacked the barbed-wire defences of Dien Bien Phu.

They suffer terrifying losses on the barbed wire, leaving hundreds of corpses behind. . . . And yet, here and there, they crawl through the gaps, or jump the defences with the help of light bamboo ladders . . . and then it's hand-to-hand fighting.[10]

Guillain reported that, at Saigon at that time, the French Command were still wondering whether, in attacking Dien Bien Phu, Vietminh had not made "a monumental mistake". Yet the fact remained that Vietminh troops had, despite "staggering" losses, captured one French stronghold in the very first attack. And, in the weeks that followed, more and more strongholds were going to be captured, till finally the area still in French hands was only 1,300 yards in diameter. The small size of the area and the high concentration of men in it—a large number among the 15,000 were by now sick and wounded—turned the place

---

[9] *Le Monde*, May 10, 1954.   [10] *Le Monde*, March 16, 1954.

into a hell in which almost every shell fired by Vietminh was a direct hit.

Navarre claimed, during those weeks, that Vietminh's artillery was the great "surprise" of the battle; that Dien Bien Phu was meant to deal with guerillas, not with a modern army. That the "surprise" was not genuine may be seen from the very grave doubts that were expressed about the Dien Bien Phu venture from the very start by General Cogny.

Thousands of gallons of US-made napalm were poured on the jungle round Dien Bien Phu by the French Air Force; but the Vietminh soldiers were so well dug-in that nothing could stop the pressure on Dien Bien Phu, and after 56 days of heavy fighting the fortress fell.

It had, throughout, been a pawn in the tortuous political game played in Paris and Geneva. How important it was for M. Bidault to keep Dien Bien Phu going may be seen from the fact that, although Dien Bien Phu should have been written off as a dead loss early in the siege, three paratroop battalions were sent there to replace the dead and wounded and to prolong the agony.

Why? Because so long as emotional tension was being maintained over Dien Bien Phu, it was easier to scream that only massive American intervention could still save the heroes fighting the Vietnam Communists and the Chinese who (various papers now claimed) were taking part in the siege—though without any evidence to support this story.

Anyway, it was an awkward story to tell, after Bidault had put forward the theory that both Russia and China were "dropping" Vietminh.

But consistency was no longer *de rigueur*. The real trouble was that those very members of the Government—and particularly Bidault and Laniel—who were now paying lip-service to "peace" and to the virtues of Geneva were also the very people who could least be trusted to pursue a peace policy.

This point was stressed by Mendès-France in his speech at the National Assembly on March 9 when he said: "Can these people be trusted to pursue a policy which is diametrically opposed to that which they have pursued up till now?"

And, as Dien Bien Phu was being built up into a symbol of the Free World's struggle against Communism, Bidault was banking more and more on American intervention.

6. "US SHIPS AND A-BOMBS ON WAY TO INDO-CHINA"

During March and April the USA attitude to Indo-China stiffened. If, in March, Eisenhower still spoke of the "awful" possibility of the USA becoming involved in the war in Indo-China, in April already

Dulles was openly threatening the Communists with direct American intervention. In any case, Dulles was obviously hoping that the war in Indo-China would continue.

It all gave rise to a struggle of great complexity during Dulles's visit to Paris, on the eve of the Geneva Conference. The main points may be summarized as follows:

(1) Without allowing himself to be wholly diverted by Indo-China, during his visit to Paris in April, Dulles pressed Bidault to sign a draft convention drawn up by the British Government, and specifying Britain's future relationship with the European Defence Community; despite objections raised by several members of the Government, Bidault authorized M. Hervé Alphand to sign it.

(2) In view of the reluctance shown by the British Government to become involved in the Indo-China war, Dulles was no longer insistent on sending a virtual Three-Power ultimatum to China, warning her against giving further help to Vietminh, but was now talking in terms of a Pacific Pact "similar to the Atlantic Pact". This, as seen by most French observers, simply meant that the war in Indo-China would become internationalized, and that France could never get out of it, without breaking various multilateral agreements.

(3) Dulles was by now scared of the feeling sweeping France in favour of ending the war in Indo-China (he was aware that even M. Pleven had, since his visit to Indo-China in February, taken a new line; that many French generals in Indo-China were against continuing the war, and that they had bluntly denied Mr Dulles's statement that his information on Chinese aid to Vietminh had come from them).

(4) Still pursuing his dreams of "Asians fighting Asians", Dulles was increasingly insistent on Americans being placed in charge of training the Bao Dai Army. By a curious "coincidence", Bao Dai, who had been telling the Americans at Saigon that he was much more wholehearted about the war than the French, arrived in Paris at the same time as Dulles. Before leaving for Paris, Dulles had had talks with the Ambassadors of Vietnam, Laos, and Cambodia in Washington. It looked as though Bao Dai might be promoted to the rank of Syngman Rhee.

But, most important of all, Dulles and Bidault agreed in April on the "principle" of American intervention. What form should this take? There were two problems: one, a long-term problem, the other, the urgent problem raised by Dien Bien Phu. To Bidault it was important that Dien Bien Phu should hold out as long as possible (hence the useless sacrifice of three more airborne battalions). The continued resistance of Dien Bien Phu would help Bidault both at Geneva and vis-à-vis the Americans: it would help him to show that France was still "worthy" of playing the leading part in the conduct of a war which nobody in France wanted any longer, but which might, with American help, continue in spite of it.

Dulles does not seem to have suggested the shipping of American troops in the near future; what was discussed were technicians, instructors, experts, and the possible dispatch to Indo-China of Chiang Kai Shek and Syngman Rhee troops, the intensified training of a bigger and better Bao Dai Army, etc. But the clear implication of it all was that the Vietnamese, Tunisians, Moroccans, Frenchmen, Koreans, Germans, Senegalese, and the rest of them would be under supreme American command. So much for the long-term plan.

But, to Bidault, this long-term planning was not enough. Dien Bien Phu could only be saved if there was urgent, large-scale intervention by the American Air Force. Whether, as a result, Dien Bien Phu was saved or not, it would mean that America was "in it".

What clearly emerges from all these tortuous talks in Paris, and, later, at Geneva, is that, although the planes and the A-bombs were already said to be on their way to Indo-China, the "war party" in the USA did not receive sufficient encouragement from a hesitant Eisenhower, who, for his own part, had been impressed by the sharp opposition shown to an "extension of the war" by the British Government, and refrained from putting the matter before Congress on April 26, as was at first planned. The war party would not, however, admit defeat right away; both before and after the fall of Dien Bien Phu the French press recorded growing or diminishing eagerness in the United States to strike out in Indo-China.

What perhaps also delayed the decision to strike was the rapid deterioration of the French position at Dien Bien Phu. This made it uncertain whether the USA Air Force could organize a gigantic air raid on the Vietminh forces around Dien Bien Phu sufficiently quickly to save the fortress. By the beginning of May all hope was gone; planes could no longer land at Dien Bien Phu, and at least half the supplies dropped were captured by Vietminh. For all that, according to the French press, Laniel and Bidault continued to send out SOS's to Eisenhower, and Radford and Van Fleet did not consider themselves beaten yet—not even if Dien Bien Phu were to fall in the next few days.[11]

During the last few weeks of Dien Bien Phu a tremendous propaganda drive was organized in the French press exalting the heroism of "the French garrison". The fact which was overlooked in France (though not in Germany) was that about one-third of the defenders of Dien Bien Phu were Germans—"mostly former SS-men", as Bourdet

[11] At the end of June US News and World Report published a detailed study of these negotiations, a study widely quoted in the French press. It transpired from this that Bidault had—with Dulles's support—strongly urged that the US Air-force make an all-out attack on the troops besieging Dien Bien Phu; but that he hated to subscribe to Admiral Radford's plan for dropping atom bombs on China which would have unleashed World War III. Thanks to British opposition, both plans were abandoned in the end.

put it perhaps rather too bluntly, "who had been released on condition that they join the Foreign Legion, where they could do some 'Viet-busting', and so let us forget the 'French-busting' they had done in the past".

Apart from 220 French officers and 1,000 French nco's there were not many French at Dien Bien Phu; the bulk of the troops were composed of colonial troops, some Vietnamese and the Legion.[12] Some of the paratroops were "non-Indo-Chinese yellows"; the awkward question asked by Bourdet was whether these were not Chiang Kai Shek men who had been interned in Indo-China since 1950.

No doubt it was easy enough and more than justified to exalt the heroism of the defenders of Dien Bien Phu, of Colonel de Castries and Geneviève de Galard, "the angel—or the Florence Nightingale—of Dien Bien Phu". The fact remains that a prominent French general described Dien Bien Phu to *France-Observateur* as a "crime, a political crime". But the build-up of all the heroism had political motives behind it. When Cardinal Spellman came to Paris in May, he said that the world had heard the "horn of Roland" being blown at Dien Bien Phu. It was almost like saying that the Infidels should be routed and Roland avenged.

Another propaganda line shot by a large part of the French press and, even more so, by the State-controlled radio was about "colossal Chinese aid"—Chinese artillery, Molotov trucks, etc. And another one still was to stress the inhumanity shown by Vietminh in not allowing the wounded to be evacuated from the fortress; in reality, everything shows that the dilatory tactics used by M. Bidault at Geneva, and his extreme reluctance to have any contact with the "rebels", the Russians and the Chinese extended to the question of securing a "humanitarian truce".[13]

Dien Bien Phu had some grotesque repercussions in Paris. At a ceremony at the Arc de Triomphe M. Laniel and M. Pleven received kicks in the pants from some men who claimed to be Indo-China war veterans; but whether war veterans or not, these men were later found to belong to a "commando" in close contact with certain police authorities (a theory supported by the fact that the police were remarkably slow in "rescuing" the two ministers from the angry crowd at the Etoile that day). It was also they who, by threatening to cause major trouble at the Opera on the night of the fall of Dien Bien Phu, induced M. Laniel to prohibit the show to be given by the Soviet Ballet (complete with Ulanova), and to invite the dancers to go back to

---

[12] How numerous the German (and other non-French) soldiers were was made apparent by the publication in the *Monde* and other papers of lists of prisoners taken by Vietminh after the fall of Dien Bien Phu.

[13] *Cf.* "Mensonges officiels sur l'évacuation des blessés", by H. de Galard: in *France-Observateur*, May 13, 1954.

Russia, even though the Comédie Française was, at that very time, playing to packed houses in Moscow.

7. THE END OF LANIEL

Meantime the Laniel Government was at sixes and sevens. Generals Ely, Salan, and Pélissier, who had been sent to Indo-China, returned from there with an extremely pessimistic report. The question they raised was whether Parliament would authorize regular French conscripts (*le contingent*) to be sent there from France.

M. Bidault, despite the reasonable cease-fire proposals made by Pham Van Dong, the chief Vietminh delegate at Geneva, and supported, up to a point, by Mr Eden, had not given up hope that the Americans might yet intervene in a big way.

The Generals were not enchanted with the idea; and thought that, in any case, the situation was so serious in the Tongking Delta with Vietminh infiltrations all over the place, that France had better hasten to agree on a cease-fire.

A part of the Government was shocked by this "defeatism" of the Generals; M. Teitgen, one of Bidault's closest MRP associates, is said to have spontaneously exclaimed: "But that would be capitulation! And it would show that we had been wrong for seven years!" A *cri de cœur*, if ever there was one. An equally "anti-defeatist" line was taken —naturally—by Bidault, as well as by Martinaud-Déplat, Maurice Schumann and Laniel.

But it was no good. The Laniel Government was on its last legs. It had public sentiment against it, and its majority in Parliament was rapidly dwindling. By the beginning of June it had a majority of only two votes. The Minister for Indo-China Affairs, M. Jacquet, in total disagreement with M. Bidault, resigned, and was replaced—of all people—by M. Fréderic-Dupont, one of the Indo-China diehards. M. Bidault's delaying tactics at Geneva, his hope for some political miracle in Washington or some military miracle in Indo-China and his reluctance to endorse Eden's "partition plan", were causing growing exasperation on all sides.

The *coup de grâce* to the Laniel Government was delivered by Mendès-France, the obvious candidate for the succession. His speech at the National Assembly on June 9 was in answer to M. Bidault's woolly speech, of which "internationalization in case the Geneva Conference fails" was the principal theme.

He began by recalling that all those who had favoured negotiations in Indo-China had for a long time been treated as "Moscow agents". He then ridiculed Bidault's "grand idea"—which was to defeat Ho

Chi Minh by making the USA "pay off China"—even though M. Bidault was in no position to commit the USA to such a course.

The rest was tragi-comedy: for several weeks at Geneva now Bidault had avoided talking to the Chinese, to neutrals like the Indians (who might be helpful) or to the Vietminh representatives.

During the six weeks that the Conference has already lasted, there wasn't a single serious talk between the two delegates most directly interested in the conflict. Many abroad suspect the sincerity and the good faith of the French delegation, and public opinion in this country has been quite right to compare the attitude of our delegation with the determination shown by the British to arrive at a settlement.

Mendès-France then attacked Bidault for having nearly started World War III:

You had a plan which was revealed at the beginning of May: the large-scale intervention of the American Air Force at the risk of provoking Chinese intervention and general war. Parliament had adjourned on April 10, but M. Laniel had undertaken to call it if there was anything new and important. The American intervention Plan had been prepared, and was about to come into action—at your request, too! The attack was to be launched on April 28, and the ships with the aircraft and the atom bombs were on the way. President Eisenhower was going to ask Congress on April 26 for the necessary authority. The French Parliament was going to be faced with a *fait accompli*. Never had any Government taken such a responsibility with such a total disregard of Parliament. (*Cheers on Left*.) Fortunately, the plan was rejected by Britain and by public opinion in the USA—at least for the time being.

Five years before, Mendès-France said, he had already told the Government of the day that French policy in Indo-China would inevitably demand more and more sacrifices and, in the end, necessitate the dispatch of French conscripts to Vietnam.

At that time military victory was possible in Indo-China, if you were willing to pay the price. But you wanted public opinion to imagine that victory could be won at a low cost. Today it is too late. Whatever you do, you will not change the course of events.

And he foreshadowed the possibility of units of the French conscript army being sent to Vietnam; but if this were done, it should only be "to give security for our soldiers who are continuing to fight there, 7,000 miles away from their homeland, in hard conditions and without any illusions". They must not be sent there to prolong the war. And it would be intolerable to send them there and put them in the hands of people who had shown such a total lack of foresight throughout the years.

As for French diplomacy, it was high time (Mendès-France said) that it stopped its present tortuous game:

It must be made obvious that what we want is not American intervention but an honourable ending to this horrible war. Well, we are not at all sure that the flattering promotion of M. Frédéric-Dupont can destroy the doubts existing about our real aims. For M. Frédéric-Dupont's argument was always that we were not sufficiently deeply involved in Indo-China! He always clamoured for "final victory", he always wanted to "crush the enemy"; this is the kind of man you have sent to Geneva to negotiate with the said enemy!

After dealing with North Africa, EDC and a variety of other problems—the whole speech was, indeed, like a condensed pre-view of his investiture speech only a few days later—Mendès-France concluded by saying that if the Laniel Government were to be succeeded merely by another one looking just like it, then it was not worth overthrowing; but if Parliament were willing to listen to the clamour for something different coming from the French towns and the French countryside, then the time was ripe for turning over a new leaf.

One often heard it said, Mendès-France concluded, that France was suffering from government instability; it wasn't true. Practically without a break, the same people had filled the same jobs since the beginning of the Fourth Republic. (What he chiefly meant was that the Government departments dealing with Foreign Affairs and Indo-China had been virtually monopolized for years past by a small group of the MRP, with Bidault or Schuman at the head of one, and Coste-Floret or Letourneau at the head of the other.) It was contrary to the will of France that adversity should cement these statues into their pedestals! (*Loud cheers on the Socialist and Gaullist benches.*)

That same night, the Laniel Government was defeated, and finally overthrown on a motion of confidence three days later. The Socialists, Communists, most of the Gaullists and half the Radicals voted against; the whole of the MRP and most of the Right voted for the Laniel-Bidault team, who had, in fact, nothing to offer other than a "Dunkirk" in Tongking or—a Third World War. Irrelevantly they muttered something about a "Far Eastern Munich", and about their downfall being "a victory for the Kremlin". Sure enough, this theme was to be taken up in a part of the US press a few days later when Mendès-France was about to become Head of the new Government.

CHAPTER TWO

THE "DISQUIETING" MENDES-FRANCE TAKES OVER

I. A DAZZLING START

BY THE middle of June 1954, the position of the Expeditionary Corps in Indo-China had become so precarious, and the "negotiations" conducted at Geneva by M. Bidault and M. Frédéric-Dupont (no more extravagant appointment than his could be imagined in the circumstances) were so slow and seemingly sterile that the need for drastic remedies had become obvious to practically everybody. Perhaps a few diehards (M. Bidault among them) were still hoping that by resorting to delaying tactics at Geneva, they might yet hold out till the time when the "interventionists" in the USA would again gain the upper hand—as they had nearly done at the end of April; but public opinion in France was now practically unanimous in favour of winding up the Indo-China war on almost any conditions.

A decisive factor in this strong outburst of feeling were the more and more frequent references to *le contingent*—i.e. to the possibility that ordinary French conscripts, *our* Pierre or *our* Jacques, might have to be sent there if there was no armistice. Anyone who, like the present writer, happened to be in provincial France about that time, knows how strong the feeling was. At Le Bugue-sur-Vézère, a small town in the Dordogne in that mid-June, there were only two topics of conversation: the two Laval boys, only sons of the retired schoolmaster, who had both been killed in Indo-China (one of them only "the other day", at Dien Bien Phu); and the fact that the *contingent* might soon have to be sent there. The death of both the Laval boys in Indo-China "would kill" their poor mother; it was a shame how young fellows like them—such *beaux garçons*, too—had been tempted to volunteer for the Indo-China army. Of course, they were well-paid there—200,000 a month; if they came home alive, they might well have each a million francs tucked away; but, as Mme. Laroumanie, the *épicière* with her three big strapping sons said: "I wouldn't have any of my sons go out to Indo-China even if they were paid a million *a month*! I'd rather Jean remained a booking-clerk at the Gare d'Austerlitz for the rest of his life!" As for being sent out there as ordinary conscripts, without any extra pay—that would be really the limit!

From the moment Mendès-France took over, the sales of newspapers at Le Bugue-sur-Vézère shot up as never before. The dead-line Mendès-France had fixed for himself for negotiating a cease-fire before July 20 seized people's imagination as nothing had done for a long time. Here at last was a man who was getting things done, and was not content to muddle along like Bidault and that "absurd" M. Laniel. It was a gamble for high stakes; would he, or wouldn't he win? It was much more exciting than the *Tour de France*—and so much more important. *Un type formidable*, people were saying. If anybody remarked (and the remark was not uncommon)—*"Oui, mais c'est un juif"*—there were three reactions I recorded at the time. One was to say that that was wholly irrelevant; he was a great French patriot, who had been a fighter pilot in the Resistance; another that it wasn't true—it was American propaganda that was spreading the story that he was a Jew; and, finally: "Well, it's just too bad that the French politicians are so stupid and inept that we have to depend on a Jew to get us out of the mess. And good luck to him!"

June 17 was, indeed, a historic date in the annals of the National Assembly. Mendès-France was in great form when he mounted the tribune to make his investiture speech. He recalled that he had favoured a cease-fire in Indo-China long ago; "it was because we had more trumps in those days, and I wanted better peace terms than what we can hope to get now".

But even now there are surrenders to which we need not agree.... France need not accept, and will not acccept a settlement which would be incompatible with her vital interests. We shall stay in the Far East; let our allies and our opponents make no mistake about it.

Then came the allusion to the fact that if the negotiations failed, it might be necessary to send parts of the French conscript army to Indo-China:

The safety of our Expeditionary Corps and the preservation of its strength are a sacred duty in which neither the Government nor Parliament will fail.

And then came the "gamble"—which so much annoyed M. Raymond Aron of the *Figaro*:

The cease-fire must come quickly. The Government I intend to form will fix for itself—and for our opponents—a time limit.... To-day is June 17. On July 20 I shall report to you on the results achieved. If no satisfactory solution has been reached, our "contract" will be cancelled, and my Government will hand its resignation to the President of the Republic.

There followed another allusion to the *contingent*; if, in the next few weeks it was necessary, for the safety of the Expeditionary Corps, to take certain measures requiring parliamentary approval, he (Mendès-France) would not hesitate to make the relevant proposals to Parliament.

This "Indo-China gamble" was the most sensational part of Mendès-France's investiture speech. The economic programme of the Government was mentioned only briefly, and closely followed the general line Mendès-France had already outlined in his investiture speech a year before.

Rather more excitement was caused by what he had to say on EDC and Germany:

After peace has been restored in Indo-China, and after the essential decisions have been taken for our economic revival, France will have to state clearly what policy she intends to pursue on the vital question of Europe. Both in respect of her friends and in respect of herself, she cannot allow the *équivoque* to continue any longer; for this is damaging to the Western Alliance.

It was necessary, he said, to put an end to all the painful doubts and hesitations over EDC, and over "the cruel prospect" of German rearmament. He clearly indicated that there was room for a "compromise" between those favouring EDC and those opposed to it, and he undertook to put certain proposals before Parliament before the summer recess, and so "give our allies that clear and constructive answer to which they have been entitled for a long time". After foreshadowing a more liberal policy in North Africa—"where we must keep the promises we have made to Tunisia and Morocco"—he repeated that the government's immediate programme fell into three stages: Indo-China settlement before July 20; an economic programme, in respect of which the Government would ask Parliament for special powers; and clear decisions to be taken in respect of "Europe".

The most awkward problem for Mendès-France (as he saw it) were the 95 Communist votes. If the Communists voted for him (and they declared their intention to do so) it would be argued, especially abroad, that he had been "invested"—at least in part—by the Communists. Although many critics later said that this was both "undemocratic" and "unconstitutional", Mendès-France declared, before the investiture vote, that he would not "count" the Communist votes; and that if there was no "constitutional majority" of 314 (after the favourable Communist votes had been deducted), he would not proceed with the formation of the Government.

Addressing M. Billoux who, on behalf of his friends, had announced that, "for the sake of peace in Indo-China", and despite many "reservations" on certain other aspects of M. Mendès-France's programme, the Communists would vote for him, the prospective premier said:

I should like to thank M. Billoux for his precious support. (*Laughter.*) But . . . he must surely know that I am determined not to count as part of my investiture majority the 95 votes he is so generously giving me. (*Cheers on Socialist and Gaullist benches.*) The Communists and I are profoundly divided on many issues; and in this case the reasons for my determination not to accept their votes appear to me decisive. What, indeed, would be the feelings of our soldiers in Indo-China if they knew that the country for which they are fighting is governed by a man who had at least partially been appointed by a party which had refused to pay homage to those who had "piously died for their country". (*Prolonged cheers on all except the Communist benches.*)

He added that at Geneva the Government would have to negotiate with the adversaries of France—those very men to whom the Communist Party had, for years, expressed its sympathy and solidarity. If the French Government had (even in part) been appointed by the Communists, it could only undermine in the eyes of the world the authority and independence of the French delegation at Geneva.

Mendès-France had again embarked on a rather reckless gamble; but he won: the Assembly gave him an overwhelming vote of confidence: 419 votes to 47. The 419 included 95 Communists, which still meant that 324 non-Communists had voted for him—or ten votes above the "constitutional majority", admittedly not a very wide margin. It is true that if he had not explicitly "rejected" the Communist votes, fewer non-Communists would have voted for him. But it was a dangerous precedent to set up; and MRP speakers did not fail to exploit it when they wondered whether, in the case of EDC, for example, the Communist votes would be "counted" or "not counted"; even many of Mendès-France's friends doubted whether, in the long run, it was a wise move. But Mendès-France's curious manœuvre had, obviously, a clear immediate object—which was to facilitate his task at Geneva, and make him "respectable" in the eyes of the USA. The Communists, needless to say, were furious. Duclos angrily referred to Mendès-France in the Lobby as a "gutless and cold-footed little Jew" (a phrase picked up with great relish by the Jewish press in the USA, and one for which Duclos was, soon afterwards, to be rapped over the knuckles by the Central Committee of the French CP). But when somebody asked Duclos if the Communists were still going to vote for Mendès, he replied: "Yes, we shall. It can't be helped."

Public opinion in the country was unquestionably favourable to Mendès, and had been tremendously impressed by his Indo-China deadline. Even many Communists thought that his objectionable attitude to them was perhaps chiefly "tactical". But whereas Parliament was fully conscious of the immense impression his "gamble" had made in the country, it felt a little uneasy about him.

As Fauvet wrote in the *Monde* before the investiture vote:

Just because he doesn't respect certain rules of the game, the man seems to worry and indispose even those who constantly complain of parliamentary routine. He didn't, before making his investiture speech, consult any of the groups—not that this really mattered, since all groups, with two or three exceptions, are so divided on most issues that nobody could commit them to voting one way or the other.... Even so, Mendès is suspected of either despising office so much that he doesn't care on how many toes he treads, or else of wanting office so desperately that he is willing to adopt, if necessary, the policy of his enemies. Everything concerning Mendès-France is not so much a matter of pure politics as a question of psychological and personal reactions.... He has the flattering, but slightly alarming reputation of being a man *hors série*, who might be accepted *intuitu personæ, intuitu rationis* without the blessing of any party.[1]

On the following day, Fauvet praised Mendès for his "courage" in rejecting the Communist votes; this, he said, had produced an ovation at the Assembly, the like of which had not been heard for a long time. Perhaps he had no choice; already the American press was saying that, by promising to vote for him, the Communists had given him "the kiss of death".[2] The first reactions in America and Germany to Mendès-France's candidature had, indeed, been distinctly hostile, while the press in Franco Spain had referred to him as "the man of the Popular Front".

In France, the right-wing press was reserved at first. Raymond Aron, in the *Figaro*, deplored the "patent medicine advertising" methods of the "cure in thirty days"; and thought the "dead-line" an "intolerable stunt of playing double-or-quits with the Government and with an international conference". But although the Socialists had refused to join the Government (they had no liking for M. Faure's economic policy), their press was enthusiastic about Mendès, and so were the "non-conformist" and "intellectual" papers like *Le Monde*, *Combat*, *Franc-Tireur*, *France-Observateur*, and the most "Mendèsiste" of all the papers, the weekly *Express*. Partly out of admiration for Mendès, and his "new technique of governing", and partly because it had, no doubt, sensed the strong currents of public opinion in his favour, a

[1] *Le Monde*, June 18, 1954.
[2] In reality, the Communists were merely following the decisions taken by their Central Committee at Drancy in October 1953 to vote for "comparatively progressive" candidates: thus, they had voted for Naegelen (Soc.) in the Presidential Election in December 1953 and for Le Troquer (Soc.) in the election of the President of the National Assembly in January 1954.

popular evening paper like *France-Soir* lent a hand in the Mendès "build-up". Before long, almost the entire press became pro-Mendès, even an "ultra-reactionary" paper like *l'Aurore* publishing PMF's wartime reminiscences as a serial!

On June 19 he formed his Government from which practically all the members of the "old gang" were excluded: Laniel, Reynaud, Queuille, Teitgen, Bidault, Martinaud-Déplat, Pleven, André Marie, Maurice Schumann, de Chevigné, and so many other of the *immobilistes* and Indo-China and North Africa diehards. The 16 Ministers included 5 Radicals, 4 Gaullists, 2 UDSR's, 4 right-wing "independents", and 1 (undisciplined) MRP; the proportion was roughly the same among the 13 Secretaries of State.[3] No doubt, the composition of this Government was enough to show how vulnerable Mendès-France would soon become, once the full effect of his "shock tactics" over Indo-China had worn off. Whichever way one looked at it, it was not a coherent government. While peace in Indo-China was No 1 target, it didn't matter; but what would happen once EDC came up for discussion? Practically all the Gaullists in the Government were determined opponents of EDC; while others, like M. Bourgès-Maunoury and M. Guérin de Beaumont, for instance, were known as strong pro-EDC men.

However, that was still a problem for the future; at the height of his popularity in June and July—both before and after the deadline of July 20—Mendès perhaps still thought that he could square the circle, and govern either with the help of "public opinion", which would strongly resent his overthrow by Parliament, or, failing that, with *alternative* majorities—the Right supporting him in some cases, and the Left in others.

He tackled Indo-China with a tremendous display of energy and virtuosity. Without wasting any time, he received Eden and Bedell Smith (the US representative at Geneva) almost the moment the Government was formed; "it's a change of method, rather than of policy", the *Monde* wrote, "and the British Foreign Office certainly prefers his methods to Bidault's". On the day after his Government was formed—Sunday, June 20—this was his time-table:

[3] Ministers: Premier and Foreign Affairs: Mendès-France (Rad.); Justice, E. Hugues (Rad.); Defence, General Koenig (Gaull.); Interior, F. Mitterrand (UDSR); Finance, Edgar Faure (Rad.); Education, Berthoin (Rad.); Public Works, Chaban-Delmas (Gaull.); Industry and Trade, Bourgès-Maunoury (Rad.); Agriculture, Houdet (Right); Associated States of Indo-China, Guy La Chambre (Right); Overseas France, Buron (MRP); Reconstruction, Lemaire (Gaull.); Labour, Claudius-Petit (UDSR); Health, Aujolat (Right); War Veterans, Temple (Right); Tunisia and Morocco, Fouchet (Gaull.).

The Secretaries of State included Guérin de Beaumont (Right, Foreign Affairs); André Monteil (MRP, Navy); Diomède Catroux (Gaull., Air); Ulver (Gaull., Budget).

9.30. Received M. Massigli, French Ambassador in London and M. Chauvel, Ambassador in Berne, and interim head of the French delegation at Geneva.

11.15. Took over Premier's office from M. Laniel.

12.10. Took over Quai d'Orsay from Bidault and had most of the higher officials presented to him.

1.30 p.m. Lunch at British Embassy with Eden, Gladwyn Jebb, and Massigli.

3.15. Further conversation with Eden.

4.0. Conference with immediate assistants, Pelabau and Georges Boris; also General Ely, Chauvel, etc.

5.05 to 6.10 p.m. Received Bedell Smith and US Ambassador Dillon.

7.30. Press conference.

That was the kind of rhythm at which Mendès-France worked—both in Paris and at Geneva—during those thirty days before the famous 20th of July. Apart from endless meetings with experts and generals in Paris, there were the series of meetings in Switzerland with Chou En Lai, with whom he agreed almost at once that there should be simultaneous negotiations for a cease-fire and for a political settlement; there were direct talks with Pham Van Dong, the Vietminh representative, and (as far as necessary) with the somewhat neglected Bao Dai representatives, as well as with Krishna Menon, the very helpful Indian delegate. Contact was constant with Eden; and on July 9 Molotov returned to Geneva. Finally—during the Mendès-Eden-Dulles talks in Paris on July 14—Mendès persuaded Dulles (who continued to sulk and refused to go to Geneva) at least to send Bedell Smith there.

During those first three weeks an enormous amount of ground had been cleared. The "finish" of July 20 was now clearly in sight. On the 16th a series of meetings of "capital importance"[4] began between Mendès, Eden, and Molotov. A last-minute hitch was caused by Cambodia; but, in the end, the Geneva agreement was signed, barely a few hours after the deadline had expired.

It had not been easy for Mendès-France to devote his undivided attention to Indo-China during those thirty days. The US Government was in an unpleasant and distrustful mood. In a personal message to President Coty, President Eisenhower had, in effect, "protested" against the overthrow of the Laniel Government, and had thought fit to remind France of her "duties" to Europe.

M. Spaak, not content to be merely a leader of little Belgium, and straining to become one of the great leaders of "Europe", albeit a "Little Europe", waited barely a week after the formation of the Mendès-France Government before he began to pester the new Premier with his project for an immediate Six-Power meeting to discuss EDC.

⁴ *Le Monde*, June 17, 1954.

Mendès had to tell him, rather sharply, that the Indo-China settlement must come first.

Bonn and Washington were both acutely worried. The pro-Adenauer press in Western Germany was saying that Mendès-France was going to "sabotage" Europe; at the beginning of July Dulles turned on once again the "agonizing reappraisal" tune; the Germans rejoiced at this renewed pressure on France, and Adenauer hastened to make an angry statement saying that if there was to be no EDC, then the only alternative was a revival of the Wehrmacht. Mendès, who had meant to reassure Adenauer by sending the pro-EDC Guérin de Beaumont to Bonn, cancelled the mission after Adenauer's truculent speech.

There were other complications. At the end of June the hard-pressed Franco-Vietnamese troops proceeded to evacuate the southern part of the Tongking Delta, and crowds of refugees started pouring into Hanoi and Haiphong—even though the French population of Hanoi was itself, by now, preparing to quit. On July 7 Mendès-France had to announce officially that the *contingent* would be sent to Indo-China if no settlement was reached by July 20. This was meant as a warning to China, and produced the first reasonably favourable reactions in the USA. Pro-Mendès papers like the *Monde* pleaded with Moscow and Peking that Mendès's failure would, sooner or later, lead to an extension of the war. But by the time Molotov returned to Geneva, it was fairly obvious that Moscow and Peking were both anxious to avoid anything of the kind. They realized that if there was no agreement by July 20, Mendès would go, and Bidault might be back in office again, and there was no guarantee that he would not ask again for 500-bomber raids on Vietminh, with Admiral Radford willing to go one better, and drop atom bombs on China. America's changing moods in these matters were unpredictable.

It is unnecessary here to discuss in detail the terms of the Geneva settlement of July 20—the demarcation line just south of the 17th parallel, complete with the transfer of Tongking to Vietminh within 300 days; the evacuation of the Vietminh forces from the south; the provisions for a general election in both zones of Vietnam in July 1956; the "regrouping" of the various forces; the "neutralization" of Laos and Cambodia, the economic and cultural rights to be preserved in Indo-China by France, etc. Many of these provisions—especially those concerning the Election—were pregnant with many future difficulties and complications; it became obvious before long that both in France and in the USA there were people who were hoping to turn South Vietnam into another "South Korea", and prevent the 1956 election, which might well unify the country under Communist rule, from taking place at all. But it was agreed in France that the agreement was not a "dishonourable" one; that, considering the precarious state of the

French forces in Indo-China, the "East" had made more concessions at Geneva than the "West", and that the net result was as good as could be expected. And the main thing was, of course, that the fighting was over, and that there would be no need to send the *contingent*.

The whole of France heaved a sigh of relief; Mendès-France was immensely popular throughout the country, and no one would believe a word of it when the MRP leaders tried to demonstrate that if they had remained in office, the result of the Geneva conference would have been not merely the same but indeed, better!

"Sirius" (Beuve-Méry) wrote in the *Monde* on July 22:

The clear common sense, the quiet determination, the perfect loyalty and, indeed, the astonishing physical endurance of Mendès-France have contributed enormously to this great achievement.... The end of hostilities in Indo-China was the *sine qua non* of a French revival. This ruinous war made it impossible for us to balance our budget.... For a long time this war cost more than all the American aid we were receiving; and even if, latterly, it began to "bring in" dollars, how could France have continued to be mistress of her own foreign policy, and shake off this new form of bondage? ... The continuous massacre of our officers and nco's was disorganizing our forces in Germany, North Africa, and France.... Our allies were aware of it, and therefore insisted, more and more, on German rearmament.... Our whole national life was poisoned by this running sore. It created a gulf of ignorance and incomprehension between a nation (which imagined that since the soldiers in Indo-China were *cadres* and volunteers, it was nothing but a "police operation against rebels") and the French forces in Vietnam which, for all their heroism, were something like mercenaries, nevertheless. The high proportion of coloured troops and the Foreign Legion only strengthened this impression.

After recalling that only too many people had made this war a profitable racket (and it was also these people who tried to denounce anyone telling the truth as a "traitor"), Beuve-Méry dealt with the latest "Munich" argument:

There is no connexion with Munich. At Munich we gratuitously abandoned a key position to Hitler and betrayed a nation ready to fight. In Indo-China, on the contrary, we persisted in fighting a useless and increasingly hopeless war.

He concluded by saying that Mendès-France should now use all his well-deserved prestige and authority for bringing about a peaceful settlement in Europe—without German rearmament; this non-rearmament of Germany should be a prelude to a general disarmament; and France, helped by England (as she was in the course of the Geneva negotiations) should do her utmost to reduce tension everywhere between East and West. Only would England be as helpful in Europe as she had been over South-East Asia? Could not France and England combine their powers of persuasion in talking to the Russians, Americans, and Germans in an effort to reach a satisfactory settlement of the German problem?

As could have been foreseen, this Anglo-French "coalition", so fruitful in the Indo-China settlement, did not apply in the case of Europe. Far from it.

There were some melancholy post-mortems on all the terrible waste of the Indo-China war; the Expeditionary Corps had, between the end of 1945 and June 1, 1954, lost 92,000 men in dead and missing, among them 19,000 French, 43,000 Indo-Chinese, 30,000 Legionnaires (French and foreign, mostly German), Africans and North Africans. One hundred and fourteen thousand had been wounded and 28,000 taken prisoner; the total effectives of the "Free World" forces were given at over 550,000, 76,000 of them French, 100,000 Indian-Chinese of the French Expeditionary Corps, 17,000 men of the Foreign Legion, 56,000 Africans and North Africans, and 310,000 Bao Dai and other "national" troops.[5]

The war had cost over 3,000 milliard francs, of which 2,385 milliards had come out of the French budget; except for 1954, France had paid the greater share of the cost.[6]

In short (allowing for the higher value of the franc in the early years of the war) something like £3,000 million had gone down the drain.

Mendès-France reported on the outcome of Geneva to the National Assembly on July 22. It was one of the great days in the parliamentary history of France. There was no open rejoicing; Mendès-France stressed that the Geneva agreements had been rendered necessary as a result of a French defeat, itself the outcome of a disastrous policy pursued for nearly eight years. In order not to poison the atmosphere, he pulled his punches and tried to take as charitable a view as possible of the "preparatory work" done by Bidault at Geneva. Bidault's criticism of the settlement was weak and rather petulant, with its harping on the "Munich" theme, and on the excessive part played by nations like

---

[5] This total figure, which is about 150,000 higher than that quoted in an earlier chapter, comprises what looks like a greatly inflated figure of over 300,000 men for the Bao Dai and other "national" Indo-Chinese armies. These had largely been formed only "on paper".

[6] The constant increase is well illustrated by the following figures of French budget expenditure on the war in Indo-China (in milliard francs):

1946....101·8	1949....177·3	1952....427·6
1947....131·3	1950....258·3	1953....403·5
1948....136·3	1951....321·0	1954....428·0

Le Monde, July 21, 1954

India in this "neutralist" settlement; for although the Indians were "neutral", Bidault said, they invariably took the Communist side when it came to the point. Various objections were also raised by M. Frédéric-Dupont who thought that the settlement merely meant that Indo-China would be abandoned to the Communists "in three stages".

Mendès-France effectively dealt with Bidault's and Frédéric-Dupont's arguments, and, on the following day, after the greater part of the Assembly—Socialists, Gaullists, Communists and Radicals—had joined in a tremendous ovation in Mendès-France's honour, the Assembly passed by 669 votes to 9 the part of the motion recording its satisfaction at the termination of hostilities in Indo-China, "largely due to the decisive action of the head of the Government", and its realization that "the cruel sacrifices were inevitable". This part of the motion added that France would defend, within the framework of the French Union and of the Geneva agreements, the French and pro-French populations in Indo-China. The next paragraph, "approving the Government's statements", was passed by 501 votes to 93, and the motion in its entirety by 462 votes to 13. The principal opposition (or abstention) came from the MRP. More charitable critics of the MRP were now saying that even if Bidault's policy at Geneva wasn't perhaps "quite as bad" as had seemed at first, the most that could have been expected from Geneva with Bidault still in charge was "another Panmunjom". (In the course of which, no doubt, the French Expeditionary Corps would have been thrown into the sea.)

2. TUNISIA: "LOYALTY AND NO MENTAL RESERVATIONS"

It will be remembered that in his investiture speech, Mendès-France declared the following three to be his "immediate" objectives: Peace in Indo-China; economic reforms; and a clear decision on EDC. But sensational developments in the Arab world upset this time-table, and were partly responsible for the virtual shelving of the economic problems—as far as Mendès-France himself was concerned.

These developments were of two orders: on the one hand, the terrorism against the French both in Tunisia and Morocco and the "counter-terrorism" by the Red Hand and other French organizations were increasing in scope and frequency; and, on the other hand, the Anglo-Egyptian Treaty, complete with the evacuation of Suez by the British, had focused world attention on the Arab World. French North Africa was the only part of this Arab world that was, not only in reality (as Libya was) under European rule, but also juridically.

Could France hope to preserve North Africa—without an ever-growing list of murders and massacres? Could a sufficient number of concessions be made to North Africa to bring about a "peaceful co-existence" between French and Arab, while preserving for France some of her old privileges?

That was the question Mendès-France bluntly put to himself and his colleagues at the end of July; and on July 31, in a manner likely to create the biggest possible "psychological shock", he flew off to Tunis, accompanied by Marshal Juin and M. Christian Fouchet, Gaullist Minister for Tunisia and Morocco. It was perhaps a good idea to start in Tunisia, the least "depressed" of the three North-African countries,[7] and one with a progressive nationalist party which was, fundamentally, less hostile to the French, and less Pan-Arab and xenophobe than the more extreme nationalists in Algeria and Tunisia. Moreover, fewer French economic interests were involved in Tunisia than in the other two countries.

The trip to Tunis had not been a sudden brainwave. In July, the terrorism had assumed particularly alarming proportions. Thus, on July 7 at Menéei-Bou-Zelfa, in the Cap Bon area, eight members of the Neo-Destour youth organizations were murdered by French terrorists. A few days later came the "retort": at Ferryville, the arsenal of Bizerta, in the heart of the European town, 11 Europeans were killed and 22 wounded by "fellaga" gunmen. On the following day, in two different places, Arabs in a Moorish café were mowed down by tommy-gun fire from French "counter-terrorists" in a car outside. And so it went on, day after day. M. Voizard, the Resident-General (though a devoted Vichyite in the past),[8] was violently upbraided and insulted by French *colons* for his "gutlessness" when he attended the funeral of the victims of the Ferryville shootings.

Before leaving for Tunis, Mendès-France not only took several hours to persuade his cabinet that he was doing the right thing, but also felt compelled to give some assurance to Senator Colonna (representative of the French in Tunisia at the Council of the Republic); and it was partly to reassure the diehards that he asked Marshal Juin to accompany him on his journey. The plans for this journey had been kept a well-guarded secret, and the news in the evening papers, on Saturday, July 31 that since that morning Mendès-France, Juin, and Fouchet were in Tunis produced in France the right "psychological shock". As in the case of Indo-China, so also in the case of Tunis, there was more and more talk of *le contingent* being sent there to fight the "terrorists", and, in this case, several battalions had actually sailed, and others were about to sail.

---

[7] "Less depressed" in the sense that, despite much economic stagnation, compared with Morocco, there was less abject poverty than in that country and a less acute problem of a starving surplus population than in Algeria.

[8] *Cf.* "Qui est Voizard?" in *L'Humanité*, September 16, 1953.

This, in the words of the *Monde*, was the international background of Mendès-France's "surprise visit" to Tunis:

The decisions taken by the Government closely follow the announcement that Suez is to be evacuated by the British. The Anglo-Egyptian treaty opens, indeed, a new era in the life of the Arab world. There is no further obstacle in the way of close co-operation between Egypt and the other Arab countries and the West. Their whole propaganda effort, however, will henceforth be concentrated on giving material and moral support to the nationalist movements in French North Africa.

The pan-Arab policy of the USA is bearing fruit. In their desire to secure Arab co-operation in the defence of the Mediterranean, the Americans have encouraged all the Arab capitals. As for the British, they ... have now returned to their traditional pro-Arab policy, under which, in the past, they gave their blessing to the Arab League, and which induced Mr Churchill to think up the Kingdoms of Jordan and Libya. . . . Trapped between the Arab bloc, determined to secure the independence of Maghreb,[9] and allies who are not at all anxious to see the trouble in North Africa going from bad to worse, France was obliged to act promptly. . . . Unfortunately, during the past few years, our governments showed only an intermittent interest in Tunisia and Morocco.[10]

The *Monde* qualified Mendès-France's spectacular visit to Tunis as "truly Churchillian" in style. While stressing that he was not giving away "any vital French interests", it observed that what was really new in Mendès-France's approach to the problem was his promise to apply the new programme "loyally and without mental reservations". This had never been said, still less done, before.

It was quick work. Soon after landing at Tunis at 10 a.m., Mendès-France drove to the Bey's palace at Carthage, and began his address to the old gentleman with the promising phrase:

Monseigneur, I come here as a friend, as a friend of Your Highness and of your country.

After deploring the clashes of interests and the bloodshed in Tunisia, and saying that General Boyer de La Tour had come to replace M. Voizard as Resident-General, Mendès-France declared that the internal autonomy of the Tunisian State had been recognized by the French Government "without mental reservations", and that the Tunisian people had reached a "degree of evolution" (an evolution to which France had been proud to contribute), in which they could manage their own affairs.

[9] The word "Maghreb", though sometimes applied to Morocco only, means, in pan-Arab terminology, the whole of French North Africa.
[10] *Le Monde*, August 1, 1954.

That is why we are prepared to transfer to Tunisian persons and Tunisian institutions the internal exercise of their sovereignty.

He then proposed that a new Tunisian government be formed which would negotiate new conventions with France, clearly defining the respective rights of the two partners.

Naturally, Mendès-France continued, it was in the common interests of the two countries that France remained in Tunisia. She was rendering the country great financial, economic, technical, and cultural services, and an important place was held in the life of the country by numerous Frenchmen, a fact which no Tunisian patriot would challenge. Moreover, the Bardo Treaty would remain in force as regards a common military and foreign policy. The French, in return for the past and present services rendered to Tunisia, would have a right to stay in Tunisia—they, as well as their children and grandchildren. They would contribute to the economic prosperity of the country.

He concluded by asking everybody in Tunisia to co-operate in putting an end to the bloodshed; but uttered a warning that any further trouble would be ruthlessly crushed.

The most important feature of Mendès-France's proposals was that a proper Tunisian government—and no longer a puppet government—be appointed, which would then negotiate new conventions with the French. Until these conventions were signed, it was still hard to say to what extent the "internal autonomy" would actually transfer the civil authority and the administration of the country to Tunisians only. Mendès had spoken a great deal of the continued "presence of the French", and of their children and grandchildren, in Tunisia.

Despite all the verbal precautions he had taken in favour of the French in Tunisia, the Rassemblement Français at Tunis refused to meet the French Premier, even though they had been reassured, to some extent, by the presence of their hero, Marshal Juin, and also by the appointment of a general as new Resident-General.

Also, on second thoughts, after Mendès had already left, they felt that his address to the Bey might have been worse.[11]

If, in the British and American press, the reactions to Mendès's visit to Tunis were unanimously favourable, the same was not the case in France. The *Figaro*, though expressing an unusual admiration for the man and his manner, was afraid of the repercussions his Tunis visit might have in Algeria and Morocco, and warned the Government against going one step beyond the "limit" Mendès-France had fixed.

Other right-wing papers, like *L'Aurore*, were much more critical, and so were the men of the North Africa Lobby, like Senator Colonna,

[11] *Le Monde*, August 3, 1954.

who declared that Mendès-France had "proposed the dissolution of the Franco-Tunisian community". What played into the hands of Mendès-France's critics was the statement made by Habib Bourguiba, the leader of the Neo-Destour, who was still interned in France, and who said that the Mendès-France proposals marked "a substantial and decisive step towards the restoration of the complete sovereignty of Tunisia".

Independence remains the ideal of the Tunisian people, but the march towards this independence will no longer be marked by a struggle between the Tunisian people and France.... This progression towards independence will be marked by a co-operation between the two peoples, a co-operation from which all thought of domination will be excluded.

M. Tahar ben Ammar, the moderate Tunisian nationalist leader, and president of the Tunisian Chamber of Agriculture, who was shortly to form the new Tunisian government, declared, for his part, that Mendès-France had given "complete satisfaction to our legitimate hopes". "We must respond with the same loyalty and sincerity."

The Tahar ben Ammar Government, which was formed on August 9, though containing four Neo-Destour members (some of whom, like Dr Moqqadem, had, only recently, returned from deportation in the South), was predominantly "moderate" and middle class, and all its members were men of French culture. One of them, Si Naceur ben Said, was an ex-officer in the French Army, who had fought in the 1914–18 war and in the Riff campaign, and enjoyed the distinction of having been the first Tunisian to be admitted to Saint-Cyr. Several, like the young M. Masmoudi, the representative of the Neo-Destour in France, had received a French university education. A Beylical decree appointed the French Resident-General Minister of Foreign Affairs, in accordance with the treaties in force.[12]

So far so good. But the negotiations with the Tunisian Government were still in the future; and meantime, in Morocco, the unrest was becoming more alarming every day. At the two main mosques at Fez —a city now in a state of constant unrest, prayers were now being said in the name of the deposed Sultan; at Port-Lyautey four Europeans were murdered on August 7; and scarcely a day passed in Casablanca without somebody being assassinated by either terrorists or "counter-terrorists". On the Right in France there was a growing tendency to blame Mendès-France for having "encouraged" all this by being "soft" with the Tunisians.

[12] The posts distributed among the Tunisian ministers were: Premier and Moslem Institutions; three Ministers of State; Tunisian Justice; Health; Labour; Agriculture; Commerce; Housing. The police remained under the control of the French military authorities. Similarly, Education and other "internal" sectors remained French departments, pending the new Conventions.

Actually, the line M. Mendès-France took on Morocco was different from that on Tunisia; he considered that the two countries were "not identical" and that "both the social and the institutional problems in Morocco were much more acute"[13]—which was, however, far from meaning that he was inclined to make concessions to Morocco similar to those made to Tunisia. On the vital dynastic issue, Mendès-France was to declare soon afterwards that there could be no question of bringing the old Sultan back.

What a month it was for Mendès-France! No sooner had he returned from Tunis than he had to deal with the Economic Reforms; there was a growing clamour for a full-dress parliamentary debate on North Africa; and, above all, it was time to prepare for the Brussels Conference on EDC, which had been fixed for August 19.

The least exciting debate was that on the economic plenary powers.

Mendès-France made a relatively short speech in which he stressed the dependence of higher wages on higher production, undertook, in this context, to examine the wage level in October, and suggested that such "re-adjustments" could take place twice a year. He thought it preferable to adopt such a method, rather than wait for strikes, and then increase wages in "chaotic conditions". He then spoke about the "reconversion" of a certain number of redundant enterprises, and of the measures the Government might take to help in this reconversion; he also attached great importance to the modernization of housing, and concluded by saying that France should "awake" economically, and that she had every opportunity of showing that she was in no sense "the sick man of Europe".

All this sounded fine, even though a little inconclusive, in comparison with Mendès-France's Opposition speeches. It was widely felt that he was too much concerned about other things at the time. Small wonder —with the EDC Conference only a week ahead! M. Edgar Faure, not very illuminating either on what the Government were planning to do with their economic plenary powers, denied that France was in a bad financial way; it was not true, as one speaker had said, that she had a current budget deficit of 1,000 milliard francs; the deficit was only one of 390 milliards.

The plenary powers were passed by 362 votes to 90; the Communists and the greater part of the Right abstained; the MRP, on the contrary, voted for Mendès-France on this occasion.

As against this, in the vote on the adjournment of the interpellations on North Africa (397 for, 114 against, 90 abstentions) the Communists and Socialists voted for Mendès, most of the MRP abstained, the Gaullists were divided, and the whole Right (as well as a few Radicals)

[13] *Le Monde*, August 10, 1954.

voted against. It looked as though Mendès-France's attempt to work with "alternative majorities" might work—at least for a time. But it wasn't a sound basis, all the same.

In any case, the North African diehards were not going to miss the chance of speaking their mind when Mendès's demand that the debate on North Africa be postponed came up for discussion on August 10. The "date-fixing" discussion developed into what was almost a full-dress debate. The *grands ténors* of the North Africa Lobby—like the Premier's "colleague" in the Radical Party, M. Martinaud-Déplat, and M. Quilici—were let loose. Martinaud-Déplat painted a lurid picture of the Neo-Destour and of their leader, Bourguiba, whose only aim, he said, was to "evict the French from Tunisia", and he thought it lamentable that Mendès-France should "negotiate with criminals". Martinaud-Déplat argued that Bourguiba had worked with Fascist Italy during the war, and quoted two letters written by him which, he said, were like a Tunisian *Mein Kampf*.

Mendès-France remarked that these "letters", published in the *Figaro* on April 6, 1952 were, to say the least, of "doubtful authority".[14]

But Martinaud-Déplat was not to be put out. He declared that Mendès had been "blackmailed" into "disastrous" concessions to Tunisia by the "terrorists"; and that the preservation of "co-sovereignty" was France's only hope in Tunisia. France, he said, should refuse to negotiate with the Neo-Destour. A Socialist, interrupting, recalled that terrorism in Tunisia had developed between 1952 and 1954—i.e. at the time when M. Martinaud-Déplat, as Minister of the Interior in the successive French Governments, was inflicting his "tough" policy on his more reasonable colleagues, notably M. Robert Schuman.

Mendès sharply dealt with Martinaud-Déplat's views on Tunisia; but, in the case of Morocco, he seemed strangely reluctant to take any decisive course. France, he said, would do her best to come to an agreement with the present Sultan H. M. Mohammed Ben Arafa. This remark was meant to convey that Mendès did not wish to antagonize the Glaoui, and that there was no question of reinstating the old Sultan. He merely "implored" all Moroccans to put an end to "all the horrible violence". This was "delaying that modern evolution of their country, which we all desire".

This meant that he preferred to ignore the Socialist speeches to the effect that the overthrow of the old Sultan had been a fatal mistake, and was at the root of all the trouble in Morocco, as well as the warning given to the Government by M. Clostermann (Gaullist), who said that

[14] The *Monde* recalled on the following day (August 12) that the *Figaro* had lost a legal action over the "Bourguiba letters", and had been ordered by the Court to publish a *lettre de rectification*.

Franco and the Moroccan leaders in the Spanish Zone—who had never recognized the deposition of Sidi Mohammed Ben Yussef—might well start another campaign in favour of the unification of Morocco under the exiled Sultan.[15]

François Mauriac was to comment with great bitterness in *L'Express* that week on Mendès-France's failure "to say the one thing that mattered".

Many of Mendès's greatest admirers were puzzled by the man. Sometimes he was so brave and bold; and at other times so timid. Was it because he could not take on too many things all at once? Or did he feel that he could carry on at all only if on some issues at any rate, he compromised with his enemies?

[15] There had already been, with the blessing of General Valino, the Spanish High Commissioner, demonstrations to that effect at Tetuan, the capital of the Spanish Zone, during the previous winter. These were followed by agitated diplomatic exchanges between Paris and Madrid. But the danger of a Spanish-inspired revolt had never been entirely eliminated. When, in 1953, I saw the "old" Sultan's son, Prince Moulay Hassan, he bitterly remarked that, in relation to the Arabs, Franco Spain was "more democratic than France".

CHAPTER THREE

SHOWDOWN ON GERMAN REARMAMENT

I. BRUSSELS AND THE DEATH OF EDC

COMPROMISE. This word was Mendès-France's *idée fixe* in the case of EDC.

This was his starting-point: for the EDC Treaty in its original form there was no majority at the National Assembly or in the country. Therefore, it would have a chance of being accepted by a substantial majority (or even by a small majority) only on condition that it was seriously amended, and met at least some of the objections of the anti-EDC people—the anti-EDC Socialists, Gaullists and Radicals. The Communists could be written off; they would be against EDC in any shape or form.

For several days—from August 12 on—the battle raged furiously inside the Mendès-France Cabinet between the supporters and opponents of EDC. There were times when it was rumoured that Mendès had capitulated to the EDC people, and that except for some slight changes in its "presentation", he was willing to throw in his whole authority in support of the EDC treaty. In that case the Gaullists would leave the Government and be replaced by pro-EDC Socialists and a few members of the MRP.[16] This proved untrue, and, already on August 13 Mendès-France produced his "compromise" in the form of additional protocols to be submitted to the Six-Power Conference at Brussels. The principal clauses of these protocols concerned the duration of the EDC treaty; the option for its signatories to leave the EDC in the event of major changes, e.g. in the composition of NATO, or in the event of German reunification. Secondly, Mendès-France proposed that for eight years the supra-national clauses of the treaty be not applied; which meant in reality that a power of veto was given during this period to each member of the council of ministers of the EDC; further, Mendès proposed that only the forces stationed in Germany would be "integrated"—which meant that there would be no German troops on French soil; and that the French system of ranks and promotions be adopted by the EDC, besides various "organizational" amendments,

[16] *Le Monde*, August 13, 1954.

concerning the administrative and judicial machinery of the European Defence Community.

All this was discussed for hours and hours at the constant succession of Cabinet meetings. On August 14, three of the Gaullist ministers, General Koenig, M. Chaban-Delmas and M. Lemaire, resigned. It was not so much a case of approving or disapproving of the "additional protocols" that were to be submitted to the Brussels Conference, as the objection to taking any decision on EDC at all, and so ruining every chance of East-West talks in the near future. At that time it still seemed probable that the Brussels Powers, after a little argument, would accept the French "protocols" in the main.

Determined anti-EDC people were praying for Mendès to fail at Brussels, but, whether he did or not, they deplored the fact that he should have agreed to go to the Brussels Conference at all: for what if he succeeded and EDC in its modified form was passed by the Assembly?

And even if he failed to get his protocols accepted, it would still show that he was not "strongminded" on the question of German rearmament; but most of his admirers liked to think that, at heart, he was. It was one of the most curious cases of collective optical delusion, which could partly perhaps be explained by the fact that some of his closest associates, like M. Georges Boris, had for years been openly opposed to EDC and to German rearmament in any form.

However, it soon became obvious that Brussels would not be a walk-over for Mendès-France.

The first most violent reactions to the Mendès-France plan came from Bonn, where the French Premier was openly accused of "sabotaging" Europe. Although the British press was less emphatic, *The Times*, in particular, thought the Mendès-France proposals unacceptable, since they implied sharp discrimination against Germany.

Towards the end of the Conference it became quite clear that there was a general Anglo-American-German gang-up against Mendès-France, with the hearty support of M. Spaak and M. Beyen, the Dutch Foreign Minister.

The last straw was Sir Winston Churchill's telegram to Adenauer on the 23rd, saying that everything would end well, and that his [Adenauer's] great statesmanly qualities would be worthily rewarded —which everybody interpreted as meaning that, whether EDC was now ratified by the French Assembly or not, Germany would be rearmed in one way or another.

It would be tedious to record in detail the Brussels negotiations; instead, it seems interesting to show how exactly the story was presented by one of the most potent "Western propagandists" in France, M. Raymond Cartier, the star reporter of *Match*, and how this popular weekly with more than a million circulation was trying to scare the life out of France with the threat of "isolation". Equally significant are Cartier's lamentations over "Europe", complete with Spaak's "moist spectacles" when "all was over". No doubt it was "all over" for Spaak, who had hoped to become one of the great personages of an integrated "Europe".

At 2.35 a.m. Paul Spaak, the chairman of the Conference declared: "Gentlemen, it is all over. . . ." His voice, as full and powerful as the man himself, had not trembled. But those present thought that the Belgian statesman's spectacles were moist.

Spaak! Yes, Spaak had made a supreme effort in the service of a cause with which he had identified himself. . . . A few hours before, when failure seemed imminent, Spaak had taken Mendès-France aside. . . . Spaak's hand was clasping Mendès's arm, as though trying to add physical strength to the power of his arguments. . . .

"The failure of this conference is a catastrophe. France will be completely isolated. There will be an EDC without her. Western Germany will rearm, and will become integrated with Benelux and the Scandinavians. She will have the fullest Anglo-American support. Can you doubt it for a moment after Churchill's telegram to Adenauer? You will be alone. Is that what you want? . . . We must, *must* make Europe. The military side isn't everything. What matters more is the integration of Europe. EDC is only a step in that direction, but if there is no EDC, then everything falls to the ground. . . ."

But no! Spaak spoke of Europe. Mendès-France replied: "Palais-Bourbon."

Enter USA. This is how Cartier continued the story:

This dialogue was interrupted when M. Spaak's *chef de cabinet* came to inform him that Mr David Bruce, the US Ambassador had arrived at the Ministry of Foreign Affairs, and was waiting in the library. Mendès-France reacted sharply. Bruce had arrived in Brussels on the previous day, and had had numerous contacts and conversations; but this was the first time he had come to the Ministry where the conference was being held. Mendès realized that here was a formidable new adversary, in addition to the five others, and that this American intrusion could only stiffen the attitude of Germany and Benelux. . . . During the Belgian-American talk, the French made no attempt to conceal their bitterness and irritation. . . .

The final efforts to patch up an agreement were half-hearted. At 11.35 p.m. there was a brief Franco-German conversation, in the course of which Dr Adenauer demonstrated to M. Mendès-France, complete with figures, that Mendès was wrong to say that there was no parliamentary majority in France in favour of EDC.

What M. Cartier discreetly failed to add was that the "figures" had been supplied to Adenauer by Robert Schuman—an elegant way of sabotaging the efforts of the French Premier at Brussels! During the following weeks there were to be many angry comments in France on this "stab in the back", and on the conspiracy of the "Black International". Similarly, M. André Philip had "tipped off" M. Spaak, his "Socialist" colleague.

How then had the violent opposition to the Mendés-France protocols crystallized? Before the Conference, the Germans had examined the fourteen pages of the protocols, and had rejected them outright. They went contrary to these two great principles of EDC—supra-nationality and equality among all its members. Adenauer was supported by the other four. No doubt Cartier was not entirely wrong in his analysis of Mendès-France's "ambiguous position" at Brussels.

It has never been possible to know, with any degree of precision, whether Mendès was pro- or anti-EDC. His thought is wrapped in reticence and contradictions. He agrees that the failure of the Treaty would be a disaster, as it would lead to a crisis in the Atlantic Alliance; but, for all that, he clearly feels no affection for the EDC treaty.... He does not use the classical arguments against EDC ("eternal Germany" or national sovereignty), but merely says Parliament will not ratify it.... Anyway, Spaak was not convinced, and ... on one occasion he exploded and accused Mendès of not being a good European.

"How can you say that," Mendès cried. "I've been a European all my life, and it is I who have dragged the treaty out of its folder, where it has been lying for years!..." Bech of Luxemburg intervened, and Spaak apologized, but, for all that, he had expressed the feeling shared by everybody at the Conference.... The feeling that Schuman and Bidault were true Europeans ... and that Mendès-France was thinking of the Malenkov proposals....

Adenauer, according to Cartier, avoided turning Brussels into the scene of a Franco-German quarrel, and therefore let Beyen, the Dutchman "demolish" Mendès-France. There was "no greater expert in the world on the EDC than Beyen, and Mendès was at a disadvantage". Later Beyen commented acidly on Mendès: "He is too intelligent to be a negotiator."

Meantime, Adenauer had gone on a sightseeing trip to Bruges.

And early the next morning the conference broke up.

After only a few hours' rest, Mendès flew to Chartwell to see Churchill, seemingly undismayed by Churchill's "unilateral message to Adenauer", as Cartier put it. Mendès's entourage (Cartier reported) denied that his sudden visit to the British Prime Minister was "a gesture of bewilderment".

But at Chartwell another disappointment was in store for him. Churchill was in excellent humour, and greatly flattered at being asked to pull Europe out of the bog. But Mendès came up against the same arguments he had already heard at Brussels. Worse still, he found that Britain's point of view was becoming identified with Germany's. . . . In the evening, a Reuter message stated that Mendès-France had got nothing out of Churchill; the latter had refused to strengthen Britain's links with EDC. He had praised EDC and had urged Mendès-France to make another effort to get it ratified in its present form, before looking for alternative solutions. The alternative solution at which he hinted was that Germany would be rearmed as a member of NATO.

And the Cartier article ended, as it had started, on a note of intimidation: France must choose: either EDC or Isolation. Or the Empty Chair, as Churchill was to call it a few months later. . . .[17]

After the failure of the Brussels Conference (a failure to which they had done their best to contribute) the "Europeans" attempted to prevent a decision from being taken on EDC; they knew that the National Assembly was in a defiant mood, and would reject the EDC Treaty in that original form in which it had emerged from Brussels. Mendès-France, nettled by the reception he had been given by the co-signatories of the Treaty, and unfavourable to it, now that the protocols had been rejected, wanted the Assembly to decide at once whether it wanted EDC or not. On a question of procedure, which, however, implied the rejection of EDC, this was rejected in the course of a stormy and highly emotional debate by 319 votes to 264. The largest nail in the coffin of EDC was hammered by M. Herriot who, in an emotional address (he was too old and frail to stand up, and spoke from his seat), dwelt on the loss of an independent policy and diplomacy that would be inherent in France's loss of control over her own army. It was this supra-national angle, rather than the German rearmament angle that was stressed in this debate. What was also stressed was the total inadequacy of the British "guarantees" to EDC.

This vote was the last great demonstration—or rather the last but one—of the French spirit of independence—the gesture of defiance thrown in the face of all those who, without taking account of her susceptibilities, were telling France what was best for *her*. In the

---

[17] The *Canard Enchaîné* published on September 8, 1954 this "imaginary conversation" between the celebrated Major Thompson, M. Pierre Daninos's hero and M. Raymond Aron, *le penseur-maison* of the *Figaro* (as it called him):

"Oh, you are English?" said Aron. "You must be very cross with us, aren't you?"

"No," I said, "what on earth makes you think that?"

"I mean our rejection of EDC."

"Not at all," I said politely. "France is a free country."

He looked like thunder.

"I say," he said, "you aren't by any chance a crypto-communist?"

"My dear sir," said the Major, "my family has voted Tory for *generations*!"

country at large, the Assembly vote caused a feeling of at least temporary elation.

Mendès-France and the other members of the Government had abstained from voting one way or the other.

What followed is very recent history, and can be told only briefly.

2. THE THREAT OF THE "EMPTY CHAIR"

The Assembly vote of August 30 caused a violent uproar in Germany, where the Adenauer press and Adenauer himself, in various statements, including one to *The Times*, proceeded to insult the French Assembly and Mendès-France himself, whom Adenauer declared to be personally responsible for what had happened. It was not only an international, but also an internal German issue; and the elections in Schleswig-Holstein showed that Adenauer and the supporters of German rearmament were losing ground.

But Dulles was not caught napping. His "lightning visits" to London and Bonn were intended to prop up Adenauer, and also to show the French where they "got off": it was explained that Mr Dulles was "too busy" to come to Paris. There was no clearer way of showing that France was "in the doghouse".

Meantime Eden had started on his "European tour"; and Mendès-France, terrified of France's "isolation", was already saying that there might, before the end of the year, be a new agreement, and that he was not the man to resort to delaying tactics. At Strasbourg, Mendès, angrily denounced by Teitgen and the other EDC *ultras*, appeared to be, to many observers, too much on the defensive—if not actually apologetic. Maurice Duverger, in the *Monde*,[18] was deploring the fact that Mendès was now in the rôle of Arbenz of Guatemala, and France in the position of a United Fruit republic. If France did not toe the line, he wrote, America would try to force her to do so.

Mendès was privately informed that German rearmament without France's consent was now on the cards.[19]

The trial of General Oberg, the head of the Gestapo, just at that time, with all its lurid details, no doubt contributed to "conditioning" French opinion against any easy acceptance of German rearmament; but neither Sir Winston nor Mr Dulles were in the least interested in Oberg.

It is quite clear that Mendès-France thought any resistance against German rearmament utterly hopeless. Already on October 5 the deci-

[18] *Le Monde*, September 22, 1954.
[19] A significant example at that stage of the British attitude to Germany (as the French saw it) was the attempt made by the War Office to prevent the publication of Lord Russell's book on Nazi atrocities.

sions of the "9" at the London Conference were published; but much more was made in England of Eden's "miraculous" concession about "British troops in Europe" than in France. "Nothing very new" was the *Monde* comment. A few days later, Mendès-France reported to the Assembly on the London talks, claiming that what had been accepted by France was "a lesser evil".

What else could he have done? From the very start he had, in any case, accepted the principle of German rearmament; if the Germans were now, with British and American support, insisting on having a General Staff, it couldn't be helped.

At Margate, the same week, Sir Winston again expressed his impatience with France, and said that any revision of the London Agreements was absolutely out of the question.

By and large, it may be said that French public opinion was, at this stage, becoming fatalistic and resigned. There was a tendency to take the view that France had duly uttered her *mot de Cambronne* on August 30; that she had thus at least avoided the pitfalls of supra-nationality, and that, before very long, she would have to give way, rather than see herself isolated from the "West". There was no great love for Britain or America—least of all at that time; but, all the same, it was, somehow, "safer" to have some Allies, however ununderstanding and even *antipathique*. Besides, German rearmament was not perhaps quite as dangerous as it would have been three or four years before. Even the *Monde* was ready to admit this when it said that twelve German divisions mattered little in a world of "atomic strategy"— except for all the old ghosts that would still haunt this army. Would the Soviet H-bomb be enough to keep the Germans in order?

But events were now moving fast. On October 23, the "14" signed the Paris agreements on the rearmament and the sovereignty of Western Germany.

Only a spectacular Soviet initiative can now stop the ratification of the Paris agreements, [wrote the *Monde* on October 26] but the latest Soviet Note is nothing. . . .

It added that there was nothing "mystical" about the West-European Union, as there had been about EDC, and that there was, therefore, likely to be less opposition to it.

Mendès-France was now certain that the Paris agreements would be ratified, provided there were no further hitches, notably over the Saar, and over armaments control; yet on the Saar, in particular, Bonn would persist in what the French called "misinterpreting the Franco-German agreement of October 23".

The row over the Saar came to a climax at the end of November, when the preamble to the ratification Bill that came before the Bundestag, gave an interpretation to the agreement which the Quai d'Orsay denounced as a deliberate "distortion".[20]

This fundamental quarrel over the Saar, and the fact that no decisions would be taken on the "armaments agency" or, better still, "pool" until the international conference on January 17 (the only agency which, even the staunchest opponents of EDC agreed, must inevitably be as supra-national as possible) greatly weakened Mendès-France's case for immediate ratification.

At least two very essential aspects of the Paris agreements had been left suspended in mid-air, while France was being urged not to waste another day before ratifying the whole thing—West-German rearmament, West-German sovereignty, the confusing Saar agreement, and all.

Since British and American Government spokesmen and practically the entire British and American press (not to mention the Adenauer press in Germany) treated the French National Assembly during those weeks as a sort of monkey-house, and Sir Winston Churchill referred, in his famous letter to Mendès-France, to these "vehement and self-centred groups", it does not seem superfluous to point out that, despite Mendès-Frances's petulant outburst on the night of December 24 that the Assembly was "not serious-minded", the debate was, in reality, one of a remarkably high standard, which faithfully reflected the anxiety and bitterness existing in the country over the whole issue.

It is possible here to quote only some of the highlights of this debate, which continued for over a week.

General Billotte, the Gaullist *rapporteur* of the Foreign Affairs Committee, without sounding enthusiastic, was favourable to the ratification of the Paris Agreements; he declared that the Political Council was more than a mere advisory body, but represented something which

---

[20] On four essential points the French and German "interpretations" widely differed: (1) The Bonn preamble denied that the Saar had been "Europeanized", and claimed that it continued to be "part of Germany". (2) The Bonn preamble claimed that the Saarlanders would, under the Franco-German agreement, hold a referendum after the signing of the Peace Treaty, and that they would then decide on "the ultimate fate of the Saar"—with the implication that the Saar would then be wholly reincorporated in Germany. France, it was explained in official Paris quarters, had made no such commitment, and had merely agreed to submit to the approval of the Saarlanders the Saar clauses of the Peace Treaty. "These clauses will have been approved by the signatories of the Treaty, who will, at France's request, have agreed to the final consolidation of the Saar's 'European' status. Bonn is trying to interpret this status as something provisional." (3) Bonn also questioned the lasting nature of the monetary and customs union between France and the Saar; and (4) deliberately overlooked the provisions against propaganda in favour of the reincorporation of the Saar in Germany.

would enable Europe to act coherently; the British contribution was important in the sense that "a certain minimum of British forces" available on the Continent would conform to a majority vote taken on this Council. The agreements also provided adequate guarantees against an excessive increase of German forces, and could limit the police forces of the signatories.

On the armaments "pool", Billotte was less precise:

The control of armaments will be particularly effective if it becomes part of the joint production of armaments. That is the field in which our determination to secure results has not yet proved sufficient. But I have the impression that the *ad hoc* conference which is to meet in Paris on January 17, will study and solve this problem.

M. PIERRE MONTELE: Can you, quite honestly and sincerely, tell us that it would be conscientious of us to vote the agreement on effectives, without first knowing anything about the conditions in which armaments are going to be controlled, distributed, and stored?[21]

Billotte replied, rather feebly, that the question had worried him, too, but that he had been reassured by "competent authorities"; moreover M. Mendès-France would no doubt have more to say on the subject.

A few hours later M. Vendroux, another *rapporteur* of the Foreign Affairs Committee dealt with the Saar agreements, and immediately drew attention to the Bonn preamble and the most disquieting way in which the Germans were "interpreting" the agreement.

It was an awkward moment for Mendès-France. He took the over-easy "legalistic" approach:

The Assembly is not called upon to vote on the German preamble, but on the text of the agreement.[22]

Later in the debate he said he would have further talks with Adenauer and if, moreover, there were to be more trouble in future, the Saar agreement could be submitted to the Hague Court for arbitration.

M. Vincent Badie, *rapporteur pour avis* of the Defence Committee dwelt on the size of the German army to be included within the NATO framework—a force with much heavier equipment than that of the French Army:

It will consist of 12 divisions of the American type, i.e. 400,000 men, including 4 divisions with 300 heavy tanks each, i.e. twice as strong as a

[21] *Débats, Assemblée Nationale,* December 20, 1954, p. 6642.
[22] *Ibid.,* p. 6653.

Hitler division, 2 mechanized and 6 motorized divisions, an air force of 80,000 men and 1,150 planes.

In theory [M. Badie said] there will be an incorporated general staff, for operational purposes; in reality, there will be an autonomous German general staff, "that ruthless machine", as the *Daily Express* has called it, "which has planned wars in Europe over the last 100 years".

There is no sign of any "armaments pool".

The British, who are very European where others are concerned, have been consistently opposed to the integration of programmes, to the control of armaments manufacture and to standardization. As for the Americans, they don't want any control of allocations, being anxious to exercise sole and arbitrary command over the "off shore" weapon.

In view of this, and the confusion over the Saar, M. Badie called for the postponement of any decision. He called attention to the "feelings of embarrassment, uneasiness and bewilderment on all the Committees of the Assembly".[23]

As though to illustrate this point, M. P.-O. Lapie, the Socialist *rapporteur pour avis* of the Committee of Industrial Production was to say the next day that his Committee had recommended ratification by 13 votes against 10 and 3 abstentions.

M. PIERRE ANDRÉ: Not brilliant, eh?

M. P.-O. LAPIE: These figures point to an enthusiasm which I would describe as moderate. (*Laughter.*)[24]

Speaking as an historian and "a student of diplomatic documents", M. Jacques Bardoux said that he had never seen such a jumble of incoherent documents in his life as the Paris agreements; they "pointed to a decline of general culture and a decay of the art of diplomacy". He thought the Assembly should not ratify the agreements, until all this mess had been sorted out, and France knew where she stood. Also, he feared that ratification could only aggravate the Cold War.

Jacques Soustelle (Gaullist) said the Paris agreements were not better, but less bad than EDC in so far as they did not "drown the French Army in a cosmopolitan puddle". But if anything needed to be supra-national, it was surely the "European armaments agency" or "armaments pool"; if it wasn't, then the USA could, at its sole discretion, raise or lower the military strength and efficiency of this or that country; in that case, West-European Union would be mere eyewash, and the whole thing would depend on the whims of the Pentagon. He added that the inclusion of Germany in NATO was liable to turn a defensive organization into an aggressive one, in view of Germany's territorial ambitions. German irridentism was a reality to which it was useless to close one's eyes.

[23] *Ibid.*, p. 6658.   [24] *Ibid.*, December 21, 1954, p. 6680.

He quoted Cyrus Sulzberger in the *New York Times* to show that France had already been "relegated to the background". And if, as the Russians had already warned France, the Franco-Soviet Pact was going to be denounced, then there were two dangers: German irridentism or a German-Soviet *rapprochement*—after Germany had become strong.[25]

Jacques Duclos (Communist) drew attention to the innumerable delegations arriving during the last few days at the Assembly from all over the country to protest against German rearmament. He attached Mendès-France.

M. Duclos: For the rest of his life he will have this terrible label attached to him. . . .
M. Bouxom (MRP): "Invested by the Communists. . . ."
M. Duclos: "Responsible for the revival of German militarism."

M. Maurice Schumann (MRP) thought that, under the Paris agreements, France was going to get "the worst of both worlds"—they would increase *both* the Russian danger and the German danger to France. He sharply criticized the "quite incomprehensible second Saar referendum". (Surprisingly, *nobody* worried about the first one!)

M. Jules Moch said that, as French Delegate to the Disarmament Commission in London, he was particularly distressed by the armaments race on which Western Europe, complete with Germany, was planning to embark—especially at a time when everything showed that if, in 1950, the Russians were in a truculent and aggressive mood, they were now genuinely in favour of a *détente*, lower armaments expenditure and peaceful co-existence.
He thought that German rearmament at this stage made little sense, and it was much more important, in this thermo-nuclear age, to try to prohibit A-bomb and H-bomb experiments (to begin with) as these represented, if persisted in, a deadly danger to humanity. He advocated top-level talks with the Russians, but realized that France was in "a painful dilemma": refusal to ratify would mean an "Atlantic crisis"; while unconditional ratification might kill the prospect of any East-West agreement. He thought, however, that the Russians would perhaps "prove more realistic than the French Communists".

M. Paul Reynaud hit the nail on the head when he said that if this debate went on for another fortnight, there wouldn't be a soul in the place to vote for the Paris Agreements! Germany (he continued) was becoming more and more nationalist, and might well enter into a deal with the Russians. If, in the past, there was genuine enthusiasm among many deputies in France for EDC, he saw no signs of any enthusiasm for the Paris Agreements.

[25] *Débats, Assemblée Nationale*, December 21, 1954, pp. 6697–6700.

M. Robert Schuman also commented on the general reluctance to ratify the Paris agreements, and admitted that the idea of "Europe" had sadly declined since 1950 when he (Schuman) had embarked on direct talks with Adenauer. But it was no use rejecting the Paris agreements on the ground that the Saar agreement, for instance, was open to criticism. The Saar agreement, whatever its contents, would work only if a faith in Europe was revived on both sides.

Then came another dramatic moment. Herriot said he would not vote for the Paris agreements. They could only encourage the militarist and reactionary elements in Germany against the peaceful and democratic elements. Moreover, neither the Saar, nor the question of armaments control had been settled. There was, on the part of the Allies, a great lack of consideration for France. Was not disarmament preferable to super-rearmament? Yet it now looked as though France was going to let Germany rearm; but with whose help was she going to disarm her later? No doubt France owed America a great deal. "But," concluded Herriot, "if I love the United States, I love France even more".[26] (*Loud cheers on most benches.*)

In the afternoon of December 23 M. Mendès-France defended the Agreements as best he could, but throughout his speech there was the suggestion that there was really no alternative to unconditional ratification: "Last September," he said, "we were one-tenth of an inch from seeing German rearmament being carried out without us, without any limits, without any control, without our consent." As regards the armaments control and the "pool" he said that "slow but certain progress" had been made in that direction, and that the British and Americans were showing themselves "less reluctant" than before to subscribe to the French views on the essential supra-nationality of the control machinery; he sincerely hoped there would be an agreement in January. He also hoped that France would become better organized economically and in other ways, lose her inferiority complex (an allusion to Soustelle's speech the day before), and so pull her weight more than she was doing now.

Jacques Soustelle: *M. le président du conseil*, I cannot let you say that my speech yesterday reflected a French inferiority complex *vis-à-vis* Germany.... That isn't the point. If the system you are proposing to us materializes, then Germany will carry more weight in Europe than we do. And the reason for this is obvious. She will become America's privileged ally on the Continent, and will receive top priority in the supply of armaments.

He added that with her territorial ambitions and her attention and

[26] *Débats, A.N.,* December 23, 1954, p. 6811.

energies concentrated in Europe (since she had no overseas territories), she would inevitably become the most dynamic and dangerous force within the Western Union.

M. Pierre Cot (Progressive) made an important point when he said that Mendès-France had hinted several times at the danger of America and England "rearming Germany without France's consent". But had it not occurred to M. Mendès-France that France could take the matter before the International Court at The Hague, which would undoubtedly confirm France's right of veto, and make the whole thing extremely awkward for Britain and the USA?

Mendès replied that it wasn't a case of safeguarding France's rights; it was a case of safeguarding the Atlantic Alliance.

And then, in the early morning hours of December 24, came the *mot de Cambronne*, when the first paragraph of the Ratification Bill authorizing the creation of a German national army was rejected by 280 votes to 259, most of the MRP as well as many Radicals and right-wing members joining the Gaullists and Communists.

It was this vote which created a violent outburst of anger in London and Washington. That that would happen was Mendès-France's first thought: "In reading the international press comments tomorrow, you will see how great the disregard is for our methods of work. . . ." And he declared that he wished the "condemned" article to come before the Assembly for a second reading, and this time the Government would make it a vote of confidence.

But this could not be done until the following Monday, December 27. Sure enough, in the interval, the British Foreign Office had gone off the deep end, ignoring the fact that responsible leaders of such widely varying opinions as Reynaud, Daladier, Maurice Schumann, Coste-Floret, Herriot, Moch, and Soustelle (not to mention the Communists and *Progressistes*) had expressed their deep anxiety over the Paris agreements—an anxiety—and a protest—that were reflected in the famous vote of December 24.

But Mendes's troubles were not yet over. The Foreign Affairs Committee rejected a "second reading" of Article 1 by 20 votes to 19 and 4 abstentions and Mendès-France was reduced to making the vote on the Bill as a whole a vote of confidence.

For three more days the debate dragged on, but no longer arousing much interest. All that needed saying had already been said, and after its demonstration of independence, a large part of the Assembly now felt tired and resigned. And, time and again, Mendès-France spoke of "foreign reactions", and of the terrible impression the rejection of the Paris agreements would make abroad. "If only every Deputy would read, as I do, the critical and often malevolent comments coming from every foreign capital! ..."[27]

It was on this note that the discussion ended. A few minutes later the whole of the Ratification Bill was adopted by 287 votes to 260.

The result was announced in complete silence. Then the Communists, shouting "*A bas la guerre*", proceeded to abuse Mendès-France, as well as Guy Mollet, who had "disciplined" all the Socialists (except eighteen) into voting for the Paris agreements.

Except for the Communists, all the major groups were divided; half the Gaullists and the greater part of the Right and Radicals had voted for the agreements, but most of the MRP had voted against. Seventy-six Deputies had abstained, among them MM. Schuman, Bidault, Paul Reynaud, and Pinay. Anyway, by a majority of 27, German rearmament had been approved. Mendès-France had won. It was now for the Senate to confirm this vote.

President Eisenhower said this was "most satisfactory news for the whole Free World".

In France, the Assembly's debate was taken very earnestly; and seldom was France *less* inclined to treat its Parliament as a monkey-house, whatever the outside world was saying.

A real insight into the workings of Mendès-France's mind is provided by the exchange of letters between him and Sir Winston Churchill only a few days later.... And it provides an even better insight into the terrible pressures to which France was subjected throughout that period by her Allies, not least by the British Government.

Mendès-France's letter of January 5, 1955 began with the words:

MY DEAR PRIME MINISTER,
As I felt able to give you an assurance during the discussions in London, the National Assembly has approved the Agreements on which the unity and cohesion of the Western Powers depend....

But, added Mendès, it had been difficult; and there were more difficulties ahead; if these difficulties were to be overcome, "the West must unceasingly demonstrate its goodwill". In an accompanying memorandum, he proposed that there be (*a*) either a French offer to the Soviet Government that the two Governments discuss the possibility of a Four-Power conference in May, i.e. after the French ratification of the Paris agreements, or (*b*) another course, which, Mendès said, he preferred: and that was that there be a joint invitation from the three Western Powers to the Soviet Government. This second solution did not explicitly provide that the Paris Agreements be ratified by the Council of the Republic first. It was over this that Churchill blew up.

[27] *Débate, Assemblée Nationale*, December 29, 1954, p. 6840.

This Churchill letter of January 12, with its threat of the Empty Chair, explains better than anything else the real background against which Mendès-France had to work. It is doubtful whether the extravagant flattery to Mendès-France personally could make up for the contempt with which Churchill treated the French Assembly and his threat, unprecedented in its harshness, to isolate France:

Thank you very much for your letter. I renew my congratulations to you on your success in the Chamber. I feel that your difficulties in dealing with all the vehement and self-centred groups must be enormous. Your courage and vitality have given me an impression of French leadership which I had not sustained since the days of Clemenceau. Pray accept my earnest compliments.

I have for some time felt a strong desire to establish a direct personal contact with the new leaders of the Soviet Government such as might lead to a fruitful four-Power conference. But these thoughts of mine received a rude check when the Soviets requested a four-Power meeting of the Foreign Secretaries, apparently with the object of stimulating opposition in the French Chamber to the ratification of EDC.

After this came the London conference and Sir Anthony Eden's initiative was there, and subsequently at Paris, crowned by the agreements which you by your determination and skill managed, though by a very small majority, to pass through the Chamber. I am well aware that the treaty has also to pass the Conseil de la République [sic] and of the many opportunities for uncertainty and delay which still remain.

I still hold most strongly to my conviction that a top-level meeting might be productive of real advantages if the time and circumstances were well chosen. . . .

Although we have every sympathy with you in your difficulties and admiration for your exertions, the fact should be accepted that I and my colleagues are wholeheartedly resolved that there shall be no meeting or invitation in any circumstances which we can foresee between the four Powers, either on the Foreign Secretaries level or on that of the heads of Governments, until the London-Paris Agreements have been ratified by all the signatories. In this we are in the closest accord with the United States. I cannot believe there is the slightest chance of any change of attitude on this point in either of our two countries. Indeed, I fear that an indefinite process of delay may well lead to the adoption of other solutions which are certainly being studied on both sides of the Atlantic.

And then—the "Empty Chair"—

I, myself, am very much opposed to the withdrawal of all American and British troops from the Continent. You may count on me to oppose to the best of my ability the strategic conception known as "peripheral". *On the other hand I should feel bound, whether as Prime Minister or as a private member, to support the policy known as "the empty chair", although this would involve large changes in the infra-structure of NATO, both mili-*

tary and political. I feel that the United States with their immense superiority of nuclear weapons and acting in association with Great Britain, the British Commonwealth, and the German Federal Republic, will be strong enough, at any rate during the next few years, to afford to the Benelux countries and our other Allies for whom we have a deep regard, and also the German Federal Republic to whom we are bound in honour, a definite and substantial security based on physical and moral deterrent power.

In this breathing space much may be achieved. But having ever since 1910 worked and fought with and for France, for whose people I have a deep affection, I should feel the utmost sorrow to see her isolated and losing her influence with the rest of the free world. I hope indeed that it will fall to you to save your country from this evil turn of fortune.

Please accept for yourself and Madame Mendès-France all my good wishes for the New Year and my earnest hopes that you may continue at the helm. —Winston S. Churchill.

It is unnecessary to quote French comments on this letter—when finally, in March 1955, it was made public—after Mendès-France had ceased to be "at the helm". These comments were not complimentary. The *Monde* uttered the word that was on so many lips: *Diktat.*

CHAPTER FIVE

WAS MENDÈS-FRANCE TOO GOOD
TO BE TRUE?

IN THE first week of February 1955, Mendès-France was overthrown by the National Assembly, in the midst of an uproar, in which the MRP and the Right, joined by the Communists, shouted abuse and insults at the man who had, for nearly eight months, put France in the limelight of international politics, and who, for some time, was more popular with the people of France than any man since de Gaulle at the time of the Liberation. An inquiry made by the IFOP (the French "Gallup") in August 1954 showed that Mendès-France was overwhelmingly popular in France; even right-wing and Communist voters put him very high in their esteem.

But August was a time when Mendès was looked upon chiefly as the man who had ended the war in Indo-China, and who had stopped the rot in North Africa, threatened at that time with anarchy, chaos, and large-scale bloodshed.

Yet was not Mendès-France one of those strange phenomena who emerge for a short time, when everything looks desperate, and who are then pushed aside, once things have "got back to normal"?

As Professor Alfred Sauvy wrote:

Political power in France is composed of a tangle of many incoherent things. From time to time, after serious setbacks, an authority emerges: the collapse of the franc brought Poincaré into power; Munich brought in Paul Reynaud; the disaster of 1940, de Gaulle; and Dien Bien Phu, Mendès-France. But anxious to return to her routine methods, France employs these people for only a short time—for just long enough to enable the country to "return to normal".[1]

The case of Mendès-France is a very strange one. He enjoyed immense popularity in the country after the Indo-China settlement and his visit to Tunis. He enjoyed the admiration of a large part of the Assembly especially among the Socialists, the greater part of the Radicals (who were now proud to claim that he was "one of us"), and many of the Gaullists—who felt much sympathy for his difficulties

[1] *L'Express*, December 18, 1954, in article entitled "Who pulls the Wires?—This is how France is 'lobbyfied'".

with what de Gaulle used to call "the system"; among many others, there was a sneaking admiration for the man; but this feeling was mingled with one of disquiet and uneasiness. As the *Monde* had rightly said from the start, it wasn't so much a political, as a personal reaction. In time, however, the number of those who frankly hated Mendès rapidly grew. It grew as his popularity in the country began to decline after Brussels, and especially after the London agreements. The left-wing intellectuals were enthusiastic supporters of Mendès at least until Brussels; after that, their attitude became lukewarm. The impression grew that the man, whom Bourdet had described as "our most serious and most lonely statesman", was again fighting a lone battle—and this time against his former admirers and—with the temporary acquiescence or even co-operation of men who had no love for him.

Some day it will perhaps be possible to tell the full story of all the wire-pulling and all the murky intrigues—ultimately designed to put an end to his rule—which typified the Mendès-France régime. Below the surface of admiration or acquiescence, there was a hard layer of uncompromising hatred against the man.

This hatred had many causes. He was upsetting many old parliamentary and administrative routines; he was governing in too "personalist" a manner, and was hoping, by using his nation-wide popularity, to enter upon many fields where angels fear to tread.

There were bitter animosities between him and the MRP—especially Bidault and Teitgen who were little short of "pathological" where Mendès was concerned—not only over major issues, but even over small things, and there was much gossip about "mutual intimidation" and "mutual blackmail". The following story from the *Canard Enchaîné* (a much more serious and well-informed political paper than its frivolous appearance suggests) is a good example of this kind of gossip:

At the Quai d'Orsay today there's a sub-team of the Mendès-France team which has been specially instructed to look for, collect, and classify all the official papers (anyway, those that can still be found) concerning Indo-China during the last seven years.

The said sub-team is believed to have collected quite a few papers showing that the MRP have deliberately missed a good many chances to make peace with Ho Chi Minh. So let's just suppose that the Reverent Fathers of the PDBP (*Parti Dien Bien Phu*, as Mauriac has rechristened the MRP) get too nasty with PMF....[2]

And the *Canard Enchaîné* related how PMF broadly hinted at this in the presence of Maurice Schumann—who promptly rushed off to the MRP headquarters, where a meeting of the Executive Committee was called. Whereupon a communiqué was published, saying that the

[2] *Le Canard Enchaîné*, July 14, 1954.

MRP's conscience was clear, and that they were not afraid of any threats and intimidation. What the communiqué did not say, the *Canard* added, was that the MRP had decided, there and then, to compile a "counter-*dossier*" to show that Mendès-France had had contacts with Vietminh for a long time.

In this battle between Mendès-France and the MRP—a still fairly polite battle at first, but then more and more poisonous, as Mendès-France's position grew weaker—there was far more "hanky-panky" and "funny business" than met the eye. The *Canard Enchaîné* was not perhaps far wrong when it attributed to some "secondary" matters the acute antipathy between Mendès and the MRP:

> If the MRP are in such a state over the loss of the Quai d'Orsay, it's because of "Europe", EDC and all that. That's the official side of it. But there's also an unofficial side. You realize that the Ministry of Foreign Affairs is also, as it were, the Ministry of Religious Affairs under the Fourth Republic.... Since the Separation Law, the Vatican has to receive the *agrément* of the Quai d'Orsay to any appointment of Bishops that it makes. For ten years (we need hardly explain) Bidault and Schuman have used this prerogative in favour of Bishops who were in the MRP line. And who were, in the dioceses, good election agents for the Party. On the whole, the trick worked very well. *Ad majorem Dei gloriam.*

Behind the façade of relative unanimity and apparent cordiality that the end of the war in Indo-China had created, the knives were being sharpened and the banana skins scattered all along Mendès-France's path.

The man was irritating and his methods were irritating to many of his political opponents, and not least his highly popular "fireside chats" on the radio; but so long as he had public opinion solidly and, indeed, enthusiastically behind him (and all reports from the towns and the countryside showed that he had—hence the relatively good grace with which his opponents swallowed the Geneva agreements) it was best to lie low.

He worked in spectacular style. Only a few days after the Indo-China vote, on July 28 (*Le Monde* related) he and his economic counsellors had worked till four o'clock in the morning drawing up a thirty-page memorandum outlining the Premier's economic doctrine. Who were these "economic counsellors"—this "brains trust"? Apart from a small "brains trust" of his personal staff and friends (many of whom, it should be added, greatly annoyed by their presence the permanent officials), there was also the Big Brains Trust which *L'Express* (a specifically Mendès-France paper more than any other) wrote up in grand style on July 17. This economic Brains Trust which, *L'Express* suggested, Mendès had specially set up, was composed of the following:

Paul Delouvrier (40), Inspecteur des Finances, secretary general of the Interministerial Committee for questions of European economic co-operation;

Etienne Hirsch (53), mining engineer, General Commissioner of the Modernization and Equipment Plan; formerly assistant to Jean Monnet;

Gabriel Ardant (49), Inspecteur des Finances, General Commissioner for Productivity; former head of the central committee for costs and yield in the Public Services;

François Bloch-Lainé, director-general of the Caisse des dépôts et des Consignations; former Director of the Treasury;

Pierre Besse (39), Inspecteur des Finances; secretary-general of the Conseil National du Crédit; professor at the Institut d'Etudes Politiques;

Cloude Gruson (43), mining engineer, Inspecteur des Finances, head of the economic and financial studies department at the Ministry of Finance (the real head of the Brains Trust);

Simon Nora (33), Inspecteur des Finances, secretary-general of the Commission des Comptes de la Nation, technical adviser to M. Mendès-France;

Jacques Duhamel (30), Inspecteur des Finances, *auditeur* at the Conseil d'Etat, etc, deputy-chief of M. Mendès-France's secretariat;

Valéry Giscard d'Estaing (28), Inspecteur des Finances, *polytechnicien*, technical counsellor in Mendès-France's secretariat.

This, according to *L'Express*, was the "basic idea" of this brains trust:

The State must take the pulse of the nation. . . . Much too complicated a process . . . but for a Keynesian "revolution" which provides that the State must have an all-round view of the nation's economy; and that since the State's primary duty is to provide full employment, it must be in a position to "regulate" this economy.

"It will soon seem quite absurd," M. Edgar Faure, Mendès-France's Minister of Finance, declared to *L'Express*, "that we should have done without this technique before"—this instrument of statistical, economic, and social analysis and deduction.

Without going into all the details of its functions (and, indeed, most of its activities were very much "behind closed doors") it should be said that this brains trust met three times a week, and was apparently of great value to Mendès-France and Edgar Faure in the economic reorganization of the country that they were said to be preparing.

But—and, indeed, there are several *buts*: Was this "Keynesian" Council as Mendèsiste as Mendès? Was there complete harmony between him and these Inspecteurs des Finances—that super-aristocracy of the French civil service, with their powerful *esprit de corps,* their traditionalism, their Big Business contacts,[3] their inevitably divided

---

[3] *France-Observateur* alleged that at least one of the members of the "brains trust" later proved to be under the influence of the *betteravier* lobby.

loyalties? Were not Mendès-France's methods, ideas, technique, and personality rubbing many of them the wrong way? It was, for instance, a well-known fact that, at the Quai d'Orsay, the MRP ministers, who had ruled the place for ten years, had left many of their "agents" there; that these reported to the MRP leaders what was "going on" under the new boss. Were not members of other Departments "disloyal" to him, too? And, finally, was it not, in the last analysis, Edgar Faure who was more responsible than Mendès for the economic reforms of the Mendès-France régime; and was it not under his influence (with the co-operation of the "brains trust") that so many of these reforms were watered down? Did not, for instance, the all-out battle that Mendès-France was planning against the Monster Booze amount to no more than an initial skirmish because of the "reticence" of many who worked with him? Even so, it was enough to mobilize against him all the huge vested interests he was proposing to disturb in a big way.

Besides, it should be remembered that, throughout his seven months in office, Mendès-France had to devote himself almost exclusively to foreign and colonial affairs, and that from the moment he declared that he would shortly take the country's economic problems in hand, his enemies moved heaven and earth to turn him out without any further delay.

There is no need to apologize to the reader for quoting again a "frivolous" paper like the *Canard Enchaîné*; despite its flippant tone, the *Canard* not only often published extremely significant facts, but also "sized up" situations with verve and brilliance. It was after Mendès-Frances's spectacular trip to Tunis that R. Tréno published this piece, which was both a reflection of the great impression Mendès-France's manner was producing in the country *at the time*, but also an excellent prophecy of why "it couldn't last":

ANOTHER COUP DE THEATRE

M. Mendès-France Proposes Internal Autonomy for the French

There is no end to the surprises Prime Minister Bang has in store for us.

The effect of the Tunisian bombshell had scarcely died down when another bombshell, even more staggering than the first, blew up with a terrific bang which echoed through the whole world.

M. Le Troquer, in overalls, was watering the flowers in the back garden of the Palais Bourbon, when suddenly ... a helicopter, followed by two more, landed on the lawn. M. Le Troquer had to jump for his life. When he recovered his senses, he saw M. Mendès-France and the members of the Government alighting from the helicopters; and Mendès-France cried: "Quick, quick, get into your presidential chair!"

"But ... just a moment ..."

"Never mind, my dear Le Troquer; let's have none of this *immobilisme*. Here's the first bunch of Deputies arriving."

Motor coaches were, indeed, beginning to pour into the yard of the Palais Bourbon; the Deputies had been picked up all over Paris, and at railway stations and airfields.

"But let me put on my evening dress," M. Le Troquer muttered.

"Never mind about that!" said Mendès-France. "For once, you can preside in your overalls," and grabbing him round the waist, PMF literally carried him to his seat. The meeting was opened.

"Ladies and gentlemen," said the Prime Minister. "It is time to act." (*Agitation among the MRP, groans from the Right, a loud snore from M. Queuille.*)

"I solemnly wish to propose that you give internal autonomy—to begin with—to the people of France."

M. Bidault (*sarcastically*): Is it to listen to this high-falutin' nonsense that you have asked us to come here?

PMF: Yes, gentlemen, we must free the French people of all their fetters. I therefore table: (1) a Bill putting an end to the privileges of the following economic monopolies: the *betteraviers*, the wine trade, the milk trade, the meat trade, etc.

A member of the Right: You mean you wish to outlaw us? You can't get away with that. (*He leaves debating hall, followed by 200 colleagues.*)

PMF (*unperturbed*): (2) a Bill providing for a Fiscal Reform under which all the rich, including the rich peasants, shall pay their taxes. (*At this point 200 more Deputies noisily leave the Hall.*)

PMF (*still unperturbed*): I also wish to reform Justice and the press. Do you know that you have to be a milliardaire in this country today before you can start a newspaper? I also wish to propose an electoral law which would free the Republic of the dictatorship of the Party committees. (*Uproar on the last occupied benches.*)

In the end, the Socialists and Communists also leave in a huff, and the only people left in the audience are a few Negro Deputies from Central Africa, who welcome the idea of giving the French internal autonomy.

Was Mendès, indeed, trying to do too much all at once? Although he was an economist first and foremost, circumstances did not allow him to devote his undivided attention to that side of things; and the economic plenary powers he received from the Assembly in August did not produce anything very sensational. It has even been suggested that the great "anti-alcohol" operation was chiefly intended to camouflage the unspectacular nature of the other innovations. Not only that—but the anti-alcoholic measures introduced in the end had been watered down: thus, the duty on spirits was increased by 20 per cent, and not by 100 per cent, as was originally intended; the original plan also provided that no drink be sold within a wide perimeter of any factory or school; but nothing was done about this; also, for fear of peasant riots in Normandy and Brittany, little was done against the *bouilleurs de crû*, the small tax-free distillers; nor were the originally-planned restrictions placed in the way of *apéritif* advertising. Mendès-France, like others before him (Pinay and René Mayer, for instance) came up against important electoral interests (e.g. the *bouilleurs de crû*, who run into millions of voters).[4]

Mendès-France was overthrown for a great number of reasons. Chief among them were: (1) he had already taken upon himself the highly unpopular ratification of the Paris Agreements; (2) his "personalism" was rubbing more and more people the wrong way; (3) he had announced his decision, before long, to change places with Edgar Faure: appoint the latter Foreign Minister, and devote himself almost entirely to the economic reorganization of the country. What all mightn't he do if he made the economic reorganization of France a full-time job? Until then, he had not done much, but what he *had* done had already provided a foretaste of the far more "terrible" things he might do—in respect of income-tax, drink, motor transport (which was ruining the railways) and other matters which deeply concerned the various "Lobbies". Of the various Lobbies, the powerful *betteravier* (sugar-beet grower) Lobby—besides some of the other Alcohol Lobbies—was the one he had alarmed and annoyed most of all. Without going into all the details of the complex "alcohol problem" in France, it is necessary here to say something about it, with special reference to the *betteraviers*.

The *régime de l'alcool* has, time and again, been denounced as the "greatest economic scandal in France". The political problem of Alcohol is personified by several lobbies—the sugar-beet lobby, the wine lobby, the apple lobby, and by the great army of *bouilleurs de crû,* composed of a powerful electoral body of about four million persons who are not only allowed to distil ten litres of pure alcohol a year, free of tax (representing 400,000 hectolitres), but who are estimated to distil at least as much again (if not twice as much) "unofficially". As a result the incidence of alcoholism is highest of all in Normandy and Brittany.

Much has been written on the disastrous effect on public health in France of the Monster Booze, with a *per capita* consumption of alcohol which, with nearly twenty litres of pure alcohol per annum, is much higher than in any other country in the world.

No doubt, medical authorities in France have differed on the question

---

[4] *Cf.* in particular a detailed study on this question by Georges Léguillon in *Esprit*, December 1954, pp. 818–34, called "L'attentisme économique". In this the author blames the disappointing results of the "anti-liquor" drive on the caution displayed by M. Edgar Faure, whom he describes as *attentiste* and *immobiliste*.

whether spirits are primarily responsible for this state of affairs; many authorities have blamed the large consumption of wine for much of the ill-health. Thus, it has been argued that if one half-bottle of wine per day is "quite harmless", people in the South and Centre of France think nothing of drinking two, three, and even more bottles of wine a day, in the common belief that "it is harmless" or even that "it's good for you". In reality, this immoderate consumption of wine creates in time what medical authorities have called *alcoolisme vinique*, different in its effects from those caused by the hard liquor of Normandy and Brittany, or by brandy, pernot, and *apéritifs*, but almost equally disastrous in the long run.

Whether, by drinking milk in public, Mendès-France tried to persuade people that milk *was* drinkable, and that wine was not an essential part of every meal, he no doubt felt that it would be unwise at that stage to be so "un-French" as to challenge wine-drinking.

What Mendès-France tried, however, to challenge (after Pinay, René Mayer and others had failed) was the extraordinary system crowned by a mysterious autonomous government office, called the "Régie des alcools". One of the principal features of this system is the State's undertaking to buy up the alcohol made of the "surplus" of sugar-beet not used up by the sugar refineries. The latter are handicapped by the simple fact that a parity has been fixed by law between the price of sugar-beet turned into sugar and that of sugar-beet turned into alcohol; and since a distillery is much cheaper to set up and to run than a sugar refinery, distillers can afford to refund some of their profits to the sugar-beet growers.[5]

The prices fixed by Parliament for both sugar-beet and the alcohol, which the State undertakes to buy, are generous and have no reference to world prices. As a result, the State in 1953 bought beet alcohol at 100 francs a litre, which was three or four times higher than the world price. There is thus an over-production of alcohol, which the State is left to "carry". Occasionally, as at the time of the Korean War, it was able to sell a large quantity of this surplus alcohol to the USA (needless to say, at a loss). The attempts—however uneconomical—made by the State to turn this alcohol into motor fuel has met with opposition from the petrol trade—a rival lobby.

The keystone of the whole structure being the price parity between beet-for-sugar and beet-for-alcohol, as well as the purchase price of the sugar-beet crop as a whole, the whole process of fixing prices, contingents of the alcohol to be bought by the State, etc, can obviously be the object of endless political wire-pulling.

The interests of 150,000 small growers and of 5,000 large "industrial"

[5] *France-Observateur*, May 13, 1954.

growers of sugar-beet are directly involved.[6] Their central organization is the CGB, the *Confédération générale des planteurs de betterave*, some of whose members carry on active propaganda in favour of alcohol motor-fuel, *apéritifs* containing beet alcohol, higher duties on imported sugar, etc. The *betteraviers'* parliamentary lobby is composed of several Deputies. Occasionally, very occasionally the press has come out with "inside stories" of how attempts, such as M. René Mayer's in 1953 to fix a poorer price for sugar-beet earmarked for distilleries and a better price for beet earmarked for sugar-refineries (so as to encourage growers to produce beet for sugar, rather than for the distillers), or to cut in half the quantities of alcohol to be purchased by the State, had invariably been defeated in Parliament, or rather, before reaching Parliament.

All these "operations" are estimated to bring in the *betteraviers* a yearly profit of some ten milliard francs out of public funds.

What then did Mendès-France do to annoy the *betteravier* lobby? He did not scrap the iniquitous system. But at least he *began* to reform it. Thus, his decrees transferred to sugar-refineries two-thirds of the beet earmarked for the distilleries and reduced the quantity of beet alcohol to be bought by the State. This represented a saving to the Treasury; it encouraged the production of sugar, instead of alcohol; and so it tended to put an end to a "social scandal", if not—*not yet*— to an "economic scandal". The decision to give free milk and sugar to school-children was a gesture which impressed mothers, but naturally annoyed the *betteravier* lobby, who found it more profitable to grow beet for alcohol than for sugar.

Not to annoy the mighty Lobby too much, Mendès, however, agreed to pay a premium of 1,500 francs on every ton of *undistilled* sugar beet. He also discouraged the wasteful use of alcohol in motor fuel, raised the cost of café licences, and increased by 20 per cent the tax on liquor. (Originally he had meant to raise it by 100 per cent.) All this was still relatively small stuff. The sacrosanct price parity between beet-for-sugar and beet-for-alcohol was left unaffected. Nevertheless, Mendès-France had done enough to scare the *betteravier* lobby, as well as the *bouilleurs de crû*, whose numbers, it was believed, he was planning to limit, and over whose stills he was proposing to set up a close control by Government inspectors. Altogether, he was beginning to annoy a part of the

---

[6] M. Paul Reynaud criticized in the Assembly Mendès-France's "operation" against the *betteraviers* as a piece of "anti-alcoholic" demagogy, adding that no beet alcohol was drunk. It was pointed out to him that this was untrue: beet alcohol went into certain *apéritifs* and "*brandys*". It is true, nevertheless, that, although it was convenient to use the *betteraviers* as targets in the "anti-booze" campaign, they were, in reality, chiefly attacked for the financial "racket" on which they had been thriving for years.

peasantry—the apple-growers in the West and the beet-growers in the North—more than anyone had done in the past.

Many measures, more far-reaching ones, which Mendès-France had in mind were not, however, applied. But the men of the Lobby were nervous, all the same, and were anxious to see the last of the Mendès-France Government. It struck many observers as particularly significant that the great attack on the Government on December 3, in connexion with the Dides Affair,[7] the *affaire des fuites* (the leakage of military secrets concerning Indo-China) should have been conducted by none other than M. Legendre, a right-wing Deputy of the Oise, and known as one of the pillars of the *betteravier* lobby. Indo-China military secrets and—sugar-beet; the connexion was so remote that Legendre's attack could only be interpreted as an attack by the *betteraviers* on the Government as such.

This attack failed; and, more generally, it was not in the interests of the Right to overthrow the Mendès-France Government before the Paris Agreements had been ratified (from their point of view, it was all the better to let Mendès associate himself with that highly unpopular step in French foreign policy); but when, about the time of this ratification, it was announced that Mendès-France intended to change places with Edgar Faure and deal himself with the country's economic reforms, the time for getting rid of the Government was close at hand.

It is highly significant that, under the influence of the *betteraviers*, the National Assembly proceeded to scrap some of the anti-alcoholic reforms Mendès had introduced barely a month after the fall of his Government; while, already, on February 15, M. Legendre and other *betteraviers* tabled a private members' Bill restoring, on a long-term basis, the full privileges of the beet-growers and the distillers, by putting

---

[7] It is impossible to deal here in detail with the *affaire Dides* with its almost inextricable tangle of plots, counter-plots, rival secret police organizations, American spies, Communist or pseudo-Communist spies, double and triple agents, newspaper tipsters and *agents provocateurs* belonging, or claiming to belong, with their "inside information", to the Communist Party, with the voluntary or involuntary indiscretions committed by persons acquainted with military secrets concerning Indo-China, etc. The purpose of "politicizing" the *affaire Dides* was a dual one: to blow up the Mendès-France Government from inside by trying to implicate in the "military leakages" M. Mitterrand, the Minister of the Interior (who had aroused undying hatred in certain quarters, notably by sacking M. Baylot, the Paris Prefect of Police), and certain persons in Mendès-France's own entourage; and, secondly (and this is where the MRP were specially interested in the *affaire*) to show that the war in Indo-China had been lost because of "treason" on the part of "tipsters" and of the left-wing journalists who had used these "tips", notably Gilles Martinet and Roger Stéphane of *France-Observateur*. Their defence was that they *had* used certain "indiscretions" because they considered it in the interests of the country to end the war in Indo-China.

the "contingent" of the Government purchases of alcohol several hundred thousand hectolitres above the figure fixed by Mendès-France.[8]

How then was Mendès-France overthrown?

Mendès's conflict with the *betteravier* lobby was a fundamental one. Almost as fundamental was his conflict with the North African diehards. No doubt, there was not much they could complain of in the case of Tunisia. Since Mendès's famous visit to Tunis, the country was settling down; the fellagas had surrendered and had allowed themselves to be disarmed and, as Mendès-France pointed out in the final debate, on February 4, 1955, the murders and assassinations in the Tunisian towns in the last few months had been *nil*, and in the Tunisian countryside, also *nil*.

In Morocco he had done nothing to annoy the diehards; and things were, indeed, just as bad as they had been—complete with terrorism and counter-terrorism.

But, early in November, a rebellion had broken out in the Aurès mountains in Algeria. The diehards now attacked Mendès not only for having "encouraged" this rebellion by the concessions he had made to the "criminals" of the Neo-Destour in Tunisia, but—much worse— for having tentatively taken out of its folder, where it had been lying safely buried since 1947, the famous *statut d'Algérie*, and for having suggested that this moderate programme of democratic reforms might be re-examined. In the end, the "grand attack" on this Algerian issue was launched on Mendès-France by a fellow Radical—who was, however, one of the pillars of the North Africa Lobby, M. René Meyer. The MRP lustily joined in this *"revanche* for Indo-China".

To add insult to injury, Mendès had, only a few days before, suddenly appointed Jacques Soustelle, the Gaullist leader, known for his "socially-minded" attitude, Governor-General of Algeria.

Not only did the diehards (rightly or wrongly) consider Soustelle too "liberal"; but they suspected Mendès of a very tricky parliamentary and political manœuvre. Had he not been hobnobbing with de Gaulle? Was he not planning a new, and fairly solid majority, based on the Gaullists, Socialists, and part of the Radicals?

Also, had not *L'Express* launched, only a fortnight before, the idea

[8] The classical argument in favour of producing all this surplus alcohol is (*a*) that it will be useful to have in case of war, and (*b*) it saves dollars, since it can be used instead of petrol, an absurd argument since the alcohol costs the State ten times more than imported petrol. The whole system is, in fact, based on the perpetuation of a war-time measure adopted in 1916. If, by 1924, the State's undertaking to help sugar-beet growers by buying up their surplus crop in the form of alcohol was meant merely as a "relief measure", the *betteravier* organization has been growing beet for the primary purpose of making alcohol, sold at exorbitant prices to the State.

of a *Nouvelle Gauche*, with the blessing of Malraux and Mauriac, and with the clear suggestion that Mendès-France alone could perform the miracle, and gradually win over to the *Nouvelle Gauche* the greater part of the Communist electorate—Malraux's favourite idea?[9]

In the *couloirs*, during that famous debate at the end of which Mendès-France was overthrown amidst animal howls of rage from the Right and the MRP, an MRP leader was saying: "It is now or never."

It was a dirty business. The MRP who, in theory, were just as "liberal" about North Africa as Mendès-France, were filled against the man with such acute personal hatred that all restraint was thrown to the winds. After Mendès-France had been overthrown on February 4 by 319 votes to 273, he did what was perhaps an ill-considered thing: he was determined to "have the last word". Instead of, as is usual, driving straight to the Elysée to hand the Government's resignation to the President of the Republic, he decided to make a "farewell speech".

After referring to North Africa, he said that he did not wish to say anything that might in any way embarrass his successors who would have to continue the work that had been started under his (Mendès-France's) Government.

"No, the work we have accomplished will not be wasted, neither in this, nor in any other field (*Loud protests from Right and Extreme Left*)... What has been done in the last seven or eight months will remain. The things we have set in motion will not stop. (*More protests.*) Men come and go, but the nation's needs remain. . . .

In so far as the admirable stenographers of the National Assembly were able to piece together what was said in the midst of the booing and the infernal uproar that followed this remark, this is what was said:

ALPHONSE DENIS (Communist): And what about German rearmament?
MENDÈS-FRANCE: . . . The nation, which is conscious of what has been done, will not forget all those hopes that were revived in it. . . . (*Loud protests on Right and Centre. Cheers on Left and a few Gaullist benches.*)
ALPHONSE DENIS: You have no business to make this speech. . . .

After M. de Menthon (MRP) and others shouted that all this was wholly out of order, the "discussion" was something like this:

THE PRESIDENT OF THE ASSEMBLY: The Premier will, in a few moments go to the Elysée. . . .
M. BOUXOM (MRP): That's all he's got to do. . . .
THE PRESIDENT OF THE ASSEMBLY: But since he asked my permission to say a few words, I saw no objection to this in the regulations of the

---

[9] A rival *Nouvelle Gauche* (or was it *Gauche Nouvelle*?), more on Popular Front lines was started about the same time by the "non-conformist" Left, among them Senator Léo Hamon, Claude Bourdet, etc.

Assembly. . . . I must ask you to show some courtesy to a Premier who has been in office for eight months. (*Cheers on Left and loud protests on Right and Centre.*)

M. Bouxom: The tribune isn't meant for personal propaganda.

Mendès-France: . . . The purpose of my brief statement is merely to facilitate (*loud protests*) the task of the next government. (*Loud cheers on Left.*) As for procedure, the Government has the right . . .

Protests on Right and Centre: There is no Government ! . . .

Mendès-France: Will you allow me to answer . . . (*Uproar.*)

M. Verdier (Socialist): Fascists !

Mendès-France: I want to tell M. de Menthon and M. Bouxom that the debate is not finished . . .

M. Mutter (Right): Yes, it is . . .

M. Bouxom: The President of the Republic is waiting for you. . . .

And so on—till this final touch:

Mendès-France: In response to the President's proposal, I hereby ask the Assembly to meet on Monday to discuss the provisional monthly estimates . . .

M. Bouxom: Full stop.

Mendès-France: You will excuse me, my dear colleague, it is not you, but I who will make the full stop. (*Violent protests on Right and Centre. . . .*) I hope that in future, thanks to the union of all patriots, and in a better climate, we shall give the country new reasons for hope, and that we shall overcome that hatred of which we have here only too often given such a sorry spectacle. *Vive la France! (Prolonged uproar on Extreme Left, Centre, and Right.)*

As Mendès-France, followed by the members of the Government, left, he was cheered by the Socialists and members on various other benches, while the booing continued among the MRP, on the Right and among the Communists.

In that unfortunate and ill-considered farewell speech, he had, however, used the *mot juste*: hatred. He was hated by the MRP because he had made fools of them over Indo-China, and had wrecked EDC; he was hated by the Communists because of German rearmament; most deeply of all, perhaps, was he hated by the "classical" Right, and by some of his own colleagues in the Radical Party—the sticks-in-the-mud on the one hand, and the "McCarthys" on the other. He was not playing the parliamentary game according to the established rules; and he had made his Government more *personalist* than anything seen since the days of de Gaulle. He thought his personal prestige could carry him through. He was too ambitious. He now wanted to tackle the whole economic structure of France, and upset all the apple-carts. He was disquieting—*that* was the word. The Right hated him with a kind of pathological hatred.

"*Regarde-les, mon âme, ils sont vraiment affreux*"; Mauriac had quoted Baudelaire to describe this hatred of the diehards for Mendès-France.

By February 1955 he had not many friends left. Those who had been most enthusiastic about Mendès-France when he put an end to the war in Indo-China found it hard to forgive him German rearmament.

On balance, Mendès-France's record still remains perhaps the most memorable one in the history of the Fourth Republic: he will always have the end of the Indo-China war to his credit, and the reversal of the ruinous policy in North Africa.

But he was not given enough time. During practically his entire term of office, foreign affairs absorbed all his attention. Britain and the USA bullied him into subscribing to *their* policy, and on terms and in conditions less favourable to France than they might have been but for the deadlines and time limits that were laid down. It was hard for him to resort to delaying tactics after he had made his reputation by being a man of quick action.

Mendès-France was turned out of office when his stock was lowest. Parliament knew that, after the ratification of the Paris Agreements, he had lost an immense amount of the support he had enjoyed in the country; and he had not yet had time to pick himself up, as perhaps he would have done, had he remained in office for two more months. The MRP deputy was right when he exclaimed: "*C'est aujourd'hui ou jamais.*" "Jamais" is a big word; but the risk that Mendès might acquire a new popularity in the country with a bold economic policy was too grave a risk to take. It was not only a matter of Africa, or a matter of sugar-beet; his manner, his personality, his "rhythm" were disturbing.

After a lengthy Cabinet crisis, following the overthrow of the Mendès-France Government, M. Edgar Faure formed the next Government—"*enfin un gouvernement de moindre E. Faure*" (*effort*)—as the wisecracking *Canard Enchaîné* remarked, perhaps a little unfairly.

The ratification of the Paris Agreements and the overthrow, a month later, of the Mendès-France Government mark the end of an epoch. The long struggle France had put up against German rearmament was over.

Before the Council of the Republic had, in turn, ratified the Paris agreements (by this time M. Faure was Premier and M. Pinay Foreign Minister) the *Monde* still went on protesting against what it called *le Diktat*, and against the determination of France's Allies to have the Agreements ratified, even though the Senators still had some reasonable complaints to make about no proper agreement having been reached over the "Armaments Agency" and the Saar.

In an article that aroused much attention, and called *Solitude de la France*, Jacques Madaule recalled all the pressures to which France had been subjected.

And so we are told that the world is sick and tired of our hesitations. If such hesitations were justified, nobody cares. Sentiment doesn't count in politics. And so we are alone, face to face with our destiny.

However, a few days later the Paris Agreements were voted by a reluctant Senate. It was done in an atmosphere of weariness and resignation.

The only consoling thought was that perhaps it no longer mattered very much. *La question est dépassée*, many were now saying. With H-bombs on both sides, what did twelve German divisions matter, after all? Germany would be just as scared of war as the rest of the world, and perhaps more so.

For a time, a weary sort of euphoria now descended on France, as on the rest of Europe. The Russians had not carried out any of the dark threats they had uttered to warn France against ratification. On the contrary, they were now more forthcoming than they had been before. They embarked on a new policy, which some thought a sign of weakness, and others a sign of devilish cunning. They took the initiative in creating a neutral Austria, and made seemingly abject apologies to Tito. They cordially invited Adenauer to Moscow; and although Adenauer swore that his heart would always be with the West, it was not certain that the whole of Germany shared his emotions. Already the Austrian Treaty had badly shaken many Germans.

This euphoria continued right into the summer, and on the eve of the "Summit" Conference of the Big Four at Geneva the *Monde* noted:

Public opinion seems to be remarkably apathetic about the coming Geneva Conference. If such a meeting had taken place a year or two years ago . . . it would have given rise to tremendous hopes. But not today. The nations of the world now consider that the H-bomb gives them a sort of "peace through fear" which is enough to keep everybody quiet.[1]

It went on to say that this, of course, wasn't good enough.

The antagonism between East and West remains complete, both in doctrinal and practical matters. Both sides are rearming at a ruinous rate, and although everybody agrees that the armaments race can only end in a collective suicide, nobody is doing anything to stop it. One day there will be a man or a team, either in the East or in the West who will yield to the

[1] *Le Monde*, July 14, 1955.

temptation of putting an end to it all. And we know what will happen then. . . .

On a short-term basis, at any rate, such pessimism seemed unwarranted in the light of the new "Geneva Spirit", to which, in an atmosphere of mutual back-slapping, the Big Four Conference gave birth. Eisenhower became the Man of Peace in the eyes of Europe, more than any man for years. Nevertheless, the question remained unanswered whether Disarmament would some day become a reality.

That depends perhaps least of all on France, and today (as the opponents of the ratification of the Paris agreements foresaw) France's weight in international affairs has, at least temporarily, greatly diminished. It was different before.

In the past, much depended on her. While the Roll-Back spirit, the Crusading spirit were strong in the United States; while German rearmament constituted (as it did from 1950 to 1953) a genuine danger, while Russia, to many, seemed ready for a "preventive" invasion of Western Europe, France did her utmost, through her hesitations, her delaying tactics, and her "disloyalty"—if it must be called what Truman once called it—to prevent the Cold War from becoming Hot. That part of her mission is now completed. In performing it, France showed a remarkable instinct of self-preservation. Paul Reynaud published a book after the war with the not altogether convincing title, *La France a sauvé l'Europe*. Today a much better case could be made out to show that French "half-heartedness" during the last ten years saved Europe from World War III. This continuous passive resistance to the Cold War becoming too Hot was, as a *chronic* factor, at least as important in averting disaster as the famous British explosion of anti-MacArthurism at the end of 1950.

What is to be France's place in the world now? In 1949 André Malraux made an impassioned speech, which concluded as follows:

When was France great? Only at those times when she was not self-absorbed. She was universalist. For the world, a great France is more than just the France of the Cathedrals, the Revolution or Louis XIV. There are countries like Great Britain—and it may be to their credit—which are great in their solitude. France has always been at her greatest when she spoke for all men; and that is why one cannot listen to her silence today without anguish.[2]

Had France then ceased to be "universal", as Sartre's hero (quoted on the first page of this book) had already said in 1940, and as Malraux was saying again ten years later? Was it true that France had become "silent"?

Has not France, on the contrary, as this whole book shows, been

[2] Postface (1949) to *Les Conquérants* (Paris, 1952), p. 245.

thinking much, and thinking hard, and carefully observing the world around her; and have not her sharply critical attitude, her scepticism, and even her moments of pessimism been a clear expression of so many of the "universal" thoughts of our time? What would the Western civilization of 1945–55 have been without France? Surely, Péguy's God is still right:

> C'est embêtant, dit Dieu, quand il n'y aura plus ces Français,
> Il y a des choses que je fais, il n'y aura plus personne pour les
> comprendre ...

Yet, if France's "universalism" shines less brightly than in the past, it is not entirely the fault of the French. Her weight in the world counts for little in the atomic age (a point overlooked by Malraux, who still likes to think in terms of Valmy and Napoleon, in whose days France was not only "radiant", but also powerful); but there is also this: only too many of France's fellow-nations today are practising a deliberate mental and intellectual autarky, no matter how low their own intellectual rations.

The fact remains, however, that France has lost physically in weight, and may lose still more in the years before us. And two questions inevitably arise: Who will win the battle that has not yet been fought out to a final finish: the battle between the lively and brilliant intelligence of the French intellectual and technical élite and (using these as symbols), Poujade, the big-mouthed successor of Doriot, and Senator Colonna, the colonialist diehard, and the unintelligent part of the *patronat*, and the fossils of French politics—the Legendres, Martinaud-Déplats and Coste-Florets? And secondly, what clear-sighted leaders will emerge to prevent, before it is too late, the loss of North Africa—a loss which would inevitably reduce France to the position of a mere medium-sized Continental Power?

1955–6 POSTSCRIPT:
INTO A NEW EPOCH—WHAT KIND OF EPOCH?

The last lines of this book are being written as France enters the dangerous year of 1956. Unlike the rest of this book, much of what follows is mere hypothesis and speculation.

Of the numerous events in the world during the latter half of 1955, two affected France most closely of all: the return of the exiled Sultan to Morocco,[1] and the Saar referendum of October 23. It is ironical to think that M. Boniface's *emmerdeur* should now be looked upon, by the very people who plotted against him and brought about his overthrow in 1953, as the one bright hope that France still has of maintaining herself in Morocco—even in a greatly reduced capacity. Events have been moving with break-neck speed. If, in August 1955, Mendès-

---

[1] See postscript to earlier chapter on Morocco, p. 630.

France thought that France would have to decide "in the next five years" whether she was to save her Empire or not, her chances of saving it have rapidly dwindled—not in five years, but in five months. *Sa Majesté le Sultan Mohammed V* (as he is now mellifluously referred to on the French radio), who was ready to eat out of France's hand in 1953 (see pp. 622 and 626), but was overthrown, none the less, as an "extremist", has now become the "moderate" (no matter how truculent and resentful he may be at heart); just as Bourguiba is now the "moderate" (perhaps a more genuine one), struggling against the new forces, represented by Salah Ben Yussef, some more xenophobe and anti-European, others more revolutionary in a social sense than anything Bourguiba himself ever represented in the course of his long struggle for Tunisia's "internal autonomy". The pressure from these new revolutionary forces is so great that even the "moderates" of the Neo-Destour are already demanding the creation of an independent Tunisian Army. Both in Tunisia and in Morocco, the nationalist struggle is showing signs of developing into a revolutionary social conflict, a revolt of the downtrodden proletariat and the starving multitudes, not only against the French, but also against the whole feudal and *caidal* system of oppression and exploitation. And the same is true of Algeria.

The second event which showed how quickly the world is changing was the Saar referendum of October 23, 1955—that wretched little First Referendum on the Saar's European Statute, the outcome of which was never even questioned. A mere formality, it was thought. All the arguing and squabbling over the Saar at the French National Assembly in December 1954 (*see* pp. 699–709) was not over the first, but over the second referendum, provided in the Mendès-France-Adenauer agreements. As for the first one, the overwhelming acceptance of the "European Statute" (seemingly so dear to the heart of "Little Europe" Adenauer), was considered a foregone conclusion. And yet, when it came to the point, two-thirds of the Saar voters rejected the European statute, and French cars were mobbed in the streets of Saarbrücken, in the midst of the time-honoured howls of *Deutsch ist die Saar.* . . .

Apart from anything else, the result of the referendum threatened to make complete nonsense of the Coal-Steel Pool, based on the careful balance of Western Germany and France-plus-Saar.

The Russians—and not only the Russians—drew quick conclusions from the Saar referendum. If the Saar cared so little for Western Integration and the European Statute and that Coal and Steel Pool (which was symbolically preparing to move its headquarters to Saarbrücken) what certainty was there that, a year or so later, Western Germany would care more for integration in the West than for a United Germany on terms which Russia would find acceptable? "No," said Molotov at the Second Geneva Conference. "No united Germany on *your* terms. Let the Germans argue it out amongst themselves." And, as the *Monde* commented:

> If Adenauer established diplomatic relations with Russia in return for 9,000 war prisoners, what mightn't Germany agree to for the "return" of the 18 million Germans of the Eastern Zone?

In the next few years, if not months, there are certain to be many spectacular changes in the world, of which the above two are among the most significant symptoms. These two "episodes" raise some far-reaching questions.

Can France still remain "present" in North Africa—with the help of the "moderates"—the Sultan Ben Yussef and Bourguiba? Or will both go "extremist" themselves, or else seek their support from abroad—though no longer from weak-kneed France, but from that stronghold of bourgeois capitalism, the United States? The French, it might be noted, were distinctly upset when

President Eisenhower congratulated the Sultan on his return, and made no mention of France. And then the Sultan asked "Ike" whether, during his convalescence, he wouldn't like a quiet holiday in Morocco? No doubt the *Canard Enchaîné* was right, in the light of all the lynchings at Rabat and Casablanca during that week of great rejoicings, to publish a cartoon showing Eisenhower phoning the Sultan and asking whether *he* wouldn't like a quiet holiday in the United States? Only that wasn't the real point of the original invitation to Eisenhower.

Is the era of colonies and protectorates over? Some Frenchmen will now say that the Dutch and Italians are lucky, and much better-off today without their colonies. "Colonies today don't bring in money," a learned French economist was recently saying, "With all the blah about under-developed countries, they merely expect money to be spent on them. For instance, it'll cost us far too much to make Algeria a habitable place for the 8 million starved or half-starved *sidis*." And he added: "Perhaps with new scientific developments, it would be much simpler if we (maybe together with the Americans) invested money in an independent Tunisia, Algeria and Morocco, and stopped worrying about our political and military *présence* all the time."

All the same, it may take a lot of "conditioning" for France to get used to the thought that she is merely a smaller Italy—or a bigger Holland. The psychological repercussions of the loss of North Africa might be very serious. Especially if, at the same time, Germany became reunited, independently of the West.

Various possibilities may be considered as to the future course of France, if that were to happen. She might well be torn by three conflicting desires:

   1. To be left alone. (Which has never really worked in practice.)
   2. Belong to the West—and much more wholeheartedly now than before.
   3. Experiment once again with "Europe", but now only as a very junior partner.

The dangers of such a partnership would not be far to seek. One may well imagine Berlin and Moscow jointly proposing some day a referendum in Alsace-Lorraine—to begin with (among the French Communists, the idea of Alsatian autonomy has cropped up from time to time in recent years).

If such a Russian-German "grouping" were ever to be formed, it seems highly probable that France would, indeed, be drawn to the West more than before—especially if the West continued to stand for certain democratic conventions of the old type.

Such a strong urge to remain in the West would be a continuation of France's conscious or unconscious *balance-of-power instinct, an instinct which, in the last analysis, largely explains the "oddness" of her behaviour in the last ten years.* Only would a sharply "Atlantic" attitude succeed at that juncture, and would there not be a revival of the old myths of a "greater Europe"—"stretching all the way to the Urals", of which de Gaulle used to speak in 1949, though in a different, a very different context?

*   *   *

The "atomic" equilibrium reached in 1954 had much to be thanked for. World War III was avoided. But this same "atomic equilibrium" (so long as it lasts) leaves room for many spectacular transformations in the world during the next few years. The economic, technical, and ideological competition between the two worlds may assume vast proportions. There may be a "local"—but still major—conflict in the Middle East; there may be an attempt at far-reaching "peaceful" penetration by Russia into many "under-developed" areas of the world; France may lose her Empire, and in Europe she might be faced with the alternatives of being overshadowed by an American-blessed—but un-united—Western Germany, or of being even more heavily overshadowed by a Russian-blessed United Germany.

Probably a *divided Germany* will, for a long time, still remain the best safeguard against major commotions in Europe. But outside Europe the commotions are inevitable.

It seems almost incongruous, against this background of world-wide change and unrest, to talk of the *petite cuisine* of French home politics.

During the last months of 1955 the French State did not present an inspiring spectacle.

The unfortunate "accidents" of Morocco and the Saar coincided in France with an almost inextricable wrangle over a new General Election. Edgar Faure (who, as late as October 6 had declared that Ben Yussef's return was "out of the question"—thus using once again that meaningless phrase which was so often used before by leaders of the 4th Republic) was now only too anxious to make friends with him, and M. Pinay was sent to St Cloud to eat humble pie. Faure declared—no doubt rightly—that these were "serious times", and that many grave decisions would have to be taken "within the next few months". Therefore a General Election was desirable in December. The major offensive against this move (which he took almost as a personal affront) was conducted by Mendès-France. He started a violent campaign in favour of the *scrutin d'arrondissement*, on the ground that a return to this pre-war system would (a) virtually eliminate the Communists from the next Assembly, and (b) make it possible for a clear "republican" majority to emerge.[1]

After weeks of hair-splitting discussions on the *pros* and *cons* of the various election systems (each deputy taking inevitably a somewhat subjective view of the problem—i.e. with reference to his own chances of being returned), the Faure Government was overthrown on November 29 by a "constitutional majority" of 318 votes. But on the following day, M. Faure took a step that no one had dared to take since Marshal MacMahon in 1877: taking advantage of an obscure article of the Constitution, which many of those who had voted against him had overlooked or not taken seriously, he decided on the dissolution of the Assembly, and the decree to that effect was duly signed by President Coty on December 1. A new election was to take place on January 2, 1956.

Apart from the personal animosity between Mendès-France and Edgar Faure, it was not easy to discover why exactly Faure had yielded to the pressure of the Right and the MRP, for he was not fundamentally a man of the Right. The fact however, remains that, with the *apparentements* system still in force, the candidates in the 1956 Election split, broadly, into three groups:

(a) The Right: the Faure-Martinaud-Déplat-René Mayer-J. P. David Radicals (most of these having been expelled from the Radical Party, they used instead the label of the RGR, the *Rassemblement des Gauches Républicaines*—a loosely-knit organization composed of Radicals and sundry Right-wing elements), and the greater part of the Gaullists;

(b) The Radicals who had accepted the "discipline" of their Vice-Premier, Mendès-France; the Socialists; the UDSR; and a small number of Gaullists;

[1] He preferred not to be reminded of 1940. The Assembly which gave Pétain his plenary powers was, for the greater part, composed of deputies who had been elected under the *scrutin d'arrondissement*. This means election without Party lists and in single-member constituencies, with a second ballot when no candidate received an absolute majority in the first.

(c) The Communists, with whom the Socialists had decided not to "associate" themselves, even at the risk of losing many seats themselves.

Again the Left forces were split in two, and there was a danger—loudly-voiced —particularly by Mendès-France—of "the majority of the chronic housing shortage, of the Moroccan *coup* of August 1953, and of Dien Bien Phu" returning to power. (Not that he had himself encouraged an *apparentement* with the Communists—far from it.) In addition to these regular political forces, an innovation in the 1956 election was provided by strong anti-parliamentary right-wing forces under Poujade.

The *apparentements* system hardly worked, and the voting was done virtually on a PR basis. 150 Communists (instead of 95) were returned; the "Republican Front" of Socialists, Mendès Radicals and a few others had nearly another 150 seats between them; the Right, MRP and "Faure Radicals" suffered some losses, and the ex-Gaullists were virtually wiped out. Instead, a new major force came into being: the Poujadists, whom few "experts" had taken seriously, but who now had 52 deputies. Started originally as a shopkeepers' protest movement against unfair and "inquisitorial" taxation, Poujadism showed, by January 1956, every sign of developing into a full-fledged Fascist movement, in which the "shopkeepers" were already being swamped by the "thugs". The 2½ million people who had voted for Poujade had done so for various reasons: most of them were mere malcontents, who were protesting not only against taxation, but also against the ineptitude of Parliament, as shown in the last year, and against the humiliations France had suffered in North Africa. But all this grousing was being canalized into Fascist channels, not least by Poujade himself, a noisy demagogue who had learned his tricks from both Hitler and Doriot. Among the "intellectual élite" of the Poujade movement could be found many former Action Française men, ex-Doriotists and plain *collabos* of the days of the German occupation.

With their clamour for the *Etats-Généraux* which, they said, would be "more representative than Parliament", the Poujadists were outspokenly anti-parliamentarian, racialist and noisily anti-semitic, with Mendès-France as their Enemy No 1. Their slogan for North Africa (where most of the French settlers are Poujadists) was simply "repression". Regardless of the clamour for lower taxes among his "shopkeepers", Poujade was willing, in short, to embark on "repression", i.e. a regular major war in Algeria. Ominously enough, practically the whole right-wing press in France proceeded to build up Poujade "*le bon Français*" (Pierre as a baby, his family, mother-in-law, etc) in the best sloppily-Nazi tradition. Poujade, determined to crush democracy and the trade unions, had many Big Business interests, as well as (naturally) the North Africa Lobby supporting him. A question widely asked in January 1956 was whether, as in 1934, so now, the Popular Front alone could not save France from Fascism; but to the Socialists and the Mendèsistes the question appeared, to say the least, premature.

In short, with Africa and Asia in a state of revolt, and with a repetition of the civil war atmosphere of the 1930's threatening France, the world has entered an epoch which will not necessarily be more restful than the precarious peace of the last ten years. And France is sure to have her share of trouble—and probably much more than her share.

THE END

A NOTE ON ALGERIA

I F, as distinct from Tunisia and Morocco, Algeria is dealt with only incidentally in the foregoing narrative, it is because, in the main, Algeria was, throughout the last ten years, a chronic, rather than an acute problem for France. That, sooner or later, the agitation in Morocco would spread to Algeria was, however, obvious to anybody acquainted with that country, where economic conditions were, on the whole, worse than in Morocco, and much worse than in Tunisia. As distinct from the other two, Algeria formed "part of France", and there were, *ipso facto*, no *interlocuteurs* i.e. no Algerian "representatives" with whom the French could, or would negotiate. The *Statut d'Algérie* of 1947 had remained a dead letter, and elections in Algeria remained one of the worst jokes in all colonial history, not least under the rule of M. Naegelen, the Socialist Governor-General of 1948–9.

What complicated matters still further was that Algerians had, soon after the war, been granted the "status" of French citizens, and hunger and over-population, especially in Kabylia, had driven hundreds of thousands of them to France, where they formed a wretched sub-proletariat, a sort of half-unemployed labour reserve, most of them living in appalling slum conditions. The "racialist" propaganda in some right-wing papers like *L'Aurore*—which tended to attribute to the "North Africans" (often quite arbitrarily) any burglaries, robberies and other crimes committed in the Paris area—assumed quite indecent proportions at times. The fact that these wretched *sidis* and *bicots* had largely been driven to France by the shocking economic conditions created in Algeria by French Big Business and by the French settlers was, naturally, overlooked.

In June 1955 a Parliamentary Commission, composed of two Socialists (M. Christian Pineau and M. Max Lejeune), one right-wing member (M. Jean-Moreau), one Gaullist (M. Jacquet), and one MRP—and a highly "colonialist" one at that—(M. de Chevigné) drew up an important report, which was published on July 1. This dealt, first of all with the rebellion that had continued, off and on, since the previous autumn. In itself, the report said, the rebellion was not a serious matter, and put the number of armed rebels at not more than 2,500. But that was not the main point:

731

Our enemies are benefiting from the mountainous terrain which is suitable for ambushes, rather than for regular warfare; and, above all, they are benefiting from the attitude of the Moslem population.... Thus the number of armed rebels is less important than the widespread support they enjoy in their guerilla activities and in their propaganda.... By harassing our army units, by organizing ambushes, by burning the crops, they have succeeded in creating a general atmosphere of insecurity.... Their leaders all seem to belong to an organization called the CRUA (*Comité révolutionnaire d'unité d'action pour l'Algérie*).

This organization, the report continued, was closely, though not "organically" connected with the two Algerian autonomist movements, the UDMA and the MTLD. The support given to the rebels by certain *oulemas* tended to give the rebellion the character of a Holy War, and so enhanced their prestige among numerous Moslem elements. Although the report denied that the rebels were receiving large quantities of arms from abroad, it claimed that numerous "well-trained agitators" had been sent by Algerian leaders living in Egypt. A great influence in Algeria was exercised by the anti-French broadcasts from Cairo Radio.

Curiously enough, the report added that, to be on the safe side, certain French settlers were taking out "insurance" by paying the rebels.

The real danger (this part of the report concluded) came not from the Aurès area, always a hot-bed of unrest, but from the movement spreading to Kabylia and the Constantinois, whence it might well spread to the whole of Algeria. There had already been some alarming symptoms of this.

Equally important was the analysis given of the economic structure of Algeria—a structure which explained the unrest and discontent among the native population.

We do not wish to underrate the great things done by France in Algeria; but we must admit that Europeans have benefited from these improvements far more than the natives. The condition of these may perhaps have improved in absolute terms, but certainly not in relative terms, i.e. in comparison with the prosperity of the Europeans.... The natives are like so many shadows moving against the background of European prosperity and artificial security. No man with any feeling for his fellow men can fail to be struck by the appalling poverty still existing in numerous regions of Algeria.... Native wages are extremely low. In the Oran region an agricultural labourer is paid 360 francs [about 1 dollar] a day, on which he usually has to feed seven or eight persons. Even with this wage, he generally works only 150 days a year; but even so, he is still a privileged person amidst the countless hordes of the wholly unemployed.

And then this comparison between the recent benefits conferred on the French settlers, with their emphasis on crops for export, and the wretched condition of the small native farmers, not to mention the landless multitudes:

The credits received by Algeria under the first Modernization and Equipment Plan have benefited chiefly the big landowners, nearly all of them Europeans, who have concentrated on growing wine and vegetables for export. These exports to France compete unnecessarily with the French home market, already suffering from a glut. On the other hand, very little has been done for the small Moslem farmers. These all live on meagre and poorly-irrigated land. The taxes paid by the big landowners are ludicrously low. We know of the case of a person owning 1,200 hectares of vineyards worth 1,200 million francs, and paying only 25,000 francs[1] a year in direct taxes.... There cannot be a *rapprochement* between Arabs and Europeans in such an atmosphere of social and fiscal injustice and inequality....

After severely criticizing the administration in Algeria which, in the last ten years, "seemed to have lost contact with the native population", and was leaving all the day-to-day work to an army of corrupt *caïds* and other Moslem stooges—whose prevarication gave the natives the most deplorable impression of French methods—the report then alluded to the wholly arbitrary and inhuman behaviour of certain law courts and especially of the Police. Although the report was carefully worded, it clearly suggested that there was some truth in the allegations made by numerous papers in France that the French police in Algeria was little better than the Gestapo, complete with third-degree methods and torture chambers.

Significantly, the report concluded by rejecting the methods advocated "in certain quarters" in favour of the wholesale extermination of native populations as the surest means of preserving Algeria for France:

Taking account of the sympathy shown for the rebels by numerous elements of the native population, certain persons have advocated the system of collective reprisals, such as the rounding-up of hostages, or the bombing of villages. We believe that such methods should be rejected absolutely, not only for humanitarian reasons, but also for political reasons. Our experience in Indo-China has shown that such methods breed hatred far more than fear, and play, in the end, into the hands of the rebels. This appears to be the view generally held by the French military leaders in Algeria, especially of the land forces.

It is certain that although Algeria is "part of France", she is likely, in the next few years, to become by far the most troublesome of the three countries of French North Africa. The population pressure is much stronger here than in either Tunisia or Morocco. Whilst Morocco today presents a major political problem, Algeria is, above all, a major

---

[1] £1,200,000 and £25 respectively.

economic problem. The October 1948 census already showed a population of 8,676,000 (including 1,040,000 Europeans)—a total increase of 1,400,000 (including 53,000 Europeans), compared with 1936.

The choice in 1956 lies, as in Tunisia and Morocco before, between a policy of liberalism and economic reforms and a policy of "repression". In his election campaign, Mendès-France insisted that Algeria was Number 1 problem, without the settlement of which it was useless to talk of a higher living standard in France, better housing conditions, or anything else; a war in Algeria would wreck any plans for improvements at home. He advocated free elections in Algeria, a land reform, immediate relief for the "starvation areas", and subsequent negotiations with "Algerian representatives". The weakness of this programme was that it did not provide for the *immediate* recognition of any Algerian representatives, or for immediate cease-fire talks with the Algerian Resistance—even though Mendès-France himself agreed that if nothing were done, there would be a major war in Algeria before the summer of 1956. The Socialists followed, more or less, the same line. The Communists (unwisely) asked that all French troops simply be withdrawn from Algeria. Which did not show much consideration for the 1,000,000 Frenchmen living in that country.

At the other extreme are the Poujadists with their programme of "repression", which can obviously lead only to a major war in Algeria. Moreover, the Poujadists, supported by the North Africa Lobby, even propose to go back on the concessions "extracted" from the French by Tunisia and Morocco in the past few years.

THE FRENCH PRESS FROM THE LIBERATION TO THE PRESENT TIME[1]

THE *Statut de la Presse*, elaborated at the time of the Liberation, and described by Albert Bayet, one of the principal left-wing ideologists of the Resistance as "*la séparation de l'Argent et de l'Idée*" was a lofty idea which, before long, came up against the hard realities of newspaper finance in a capitalist society.

Although the various Resistance organizations (as their critics put it) "grabbed" and "helped themselves" to the offices and printing-plants of the *collabo* press, and although the authorization to print a newspaper and the allocations of newsprint were for some years after the Liberation in Government hands, this "ideal" system, conforming to the principle laid down by the CNR Charter, did not last long. It was no doubt an interesting experiment to try to have a press "without any financial capital behind it", and to allow each authorized paper to continue publication as long as it managed to make ends meet; but the system just did not work. Before long it was realized that some papers did much better than others; and by 1947, at any rate, it became clear that the financing of a daily created precisely the same problems as before the war. By 1948 Big Business gained control of a large part of the French press.

There were many reasons why the system proved unworkable. During the 1944–6 period all papers appeared on two, or at most, four pages, and the advertising revenue was practically nil. At that time there was a keen interest in "the battle for the New France", and many of the "Resistance" papers succeeded in living on their sales. Others, however, very quickly failed, and managed to keep going (until their allocation of newsprint was reduced) by selling their surplus newsprint in the black market.

At the end of 1945 there were 39 daily papers in Paris (23 morning, 10 evening, and 6 "special"—sports, finance, etc); by the middle of 1950 there were only 20 (11 morning, 5 evening, 4 "special"), a figure

---

[1] Most of the figures quoted below are from the special number of *NEF*, *La Presse, IV-e pouvoir* (September 1950), and from the excellent special studies in *L'Observateur*, April 13, 1950, April 19, 1951, December 25, 1952, February 5, 1953, February 12, 1953, July 23, 1953, July 12, 1955, etc.

that is still lower today, 2 mornings—*L'Aube* and *Ce Matin*—and one evening—the Communist *Ce Soir*—having since disappeared. Similarly, between 1948 and 1950 4 other dailies had stopped publication—*L'Époque*, *L'Ordre*, *Le Pays*, and *La France Libre*, not to mention the hecatomb in 1946–7 of numerous ephemeral dailies that had come into existence about the time of the Liberation.

If, during the first few years after the Liberation, there was a general desire to read "political" papers, it became apparent in 1948–9, as things began to settle down, that more and more people wanted to be simply informed and "entertained".

This is apparent from the following table showing the actual sales (*ventes*) (as distinct from printings [*tirages*])[2] of the Paris dailies between March 1948 and October 1952:

| | (In thousands of copies) | | | | | |
| | March | | | Oct. | | |
	'48	'49	'50	'51	'52	Gain or Loss
Le Parisien Libéré	299	323	392	408	484	+ 185
L'Aurore	189	267	290	276	283	+ 94
Le Figaro	303	326	356	352	369	+ 66
France-Soir	501	462	538	588	706	+ 205
Franc-Tireur	276	226	187	140	96	− 180
L'Humanité	292	219	200	167	141	− 151
Le Populaire	77	36	25	24	16	− 61
Ce Matin	125	164	135	107	81	− 44
Libération	136	109	104	106	94	− 42
Combat	69	69	59	51	46	− 23
Paris-Presse	354	320	315	213	137	− 217
Ce Soir	303	214	199	114	81	− 222
Le Monde	146	137	134	124	117	− 29

To these should be added the conservative Catholic daily, *La Croix*, with a steady, almost unvarying sale (nearly all to postal subscribers) of between 150,000 and 160,000, and a few "special" dailies, such as the financial paper *L'Information*, or the sports paper *L'Equipe*.

Several important facts emerge from the above table: in the first place, the sharp rise in the *presse d'information* and the sharper decline of the *presse d'opinion*.

The *Parisien Libéré* and *L'Aurore* are the so-called "*concierge's* papers", with much of their space given to headlines, pictures, crime stories, sports, etc—popular dailies, though with a strong right-wing slant in their news and editorial comments. (It should, of course, be emphasized that as distinct from some British dailies, there are no

[2] The number of "unsolds" is unusually high in France; if, before the war, it is estimated to have amounted to about 10 or 12 per cent, the average of "unsolds" in 1948–9 was around 25 per cent; 35 or even 40 per cent in the case of some of the moribund papers.

French dailies which are almost *entirely* given to "entertainment" and crime.)

The *Figaro*, also right-wing, and very much the organ of the conservative bourgeoisie, is in a higher "class" than the *Parisien Libéré* or *L'Aurore*; apart from the sometimes surprisingly non-conformist editorials of François Mauriac (who, more or less, dropped out after 1953), the *Figaro* is ultra-conservative, violently anti-Communist, anti-Soviet, and pro-American. Its commercial success as a newspaper may partly be attributed to its size (usually sixteen pages) and to the publication of "exclusive" serials like the War Memoirs of General Giraud, Winston Churchill, Skorzeny (the SS-man who organized the kidnapping of Mussolini), and lengthy *reportages* in various parts of the world. When newsprint stopped being rationed, the *Figaro* benefited from its financial capacity of giving the politically more-or-less indifferent reader his money's worth. (The same is partly also true of *L'Aurore* and *Le Parisien Libéré*.)

The principle of giving people their money's worth also underlies the rapid rise of the popular Paris evening paper, *France-Soir*, the successor of the pre-war *Paris-Soir*. What, however, distinguishes *France-Soir* from the "sillier" morning papers like *L'Aurore* and the *Parisien Libéré*, and, even more so, from the London evening papers (which carry practically no news at all) is the high standard of most of its reporting, and the intelligent interest shown by this popular evening paper (and, consequently, by its readers) in world affairs. It has a large staff of correspondents abroad, runs usually two pages of foreign news, and often sends its star reporters (Gordey, Segonzac, etc) on long journeys to foreign countries. Its coverage of international conferences is usually informative, accurate, and very readable (and not simply based on official hand-outs, which is the case of so much of the foreign news coverage in the British press since the war). Except for occasional anti-Communist spurts, *France-Soir* does not ram any violent political line down the reader's throat.

Ce Matin, which no longer exists, was strongly Gaullist at one time, but proved redundant around 1951.

Paris-Presse, the chief rival of *France-Soir* as a popular evening paper, was also Gaullist at one time; then it attempted to be "different" from *France-Soir* by becoming more "highbrow", and hoped to win over some readers from *Le Monde*; in this it failed; since it is now chiefly owned by the same people as *France-Soir,* and is not very different from it in any major respect, it does not seem to serve any distinct purpose. Except that it is more "right-wing".

The papers that suffered most from the inequality in financial resources, from the growing lack of interest in "pure politics", and from people's desire to be entertained and to get their money's worth are, of course, the Party papers and the papers financially unable to print on more than 4, 6, or 8 pages. The MRP Party paper, *L'Aube*, had to cease publication in 1952; the Communist Party paper, *L'Humanité* declined steadily, losing more than half its circulation between 1948 and 1952, and declining to around 100,000 copies since; the specifically Communist evening paper, *Ce Soir*, closed down in 1953, owing chiefly to the competition of the more opulent and varied *France-Soir*. (It has also been observed that, among the working-class, a purely sports paper like *L'Equipe* has eaten severely into the circulation of *L'Humanité*.) The official organ of the Socialist Party, *Le Populaire* has been kept barely alive (at the ludicrously low level of barely over 15,000) by the help of foreign well-wishers.

It should, however, be added that both the Communist *Humanité* and the Socialist *Populaire* benefit from the virtual absence of regular Sunday papers by bringing out their *Humanité-Dimanche* and their *Populaire-Dimanche*, the former with a circulation of 500,000, the latter with one of 70,000. They are "magazines", rather than news-papers.

Libération (editor, Emmanuel d'Astier), which is "*progressiste*" but not officially Communist, and is technically a better-produced paper than *L'Humanité*, has declined much less than most left-wing papers; many habitual Communist readers find it more "readable" than *L'Humanité*. *Franc-Tireur*, which was almost wholly Communist until 1947, rapidly changed by the end of 1948, to an "Atlantic" and strongly anti-Communist line, after the split on its staff, as a result of which the Communists were eliminated. In 1954, Tréno, disagreeing with Georges Altman and Charles Ronsac on German rearmament, also left, devoting himself entirely to the *Canard Enchaîné*.

Combat was, at least until recently, the favourite paper of the non-conformist left-wing intellectuals; though controlled by M. Smadja, a Tunisian-Jewish business man since 1950, its staff have, in the main, managed to preserve its left-wing intellectual traditions. However, it has lost the great significance it had in the past, when it tried, as late as 1949, to remain the last specifically "Resistance" paper.

The *Monde*, despite its small circulation, is by far the most influential paper in France, and one which has expressed, more consistently than any other, the "reservations" of French public opinion *vis-à-vis* "Atlantic conformism". It is not a rich paper, is practically self-supporting, and is not known to have any powerful financial interests behind it. Despite numerous attempts, both from inside the paper and from outside, to bring pressure to bear on its editor, M. Beuve-Méry, or even to eliminate him, he has quietly stuck to his guns, often with the tacit approval of various members of the successive governments. The *Monde* is so important an institution in French public life that all attempts to give it a more "conformist" character, or to set up news-papers in competition with it, have invariably failed so far.

For news-coverage (it has several first-class correspondents abroad), for *reportages*, for its political analysis of both home and international events, the *Monde* probably comes closer than any paper today to the ideals set down by the late C. P. Scott of the *Manchester Guardian*. Its pages on literature, art, music and the theatre are also of a very high standard.

The question of "who owns the press" can only be briefly dealt with here. The outstanding fact is that all the big-circulation newspapers are owned by financial groups, many of which were already active in this field before the war.

L'Aurore is controlled by M. Marcel Boussac, one of France's "textile kings"; 50 per cent of the capital of the *Figaro* is said to be owned by another "textile king", M. Prouvost, who also owns the immensely successful illustrated weekly, *Paris-Match*; another important share-holder of the *Figaro* is M. Ferdinand Béghin (Crédit du Nord and Béghin Sugar Refineries); *Paris-Presse* was founded by M. and Mme Phillippe Barrès as a Gaullist paper; in 1949 they sold half the shares to Holpa, an annex of Hachette; thus Hachette controls both the popular Paris evening papers, its interests being represented on *France-Soir* by MM. Schoeller, Corniglion-Molinier, and Bleustein.

An even greater concentration of capital is to be found in the case of the illustrated weeklies, the women's magazines (the so-called *presse du cœur*) and the children's magazines.

Two hundred weeklies are published in Paris, ranging from the serious political weekly to the quasi-pornographic one. The approximate circulation of the principal weeklies is: *Paris-Match*, over a million (only 208,000 in 1948); *France-Dimanche* (460,000 in 1953, as against 630,000 in 1948); *Samedi-Soir* (respectively, 342,000 and 672,000);[3] two other popular illustrated weeklies, *Blanc-et-Noir* and *Point de Vue* (about 150,000 each); *France Nouvelle* (Communist—65,000 in 1953, as against 109,000 in 1948); *Lettres Françaises* (Communist—45,000 in 1953, as against 100,000 in 1948); *Humanité-Dimanche* (500,000 in 1954); *Carrefour*, which, as the principal Gaullist weekly, exceeded 150,000 in 1948, but was down to some 75,000 in 1953; *La Vie Ouvrière* (CGT fortnightly—still had a circulation of 258,000 in 1952). Among art and literary papers should be mentioned *Arts* (60,000 in 1952); *Nouvelles Littéraries* (75,000); *Figaro Littéraire* (127,000); and finally that French "institution", the left-wing satirical weekly *Le Canard Enchaîné*

---

[3] Both these are roughly printed and crude "sensational" papers of the "magazine" type, which have obviously suffered from the competition of *Match*, modelled on *Life* Magazine, and very well produced. Its attitude is "Atlantic" and very anti-Communist.

(111,000 in 1952, against 213,000 in 1948). Among recent political weeklies, *L'Express* (founded in 1953) claimed in 1955 a circulation of about 150,000, and *France-Observateur* (founded in 1950) one of some 50,000. The two ultra-reactionary weeklies, *Rivarol* and *Aspects de la France* have each between 30,000 and 40,000 readers.

Moreover, numerous monthlies are published in Paris, among them many of great political influence and literary importance, notably *Esprit, Temps Modernes, La Table Ronde, La Nouvelle NRF*, the "pro-American" *Preuves*, besides the more "old-fashioned" *Revue des Deux Mondes, Revue de Paris, Mercure de France*, etc, besides scores of more specialized monthlies.

A special place is held by "digests": *Sélection du Reader's Digest* (over 1 million copies), *Constellations* (500,000), its "genuinely French" rival, and many others.

Despite this multitude of publications, the total paper consumption in France is much lower, per head of population, than in several other countries: if, in 1951, the USA consumed over 5 million tons, and the UK 697,000 tons, France consumed only 270,000 tons.[4] Not only are British and American papers larger, but much fewer copies of the daily press are actually sold in France than in Britain; the price has much to do with it. In 1955 the ordinary daily in France cost 15 francs, or about 4d, and it is worth noting that between 1948 and 1952 the number of copies of the Paris dailies sold declined from 3,650,000 to 2,883,000, a loss of 770,000 readers, who were not sufficiently interested to pay a higher price for their newspaper.

As distinct from Britain, where all the London dailies (total circulation about 16 millions) have a "national" circulation, the Paris press meets with severe competition from the provincial press—and, indeed, a good deal more than it did before the war. The division of France into an occupied and an unoccupied zone during the war, and the transport difficulties for some time after the Liberation have something to do with the failure of the Paris press to recapture the whole of its provincial public.

In 1950 the total printing of the French daily press was 10·8 million copies, i.e. nearly the same as in 1939; but this represented nearly 2 million fewer Paris papers than in 1939 and 1¾ million more copies of the provincial press.

But the real *sales* of the total French press between 1939 and 1950 showed that these had declined from 9,680,000 copies to 8,640,000—the loss of over 1 million readers.

The total *printing* of the daily provincial press amounted in June 1950 to 7·2 million copies, but in June 1952 to only 6·2 million copies,

---

[4] *UNESCO: L'information à travers le monde.* (Paris, 1951.)

without, however, the Paris press having made much headway in the provinces in the meantime.

Taking account of the "unsolds", it is probable that the total number of provincial dailies *sold* must be about 4½ to 4¾ million or over a million more than the total of the Paris dailies sold.[5]

As in Paris, so in the provinces, one observes certain parallel developments since 1945: the sharp decline of the specifically political paper, and the rise of the *journal d'information*; the disappearance of numerous dailies (total number of provincial dailies in 1946, 175; in 1952, 127), and a general decline in the number of copies sold.

If, in 1945, the Communists were publishing 32 daily provincial papers with a printing of 1,730,000, they were printing only 14 papers in 1952, with 650,000 copies; the Socialist press declined in the same period from 32 papers with 1·7 million copies to 14 papers with 1·1 million copies; the MRP press from 22 papers and 1·3 million copies to 8 papers with 670,000 copies; The RPF press, after a sharp rise in 1948 dwindled to a mere 140,000 copies in 1952. The Radical press alone rose from 320,000 copies in 1945 to 630,000 in 1952. On the other hand, the *journaux d'information* without a specific political label rose from a mere 810,000 copies (and 16 papers) in 1945 to 2,640,000 copies (and 29 papers) in 1952.

It does not, of course, follow from this that these *journaux d'information* are of no political consequence; thus *Ouest-France* (Rennes), though classified as a *journal d'information*, with a circulation throughout the West of France of over 450,000 copies, is an organ of militant clericalism with considerable political weight. Others, like the *Progrès de Lyon* (circulation, 303,000), or the *Sud-Ouest* of Bordeaux (280,000); or the *Dépêche du Midi* (224,000) Toulouse (successor of the old *Dépêche*) tend to be "conformist" in their attitude to the international scene. What they all have in common is the considerable space they give to local news—a field in which the Paris press is unable to compete.

A few words should be said about women's and children's papers in France. In the last few years, these have shown a spectacular development, compared with pre-war days. In 1947 there was still practically no *presse de cœur*; today its circulation is estimated at about 4 million copies. Principal among the women's journals are (figures for July 1952): *Elle* (600,000); *Confidences* (740,000); *Nous Deux* (1,227,000); *A Tout Cœur* (287,000); *Intimité* (575,000); *Madrigal* (316,000); and many more. The two great brains behind many of these publications are the Italian, M. Del Duca, and M. Paul Winkler, both of whom are the principal originators of the cartoon strips in the French Press (the latter through the Opera Mundi agency). *Confidences*, as well as the chil-

[5] Unfortunately, on the actual *sales* of the provincial press no exact figures are available.

dren's magazines *Robinson*, *Mickey*, *Donald*, the popular medical weekly, *Votre Santé*, were started by Winkler; all of these are now owned by Edi-Monde, 70 per cent of whose capital is owned by Hachette.

There is also a large Children's Press in France today, running into millions of copies. Principal among them are (1953 figures):

Mickey, 400,000	*Petit Sheriff*, 73,000
Donald, 100,000	*Benjamin*, 90,000
Tarzan, 155,000	*Vaillants*, 114,000
Tarzan (Collection), 80,000	*Lisette*, 158,000
L'Intrépide, 118,000	*Equipe J.*, 130,000
Ames Vaillantes, 101,000	*France-Jeux*, 91,000
Cœurs Vaillants, 277,000	*Coq Hardi*, 80,000
Bayard, 153,000	*Bernadette*, 212,000

It is interesting to observe that there are no horror comics for children in France. In 1949 a *Commission de surveillance des publications pour enfants* was set up comprising representatives of family organizations, publishers, educationists, and officials of the Ministries of Health, Education, Justice, and Information. The work of this Government-sponsored "vigilance committee" has been salutary, on the whole. Their terms of reference have been sufficiently wide to enable them to exclude pornography, sadism, the apologia of banditism, sharp international hatred, and other features familiar to readers of American horror comics from children's papers and books in France. In 1952 the Commission compiled such a damaging *dossier* against one of the "Superman" type of publications that this decided to go out of business for a time, and did not reappear until some months later in a relatively anodyne form.

A number of the children's journals (e.g. *Cœurs Vaillants*, *Ames Vaillantes*, *Bernadette*, etc) are supported by the Church.

Note 1. Many interesting details on who owns the press are to be found in *La France et les Trusts*, a special issue (1954) of *Economie et Politique*.

Note 2. The weekly *Express* became, in October 1955, a morning daily. Outwardly modelled on the London *Daily Mirror*, it is politically important, thanks to the regular articles by P. Mendès-France, F. Mauriac, A. Camus, A. Sauvy and F. Mitterrand. At the end of October its circulation was said to be about 60,000, half of it in Paris. In November it already printed 150,000. Its policy is *Mendèsiste*.

BIBLIOGRAPHY

This list of titles, while it does not claim to be exhaustive, contains most of the books relevant to the foregoing narrative. It is divided into five sections:

1. A short list of books relating to the immediate pre-war years and dealing with matters directly or indirectly referred to in this work.

2. A list of the more important and significant books relating to the 1940–4 period, some written at the time, others written in retrospect (here, for the reader's convenience, most titles are followed by the following letters to indicate the nature of the book and the author's point of view; COL — collaborationist; PV = pro-Vichy; AV = anti-Vichy; QC = quasi-collaborationist; QV = quasi-Vichyite; G = Giraudist; R = Resistance or pro-Resistance; AR = anti-Resistance; PC = pro-Communist; AC = anti-Communist; F = factual; T = trial record. In the case of foreign books or in cases hard to classify the title is not followed by any letter).

3. A list of books and publications relating to the post-war period (classification being more difficult than for the 1940–4 period, the only possible simple distinction to make was to list the Communist books separately).

4 and 5. Short bibliographies on North Africa and Indo-China.

All books are published in Paris, unless otherwise stated.

1. Pre-War

Berl, E. *La politique et les partis* (1932).
Bernanos, G. *Scandale de la vérité* (1939).
   Les grands cimetières sous la lune (1938).
Blum, L. *Radicaux et Socialistes* (1936).
   La jeunesse et le socialisme (1936).
   Socialisme et bolchévisme (1936).
Brasillach, R. *Les quatre jeudis; images: d'avant-guerre* (1944).
Brogan, D. W. *The Development of Modern France* (London, 1940).
Caillaux, J. *Mes mémoires*, 3 vols (1943–4).
Céline, L.-F. *Bagatelles pour un massacre* (1937).
Chavineau, Gén. *L'invasion est-elle possible?* Préface du Maréchal Pétain (1938).
Coulondre, R. *De Staline à Hitler* (1950).
Déat, M. *Perspectives socialistes* (1930).
Doriot, J. *C'est Moscou qui paie* (1937).
   La France ne sera pas un pays d'esclaves (1936).
Drieu La Rochelle, *Gilles* (1938).
Gaulle, Ch. de. *Le fil de l'épée* (1932).
   Vers l'armée de métier (1934).
Giraudoux, J. *Pleins pouvoirs* (1939).
Lapaquellerie, Y. *Edouard Daladier* (s.d.).
Martet, J. M. *Clemenceau peint pas lui-même* (1928).
   Les silences de M. Clemenceau (1929).
Millet, P. *Doriot et ses compagnons* (1937).
Min. des Aff. Etr. *Le livre jaune français. Documents diplom. 1938–9* (1940).
Pannetier, Odette. *Pierre Laval* (1936).
Poincaré, R. *Au service de la France*, 10 vols (1923–9).
Recouly, R. *Le mémorial de Foch* (1929).
Reynaud, Paul. *Jeunesse, quelle France veux-tu?* (1936).
Suarez, G. *Briand*, 5 vols (1941–4).

TARDIEU, ANDRÉ. *L'heure de la décision* (1934).
  Le souverain captif (1936).
  La profession parlementaire (1937).
THOREZ, M. *Fils du peuple* (1936).
WERTH, ALEXANDER. *France in Ferment* (London, 1934).
  The Destiny of France (London, 1937).
  France and Munich; Before and After the Surrender (London, 1939).
WEYGAND. *Comment élever nos fils?* (1937).

2. WAR, OCCUPATION, VICHY AND RESISTANCE

ABETZ, O. *D'une prison* (1949).
  Une politique franco-allemande (1952).
ARAGON. *Le crève-coeur* (1945).
D'ARGENSON. *Pétain et le Pétinisme* (1952). AV.
ARON, ROBERT. *Histoire de Vichy* (1953).
ARON, RAYMOND. *De l'armistice à l'insurrection nationale* (1945). R.
d'ASTIER, E. (de la Vigerie). *Sept fois sept jours* (1947). R.
AUBRAC, LUCIE. *La Résistance: naissance et organisation* (1945). R, PC.
AUDOUIN-DUBREUIL, COL. L. *La guerre en Tunisie* (Nov. 1942 à Mai 1943) (1945). F.
AURIOL, VINCENT. *Hier, demain*, Vol I (1945). AV.
AVELINE, C. *Le temps mort* (1945). R.
BARADUC, J. *Dans la cellule de Pierre Laval* (1948).
BARRÈS, PHILIPPE. *Charles de Gaulle* (1944). R.
BELLEVAL. *Le cri de la France* (1951). PV.
BENJAMIN, RENÉ. *Le grand homme seul* (1943). PV.
BENOIST-MÉCHIN. *Ce qui demeure* (1942). COL.
  La moisson de Quarante (1941). COL.
BÉNOUVILLE, GUILLAIN DE. *Le sacrifice du matin* (1945). R.
BERGE, F. *Le Pétinisme, étrange vertu* (1945). AV.
BERNANOS, G. *Les enfants humiliés* (1949). R.
  Lettre aux Anglais (1946). R.
BLOCQ-MASCART, M. *Chronique de la Résistance* (1945). R.
BOST, P. *La haute fourche* (1945). R.
BOURDAN, P. *Carnet de retour avec la division Leclerc* (1945). R.
CARCOPINO, JÉRÔME. *Souvenirs de sept ans* (1937–44) (1953). PV.
CASSIUS. *La vérité sur l'affaire Pétain* (1945). PV.
CHURCHILL, W. S. *The Second World War*, 6 vols (London).
Ciano Diary, The, 1939–43 (London, 1947).
COBLENTZ, P. *Georges Mandel* (1946). R.
CRUSOË (Lemaigre-Dubreuil). *Vicissitudes d'une victoire* (1946). G.
DANSETTE, A. *Histoire de la Libération de Paris* (1946). F.
DARLAN, ALAIN. *L'Amiral Darlan parle . . .* (1952). AR.
DESCHAUMES, GUY. *Vers la Croix de Lorraine* (1946). R.
DESGRANGES, ABBÉ. *Les crimes masqués du Résistantialisme* (1948). AR.
DESTAING, PH. *Missions en France* (1945). R.
DRESSE, P. *Léon Daudet vivant* (1947).
DUHAMEL, G. *Civilisation française* (1944).
  Chroniques des saisons amères (1944).
DUNAN, R. *"Ceux" de Paris: Août 1944* (Genève, 1945). R.
EISENHOWER, GEN. D. *Crusade in Europe* (London, 1948).
ELUARD, P. *Le rendez-vous allemand* (1945). R.
FABRE-LUCE, ALFRED. *Journal de la France*, Vol I (1941). COL.
  Journal de la France, Vol II (1942). COL.
  Journal de la France (revised edition) (Genève, 1945). PV.
  Le mystère du Maréchal Pétain (Genève, 1945). PV.
  Au nom des silencieux (Genève, 1945). PV.
FAURE, PAUL. *De Munich à la V-e République* (1947). PV.
GALTIER-BOISSIÈRE, J. *Mon journal sous l'Occupation* (1944).

GAMELIN, GÉN. *Mémoires*. 2 vols (1947-8).
GARAUDY, ROGER. *L'église, le Communisme et les chrétiens* (1949). PC, AV.
GAULLE, CH. DE. *Discours aux Français*, 2 vols (1945). R.
 Mémoires de Guerre, Vol I: "L'appel." (1954). R.
GIRAUD, GEN. *Mémoires* (1949). G.
GIRAUDOUX, J. *Sans pouvoirs* (1946).
 L'Armistice à Bordeaux (Monaco, 1945).
GOURFINKEL, NINA. *L'autre patrie* (1953). R.
HÉROLD-PAQUIS, J. *Mémoires: Des illusions . . . désillusion* (1948). COL.
HERRIOT, E. *Episodes 1940-44* (1950).
HITLER, A. *Discours 1939-41* (1942).
HUDDLESTON, SISLEY. *Terreur 1944* (1947). AR, PV.
ISORNI, J. *Le procès de Robert Brasillach* (1946).
JAFFRÉ, Y. F. *Les derniers propos de Pierre Laval* (1953).
JUNIUS. *Les Oligarques* (1945). R.
KAMMERER, ALBERT. *La tragédie de Mers-el-Kébir* (1945). F.
 Du débarquement africain au meurtre de Darlan (1949). F.
Laval parle . . . (1948).
LEAHY, W. D. *I Was There* (London, 1950).
LENORMAND, M. H. *Vers le régime corporatif* (1943). PV.
LUCHAIRE, CORINNE. *Ma drôle de vie* (1949). COL.
MALLET, A. *Pierre Laval*, 2 vols (1955). F.
MARTIN DU GARD, MAURICE. *Chronique de Vichy, 1940-44* (1948). QV.
MARITAIN, JAQUES. *A travers le désastre* (1945). R.
 A travers la victoire (1945). R.
MASSIS, H. *Les idées restent* (Lyon, 1941). PV.
MAUDRU, P. *Les six glorieuses de Paris* (1944). R.
MAULNIER, THIERRY. *La France, la guerre et la paix* (Lyon, 1942). PV.
MAURIAC, FRANÇOIS. *Le Cahier Noir* (1947). R.
MAURRAS, C. *La seule France* (Lyon, 1941). PV.
MAZÉ, P. et GÉNÉBRIER, R. *Les grandes journées du procès de Riom* (1945). T.
MENTHON, F. DE. *Vers la 4-e République* (1946). R.
MICHEL, HENRI. *Histoire de la Résistance* (1950). R, F.
MONTIGNY, J. *Toute la vérité sur un mois dramatique de notre histoire* (Clermont-Ferrand
 1940). PV, QC.
 La défaite (1941). PV, QC.
MONZIE, ANATOLE DE. *Ci-devant* (1941). QV.
 Pétition pour l'Histoire (1942).
 La saison des juges (1942).
MORNET, PROCUREUR-GÉNÉRAL. *Quatre ans à rayer de notre histoire* (1949).
MOULIN DE LABARTHÈTE, H. DU. *Le temps des illusions* (Genève, 1945). PV.
MUSELIER, VICE-AMIRAL. *De Gaulle contre le Gaullisme* (1946). R.
NACHIN, L. *Charles de Gaulle, Général de France* (1944). R.
NÉRET. *Pour aller à la terre. Guide pratique complet* (1941). PV.
NICOLLE, P. *Cinq mois d'Armistice*, 2 vols (1947). PV.
Jean Oberlé vous parle (1945). R.
PASSY, COLONEL. *Souvenirs*, 2 vols (1946-7). R.
PAULHAN, J. *Lettre aux directeurs de la Résistance* (1952). AR.
PERTINAX. *Les Fossoyeurs*, 2 vols (New York, 1943). AV.
Le procès de Charles Maurras (1945). T.
Le procès du Maréchal Pétain, 2 vols (1945). T.
Le procès de Pierre Laval (1945). T.
Le procès de Benoist-Méchin (ed. J. D. Aujol) (1947). T.
Les procès de la Collaboration F. de Brinon, Darnand, Luchaire (1948). T.
Les procès de la Radio: Ferdonnet et Hérold-Paquis (1947). T.
RÉMY. *Mémoires d'un agent secret de la France Libre* (Monte Carlo, 1946). R.
 Comment meurt un réseau (Monte Carlo, 1947). R.
 Une affaire de trahison (Monte Carlo, 1947). R.
REYNAUD, PAUL. *La France a sauvé l'Europe*, 2 vols (1947).
ROSSI, A. *Les Communistes français pendant la drôle de guerre* (1951). AC.

ROUGIER, L. *Mission secrète à Londres* (Genève, 1946). PV.

ROULLEAUX-DUGAGE, J. *Deux ans d'histoire secrète en Afrique du Nord* (1945).

SAINT-BERNARD. *Conseils au Pape* (1945). R.

SALIÈGES, MGR., *Archevêque de Toulouse. Paroles . . .* (1945). R.

SECRÉTARIAT D'ETAT À L'ECONOMIE NATIONALE ET AUX FINANCES. *L'action économique en France depuis l'Armistice* (Mâcon, 1941). PV.

SOULAIROL, J. *Charles de Gaulle, le Libérateur* (1944). R.

SOUSTELLE, J. *Envers et contre tout*, Vol I: "De Londres à Alger (1947). R.
Envers et contre tout, Vol II: "D'Alger à Paris (1950). R.

SPEARS, GEN. *The Fall of France* (London, 1954).

STÉPHANE, ROGER. *Chaque homme est lié au monde* (1946). R.

SUAREZ, GEORGES. *Le Maréchal Pétain* (1940). COL.

TEXCIER, J. *Ecrit dans la nuit* (1945). R.

THOMSON, DAVID. *Two Frenchmen: Laval and de Gaulle* (London, 1951).

VAILLAND, R. *Drôle de jeu* (1945). R, PC.

VALLÉRY-RADOT, R. *La Franc-Maçonnerie vous parle* (1941). PV.

VANINO, M. *De Rethondes a l'Ile d'Yeu* (1952). AV.

VERCORS. *Le silence de la mer* (1945). R.

VIALATOUX, J. *Le problème de la légitimité du pouvoir* (1945). AV.

WEIL-CURIEL, A. *Le jour se lève à Londres* (1945). R.

WERTH, ALEXANDER. *The Last Days of Paris* (London, 1940).

WEYGAND. *Mémoires: Rappelé au service* (1950) PV.

(Note: Although the publication dates of many of the "R" (i.e. Resistance) books are given as 1944, '45, '46, or '47, these are in many cases the dates of post-Liberation reprints (e.g. Vercors' *Silence de la mer* or Mauriac's *Cahier Noir*). These, like many others, originally appeared clandestinely during the Occupation.

3. POST-WAR FRANCE

Following are the most important and significant papers and periodicals since the Liberation:

DAILY NEWSPAPERS: *L'Aube* (until 1952), *Combat, Le Figaro, Franc-Tireur, France-Soir, L'Humanité, Le Monde.* (Highly valuable to the student are also the parliamentary debates and parliamentary documents published by the *Journal Officiel*.)

WEEKLIES: *Carrefour, Le Canard Enchaîné, L'Express* (since 1953), *France-Observateur* (since 1950[1]), *Paris-Match* (since 1947), *Témoignage Chrétien, Lettres Françaises* (Com.), *Action* (until 1952, Com.), *La Tribune des Nations, Perspectives* ("newsletter").

MONTHLIES: *Esprit, Temps Modernes,*[2] *La Table Ronde, Terre Humaine* (until 1953), *Cahiers du Communisme, La Revue Socialiste, Politique Etrangère, Preuves, Cahiers Internationaux* (near Com.), *Europe* (near Com.), *La Nouvelle Critique* (Com.), besides the more "old-fashioned" *Revue des Deux Mondes, Revue de Paris, Revue Politique et Parlementaire,* etc.

BI-MONTHLY: *Année politique et économique* (Ed. by B. Lavergne and J. Gascuel).

ANNUALS: *L'Année Politique, Statistique générale de la France* (both very useful).

BIOGRAPHICAL REFERENCE BOOK: *Dictionnaire biographique français contemporain,* 1st ed. 1950, 2nd ed. 1954 (inadequate).

[1] Called *L'Observateur* till 1953.

[2] These two monthlies often produce remarkable special single or double numbers constituting valuable monographs, such as *Esprit's* special numbers on the Marshall Plan, Marxist doctrine, working-class conditions in France, educational problems, the mechanism of the French state, housing, North Africa, Indo-China, etc, or the *Temps Modernes'* similar special issues on North Africa, Indo-China, The French Left, etc. These "symposia" are often more valuable than any one-man books on the subject. (See also NEF symposia listed under "books".)

SELECTION OF SIGNIFICANT BOOKS RELATING TO POST-WAR FRANCE[1]

(a) Non-Communist

ARON, RAYMOND. *L'homme contre les tyrans* (1946).
  Le grand schisme (1948).
AURIOL, VINCENT. *Hier, demain*, Vol II (1945).
AYMÉ, MARCEL. *Le confort intellectuel* (1948).
BARDÈCHE, M. *Lettre à François Mauriac* (1947).
BEAUVOIR, SIMONE DE. *Les Mandarins* (1954).
BEUVE-MÉRY, H. *Réflections politiques* (1951).
BLUM, LÉON. *A l'échelle humaine* (1945).
BURNHAM, J. *Contenir ou libérer. Postface de Raymond Aron* (1952).
CAMUS, ALBERT. *L'homme révolté* (1951).
CHAPMAN, B. *French Local Government* (London, 1953).
CHAPMAN, B. *The Prefects and Provincial France* (London, 1955).
DAVIDSON, JEAN. *Correspondant à Washington* (1954).
DOMENACH, J. M. *La propagande politique* (1949).
DZELEPY, C. N. *Mourir pour l'Allemagne?* (1955).
ECONOMIE ET POLITIQUE. *La France et les Trusts* (1954). (Near-Com.
FABRE-LUCE, A. *Journal de l'Europe*, 1946–47 (Genève, 1947).
FARGE, YVES. *Le pain de la corruption* (1947). (Black market.)
  Le sang de la corruption (1951). (Korea.)
FAUVET, J. *Partis Politiques en France* (1951).
GALTIER-BOISSIÈRE, J. *Mon journal depuis la Libération* (1945).
  Mon journal dans la drôle de paix (1947).
  Mon journal pendant la grande pagaie (1950).
GORDEY, MICHEL. *Visa pour Moscou* (1952).
ISMAY, LORD. *NATO, The First Five Years 1949–54* (1955).
LAVERGNE, BERNARD. *Le Plan Schuman* (1952).
  L'Armée Européenne (1952).
MALRAUX, ANDRÉ. *Les conquérants* (avec Postface, 1949) (1953).
MATTHEWS, RONALD. *The Death of the Fourth Republic* (London, 1954).
MARABUTO, P. *Les partis politiques et les mouvements sociaux sous la 4-e République* (1948).
MENDÈS-FRANCE, P. *Gouverner c'est choisir* (1953).
  Sept mois dix-sept jours (1955).
  Dire la vérité: causeries de samedi (1955).
MENDÈS-FRANCE, P. et ARDANT, G. *La science économique et l'action* (Unesco, 1954).
MOLLET, GUY. *Nous travaillons pour la bonne cause* (1948).
NEF. *La Radio* (1950).
  Tableau politique de la France (1951).
  Le socialisme française, victime du marxisme? (1953).
  La presse, IV-e pouvoir (1950).
  Le problème allemand (1952).
  Le franc, mythe et réalité (1953).
OEEC. *European Payments Union* (June 1954).
  Progress and the problems of European Economy (5th annual report, January 1954).
  From Recovery towards Economic Strength (6th annual report, 1955).
  Economic Conditions in France, 1953.
  Economic Conditions in France, 1954.
Paix et Liberté: Défendre la vérité (Anti-Communist pamphlets published every ten days since 1951).
PICKLES, D. *French Politics* (London, 1952).
PRÉLOT, M. *Précis de droit constitutionnel* (1953).
Le Procès Kravchenko contre "Les Lettres Françaises". Compte-rendu sténographique. La Jeune Parque (Paris, 1949).
REYNAUD, PAUL. *Le destin hésite* (1946).
RICHARD, MARTHE. *Faire face* (1947).

[1] In view of their political significance, a number of novels, plays and other literary works are included in this bibliography.

ROURE, RÉMY. *La 4-e République: naissance ou avortement d'un régime?* (1948).
SARTRE, JEAN-PAUL. *Situations I, II et III* (1947–50).
    Le Diable et le Bon Dieu (1951).
    Les chemins de la liberté, 3 vols (1947–50).
    Les mains sales (1948).
SARTRE, JEAN-PAUL (editor). *L'affaire Henri Martin* (1952).
SARTRE, ROUSSET, ROSENTHAL. *Entretiens sur la politique* (1948).
SAUVY, A. *Le pouvoir et l'opinion* (1949).
TERSEN, E., DAUTRY, J. [etc.]. *L'Europe, mythes et réalités* (1954).
VIVANTS, LES. *Cahiers . . . des prisonniers et déportés,* 3 vols (1945–6).
WILLIAMS, P. *Politics in Post-War France* (London, 1954).
WEYGAND. *Défense de l'Europe* (1953).

(b) Communist

ARAGON. *Le nouveau creve-coeur* (1948).
    Les Communistes, 6 vols (1949–51).
    L'homme communiste, 2 vols. (1947 et 1953).
CASANOVA, L. *Le parti communiste, les intellectuels et la nation* (1949).
COGNIOT, G. *Réalité de la nation* (1950).
COURTADE, P. *Jimmy* (1951).
    La rivière noire (1953).
DAIX, P. *Classe 42* (1952).
DUCLOS, J. *Ecrits de prison* (1952).
ELUARD, P. *Poèmes pour tous* (1953).
FIGUÈRES, L. *Je reviens du Vietnam libre* (1950).
FRÉVILLE, J. *La nuit finit a Tours* (1951).
GAMARRA, P. *Les lilas de Saint-Lazare* (1951).
GARAUDY, R. *Une littérature de fossoyeurs* (1949).
KANAPA, J. *Le traître et le prolétaire* (1951).
Meeting of the Information Bureau of Communist Parties in Poland, September 1947 (Moscow, 1948).
Meeting of the Information Bureau of Communist Parties in Hungary, November 1949 (Moscow, 1950).
STIL, ANDRÉ. *Le premier choc* (1951).
THOREZ, M. *Oeuvres complètes,* 14 vols (1949–55) (more to come).
    Une politique de grandeur française (1945).
    Also numerous pamphlets by Aragon, Garaudy, Elsa Triolet, Roger Vailland, Kanapa, Pierre Hervé, Pierre Courtade, Georges Cogniot, etc.

4. BOOKS, ETC, ON NORTH AFRICA

BERNARD, AUGUSTIN. *L'Algérie* (1930).
ESQUER, J. *Histoire de l'Algérie* (1950).
GUÉRIN, D. *Pitié pour le Maghreb* (1953).
    Au service des colonisés (1954).
JULIEN, C. A. *L'Afrique du Nord en marche* (1952).
    Histoire de l'Afrique du Nord (1931).
Du Manifeste à la République Algérienne (UDMA, Alger, 1948).
MITTERRAND, F. *Aux frontières de l'Union Française.* Préface de P. Mendès-France (1953).
MAUROIS, A. *Lyautey* (1931).
NEF. *Maroc et Tunisie* (1953).
PARENT, PIERRE. *Le problème marocain en 1949* (Toulouse, 1949).
    La vérité sur le Maroc (Toulouse, 1952).
Le problème algérien. (MTLD pamphlets) (Alger, 1951–4).
ROUS, J. *Tunisie, Attention!* (1952).
SEBAG, G. *La Tunisie* (1952).

5. Books on Indo-China

BOUTBIEN, L. *Je reviens d'Indochine* (1950).
DECOUX, AMIRAL. *A la barre d'Indochine* (1949).
DEVILLERS, P. *Histoire du Viet-Nam de 1940 à 1952* (1952).
DESPUECH, J. *Le trafic des piastres* (1953).
FIGUÈRES, L. *Je reviens du Vietnam libre* (1950).
GOROU, PIERRE. *L'avenir de l'Indochine* (1947).
KILIAN, ROBERT. *Les fusiliers marins en Indochine* (1948).
BOURGEOIS, J. Le. *Saigon sans la France* (1949).
MARCHAND, COL. *L'Indochine dans le cadre de l'Asie et ses problèmes actuels* (1949).
MARTIN, FRANÇOISE. *Heures tragiques au Tonkin* (1949).
MUS, PAUL. *Le Vietnam: Sociologie d'une guerre* (1952).
VIOLLIS, ANDRÉE. *S.O.S. Indochine* (1932, nouvelle édition 1945).

LIST OF THE PRINCIPAL ABBREVIATIONS USED

AF—Action Française. (Anti-republican—originally Royalist—movement and paper of same name.)

AFL—American Federation of Labor.

AFP—Agence France-Presse. (Quasi-Official French news agency.)

AN—Assemblée Nationale.

BCRA—Bureau Central de Renseignements et d'Action. (De Gaulle's Intelligence organization in London.)

CAD—Comités d'Action contre la Déportation. (Resistance organization.)

CFLN—Comité Français de Libération Nationale. (The French Liberation Committee at Algiers in 1943–44.)

CFTC—Confédération Française de Travailleurs Chrétiens. (Catholic trade union federation.)

CGT—Confédération Générale de Travail. (French trade union federation, mostly Communist since 1947.)

CGT-FO—CGT (as above)—Force Ouvrière. (Predominantly Socialist trade union federation, created after 1947 split in CGT.)

CIO—Congress of Industrial Organizations. (US trade union federation.)

CNR—Comité National de la Résistance.

COMAC—Comité d'action militaire. (Military action committee of the CNR.)

CP—Communist Party.

CRS—Compagnies Républicaines de Sécurité. (Militarized police, successor of the pre-war *Garde Mobile*.)

CSAR—Comité secret d'action révolutionnaire. (Secret terrorist right-wing organization active in 1937–39; also known as Cagoulards.)

EDC—European Defence Community. (CED in French.)

ERP—European Recovery Programme. (Usually known as "Marshall Aid".)

FFI—Forces Françaises de l'Interieur. (French home army chiefly created by the Resistance.)

FN—Front National. (Predominantly Communist Resistance organization.)

FT-PF—Francs-Tireurs-Partisans Français. (Guerilla organization of the Front National.)

ICFTU—International Confederation of Free Trade Unions. (Non-Communist.) (CISL in French.)

LVF—Légion des Volontaires Français. (French Legion fighting for Germany on the Russian Front.)

MLN—Mouvement de Libération Nationale. (Chiefly non-Communist Resistance organization, formed after the Liberation.)

MRP—Mouvement Républican Populaire. (Catholic Party formed at the Liberation by Bidault, Teitgen, etc.)

MTLD—Mouvement pour le Triomphe des Libertés Démocratiques. (Algerian nationalist party, more left-wing than the UDMA. Its leader, Messali Hadj, has been interned in France for years.)

MUR—Mouvements Unis de la Résistance. (Amalgamated Resistance movements—mostly non-Communist—originally in Vichy France.)

MURF—Mouvement Unifiéde Résistance Française. (See p. 265.)

NRF—*Nouvelle Revue Française.*

OCM—Organization Civile et Militaire. (Non-Communist Resistance Organization.)

OEEC—Organization for European Economic Co-operation.

PC—Parti Communiste. (French Communist Party.)

PPF—Parti Populaire Français. (Doriot's pro-Nazi party.)

RDR—Rassemblement Démocratique Révolutionnaire. (J. P. Sartre's abortive "movement" of 1948–49.)

RPF—Rassemblement du Peuple Français. (De Gaulle's "mass" movement of 1947–53.)

SFIO—Section Française de l'Internationale Ouvrière. (Official description of the French Socialist Party.)

SOE—Secret Operations Executive. (British war-time organization.)

SOL—Service d'ordre Légionnaire. (See p. 125.)

STO—Service de Travail Obligatoire. (Compulsory Labour Service in Germany.)

UDMA—Union Démocratique du Manifeste Algérien. ("Moderate" Algerian Nationalist Party under Ferhat Abbas.)

UDSR—Union Démocratique et Socialiste de la Résistance. (Now a small parliamentary party comprising M. Pleven, Claudius-Petit, Mitterrand, etc.)

UGTT—Union Générale des Travailleurs Tunisiens. (Tunisian trade union federation.)

URAS—Union Républicaine d'Action Sociale. (Title adopted by "orthodox" Gaullist parliamentary group after the split of 1952.)

WFTU—World Federation of Trade Unions. (Predominantly Communist.)

INDEX

Date Due

APR 6 '61	DEC 4 '72	
APR 19 '61	AP 13'78	
DEC 12 '61		
JAN 3 '62		
JAN 17 '62		
APR 4 '62		
APR 22 '65		
OCT 13 '65		
FEB 29 '69		
MAR 20 '69		
APR 23 '69		
APR 28 '69		
APR 21 '70		
MAY 5 '70		
MAY 5 '71		
MAR 1 '72		
MAR 18 '72		
NOV 18 '72	PRINTED IN U. S. A.	